ASYLUM AND HUMAN RIGHTS APPEALS HANDBOOK

ASYLUM AND HUMAN RIGHTS APPEALS HANDBOOK

ANNA KOTZEVA

Barrister, 1 Temple Gardens

LUCY MURRAY

Barrister, 33 Park Place

ROBIN TAM QC

Barrister, 1 Temple Gardens

Consultant Editor

IAN BURNETT QC

Barrister, 1 Temple Gardens

OXFORD

UNIVERSITY PRESS

OXFORD

UNIVERSITY PRESS

Great Clarendon Street, Oxford OX2 6DP

Oxford University Press is a department of the University of Oxford.
It furthers the University's objective of excellence in research, scholarship,
and education by publishing worldwide in

Oxford New York

Auckland Cape Town Dar es Salaam Hong Kong Karachi
Kuala Lumpur Madrid Melbourne Mexico City Nairobi
New Delhi Shanghai Taipei Toronto

With offices in

Argentina Austria Brazil Chile Czech Republic France Greece
Guatemala Hungary Italy Japan Poland Portugal Singapore
South Korea Switzerland Thailand Turkey Ukraine Vietnam

Oxford is a registered trade mark of Oxford University Press
in the UK and in certain other countries

Published in the United States
by Oxford University Press Inc., New York

British Library Cataloguing in Publication Data

Data available

Library of Congress Cataloging in Publication Data

Data available

Typeset by Cepha Imaging Private Ltd., Bangalore, India
Printed in Great Britain
on acid-free paper by
Ashford Colour Press Ltd., Gosport, Hampshire

ISBN 978-0-19-928942-4

1 3 5 7 9 10 8 6 4 2

FOREWORD

There can be no doubt that a handbook such as this is a most useful addition to the material to which any practitioner in this field should have access. There is much new case law which has to be taken into account and there is no reason to believe that there will be any brake on necessary judicial activity. This is particularly the case because new legislation on asylum and immigration has been virtually an annual event. Such legislation, particularly in connection with anti-terrorism measures, has often been less than clear and a response to a perceived immediate problem. While it is to be hoped that that trend will not continue, experience suggests it will. As I write this, the observations of politicians and the outcry in the media in relation to the Chindamo case, involving the murderer of teacher Philip Lawrence, suggests that we may be in for more legislation.

The standard textbooks on immigration are now of a substantial size. An affordable handbook which concentrates on asylum and human rights issues in the context of immigration is to be welcomed. Especially valuable is the part dealing with appeal rights since it is often apparent to a judge of the Administrative Court that the extent of appeal rights and limitations on them are not properly understood.

I am also pleased to see the models set out in the appendix. Clarity and succinctness in presenting appeals and judicial review applications are most important. If there is a good point, it should not be hidden amid a welter of bad points and length of grounds cannot by themselves indicate that there must be something worth arguing. Those together with the practice notes will be particularly useful.

I am most happy to commend this handbook. I am, I am bound to say, only concerned that legislative activity coupled with the output of domestic and European courts do not overtake its content before it has become well thumbed through much use.

Mr Justice Collins
Lead Judge
Administrative Court
August 2007

PREFACE

Asylum and human rights cases arising from immigration decisions continue to occupy a great deal of the time of the growing army of Immigration Judges, both full time and part time. Despite the best endeavours of successive Home Secretaries who have introduced waves of immigration legislation, the burden of such cases in the Administrative Court and Court of Appeal shows no sign of reducing. It is in the immigration field that many of the principles of law that inform and explain the Human Rights Act have developed. The steady stream of cases emerging from the House of Lords is testimony to that.

Whilst the domestic courts attempt to keep pace with immigration legislation, the Strasbourg Court has continued to interpret the Convention as a living instrument and found new ways to apply its terms, especially in cases which spring from decisions to remove an alien to a non-ECHR state where human rights standards are in general less exacting and where particular fears about treatment are evident.

Keeping pace with all these developments is a difficult task. The aim of the authors of this handbook is to assist those who have to deal with asylum and human rights cases on a daily basis by providing a manageable but comprehensive body of material and commentary on the main issues that are likely to arise, including information on relevant Home Office policies and practice notes which focus on the points which are often likely to arise.

It has been possible to reflect the decision on the House of Lords in *Huang v Secretary of State* [2007] UKHL 7 in the text together with the extremely useful exposition of its impact found in *AG (Eritrea) v Secretary of State* [2007] EWCA Civ 80. The correct approach of the AIT to its task when considering proportionality on an appeal is thus settled. And the House of Lords has clarified the whole question of exceptionality when considering claims under Article 8.

In their recent decisions, which include *Razgar, Ullah,* and *Bagdanovicius* as well as *Huang,* the judges of the House of Lords have sought to explain in relatively simple terms how decision makers, the appellate authority, and practitioners should approach claims which rely upon the Convention to resist removal. The hope, if not the confident expectation, is that the application of the Convention to removal decisions will now settle down into well-understood and easily applied principles.

Ian Burnett QC
1 Temple Gardens
London
August 2007

CONTENTS—SUMMARY

CONTENTS

Contents

LIST OF ABBREVIATIONS

AIT   Asylum and Immigration Tribunal
CIPU   Country Information and Policy Unit
CLR   Controlled Legal Representation
CLS   Community Legal Services
CPR   Civil Procedure Rules
ECHR   European Convention on Human Rights
ECtHR   European Court of Human Rights
HRA   Human Rights Act 1998
IAA   Immigration and Asylum Act 1999
IAT   Immigration Appeal Tribunal
IND   Immigration and Nationality Directorate
NAM   New Asylum Model
NASS   National Asylum Support Service
NIAA   Nationality, Immigration and Asylum Act
OEM   Operational Enforcement Manual
SEF   Statement of Evidence Form
UDHR   Universal Declaration of Human Rights

TABLE OF CASES

TABLE OF STATUTES

TABLE OF STATUTORY INSTRUMENTS

Note that references to page numbers indicate that the article or rule is reproduced on that page.

TABLE OF EUROPEAN LEGISLATION

CONVENTIONS

TABLE OF INTERNATIONAL LEGISLATION

1

INTRODUCTION

Supposedly unmeritorious asylum seekers, and their alleged abuses of the United **1.01** Kingdom's immigration and welfare systems, have now been a staple topic for sections of our news media for some years. Yet the explosion in asylum and human rights cases is a comparatively recent phenomenon when compared with the stream of immigrants who for decades have been coming to this country with official approval or encouragement.

A review of the Immigration Appeal Reports for 1987 shows that of just under 70 **1.02** reported cases, only seven had an asylum context under the Refugee Convention (and some of those cases concerned only bail), and in only one other case were arguments based directly on the European Convention on Human Rights (ECHR). A large proportion of the rest were 'family' cases. Even so, in those cases, as in most of the remainder, the arguments usually concerned the requirements of the Immigration Rules. This illustrates how the focus of immigration litigation lay elsewhere, both in the appellate structure set up by the Immigration Appeals Act 1969 adopted by the Immigration Act 1971, and in the judicial review jurisdiction. Asylum cases were then only a small proportion of the workload.

Home Office statistics for the following years show how rapidly this area has **1.03** grown. In 1989, there were 11,640 principal applications for asylum (excluding dependants). Over the following nine years, the number of applications varied between the low twenties and mid forties of thousands of cases, averaging a little under 35,000 a year. But in 1999 to 2002, there was a blunt peak of applications, with 71,160, 80,315, 71,025, and 84,130 applications made in each of those years respectively, before numbers began a distinct decline. During those heavy years, the administrative decision-making system became swamped and overloaded, the after-effects of which are still being felt today.

The change in focus has also been reflected in the pace and nature of statutory **1.04** change. In 1987, the Immigration Act 1971 remained the only substantive Act governing immigration, and it had not yet been amended by a statute dealing specifically with immigration. A number of relatively minor changes had been necessitated by such events as the overhaul of the system of British nationality and legislative provision for the Channel Tunnel, and this approach was continued by the modest amendments brought about by the Immigration Act 1988. Five further years elapsed before the next immigration-specific statute, the Asylum and Immigration Appeals Act 1993. Its title would not disappoint its reader: it extended the immigration appeals system to the general run of asylum cases for the first time. The pace of statutory change since then has been relentless. Further Acts followed in 1996, 1999, 2002, 2004, and 2006, with the titles of all of these statutes containing the word 'Asylum'. And at the time of writing a Criminal Justice and Immigration Bill is before Parliament.

1.05 Another major statutory change occurred during this period. In 1987, the prospect of the 'incorporation' of the European Convention on Human Rights into the United Kingdom's domestic law remained at best a distant possibility. Ultimately, another decade was to pass before the political landscape changed in favour of that idea. On 2 October 2000, the Human Rights Act 1998 came into force. For the first time, those seeking to enter or remain in the United Kingdom could rely directly on ECHR rights to support their claims. Immigration cases became one of the areas in which ECHR issues were commonly argued and decided, with much litigation progressing to the higher courts for definitive decision and important guidance. In some respects, the ECHR seemed potentially to offer a wider scope for claims to enter or remain on human rights grounds, in particular because of the 'absolute' nature of the protection afforded by Article 3, which is not beset by many of the technical issues raised by the Refugee Convention. Other articles of the ECHR also provided fruitful scope for argument, at least while domestic jurisprudence on the ECHR remained less developed. Consequently, ECHR arguments sometimes took on a substantially higher profile than asylum arguments under the Refugee Convention.

1.06 Perhaps the most telling consequence of the change in focus was introduced by the 2004 statute, the Asylum and Immigration (Treatment of Claimants etc) Act 2004. During its passage through Parliament, the most controversial proposal contained in the Bill was a radical overhaul of the asylum appeals system. The chief aim was to effect a change from the two-tier system of appeals to Adjudicators and then the Immigration Appeal Tribunal, originally set up by the 1969 Act, to a single-tier system, in the belief that this would produce a faster and cheaper system. Much heat was generated by a debate over an allied proposal to restrict the right of further appeal to the higher courts, which many considered was objectionable on constitutional as well as more pragmatic grounds. That proposal was eventually abandoned. But the change to the single-tier system survived and remained in the Act as passed, as did the name chosen for the new appellate body: the Asylum and Immigration Tribunal.

As the volume of work in this jurisdiction has grown, so has the number of prac- **1.07** titioners involved in it. Inevitably, many of these practitioners will not specialize exclusively in the field of asylum and human rights. Accordingly, this work aims to provide a guide to the main principles and issues which might be encountered when conducting a case in this field. The first part of the book deals with the substantive law on which claims against removal on asylum or human rights grounds might be based. First, the comparatively settled principles relating to the Refugee Convention are covered. Next, the two key articles of the ECHR for immigration cases are considered in turn: Article 3, which protects against torture and inhuman or degrading treatment or punishment, and Article 8, which protects private and family life, home, and correspondence. Then consideration is given to the other articles of the ECHR which can, exceptionally, form the basis of claims not to be removed. The second part of the book goes on to consider questions of procedure and practice: the rights of appeal and the complex procedural routes that an appeal might take; certification and removal; and detention, along with bail and other modes of challenging detention. Finally, there is discussion of the likely path of future reforms, and a selection of the most useful sources and materials. Thanks must go to Alan Payne and John-Paul Waite at 5 Essex Court for their contribution towards the model pleadings and skeleton arguments. Although few cases in this field could be described as simple, this text should as a whole provide sufficient assistance for dealing with relatively straightforward examples.

2

ASYLUM

A. History of the Refugee Convention

After the establishment of the United Nations in 1945, one of its most immediate **2.01**
concerns was the question of the refugees displaced by the Second World War.
On 12 February 1946, the General Assembly referred the problem to the
Economic and Social Council, recognizing the urgency of the problem and the
necessity to distinguish between genuine refugees and 'war criminals, quislings
and traitors'.[1] The outcome was the creation of a temporary agency, the International Refugee Organization, established by a General Assembly resolution on
15 December 1946,[2] whose primary function was to assist genuine refugees and
displaced persons either to return to their countries of nationality or former
habitual residence, or to find new homes elsewhere.

---

[1] General Assembly resolution 8 (I).
[2] General Assembly resolution 62 (I).

2.02 Another early act of the General Assembly was the adoption and proclamation of the Universal Declaration of Human Rights (UDHR) on 10 December 1948,[3] Article 14 of which provided:

> (1) Everyone has the right to seek and to enjoy in other countries asylum from persecution.
> (2) This right may not be invoked in the case of prosecutions genuinely arising from non-political crimes or from acts contrary to the purposes and principles of the United Nations.

2.03 On 3 December 1949, the General Assembly decided to establish a High Commissioner's Office for Refugees with effect from 1 January 1951 to provide protection for refugees who had been the concern of the International Refugee Organization after the termination of its activities, and for such other persons as the General Assembly might from time to time determine.[4] The General Assembly asked the Economic and Social Council to prepare a structure for the High Commissioner's Office, and also to make recommendations to the General Assembly about the definition of the term 'refugee'.

2.04 Thus the General Assembly passed two resolutions on 14 December 1950. It adopted the Statute of the Office of the United Nations High Commissioner for Refugees (UNHCR), thus establishing the UNHCR.[5] The Economic and Social Council having prepared a draft 'Convention relating to the Status of Refugees', the General Assembly also decided to convene a conference of plenipotentiaries to complete the drafting of, and to sign, both a convention relating to refugees and a protocol relating to the status of stateless persons.[6]

2.05 Article 1 of the draft Convention, dealing with the definition of the term 'refugee', was annexed to the resolution. Article 1A contained the basic definition of the term, setting out two alternative ways in which an individual might fall within the term. Article 1A(1) listed a number of prior arrangements under which individuals might have been considered refugees, including decisions taken by the International Refugee Organization; such individuals were included in the term 'refugee'. Article 1A(2) also contained an alternative qualification in the following terms:

> As a result of events occurring before 1 January 1951, and owing to well-founded fear of being persecuted for reasons of race, religion, nationality or political opinion, is outside the country of his nationality and is unable or, owing to such fear or for reasons other than his personal convenience, is unwilling to avail himself of the

---

[3] General Assembly resolution 217 A (III).
[4] General Assembly resolution 319 (IV).
[5] General Assembly resolution 428 (V).
[6] General Assembly resolution 429 (V).

protection of that country; or who, not having a nationality and being outside the country of his former habitual residence, is unable or, owing to such fear or for reasons other than personal convenience, is unwilling to return to it;

In the case of a person who has more than one nationality, the above term 'the country of his nationality' shall mean any of the countries of which he is a national, and a person shall not be deemed to be lacking the protection of the country of his nationality if, without any valid reason based on well-founded fear, he has not availed himself of the protection of one of the countries of which he is a national.

The conference of plenipotentiaries took place from 2 to 25 July 1951 in Geneva, **2.06** and the Convention was adopted on 25 July 1951. The final act of the conference was signed three days later, on 28 July 1951.[7] The Convention entered into force on 24 April 1954.

Almost all of the draft of Article 1A was adopted by the conference. The confer- **2.07** ence also inserted, as Article 1B, a provision which permitted Contracting States to specify on signature, ratification, or accession whether they wished the words 'events occurring before 1 January 1951' to mean 'events occurring in Europe before 1 January 1951' or 'events occurring in Europe or elsewhere before 1 January 1951'. Whichever option any individual Contracting State chose, the temporal scope of the Convention was clearly identified.[8]

Over the following years, the limitation that the temporal scope of the Convention **2.08** imposed on the protection afforded by it became increasingly evident, with new situations arising in which refugees (in the colloquial sense) did not fall within the Convention. A draft Protocol to the Convention was prepared and submitted to the General Assembly of the United Nations. States Parties to the Protocol would undertake to apply the operative parts of the Convention (Articles 2 to 34) to any individual falling within a revised definition of the term 'refugee' that removed the temporal limitation. This was achieved by omitting the words 'As a result of events occurring before 1 January 1951 and' and 'as a result of such events' from Article 1A(2), resulting in this revised definition of 'refugee':

Owing to well-founded fear of being persecuted for reasons of race, religion, nationality, membership of a particular social group or political opinion, is outside the country of his nationality and is unable or, owing to such fear, is unwilling to avail himself of the protection of that country; or who, not having a nationality and being outside the country of his former habitual residence, is unable or, owing to such fear, is unwilling to return to it.

---

[7] An account of the *travaux préparatoires* (other than in relation to Article 1) can be found in P Weis (ed), *The Refugee Convention, 1951*.

[8] In the event, only Congo, Madagascar, Monaco, and Turkey chose the geographical limitation to events occurring in Europe.

2.09 On 16 December 1966, the General Assembly took note of this Protocol and requested the Secretary-General to transmit it to various States with a view to enabling them to accede to the Protocol.[9] The Protocol entered into force on 4 October 1967.[10] In addition to the revised definition of the 'refugee', the Protocol provided that States Parties to the Protocol would apply the Convention without geographical limitation, except where a choice under Article 1B of the Convention to limit its application to events occurring in Europe had already been made by a State Party and remained in place.

2.10 It was this historical process that produced the form of the definition of 'refugee' that is in general use today. As the United Kingdom is a Party to both the Convention and the Protocol, it is the revised definition of the term 'refugee' which is relevant to this book.

2.11 As the Convention does not provide for a supra-national court to pronounce definitively on its meaning (unlike, for example, the position in relation to the European Convention on Human Rights), the interpretation of the Convention sometimes raises difficult issues for practitioners and judicial bodies. Some of the questions of interpretation raised by individual cases are not straightforward. The UNHCR publishes a number of documents and papers, including the *Handbook on Procedures and Criteria for Determining Refugee Status*, and a series of *Guidelines on International Protection*. Although these publications may be taken into account by courts as persuasive material in favour of one interpretation rather than another, they are neither definitive nor binding.[11]

B. The Key Provisions of the Refugee Convention

2.12 For the purposes of this book, the key provisions of the Refugee Convention are Articles 1 and 33 of the Convention, as they respectively define who is a 'refugee' and set out the core immigration law protection provided by the Convention to refugees, namely an obligation not to remove a refugee to a place where he might suffer harm of a type against which the Convention was intended to guard. In a small number of cases, Article 32 of the Convention may be of relevance.

---

[9] General Assembly resolution 2198 (XXI). On the same day, the General Assembly adopted the International Covenant on Economic, Social and Cultural Rights (ICESCR), the International Covenant on Civil and Political Rights (ICCPR), and the Optional Protocol to the ICCPR.

[10] As of 1 December 2006, there were 147 States Parties to either the Convention or the Protocol or both. This included three States Parties to the Convention only, and three States Parties to the Protocol only.

[11] An example can be found in the seminal case of *R v Home Secretary, ex parte Sivakumaran* [1988] 1 AC 958. The House of Lords decided that a fear of persecution was well founded if it was objectively justified, expressly rejecting the view espoused by the UNHCR, set out in the *Handbook*, that such a fear was well founded so long as subjectively it was reasonably held.

Article 1 has six sub-divisions. As has been mentioned, Article 1A contains **2.13** the two alternative ways in which an individual might fall within the term 'refugee'. Article 1A(1) is the first of these definitions, and includes in the term any person who:

> Has been considered a refugee under the Arrangements of 12 May 1926 and 30 June 1928 or under the Conventions of 28 October 1933 and 10 February 1938, the Protocol of 14 September 1939 or the Constitution of the International Refugee Organization.

These individuals have been described as 'statutory refugees'. As is obvious from the static definition, 'statutory refugees' will in due course become a purely historical category.

A second sub-paragraph to Article 1A(1) makes clear that the two alternative **2.14** definitions are not mutually exclusive:

> Decisions of non-eligibility taken by the International Refugee Organization during the period of its activities shall not prevent the status of refugee being accorded to persons who fulfil the conditions of paragraph 2 of this section.

An individual might qualify as a refugee under Article 1A(2) even if he did not qualify under Article 1A(1) because the International Refugee Organization had decided that he was not eligible.

The second definition, in its revised form, is that which is of most relevance **2.15** today. Article 1A(2) (when applied as provided by the Protocol) includes in the term 'refugee' any person who:

> Owing to well-founded fear of being persecuted for reasons of race, religion, nation-ality, membership of a particular social group or political opinion, is outside the country of his nationality and is unable or, owing to such fear, is unwilling to avail himself of the protection of that country; or who, not having a nationality and being outside the country of his former habitual residence, is unable or, owing to such fear, is unwilling to return to it.

Following the Protocol, Article 1B is no longer relevant to the United Kingdom, **2.16** which did not choose the geographic limitation to events occurring in Europe when originally becoming a Party to the Convention, and which thus now applies the Convention without geographical limitation in accordance with the Protocol.

The remainder of Article 1 consists of four provisions which disapply the **2.17** Convention to the individuals who fall within them. They are sometimes collectively referred to as the exclusion clauses, although individual clauses are sometimes referred to by other names. In summary, Article 1C excludes individu-als who no longer need the protection of the Convention because of some change of circumstances; Article 1D excludes individuals who are receiving protection or assistance from United Nations organs or agencies other than the UNHCR; Article 1E excludes individuals who are treated by their country of residence as if they were nationals of that country; and Article 1F excludes those who do not deserve international protection because of their own acts.

2.18 Article 33(1) is the core immigration law protection to refugees, as it provides:

> No Contracting State shall expel or return ('*refouler*')[12] a refugee in any manner whatsoever to the frontiers of territories where his life or freedom would be threatened on account of his race, religion, nationality, membership of a particular social group or political opinion.

2.19 But this is subject to an important exception, set out in Article 33(2):

> The benefit of the present provision may not, however, be claimed by a refugee whom there are reasonable grounds for regarding as a danger to the security of the country in which he is, or who, having been convicted by a final judgment of a particularly serious crime, constitutes a danger to the community of that country.

This is not an exclusion clause in the same way as Articles 1C–1F. Those clauses disapply the whole of the Convention in relation to the individuals concerned. Article 33(2) merely excepts the relevant individuals from the benefit of the 'non-*refoulement*' provision of Article 33(1). The individual may continue to be a 'refugee' within the meaning of the Convention, even if he can no longer claim protection from *refoulement* under Article 33(1).

2.20 Finally, Article 32 of the Convention may be of relevance in a small number of cases. This provides some procedural protection for refugees lawfully in the territory of a Contracting State. It is obvious that this applies to those who have been admitted and are legally resident in the country concerned, and not to those who are seeking admission. Article 32(1) provides that such refugees may not be expelled save on grounds of national security or public order, and the remainder of the Article goes on to provide:

> (2) The expulsion of such a refugee shall be only in pursuance of a decision reached in accordance with due process of law. Except where compelling reasons of national security otherwise require, the refugee shall be allowed to submit evidence to clear himself, and to appeal to and be represented for the purpose before competent authority or a person or persons specially designated by the competent authority.
>
> (3) The Contracting States shall allow such a refugee a reasonable period within which to seek legal admission into another country. The Contracting States reserve the right to apply during that period such internal measures as they may deem necessary.

---

[12] Various French–English dictionaries suggest meanings of '*refouler*' such as 'to force back', 'to turn away', 'to turn back', 'to push back', and 'to block out'. In many ways, the word '*refoulement*' has become accepted shorthand in this context for the concept of sending a refugee or asylum seeker back to a country in which they might be harmed.

However, in the cases of refugees in the United Kingdom to which this provision applies, the appeals system should automatically provide the required procedural protection.

C. Implementation of Convention in United Kingdom Law

The Convention has not been directly incorporated into United Kingdom law **2.21** and there are many aspects of the Convention which until recently have not been reflected in explicit statutory provisions. Many parts of the protection afforded by the United Kingdom to refugees have been provided by practice rather than strict legal obligation.

For example, although recognition as a refugee entails a number of practical ben- **2.22** efits to the individual,[13] there were no statutory provisions providing for formal recognition of refugee status, nor for its renewal, expiry, revocation, or cessation. Instead, immigration benefits were conferred by the grant of immigration status within the normal immigration system, with the Immigration Rules providing some limited guidance about what should be done.[14] Other benefits, such as access to welfare benefits, were provided under statutes of general application dealing with such benefits. The provision of refugee travel documents, as required by the Convention,[15] did not have any statutory backing at all.

Indeed, historically, the only express acknowledgement in immigration materials **2.23** of the importance of the Refugee Convention to asylum matters was a reference in the Immigration Rules. In 1993, that reference was put on a statutory basis. Section 2 of the Asylum and Immigration Appeals Act 1993 provides that:

> Nothing in the immigration rules (within the meaning of the 1971 Act) shall lay down any practice which would be contrary to the Convention.

This section has been prospectively repealed, but no effective date has yet been announced.

In 2004, an EC Directive was issued,[16] which laid down minimum standards for **2.24** the qualification and status of third country nationals or stateless persons as refugees or as persons who otherwise need international protection, and the content of the protection granted. Where it has been considered necessary to take any

---

[13] See, for example, Articles 12–30 of the Convention.

[14] At times, the benefits conferred were even inconsistent with the provisions of the Immigration Rules. For many years, it was the practice to grant refugees indefinite leave to enter or remain immediately on recognition, notwithstanding the express provisions of the Immigration Rules that only limited leave to enter or remain should be granted.

[15] Article 28 of the Convention.

[16] Council Directive 2004/83/EC, known as the 'Qualification Directive'.

action, this Directive has been transposed into domestic law in part by amendments to the immigration rules, and in part by the introduction of the Refugee or Person in Need of International Protection (Qualification) Regulations 2006,[17] which came into force on 9 October 2006. These measures have now statutorily codified many of the matters which were previously a matter of practice or less explicitly set out in statutory materials. Importantly, they now include statutory backing (in the Immigration Rules) for the issue of a United Kingdom residence permit when refugee status is recognized, and for the issue of refugee travel documents.

2.25 For the purposes of this book, immigration status is the most important aspect of the implementation of the Convention. If an individual is recognised as a refugee, he is granted leave to enter or remain in the United Kingdom, which protects him from *refoulement* contrary to Article 33(1) of the Convention. If the individual contests the Secretary of State's decision that he is not a refugee, this is done by the device of a right of appeal against the consequent immigration decision (usually a refusal of leave to enter or remain) on the ground that removal of the individual from the United Kingdom in consequence of that refusal of immigration status would breach the United Kingdom's obligations under the Refugee Convention.[18] If the individual is in fact a refugee and the Secretary of State's decision is wrong, the individual would most likely succeed on appeal on the basis that such removal would be in breach of Article 33(1) of the Convention.

2.26 The immigration appeals system thus provides a mechanism by which the question of whether the individual is or is not a refugee can be considered again, independently of the Secretary of State, even if the statute does not make that question the central issue in the appeal.[19] But the focus of the statute cannot be ignored, and in general there is no free-standing appeal against a refusal of recognition as a refugee.[20]

2.27 Similarly, if an individual ceases to be a refugee according to the Convention, his status under United Kingdom law does not automatically change. Further action

---

[17] SI 2006/2525.

[18] Section 84(1)(g) of the Nationality, Immigration and Asylum Act 2002.

[19] *Saad, Osorio and Diriye v Home Secretary* [2002] INLR 34.

[20] *Massaquoi v Home Secretary* [2001] Imm AR 309. The main exception is the 'upgrade' appeal, now under s 83 of the 2002 Act. If an upgrade appeal right had existed at the time of the Secretary of State's decisions in *Saad, Osorio and Diriye*, the Court of Appeal might not have had to embark on reasoning of significant contortion. It seems likely that the Court of Appeal did so in order to preserve the possibility of an appeal that could decide the question of whether the individual was a refugee, within the structure of the appeal rights then provided by s 8 of the Asylum and Immigration Appeals Act 1993.

to alter his immigration status, for example, is required if the individual is to be removed simply because he has been, but has now ceased to be, a refugee.[21] Only when the individual's immigration status has been appropriately changed can he be removed from the United Kingdom.

A corollary is that a person who is recognised as a refugee but later ceases to be a **2.28** refugee within the meaning of the Convention may find that his substantive status does not in fact change. For example, an individual who was granted indefinite leave to remain in the United Kingdom on recognition of his refugee status does not automatically lose that immigration status if he ceases to be a refugee because it is now safe for him to return home.[22] Unless the Secretary of State takes some action to revoke that indefinite leave to remain or otherwise to terminate it,[23] the individual will continue to enjoy the rights attaching to the grant of indefinite leave.

D. Article 1A(2)—Introduction

Article 1A(2) of the Convention provides the well-known test that a refugee is a **2.29** person who 'owing to well-founded fear of being persecuted for reasons of race, religion, nationality, membership of a particular social group or political opin-ion, is outside the country of his nationality and is unable or, owing to such fear, is unwilling to avail himself of the protection of that country; or who, not having a nationality and being outside the country of his former habitual residence, is unable or, owing to such fear, is unwilling to return to it'.

Although the drafting of this clause, like that of many international treaties, may **2.30** be regarded as imprecise, the House of Lords has approved an analysis which breaks this down into four categories of refugee:

(1) nationals who are outside their country owing to a well-founded fear of per-secution for a Convention reason, and are unable to avail themselves of the protection of their country;

(2) nationals who are outside their country owing to a well-founded fear of perse-cution for a Convention reason, and, owing to such fear, are unwilling to avail themselves of the protection of their country;

(3) non-nationals who are outside the country of their former habitual residence owing to a well-founded fear of persecution for a Convention reason and are unable to return to their country; and

---

[21] See s 76 of the Nationality, Immigration and Asylum Act 2002.

[22] See the section below on Article 1C of the Convention, the cessation clause.

[23] A topical recent example is the making of decisions to deport a number of recognised refugees on national security grounds, because inter alia they are no longer refugees within the meaning of the Convention, having become excluded by the operation of Article 1F.

(4) non-nationals who are outside the country of their former habitual residence owing to a well-founded fear of persecution for a Convention reason, and, owing to such fear, are unwilling to return to their country.[24]

2.31 In each of these categories, the asylum seeker must satisfy two separate tests, which can be called the 'fear test' and the 'protection test'.[25] The 'fear test' is common to all four categories, and is the focus of dispute and argument in the overwhelming majority of asylum cases. The 'protection test' is relatively seldom of separate importance. It is couched in different language for those with no nationality (ie categories (3) and (4)), for obvious reasons.

2.32 The 'fear test' relates only to a current well-founded fear of persecution. A historic well-founded fear of persecution, which is either no longer held or no longer well founded, will not suffice to constitute an individual a refugee, even if the individual remains unable to avail himself of the protection of his country.[26] Of course, a historic well-founded fear of persecution may well provide evidence of a current well-founded fear. And if the Secretary of State accepts that the individual had a historic well-founded fear of persecution which the Secretary of State contends has now ceased, he may have to discharge an evidential burden to establish that the individual can now safely be returned home.[27]

2.33 A situation can arise in which an asylum seeker may return home voluntarily without attracting any risk of persecution, but a risk of persecution might arise if they refused to return home voluntarily and had to be compulsorily removed there. Such an asylum seeker is not 'outside their country owing to a well-founded fear of persecution' and does not qualify for refugee status.[28]

---

[24] *Adan v Home Secretary* [1999] 1 AC 293, 304C–E per Lord Lloyd.

[25] At 304E per Lord Lloyd.

[26] At 308B–D per Lord Lloyd.

[27] *Arif v Home Secretary* [1999] Imm AR 271, 276 per Simon Brown LJ; affirmed at para 66 of *Hoxha v Home Secretary* [2005] 1 WLR 1063 per Lord Brown, who emphasized that the evidential burden was only 'to place before the appellate authority sufficient material to satisfy them of that critical fact'. It would be an error to confuse this with a burden of proving that the asylum seeker is not a refugee; the existence of an evidential burden on the Secretary of State does not alter the normal position that the asylum seeker must establish that he is a refugee. Article 4(4) of the Directive, which has not been transposed, provides:

The fact that an applicant has already been subject to persecution or serious harm, or to direct threats of such persecution or such harm, is a serious indication of the applicant's well-founded fear of persecution or real risk of suffering serious harm, unless there are good reasons to consider that such persecution or serious harm will not be repeated.

[28] *AA v Home Secretary* [2007] 2 All ER 160 at para 99.

E. Well-founded Fear of Persecution

The standard to which the elements of the refugee test have to be established **2.34**
has been the source of controversy, and parts of the legal tests are still often
misunderstood.

The burden of proof rests on the asylum seeker to establish his case. This is not **2.35**
controversial. Issues more commonly arise in relation to the standard of proof.
However, difficulties are often caused by two matters. First, the terms 'burden of
proof' and 'standard of proof' are often used incorrectly. They refer to different
concepts, but confusion is sometimes caused by imprecision. Second, because of
the approach in asylum cases to the 'proof' of past and present events, and because
of the evaluation of the future which is the central task of a decision maker in asylum cases, it is probably not apt to speak of a standard of 'proof' in any event, as
the task is more one of assessment than 'proof' of the type seen in conventional
common law litigation.

The central issue in most asylum cases is whether the individual's fear of perse- **2.36**
cution is well founded. The House of Lords has definitively held that a fear of
persecution is well founded if there is shown, objectively, to be a reasonable
degree of likelihood that the applicant would be persecuted if returned to his
own country.[29] There is little, if any, difference between the phrase 'a reasonable
degree of likelihood' and the phrases 'a reasonable chance', 'substantial grounds
for thinking', and 'a serious possibility'.[30]

However, this decision relates to the question which should be asked about the **2.37**
future and about what might happen to the asylum seeker were he returned to his
own country. The decision does not assist with the trickier practical question
about the approach that should be adopted to the evidence available about historical or current events, on the basis of which that assessment about the future is
likely to be made. The evidence about the past or the present may be fragile, frag-
mentary, or obviously unreliable. Conventional common law litigation requires
such past or present events to be proved on the balance of probabilities. Many
asylum seekers would not be able to satisfy such a standard of proof.

In an early asylum case, the High Court held that if a court is obliged to make an **2.38**
informed guess as to what might happen in the future, as in relation to an assessment about the future likelihood of persecution, it can do so only on the basis of

---

[29] *R v Home Secretary, ex parte Sivakumaran* [1988] 1 AC 958, 994F–G per Lord Keith.
[30] *Fernandez v Government of Singapore* [1971] 1 WLR 987, 994H per Lord Diplock.

the facts proved on the balance of probabilities.[31] But when the Immigration Appeal Tribunal came to consider this issue, it decided (by a majority) that the assessment of future risk was not a two-stage process of finding the facts by applying the balance of probabilities, then making an assessment on the basis of proved facts; rather it was a single-stage process of evaluating all the evidence for what it is worth.[32] That decision appears to have been inconsistent with the earlier High Court decision. But the Court of Appeal has since approved the Tribunal's approach.[33]

2.39 It is important to note that this approach does not apply a 'lower standard of proof' to past or current facts. Past or current facts are not to be treated as true (ie as having occurred or as occurring) as soon as it has been established that there is a reasonable degree of likelihood that they have occurred (or are occurring). The Court of Appeal was at pains to note that the Tribunal's approach had not been to apply 'the lower standard of proof set out in *Sivakumaran* . . . both to the assessment of accounts of past events and the likelihood of persecution in the future'.[34] As Brooke LJ said: 'This approach does not entail the decision-maker (whether the Secretary of State or an adjudicator or the Immigration Appeal Tribunal itself) purporting to find "proved" facts, whether past or present, about which it is not satisfied on the balance of probabilities. What it does mean, on the other hand, is that it must not exclude any matters from its consideration when it is assessing the future unless it feels that it can safely discard them because it has no real doubt that they did not in fact occur (or, indeed, that they are not occurring at present). Similarly, if an applicant contends that relevant matters did not happen, the decision-maker should not exclude the possibility that they did not happen (although believing that they probably did) unless it has no real doubt that they did in fact happen.'[35] Or, as Sedley LJ put it: 'No probabilistic cut-off operates here: everything capable of having a bearing has to be given the weight, great or little, due to it.'[36]

2.40 Thus, if the evidence suggests that an assertion about a past or present event may be true, but the evidence is not strong enough to show that the assertion is more likely than not to be true, then the decision-maker is not to take the assertion as having been proved to be true. The decision maker must take the assertion

---

[31] *R v Immigration Appeal Tribunal, ex parte Jonah* [1985] Imm AR 7, 11 per Nolan J, who based his view on a dictum of Lord Diplock at 993H–994A of *Fernandez*.

[32] *Kaja v Home Secretary* [1995] Imm AR 1.

[33] *Karanakaran v Home Secretary* [2000] 3 All ER 449, 469d–f per Brooke LJ. The approach set out in *Karanakaran* has since been approved by the House of Lords in *R (Sivakumar) v Home Secretary* [2003] 1 WLR 840.

[34] At 459g–j.

[35] At 469h–j.

[36] At 479d.

into account only as something that may have been (or may be) true. The importance of this Court of Appeal decision is that the decision maker is not entitled
to disregard the assertion entirely on the basis that it is taken to be unproved
and therefore untrue, as would be the position in conventional common law
litigation.

F. Persecution

Persecution connotes very serious ill-treatment. The High Court has applied the **2.41**
dictionary definitions of 'to pursue, hunt, drive' and 'to pursue with malignancy
or injurious action; esp to oppress for holding a heretical opinion or belief'.[37] But
this was tempered with the pragmatic view that 'considerations of policy may
require a stringent test to be adopted if this country is not to be flooded with
those claiming political asylum'.

A human rights-based analytical approach has since gained currency, based on **2.42**
the view of Professor James Hathaway that persecution is 'the sustained or systemic failure of State protection in relation to one of the core entitlements
which has been recognised by the international community'.[38] This general
approach has now been accepted by the House of Lords on several occasions,[39]
although it has been pointed out in the Court of Appeal that 'these words give no
very clear place to the requirement of gravity or seriousness'.[40]

Thus, the approach does not itself answer the question in any particular case. **2.43**
Whether a certain level of ill-treatment amounts (or would amount) to persecution still depends on the severity of the ill-treatment, which may be capable
of being assessed by reference to the importance of the right which is being
(or would be) violated,[41] the nature of the violation, its frequency, duration, or
persistence. In extreme cases, even a threat of ill-treatment might be sufficient to
amount to persecution. But in other cases, a realistic look at what may happen
after the asylum seeker's removal can show that ill-treatment of the required level
of severity is too unlikely to occur because of his individual characteristics or

---

[37] See *ex parte Jonah* at 13 per Nolan J.
[38] *The Law of Refugee Status* (1991) at p 112.
[39] *Horvath v Home Secretary* [2001] 1 AC 489, 495F–G per Lord Hope; *Sepet v Home Secretary*
[2003] 1 WLR 856 at para 7 per Lord Bingham; *R (Ullah) v Special Adjudicator* [2004] 2 AC 323 at
para 32 per Lord Steyn.
[40] *Amare v Home Secretary* [2006] Imm AR 217 at para 31 per Laws LJ.
[41] Hathaway divides the core human rights into three categories and suggests that each category
may require a different type of breach in order to constitute persecution.

behavioural patterns, even if other apparently similar people might be more likely to attract ill-treatment because they are more open or demonstrative.[42]

2.44   The Directive also contains guidance about what acts may be sufficiently serious as to constitute persecution. As transposed, it provides that:

> (1) In deciding whether a person is a refugee an act of persecution must be:
> > (a) sufficiently serious by its nature or repetition as to constitute a severe violation of a basic human right, in particular a right from which derogation cannot be made under Article 15 of the Convention for the Protection of Human Rights and Fundamental Freedoms; or
> > (b) an accumulation of various measures, including a violation of a human right which is sufficiently severe as to affect an individual in a similar manner as specified in (a).
> (2) An act of persecution may, for example, take the form of:
> > (a) an act of physical or mental violence, including an act of sexual violence;
> > (b) a legal, administrative, police, or judicial measure which in itself is discriminatory or which is implemented in a discriminatory manner;
> > (c) prosecution or punishment, which is disproportionate or discriminatory;
> > (d) denial of judicial redress resulting in a disproportionate or discriminatory punishment;
> > (e) prosecution or punishment for refusal to perform military service in a conflict, where performing military service would include crimes or acts falling under regulation 7.[43]

2.45   However, in all cases, unless a core human right is (or would be) violated by the ill-treatment complained of, the ill-treatment would not constitute persecution.[44]

2.46   A consequence of this human rights-based approach is that persecution requires some failure of the State to protect the individual against ill-treatment, for only then is there a 'sustained or systemic failure of State protection'. It has been said that 'persecution = serious harm + the failure of State protection'.[45] A well-founded

---

[42] See *Jain v Home Secretary* [2000] Imm AR 76, where it was argued that a homosexual in India might be at risk of ill-treatment if he were handed over to the police for prosecution for committing a homosexual act, thus making it risky for him to live openly in a homosexual relationship. But the reality was that he who would seek an adult male partner and his homosexual practices would be conducted in private with that partner. And there had been no known charges of or convictions for sodomy in recent years. Thus the risk of ill-treatment was judged to be too low to qualify him for refugee status.

[43] Part of Regulation 5.

[44] *Sepet v Home Secretary* [2003] 1 WLR 856, in which the House of Lords held that there is no internationally recognised core right to be exempted from performing compulsory military service, so that punishment for failing to do so is not persecution.

[45] *R v Immigration Appeal Tribunal, ex parte Shah* [1999] 2 AC 629, 653G per Lord Hoffmann, who also observed: 'What is the reason for the persecution which the appellants fear? Here it is important to notice that it is made up of two elements. First, there is the threat of violence to Mrs Islam by her husband and his political friends and to Mrs Shah by her husband. This is a personal affair, directed against them as individuals. Secondly, there is the inability or unwillingness of the State to do anything to protect them. There is nothing personal about this. The evidence was that

fear of serious ill-treatment at the hands of fellow citizens[46] will in itself not suffice to constitute an individual a refugee. He would have to show, in addition, 'a failure by the State to make protection available against the ill-treatment or violence which the person suffers at the hands of his persecutors'.[47] This principle has now been incorporated into the Directive.[48]

The House of Lords has approved a test of the level of State protection which **2.47** would satisfy the Refugee Convention, which had been propounded by Stuart-Smith LJ in the Court of Appeal in the following terms:

> In my judgment there must be in force in the country in question a criminal law which makes the violent attacks by the persecutors punishable by sentences commensurate with the gravity of the crimes. The victims as a class must not be exempt from the protection of the law. There must be a reasonable willingness by the law enforcement agencies, that is to say the police and the courts, to detect, prosecute and punish offenders. It must be remembered that inefficiency and incompetence is not the same as unwillingness, unless it is extreme and widespread. There may be many reasons why criminals are not brought to justice including lack of admissible evidence even where the best endeavours are made; they are not always convicted because of the high standard of proof required, and the desire to protect the rights of accused persons. Moreover, the existence of some policemen who are corrupt or sympathetic to the criminals, or some judges who are weak in the control of the court or in sentencing, does not mean that the State is unwilling to afford protection. It will require cogent evidence that the State which is able to afford protection is unwilling to do so, especially in the case of a democracy.[49]

Despite a certain amount of criticism from outside the United Kingdom, the **2.48** House of Lords appears to stand by this decision. It has applied a similar approach to the question of serious ill-treatment, of a level of severity that might breach Article 3 of the European Convention on Human Rights, by citizens not acting on behalf of the State; that is insufficient to found a claim for protection under Article 3 because a breach of Article 3 would only be constituted by a State failure

---

the State would not assist them because they were women. It denied them a protection against violence which it would have given to men. These two elements have to be combined to constitute persecution within the meaning of the Convention.'

[46] Such persecutors are often referred to as 'non-State agents of persecution'. This phrase has sometimes given rise to misunderstanding. The feared actions of such individuals can give rise to a claim for asylum even if their actions are nothing to do with the State and they do not act on behalf of the State. They are not 'agents' in the sense of 'principal and agent'. They might be regarded as 'agents' only in the sense of 'cleaning agents'—simply the means by which something occurs. The Directive and Regulations have now adopted the alternative term 'non-State actors'.

[47] *Horvath v Home Secretary* [2001] 1 AC 489, 497H per Lord Hope.

[48] Transposed into Regulation 3(c); see also Regulation 4(1).

[49] *Horvath v Home Secretary* [2000] INLR 15, 26B–E per Stuart-Smith LJ, who dissented in the result in the Court of Appeal. Not surprisingly, this has become generally known as the '*Horvath* test'.

to provide reasonable protection.[50] And in any event the test has now been incorporated, in a summarized form, into the Directive.[51]

2.49 The view has been expressed that such protection can be provided only by an entity which is capable of granting nationality to a person in a form recognised internationally. In relation to Kosovo after the intervention of the United Nations, protection was provided by international organizations which had acquired the duty to do so under international law, and which were also operating with the consent of the State concerned. At least on these grounds, the protection being provided was capable of satisfying the '*Horvath* test'.[52]

2.50 But in relation to the Kurdish Autonomous Region in the north of Iraq, which was not controlled by Saddam Hussein's regime (prior to its removal) but mainly by two Kurdish political parties, the Court of Appeal considered that the protection available there would not be regarded as being provided by such an entity and would therefore fall to be disregarded. However, it did not have to decide this issue, and the decision itself was later nullified for technical reasons.[53]

2.51 Nevertheless, the Directive may now have reversed this position. Article 7 of the Directive[54] provides that protection can be provided by the State or by 'parties or organisations, including international organisations, controlling the State or a substantial part of the territory of the State'. This language appears to cover the situation in the Kurdish Autonomous Region as well as that in Kosovo. However, the factual situations in which this issue arises will always be unusual, and it may be some time before there is another opportunity to test whether the law has in fact changed.

G. Causation—'For Reasons Of'

2.52 It is obvious from the terms of Article 1A(2) that the asylum seeker must demonstrate that the persecution that he fears is (or would be) caused by one or more of the five 'Convention reasons', namely race, religion, nationality,

---

[50] See *R (Bagdanavicius) v Home Secretary* at paras 24–25 per Lord Brown; see also paras 29–30 in respect of the Refugee Convention.

[51] See Regulation 4(2).

[52] *Canaj v Home Secretary* [2001] EWCA Civ 782, [2001] INLR 342, which is to be read with *R (Vallaj) v Special Adjudicator* [2001] INLR 455.

[53] *Gardi v Home Secretary* [2002] EWCA Civ 750, [2002] INLR 499. The actual decision was later nullified because the appeal should have been to the Scottish Court of Session rather than to the English Court of Appeal—see [2002] EWCA Civ 1560, [2002] INLR 557. But the Scottish Court of Session has adopted the reasoning of the Court of Appeal in a decision—*Saber v Home Secretary* [2003] ScotCS 360—which is now the subject of an appeal to the House of Lords.

[54] Transposed into Regulation 4.

membership of a particular social group, or political opinion. This is reflected by the Directive.[55]

In most asylum cases, the issue of causation does not present a separate problem. **2.53** To the extent that there is any causation issue, it is usually intimately bound up in examining the question whether any 'Convention reason' is relevant to the case, and therefore considered as a single issue alongside 'Convention reason'. However, there are special cases in which causation may have to be analyzed in some detail. Often, this is closely linked to problems about the identification of a relevant 'Convention reason', frequently the identification of a 'particular social group'.

The most frequently cited example of a causation problem is that of the 'Jewish **2.54** shopkeeper',[56] which has been used repeatedly by the courts to illustrate or test propositions relating to causation. The importance of the formula 'persecution = serious harm + the failure of State protection' is highlighted by this example. The harm caused to the Jewish shopkeeper was not caused by a Convention reason but by business rivalry and personal enmity. But the refusal by the State to protect and deter was based on a Convention reason. This was sufficient for the resultant persecution to be regarded as caused by a Convention reason.

This detailed analysis was necessary, because a simple 'but for' test was said to be **2.55** an oversimplification. An example of a situation where a 'but for' test would be satisfied is that of women who are particularly vulnerable to attack by marauding men during a time of civil unrest and disorder, because the attacks are sexually motivated or because the women are thought to be weaker and less able to defend themselves. But the government is unable to protect these women simply because its writ does not run in that part of the country. The government is therefore equally unable to protect men, and there is no discrimination between men and women in this regard. Although the women would not fear such attack 'but for' the fact that they are women, they are not being persecuted by reason of their sex; the 'but for' test is not enough to establish causation. However, the difference between this example and the case of wives in Pakistan fearing domestic violence[57] is not immediately obvious. The distinction appears to be that in the latter case, there was a discriminatory denial of protection by the State which withheld it from women. In contrast, even though the 'marauding men' are attacking women on a discriminatory basis in the former case, they are doing so when State

---

[55] See Regulation 5(3).
[56] See *ex parte Shah* [1999] 2 AC 629, 653G–654D per Lord Hoffmann.
[57] That is, the facts of the cases in *ex parte Shah*, in which Lord Hoffmann gave the example of the situation in which a 'but for' test is insufficient at 654F–H.

protection is not being discriminatorily denied to those women, as a non-functioning State is not providing protection to anyone.

2.56 These examples demonstrate why it can safely be said that when questions of causation arise that require such analysis, the difficulties that they (and their relationship with the relevant Convention reasons) pose are some of the most intractable and least comprehensible problems in relation to the Refugee Convention.

2.57 Sometimes, there may be more than one reason for the feared ill-treatment, and the reason may appear to be different depending on whose viewpoint it is seen from. The motives of those carrying out the ill-treatment may have nothing to do with any of the Convention reasons; conversely, the asylum seeker may have reasonable grounds for perceiving a discriminatory effect against him because of one of the Convention reasons. The House of Lords has suggested that these difficulties can be set aside if a simple test is adopted: What is the 'real cause' or the 'effective cause' of the ill-treatment? Is it one of the Convention reasons?[58]

H. Convention Reason

2.58 The Directive makes specific provision for the interpretation of some of the Convention reasons. So, for example, 'race' includes colour, descent, and membership of an ethnic group.[59] 'Religion' includes the holding of theistic, non-theistic, and atheistic beliefs, the participation in, or abstention from, formal worship in private or in public, either alone or in community with others, other religious acts or expressions of view, or forms of personal or communal conduct based on or mandated by any religious belief.[60] And 'nationality' is not confined to citizenship (or its lack) but includes, for example, membership of a group determined by its cultural, ethnic, or linguistic identity, common geographical or political origins, or its relationship with the population of another State.[61] The Directive also provides that the concept of political opinion includes the holding of an opinion, thought, or belief on a matter related to potential actors of persecution and to their policies or methods, whether or not that opinion, thought, or belief has been acted upon by the asylum seeker.[62]

2.59 The Directive also codifies the imputation principle. It has long been acknowledged that the protection of the Refugee Convention extends to an individual whose State persecutes those who hold a particular political opinion and which

---

[58] *Sepet v Home Secretary* at para 22 per Lord Bingham.
[59] Regulation 6(1)(a).
[60] Regulation 6(1)(b).
[61] Regulation 6(1)(c).
[62] Regulation 6(1)(f).

would wrongly believe that the individual holds that political opinion even if he does not. The political opinion wrongly imputed to the individual by the persecuting State is sufficient to allow the persecution to be regarded as caused by the Convention reason of 'political opinion'. The Directive now expressly provides that 'In deciding whether a person has a well-founded fear of being persecuted, it is immaterial whether he actually possesses the racial, religious, national, social or political characteristic which attracts the persecution, provided that such a characteristic is attributed to him by the actor of persecution'.[63] It is notable that this codification expressly applies the imputation principle to the other Convention reasons and is not limited to political opinion.

2.60 The Convention reason of political opinion may be linked to asylum claims based on a requirement to perform compulsory military service. However, the consequences of such a requirement have often been discussed without much express linkage to the Convention reason which may be applicable. Ordinarily, a universal requirement to perform compulsory military service, and the prospect of punishment for refusing to do so, cannot form the basis of an asylum claim. This is so even if the individual is a genuine conscientious objector to all forms of military service, or if he objects to performing certain kinds of military service on political grounds, because there is no internationally recognised right to object to performing military service on these grounds.[64] It appears that an individual might be able to claim refugee status on the basis of a requirement to perform military service only if such service would or might require him to commit atrocities or gross human rights abuses or participate in a conflict condemned by the international community.[65] It has also been suggested that a claim might be made if refusal to serve would earn grossly excessive or disproportionate punishment, but if excessive punishment would not be imposed on the asylum seeker on a basis which discriminates against him for one of the Convention reasons, it is difficult to see how it would amount to persecution for a Convention reason.

2.61 Political opinion has also sometimes been invoked by those who fear retribution for taking some action against violent or powerful criminals, sometimes individuals holding positions of State authority. But doing so will not necessarily result in the individual being regarded as holding a political opinion or having a political opinion imputed to him. The retribution may simply be by criminals

---

[63] Regulation 6(2).
[64] *Sepet v Home Secretary* [2003] 1 WLR 856 at para 20 per Lord Bingham.
[65] Para 8 per Lord Bingham, and see the decision of the Court of Appeal in *Krotov v Home Secretary* [2004] 1 WLR 1825.

against an individual who is able to cause them damage, perhaps by giving evidence about what they have witnessed.[66]

2.62 Difficulties about Convention reasons can arise in the context of civil war. It is obvious that the normal incidents of a civil war may bring a risk of serious ill-treatment, but this cannot itself found a claim to refugee status. This is so even if the civil war is clan based, the asylum seeker belongs to one clan, and the ill-treatment would be at the hands of an opposing clan; or if the civil war is being fought on political, religious, or racial grounds. It has been decided that in a state of civil war between clans, an asylum seeker must be able to show that he is at greater risk of ill-treatment than other members of his clan. There must be a 'differential impact' on him, in other words a fear of persecution for Convention reasons over and above the ordinary risks of clan warfare.[67]

2.63 The most difficult of the Convention reasons is 'membership of a particular social group'. It was introduced at a late stage of the drafting of the Refugee Convention, and the *travaux préparatoires* are uninformative.[68] Courts have experienced substantial difficulties in interpreting this phrase, and various approaches have been suggested over the years. But a number of general principles are clear.

2.64 First, this Convention reason must cover different ground from the other four, otherwise it would have no separate life and its inclusion in the list of Convention reasons would be meaningless. But it was not intended to be a catch-all provision allowing anyone who might suffer sufficiently severe ill-treatment to qualify as a refugee.[69] The existence of a limited list of Convention reasons shows that the Convention was not intended to protect everyone who might suffer ill-treatment. It would be wrong to regard 'particular social group' as 'an all-encompassing residual category'.[70]

2.65 Second, it has now been definitively decided that there is no requirement of 'cohesiveness, cooperation or interdependence', or of voluntary association.[71] Suggestions of such a requirement had in mind 'particular social groups' such as trade union activists, but it would exclude such groups as homosexuals or women which have now both been recognised as capable of constituting 'particular social groups', if circumstances in the asylum seeker's country warrant such a finding.

---

[66] See *Suarez v Home Secretary* [2002] 1 WLR 2663, which also demonstrates that where the criminals are not acting with State authority, the State may also be found to be providing sufficient protection for the asylum seeker so that he does not need refugee status.

[67] *Adan v Home Secretary* [1999] 1 AC 293, 308E–H and 311E–F per Lord Lloyd.

[68] See *ex parte Shah* at 638G–H per Lord Steyn and 650G per Lord Hoffmann.

[69] See *ex parte Shah* at 643B–C per Lord Steyn.

[70] See *ex parte Shah* at 643A–C per Lord Steyn.

[71] See *ex parte Shah* at 643F–G per Lord Steyn and 651G–652B per Lord Hoffmann.

Nevertheless, cohesiveness may evidence the existence of a 'particular social group'.[72]

Third, the remainder of the list of Convention reasons are common grounds on which individuals might be discriminated against.[73] Protection against unjustified discrimination is at the core of the protection afforded by the Refugee Convention. So any 'particular social group' must be one that is discriminated against by the society concerned. **2.66**

Fourth, the group must exist independently of, and not be defined by, the feared persecution, otherwise, circular reasoning would be involved when relying on the persecution to prove the existence of the 'particular social group'.[74] But a combination of the fact that a 'particular social group' may be identifiable because it is discriminated against, and the fact that all or some[75] members of that 'particular social group' are at risk of persecution because of their membership of it, does not in itself infringe this principle. The key question may be whether the members of the group share any characteristics other than the risk of persecution.[76] **2.67**

The Directive has also made an attempt to deal with this issue. As transposed it provides that: **2.68**

> a group shall be considered to form a particular social group where, for example,
> (i) members of that group share an innate characteristic, or a common background that cannot be changed, or share a characteristic or belief that is so fundamental to identity or conscience that a person should not be forced to renounce it, and
> (ii) that group has a distinct identity in the relevant country, because it is perceived as being different by the surrounding society.[77]

It also provides that:

> a particular social group might include a group based on a common characteristic of sexual orientation but sexual orientation cannot be understood to include acts considered to be criminal in accordance with national law of the United Kingdom.[78]

---

[72] See *ex parte Shah* at 643G per Lord Steyn.

[73] See *ex parte Shah* at 643A–B per Lord Steyn, 651A–F per Lord Hoffmann, and 656E–F per Lord Hope.

[74] See *ex parte Shah* at 639G–640B per Lord Steyn and 656G–H per Lord Hope.

[75] It is clear that the fact that some members of a 'particular social group' may not be at risk of persecution does not mean that those who are at risk of persecution cannot be at risk for reasons of their membership of that 'particular social group'— see, for example, *ex parte Shah* at 653H per Lord Hoffmann. But it must also be the case that if only some members of a 'particular social group' are at risk of persecution, questions could be asked as to whether they truly are at risk because of their membership of the 'particular social group', or whether they are at risk for some other 'real reason' or 'effective reason'.

[76] See *ex parte Shah* at 645C–E per Lord Steyn and 658A–D per Lord Hope, and *K v Home Secretary* [2007] 1 AC 412 at para 120 per Lord Brown.

[77] Regulation 6(d).

[78] Regulation 6(e).

However, the Regulations do not contain any text corresponding to the part of the Directive that provides that 'Gender related aspects might be considered, without by themselves alone creating a presumption for the applicability of this Article'.[79] It seems likely that this is because this part of Article 10(1)(d) is not as prescriptive in its language as the earlier parts, and does not require any specific legislative transposition beyond what the courts have decided in relation to gender-related persecution.

2.69   The question of whether and in what circumstances membership of a family can constitute the Convention reason of 'membership of a particular social group' has been troublesome. The family is obviously capable of being regarded as a social group.[80] The royal (Bourbon) family in France at the time of the French Revolution has frequently been cited as an example of a family whose members could be said to have had a well-founded fear of persecution for the Convention reason of 'membership of a particular social group'. But more difficulty is caused in situations where, for example, one individual suffers or fears serious ill-treatment for a plainly non-Convention reason, like resisting the demands of drug traffickers or other criminals, and other members of his family are similarly threatened simply because they are related to him. The Court of Appeal took the view that the family members were not being threatened for reasons of being members of his family and therefore not members of a 'particular social group'. This was a causation issue: the family members risked ill-treatment because of their connection with the first individual, not because of their membership of the family, as those making the threats might equally have decided to target business partners or employees of the first individual.[81] But the House of Lords has now disapproved this decision; in this situation, the family members could qualify as refugees because membership of the family was in fact the reason for the risk of persecution,[82] and it is not an unacceptable anomaly that the first individual does not qualify.[83]

2.70   It is also now established that women can constitute a 'particular social group'. This depends on the conditions in the asylum seeker's country. In a case concerning Pakistan, the House of Lords were divided about whether, on the evidence,

---

[79] The last part of Article 10(1)(d) of the Directive.

[80] For example, Article 23(1) of the ICCPR states that the family 'is the natural and fundamental group unit of society and is entitled to protection by society and the State'.

[81] *Quijano v Home Secretary* [1997] Imm AR 227.

[82] *K v Home Secretary* [2007] 1 AC 412, para 21 per Lord Bingham and paras 42–52 per Lord Hope.

[83] At para 45, Lord Hope said: 'The ties that bind members of a family together, whether by blood or by marriage, define the group. It is those ties that set it apart from the rest of society. Persecution of a person simply because he is a member of the same family as someone else is as arbitrary and capricious, and just as pernicious, as persecution for reasons of race or religion. As a social group the family falls naturally into the category of cases to which the Refugee Convention extends its protection.'

the 'particular social group' of which the asylum seekers were members was the group of 'women in Pakistan', against whom there was strong discrimination, tolerated by the state, to the extent that they were unprotected against the consequences of the allegations of infidelity made against them by their estranged husbands; or a narrower group described by the coincidence of three characteristics which set the appellants apart from the rest of society, namely their gender, the suspicion of adultery, and their unprotected status in Pakistan.[84] A similar difficulty arose in relation to Sierra Leone, in which most women suffer female genital mutilation but most undergo the procedure willingly as part of initiation into adulthood. None of the House of Lords rejected either a wider group of 'women in Sierra Leone', against whom there was widespread discrimination, or a narrower group of 'uninitiated intact women in Sierra Leone', who were the group at risk of persecution but who shared other common characteristics. But there was a division about which group was preferable, and why.[85]

Finally in this section, it is now recognised that homosexuals can also constitute a 'particular social group'. After Lord Steyn made a number of firmly stated obiter remarks[86] accepting the correctness of a New Zealand decision which accepted this proposition,[87] there has been no further challenge in the UK to the proposition.[88] The difficulties posed by asylum claims by homosexuals no longer concern whether they could constitute a 'particular social group', but rather tend to revolve around whether the ill-treatment that they might suffer would be sufficiently serious as to amount to persecution, particularly when judged against the degree to which they might suffer by exercising self-restraint or self-denial in order to avoid overt forms of ill-treatment.[89]   **2.71**

I. Internal Relocation

It has long been recognised, in relation to the Refugee Convention, that an individual who has a well-founded fear of persecution in the part of his country of origin in which he has his home is not a refugee if there is another part of the country to which he can go where he will be safe. Paragraph 91 of the UNHCR *Handbook* provided: **2.72**

> The fear of being persecuted need not always extend to the whole territory of the refugee's country of nationality. Thus in ethnic clashes or in cases of grave

---

[84] See *ex parte Shah* [1999] 2 AC 629.
[85] *K v Home Secretary* [2007] 1 AC 412, in which Lord Bingham and Lady Hale preferred the wider group and Lord Hope, Lord Rodger, and Lord Brown preferred the narrower group.
[86] *Ex parte Shah* at 643C–F.
[87] *In re G J* [1998] INLR 387.
[88] See *Jain v Home Secretary* [2000] Imm AR 76.
[89] *Amare v Home Secretary* [2006] Imm AR 217.

disturbances involving civil war conditions, persecution of a specific ethnic or national group may occur in only one part of the country. In such situations, a person will not be excluded from refugee status merely because he could have sought refuge in another part of the same country, if under all the circumstances it would not have been reasonable to expect him to do so.

2.73 The Court of Appeal has recognised that this approach is based on the principle that the Refugee Convention offers surrogate protection of an individual's human rights by the international community when his own country cannot afford him protection within its own frontiers. So if the home state can afford 'a safe haven', 'relocation', 'internal protection', or 'an internal flight alternative' where the claimant would not have a well-founded fear of persecution for a Convention reason, then international protection is not necessary.[90]

2.74 The Qualification Directive has now codified this principle in Article 8(1), which provides:

> As part of the assessment of the application for international protection, Member States may determine that an applicant is not in need of international protection if in a part of the country of origin there is no well-founded fear of being persecuted or no real risk of suffering serious harm and the applicant can reasonably be expected to stay in that part of the country.[91]

It is thus clear that the question of whether internal relocation is possible is part of the question of whether the individual is a refugee.[92]

2.75 As a matter of logic, there is no reason why this principle should not apply also to claims for protection under the European Convention on Human Rights. The Immigration Rules now contain at least partial recognition that this is so, as paragraph 339O also makes corresponding provision in relation to 'humanitarian protection', one of the vehicles by which ECHR protection is delivered. But as Refugee Convention and ECHR claims generally march hand-in-hand, it seems unlikely that there will be much separate case law specifically in relation to 'internal relocation' under the ECHR.

2.76 The 'internal relocation' principle has not been applied with all the rigour with which it might. For example, the Court of Appeal has pointed out that 'In theory it might be possible for someone to return to a desert region of his former country, populated only by camels and nomads'.[93] But it has been tempered with

---

90 *R v Home Secretary, ex parte Robinson* [1998] QB 929, 939D–H per Lord Woolf MR giving the judgment of the court. This principle is applicable only where the individual's home area is unsafe for him—see *Canaj v Home Secretary* [2001] INLR 342 at paras 30–33 per Simon Brown LJ.

91 Council Directive 2004/83/EC. Article 8 has been transposed into domestic law by para 339O of the Immigration Rules.

92 See *Robinson* at 941D–G and 942E–G.

93 See *Karanakaran v Home Secretary* [2000] 3 All ER 449, 456g–h per Brooke LJ.

'a small amount of humanity'.[94] For it to apply, it must be reasonable to expect the individual to move to and stay in that 'safe haven'. Various criteria have been suggested against which this can be assessed, including whether it is practicable to gain access to the safe haven, or whether there would be great physical danger or undue hardship in travelling there or staying there.[95] The general circumstances in the safe haven and the personal circumstances of the individual must be taken into account.[96]

A pithy test of Canadian origin has been approved by the Court of Appeal and has **2.77** become the most widely used encapsulation: Would it be 'unduly harsh' to expect the individual to move to the safe haven?[97] When setting out this test, the Canadian court observed that while individuals should not be compelled to cross battle lines or hide out in an isolated region of their country, like a cave in the mountains, a desert, or jungle, it would not be enough for them to say that they do not like the weather in a safe area, or that they have no friends or relatives there, or that they may not be able to find suitable work there. The test is a 'very rigorous' one.[98]

However, even though that test is capable of easy statement, its application has **2.78** not been free from difficulty. It is now clear that the question whether it would be 'unduly harsh' to relocate him to the safe haven is to be judged by comparing conditions in the individual's home area with conditions in the safe haven.[99] But, after considerable debate, a suggestion that consideration must be given to whether the quality of protection in the safe haven meets basic norms of civil, political, or socio-economic human rights has now been definitively rejected.[100] In doing so, the House of Lords has also commended, as guidance on the approach to reasonableness and undue harshness, the UNHCR Guidelines on International Protection No 4: 'Internal Flight or Relocation Alternative'.[101] In particular, Lord Bingham referred to the general question: 'Can the claimant, in the context of the country concerned, lead a relatively normal life without facing undue hardship?'[102]

---

[94] *Karanakaran v Home Secretary* [2000] 3 All ER 449, 456g per Brooke LJ.

[95] See *Robinson* at 940a–b per Brooke LJ.

[96] Article 8(2) of the Qualification Directive and paragraph 339O(ii) of the Immigration Rules.

[97] Taken from *Thirunavukkarasu v Canada* (1993) 109 DLR (4th) 682, 687 per Linden JA, approved in *ex parte Robinson* at 943C–D.

[98] See *Karanakaran v Home Secretary* [2000] 3 All ER 449, 456j per Brooke LJ.

[99] *E v Home Secretary* [2004] QB 531 at para 67.

[100] By the Court of Appeal in *E v Home Secretary* [2004] QB 531 at paras 38–39 and 64–67 per Simon Brown LJ, and by the House of Lords in *Januzi v Home Secretary* [2006] 2 AC 426 at paras 15–20 per Lord Bingham, para 45 per Lord Hope; and para 67 per Lord Carswell.

[101] Published on 23 July 2003—see *Januzi v Home Secretary* [2006] 2 AC 426, para 20 per Lord Bingham.

[102] Paragraph 7(ii)(a) of the Guidelines. Attention was also drawn to paras 28 and 29.

2.79 Complicated questions of the burden and standard of proof in relation to 'internal relocation' have from time to time been raised. But because 'internal relocation' is part of the question of whether the individual is a refugee, it is clear that a conventional approach can be taken. If possible 'internal relocation' is an issue, the asylum seeker must show that it is not a viable option for him. The assessment of safety in any putative 'safe haven' can be carried out on conventional lines.

2.80 The most complex questions have been suggested in relation to the question of reasonableness. For example, the test 'Is there a serious possibility that it would be unduly harsh to relocate him to the safe haven?' has been proposed. But it has been decided that this question should be approached as a single simple question: 'Would it be unduly harsh to relocate him to the safe haven?'[103]

2.81 All this has led the Court of Appeal now to be able to distil five propositions as guidance:

(a) The starting point must be conditions prevailing in the place of habitual residence.

(b) Those conditions must be compared with the conditions prevailing in the safe haven.

(c) The latter conditions must be assessed according to the impact that they will have on a person with the characteristics of the asylum seeker.

(d) If under those conditions the asylum seeker cannot live a relatively normal life according to the standards of his country, it will be unduly harsh to expect him to go to the safe haven.

(e) Traumatic changes of lifestyle, for instance from a city to a desert, or into slum conditions, should not be forced on the asylum seeker.[104]

2.82 If care is not taken, there is a risk of confusion between concepts relating to 'internal relocation' and similar but distinct questions arising from the practicalities of returning an individual to his country of origin if he is not a refugee. By definition, the asylum seeker whose asylum claim is under consideration is not then taking advantage of any 'internal relocation' option available to him in his country of origin. But the availability of such an option means that he is not a refugee, even if (for example) he cannot at that time be returned to the safe haven for reasons that do not affect its safety or the reasonableness of a relocation there.[105] It is therefore important, when considering whether the individual is a refugee, to address the issues that properly relate to 'internal relocation'.

---

[103] See *Karanakaran* at 470d–e per Brooke LJ.

[104] *AH (Sudan) v Home Secretary* [2007] EWCA Civ 297 at para 33.

[105] As is made clear by Article 8(3) of the Qualification Directive and rule 339O(iii) of the Immigration Rules.

J. Article 1C—Cessation

A person who is a refugee at one point in time may not necessarily require protec- **2.83**
tion for ever. One of the constants in life is change. Circumstances may change
so that a person who once needed protection no longer requires it. Article 1C
specifies a number of circumstances in which a refugee ceases to be a refugee,
namely:

(1) He has voluntarily re-availed himself of the protection of the country of his
    nationality; or
(2) Having lost his nationality, he has voluntarily re-acquired it; or
(3) He has acquired a new nationality, and enjoys the protection of the country of
    his new nationality; or
(4) He has voluntarily re-established himself in the country which he left or outside
    which he remained owing to fear of persecution; or
(5) He can no longer, because the circumstances in connection with which he has
    been recognized as a refugee have ceased to exist, continue to refuse to avail
    himself of the protection of the country of his nationality;
Provided that this paragraph shall not apply to a refugee falling under section A(1)
of this article who is able to invoke compelling reasons arising out of previous persecution for refusing to avail himself of the protection of the country of nationality;
(6) Being a person who has no nationality he is, because the circumstances in con-
    nection with which he has been recognized as a refugee have ceased to exist, able
    to return to the country of his former habitual residence;
Provided that this paragraph shall not apply to a refugee falling under section A(1)
of this article who is able to invoke compelling reasons arising out of previous persecution for refusing to return to the country of his former habitual residence.[106]

The House of Lords considers that Article 1C(5) applies only to an individual **2.84**
who has already been formally recognised as a refugee.[107] But its reasoning does
not appear to be capable of being limited to Article 1C(5) (and the similarly
worded Article 1C(6))—it is likely to apply to all of the situations encompassed
in Article 1C. If any of these situations applies to an individual, he is excluded
from the benefit of the whole of the Convention because the Convention simply
ceases to apply to him. As well as being described as an exclusion clause, this
Article is often referred to as the cessation clause, for obvious reasons. But the
potential effect on the individual of the operation of this clause means that it
should be used only if there is demonstrably good and sufficient reason.[108]

---

[106] Article 1C is effectively reproduced in Article 11(1) of the Directive, but this has not been
transposed.
[107] *R (Hoxha) v Special Adjudicator* [2005] 1 WLR 1063 at paras 60–67 per Lord Brown.
[108] See *Hoxha* at para 65 per Lord Brown.

2.85   The first four situations reflect the underlying purpose of the Refugee Convention, which is to provide surrogate protection for basic human rights to those whose own countries cannot or will not provide such protection. If the individual has voluntarily re-availed himself of the protection of his own country, or has voluntarily acquired the protection of another country by becoming its national, then he has no further need for the surrogate protection provided by the Refugee Convention.

2.86   Of course, care should be taken to ensure that the individual has genuinely re-acquired the protection of that country. Formal acts, such as applying for a passport renewal or obtaining an official document such as a birth certificate, may not amount to re-acquisition. Similarly, a brief visit by the individual to his country of origin in exceptional circumstances may not amount to re-establishment; a necessary visit to a sick relative may not be inconsistent with a continuing and well-founded fear of persecution in the country of origin.

2.87   The last two situations[109] may raise more difficulty, because they exclude an individual from the benefits of the Convention when an objective appraisal of the circumstances in his own country shows that he no longer needs surrogate protection, even if the individual himself continues to consider that he does require it or is otherwise unwilling to return to his own country. The *Handbook* and the *Guidelines* suggest that the change of circumstances causing the loss of refugee status must be fundamental and not merely transitory,[110] and that the change should apply across the entire territory of the refugee's own country. As at the beginning of 2005, the United Kingdom had only ever invoked Article 1C(5) on one occasion to remove a previously recognised refugee.[111] It remains to be seen whether Article 1C(5) is relied on to any greater extent in the future, in the light of the domestic statutory provisions which have now been expressly made to withdraw the benefits of refugee status from individuals in respect of whom the cessation clause has operated.

2.88   Articles 1C(5) and (6) (which relate respectively to individuals who have a nationality and individuals who do not) each contain a proviso, which excludes the cessation effect of Articles 1C(5) and (6) from those who fall within the terms of the proviso. It has now been established that the proviso applies only to 'statutory refugees' falling within Article 1A(1), as the terms of the provisos suggest.[112]

---

[109]   These situations are discussed in the UNHCR's *Guidelines on International Protection No. 3: Cessation of Refugee Status under Article 1C(5) and (6)*.

[110]   This is reflected in Article 11(2) of the Directive, which has not been transposed.

[111]   See *Hoxha* at para 84 per Lord Brown.

[112]   See *Hoxha* at paras 67–85 per Lord Brown.

K. Article 1D—UNRWA

At the date of the signing of the Refugee Convention, on 28 July 1951, a substan- **2.89** tial number of individuals were already receiving protection and assistance from organs and agencies of the United Nations other than the UNHCR. Article 1D excludes these individuals from the benefit of the Refugee Convention, but with a proviso that if and when that protection ceases, then those individuals are automatically entitled to the benefits of refugee status under the Refugee Convention:

> This Convention shall not apply to persons who are at present receiving from organs or agencies of the United Nations other than the United Nations High Commissioner for Refugees protection or assistance.
>
> When such protection or assistance has ceased for any reason, without the position of such persons being definitively settled in accordance with the relevant resolutions adopted by the General Assembly of the United Nations, these persons shall ipso facto be entitled to the benefits of this Convention.[113]

There was a possibility that this proviso, with its automatic conferment of the **2.90** benefits of refugee status, might be invoked by many individuals claiming to have been receiving some protection and assistance from other United Nations organs or agencies. However, it has now been established that in practice Article 1D applies only to those who were registered as receiving assistance from the United Nations Relief and Works Agency (UNRWA) on that date. Everyone else must establish their entitlement to refugee status in the usual way under Article 1A(2).[114]

L. Article 1F—Exclusion of Undeserving Individuals

Article 1F excludes individuals who, for one reason or another, do not deserve **2.91** refugee status for reasons of their personal conduct, even if they might other- wise satisfy the definition of refugee. Common to all three situations covered by Article 1F is a low standard of proof: the Convention does not apply if 'there are serious reasons for considering that' the individual has committed acts of the type mentioned. Further, exclusion is mandatory; the words used are that the provi- sions of the Convention 'shall not apply' to such individuals.[115] And there is no

---

[113] The Directive effectively sets out in full the provisions of Articles 1D, 1E, and 1F, but the Regulations merely refer to those clauses when providing that a person is not a refugee if he falls within them—see Regulation 7(1).

[114] *El-Ali v Home Secretary* [2003] 1 WLR 95.

[115] See the decisions of the Immigration Appeal Tribunal in *Gurung v Home Secretary* [2003] INLR 133 and *KK v Home Secretary* [2005] INLR 124. In *Gurung*, the Tribunal gave general guid- ance on the proper approach to exclusion under Article 1F.

question of balancing the gravity of the crimes committed against the likely danger to the individual if he is returned to his own country.[116] It is also important to note that Article 1F(b) expressly includes both geographical and temporal limits on the acts which might serve to exclude the individual from the protection of the Convention, but Articles 1F(a) and 1F(c) contain no such limits.

2.92 Article 1F(a) excludes those who have committed a crime against peace, a war crime, or a crime against humanity, as defined in the international instruments drawn up to make provision in respect of such crimes. These are listed in Annex VI of the *Handbook*. There have been few United Kingdom cases involving Article 1F(a), but more appear in the Australian and Canadian jurisprudence.

2.93 Article 1F(b) excludes those who have committed a serious non-political crime outside the country of refuge prior to admission to that country as a refugee. The distinction between political and non-political crimes is liable to give rise to difficulty in this context as much as in extradition cases. The House of Lords has given guidance in the context of a terrorist act committed by the individual in his own country before arriving in the United Kingdom.[117] Lord Lloyd (with whom Lord Keith and Lord Browne-Wilkinson agreed) considered that a political crime had to be sufficiently closely and directly linked to the political purpose and not too remote from it. Regard had to be had to the means used to achieve the political end, in particular whether the crime was aimed at a military or governmental target on the one hand or a civilian target on the other. In either event regard had to be had as to whether it was likely to involve the indiscriminate killing or injuring of members of the public.[118]

2.94 Article 1F(c) excludes those who have committed acts contrary to the purposes and principles of the United Nations. This part of Article 1F has received renewed attention in the last decade, particularly because of the upsurge in international terrorism. The purposes and principles of the United Nations are set out in Articles 1 and 2 of its Charter. However, the list is not of much assistance in deciding whether a particular type of act is or is not to be regarded as contrary to the purposes and principles of the United Nations.

2.95 In Canada, the Supreme Court has rejected the argument that drug trafficking is contrary to the purposes and principles of the United Nations.[119] The majority of the court considered that 'the purpose of Article 1F(c) can be characterized in the

---

[116] See s 34(1) of the Anti-Terrorism, Crime and Security Act 2001.

[117] *T v Immigration Officer* [1996] AC 742.

[118] The Directive appears to add a gloss to this guidance, in providing that 'particularly cruel actions, even if committed with an allegedly political objective, may be classified as serious non-political crimes'—see Article 12(2)(b), which has been transposed into Regulation 7(2)(a).

[119] *Pushpanathan v Canada (Minister of Citizenship and Immigration)* [1998] 1 SCR 982.

following terms: to exclude those individuals responsible for serious, sustained or systemic violations of fundamental human rights which amount to persecution in a non-war setting'.[120] But there were no international law materials indicating that drug trafficking was contrary to the purposes and principles of the United Nations,[121] and there was 'simply no indication that the drug trafficking comes close to the core, or even forms a part of the corpus of fundamental human rights'.[122]

But it is now well established in the United Kingdom that terrorism is contrary to the purposes and principles of the United Nations.[123] In contrast to the provisions relating to drug trafficking, United Nations materials relating to terrorism repeatedly use formulae such as 'Acts, methods and practices of terrorism constitute a grave violation of the purposes and principles of the United Nations, which may pose a threat to international peace and security, jeopardize friendly relations among States, hinder international cooperation and aim at the destruction of human rights, fundamental freedoms and the democratic bases of society'.[124] It has also been established that Article 1F(c) is not concerned only with individuals holding some position of authority within a State or otherwise acting on behalf of a State, and that acts may fall within Article 1F(c) even if they were purportedly committed for political reasons or in purported pursuance of a right of self-determination.[125] In the case of a person connected with terrorism, Article 1F(c) may operate against him after he has been formally recognised as a

2.96

---

[120] See para 64.

[121] See para 69.

[122] See para 72. The court was prepared to consider finding, as a 'category of acts which fall within the scope of Article 1F(c) [. . .] those which a court is able, for itself, to characterize as serious, sustained and systemic violations of fundamental human rights constituting persecution. . . . Where the rule which has been violated is very near the core of the most valued principles of human rights and is recognized as immediately subject to international condemnation and punishment, then even an isolated violation could lead to an exclusion under Article 1F(c). The status of a violated rule as a universal jurisdiction offence would be a compelling indication that even an isolated violation constitutes persecution'—see para 70.

[123] *Singh and Singh v Home Secretary* (SIAC, 31 July 2000, unreported) and *KK v Home Secretary* [2005] INLR 124.

[124] Para 2 of the Declaration on Measures to Eliminate International Terrorism, United Nations General Assembly resolution 49/60 (1994). At para 68 of *Pushpanathan*, the Canadian Supreme Court noted this feature of such materials, and contrasted this with the position relating to drug trafficking.

[125] *Singh and Singh v Home Secretary* (SIAC, 31 July 2000, unreported) and *KK v Home Secretary* [2005] INLR 124. At para 68 of *Pushpanathan*, the Canadian Supreme Court had said: 'Although it may be more difficult for a non-state actor to perpetrate human rights violations on a scale amounting to persecution without the state thereby implicitly adopting those acts, the possibility should not be excluded *a priori*. As mentioned earlier, the Court must also take into consideration that some crimes that have specifically been declared to contravene the purposes and principles of the United Nations are not restricted to state actors.'

refugee in ignorance of that connection,[126] or where his connection with terrorism post-dates formal recognition as a refugee.[127]

M. Practice and Procedure Note

2.97   *Assembling the claim*   At the outset, practitioners should aim to assemble a clear and coherent account of the claimant's reasons for seeking protection. This may not be an easy task, particularly if there are language difficulties, if the claimant is traumatized and unwilling to discuss matters with his representatives, or if there are time pressures. But if a full and comprehensible account is presented at the beginning, and it is consistently related, there will be less scope for suggestions that the account has developed between successive occasions on which it was told.

2.98   *Credibility*   It is important to try to avoid giving the impression that the account has developed, because the central issue in many, if not most, claims is the question of whether the claimant is credible. A story that changes, or becomes fuller, each time it is told is the type of story that is liable to be disbelieved on the grounds that those changes indicate that the claimant is making it up as he goes along. This is particularly so if the changes appear to have been produced to deal with particular lines of probing questioning at an earlier stage of the claim, or if the new parts of the account could reasonably have been expected to have been recalled earlier by the claimant and there is no reason why he did not remember them at the outset. An asylum policy instruction on credibility indicates the types of approach and analysis that may be taken when assessing credibility.[128]

2.99   *Testing the claimant's account*   It is therefore a vital part of the practitioner's task to test the account that the claimant is giving, preferably in advance of any interviews— and certainly before the substantive asylum interview. As always when taking instructions from a client, the practitioner should be asking himself: What is missing from this story? Where are the gaps? What has not yet been explained clearly? Are there any areas of muddle in the story? When the claimant describes his reaction to an

---

[126]   *C v Home Secretary* (SIAC, 29 October 2003, unreported).

[127]   *Y v Home Secretary* (SIAC, 24 August 2006, unreported) and *Othman v Home Secretary* (SIAC, 26 February 2007, unreported). In these decisions, SIAC doubted the correctness of the argument, based on a dictum in *Pushpanathan*, that acts falling within Article 1F(c) but committed after formal recognition of refugee status cannot be taken into account under Article 1F(c) and can only be taken into account under Article 33(2). This view has now been affirmed by the Court of Appeal in *MT (Algeria) & Ors v Home Secretary* [2007] EWCA Civ 808 (which included the appeal from *Y v Home Secretary*).

[128]   <http://www.ind.homeoffice.gov.uk/documents/asylumpolicyinstructions/apis/credibility.pdf?view=Binary>

event or a situation, was that a reasonable reaction? Would a reasonable person have done what the claimant says he did? If not, or if that is unclear, why did he do what he did? The practitioner should not be shy of 'shaking the tree' in this way, and if necessary, doing so firmly. It is better that any difficulties are made apparent at this stage, than that the claimant is left exposed to similar questioning for the first time during the substantive asylum interview. It should be remembered that the claimant's account, for these purposes, includes the whole of the journey to the United Kingdom and the way in which the claim for protection was first made; implausibilities in the route of escape or in the account of the journey to this country can undermine the credibility of the entire account.

Supporting evidence   The claimant's account may suggest points on which support- **2.100** ing evidence might be capable of being obtained. The practitioner should always be asking himself: Might there be a document that evidences this part of the account? Does the claimant know whether or not there is one? Who is likely to have any such documents? Can they be sent to the United Kingdom? But the practitioner should also be alive to the possibility that such documentary support is not genuine. Is it reasonable for the person who is said to have such a document actually to have possession of it? Where did that document come from? How did that person get hold of it? For example, a claimant might say that he is wanted by the police, and that there is an arrest warrant to demonstrate that. But who has possession of it? Why would that person have the arrest warrant, or a copy of it? Where did that person get it from? Cogent answers to these questions may help to avoid the suggestion that the documentary evidence is a fabrication, because the person who has possession of it would not be in a position to hold the genuine article.

Independent reporting   Sometimes, a claimant's account will give rise to the possi- **2.101** bility that the events he describes have been independently reported, for example in a local newspaper. Practitioners should always consider this possibility, and should ask whether any such reports can be obtained. But again, there is always the possibility that what is proffered is not genuine. Consideration must be given to the form in which any such report is produced. Production of an original newspaper, for example, means that it is less likely to be the subject of an allegation that it has been forged; photocopies of a purported newspaper, however, may be the subject of such a contention—and some forgeries have been detected when the alleged 'newspaper' is unknown to reliable sources or the photocopies produced in support of the claim do not match the style or layout of the real newspaper from which the report was said to have come.

Expert evidence   Practitioners should also be alive to the possible need to obtain **2.102** expert evidence to support a claim. This will not be necessary or justifiable in many cases, particularly given the limits of what an expert can properly contribute to the process. In addition, some of the experts who regularly assist claimants are not genuinely independent but bring an obvious point of view to bear on all that they say. Although a claimant might perceive such an 'expert' to have a superficial appeal, experienced practitioners will know that this approach can be positively harmful to the client, especially if expert evidence was not really needed in any event and the 'expert' is simply trying to add more eggs to the pudding. But there are situations in which an expert may well be genuinely needed—for example, if the claimant's claim is unusual and the generally available background country information does not properly cover the area relevant to the claim. Even then, the claimant may be best assisted if the chosen expert is given a well-defined brief to work to; if the instructions are too diffuse, the expert may be tempted to trespass into areas where he should not go.

2.103 *Legal analysis* It is also important that practitioners bring their legal expertise to bear on the case. When the claimant's account is analyzed, from whom does he really fear persecution or ill-treatment? Is there more than one claimed source of ill-treatment? If so, do these need to be considered separately, almost as separate claims arising out of the same factual account? What persecution or ill-treatment does the claimant fear? How severe is it? How likely is it to occur? As far as any Refugee Convention claim is concerned, does the claim fall within one of the Convention reasons?

2.104 *Home Office policy instructions* It will also be useful for the practitioner to have an eye on the Home Office's policy instructions on dealing with claims, most importantly that concerning the assessment of the asylum claim.[129] Also, in a case in which gender issues may be relevant, the relevant instruction may help in the presentation of the claim.[130]

2.105 *Home Office country information* The Home Office regularly publishes reports on the countries from which most asylum seekers come to the UK.[131] These reports are intended to be a neutral collection of (for the most part) publicly available information about the country, organised into a coherent and consistent structure. The information is sourced, so that the original source can be checked; the report is as much as anything a collection of signposts to the underlying evidence that is available. In addition, country-specific asylum policy is published from time to time in respect of countries which warrant the formulation of policy, in the form of Operational Guidance

---

[129] <http://www.ind.homeoffice.gov.uk/documents/asylumpolicyinstructions/apis/assessingtheclaim.pdf?view=Binary>

[130] <http://www.ind.homeoffice.gov.uk/documents/asylumpolicyinstructions/apis/genderissueintheasylum.pdf?view=Binary>

[131] <http://www.homeoffice.gov.uk/rds/country_reports.html>

Notes[132] and Country Policy Bulletins.[133] These are useful documents, because they often form a large part of the information before caseworkers when making decisions on claims. (They are often also the core of the country evidence in an appeal hearing.)

Other sources of guidance and evidence Other guidance, and more general back-   **2.106**
ground information, can be obtained from a number of well-known sources. The publications side of the website of the United Nations High Commissioner for Refugees is one good source and has a good search engine which will reveal both policy documents and factual and evidential material.[134] The State Department of the United States publishes an annual human rights report, which includes a section in relation to every country.[135] But before being lured into the detail of the report about the claimant's country, it is often instructive first to read the report about the United Kingdom, which gives a flavour of the way in which these reports use language to describe everyday events. Other organisations whose reports are frequently relied on include Amnesty International[136] and Human Rights Watch,[137] both of which publish annual and other reports.

---

[132] <http://www.ind.homeoffice.gov.uk/documents/countryspecificasylumpolicyogns/>
[133] <http://www.ind.homeoffice.gov.uk/documents/countryspecificpolicybulletins/>
[134] <http://www.unhcr.org/publ.html>
[135] <http://www.state.gov/g/drl/rls/hrrpt/>
[136] <http://web.amnesty.org/library/engindex>
[137] <http://www.hrw.org/countries.html>

3

ARTICLE 3 OF THE EUROPEAN CONVENTION ON HUMAN RIGHTS (PROHIBITION OF TORTURE AND INHUMAN OR DEGRADING TREATMENT)

A. Application of the Convention by the Domestic Courts and the Use of Strasbourg Jurisprudence

3.01 Under section 6(1) of the Human Rights Act 1998 (HRA), it is unlawful for a public authority to act in a way which is incompatible with a right protected under the European Convention on Human Rights, as translated into domestic law rights by the HRA. The translated Convention provisions are Article 2 (right to life), Article 3 (prohibition of torture), Article 4 (prohibition of slavery and forced labour), Article 5 (right to liberty and security), Article 6 (right to a fair trial), Article 7 (no punishment without law), Article 8 (right to respect for private and family life), Article 9 (freedom of thought, conscience, and religion), Article 10 (freedom of expression), Article 11 (freedom of assembly and association), Article 12 (right to marry), Article 14 (prohibition of discrimination), as well as Articles 16 to 18 and parts of the First and Sixth Protocols, which are less relevant in the immigration context.

3.02 Without a doubt, the Articles of greatest interest to immigration and asylum practitioners are Articles 3 and 8, due to their wide scope of potential applicability. For example, it is difficult to conceive of an asylum claim where it would not be appropriate to consider whether the immigration decision to expel the applicant would also be contrary to Article 3. This chapter examines the many varied situations in which Article 3 claims arise, and reviews the extensive domestic jurisprudence which has grown rapidly since the introduction of the HRA and has refined the exact limits to such protection. The most significant aspects of Article 8 in the context of asylum claims will be examined in Chapter 4. Again this is an area of great judicial activity, with an ever expanding level of complexity, in particular with regard to the margin of discretion allowed to the original decision maker in balancing the right to family and private life against other interests justifying the interference with such rights, and the intensity of the judicial oversight into this original decision. By contrast, the domestic jurisprudence in relation to other ECHR Articles is less well developed. The main reasons for this, together with an analysis of the available domestic and European Court of Human

Rights (ECtHR) case law on other Articles of relevance to asylum cases, will be the subjects of Chapter 5.

The duty not to act incompatibly with the ECHR rests on public authorities. **3.03**
A 'public authority' under the HRA includes a court or tribunal[1] and 'any person certain of whose functions are functions of a public nature'.[2] Immigration officers, who take immigration decisions such as refusals of leave to enter, removal directions, and immigration detention decisions, as well as the Secretary of State in making immigration decisions and decisions to refuse asylum; are clear examples of public authorities caught by the HRA provisions. The Courts and the Asylum and Immigration Tribunal (AIT) would similarly have a duty under section 6(1) of the HRA to act compatibly with protected ECHR rights.

Additionally, section 3 of the HRA mandates that so far as it is possible to do so, **3.04**
primary and subordinate legislation must be read and given effect in a way which is compatible with ECHR rights. If the legislation does not permit such an interpretation, then the High Court and higher courts may make a declaration of incompatibility.[3] However, such declaration does not invalidate the legislative provision challenged and is not binding on the parties to the proceedings.[4] Whilst practitioners may seek to challenge asylum legislation,[5] in particular the statutory instruments seeking to implement such legislation, the focus of this chapter relates to the much more common challenges to individual immigration decisions, accompanying a refusal of asylum.

Duty to take Strasbourg case law into account

Courts and the AIT are bound by section 2(1) of the HRA to take into account **3.05**
judgments, decisions, declarations, or advisory opinions of the European Court of Human Rights. The much more restricted appeals structure introduced by the Asylum and Immigration Act 2004 (AIA) underlines the importance of practitioners preparing detailed and comprehensive skeleton arguments, written submissions, or grounds of appeal. In assisting the Courts and the AIT in fulfilment of the duty to take Strasbourg jurisprudence into account, practitioners

---

[1] HRA s 6(3)(a).

[2] HRA s 6(3)(b), but see s 6(3), (4), and (5) for certain limitations (if the public nature functions, but the nature of the act complained of being private; and Houses of Parliament, save for the House of Lords exercising its judicial functions).

[3] HRA s 4.

[4] HRA s 4(6).

[5] See, for example, *Javad Nasseri v SSHD* [2007] EWHC 1548 (Admin) QBD (Admin), which declared the provisions of the Asylum and Immigration (Treatment of Claimants, etc) Act 2004 Schedule 3 paragraph 3 incompatible with Article 3, because they operated to prevent the Secretary of State or the Court from investigating a potential breach of Article 3.

and Presenting Officers alike should be aware of the scope of such duty. In relation to this question Lord Bingham in *R (Ullah) v Special Adjudicator* [2004] 2 AC 323, 350, para 20, held:

> In determining the present question, the House is required by section 2(1) of the Human Rights Act 1998 to take into account any relevant Strasbourg case law. While such case law is not strictly binding, it has been held that courts should, in the absence of some special circumstances, follow any clear and constant jurisprudence of the Strasbourg court: *R (Alconbury Developments Ltd) v Secretary of State for the Environment, Transport and the Regions* [2003] 2 AC 295, para 26. This reflects the fact that the Convention is an international instrument, the correct interpretation of which can be authoritatively expounded only by the Strasbourg court. From this it follows that a national court subject to a duty such as that imposed by section 2 should not without strong reason dilute or weaken the effect of the Strasbourg case law. It is indeed unlawful under section 6 of the 1998 Act for a public authority, including a court, to act in a way which is incompatible with a Convention right. It is of course open to member states to provide for rights more generous than those guaranteed by the Convention, but such provision should not be the product of interpretation of the Convention by national courts, since the meaning of the Convention should be uniform throughout the states party to it. The duty of national courts is to keep pace with the Strasbourg jurisprudence as it evolves over time: no more, but certainly no less.

Limitations on expansive interpretation

3.06   Thus, in pursuing their interpretative obligations, the Courts and the AIT must not stray into the realm of an expansive interpretation of ECHR rights, beyond that established in the jurisprudence of the ECtHR. In particular the House of Lords in another case (*N (FC) v SSHD* [2005] UKHL 31, (2005) 2 WLR 1124) cautioned against too liberal an approach to the interpretation of the Convention so as to enlarge its express obligations on humanitarian principles. The Convention is a living instrument, but enlargement of the scope in its application in one contracting state is an enlargement for all other signatory states. Therefore the Courts must always consider whether the enlargement of the express terms of the Convention through interpretation is one which the contracting parties would have accepted and agreed to be bound by. In *N(FC) v SSHD* Lord Hope cited with approval the following passage from the speech of Lord Bingham of Cornhill in *Brown v Stott* [2003] 1 AC 681, 703:

> The language of the Convention is for the most part so general that some implication of terms is necessary, and the case law of the European Court shows that the court has been willing to imply terms into the Convention when it was judged necessary or plainly right to do so. But the process of implication is one to be carried out with caution, if the risk is to be averted that the contracting parties may, by judicial interpretation, become bound by obligations which they did not expressly accept and might not have been willing to accept.

Bearing in mind the above general principles, perhaps the most important issue **3.07** for decision makers, be they primary or at appellate level, and hence for practitioners presenting cases, concerns the level of proof in establishing that a decision would breach ECHR Article 3 rights. In the asylum context Article 3 claims are likely to involve prospective breaches. Further, they are likely to occur through the act of returning the applicant to another country where he would be at risk of treatment prohibited by Article 3. Such receiving State would usually not be a party to the ECHR. Additionally the applicable test has been subject to refinement due to a further level of complexity arising in cases where the inhuman treatment is not inflicted by State agents of the receiving State but by non-State actors. These matters are considered in detail in the section below.

B. Article 3 and Burden and Standard of Proof

Article 3 of the European Convention on Human Rights states: **3.08**

> No one shall be subjected to torture or to inhuman or degrading treatment or punishment.

This right is absolute, there are no qualifications to it, and States may not dero- **3.09** gate from it on national security[6] or other grounds. Thus in cases of deportation or removal of suspected terrorists, the protection afforded by Article 3 is wider than that provided by the Refugee Convention. The activities of the individual in question, however undesirable or dangerous, have been held to be an irrelevant consideration.[7]

Limitations on a State's sovereign right to control entry

Under international law a State has the right to control the entry and exit of for- **3.10** eign nationals into and out of its territory. However, a State party to the European Convention on Human Rights is taken to have agreed to restrict the free exercise of this right to control entry and exit to the extent of the obligations accepted by that State under the ECHR. In the international law context this springs from the obligation under Article 1 of the ECHR to 'secure to everyone within [the signatory state's] jurisdiction the rights and freedoms defined in Section I of this Convention'. By expelling an individual to another State, the act of removal is regarded as an event which engages the responsibility of the expelling State for the foreseeable consequences of ill-treatment in the receiving State.[8] The same

---

[6] Under ECHR art 15.

[7] See *Chahal v United Kingdom* (1997) 23 EHRR 413. The ECtHR has been asked to revisit this question of balance in the case of *NS v Italy* argued in July 2007.

[8] See *Pretty v UK* (2002) 35 EHRR 1, para 53—the relevant treatment is the act of expulsion.

applies in cases where the removal is not directly to the State where Article 3 ill-treatment is likely to occur but to another State, even if that other State is an ECHR signatory, from where the applicant might yet be expelled.[9]

Distinction between foreign and domestic cases

3.11 The House of Lords in *Ullah v SSHD* [2004] UKHL26, [2004] 2AC 323 drew a distinction between 'foreign' and 'domestic' cases. Challenges to immigration decisions are usually characterized as 'foreign cases' as the violation of the Convention complained of does not arise from the State infringing the claimant's ECHR rights within its own territory but in removing the claimant to another territory, which gives rise to the risk of ill-treatment in that other territory.[10]

3.12 The House of Lords confirmed that possible reliance in foreign cases on ECHR Articles 2, 4, 5, 6, 7, and 8 could not be ruled out in the light of the current state of Strasbourg jurisprudence. However, it was hard to think that a person could successfully resist expulsion in reliance on Article 9 (freedom of thought, conscience, and religion), on which the appeals before the House were founded, without that person being entitled either to asylum on the ground of a well-founded fear of persecution for reasons of religion, or being able to resist expulsion in reliance on Article 3. Therefore, although there remained the possibility in principle that expulsion may be restrained on Article 9 grounds, the main focus in most cases would remain on Article 3.

Standard of proof in foreign cases

3.13 In cases where the claimant alleges that his expulsion to another territory would violate his ECHR Article 3 rights on the grounds of a risk of ill-treatment at the hands of the receiving State, the standard of proof is whether 'substantial grounds have been shown for believing in the existence of a real risk of treatment contrary to Article 3' (see *Soering v United Kingdom* (1989) 11 EHRR 439 para 91, *Cruz Varas v Sweden* (1991) 14 EHRR 1 para 75 and 82, *Vilvarajah v United Kingdom* (1992) 14 EHRR 248 para 103). In *Chahal v United Kingdom* (1997) 23 EHRR 413 para 80 the ECt used slightly different language to the same effect:

> The prohibition provided by Article 3 against ill-treatment is equally absolute in expulsion cases. Thus, whenever substantial grounds have been shown for believing that an individual would face a real risk of being subjected to treatment contrary to Article 3 if removed to another State, the responsibility of the Contracting State to

---

[9] See *TI v UK* [2000] INLR 211.

[10] For an unusual example of a 'domestic case' with regard to the actions of British forces in a military detention facility abroad see *R (on the appln of Al-Skeini & Ors) v SSHD* [2007] UKHL 26. The House of Lords held that s 6 of the HRA should be interpreted as applying not only when a public authority acted within the UK but also when it acted within the jurisdiction of the UK for the purposes of ECHR Article 1, even if outside the physical territory of the UK.

safeguard him or her against such treatment is engaged in the event of expulsion (see [*Vilvarajah v United Kingdom* (1991) 14 EHRR 248 at] para 103). In these circumstances, the activities of the individual in question, however undesirable or dangerous, cannot be a material consideration.

This test has been adopted by the domestic courts, although formulated slightly differently:

> In relation to Article 3, it is necessary to show strong grounds for believing that the person, if returned, faces a real risk of being subjected to torture or to inhuman or degrading treatment or punishment. (See Lord Bingham's speech in *Ullah* at para 24)

3.14 Therefore the AIT has to assess, just as the Secretary of State would have done initially, whether on the totality of the evidence there are substantial grounds for believing that there is a real risk of the applicant suffering torture or inhuman or degrading treatment or punishment if removed now. In performing this task, the AIT has to take into account the objective background country material and any evidence personal to the applicant, be it his oral testimony, medical reports, or documentary evidence in relation to past events. If the AIT reaches the conclusion that such a real risk exists then the appeal should be allowed, as the immigration decision is not in accordance with the law (section 84(1)(c) and (g) and section 86(3)(a) NIAA 2002 as amended).

3.15 The question in each case is concerned with the circumstances that the individual himself will face on return. That is clear from established ECtHR case law. Generic evidence alone will not suffice (see *Mamatkulov v Turkey* (2005) 41 EHRR 25 at paras 72–73). In *Chahal*, the Court's conclusion was based on specific, corroborated (and to an extent uncontroverted) evidence of the activities of the Punjabi police, who were the specific source of the alleged risk to the individual, and not on generic in-country material (see paras 99–103). So mere generic allegations that do not relate to the specific circumstances of the individual will not suffice. In *Kaldik v Germany* (Application No 28526/05), for example, the complaints were inadmissible due to the lack of evidence specific to the individuals showing a risk of treatment contrary to Article 3 on return.

3.16 This approach is consistent with that taken by the United Nations Committee Against Torture. It is clear from the ECtHR's decision in *Soering* that it drew inspiration for its decision from the text of Article 3 of the United Nations Convention Against Torture, which provides:

> 1. No State Party shall expel, return ('*refouler*') or extradite a person to another State where there are substantial grounds for believing that he would be in danger of being subjected to torture.
>
> 2. For the purpose of determining whether there are such grounds, the competent authorities shall take into account all relevant considerations including, where applicable, the existence in the State concerned of a consistent pattern of gross, flagrant or mass violations of human rights.

3.17 In *Khan v Canada* (15/11/94, Communication 15/1994), the Committee said:

> 12.2 … The Committee must decide, pursuant to paragraph 1 of Article 3, whether there are substantial grounds for believing that Mr Khan would be in danger of being subject to torture. In reaching this conclusion, the Committee must take into account all relevant considerations, pursuant to paragraph 2 of Article 3, including the existence of a consistent pattern of gross, flagrant or mass violations of human rights. The aim of the determination, however, is to establish whether the individual concerned would be personally at risk of being subjected to torture in the country to which he would return. It follows that the existence of a consistent pattern of gross, flagrant or mass violations of human rights in a country does not as such constitute a sufficient ground for determining that a person would be in danger of being subjected to torture upon his return to that country; additional grounds must exist that indicate that the individual concerned would be personally at risk. Similarly, the absence of a consistent pattern of gross violations of human rights does not mean that a person cannot be considered to be in danger of being subjected to torture in his specific circumstances.

3.18 These principles, taken together with the words 'substantial grounds' in the ECtHR's formulation of the legal test (or strong grounds in *Ullah*), illustrate that the threshold of demonstrated risk has not been set at a very low level. The ECtHR has repeatedly stated that evidence of a mere possibility does not suffice for these purposes (see, for example, *Vilvarajah* at para 111). The fact that the ECtHR does not regard the threshold as low is illustrated by the decision history of the court: in its entire history, the ECtHR has only ever found a breach of Article 3 in removal cases on nine occasions (including at least one—*Ahmed v Austria* (1996) 24 EHRR 278—in which the issue was in effect conceded), notwithstanding the fact that Article 3 is cited in nearly all such cases.

3.19 In relation to the evidence to be considered by the Court, the ECtHR has made the following observations:

> … it would be too narrow an approach under Article 3 in cases concerning aliens facing expulsion or extradition if the Court, as an international human rights court, were only to take into account materials made available by the domestic authorities of the Contracting State concerned without comparing these with materials from other, reliable and objective sources. … (G)iven that the applicant has not yet been expelled, the material point in time is that of the Court's consideration of the case. Even though the historical position is of interest in so far as it may shed light on the current situation and its likely evolution, it is the present conditions which are decisive and it is therefore necessary to take into account information that has come to light after the final decision taken by the domestic authorities …[11]

---

[11] *Salah Sheekh v Netherlands*, Application No 1948/04, Judgment, 11 January 2007, para 136.

This is the consistent approach of the ECtHR. So too in the domestic context, the time at which the AIT should assess the evidence is at the date of its hearing (see *Ravichandran v Home Secretary* [1996] Imm AR 97).

The burden of establishing that relevant substantial grounds exist rests on the **3.20** appellant.

Standard of proof of past ill-treatment

Where an allegation of treatment contrary to Article 3 is made against a State **3.21** Party to the Convention, the European Court of Human Rights requires proof beyond reasonable doubt.[12] That standard has no part to play in cases where it is alleged that removal will expose a person to a risk of treatment prohibited by Article 3 in a third country because the decision maker (and eventually the ECtHR) is concerned with an evaluation of future risk. That does not necessarily depend upon proof of past facts to any particular standard.

In relation to past events, including claims of past ill-treatment, the Home Office, **3.22** the AIT, and the Courts have adopted the approach taken in asylum cases—see *Karanakaran v Secretary of State for the Home Department* [2000] 3 All ER 449, [2000] INLR 122, CA and *Demirkaya v SSHD* [1999] Imm AR 498, where the Court held:

> Where evidence of past maltreatment exists, however, it is unquestionably an excellent indicator of the fate that may await an applicant on return to her home. . . . In sum, evidence of individualised past persecution is generally a sufficient, though not a mandatory, means of establishing prospective risks.

When evalutation of all risks on arrival at an airport is impossible at the date of hearing

There are limited circumstances in which an evaluation of future risk cannot be **3.23** made at the date of the appeal hearing because of uncertainty about what will happen to an appellant on his arrival in his home country, particularly where the Secretary of State has not issued removal directions. This issue arose in relation to a failed asylum seeker from Somalia in *Gedow, Abdulkadir and Mohamed v SSHD* [2006] EWCA Civ 1342. Somalian cases raise complicated questions concerning 'clan' membership and its impact upon safety on return, especially making the journey from Mogadishu airport to the city or elsewhere in Somalia. The Court of Appeal accepted that there could be real risks associated with the return from the airport to the applicant's home, even where the failed asylum seeker is from a majority clan and thus prima facie safe. However, in Somali cases

---

[12] *Labita v Italy*, 6 April 2000, Reports of Judgments and Decisions 2000-IV, para 121.

it was unrealistic at the time of refusal of asylum for the Secretary of State to make firm removal plans. Undertakings as to the mode of return were found to be unnecessary. But the Secretary of State had to give the applicant advance notice of when and to where he would be returned, to enable him to make appropriate arrangements for protection on his journey from the airport to his home. Immigration judges were unable at the time of the asylum and human rights appeal hearing to deal with all issues relating to risk on return at the airport. They did have the power to specify what was to be done by the Secretary of State to prevent a real risk of Article 3 breach arising in an enforced return.

3.24 This outcome would be surprising were it not for the additional opportunity to challenge the removal directions once these are issued by the Secretary of State.

Greater scrutiny in foreign cases where infringements are not inflicted by the receiving State

3.25 However, difficulties in applying the 'real risk' test arise from the fact that breaches of ECHR Article 3 may occur in many different contexts. The clearest instances of violations arise in cases where the proscribed forms of treatment arise from intentionally inflicted acts of the public authorities in the receiving State or from those non-State actors against whom the authorities of the receiving country cannot or are unwilling to afford protection. However, often the source of the risk of proscribed treatment does not engage the responsibility of the State authorities of the receiving state either directly or indirectly. Examples include cases where the claimant is at risk of committing suicide during or after removal, or cases where his state of mental or physical health is such that there is a risk on return of consequences so extreme as to amount to a violation of ECHR Article 3. In these cases, in light of the absolute character of the protection afforded by ECHR Article 3, the decision maker and the courts are not precluded from finding a violation.

> In any such contexts, however, the Court must subject all the circumstances surrounding the case to a rigorous scrutiny, especially the applicant's personal situation in the expelling State (see the judgment of the ECtHR in *D v United Kingdom* (1997) 24 EHRR 323 para 49).

'Anxious scrutiny' as cases are exceptional

3.26 This rigorous scrutiny in 'foreign' or 'expulsion' cases arises from the fact that the restriction, imposed by ECHR Article 3 on the power of the State to expel aliens in cases where the claimant's removal would sufficiently exacerbate the suffering flowing from a naturally occurring illness, is exceptional. The House of Lords in *N (FC) v SSHD* [2005] UKHL 31, (2005) 2 WLR 1124 held that notwithstanding that ordinarily a State is entitled to expel or deport aliens in the interests of immigration control, the exercise of such power may itself in some circumstances constitute Article 3 ill-treatment.

2) . . . This will be so if the applicant would be at substantial risk of Article 3 ill-treatment in the receiving country (. . .) or *even exceptionally* (as on the facts of *D* itself) if the applicant's removal would sufficiently exacerbate the suffering flowing from a naturally occurring illness (. . .). [emphasis added]

3) In this latter exceptional class of case the Court will assess whether the applicant's removal is itself properly to be characterised as Article 3 ill-treatment in the light of the applicant's present medical condition. The mere fact that the applicant is fit to travel, however, is not of itself sufficient to preclude his removal being characterised as Article 3 ill-treatment.

4) An alien otherwise subject to removal cannot in principle claim any entitlement to remain in order to benefit from continuing medical, social or other assistance available in the contracting state.

(per Lord Brown, *N (FC) v SSHD*, para 80)

Therefore 'foreign' cases raising Article 3 are exceptional as the violations are **3.27** likely to occur in the receiving State. Second, the level of scrutiny is even higher where the alleged inhuman or degrading treatment is not the direct or indirect responsibility of the public authorities of the receiving State but results from some naturally occurring illness. This arises from the fact that such cases represent 'an extension of an extension' to the ECHR Article 3 obligations of signatory states.[13]

As Lord Brown observed in *N (FC) v SSHD*, one must 'recognise that it is indeed **3.28** positive obligations for which the appellant here must necessarily be contending. It is quite unreal to treat this Article 3 complaint for all the world as if all that is required to safeguard the appellant's health is that the State refrain from deporting her. Realistically what she seeks is continuing treatment for her condition and it is necessarily implicit in her case that the State is bound to provide it. There would simply be no point in not deporting her unless her treatment here were to continue.'

For a further discussion of the scope of Article 3 protection from removal where the direct responsibility of the State is not engaged, please see below.

C. Inhuman and Degrading Treatment and Punishment

Treatment is inhuman or degrading if, to a seriously detrimental extent, it denies **3.29** the most basic needs of any human being.[14]

---

[13] Per Lord Brown, *N (FC) v SSHD* [2005] UKHL 31, (2005) 2 WLR 1124, para 87.
[14] Per Lord Bingham in *R (on the appln of Limbuela & Ors) v SSHD* [2005] UKHL 66, (2006) 1 AC 396, para 7.

Minimum level of severity

3.30 Ill-treatment must attain a minimum level of severity for it to fall within the scope of Article 3. The assessment of this minimum is relative: it depends on all the circumstances of the case, such as:

(1) the duration of the treatment,

(2) its physical and mental effects, and

(3) in some cases, the sex, age, and state of health of the victim.[15]

3.31 In respect of a person deprived of his liberty, recourse to physical force which has not been made strictly necessary by his own conduct diminishes human dignity and is in principle an infringement of Article 3 rights.[16] Additionally, where an individual has been taken into police custody in good health but is found injured at the time of release, it is incumbent on the State to provide a plausible explanation of how those injuries were caused. Should it fail to do so, a clear Article 3 issue would arise.[17] If the injuries were unlawfully inflicted, the authorities of the State are obliged to investigate in order to enable prosecution and compensation.[18] Conditions of detention, such as serving a lengthy prison sentence in unsanitary and overcrowded conditions,[19] could amount to degrading treatment.

3.32 In order for a punishment or treatment associated with it to be 'inhuman' or 'degrading', the suffering or humiliation involved must in any event go beyond the inevitable element of suffering or humiliation connected with a given form of legitimate treatment or punishment.

3.33 Another factor to be taken into consideration is whether the purpose of the treatment was to humiliate or debase the victim.[20] However, the absence of any such purpose does not conclusively rule out a violation of Article 3. Treatment has been held by the Strasbourg Court to be 'inhuman' because it was premeditated, was applied for hours at a stretch, and caused either actual bodily injury or intense physical and mental suffering.

---

[15] *Ireland v United Kingdom* (1978) 2 EHRR 25, para 162.

[16] See *Labita v Italy* judgment of 6 April 2000, *Reports of Judgments and Decisions* 2000-IV, para 120, *Tekin v Turkey* judgment of 9 June 1998, *Reports* 1998-IV, pp 1517–18, paras 52 and 53, and *Assenov & Ors v Bulgaria* judgment of 28 October 1998, *Reports* 1998-VIII, p 3288, para 94.

[17] *Selmouni v France* (1999) 29 EHRR 403, para 87.

[18] *Aksoy v Turkey* (1997) 23 EHRR 553.

[19] *Kalashnikov v Russia* (2003) 36 EHRR 34. No allowance was made for the economic difficulties facing Russia in providing a higher standard of detention facilities. See also a later case, where the Court of Appeal concluded that it was open to the AIT to find that conditions had improved to the extent that they fell outside the ambit of Article 3—*Batayav v SSHD* [2005] EWCA Civ 366.

[20] See *V. v the United Kingdom* [GC], no 24888/94, para 71, ECHR 1999-IX.

The ECtHR and Commission have held the following to amount to inhuman **3.34** treatment or punishment:

- being subjected to death row phenomenon;[21]
- being sentenced to death following an unfair trial;[22]
- interrogation techniques causing psychological damage;[23]
- the threat of torture;[24]
- denial of food and water in detention;[25]
- stoning, flogging, and other Sharia law[26] punishments;
- incommunicado detention, prolonged sun exposure at high temperatures, and the tying of hands and feet in painful positions;[27]
- beating, kicking, robbing, intimidation and harassment, forced labour, killing the applicant's father, and raping his sister;[28]
- detaining an unaccompanied five year old for two months in a detention centre in the same conditions as adults, with no one assigned to look after her and no measures being taken to ensure that she received proper counselling and educational assistance.[29] The treatment of the applicant's mother, who was in a different country, and who was informed merely that her daughter had been detained and provided with a telephone number where she could be reached, was also held to attain the minimum level of severity.[30]

Degrading treatment and punishment

'Degrading' treatment has been found where the acts for which the State was **3.35** responsible were such as to arouse in the victims feelings of fear, anguish, and inferiority capable of humiliating and debasing them.[31]

Examples where degrading treatment or punishment has been found by the **3.36** Courts include:

- real risk of persistent sexual abuse (*A v SSHD* [2003] EWCA Civ 175, CA);

---

21 *Soering v United Kingdom* (1989) 11 EHRR 439.
22 *Ocalan v Turkey* (2003) 37 EHRR 10; see also *Bader & Ors v Sweden*, Application No 13284/04, Judgment, 8 November 2005, final on 8 February 2006, para 41.
23 *Ireland v United Kingdom* (1978) 2 EHRR 25.
24 *Campbell and Cosans v United Kingdom* (1982) 4 EHRR 293.
25 *Cyprus v Turkey* (1984) 4 EHRR 482.
26 *Jahari v Turkey* [2001] INLR 136.
27 *Said v Netherlands*, Application No 2345/02, Judgment, 5 July 2005, final on 5 October 2005.
28 *Salah Sheekh v Netherlands*, Application No 1948/04, Judgment, 11 January 2007, para 146.
29 *Mayeka and Mitunga v Belgium*, Application No 13178/03, Judgment, 12 October 2006.
30 Ibid.
31 *Pretty v United Kingdom* (2002) 35 EHRR 1, para 52.

- racially discriminatory treatment on the basis of government policy, intended to achieve a result which was degrading to the individuals (*Cyprus v Turkey* Application No 25781/94, 10 May 2001, ECtHR);

- detention in conditions of serious overcrowding, in the absence of sleeping facilities for a prolonged time (*Dougoz v Greece* (2002) 34 EHRR 61; also see *Kalashnikov v Russia* (2003) 36 EHRR 34);

- policeman birching of a boy aged 15 (*Tyler v United Kingdom* (1978) 2 EHRR 1), cf headmaster using a slipper to hit a pupil was held not to be a violation of Article 3 in *Costello-Roberts v United Kingdom* (1995) 19 EHRR 112;

- weekly strip searches of a high-security remand prisoner, taken together with other security measures (*Van der Ven v Netherlands* Application No 50901/99, 4 February 2003).

D. Torture

3.37 The ECHR does not contain a definition of 'torture'. By contrast, the UN Convention Against Torture defines the term as:

> ... any act by which severe pain or suffering, whether physical or mental, is intentionally inflicted on a person for such purposes as obtaining from him or a third person information or a confession, punishing him for an act he or a third person has committed or is suspected of having committed, or intimidating or coercing him or a third person, or for any reason based on discrimination of any kind, when such pain or suffering is inflicted by or at the instigation of or with the consent or acquiescence of a public official or other person acting in an official capacity. It does not include pain or suffering arising only from, inherent in or incidental to lawful sanctions.

3.38 In the context of the European Convention on Human Rights there is no requirement that the treatment be inflicted by State authorities in order for it to amount to torture. However, State complicity in the ill-treatment would lead more readily to the treatment being found to amount to torture.

3.39 The European Court of Human Rights has described torture as 'deliberate inhuman treatment causing very serious and cruel suffering'.[32] The distinction between inhuman or degrading treatment and torture in Article 3 has been held to derive from a difference in intensity of the suffering inflicted.[33] The classification of certain treatment as torture would attach 'a special stigma to deliberate inhuman treatment causing very serious and cruel suffering'.[34] The deliberate

---

[32] *Ireland v United Kingdom* (1978) 2 EHRR 25, para 167.
[33] *Ireland v United Kingdom*; ibid.
[34] Ibid, para 167.

infliction of the suffering is also an important distinguishing factor. Torture cannot happen inadvertently or unintentionally.

Lack of evidence that the ill-treatment is inflicted with a view to extract information or a confession does not prevent the classification of the ill-treatment as torture, provided that its deliberate infliction and severity were established.[35] **3.40**

The Convention as a living instrument has had to adapt to present-day conditions, and past classification of certain treatment as 'inhuman and degrading' does not necessarily mean that it would not be classified as 'torture' when next examined by the European Court of Human Rights.[36] **3.41**

Examples of cases where treatment has been accepted to amount to torture by the European Court of Human Rights include: **3.42**

- *Aksoy v Turkey* (1997) 23 EHRR 553
- *Aydin v Turkey* (1997) 25 EHRR 251 (rape)
- *Selmouni v France* (1999) 29 EHRR 403 (buggery with a truncheon, threats with blow torches and a syringe, urinating on the prisoner after ordering him to suck the police officer's penis, punches in the face, hair pulling, and other cruel and degrading acts).
- *Ciorap v Molova*, Application No 00012066/02, 19/06/07 (repeated force-feedings, not prompted by valid medical reasons but aiming to force the claimant to abandon his protest and performed in such a way as to cause great unnecessary physical pain and humiliation).[37]

Evidence obtained under torture may not be used in the Courts

In *A & Ors* [2005] UKHL 71 the House of Lords considered the issue of whether the Special Immigration Appeals Commission (SIAC) may receive evidence which has or may have been procured by torture inflicted, in order to obtain evidence, by officials of a foreign State without the complicity of the British authorities. Potentially such evidence could have been used in appeal hearings before SIAC. **3.43**

The Secretary of State had stated that as a matter of policy it was not his intention to rely on evidence which he knew or believed to have been obtained by torture **3.44**

---

[35] *Aydin v Turkey* (1997) 25 EHRR 251, paras 85 and 86.

[36] See dicta to this effect in *Selmouni v France* (1999) 29 EHRR 403 at para 101.

[37] The Court noted, however, that a therapeutically necessary measure, including force-feeding to save a life, could not, in principle, be regarded as inhuman and degrading treatment. However, medical necessity had to be convincingly shown and the manner in which a person was subjected to force-feeding must not exceed the threshold of the minimum level of severity under Article 3.

in a third country, and that he had not done so in any of the cases before SIAC. However, he argued that the use of such evidence was not precluded by law. He pointed to a serious anomaly if an exclusionary rule were applied. In deciding on administrative action (including whether to deport someone) it was accepted by the House of Lords that the Secretary of State could take account of all information available to him, whatever its supposed source. The Secretary of State argued that to exclude that same material from the consideration of a court determining the legality of that action would result in a serious mismatch.

3.45 Their Lordships spoke with one voice on the condemnation of torture in English common law, as well as in the ECHR, which the UK had adopted. Torture and genocide were crimes against international law which every State was obliged to punish, wherever they may have been committed. The unanimous conclusion of the House of Lords was that there was a deeply embedded exclusionary principle, which compelled the exclusion of 'third-party' 'foreign' torture evidence as 'unreliable, unfair, offensive to the ordinary standards of humanity and decency and incompatible with the principles which should animate a tribunal seeing to administer justice', in the words of Lord Bingham.[38] The House of Lords took into account that development of the common law should be in harmony with the UK's international obligations. The latter included compliance with the Torture Convention, Article 15 of which mandated that:

> Each State Party shall ensure that any statement which is established to have been made as a result of torture shall not be invoked as evidence in any proceedings, except against a person accused of torture as evidence that the statement was made.

3.46 With regard to the practical application of the exclusionary principle, however, on whom lies the burden of showing that evidence was obtained under torture, and to what standard must he prove it? On this central issue, which would define how effectively the right could be enforced, the House of Lords was split. The majority recognised that it was unrealistic to expect the detainee to prove anything, given that he is denied access to so much of the information to be used against him at a SIAC hearing. All reasonably expected of him was to raise the point about whether evidence against him was obtained from third parties under torture abroad. It was then to SIAC to decide. The majority held that:

> . . . SIAC should refuse to admit the evidence if it concludes that the evidence was obtained by torture.[39]

---

[38] The ECtHR has also held that the use of evidence obtained under torture rendered a complainant's criminal trial unfair under Article 6(1)—see *Misha Harutyuntan v Armenia* (2007), Application No 00036549/03, 28/6/2007.

[39] Per Lord Hope, paragraph 118.

In applying this test, SIAC should apply the standard of proof 'on the balance of **3.47** probabilities' rather than the higher criminal standard of 'beyond reasonable doubt'. Therefore evidence would be excluded if SIAC concludes it is more likely than not to have been obtained by torture abroad. However, 'if SIAC is left in doubt as to whether the evidence was obtained in this way, it should admit it. But it must bear its doubt in mind when it is evaluating the evidence'.[40]

In reaching this conclusion the majority relied on the wording of Article 15 of **3.48** the Torture Convention which is quoted above, which sets out the exclusionary principle as extending to any statement that 'is established' to have been made under torture.

Thus, in the opinion of the majority, even if the detained person were able to **3.49** introduce a reasonable doubt in the minds of the SIAC judges, that would not be sufficient to exclude the evidence under the exclusionary rule applicable to torture evidence.

The minority, Lords Bingham, Nicholls, and Hoffmann, in a House of Lords **3.50** constituted of seven Law Lords, dissented on this very important issue. The test adopted by the majority was said to 'undermine the practical efficacy of the Torture Convention and deny detainees the standard of fairness to which they are entitled under Article 5(4) and 6(1) of the European Convention'.[41]

The alternative test proposed by the minority would have seen appellants **3.51** adducing some plausible reason why evidence may have been procured under torture, which could be shown by pointing to the fact that the evidence is likely to have originated from a country which is known to practise torture. SIAC's inquiry thereafter would focus on 'whether the evidence has, or whether there is a real risk that it may have been, obtained by torture'.[42] Proof on the balance of probabilities was not required. The majority recognised that this approach would have the effect of excluding evidence that was in fact untainted. That is because an inquiry into the precise circumstances in which evidence was obtained from a detainee in a foreign country would be unlikely to deliver a clear result.

---

[40] Ibid.
[41] Per Lord Bingham, paragraph 62.
[42] Per Lord Bingham, paragraph 56. Put another way (within the same paragraph): 'If SIAC is unable to conclude that there is not a real risk that the evidence has been obtained by torture, it should refuse to admit the evidence.'

E. Spectrum of Article 3 Cases and the Scope for State Action

Distinction between State violence (Category A) cases and other cases (Category B)

3.52 In considering the application of Article 3 in the asylum context, domestic analysis of the ECHR jurisprudence h7as revealed several fundamental distinctions. One such distinction arises between breaches of Article 3 which consist of violence by State servants (labelled 'Category A' by Laws LJ,[43] who first drew the distinction in *Limbuela v SSHD* [2004] EWCA Civ 540, [2004] QB 1440 CA and breaches which consist of acts or omissions by the State which expose an individual to suffering inflicted by third parties or by circumstance, such as the absence of effective medical facilities ('Category B' cases). The majority of cases that arise under Article 3 are concerned with the suggestion that an individual is at risk from the authorities in his home state and are thus 'Category A' in Laws LJ's lexicon.

Historically, Category A was the paradigm case, with the European Court of Human Rights expanding the application of Article 3 to cover other situations which arise. Category B cases include those where the risk does not come from State actors, but the State is either unwilling or unable to provide protection. In addition it encompasses those rare cases where Article 3 is invoked not because of any feared action but because of the general circumstances that will be faced on return, typically connected with the availability of medical treatment.

3.53 According to Laws LJ's analysis in *Limbuela v SSHD* [2004] EWCA Civ 540, [2004] QB 1440 CA, cases under Article 3 can be seen to fall within a spectrum. Violence authorized by the State but unauthorized by law is at one end of the spectrum.[44] Such acts are absolutely forbidden and represent the worst type of Category A case. At the other end of the spectrum are decisions made pursuant to a 'lawful policy', which expose the individual to a marked degree of suffering, not caused by violence but by the circumstances in which he finds himself in consequence of the decision. In that case the decision is lawful unless the degree of suffering which is indirectly inflicted reaches such severity that the court is bound to limit the State's right to implement the policy on Article 3 grounds.

3.54 There is no bright point on this spectrum, which would readily determine whether any particular set of facts comprises an Article 3 breach or not. The Courts

---

[43] Laws LJ gave a dissenting speech in *Limbuela*; however, his exposition of the law was cited by the House of Lords in *N (FC) v SSHD*.

[44] One example of State coercion and use of force authorized by law is lawful arrest.

would have to use various factors to determine where this dividing line is. Such factors will include the severity of the threatened suffering, its origin in violence or otherwise, and the nature of the government's reasons for or purpose of its actions.

The constraints and obligations on States imposed in the spectrum of different types of case arising under Article 3 have been expressed as follows:[45] **3.55**

(1) Unlawful violence which is authorized by the State is absolutely forbidden. There are no exceptions to the prohibition.

(2) Unlawful violence by State servants which is unauthorized is also forbidden, as is all unlawful violence. Here, however, the State's duty under Article 3 lies in prevention before the event and where prevention fails, investigation, sanction, and punishment afterwards. The State enjoys a measure of judgement in the elaboration of measures to serve the aims of prevention and sanction. The closer the State's responsibility to the affected individual, the narrower will be the measure of judgement which is allowed by the law.

(3) Where Article 3 is deployed to challenge the consequences of 'lawful government policy' whose application consigns an individual to circumstances of serious hardship, Article 3 operates as a safety net, confining the State's freedom of action only in exceptional or extreme cases.

Laws LJ's spectrum analysis set out above was received with caution by the House of Lords in *Limbuela*.[46] Lord Hope's reservations about the spectrum analysis were two-fold. First, the only classification in the ECHR jurisprudence was the result of recognition that Article 3 may require States to provide protection against inhuman or degrading treatment for which they themselves are not directly responsible.[47] This was also the concern of Baroness Hale.[48] Second, spectrum analysis may inadvertently introduce by the back door considerations of proportionality in cases of 'legitimate government policy'. As Lord Hope remarked: 'proportionality, which gives a margin of appreciation to states, has no part to play when conduct for which it is directly responsible results in inhuman or degrading treatment or punishment. The obligation to refrain from such conduct is absolute.'[49] The real issue on which decision makers and courts should **3.56**

---

[45] Per Laws LJ in *Limbuela*, para 77.

[46] *R (on the appln of Limbuela & Ors) v SSHD* [2005] UKHL 66, (2006) 1 AC 396, per Lord Hope at para 53, and Baroness Hale at para 77, cf Lord Brown at para 89.

[47] Ibid, para 53.

[48] Baroness Hale identified two situations in the ECHR case law when the State can be held responsible for a person's suffering—when it itself subjected that person to such suffering, and where it should have intervened to protect a person from suffering inflicted by others. *R (on the appln of Limbuela & Ors) v SSHD* [2005] UKHL 66, (2006) 1 AC 396, para 77.

[49] Ibid, para 55.

focus is whether the State is properly to be regarded as responsible for the conduct that is prohibited by Article 3.[50]

3.57 In contrast, Lord Brown in *Limbuela* found Laws LJ's analysis useful, as it highlighted the many different considerations in play and the need in all but the clearest of cases 'to look at the problem in the round'.[51]

3.58 Bearing in mind the caution not to introduce proportionality as a consideration into the spectrum analysis, it can be usefully deployed to analyze Article 3 cases. Below are some practical examples within the various categories of the spectrum analysis.

3.59 Punishment by amputation for theft is likely to be characterized as unlawful violence authorized by the State, being inhuman punishment. The focus of inquiry is likely to centre on the credibility of the claim that the applicant has committed the offence for which the punishment might be available, the authorities' awareness of the crime, and the likelihood of prosecution and execution of the punishment. Equally, torture or beatings authorised by the State would fall within this category.

3.60 Beatings and humiliation whilst in detention, where formally such treatment is forbidden in the detaining State, are likely to fall within the second category of unlawful violence by State servants. If an applicant's case is that such ill-treatment is routine and widespread, the case is likely to be argued with an emphasis on the State's complicity in failing to prevent such ill-treatment in its prisons (or the particular detention facility), despite its prior knowledge. This is a common basis for suggesting that the Article 3 risk on return is made out. There are occasions where a past incident cannot be shown to fit into a pattern of mistreatment of detainees. Then the focus of the inquiry would lie in establishing whether the State has failed to take remedial action, such as punishing the culprits. Such a failure would be predicated on its being shown that the State knew of the incident.

3.61 Cases where 'lawful government policy' consigns an individual to circumstances of serious hardship include those where an applicant would be lawfully detained on return, but in harsh prison conditions. This would fall within Laws LJ's third category. The type of evidence which will be required to substantiate such a claim was considered by the AIT in *LJ (China—Prison Conditions) China* [2005] UKIAT 00099 (10 May 2005). To establish that on return to China, after making an unsuccessful claim for asylum in the United Kingdom, one was reasonably likely to be (a) imprisoned or subjected to administrative detention for having left unlawfully, and (b) whilst imprisoned subjected to Article 3 ill-treatment,

---

[50] Ibid, para 53.
[51] Ibid, para 89.

clear evidence would be required from bodies such as Amnesty International, Human Rights Watch, or the Canadian Immigration and Refugee Board to the effect that other persons whose histories and circumstances were reasonably comparable with those of the individual concerned had, on their return in the comparatively recent past, been imprisoned or detained *and* subjected to such maltreatment in sufficient numbers and/or with sufficient frequency. It was insufficient to rely on a general statement in the US State Department Report to the effect that conditions in Chinese prisons and administrative detention facilities were 'harsh and frequently degrading'. The ECtHR has also condemned conditions in Russian prisons in a number of cases. Where detention on expulsion is reasonably likely, an investigation of prison conditions in the receiving State on behalf of the appellant will often be called for.

Where the threatened harm emanates from non-conforming behaviour by official agents, in Article 3 cases the approach adopted by the majority of the Court of Appeal in the asylum case of *Svazas v Secretary of State for the Home Department* [2002] 1 WLR 1891 should be applied by analogy. In such cases, the question remains as to whether or not the State can properly be said to be providing sufficient protection.[52] However, **3.62**

> (w)hen, . . ., one comes to address the question in this context rather than in the context of ill-treatment exclusively by non-state agents, one must clearly recognise that the more senior the officers of state concerned, and the more closely involved they are in the refugee's ill-treatment, the more necessary it will be to demonstrate clearly the home state's political will to stamp it out and the adequacy of their systems for doing so and for punishing those responsible, and the easier it will be for the asylum seeker to cast doubt upon their readiness, or at least their ability, to do so.[53]

Sedley LJ put the question for the decision maker in cases of systematic persecution by agents of a State which repudiates their acts as follows: **3.63**

> . . . that a state which, however anxious to halt abuse, does not act promptly and effectively to stop its officials persecuting citizens on Convention grounds will not be affording protection of which the victim is able or, in view of his fear, willing to avail himself. . . . Rather than require to be satisfied that the state is actively or passively complicit in persecution by other citizens, the decision-maker in a case like the present (which does not concern isolated rogue activity) is faced with the state's undoubted responsibility and must examine what the state is doing about it.[54]

Whether reasonable protection is available from the State authorities against non-State agents on return is context dependent. In particular, the standards applicable differ between returnees as members of the public and returnees who were **3.64**

---

[52] *Svazas v SSHD* [2002] 1 WLR 1891, per Simon Brown LJ, para 54.
[53] Ibid.
[54] Per Sedley LJ, para 22.

previously law enforcement officers. Thus in *R (on the appln of Gedara) v SSHD* [2006] EWHC 1690 (Admin), the applicant had been apprehending rebels in Sri Lanka, within the terms of his employment with the police. He had been issued with a pistol and hand grenade for self-protection. In such circumstances it could not be argued that the receiving State was unwilling to provide him with practical protection. A State was entitled to require soldiers and police to face a heightened risk of harm so that it could provide practical protection to the public.

F. State Protection and Non-State Actors

3.65 Where the violence or other ill-treatment is threatened not by the State itself but by non-State actors such as criminal gangs, the ECtHR has not excluded the possibility that Article 3 may prevent removal. In *HLR v France* (1996) 26 EHRR 29 at para 50 the Court said:

> Owing to the absolute character of the right guaranteed, the court does not rule out the possibility that the Convention may also apply where the danger emanates from persons or groups of persons who are not public officials. However, it must be shown that the risk is real and that the authorities of the receiving state are not able to obviate the risk by providing appropriate protection.

3.66 The House of Lords in the case of *R (on appln of Bagdanavicius & Anor) v SSHD* [2005] UKHL 38, (2005) 2 AC 668 considered such a case. The issue identified by Lord Brown, who gave the only speech, was formulated as follows (para 11):

> To avoid expulsion on Article 3 grounds must the applicant establish only that in the receiving country he would be at real risk of serious harm from non-state agents or must he go further and establish too that the receiving country does not provide for those within its territory a reasonable level of protection against such risk?

In short, the answer to the question was that the applicant had to go the step further. Lord Brown resolved the issue in the following terms:

> The . . . argument has been bedevilled by a failure to grasp the distinction in non-state agent cases between on the one hand the risk of serious harm and on the other hand the risk of treatment contrary to Article 3. In cases where the risk 'emanates from intentionally inflicted acts of the public authorities in the receiving country' (the language of para 49 of *D v United Kingdom* 24 EHRR 423, 447), one can use those terms interchangeably: the intentionally inflicted acts would without more constitute the proscribed treatment. Where, however, the risk emanates from non-state bodies, that is not so: any harm inflicted by non-state agents will not constitute Article 3 ill-treatment unless in addition the state has failed to provide reasonable protection. If someone is beaten up and seriously injured by a criminal gang, the member state will not be in breach of Article 3 unless it has failed in its positive duty to provide reasonable protection against such criminal acts.

In so concluding, the House of Lords achieved symmetry between the approach **3.67** under Article 3 and that under the Refugee Convention: see *Horvath v Secretary of State for the Home Department* [2001] 1AC 489.[55]

Part of the difficulty in this area was the use by the ECtHR, in the passage quoted **3.68** above from *HLR,* of the word 'obviate' in connection with the risk from non-State agents. Obviate would normally mean 'do away with' or something similar. To apply that meaning to a risk would suggest a requirement to guard absolutely against the risk. The House of Lords considered that the ECtHR could not have meant that. It endorsed the reasoning of Sedley LJ in *McPherson v SSDH* [2002] INLR 139, 147, where he found that the apparent requirement that the protection is sufficient to obviate the risk entirely 'cannot be right. What the state is expected to do is take reasonable measures to make the necessary protection available'.

Assurances by the receiving State

In national security cases of expulsion considered on appeal by SIAC, a number **3.69** of cases have involved assurances from foreign governments given to the UK government as to the treatment and conditions in detention and other relevant matters for assessing the risk on return. In such cases, SIAC has held that it can evaluate the credibility of such assurances—*BB v SSHD,* [2006] UKSIAC 39/2005 (5 December 2006), para 5, and *Y v SSHD* [2006] UKSIAC 36/2005 (24 August 2006), para 391. Depending on the circumstances of the case, a bilateral assurance of this kind is capable of reducing the risk which a deportee faces on return to an acceptable level.[56]

This conclusion is consistent with the approach of both the ECtHR and the UN **3.70** Committee Against Torture which have regularly taken into account such assurances in evaluating the risks which an individual will face on expulsion.[57]

In *Y v SSHD* the Special Immigration Appeals Commission recognised that **3.71** assurances are not usually sought unless there is a prospect that the treatment to be guarded against will occur. Where that treatment was already forbidden by a State's domestic law and international obligations, there had to be something

---

[55] For an ECtHR case where there was a finding of insufficient State protection in the DRC for an infiltrator and informant in Mobutu's special protection force, see *N v Finland* (Application No 38885/02), Judgment, 26 July 2005, final 30 November 2005.

[56] *Y v SSHD* [2006] UKSIAC 36/2005 (24 August 2006), para 392. The correctness of this approach was not doubted by the Court of Appeal, who allowed an appeal and remitted the case for reconsideration on other grounds.

[57] Eg *Chahal* at para 105; *Mamatkulaov v Turkey; Chamaiev v Georgia* Application No 36378/02 and *F v United Kingdom* Application No 36812/02 all in the ECtHR, and *Hannan Attia v Sweden* Comm No 199/2002 and *Agiza v Sweden* CAT/C/34/D/233/2003 in UNCAT.

about the assurances, sufficient to show that the promise to do that which the State has already agreed to do or is bound to do will be honoured rather than breached in this instance. SIAC held that this may come from the *person* giving the assurances, the *terms* of it, the *circumstances of the country*, *monitoring*, the political and diplomatic *incentives* to adhere to it, or the potential *penalties or consequences for a breach*, or from a combination of some or all of these factors.

3.72 These criteria, which SIAC is likely to apply to assurances by the receiving State, are set out in *BB v SSHD* as follows:

> Without attempting to lay down rules which must apply in every case, we believe that four conditions must, in general, be satisfied:
> (i) the terms of the assurances must be such that, if they are fulfilled, the person returned will not be subjected to treatment contrary to Article 3;
> (ii) the assurances must be given in good faith;
> (iii) there must be a sound objective basis for believing that the assurances will be fulfilled;
> (iv) fulfilment of the assurances must be capable of being verified.

3.73 The ECtHR has also taken into account the absence of a receiving State assurance in finding that an applicant had a well-founded fear that the death sentence against him would be executed if he was forced to return to Syria. In *Bader & Ors v Sweden*, Application No 13284/04, Judgment, 8 November 2005, final on 8 February 2006, it held (at para 45):

> More importantly, the Court notes that the Swedish Government have obtained no guarantee from the Syrian authorities that the first applicant's case will be re-opened and that the public prosecutor will not request the death penalty at any retrial.

Further, the Court of Appeal in *MT (Algeria) & Ors v SSHD* [2007] EWCA Civ 808 has upheld SIAC decisions to accept government assurances.

3.74 The UK government is most likely to seek assurances of foreign States about the detention and treatment on return of particular individuals in national security cases or in those where the question of the death penalty arises. It is settled government policy that it will not return someone to face a real risk of execution. Nonetheless, the impact of assurances from foreign governments may fall to be considered in a whole range of circumstances. These include conditions of detention and fair trial issues under Article 6.

Internal flight/internal relocation

3.75 The risk of treatment on return contrary to Article 3 may be lowered to an acceptable level by the availability of relocation internally within the receiving country. Underlying the factual assessment by the ECtHR in *Chahal* was the question of whether he would be safe if he returned to India somewhere other than the Punjab. The ECtHR has decided that there must be some minimum guarantees before the internal flight alternative can be relied on to defeat a claim under Article 3:[58]

> The Court considers that as a precondition for relying on an internal flight alternative, certain guarantees have to be in place: the person to be expelled must be *able to travel to the area* concerned, *to gain admittance and be able to settle there,* failing which an issue under Article 3 may arise, the more so if in the absence of such guarantees there is a possibility of the expellee ending up in a part of the country of origin where he or she may be subjected to ill-treatment.

This approach is echoed by the House of Lords in the asylum cases of *Januzi and Hamid v SSHD* [2006] UKHL 5, [2006] 3 All ER 305. Lord Hope stressed that the question of whether a person is not a refugee due to the availability of an internal flight alternative is: **3.76**

> . . . whether it would be unduly harsh to expect a claimant who is being persecuted for a Convention reason in one part of his country to move to a less hostile part before seeking refugee status abroad. The words 'unduly harsh' set the standard that must be met for this to be regarded as unreasonable. If the claimant can live a relatively normal life there judged by the standards that prevail in his country of nationality generally, and if he can reach the less hostile part without undue hardship or undue difficulty, it will not be unreasonable to expect him to move there.[59]

G. Medical Conditions and Insufficiency of Treatment

Human rights challenges to immigration decisions frequently arise in HIV/AIDS cases, where the humanitarian imperatives are extremely pressing. A common feature in all such cases is that the claimant faces a significantly shortened expectation of life if deported. In *N (FC) v SSHD* [2005] UKHL 31, (2005) 2 AC 296 the House of Lords considered the application of ECHR Article 3 in the context of removal of a failed asylum seeker suffering from HIV/AIDS to a country where access to medical facilities and treatment would be difficult. The claimant's condition had stabilized with treatment in the United Kingdom and with such treatment she would have been able to survive for decades. Without it, her prognosis was poor and she was unlikely to live beyond two years. In short the claimant was in a predicament sadly typical of failed asylum seekers who were afflicted with HIV/AIDS. **3.77**

---

[58] *Salah Sheekh v Netherlands*, Application No 1948/04, Judgment, 11 January 2007, para 141 (emphasis added).
[59] *Januzi and Hamid v SSHD* [2006] UKHL 5, [2006] 3 All ER 305, para 47.

The Strasbourg cases

3.78 The ECtHR has considered the issue of removal to poor medical conditions on a number of occasions. In *D v United Kingdom* (1997) 24 EHRR 423 this Court for the first time held that Article 3 is capable of being engaged in cases where the source of the risk of proscribed treatment in the receiving country stems from factors which cannot engage either directly or indirectly the responsibility of the public authorities of that country, or which, taken alone, do not in themselves infringe the standards of the ECHR. The Court stated that:

> The Court notes that the applicant is in the advanced stages of a terminal and incurable illness. At the date of the hearing, it was observed that there had been a marked decline in his condition and he had to be transferred to a hospital. His condition was giving rise to concern. The limited quality of life he now enjoys results from the availability of sophisticated treatment and medication in the United Kingdom and the care and kindness administered by a charitable organisation. He has been counselled on how to approach death and has formed bonds with his carers. (paragraph 51)

> The abrupt withdrawal of these facilities will entail the most dramatic consequences for him. It is not disputed that his removal will hasten his death. There is a serious danger that the conditions of adversity which await him in St Kitts will further reduce his already limited life expectancy and subject him to acute mental and physical suffering. Any medical treatment which he might hope to receive there could not contend with the infections which he may possibly contract on account of his lack of shelter and of a proper diet as well as exposure to the health and sanitation problems which beset the population of St Kitts. While he may have a cousin in St Kitts, no evidence has been adduced to show whether this person would be willing or in a position to attend to the needs of a terminally ill man. There is no evidence of any other form of moral or social support. Nor has it been shown whether the applicant would be guaranteed a bed in either of the hospitals on the island which, according to the Government, care for AIDS patients. (paragraph 52)

> In view of these exceptional circumstances and bearing in mind the critical stage now reached in the applicant's fatal illness, the implementation of the decision to remove him to St Kitts would amount to inhuman treatment by the respondent State in violation of Article 3. (paragraph 53)

3.79 This case marked a significant extension of the scope of Article 3 protection that might be relied upon in an immigration case. In his contribution to the *2nd Colloquy on the European Convention on Human Rights and the protection of refugees, asylum-seekers and displaced persons* (Strasbourg, 19–20 May 2000), Judge Lorenzen of the ECtHR noted the difficulty presented by the judgment in *D*:

> . . . this type of case presented a challenge to the Court, which was not easily solved. On the one hand, no one could reasonably deny that compelling humanitarian considerations demanded that persons suffering from serious diseases should be given appropriate treatment that was unavailable in their country of origin. The protection under Article 3 was consistently held to be absolute in the case-law

of the Court: those in need of it were entitled to it despite individual circumstances, such as, for example, the fact that the applicant's stay in the host country was short. On the other hand the consequences of granting an absolute right for seriously ill persons to remain in the host country to get treatment, provided they had managed to set foot there, was very far reaching. (p 28)

The approach of the Court and Commission after *D* has been to emphasize the **3.80** principle that aliens are not entitled to remain in a contracting State in order to continue to benefit from medical, social, or other forms of assistance provided by that State, and to focus on whether the condition of the individual has reached a critical or terminal stage. See, for example, *BB v France* (9 March 1998), RJD 1998-VI (p 2596); *Henao v Netherlands* Application No 13669/03; *Karara v Finland* Application No 40900/98 (29 May 1998); *MM v Switzerland* Application No 43348/98 (14 September 1998); *Tatete v Switzerland* Application No 41874/98 (18 November 1998); *SCC v Sweden* Application No 46553/99 (15 February 2000); *Ndangoya v Sweden* Application No 17868/03(22 June 2004).

In *Bensaid v United Kingdom* (2001) 33 EHRR 205 the ECtHR was concerned **3.81** with an Article 3 case in relation to an Algerian national who sought to resist his removal from the United Kingdom on the basis of the lack of psychiatric facilities in Algeria. The ECtHR found no violation of Article 3. It observed:

> The fact that the applicant's circumstances in Algeria would be less favourable than those enjoyed by him in the United Kingdom is not decisive from the point of view of Article 3 of the Convention. (paragraph 38)

And if further observed that:

> [It] accepts the seriousness of the applicant's medical condition. Having regard, however, to the high threshold set by Article 3, particularly where the case does not concern the direct responsibility of the contracting state for the infliction of harm, the court does not find that there is a sufficiently real risk that the applicant's removal in these circumstances would be contrary to the standards set by Article 3. It does not disclose the exceptional circumstances of the *D* case, where the applicant was in the final stage of a terminal illness, AIDS, and had no prospect of medical care or family support on expulsion to St Kitts. (paragraph 40)

The decision of the House of Lords in *N*

The House of Lords considered the jurisprudence of the ECtHR on the applica- **3.82** tion of Article 3 in relation to deportations/removals of persons with HIV/AIDS. It concluded unanimously that there was no breach of Article 3.

The House of Lords acknowledged that: **3.83**

> . . . it is not the words of Article 3 of the Convention that we are being asked to construe but the jurisprudence of the European Court of Human Rights in Strasbourg which explains the application of that Article in its decision in *D v United Kingdom*

(1997) 24 EHRR 423. There is no question in this case of the appellant having been subjected to inhuman or degrading treatment in this country. Nor has it been suggested that there is any risk of her being subjected to any of the forms of treatment that Article 3 proscribes from intentionally inflicted acts of the public authorities in Uganda or from those of non-state agents in that country against which the authorities there are unable to afford her appropriate protection. We are dealing here with a decision of the Strasbourg court which created what the Court of Appeal rightly accepted was an 'extension of an extension' to the Article 3 obligation . . . . [per Lord Hope at para 23]

3.84 Having considered the existing case law of the ECtHR in some detail, the House of Lords identified the following propositions that could be drawn from that jurisprudence.

3.85 The fundamental nature of the Article 3 guarantees applies irrespective of the reprehensible conduct of the applicant. It makes no difference however criminal his acts may have been or however great a risk he may present to the public if he were to remain in the expelling State's territory: see Lord Hope at para 48; Lord Brown at para 80(1).

3.86 Notwithstanding that ordinarily a State is entitled to extradite, expel or deport aliens, whether to honour extradition treaties, combat crime, safeguard its own population, or more generally in the interests of immigration control, the exercise of such a power may itself in certain circumstances constitute Article 3 ill-treatment: see Lord Brown at para 80(2).

3.87 Aliens who are subject to expulsion cannot claim any entitlement to remain in the territory of a contracting State in order to continue to benefit from medical, social, or other forms of assistance provided by the expelling State. For an exception to be made where expulsion is resisted on medical grounds the circumstances must be exceptional: see Lord Nicholls at paras 15 and 17; Lord Hope at para 48; Lady Hale at paras 62 and 63.

3.88 In assessing whether the circumstances of a particular individual are sufficiently 'exceptional' to engage Article 3, the ECtHR has always singled out for special attention the applicant's present personal situation in the expelling State: see Lord Hope at para 31; Lady Hale at paras 65 and 68; Lord Brown at para 80(4).

3.89 For the circumstances to be, as it was put in *Amegnigan v The Netherlands*, 'very exceptional' it would need to be shown that the applicant's medical condition had reached such a critical stage that there were compelling humanitarian grounds for not removing him to a place which lacked the medical and social services which he would need to prevent acute suffering while he was dying: see Lord Hope at para 50; Lady Hale at para 69; Lord Brown at paras 93 and 94.

The difference between the medical treatment available in the receiving State **3.90** as compared with that available in the expelling State is not determinative. It is sufficient if treatment for HIV/AIDS and/or family support is, in principle, available in the receiving State: see Lord Hope at paras 35, 42, 43, 48, and 50; Lady Hale at para 68; Lord Brown at para 85.

What made *D*'s circumstances 'exceptional' was that he: **3.91**

a. 'was dying and beyond the reach of medical treatment then available': see Lord Nicholls at para 15;
b. was already terminally ill while still present in the territory of the expelling State: see Lord Hope at para 36;
c. was dying, so that it would be inhuman to send him home to die unless the conditions there would be such that he could do so with dignity: see Lady Hale at paras 68 and 69;
d. 'appeared to be close to death; . . . The critical question there was accordingly where and in what circumstances *D* should die rather than where he should live and be treated. *D* really did concern what was principally a negative obligation, not to deport *D* to an imminent, lonely, and distressing end.': see Lord Brown at para 93.

It thus appears that for an applicant of this sort to make good an Article 3 claim, **3.92** he will need to be close to death and unable to meet his death with dignity unless his removal is prevented.

The reality is that *D* was a case which presented considerable conceptual difficul- **3.93** ties and it has been the subject of attenuation ever since.

On the above tests, an allegation of breach of Article 3 in 'medical cases', involv- **3.94** ing claimants' State of health and the insufficiency of medical treatment in the receiving State, is rarely likely to succeed in practice. Any change to the law is likely to be heralded by the ECtHR. However, powerful policy reasons militate against such a development. As Lord Hope said in *N (FC) v SSHD*, the effect of affording all those in the appellant's condition a right to remain until such time as the standard of medical facilities available in their home countries for the treatment of HIV/AIDS had reached that which is available in Europe

> would risk drawing into the United Kingdom large numbers of people already suffering from HIV in the hope that they too could remain here indefinitely so that they could take the benefit of the medical resources that are available in this country. This would result in a very great and no doubt unquantifiable commitment of resources which it is, to say the least, highly questionable the States Parties to the Convention would ever have agreed to. The better course, one might have thought, would be for States to continue to concentrate their efforts on the steps which are currently being taken, with the assistance of the drugs companies, to make the necessary medical

care universally and freely available in the countries of the third world which are still suffering so much from the relentless scourge of HIV/AIDS.

3.95 The House of Lords, however, did draw attention to the fact that the Secretary of State had a wide administrative discretion in respect of removal, which could be exercised in the appellant's favour. This might indicate an inevitable consequence in similar cases, namely the filing of case-specific requests that the Secretary of State exercise his discretion to grant leave to remain on compassionate grounds. On the current tests, such applications are more likely to meet with success than appeals in reliance on Article 3.

3.96 Two medical cases applying the House of Lords' guidance in *N v SSHD* (2005) UKHL 31 illustrate the difficulties which face applicants relying on medical grounds under Article 3 to resist removal. In the first case, *ZT v SSHD* [2005] EWCA Civ 1421, the appellant attempted to resist removal to Zimbabwe on the basis of Articles 3 and 8 due to her medical condition (being HIV-positive, with likelihood of survival of less than two years if returned). The Court of Appeal held that the test set out in *N v SSHD* (2005) UKHL 31, that exceptional circumstances were required to prevent a removal, made it a matter for the judgment of the AIT, once it had correctly directed itself as to the requisite standard. No error could be shown in the refusal to accept that a case was exceptional, unless the AIT had rejected a plain, obvious, and uncontroversial issue that took the case out of the limitations set out in *N*.

3.97 The second illustrative case in which *N v SSHD* (2005) UKHL 31 was applied by the Court of Appeal is *Mukarkar v SSHD* [2006] EWCA Civ 1045, Times, 16 August 2006. The Court of Appeal reiterrated that the threshold of suffering or degradation required to engage Article 3 was very high. Mukarkar's medical condition was not life threatening and there was no basis for concluding that his family or the authorities in the receiving state, Yemen, would leave him unsupported. The appeal was, however, allowed on the basis of Article 8.

3.98 *CA v SSHD* [2004] EWCA Civ 1165 is an example of a case where a medical claim succeeded. The applicant, an HIV-positive pregnant woman, successfully argued before an adjudicator that her Article 3 rights would be breached if she were to be returned to Ghana, as her unborn child would face a risk of contracting AIDS. The adjudicator allowed the appeal, directing that the applicant be granted leave to remain for two years. The AIT's reversal of this decision was held to be wrong by the Court of Appeal, as the AIT jurisdiction was limited to a point of law, and there had been no material error of law in the adjudicator's decision. The risk to the applicant's child if it was returned to Ghana was that it might contract AIDS and die. If a mother had to witness that, it would constitute an inhuman treatment to her in excess even of any experience or suffering as a result of herself developing AIDS. The Court of Appeal thus reinstated the decision of the adjudicator.

Finally, in *R (on the appln of DB) v SSHD* [2005] EWHC 59 (Admin) the Immi-   **3.99**
gration Appeal Tribunal (IAT) decision not to extend time for an appeal was quashed. The applicant suffered from HIV and leprosy and was treated with a combination of drugs not available in Uganda. The Administrative Court found that he had an arguable case that his return to Uganda would be a breach of his Article 3 rights. The matter was remitted to the IAT to consider whether it would be unjust not to extend time.

Home Office policies and guidance

On entry and after entry Immigration and Nationality Directorate (IND) poli-   **3.100**
cies in cases where the applicant is suffering from HIV/AIDS are set out in the Immigration Directorates' Instructions, Chapter 1 Section 8,[60] which at the time of writing (March 2007) comprised the February 2007 version. In summary, in 'on entry' cases, where the passenger is suffering from AIDS, HIV, or any other serious illness, that will not in itself be sufficient to justify refusal on public health grounds alone if the person satisfies the Immigration Rules. In 'after entry' cases the policy is stated as follows:

> 3.1 **Policy**
>
> The fact that a person is suffering from a serious illness is not in itself grounds for refusing entry clearance or leave to remain if the person concerned otherwise quali-fies under the Immigration Rules. Equally, the fact that an applicant is suffering from a serious illness is not in itself sufficient grounds on which to justify the grant of Discretionary Leave in accordance with API Chapter 5, section 5 where the requirements of the Rules are not met.

Guidance on the assessment of claims under Articles 3 and 8 appears in the same document at paragraph 3.4.[61]

In the context of removals the Operational Enforcement Manual, Section D,   **3.101**
deals with HIV/AIDS cases at Chapter 36 (Extenuating Circumstances), para-graph 36.9.[62] The guidance stipulates that as well as obtaining the relevant medi-cal information from the applicant, reference should be made to the Country Information and Policy Unit (CIPU) country officer to establish whether the medication or treatment is available (or affordable) in the country of origin. If such information is unavailable, further inquiries will be made abroad via the

---

[60] <http://www.ind.homeoffice.gov.uk/documents/idischapter1/>. See section 10—Human Rights.
[61] Unavailable as of March 2007, as withdrawn for updating.
[62] Chapter 36 can be accessed through <http://www.ind.homeoffice.gov.uk/documents/oemsectiond/>.

Foreign and Commonwealth Office. The details from the treating consultant which are envisaged comprise:

- confirmation that the applicant has AIDS or is HIV positive;
- his life expectancy;
- the nature and location of the treatment he is receiving;
- his fitness to travel if required to leave the country.

The UK's obligations under Article 3 of the ECHR will be engaged in all medical cases where the following requirements are satisfied:
- the UK can be regarded as having assumed responsibility for a person's care, and
- there is credible medical evidence that return, due to a complete absence of medical treatment in the country concerned, would significantly reduce the applicant's life expectancy, and
- subject them to acute physical and mental suffering.

Case law has confirmed that the circumstances in which an individual can resist removal on Article 3 related medical grounds will be exceptional.

A person who is subject to removal cannot in principle claim any entitlement to remain in the UK in order to continue to benefit from medical, social or other forms of assistance provided. Where similar treatment may not be available to a person in their home country because of its cost, this does not amount to a claim of inhuman or degrading treatment. However, to attempt to remove someone to a country where there is a complete absence of treatment, facilities or social support which could result in an imminent and/or lingering death and cause acute physical and mental suffering would be very likely to engage our obligations under Article 3. (emphasis added)

Checklist for Article 3 medical cases

1. Has the applicant's medical condition reached such a critical stage that there are compelling humanitarian grounds for not removing him? In other words, is he dying?

2. Could it be said that medical treatment is not available in the receiving State at all? If such a proposition is being advanced, detailed and objective medical evidence is likely to be required to prove it.

3. If there is some medical care available in the receiving State, proof would be required to show that it would be insufficient to prevent acute suffering while the applicant is dying.

4. In addition the availability of social services should be considered. First, objective evidence should be adduced as to State provision of social services, which the applicant will need. Additionally, evidence will be required as to the amount and quality of family support the applicant can expect once expelled.

5. Overall, if removed, is the applicant likely to experience acute suffering? The minimum level of severity requirement has to be satisfied (although Their Lordships' reasoning implies a higher standard in such cases).

6. Overall, can the case be classed as 'very exceptional'? Practitioners should consider how a case could be distinguished from other cases where the applicant suffers from the same medical condition. Consider Home Office policies.

H. Suicide Risk

In the case of *J v SSHD* [2005] EWCA Civ 629 the Court of Appeal considered **3.102** the application of Article 3 in a case where the claimant had been subjected to torture by the Sri Lankan authorities, mistreatment by the LTTE, suffered from post-traumatic stress disorder, and had attempted suicide.

The Court of Appeal found that it was necessary to draw a clear distinction **3.103** between 'foreign cases' and 'domestic cases'. The risk of a violation of Article 3 or Article 8 had to be considered in relation to three stages: (i) when J was informed that a final decision had been made to remove him to Sri Lanka, which was a domestic case; (ii) when he was physically removed by airplane to Sri Lanka, which was better classified as a domestic case; and (iii) after he had arrived in Sri Lanka, which was a foreign case.

Foreign cases

In relation to foreign cases, the relevant test was whether there were strong **3.104** grounds for believing that the person, if returned, faced a real risk of torture, inhuman or degrading treatment, or punishment. A different test was not required in cases where the Article 3 breach relied on was a risk of suicide or other self-harm. The Court stressed that 'real risk' imposed a more stringent test than merely that the risk must be more than 'not fanciful'. The test could be amplifed as follows.

Level of severity

First, the test requires an assessment to be made of the severity of the treatment **3.105** which it is said that the applicant would suffer if removed. This must attain a minimum level of severity and would depend on all the circumstances of the case. But the ill-treatment must 'necessarily be serious' such that it is 'an affront to fundamental humanitarian principles to remove an individual to a country where he is at risk of serious ill-treatment'.

Causal link

Second, a causal link must be shown to exist between the act or threatened act of **3.106** removal or expulsion and the inhuman treatment relied on as violating the applicant's Article 3 rights. The removal must have 'as a direct consequence the exposure of an individual to proscribed ill-treatment' and the examination of the Article 3 issue 'must focus on the foreseeable consequences of the removal'.

Particularly high threshold in foreign cases

Third, in the context of a foreign case, the Article 3 threshold is particularly high **3.107** simply because it is a foreign case. It is even higher where the alleged inhuman treatment is not the direct or indirect responsibility of the public authorities of the receiving State, but results from some naturally occurring illness, whether physical or mental.

Article 3 claim can in principle succeed in a suicide case

3.108 Fourth, an Article 3 claim can in principle succeed in a suicide case.

Whether fear of ill-treatment causing suicide risk is well founded is a relevant consideration

3.109 Fifth, in deciding whether there is a real risk of a breach of Article 3 in a suicide case, a question of importance is whether the applicant's fear of ill-treatment in the receiving State upon which the risk of suicide is said to be based is objectively well founded. If the fear is not well founded, that will tend to weigh against there being a real risk that the removal will be in breach of Article 3.

Mechanisms to reduce risk of suicide

3.110 Sixth, a further question of considerable relevance is whether the removing and/ or the receiving State have effective mechanisms to reduce the risk of suicide. If there are effective mechanisms, that too will weigh heavily against an applicant's claim that removal will violate his or her Article 3 rights.

Domestic cases

3.111 In domestic cases, the same considerations as in foreign cases applied, but the approach was somewhat different because the concern to avoid or minimize the extra-territorial effect of the ECHR was absent. A question of particular significance in domestic cases was whether the removing or receiving State had effective mechanisms to reduce the risk of suicide. The Court of Appeal explained that its earlier decision in *Soumahoro v SSHD* [2003] EWCA Civ 840, [2003] Imm AR 529 did not expound a different test. In that case, on its facts, it was necessary to show the proposed removal significantly increased any suicide risk that was already present. However, this became factually relevant in *Soumahoro* only where there was a risk of suicide both in the UK and in the receiving State.

3.112 A real risk that an individual is likely to commit suicide in the United Kingdom as a result of immigration action would be likely to generate an argument that a positive duty arises in the sense discussed in *Osman v United Kingdom* (1998) 29 EHRR 246 at paragraphs 115 and 116 (and see Lord Carswell's consideration of those paragraphs in *In re: Officer L* [2007] UKHL 36).

3.113 In considering the facts in *J v SSHD* [2005] EWCA Civ 629 the Court of Appeal held that the IAT had correctly determined that there was no real risk of a breach of Article 3 in respect of the removal of the appellant, because there was no real risk that he would respond to the removal decision by committing suicide in the UK before removal, whilst en route to Sri Lanka, or following arrival. The IAT was entitled to conclude that any suicide attempts would be adequately managed in the UK by the relevant medical authorities and J's uncle. In relation to the risk of suicide en route, it was entitled to infer that J's uncle, in cooperation with the medical and immigration authorities, would help J make suitable arrangements for his return to Sri Lanka. Finally, the IAT was entitled to find that the appellant would have been cared for in Sri Lanka and that his fears of ill-treatment on return to Sri Lanka were without foundation. In each case the risk was below the Article 3 threshold.

Given the approach the Court of Appeal adopted, it is unlikely that in any but a **3.114** very small minority of cases there could be any prospect of successfully arguing that Article 3 would be breached through the applicant committing suicide in the UK prior to his removal. Unless any specific grounds are established for contending that the medical and immigration authorities would not be able to prevent suicide attempts prior to and during removal, the contrary inference is likely to be drawn. However, rather than being able to rely on unsupported presumptions of fact, it is likely that the Secretary of State will be asked to provide statistics to justify such an inference under the Freedom of Information Act 2000. The most relevant statistics would relate to the number of persons who had been identified as being at risk of suicide prior to travel, and amongst them, those who attempted and committed suicide prior to and after commencement of travel.

The guidance in *J v SSHD* on Article 3 claims based on suicide risk during and **3.115** after return has been applied in a number of cases subsequently, most frequently in relation to challenges to certification by the Secretary of State. The Court of Appeal in *R (on the appln of Tozlukaya) v SSHD* [2006] EWCA Civ 379 held that an increased risk of suicide was not itself a breach of Article 3, although it was capable of being a breach in some circumstances. The test remained whether there was a real risk of inhuman or degrading treatment on return. The effectiveness of mechanisms to reduce the risk of suicide in the receiving State had to be examined. The measures in the UK to protect against the risk of suicide, including removal with suitably qualified escorts, were reasonable. The Court also accepted evidence that appropriate measures would be taken by the German authorities at the airport and later to protect against the risk of suicide. Thus an increase in the risk of suicide due to removal was not sufficient to bring the case to the Article 3 threshold, even though the risk was severe and likely to continue.

A challenge on Article 3 grounds to the system of detaining and removing **3.116** those who were at risk of suicide or self-harm failed in *R (on the appln of X) v SSHD* [2006] EWHC 1208 (Admin).

3.117 Conversely, the applicant in *R (on the appln of Kurtaj) v SSHD* [2007] EWHC 221 (Admin) successfully argued before the Administrative Court that his further representations amounted to a fresh claim. *Kurtaj* was diagnosed with paranoid schizophrenia, following the dismissal of his claim by the IAT. The medical evidence stated that without medication the applicant would suffer a recurrence of debilitating symptoms and his risk of suicide would rise to 50 per cent. The Court held that this *could* amount to sufficiently serious ill-treatment to comprise an affront to fundamental humanitarian principles to remove him. Further, it was unlikely that there was a real prospect of the AIT concluding that Albania, the receiving State, had effective mechanisms to reduce the risk of suicide.[63] Therefore the Court concluded that the further representations constituted a fresh claim, as the Secretary of State was not entitled to conclude that the applicant had no realistic prospect of success before an immigration judge.[64]

3.118 In *AJ (Liberia) v SSHD* [2006] EWCA Civ 1736 the applicant succeeded on appeal, where the Court of Appeal was unable to see any evidence to support the AIT's conclusion that the applicant would obtain the necessary medication in Liberia on return. The difficulty was compounded by the AIT's finding that the applicant could take a supply of medication with him, which appeared to be entirely unsupported by evidence. As the AIT's reasoning on the availability of medicine was not properly based upon evidence, it was found to be flawed in law and the case was remitted to the AIT.

3.119 Practitioners should note the IND Policy on Suicide Threats,[65] which provides for specific measures to minimize the risk of suicide or self-harm. For example, under the policy, detained persons should be assessed by a nurse for risk of self-harm or suicidal behaviour within two hours of admissions and seen by a doctor within 24 hours, and care plans and Prison Service suicide prevention procedures (F2052 SH) are to be set up. For non-detained asylum seekers who have produced credible evidence that they are at risk of suicide, notification of adverse immigration decisions are to take place in accordance with a procedure, which includes prior notification of the individual's legal representatives.

3.120 In relation to 'foreign' cases, it is difficult to see why the absence of well-founded fear of persecution should necessarily detract from or negate the reality of

---

63 *AJ (Liberia) v SSHD* [2006] EWCA Civ 1736.

64 This being the second stage of the fresh claim test. The Secretary of State's view of the merits of the alleged fresh claim is the starting point for evaluation of the prospects of success of such claim (*WM (Democratic Republic of Congo) v SSHD* (2006) EWCA Civ 1780). Secondly, the Secretary of State had to ask himself how an appeal in front of an immigration judge might fare (*R (on the appln of Razgar) v SSHD* (2004) UKHL 27, (2004) 2 AC 368).

65 IDI's Chapter 1, Section 10, subsection 8, available at <http://www.ind.homeoffice.gov.uk/documents/idischapter1/>.

suicide risk. A schizophrenic who wholly without foundation believes that if removed to Ruritania he would be subject to such horrendous tortures that he would rather commit suicide would be at no greater risk of suicide if his fears of torture were true. The only way in which it seems the absence of objective justification of the applicant's fear should weigh against there being a real risk of removal amounting to breach of Article 3 would be in cases where the decision maker concludes that the applicant is actually aware that his claimed fear is not well founded. Hence the decision maker is unlikely to conclude that there is a real risk of suicide on return, as the applicant would be found to be unreliable.[66] To reach such a conclusion, the Court, AIT, or Secretary of State may have to disagree with the medical assessment of psychiatric experts. This is less likely to happen where the only medical evidence available supports the applicant's case. Different considerations would apply should the Secretary of State obtain his own psychiatric reports, the conclusions of which are at variance with the applicant's and do not support the inference of a real risk of suicide on return.

However, even if the only report produced is the one on which the applicant **3.121** relies, and its conclusions are that there is a high risk of suicide on return, this conclusion would not necessarily be accepted by the AIT or the courts. For instance, in *KK v SSHD* [2005] EWCA Civ 1082, the Court of Appeal found that the IAT was entitled to reach the conclusion that there was a sufficient Roma community in Serbia for K to return there with adequate support to assist his depressive and suicidal condition, without a breach of Articles 3 or 8. The IAT had reached the view that there would be no breach of the applicant's human rights despite the medical report adduced in the case setting out a high risk of suicide on return. The Court of Appeal accepted that great care must be taken in evaluating medical evidence and the IAT was not obliged to accept the doctor's view with respect to risk. To do so did not necessarily entail criticism of the doctor. As to the experience of doctors reporting on suicide risk, the Court of Appeal commented:

> 29. The fourth submission is that the reference near the end of paragraph 28 to Dr Laudin not having had the experience of people who committed suicide was an unfair one. I would accept that it is somewhat harsh upon the doctor. It may be that her successful treatment is the reason why she has not had patients who have committed suicide. Nevertheless, the point is not without significance and the Tribunal were entitled to make it. A doctor with broader experience in this respect, unfortunate though that experience may be, could be in a stronger position to assess risk in an existing case and the comment was one the Tribunal were entitled to make.

---

[66] The Court of Appeal in *KK v SSHD* [2005] EWCA Civ 1082 seems to have adopted such a credibility-based approach—see paragraph 27 of the judgment.

3.122 Any expert's report develops the material expert opinion by reference to facts which are assumed to be correct. If the facts found by the decision maker are different from those assumed by the expert, the value of the resulting opinion will soon diminish.

3.123 Further development of the case law in this highly contentious area can be anticipated, including further guidance from the courts as to the quality of the medical evidence which has to be presented in support of similar claims.

Inter-relationship with Article 8[67]

3.124 Finally, cases involving a risk of suicide on removal are equally likely to involve Article 8 considerations. Whilst specific arguments in relation to Article 8 should be made in addition to those relating to Article 3, and the AIT should address them separately, failure by the AIT to do so is unlikely to lead to a successful appeal.[68] In *KK v SSHD* [2005] EWCA Civ 1082 the absence of differentiation between Article 3 and Article 8 considerations in the IAT judgment was not sufficient ground for the IAT decision to be disturbed by the Court of Appeal. This conclusion was reached on the basis of analysis of the House of Lords judgment in *N v SSHD* [2005] 2 AC 296, which required very exceptional circumstances to exist, in cases not involving direct state responsibility, before Article 3 protection or Article 8 protection can render unlawful a decision to return an applicant to his own country.

3.125 In principle rights protected by Article 8 can be engaged by the foreseeable consequences for health of removal from the United Kingdom pursuant to an immigration decision, even where such removal does not violate Article 3, if the facts relied on by the applicant are sufficiently strong. Such cases will be rare. In *R (on the appln of Razgar) v SSHD* [2004] UKHL 27, (2004) 2 AC 368, Baroness Hale observed:

> There clearly must be a strong case before the Article is even engaged and then a fair balance must be struck under Article 8(2). In striking that balance, only the most compelling humanitarian considerations are likely to prevail over the legitimate aims of immigration control or public safety. The expelling state is required to assess the strength of the threat and strike that balance. It is not required to compare the adequacy of the health care available in the two countries. The question is whether removal to the foreign country will have a sufficiently adverse effect upon the applicant. (paragraph 59)

3.126 *Mukarkar v SSHD* [2006] EWCA Civ 1045 is an example of a case where a claim failed under Article 3 but succeeded under Article 8.

---

[67] Article 8 is considered in detail in Chapter 4.
[68] *KK v SSHD* [2005] EWCA Civ 1082, paragraph 49.

I. Removal to Conditions of Extreme Poverty or Upheaval

Cases arise where, in addition to its being suggested that an individual will be **3.127** subjected to torture or ill-treatment if returned to his home country, the conditions prevailing there are such as to make his return unlawful irrespective of the more conventional complaints. It might be suggested that the humanitarian conditions are so harsh that to expose anyone to them would breach Article 3.

We have seen that where a case does not concern the direct responsibility of **3.128** the contracting State for the infliction of harm, the threshold set by Article 3 is particularly high: *Bensaid v United Kingdom* Application No 44599/98 at para 40; *D v United Kingdom* supra. Just as a foreign national has no right to the medical treatment available in his host country, neither does he have a right to the standards and conditions of living such that his removal to a less satisfactory environment would breach a convention right. The Court has not previously considered the effect of Article 3 in expulsion cases in circumstances where the allegation is one of return to dreadful humanitarian conditions. The analysis of the Court in cases concerning individuals suffering from serious illness who faced removal to countries with less developed medical facilities bears conceptual similarities to this type of case. Absent some exceptional factor of the same magnitude, albeit in a different context from the medical cases, relevant to the individual and the circumstances he would face on return, poor humanitarian conditions in the country to which an alien will be expelled are unlikely to breach Article 3.

J. Destitution/Refusal of Asylum Support

The refusal of accommodation and financial support to destitute asylum seekers **3.129** was subject to numerous challenges in the Courts when the provisions of the 2002 Act enabling refusal of support in late claims came into effect.

The following decisions summarize the state of the case law in this area. **3.130**

R (on the appln of Q & Ors) v SSHD [2003] 3 WLR 365

In *Q* the Master of the Rolls cited with approval the decision of the ECtHR in **3.131** *Pretty v UK* 35 EHRR 1, paragraph 52:

> As regards the types of 'treatment' which fall within the scope of Article 3 of the Convention, the court's case law refers to 'ill-treatment' that attains a minimum level of severity and involves actual bodily injury or intense physical or mental suffering. Where treatment humiliates or debases an individual showing a lack of respect for,

or diminishing, his or her human dignity or arouses feelings of fear, anguish or inferiority capable of breaking an individual's moral and physical resistance, it may be characterised as degrading and also fall within the prohibition of Article 3. The suffering which flows from naturally occurring illness, physical or mental, may be covered by Article 3, where it is, or risks being, exacerbated by treatment, whether flowing from conditions of detention, expulsion or other measures, for which the authorities can be held responsible.

3.132 In *Q* the Court of Appeal further held:

> 61 . . . The 'real risk' test is one that the Strasbourg court has applied in the case of removal to a country in circumstances where the removing state will no longer be in a position to influence events. We do not believe that it is an appropriate test in the present context.

> 62 Some who claim asylum may already be in a condition which verges on the degree of severity capable of engaging Article 3 described in *Pretty v United Kingdom*. For those section 55(5) of the 2002 Act will permit and section 6 of the Human Rights Act 1998 will oblige the Secretary of State to provide or arrange for the provision of support. What of the others? Their fate will be uncertain. . . .

> 63 . . . It is not unlawful for the Secretary of State to decline to provide support unless and until it is clear that charitable support has not been provided and the individual is incapable of fending for himself. . . . He must, however, be prepared to entertain further applications from those to whom he has refused support who have not been able to find any charitable support or other lawful means of fending for themselves. . . .

Limbuela v SSHD [2004] EWCA Civ 540, [2004] QB 1440, (2004) 3 WLR 561

3.133 In the case of *Limbuela v SSHD* [2004] EWCA Civ 540, [2004] QB 1440, (2004) 3 WLR 561, the Court of Appeal considered the extent of the Secretary of State's obligations to those who fell through the safety net provided for destitute asylum seekers by the Immigration Acts by reason of their asylum applications not being made as soon as reasonably practicable. The question raised by the appeals concerned the level of destitution such individuals must sink to before their suffering or humiliation reaches the 'minimum level of severity' to amount to 'inhuman or degrading treatment' under Article 3. The majority of the Court of Appeal declined to interfere with the conclusions of the Administrative Court judges that the Home Secretary should have provided the three asylum seekers with asylum support.

3.134 After the Court of Appeal judgment the National Asylum Support Service (NASS) adopted a less restrictive approach when assessing whether someone has applied for asylum as soon as 'reasonably practicable'.[69] Generally only those who

---

[69] From 28 June 2004 NASS was likely not to deny support to those who applied for asylum a couple of days after arrival in the UK, or to those who could not adduce documentary evidence of their arrival.

claimed asylum after being in the UK for long periods of time were likely to fall outside the support provisions.[70]

R (on the appln of Limbuela & Ors) v SSHD [2005] UKHL 66, (2006) 1 AC 396

The Secretary of State was unsuccessful in a further appeal to the House of Lords. **3.135** Lord Bingham found that the Secretary of State's duty to provide support under section 55(5)(a) arose:

> . . . when it appears on a fair and objective assessment of all relevant facts and circumstances that an individual applicant faces an imminent prospect of serious suffering caused or materially aggravated by denial of shelter, food or the most basic necessities of life. Many factors may affect that judgment, including age, gender, mental and physical health and condition, any facilities or sources of support available to the applicant, the weather and time of year and the period for which the applicant has already suffered or is likely to continue to suffer privation.[71]

Lord Bingham continued:

> It is not in my opinion possible to formulate any simple test applicable in all cases. But if there were persuasive evidence that a late applicant was obliged to sleep in the street, save perhaps for a short and foreseeably finite period, or was seriously hungry, or unable to satisfy the most basic requirements of hygiene, the threshold would, in the ordinary way, be crossed.[72]

The test was similarly formulated by Lord Hope: **3.136**

> Withdrawal of support will not in itself amount to treatment which is inhuman or degrading in breach of the asylum-seeker's Article 3 Convention right. But it will do so once the margin is crossed between destitution within the meaning of section 95(3) of the 1999 Act and the condition that results from inhuman or degrading treatment within the meaning of the Article.[73]

The withdrawal of support was an intentionally inflicted act for which the **3.137** Secretary of State is directly responsible. He is also responsible for all the consequences flowing from that act, bearing in mind the nature of the regime which does not allow asylum seekers the ability to earn money, as they could not seek employment for at least 12 months.[74]

---

[70] A new NASS Eligibility and Assessment Team (NEAT) was established, with a primary purpose to make section 55 and 95 decisions in relation to the provision of NASS support. Applicants would complete a level 1 screening form and the NASS 1 application form. Where the information contained in these documents was insufficient for a decision, the applicant would be invited to attend a level 2 interview, before a s 55 decision was made.

[71] *R (on the appln of Limbuela & Ors) v SSHD* [2005] UKHL 66, (2006) 1 AC 396, para 8.

[72] Ibid, para 9.

[73] Ibid, para 57.

[74] Ibid, para 56. See also *R (Q & Ors) v SSHD* [2004] QB 36, 69, para 57.

3.138 In relation to the question when the support under section 55(5)(a) is to be provided, the House of Lords stressed that that section provided the Secretary of State with the power to 'avoid' a breach of Article 3. He should not wait until the degree of severity which amounts to a breach of Article 3 has been reached. As soon as the asylum seeker makes it clear that there is an imminent prospect that a breach of the Article will occur because the conditions which he is having to endure are on the *verge* of reaching the necessary degree of severity, the Secretary of State has the power under section 55(5)(a), and the duty under section 6(1) of the Human Rights Act 1998, to act to avoid it.[75]

Availability of support from other sources

3.139 Difficult questions arise in cases where legislation places an independent duty on a different body, such as a local authority, to provide accommodation. In such circumstances, is the Secretary of State under an obligation to provide NASS accommodation under the IAA 1999? The case of *R (on the appln of O) v Haringey LB and SSHD* [2004] EWCA Civ 535, (2004) 2 FLR 476, 2004 LGR 672 considered the position where the local authority was obliged to provide accommodation to a disabled mother under section 21(1)(a) National Assistance Act 1948, and the children had the means of obtaining support under section 17 or section 20 of the Children Act 1989. The Court of Appeal found that under section 95(4) of the 1999 Act in considering whether the claimant was destitute, the family had to be viewed as a unit. Although accommodation was available to the mother under section 21 of the 1948 Act, and the children had rights to accommodation under the 1989 Act, neither of these sets of legislative provisions had the effect that accommodation was available to her and her children *taken together*. Therefore the applicant was destitute within the meaning of section 95 of the 1999 Act. Further, any deficiency in essential living needs was held to be sufficient to bring an asylum seeker within the NASS scheme. Therefore the fact that some of those needs were met from other sources did not prevent the asylum seeker from being treated as destitute for the purpose of section 95. Once the asylum seeker was within the scheme, the availability of other resources was taken into account in deciding what provision was required from NASS.

3.140 On the facts in *O*, the Court of Appeal held that the judge was right to find the family was destitute within the meaning of section 95 of the 1999 Act and hence entitled to support under the NASS scheme. However, he was in error in concluding that the total responsibility fell on the Secretary of State, as the duty of the local authority under section 21 of the 1948 Act remained, notwithstanding the NASS scheme, which should be taken into account in determining the support to be provided under that scheme. In effect the accommodation for the

---

75 Ibid, para 62.

family was likely to be provided by the local authority and the Secretary of State was to contribute towards the cost of accommodating the children, according to a sensible arrangement between them.

Home Office policies and practice, further resources

For further detailed consideration of the law and practice in relation to accommodation and support for asylum seekers, practitioners are referred to: **3.141**

- Willman, S Knafler, and S Pierce, with Al Stanley, *Support for Asylum-seekers: A Guide to Legal and Welfare Rights* (London: Legal Action Group, 2004)
- The section of the IND website dealing with NASS support can be found at: <http://www.ind.homeoffice.gov.uk/applying/asylum_support>. The site allows access to the current version of the application forms for NASS support and s 4 support, as well as guidance notes and particular policies (eg on the provision of support for failed asylum seekers from Iraq under s 4 of the IAA 1999).

For example, the policy bulletins section[76] provides the following information on the policies current at March 2007:

Access to support (PBs 4, 11, 23, 37, 67, 70, 71, 73, 75, 76, 78, 79, 80, 83, 84, New 87) <http://www.ind.homeoffice.gov.uk/documents/accesstosupport/>

    I. Policy Bulletin 4—Using threshold tables (142.0 K)
   II. Policy Bulletin 11—Mixed households (77.03 K)
  III. Policy Bulletin 23—Asylum support appeals process (93.84 K)
  IV. Policy Bulletin 37—Maternity payments (80.15 K)
   V. Policy Bulletin 67—Overpayments (47.42 K)
  VI. Policy Bulletin 70—Domestic violence (46.96 K)
 VII. Policy Bulletin 71—Section 4 of the Immigration and Asylum Act 1999 (56.64 K)
VIII. Policy Bulletin 73—Provisions of emergency accommodation (46.23 K)
  IX. Policy Bulletin 75—Section 55 (late claims) 2002 Act guidance—revised version (231.63 K)
   X. Policy Bulletin 76—Asylum support applications from nationals of a European Economic Area State or from persons who have refugee status abroad (New) (76.53 K)
  XI. Policy Bulletin 78—Additional payments to pregnant women and children (47.18 K)
 XII. Policy Bulletin 79—Section 57 (applications for support: false or incomplete information) 2002 Act guidance (67.69 K)

---

[76] <http://www.ind.homeoffice.gov.uk/applying/asylum_support/policybulletins>—accessed on 20 March 2007.

XIII. Policy Bulletin 80—Back payment on asylum support (131.58 K)

XIV. Policy Bulletin 83—Duty to offer support, family unity, vulnerable persons, withdrawing support (38.66 K)

 XV. Policy Bulletin 84—Entertaining a further application for support (45.6 K)

XVI. Policy Bulletin 87—The Civil Partnership Act 2004 (54.54 K)

Children (PBs 33, 29) <http://www.ind.homeoffice.gov.uk/documents/children/>

  I. Policy Bulletin 29—Transition at age 18 (81.44 K)

 II. Policy Bulletin 33—Age disputes (37.0 K)

Disbenefited (PB 53) <http://www.ind.homeoffice.gov.uk/documents/disbenefited/>

I. Policy Bulletin 53—Temporary support for NASS eligible disbenefited singles (or childless couples) (41.02 K)

Dispersal (PB 31) <http://www.ind.homeoffice.gov.uk/documents/dispersal/>

I. Policy Bulletin 31—Dispersal guidelines (45.08 K)

General (PB's 23, 47, 64, 72, 81, 86, 82) <http://www.ind.homeoffice.gov.uk/documents/general/>

    I. Policy Bulletin 23—Asylum support appeals process (93.84 K)

   II. Policy Bulletin 47—Judicial review (59.37 K)

  III. Policy Bulletin 64—Has been withdrawn. In the interim please use the 'Bail flowcharts' below for assistance in deciding support arrangements for bail cases. (41.87 K)

   IV. Bail flowchart—The applicant was not already in IND accommodation before being taken into detention (67.82 K)

    V. Bail flowchart—The applicant was already in IND accommodation before being taken into detention (68.58 K)

   VI. Bail flowchart—The applicant has already been released from immigration or police detention and now wishes to access IND accommodation as a bail address (62.12 K)

  VII. Policy Bulletin 72—Employment & voluntary activity (42.72 K)

 VIII. Policy Bulletin 81—Racist incidents (58.68 K)

   IX. Policy Bulletin 82—Asylum seekers with care needs (111.05 K)

Medical (PBs 19, 43, 59—under review, 85) <http://www.ind.homeoffice.gov.uk/documents/medical/>

  I. Medical Foundation cases—<http://www.ind.homeoffice.gov.uk/documents/consideringanddecidingtheclaim/guidance/medicalfoundation.pdf?view=Binary>

 II. Policy Bulletin 43—HC2 certificates (89.58 K)

III. Policy Bulletin 59—Help with the cost of funerals (111.5 K)

IV. Policy Bulletin 85—Dispersing asylum seekers with health care needs (225.58 K)

Travel (PBs 17, 28) <http://www.ind.homeoffice.gov.uk/documents/travel/>

I. Policy Bulletin 17 (30.82 K)—Failure to travel

II. Policy Bulletin 28—Providing travelling expenses and reimbursing essential travel (121.1 K)

K. Dispersal

Domestic cases raising Article 3 could arise in the context of the provision of **3.142** benefits and accommodation to asylum seekers. For example, in *Gezer v SSHD* [2004] EWCA 1730 the Court of Appeal considered an Article 3 challenge to the Secretary of State's decision to disperse the appellant and his family to a Glasgow estate, where they suffered racially motivated attacks, which were accepted by the respondent to constitute ill-treatment sufficiently serious to cross the Article 3 severity threshold. The fundamental question in the appeal was the rigour or intensity of the duty of the State to protect an individual from ill-treatment, failing which a breach of Article 3 would be established. In the leading judgment Laws LJ recalled the spectrum of instances in which Article 3 might be engaged, postulated in *Limbuela*, between the worst class of cases where State-sponsored violence is absolutely prohibited (call this end of the spectrum *A*) and, at the other end of the spectrum (*Z*), 'a decision made in the exercise of lawful policy, which however may expose the individual to a marked degree of suffering, not caused by violence but by the circumstances in which he finds himself in consequence of the decision'. Therefore the spectrum ranged from those instances where the State enjoyed no power of discretion or judgment but was simply forbidden to cause or perpetrate the act which would violate Article 3, to those where the State might enjoy a considerable margin of discretion as to the adoption and exercise of policy notwithstanding that the action taken *might be* sufficiently grave to meet the Article 3 threshold of severity. In deciding that the dispersal decision fell near the *Z* end of the spectrum, Laws LJ took into account the following relevant factors:

(1) First that the case was plainly not one involving acts of violence by State officials.

(2) However, it did concern violence, albeit violence by non-State actors, and not illness or destitution.

(3) Third, the appeal did not involve the use of State power to compel the appellant into a particular situation to his detriment, but rather the offer of

material assistance to him, which he was free to decline. There *was* a choice to be made by the appellant, however bleak and difficult refusal of the support might have been.[77] This latter factor was found to point to a place towards the end of the spectrum which did not engage Article 3.

3.143 The unanimous conclusion of the Court was that no Article 3 infringement had been established, as the Secretary of State, through NASS, enjoyed a wide margin of discretion as to the administration of the statutory support. He was not required to make special inquiries to save the appellant from harm. Any other conclusion would have given rise to a duty to pick accommodation suitable to the particular asylum seeker, which was not provided for in the legislation governing asylum seekers' support and, further, was not required by Article 3.

3.144 In considering the strength of an Article 3 argument, particularly in the domestic type of case, practitioners could usefully adopt the analysis in *Gezer* (see Table 3.1).

3.145 It should be noted that the House of Lords in *N (FC) v SSHD* did consider the analysis adopted by the Court of Appeal in *Gezer* and endorsed the categories and sub-categories of Article 3 cases falling within a spectrum (as set out at paragraphs 24–29 of *Gezer*). Their Lordships further endorsed the analysis that the kind of action required in any given case to exonerate the State from liability under Article 3 would reflect but is not necessarily identical with the distinction between the different categories.

Table 3.1 Article 3 Domestic cases—duty on the State

	Check list for practitioners
1.	Where in the spectrum do the circumstances of the case fall: Between 'A' (State-sponsored violence) and 'Z' (a marked degree of suffering, not caused by violence but by the circumstances in which he finds himself in consequence of a decision pursuant to a lawful policy)? Consider: a. Does the case involve acts of violence by State officials? b. Does it involve violence by non-State actors? c. Does it involve a condition arising as a result of illness or destitution?
2.	Does the case involve the use of State power to compel the appellant into a particular situation to his detriment? Does the individual have a choice or opportunity to avoid the ill-treatment?
3.	Does the impugned decision arise in a context where the State enjoys a considerable margin of discretion as to the adoption and exercise of policy?

---

[77] Elias J dissenting on this point, para 57.

L. Practice and Procedure Note

Dealing with medical evidence

Before sending instructions to a medical expert, practitioners should assess the exact **3.146** purpose of the medical evidence which they will seek to adduce. The purposes of a medical report would vary, the following being the most common:

To corroborate the applicant's account of past ill-treatment or torture. The range of **3.147** reports would include reports by plastic surgeons or orthopaedic surgeons on scarring and other physical injuries and their attributability, and reports of psychological illnesses and their causation from past ill-treatment.

To give a current diagnosis of a medical condition and a prognosis on the alternative **3.148** bases of continued treatment in the UK, and in the absence of treatment or with limited treatment on return. Such cases have little prospect of success on Article 3 grounds, unless they are of the most exceptional nature.[78] However, should such a case be pursued, thorough preparation and in particular carefully tailored medical evidence would be crucial. Involvement of a country expert is likely to be required. The country expert could comment on the availability of the type of treatment which the applicant requires and is likely to require in the near future. Once the country report is received, the medical report can be finalized, with a prognosis being given in accordance with the available treatment in the country of return. The medical expert should additionally be asked to comment on the level of suffering the applicant is likely to undergo in the absence of treatment or with the limited treatment available and its duration.

A medical report may also assist in explaining difficulties which the applicant may **3.149** encounter in giving evidence. The most obvious example would relate to traumatized individuals not being able to give an ordered historical account of their ill-treatment, being unable to concentrate, or breaking down during questioning in the appellate proceedings or in the Home Office interview. Where the medical opinion is that exposure to cross-examination would pose an unacceptable risk to the applicant's health, such as re-traumatizing him or severely exacerbating his current condition, then the decision is likely to be made not to call the applicant to give oral evidence at the hearing. The medical report would give invaluable support to such a decision, and would not leave the applicant exposed to an adverse credibility inference from the fact that the evidence has not been tested by cross-examination.

Finally, a medical report may also relate directly to the reality of the risk of Article 3 ill- **3.150** treatment and meeting the minimum level of severity threshold, for example in cases

---

[78] See section G above.

where a psychological condition would cause the applicant to be less robust in withstanding interrogation.

An illustration

3.151   In *Ladji Diaby v SSHD* [2005] EWCA Civ 651, the Court of Appeal dealt with a case where the adjudicator appeared to have made his decision on credibility without taking into account anything in a psychiatric report and a general practitioner's report sent in after the hearing. The respondent Secretary of State had conceded before the IAT that that approach amounted to an error of law. However, as the IAT did not have the medical reports before it, it proceeded on the assumption that they contained nothing relevant to credibility. It ruled that the applicant had to establish that the error of law was material, but had failed to do so. On appeal the Court of Appeal held that the IAT was wrong to proceed on the assumption that the medical evidence contained nothing material. The medical reports gave some indication that D's scarring and eye problems were consistent with his being injured in the way he alleged. Further, the fact that D suffered from post-traumatic stress was at least a possible explanation for D's breakdown during the hearing, rather than the adjudicator's conclusion that it was caused by D's realization that he had been giving inconsistent accounts. It was possible that the adjudicator might have reached a different conclusion on credibility if he had approached the question of credibility giving proper consideration to the medical reports and without forming a view about credibility before taking their contents into account. The case was remitted to be reconsidered by a different tribunal.

Choosing the medical expert

3.152   It is important that the choice of medical expert is made on the basis of the qualifications of the expert to give evidence in the medical field required. Previous experience in examining or treating asylum seekers and torture victims would also be an advantage. Practitioners would need to ensure that the expert is familiar with the standards of proof in asylum and human rights cases and the purpose for which their professional opinion is sought. With regard to the report, there is little use in obtaining a standard document with at most a paragraph relating to the particular circumstances of the case in hand and a generalized conclusion that the applicant is likely to suffer from Post-Traumatic Stress Disorder (PTSD). Such reports have been subject to severe criticism from the IAT and the courts, and are likely to detract from, rather than support, the applicant's claim. One way of ensuring that the expert reveals the criteria according to which the diagnosis is made (eg DSM IV[79] or ICD 10[80] diagnostic indices

---

[79] Diagnostic and Statistical Manual of Mental Disorders (DSM IV).
[80] Composite International Diagnostic Interview (ICD 10).

in relation to Post-Traumatic Stress Syndrome, for example) is to request in the instructions that the expert does so.

The Medical Foundation

The Medical Foundation is a well-respected source of medical evidence, in particular **3.153** for its expertise in dealing with torture survivors. Even if it is not possible to obtain a report from the Medical Foundation, which often has excessively long waiting lists, it would be advisable that its *Guidelines for the Examination of Survivors of Torture* (2nd edition) are consulted, and any physician who is independently instructed to prepare a medical report is referred to them. Additionally, the Home Office Good Practice Guidance in relation to interviewing alleged victims of torture stipulates that caseworkers may wish to explore matters from the following list, which the Medical Foundation considers interviewers should attempt to establish:

- the method of torture used;
- any equipment employed;
- the place where the torture took place;
- the duration of the ill-treatment;
- the frequency of abuse;
- the number of individuals involved in the torture;
- the immediate effects of the torture on the individual;
- the ongoing effects of torture, including the presence of scars; and
- the need for medical assistance, both immediately following the torture and in any continuing treatment.

Good practice would suggest that these matters, if not addressed in interview, should be explored by practitioners prior to obtaining a medical expert and details of the applicant's evidence on these issues should be included in the instructions to the medical expert.

Home Office policies and guidance

The Home Office policies and guidance to caseworkers in relation to dealing with **3.154** medical cases are set out in the following locations of the IND website.

Asylum Policy Unit Notices

Applications raising Article 3 medical grounds (18.5 K)[81]

---

[81] <http://www.ind.homeoffice.gov.uk/documents/asylumpolicyinstructions/apunotices/ applicationsraisingarticle3.pdf>—accessed on 20 March 2007.

Asylum Policy Instructions

ECHR—European Convention on Human Rights (357.52 K)[82]

Asylum Process Manual[83]

Chapter 2—Considering applications[84]

- Medical Foundation cases (77.92 K)[85]
- Conducting asylum interviews (269.85 K)[86]
- Medical evidence (non-Medical Foundation cases) (72.52 K)[87]
- Interviewing alleged victims of torture: good practice (53.92 K)[88]

Immigration Directorate's Instructions (IDIs)

<http://www.ind.homeoffice.gov.uk/documents/idischapter1> (Section 10 deals with case consideration of Human Rights Articles, further representations, and the IND Policy on Suicide Threats. Section 10 was updated in December 2006.)

M. Practice and Procedure Note

Country Guideline Determinations/starred appeals

3.155 Test cases pertaining to the risk on return for particular groups, or 'Country Guideline Determinations', were recognised by the Court of Appeal to embody 'the somewhat exotic doctrine of a factual precedent'. In *S & Ors v SSHD* [2002] EWCA Civ 539 Laws LJ observed:

> 26. . . . the notion of a judicial decision which is binding as to *fact* is foreign to the common law, save for the limited range of circumstances where the principle of *res judicata* (and its variant, issue estoppel) applies. . . . This principle has been evolved . . . to avoid the vice of successive trials of the same cause or question between the same parties. By contrast, it is also a principle of our law that a

---

[82] <http://www.ind.homeoffice.gov.uk/documents/asylumpolicyinstructions/apis/echr.pdf>— accessed on 20 March 2007.

[83] The Asylum Process Manual (APM) constitutes the Immigration and Nationality Directorate's official staff instructions relating to the operational processes for handling asylum claims and asylum-related applications.

[84] <http://www.ind.homeoffice.gov.uk/lawandpolicy/opprocesses/>—accessed on 20 March 2007. Chapter 2—Considering applications.

[85] <http://www.ind.homeoffice.gov.uk/documents/chapter2/apmsections/ medicalfoundationcases.pdf>—accessed on 20 March 2007.

[86] <http://www.ind.homeoffice.gov.uk/documents/chapter2/apmsections/ conductingasyluminterviews.pdf>—accessed on 20 March 2007.

[87] <http://www.ind.homeoffice.gov.uk/documents/chapter2/apmsections/medicalevidence. pdf>—accessed on 20 March 2007.

[88] <http://www.ind.homeoffice.gov.uk/documents/chapter2/annexes/ interviewingallegedvictims>—accessed on 20 March 2007.

party is free to invite the court to reach a different conclusion on a particular factual issue from that reached on the same issue in earlier litigation to which, however, he was a stranger. The first principle supports the public interest in finality in litigation. The second principle supports the ordinary call of justice, that a party have the opportunity to put his case: he is not to be bound by what others might have made of a like, or even identical case.

27. The stance taken by the IAT here, to lay out a determination intended in effect to be binding upon the appellate authorities as to the factual state of affairs in Croatia absent a demonstrable change for the worse vis-à-vis the plight of Serbs, to an extent sacrifices the second principle to the first. By no means entirely: an applicant will of course be heard on any facts particular to his case and (as the IAT made clear) evidence as to any deterioration in the state of affairs in Croatia would be listened to. Otherwise, however, the debate about the conditions in Croatia generally affecting Serbian returnees or potential returnees has been had and is not for the present to be had again.

28. While in our general law this notion of a factual precedent is exotic, in the context of the IAT's responsibilities it seems to us in principle to be benign and practical. Refugee claims vis-à-vis any particular State are inevitably made against a political backdrop which over a period of time, however long or short, is, if not constant, at any rate identifiable. Of course the impact of the prevailing political reality may vary as between one claimant and another, and it is always the appellate authorities' duty to examine the facts of individual cases. But there is no public interest, nor any legitimate individual interest, in multiple examinations of the state of the backdrop at any particular time. Such revisits give rise to the risk, perhaps the likelihood, of inconsistent results; and the likelihood, perhaps the certainty, of repeated and therefore wasted expenditure of judicial and financial resources upon the same issues and the same evidence.

The Court of Appeal, however, recognized that as a safeguard the duty to give rea- **3.156** sons should be applied with particular rigour, which led to the remittal of the test cases in *S & Ors*.

The usefulness of general assessment of the background evidence in detailed test **3.157** cases in relation to particular issues or groups was also stressed by the Court of Appeal in *Shirazi* [2003] EWCA Civ 1562, where Sedley LJ observed:

I accept readily that it is not a ground of appeal that a different conclusion was open to the tribunal below on the same facts, nor therefore that another tribunal *has* reached a different conclusion on very similar facts. But it has to be a matter of concern that the same political and legal situation, attested by much the same in-country data from case to case, is being evaluated differently by different tribunals. The latter seems to me to be the case in relation to religious apostasy in Iran. The differentials we have seen are related less to the differences between individual asylum-seekers than to differences in the Tribunal's reading of the situation on the ground in Iran. This is understandable, but it is not satisfactory. In a system which is as much inquisitorial as it is adversarial, inconsistency on such questions works against legal certainty. That does not mean that the situation cannot change, or that an individual's relationship to it does not have to be distinctly gauged in each case. It means that in any one period a judicial policy (with the flexibility that the word implies) needs to be adopted on the effect of the in-country data in recurrent classes of case.

Practitioners' checklist

3.158   Practitioners should consider reported IAT/AIT and Court of Appeal case law to identify any case law pertaining to background conditions:

3.159   Is the decision expressed in terms to be determinative of the background situation
with respect to a particular group? If this is not so, the Tribunal is unlikely to treat it as
such. Usually IAT/AIT decision of general application would be starred.

3.160   How recent is the decision? If considerable time has elapsed between the date of the
starred country guidance determination and the claim/appeal under consideration,
then arguments that the political/background situation have changed would have a
much stronger chance of success.

3.161   Have there been significant changes in the political/background situation since the
starred decision (eg have there been elections, a change of government, resurgence
of violence, etc)?

3.162   Are there facts particular to the present case which make the risk of persecution/
Article 3 ill-treatment higher, even in the light of the background conclusions in the
starred decision? Such specific factors should be clearly identified for the Tribunal.

3.163   In considering an appeal, have the factors particular to the case been considered and
have sufficient reasons been given?

3.164   Currently the AIT website contains a useful spreadsheet with Country Guideline
Determinations.[89] The determinations are divided by country, with a date indicating
when they were added to the list. In addition the list is kept up to date with outdated
cases being removed and a note of the date of their deletion being kept. Thus, identification of reliable Country Guideline Determinations and avoidance of reliance on
old and outdated determinations is considerably simplified for practitioners. Like any
compilation, the usefulness of the list would be commensurate with the regularity of
updating and review. Therefore it is important that practitioners do assess Guideline
Determinations for potential use in their cases according to the criteria identified
above.

3.165   In *R (Iran) & Ors v SSHD* [2005] EQCA Civ 982, the Court of Appeal held that a failure
without good reason to apply a relevant country guidance decision might constitute
an error of law. For a further Court of Appeal case where the application of country
guidance cases by the AIT was considered, see *Ariaya and Sammy v SSHD* [2006]
EWCA Civ 48.

---

[89] As well as other starred determinations—see spreadsheets available at <http://www.ait.gov.uk/
practice_directions/case_law.htm>.

Appellants may still succeed in establishing real risk of Article 3 ill-treatment despite **3.166** general country guidance revealing generalized improvement in the security situation. For example in *AM (Risks in Bujumbura area) Burundi* [2005] UKAIT 00123 the AIT found that the Adjudicator misdirected himself in law in failing properly to analyze the *SS Burundi CG* [2004] UKIAT 0029 decision and failing to explain why the appellant would not be at risk in her home area.

Home Office Policy on particular countries can be found in Operation Guidance Notes (OGNs) **3.167** at: <http://www.ind.homeoffice.gov.uk/documents/countryspecificasylumpolicyogns/>.

Robinson exception to consideration of obvious points of law not in the Grounds of Appeal

For the AIT to entertain an appeal on a point of law, it had to be discernible in the **3.168** grounds of appeal when the permission to appeal was given.[90]

The *Robinson* rule[91] in asylum cases provides an exception to this general require- **3.169** ment. The *Robinson* rule requires the AIT to pursue an obvious point of law relating to the Refugee Convention favourable to the asylum seeker even though it has not been raised by him in the grounds of appeal. This obligation arises from the duty of the courts to give anxious scrutiny to an asylum claim and to prevent the UK from being in breach of its international obligations under the Refugee Convention. The *Robinson* rule usually applies in favour of the applicant. Exceptionally, however, it applies in favour of the Secretary of State, by enabling the Court to consider whether a person is expressly excluded from the Refugee Convention by Art 1F(b), due to having committed a serious non-political crime, even where the Secretary of State's grounds of appeal do not include the point.[92]

In respect of human rights appeals, the Court of Appeal has held that the rationale of **3.170** the *Robinson* rule ought to apply equally to the ECHR:

> The significance of *Robinson* is in its demonstration of the role of the courts and the Tribunal in ensuring that the United Kingdom does not fall foul of the Refugee Convention, even where an obvious point of Convention law has been missed by the practitioners. It surely applies on the same basis to the ECHR, where the argument is even stronger because, by section 6 of the Human Rights Act 1998, it is unlawful for a public authority to act in a way which is incompatible with an ECHR right and courts and the Tribunal are 'public authorities' for this purpose: section 6(3)(a). (*AM (Serbia) & Ors v SSHD* [2007] EWCA Civ 16, para 29)

---

[90] *Miftari v SSHD* (2005) EWCA Civ 481, *R (Iran) v SSHD* [2005] EWCA Civ 982, Times, 19 August 2005, and *ZT v SSHD* (2005) EWCA Civ 1421.
[91] *R (on the appln of Robinson) v SSHD* (1997) 3 WLR 1162.
[92] *A (Iraq) v SSHD* (2005) EWCA Civ 1438, The Independent, 6 December 2005.

This finding is *obiter*. However, its rationale is compelling, and it is likely to be followed in future cases where the point arises for decision.

However, the extension of the *Robinson* rule to human rights appeals cannot avail the Secretary of State, as there would be no potential breach of the State's international obligations if relief is improperly allowed under an ECHR Article. (See *GH (Afghanistan) v SSHD* [2005] EWCA Civ 1603.)

4

ARTICLE 8 OF THE EUROPEAN CONVENTION ON HUMAN RIGHTS (RIGHT TO RESPECT FOR PRIVATE AND FAMILY LIFE)

Article 8 of the ECHR provides:

(1) Everyone has the right to respect for his private and family life, his home and his correspondence.

(2) There shall be no interference by a public authority with the exercise of this right except such as is in accordance with the law and is necessary in a democratic society in the interests of national security, public safety or the economic well-being of the country, for the prevention of disorder or crime, for the protection of health or morals, or for the protection of the rights and freedoms of others.

A. Rights Protected

4.01 The rights protected by Article 8, namely the right to respect for private and family life, one's home, and correspondence, are less clearly defined than the rights under Article 3 as considered in the previous chapter. Additionally, the rights protected under Article 8 are qualified rights, and interference with such rights by the State in the immigration context, if compliant with the criteria set out within Article 8(2), would not entail an infringement of those rights. Therefore practitioners will need to adopt a methodical approach to the identification of the rights protected by ECHR Article 8 and a similarly clear analysis of the permissible interferences with such rights, set in the context of the supervisory powers of the appellate authorities. This chapter aims to follow this structure, with a concluding exposition and analysis of the current Home Office policies in this area.

Family life and private life

Domestic and foreign cases in the Article 8 context

4.02 In *Ullah*[1] Lord Bingham drew a distinction between 'domestic cases' and 'foreign cases'. Domestic cases were defined as those 'where a State is said to have acted within its own territory in a way which infringes the enjoyment of a Convention right by a person within that territory'. Foreign cases constituted such cases 'in which it is claimed that the conduct of the State in removing a person from its territory (whether by expulsion or extradition) to another territory will lead to a violation of the person's Convention rights in that other territory'. Therefore in domestic cases the contracting state is directly responsible for the breach of Convention rights through its own act or omission. In contrast, in foreign cases the contracting State's responsibility is engaged because of the real risk that its conduct in expelling the person will lead to a gross invasion of his most fundamental human rights. The concept of a threshold related to the seriousness of the violation or the importance of the right involved does not exist in domestic cases. In such cases, the State must always act in a way which is compatible with Convention rights.

4.03 In the context of Article 8, Lord Bingham in *Ullah* referred to a third, hybrid, category, where 'the removal of a person from country A to country B may both violate his right to respect for his private and family life in country A and also violate the same right by depriving him of family life or impeding his enjoyment of private life in country B'. He considered those cases to be closer to 'domestic cases'. In such cases, therefore, there was no threshold test of humanitarian affront. However, as the Article 8 right is qualified, what may happen in the foreign country is relevant to the proportionality of the proposed expulsion.

---

[1] *Ullah* (2004) 2 AC 323.

Family life, private life, and 'health cases'

In *R (on the appln of Razgar) v SSHD*[2] Baroness Hale drew the following distinc-   **4.04**
tions between the different types of Article 8 cases in the immigration and expulsion context:

(1) Expulsion severing family links

Most commonly, the person to be expelled has established a family life in the
contracting state. His expulsion will be an interference, not only with his own right
to respect for his private and family life, but also with that of the other members of
his core family group: his spouse (or perhaps partner) and his children. The
Strasbourg court regards its task as to examine whether the contracting state has
struck a fair balance between the interference and the legitimate aim pursued by the
expulsion. The reason for the expulsion and the degree of interference, including
any alternative means of preserving family ties, will be explored and compared.
(para 44)

Interference with such right may be permissible if the interference is for one of
the following reasons, either expressly or impliedly envisaged within Article 8(2):

(a) 'Sometimes, the reason for expulsion will be immigration control, which is a
    legitimate aim "in the interests of the economic well-being of the country".[3]
    (para 45)

(b) 'Sometimes, the legitimate aim will be "the prevention of disorder or crime".
    This has arisen in a long line of cases concerning people who have lived in the
    contracting state since childhood but remain liable to expulsion if they
    commit serious crimes'.[4] (para 46)

(c) 'Protection of the rights and freedoms of others' is another legitimate aim
    which may justify interference with Article 8 rights. Thus, in the context of
    child abduction proceedings under the Hague Convention, the Family
    Division of the High Court in *S v B and Y (A child)*[5] considered that although
    an order for a child's return to New Zealand might interfere with the mother's
    right to respect for family life under Article 8, that order would be in accor-
    dance with the law and have a legitimate aim under Article 8(2). The order
    would be made for the protection of the rights and freedoms of others, namely
    the child's and the father's corresponding rights, to which the Hague
    Convention, by its structure and terms, accorded paramount importance. On

---

[2] *R (on the appln of Razgar) v SSHD* [2004] UKHL 27, (2004) 2 AC 368.
[3] See *Berrehab v The Netherlands* (1988) 11 EHRR 322 and *Ciliz v The Netherlands* [2000] 2 FLR
469 as examples of cases where the interference was disproportionate, as in neither case was there an
alternative means of preserving or establishing family ties between father and child.
[4] See *Moustaquim v Belgium* (1991) 13 EHRR 802, *Beldjoudi v France* (1992) 14 EHRR 801,
Nasri v France (1995) 21 EHRR 458, *Jakupovic v Austria* (2003) 38 EHRR 595.
[5] *S v B and Y (A child)* [2005] EWHC 733 (Fam), The Times, 17 May 2005.

the facts of the case, an order was made that the mother return the child to New Zealand.

These were all cases in which deportation would be an interference with the right to respect for the private or family life which the applicant had established in the expelling state. Conditions in the receiving state were relevant only for the purpose of assessing proportionality. Could that family life be established or continue elsewhere? The effect upon the spouse or child left behind had to be considered and might well be determinative. The Court is unsympathetic to actions which will have the effect of breaking up marriages or separating children from their parents. (para 50 in *Razgar*)

(2) Entry clearance cases—to continue a family life
The other type of domestic Article 8 case arises where there is no question of expulsion but immigration control prevents other close family members joining a spouse or parents living in the contracting state. (para 51)

Thus in the Article 8 context, an applicant would be arguing that failure to grant entry clearance to a family member would amount to an interference with the right to respect of his family life. In this context, any potential interference is likely to be justified and proportionate to the legitimate aim of upholding immigration control, if the family member seeking admission does not meet the requirements of the immigration rules.

(3) Private life cases—'foreign cases' and 'hybrid cases'
'Private life' cases, as opposed to 'family life' cases, arise most commonly in circumstances where the applicant alleges that there will be an infringement to his right to a private life, on the basis that expulsion would affect one's health through withdrawal of treatment received in the host country or otherwise.

Baroness Hale referred to such cases as 'health cases', ie where 'the applicant's health needs are being properly or at least adequately met in this country and the complaint is that they will not be adequately met in the country to which he is to be expelled'. *Bensaid v United Kingdom*[6] was such a case, with Baroness Hale's analysis of it in *Razgar* categorizing it essentially as a hybrid case.[7] The 'foreign' aspect of it was the difficulty in accessing appropriate psychiatric treatment in Algeria. This fell mainly to be dealt with under Article 3. However, the ECtHR did not rule out that it might be dealt with under Article 8 if the threat to moral integrity was sufficiently severe. Baroness Hale considered that the 'high threshold' to be satisfied in relation to Article 3 would logically apply to Article 8 too. The 'domestic' aspect of the case might have been the dislocation of the

---

[6] *Bensaid v United Kingdom* (2001) 33 EHRR 205.
[7] At para 58 of the judgment.

applicant's private life here caused by removing him, but that was clearly justified under Article 8(2). Baroness Hale held:

> Although the possibility cannot be excluded, it is not easy to think of a foreign health care case which would fail under Article 3 but succeed under Article 8. There clearly must be a strong case before the Article is even engaged and then a fair balance must be struck under Article 8(2). In striking that balance, only the most compelling humanitarian considerations are likely to prevail over the legitimate aims of immigration control or public safety.

On the facts in *Razgar* Baroness Hale dissented, agreeing with the Secretary of State's certification of the claim as manifestly unfounded.

Lord Bingham, delivering the leading majority opinion in *Razgar*, similarly considered that *Bensaid* clearly established that reliance may be placed on Article 8 to resist an expulsion decision, even where the main emphasis is not on the severance of family and social ties which the applicant has enjoyed in the expelling country but on the consequences for his mental health of removal to the receiving country. In such circumstances, however, the threshold for successful reliance on Article 8 was high. **4.05**

The majority in *Razgar* agreed with Lord Bingham, who held at para 10 that: **4.06**

> ... the rights protected by Article 8 can be engaged by the foreseeable consequences for health of removal from the United Kingdom pursuant to an immigration decision, even where such removal does not violate Article 3, if the facts relied on by the applicant are sufficiently strong.

However, Lord Bingham was at pains to stress that:

> It would seem plain that, as with medical treatment so with welfare, an applicant could never hope to resist an expulsion decision without showing something very much more extreme than relative disadvantage as compared with the expelling state.

Aspects of private life

In *Bensaid v United Kingdom*[8] the ECtHR held (at para 47): **4.07**

> Private life is a broad term not susceptible to exhaustive definition. The Court has already held that elements such as gender identification, name and sexual orientation and sexual life are important elements of the personal sphere protected by Article 8. Mental health must also be regarded as a crucial part of private life associated with the aspect of moral integrity. Article 8 protects a right to identity and personal development, and the right to establish and develop relationships with other human beings and the outside world. The preservation of mental stability is in that context an indispensable precondition to effective enjoyment of the right to respect for private life.

---

[8] *Bensaid v United Kingdom* (2001) 33 EHRR 205.

4.08   In *Pretty v United Kingdom*[9] the ECtHR held that private life encompassed 'the physical and psychological integrity of a person'. Additionally, 'Article 8 also protects a right to personal development, and the right to establish and develop relationships with other human beings and the outside world' (para 61).

4.09   The multi-faceted potential scope of the right to respect for one's 'private life' as protected by Article 8 can be encompassed by the following formulation by Lord Bingham in *R (on the appln of Razgar) v SSHD*:[10]

> Elusive though the concept is, I think one must understand private life in Article 8 as extending to those features which are integral to a person's identity or ability to function socially as a person.[11]

Home

4.10   The domestic jurisprudence in relation to the rights other than private and family life, protected by Article 8, is not as well developed in the asylum context, but is also likely to be of much less relevance in that sphere. The right to respect for one's home, if engaged in the immigration context, is likely to be encompassed within the private life rights and dealt with according to the stages as set out in the House of Lords' decision in *Razgar* (see below).

4.11   The right to respect for one's home has been subject to litigation in the domestic context outside the immigration sphere. The case discussed below can be seen as an illustration of the uncertain boundaries of the protection offered by the broadly defined Article 8 in areas covered by extensive legislation, such as landlord and tenant law.

4.12   In *Harrow LBC v Tarik Mahmood Qazi*,[12] the claimant's tenancy was brought to an end by his wife, a joint tenant, having given notice to quit. He applied for a sole tenancy but the application was refused on the basis that he was not entitled to family-sized accommodation as a single person. The council took possession proceedings, with the following outcomes in the appeals process:

(1)   The County Court made a possession order rejecting the claimant's defence under Article 8 on the basis that the house was not Q's home because he had no legal or equitable right or interest in the house.

---

[9] *Pretty v United Kingdom* (2002) 35 EHRR 1.

[10] *R (on the appln of Razgar) v SSHD* [2004] UKHL 27, (2004) 2 AC 368.

[11] As an example, in *Ullah,* Lord Steyn referred to the expulsion of a homosexual to a country where, short of persecution, he might be subjected to a flagrant violation of his Article 8 rights. Lord Steyn noted that in *Z v Secretary of State for the Home Department* [2002] Imm AR 560 this point had come before the Court of Appeal, with Schiemann LJ (with whom the other members of the court agreed) not being prepared to rule out such an argument. In Lord Steyn's view he was right not to do so.

[12] *Harrow LBC v Tarik Mahmood Qazi* [2003] UKHL 43, (2004) 1 AC 983.

(2) The Court of Appeal allowed an appeal holding that Article 8 was engaged even though Q's tenancy had been terminated. The question whether the interference with Q's Article 8 rights was justified under Article 8(2) was remitted to the County Court.

(3) The House of Lords held by a majority that when proceedings were issued and possession was ordered, the house was Q's home within the meaning of Article 8. Residential accommodation occupied by a former tenant whose tenancy had expired by operation of law was that person's home within the meaning of Article 8. However, the Article did not give one a right to a home, but only a right to respect for a person's home as an aspect of his right to private life. The right to respect for the home under Article 8(1) was not violated by an application of the law that enabled a public authority landlord to exercise its right to recover possession following service of a notice to quit which had terminated the tenancy. The exercise of this right by the landlord was with a view to making the premises available for letting to others on the housing list. The case law of the European Court of Human Rights showed that contractual and proprietary rights to possession could not be defeated by a defence based on Article 8. Thus the County Court did not have to consider whether any interference was permitted by Article 8(2). Lords Bingham and Steyn dissented on the basis that seeking possession of residential property was an interference with Article 8 rights, and the issue of justification should be remitted for consideration by the County Court.

In the asylum context, the most likely application of the right to respect for one's **4.13** home would be in relation to challenging detention or reception conditions, and even then infrequently. A different case from outside the asylum context reveals the focus of the judicial inquiry to be on the issue of arbitrariness or otherwise of the decision-making process through which the amenities enjoyed in relation to one's home are reduced. In *Lough & Ors v First Secretary of State & Anor*,[13] landowners appealed against a decision refusing an application to challenge the decision of a planning inspector. Planning permission had been granted for the development of a 20-storey building, which was claimed would result in loss of privacy, overlooking, loss of light, loss of a view, and interference with television reception, which were argued to be of sufficient gravity to engage Article 8. The Court of Appeal held that Article 8 required respect for the home but created no absolute right to amenities currently enjoyed. The authorities had a discretion in striking a fair balance between competing interests and the planning inspector had struck a balance that was in accordance with the requirements of Article 8. The Court's attention was focused on whether there was arbitrariness in the

---

[13] *Lough & Ors v First Secretary of State & Anor* [2004] EWCA Civ 905, (2004) 1 WLR 2557.

procedure followed. The procedure was found not to be arbitrary and there were reasonable and appropriate measures taken to secure the appellants' rights in accordance with Article 8(1) in the decision-making process.

Correspondence

4.14 Similarly, the right to respect for one's correspondence is unlikely to arise in the immigration and removals context, save, perhaps, as an incidental issue in relation to legally privileged or confidential correspondence of detained asylum seekers. In that sphere, practitioners are referred to domestic case law, dealing with the rights of prisoners, where the Article 8 issues protecting the confidentiality of correspondence have been examined by the Courts, for example:

(a) *R v SSHD ex p Daly* [2001] UKHL 26, (2001) 2 AC 532, where the blanket policy of routinely excluding all prisoners whilst their privileged correspondence was searched was found to be an infringement of the Article 8 right to maintain the confidentiality of privileged legal correspondence, which was disproportionate to the legitimate public objectives of excluding them.

(b) *R (on the appln of Szuluk) v Governor of Full Sutton Prison & SSHD* [2004] EWCA Civ 1426, Independent, 4 November 2004, where *Daly* was distinguished, and the Court of Appeal found that the reading of the applicant's medical correspondence in that case was necessary in a democratic society for the prevention of crime and the protection of the rights and freedoms of others. There was no less invasive measure available to the prison service, and the proportionality of the interference was further underlined by the risk of abuse being mitigated through the authenticity of the correspondence being checked by the prison medical officer. Furthermore, the process by which the measure was decided upon was not arbitrary.

Interference and legitimate aim

4.15 Once the relevant right has been identified and classified, for example the right to respect for family life, the subsequent steps for consideration of an Article 8 claim in the immigration context have been identified by the House of Lords in *Razgar*[14] to be as follows:

(1) Will the proposed removal be an interference by a public authority with the exercise of the applicant's right to respect for his private or (as the case may be) family life?

(2) If so, will such interference have consequences of such gravity as potentially to engage the operation of Article 8?

---

[14] *Razgar* [2004] UKHL 27, (2004) 2 AC 368.

(3) If so, is such interference in accordance with the law?

(4) If so, is such interference necessary in a democratic society in the interests of national security, public safety, or the economic well-being of the country, for the prevention of disorder or crime, for the protection of health or morals, or for the protection of the rights and freedoms of others?

(5) If so, is such interference proportionate to the legitimate public end sought to be achieved?

These steps are to be followed by the original decision makers, subsequently by the appellate authority and the Courts.

'Interference', 'minimum level of severity', and 'in accordance with the law'

As a prerequisite to arguing for or finding that an interference exists, practitioners **4.16** and decision makers would have to examine the effect of the decision of the executive on the right claimed. For example, it might be arguable that in circumstances where the applicant's family can travel with him and settle in the country of return, no such interference can be shown. Case analysis is unlikely to stop at this stage, as inevitably there would be aspects of private life in the host country with which removal would interfere. However, such interference with 'private life' may fail the second test above, namely the *de minimis* principle. The conduct must attain a minimum level of severity to engage the Convention.[15]

Where removal is proposed in pursuance of a lawful immigration policy and is **4.17** provided for within the Immigration Rules and/or legislation, questions (3) and (4) of the *Razgar* test above will almost inevitably have an affirmative answer. The State has a right under international law to control the entry of non-nationals into its territory.[16] This right is subject to the State's treaty obligations, and hence an interference with the rights protected under ECHR Article 8(1) has to be lawful, justified on the grounds of a legitimate aim identified within Article 8(2), and proportionate to that aim. The ECtHR and domestic courts have recognized that upholding immigration control is a legitimate aim within Article 8(2), which, if analyzed, is most often based on 'the interests of the economic well-being of the country'.

However, if the Secretary of State were to refuse entry with the motive of prevent- **4.18** ing the enjoyment of family life because, for instance, of a policy of opposing the intermarriage of UK citizens with aliens, an infringement of Article 8 is almost certain to be found. (See *R v SSHD ex p Farrakhan*[17] where this hypothetical example was discussed.)

---

[15] See, for example, *Costello-Roberts v United Kingdom* (1993) 19 EHRR 112.
[16] See *R v SSHD ex p Mahmood* (2001) 1 WLR 840, and *Ullah* (2004) 2 AC 323.
[17] *R v SSHD ex p Farrakhan* [2002] EWCA Civ 606, (2002) 3 WLR 481, CA, para 38.

4.19 In one of the earliest domestic decisions on Article 8—*R v SSHD ex p Mahmood*[18]— Lord Phillips, MR, having reviewed the ECtHR jurisprudence, summarized the applicable principles as follows:

(1) A State has a right under international law to control the entry of non-nationals into its territory, subject always to its treaty obligations.

(2) Article 8 does not impose on a State any general obligation to respect the choice of residence of a married couple.

(3) Removal or exclusion of one family member from a State where other members of the family are lawfully resident will not necessarily infringe Article 8 provided that there are no insurmountable obstacles to the family living together in the country of origin of the family member excluded, even where this involves a degree of hardship for some or all members of the family.

(4) Article 8 is likely to be violated by the expulsion of a member of a family that has been long established in a State if the circumstances are such that it is not reasonable to expect the other members of the family to follow that member expelled.

(5) Knowledge on the part of one spouse at the time of marriage that rights of residence of the other were precarious militates against a finding that an order excluding the latter spouse violates Article 8.

(6) Whether interference with family rights is justified in the interests of controlling immigration will depend on
 (i) the facts of the particular case, and
 (ii) the circumstances prevailing in the State whose action is impugned.

4.20 This reflects the ECtHR jurisprudence on Article 8 in the immigration context, which was summarized in *Poku v United Kingdom*[19] by the Commission as follows:

Whether removal or exclusion of a family member from a contracting state is incompatible with the requirements of Article 8 will depend on a number of factors:

(1) The extent to which family life is effectively ruptured.

(2) Whether there are insurmountable obstacles in the way of the family living in the country of origin of one or more of them.

(3) Whether there are immigration control factors, for example a history of breaches of immigration law.

(4) Considerations of public order, such as serious or persistent offences, which weigh in favour of exclusion.

Entry clearance aspects of the legitimate aim of upholding immigration control

4.21 *Mahmood*—**Jumping the Queue:** Another facet of upholding immigration control requires consistency of approach and procedure for all applicants under

---

18   *R v SSHD ex p Mahmood* (2001) 1 WLR 840.
19   *Poku v United Kingdom* (1996) 22 EHRR CD 94 at 97–8.

the immigration rules. Thus another principle identified by the Court of Appeal in *Mahmood*[20] is that a person already in the United Kingdom who requires entry clearance to come here and is not currently in possession of such entry clearance should return to his home country and make application from there. Laws LJ said (at para 26):

> No matter that the immigrant in the individual case, *having arrived here without the required entry clearance*, may be able to show that he would have been entitled to one, or even, as was the case in *ex p Hashim*, that the Home Office actually accepts that he meets the rule's substantive requirements; it is simply unfair that he should not have to wait in the queue like everyone else. At least it is unfair unless he can demonstrate some exceptional circumstance which reasonably justifies his jumping the queue.

Such exceptional circumstances were established in the case of *Abbas v SSHD* **4.22** [2005] EWCA Civ 992, where the applicant was in poor health. On the very particular facts of that case, requiring her to return to Iraq, from where she would have to travel to Syria or Jordan in order to make an entry clearance application to join her husband in the UK, was found to be disproportionate to the pursuit of the legitimate aim of immigration control, and justified the applicant in effect 'jumping the queue'.

SB (Bangladesh)—**Is jumping the queue still relevant?** This exceptionality **4.23** requirement to 'jumping the queue' is unlikely to be strictly applied in considering the future entry clearance prospects in Article 8 claims, where the applicant is in the UK.

First, the House of Lords in *Huang & Ors v SSHD*[21] at para 20 stated that there **4.24** was no 'exceptionality' test to be applied generally in Article 8 cases.[22] The AIT had to decide for itself the issue of proportionality of the interference with the Article 8 right, taking into account all relevant considerations. Nonetheless it will be a rare case that is made under Article 8 that does not fall within the rules.

Second, case law from the Court of Appeal has discouraged speculation as to the **4.25** likelihood of success of future entry clearance applications, recognizing the risk of unfairness to an appellant as an entry clearance officer might take a different view of the facts or the law, and the rules or the facts of the case might change by the time the future entry clearance application is considered. In *SB (Bangladesh) v SSHD*[23] the AIT had dismissed the applicant's Article 8 claim as it considered she could re-enter the UK effectively permanently under the Immigration Rules, as one of her children was under 18. The Court of Appeal held that it was not

---

[20] *R v SSHD ex p Mahmood* (2001) 1 WLR 840.
[21] *Huang & Ors v SSHD* [2007] UKHL 11.
[22] For further discussion and analysis of the House of Lords judgment, see further below.
[23] *SB (Bangladesh) v SSHD* [2007] EWCA Civ 28.

appropriate for the AIT to determine whether the applicant satisfied the requirements of the rules, when no entry clearance application had been made. This was to be decided in the future by an entry clearance officer and not by the AIT, whose task was to decide a different question, at a different time, in a different country, and in different circumstances. The Court of Appeal found it somewhat paradoxical if the stronger an appellant's perceived case for entry clearance under the rules, the more likely removal was. It would also be unfortunate in terms of time, effort, and expense, if when deciding on the proportionality under Article 8, the AIT had to consider as a matter of course the likelihood of success on a subsequent putative application for entry clearance. There was obvious risk of unfairness to an appellant in such a course of action.

4.26 **Analysis of entry clearance aspects has to be rigorous:**   Whether *SB (Bangladesh)* heralds a new approach to future entry clearance considerations within the proportionality analysis in Article 8 remains to be seen. However, even if the AIT and the courts continue to consider the prospect of success of entry clearance applications as a factor in assessing proportionality, the analysis has to be rigorous to withstand scrutiny. Thus, in *Rashed Azez v SSHD*[24] the Court of Appeal remitted a case for re-consideration, on the basis that an integral part of the proportionality analysis under Article 8(2) was missing from the IAT's decision. The IAT had failed to consider that in requiring the applicant to leave the UK to apply for entry clearance, he would have to make his own way to Iraq, in the absence of removal directions; the IAT had failed to consider the documents the applicant would require to travel to Jordan, from where entry clearance could be obtained; and finally there were no findings on the route of travel between Iraq and Jordan and its safety. Failure to take into account and analyze all these factors amounted to an error of law.

4.27 A further factor for appellate authorities to consider is the length of time it could take for an entry clearance application to be processed. In *Mukarkar v SSHD*,[25] where removal was resisted on medical grounds, the Court of Appeal held that the adjudicator had not been prepared to assume that any return to Yemen to apply for entry clearance would be for only a few months so that it could be expected that one of the applicant's children would go with him for that period. The timescale likely to be involved and its consequences for the applicant's care in the meantime were relevant considerations, properly taken into account on appeal.

---

24 *Rashed Azez v SSHD* (2006) CA Civ (22 June 2006).
25 *Mukarkar v SSHD* [2006] EWCA Civ 1045.

Conversely, appellants often argue that, if removed, they are unlikely to satisfy **4.28**
the entry clearance requirements under the Rules, when they attempt to re-enter.
Such contentions are unlikely to succeed in bolstering an Article 8 claim. Further,
in such cases the Court of Appeal has ruled that appellate authorities should not
embark on an examination of the likelihood of entry clearance being granted. In
R (On the app of Ekinci) v SSHD,[26] the Court of Appeal accepted that the outcome of the envisaged entry clearance application is not to be pre-judged, further
accepting the Secretary of State's argument that whether or not the appellant will
qualify for entry clearance is immaterial—it should be decided not at the removal
stage but when the applicant comes to apply for entry clearance. Even if the
applicant fails to qualify under the rules, the ECO could refer the application
to the Secretary of State who has discretion to admit someone outside the rules,
with attendant rights of appeal. Simon Brown LJ found that '(i)t would be a
bizarre and unsatisfactory result if, the less able the applicant is to satisfy the full
requirements for entry clearance, the more readily he should be excused the need
to apply'.

Similarly, in *MM (Nigeria) v SSHD*,[27] the Court of Appeal upheld the IAT's **4.29**
reversal of a decision by an adjudicator. The adjudicator had held that Article 8
would be breached due to a real possibility that future entry clearance would be
denied as the applicant had no remaining relatives in Nigeria and would have a
failed application on her record. The Court of Appeal held the latter to be just
speculations. Interestingly, however, the Court of Appeal did not find the Secretary of State's implied assertion that entry clearance *would* be granted, making
removal proportionate, to amount to speculation. Should a similar situation arise
in the future, the Court of Appeal is perhaps more likely to follow its approach in
Akaeke v SSHD,[28] namely that courts should be cautious about interfering with
decisions on matters within the expertise and competence of specialist tribunals,
including immigration tribunals. Thus first instance appellate decisions on proportionality favourable to an applicant are less likely to be disturbed on appeal,
unless an error of law is shown.[29]

Burden of proof and potential future issues on lawfulness of interference

The expressions 'in accordance with the law' in Article 8(2) and 'prescribed by **4.30**
law' in Articles 5(1), 5(1)(b), 10(2), and 11(2) are to be understood as bearing the

---

[26] *R (on the appln of Ekinci) v SSHD* [2003] EWCA Civ 765.
[27] *MM (Nigeria) v SSHD* [2007] EWCA Civ 44.
[28] *Akaeke v SSHD* [2005] EWCA Civ 947.
[29] For a decision where the proportionality analysis was held to be a judgment for the tribunal of
fact, normally raising no issues of law, see *Mukarkar v SSHD* [2006] EWCA Civ 1045.

same meaning.[30] This lawfulness requirement is a very important feature of the rule of law. In the words of Lord Bingham:

> The exercise of power by public officials, as it affects members of the public, must be governed by clear and publicly-accessible rules of law. The public must not be vulnerable to interference by public officials acting on any personal whim, caprice, malice, predilection or purpose other than that for which the power was conferred. This is what, in this context, is meant by arbitrariness, which is the antithesis of legality. This is the test which any interference with or derogation from a Convention right must meet if a violation is to be avoided.[31]

4.31 The onus of showing that the interference with an applicant's Article 8 protected rights is legitimate lies with the decision maker, thus in asylum cases—the Secretary of State. In the immigration context, this has not caused many problems, as the relevant decisions, concerning removal or deportation for example, are inevitably held to have a legitimate aim of upholding the system of immigration control, thus moving the focus of inquiry to the next element—proportionality of the measure.

Proportionality

No deference due to the Secretary of State's decision on proportionality

4.32 Having established the right protected under Article 8 and the fact that an immigration decision would interfere with such right, the interference being justified on the grounds of immigration control, the next issue for consideration by the Secretary of State, and on appeal by the AIT and the courts, is the proportionality of the measure to the legitimate public aim.

4.33 Four and a half years after the entry into force of the Human Rights Act, introducing directly enforceable Article 8 obligations on the State, and the availability of rights of appeal on human rights grounds in the asylum field, the Court of Appeal ruled on the issue as to whether deference to the Secretary of State's decision on proportionality issues is appropriate in appellate proceedings. *Huang & Ors v SSHD*,[32] discussed in more detail below, established that where the appellate body[33] is not called upon to pass judgment on government policy, there is no basis upon which it should defer to the Secretary of State's judgment on proportionality

---

[30] *R (on the appln of Gillan) v MPC and SSHD* [2006] UKHL 12, (2006) 2 WLR 537, para 31, per Lord Bingham.

[31] *R (on the appln of Gillan) v MPC and SSHD* [2006] UKHL 12, (2006) 2 WLR 537, para 34, per Lord Bingham.

[32] *Huang & Ors v SSHD* [2005] EWCA Civ 105, [2006] QB 1.

[33] In *Huang* the analysis concerned the correct approach to be adopted by adjudicators on appeal. However, the same approach would hold for determinations by the AIT, set up under the 2004 Act. This was recognized by the House of Lords judgment in *Huang v SSHD* [2007] UKHL 11, paras 2, 10, and 11.

in any individual case. This conclusion was upheld by the House of Lords' judgment in *Huang & Ors v SSHD*.[34] Their Lordships unanimously held the task of the appellate immigration authorities[35] on appeal on a Convention ground against a decision refusing leave to enter or remain to be:

> . . . to decide whether the challenged decision is unlawful as incompatible with a Convention right or compatible and so lawful. It is not a secondary, reviewing, function dependent on establishing that the primary decision-maker misdirected himself or acted irrationally or was guilty of procedural impropriety. The appellate immigration authority must decide for itself whether the impugned decision is lawful and, if not, but only if not, reverse it. This is the decision reached by the Court of Appeal (Judge, Laws and Latham LJJ) in these conjoined appeals, and it is correct: [2005] EWCA Civ 105, [2006] QB 1. (para 11)

On a human rights appeal, the AIT is not reviewing the decision of the Secretary of State or other primary decision maker. It is itself deciding whether or not it is unlawful to refuse leave to enter or remain, and this is done on the up-to-date facts, as known at the time of the appellate hearing.[36] Appropriate weight is to be given to the judgement of a person with responsibility for a given subject matter, as occurs in all judicial decision making, but that is not accurately described as 'deference'. **4.34**

The relevant question for the AIT

As already indicated, the House of Lords in *Huang* defined the ultimate question for the appellate immigration authority as follows: **4.35**

> . . . whether the refusal of leave to enter or remain, in circumstances where the life of the family cannot reasonably be expected to be enjoyed elsewhere, taking full account of all considerations weighing in favour of the refusal, prejudices the family life of the applicant in a manner sufficiently serious to amount to a breach of the fundamental right protected by Article 8. (para 20)

If the question is answered in the affirmative, the refusal of leave is unlawful and the AIT must so decide. **4.36**

No test of 'exceptionality'

The House of Lords in *Huang* specifically ruled that it was not necessary to ask the additional question, whether the case meets an exceptionality test.[37] According to the Court of Appeal decision in *Huang*, in the normal asylum and immigration **4.37**

---

[34] *Huang & Ors v SSHD* [2007] UKHL 11.
[35] Adjudicators, IAT, and immigration judges in the AIT.
[36] *Huang v SSHD* [2007] UKHL 11, para 13. The House of Lords recognized that the essential effect of the appellate provisions remains the same, despite the introduction of a single, unified, appellate body—the AIT (see *Huang*, para 10).
[37] *Huang v SSHD* [2007] UKHL 11, para 20.

case, when faced with an Article 8 claim where the applicant has no claim under the Immigration Rules, the task of the appellate body is to see whether an exceptional case has been made out such that the requirement of proportionality requires a departure from the relevant Rule on the particular facts. The House of Lords found this 'exceptionality test' not to be a legal test. It originated in an observation by Lord Bingham in *Razgar*:[38]

> Decisions taken pursuant to the lawful operation of immigration control will be proportionate in all save a small minority of exceptional cases, identifiable only on a case by case basis.

4.38 The House of Lords in *Huang* explained that '(h)e was there expressing an expectation, shared with the Immigration Appeal Tribunal, that the number of claimants not covered by the Rules and supplementary directions but entitled to succeed under Article 8 would be a very small minority. That is still his expectation. But he was not purporting to lay down a legal test.'[39]

4.39 The 'exceptionality' test, with its roots in *Razgar* and the Court of Appeal decision in *Huang,* had formed the basis of many decisions in the AIT. In a number of cases following the decision of the House of Lords in *Huang* the Court of Appeal has sought to explain or clarify what was meant and how it should be applied. The question arose as to whether decisions of the AIT which adumbrated a test based on exceptionality were necessarily flawed and should be remitted for reconsideration without more. In *AG (Eritrea) v SSHD*[40] the Court of Appeal refused to remit the case by consent, but instead took the opportunity to examine the law applicable in Article 8 cases with a view to providing authoritative guidance for the future.

4.40 The facts in *AG* were unremarkable, raising claims based under both Article 3 and Article 8. The Court considered that the original Adjudicator had gone wrong in his consideration of Article 3. In para 14 of the judgment of the Court, Sedley LJ set out why it had been thought inappropriate to remit the case under Article 8 without more, and then analyzed the correct approach in such cases, by reference to the authorities as follows:

a) The starting point in para 17 of Lord Bingham's speech in Razgar (see above).

b) The fifth step in the sequence identified by Lord Bingham, namely proportionality, involved a recognition that 'decisions taken pursuant to the lawful

---

38 *Razgar* [2004] 2 AC 368, at 374F.
39 *Huang v SSHD* [2007] UKHL 11, para 20.
40 *AG (Eritrea) v SSHD* [2007] EWCA Civ 801.

operation of immigration control will be proportionate in all save a small minority of exceptional cases [20].

c) It was this observation that led Laws LJ in *Huang* to focus on the exceptionality in para 59 of his judgment [21].

Neither *Razgar* nor *Huang* used the expression in the sense that exceptionality **4.41** was a legal test in Article 8 cases; rather it was the probable consequence of an evaluation of proportionality under Article 8 (2) in the context of immigration decisions [22]:

> The effect of their Lordships' decision (and if we may say so the intended effect of this court's decision) in *Huang* has thus not been to introduce a new interpretation of Article 8 but to clarify and reiterate a well understood one. While its practical effect is likely to be that removal is only exceptionally found to be disproportionate, it sets no formal test of exceptionality and raises no hurdles not contained in the Article itself [25].

The Court of Appeal also took time to explain Lord Bingham's reference to a **4.42** 'minimum level of security' in the context of Article 8. To engage Article 8 (1) the interference must be real, but it is not especially high [28].

The judgment of the Court then considered a number of other cases which had **4.43** followed *Huang* in the House of Lords. It commended the approach of Buxton LJ in *MT (Zimbabwe)*[41] who said:

> However the matter is expressed there is no doubt that the interests of family life will not usually prevail over the interests of immigration control. The difficulty is in expressing that general understanding in any sort of guiding rule or principle. To speak of 'exceptional' or 'rare' cases does nothing to explain what principle should be applied in identifying such cases; and that, it seems to me with respect, is what the House of Lords warned of in *Huang*.

Buxton LJ also adopted a passage from the judgment of Carnworth LJ in *Mukartar*, with which the Court in *AG* expressly agreed:

> In normal circumstances interference with family life would be justified by the requirements of immigration control. However, it is recognized that a different approach may be justified in a small minority of exceptional cases identifiable only on a case by case basis (per Lord Bingham, *Razgar*). The House of Lords has declined to lay down a more precise legal test. Accordingly, whether a particular case falls within that limited category is a question of judgement for the tribunal of fact, and normally raises no issue of law.

That approach was consistent also with the decision in *KR (Iraq)* [2007] EWCA Civ 514, but not with that in *PO (Nigeria)* [2007] EWCA Civ 438 upon which reliance can no longer be placed.

---

[41] *MT (Zimbabwe)* [2007] EWCA Civ 455.

4.44   Finally, the Court of Appeal, reviewed the ingredients of proportionality and made the telling observation that even if the AIT applied the wrong test in law in determining a question under Article 8, there would be many cases in which it was plain that the decision to remove was not disproportionate and so an appeal to the Court of Appeal would not go anywhere.

Relevant factors to take into account on proportionality

4.45   There are numerous factors which may arise in individual cases, which would be of relevance to the issue of proportionality. No exhaustive or prescriptive analysis is possible or indeed desirable, as it is important that decision makers as well as the appellate bodies retain the flexibility to respond in their analysis of proportionality issues to the multifarious circumstances of individual cases. In the words of the Court of Appeal in *AG (Eritrea) v SSHD*:[42]

> What matters is not that courts and tribunals should adopt a set formula for determining proportionality, but that they should have proper and visible regard to relevant principles in making a structured decision about it case by case. It is not sufficient, as still happens, for the Tribunal simply to characterise something as proportionate or disproportionate: to do so may well be a failure of reasoning amounting to an error of law.[43]

4.46   **General factors**: The House of Lords in *Huang v SSHD*[44] found that certain general factors will almost always have to be considered. Amongst them was the general administrative desirability of applying known rules for a workable, predictable, consistent, and fair immigration control system; the damage to good administration and effective control if a system is perceived by applicants internationally to be unduly porous or unpredictable; the need to discourage non-nationals admitted to the country temporarily from believing that they can commit serious crimes and yet be allowed to remain; the need to discourage fraud, deception, and deliberate breaches of the law; and so on.

4.47   **Specific factors on which Secretary of State has expertise**: Further and more specific factors may need to be taken into account, such as the Secretary of State's judgment that deportation was a valuable deterrent to actual or prospective drug traffickers (see *Samaroo v SSHD*[45]). The House of Lords in *Huang* viewed the giving of weight to factors such as these not as deference to the Secretary of State's decision. It was simply 'the ordinary judicial task of weighing up the competing considerations on each side and according appropriate weight to the judgment of

---

[42] *AG (Eritrea) v SSHD* [2007] EWCA Civ 801.
[43] *AG (Eritrea) v SSHD* [2007] EWCA Civ 801, para 37.
[44] *Huang v SSHD* [2007] UKHL 11.
[45] *Samaroo v SSHD* [2001] EWCA Civ 1139, [2002] INLR 55.

a person with responsibility for a given subject matter and access to special sources of knowledge and advice'.[46]

Factors specific to the applicant: Matters such as the age, health, and vulnera- **4.48**
bility of the applicant, the closeness and previous history of the family, the applicant's dependence on the financial and emotional support of the family, the
prevailing cultural tradition and conditions in the country of origin, and many
other factors may all be relevant.[47] For example, an applicant's mental illnesses
and the events which caused them (such as her own rape and witnessing the rape
of her sister) were relevant to the nature and depth of the applicant's reliance on
her brother and their bond.[48]

The further illustrations below merely attempt to highlight some other factors on **4.49**
the issue of proportionality identified and dealt with by the courts. It should be
noted that their treatment is on a case-by-case basis, and although some pro-
nouncements on issues of principle can be identified, they would not necessarily
hold fast in all circumstances. Of particular note is the different treatment the
factor of delay in decision making and the need to show prejudice have received
as relevant considerations in the assessment of proportionality.

EEA rights: Existence of rights under European Economic Area agreements **4.50**
and related legal provisions may constitute relevant factors in the consideration
of proportionality. However, this is likely to be of importance in a limited number
of cases, as the rights under the EEA Regulations would usually afford applicants
much greater protection against removal, and in effect the Article 8 considerations would be taken into account only if the Regulations themselves permit
removal. Thus the AIT in *RI (EC law–Chen–effect on proportionality) Uganda*[49]
held that the appellant did not benefit from any rights under European law,
which 'might affect the assessment of proportionality under Article 8'.[50] On the
facts of that case the appellant's son, although an EEA national, was not exercising Treaty rights in the UK. The appellant's fiancé was exercising Treaty rights,
but the appellant was not a 'family member' of his as defined by Regulation 6 of the
EEA Regulations 2000, as she was not married to him. In contrast, in *Machado v
SSHD*[51] the appellant was a foreign national married to an EU national with a
right of establishment in the United Kingdom. The issue for the Court of Appeal
concerned the correct approach of appellate bodies to a decision of the Home
Secretary to deport such an appellant on public policy grounds under reg 21(3)(b)

---

[46] *Huang v SSHD* [2007] UKHL 11, para 16.
[47] Ibid, para 18.
[48] *R (on the appln of X) v SSHD* [2006] EWHC 1208 (Admin).
[49] *RI (EC law–Chen–effect on proportionality) Uganda* [2005] UKAIT 00125.
[50] See para 24 of the judgment.
[51] *Machado v SSHD* [2005] EWCA Civ 597.

of the Regulations. The Court found that the standard of review of the Secretary of State's decision was as set out in *Huang* and was not merely a *Wednesbury* review. The IAT should have addressed the issues of whether the appellant's conduct manifested a present and serious threat to the public interest and, if so, whether it was proportionate in all the circumstances to deport him. The IAT had further erred in considering the interference with the appellant's Article 8 rights as a separate issue rather than including it in the evaluation of the proportionality of deportation of the spouse of an EU national who was in the United Kingdom as of right under the EEA Regulations. The matter was remitted to a differently constituted tribunal.

4.51 **Effect on other family members:** As stressed by Jack J in *R (AC) v Immigration Appeal Tribunal,*[52] and as cited with approval by the Court of Appeal in *Betts v SSHD,*[53] the effect of the appellant's removal on others in his family might have an effect on an appellant, nonetheless it is the consequence to the appellant which is the relevant consequence for Article 8 purposes. In *Betts* the Adjudicator had held that the appellant, who entered the UK in 1997 following a military coup in Sierra Leone, had established a private and family life in the UK, his mother and sister having obtained indefinite leave to remain, and his father having registered as a British citizen. Despite the Adjudicator's finding that to return him to Sierra Leone would be a disproportionate interference with his Article 8 rights, the IAT had held that the appellant's case was not exceptional. In his Grounds of Appeal the appellant argued that the Adjudicator had made no error of law and hence the IAT should not have interfered with his decision. The Court of Appeal held that the IAT was entitled to conclude that the Adjudicator had allowed his judgment to be affected unduly by the effect of the appellant's removal on the remainder of his family. The Adjudicator had not suggested (on the previously applicable test by the Court of Appeal in *Huang*) that the effect on the family amounted to an exceptional circumstance, which implied that the effects of removal on the applicant would not have amounted to an exceptional circumstance. Exceptionality not being a legal test, according to the House of Lords' judgment in *Huang*, the outcome of a similar case now is likely to be different. However, the effect on the applicant remains the focus for the Secretary of State and the AIT.

4.52 In *Dbeis & Ors v SSHD*[54] the effect of removal on a disabled family member was considered at greater length, although ultimately the appellant was unsuccessful in her Article 8 claim. One of the appellant's sons suffered from cerebral palsy, and she argued that he would receive a better education in the UK than he would

---

52 *R (AC) v Immigration Appeal Tribunal* [2003] EWHC 389 (Admin), [2003] INLR 507.
53 *Betts v SSHD* [2005] EWCA Civ 828.
54 *Dbeis & Ors v SSHD* [2005] EWCA Civ 584.

in Lebanon, to where the Secretary of State proposed to return the family. The Court of Appeal considered evidence obtained since the decision of the IAT which showed that, if returned, the son was likely to be deprived of the higher standard of educational support which he could expect in the UK. However, according to the authorities, that did not amount to an exceptional case sufficient to override immigration control. There was nothing in the relevant material which in any way undermined the Adjudicator's conclusions or demonstrated an 'exceptional' case within the terms described in *Razgar v SSHD*.[55] Although this reasoning was based on the requirement of 'exceptionality', now specifically ruled not to be a legal requirement (see the House of Lords in *Huang*), the outcome of the case is likely to have been the same on the correct test, as the balance between the rights of the individual and the policy requirements of immigration control had weighed against the applicant.[56]

Delay: Delay as a factor to be taken into account within the assessment of proportionality of the interference with Article 8 rights is a contentious topic, subject to much recent litigation. The general trend in the decisions appears to be towards a restriction in the circumstances and the extent to which delay in the decision-making process can benefit applicants in the assessment of proportionality, after some early generous decisions. **4.53**

The position most likely to be adopted by the courts as reflecting the requirements of the ECHR is as stated in *MB (Huang–proportionality–Bulletins) (Croatia)*[57] by the President of the AIT, Ouseley, J: **4.54**

> It is very difficult to envisage a case in which the removal of someone who has no claim to enter and no claim for international protection would be disproportionate merely because of a delay in decision-making, which had had no disadvantage as in *Shala* or which had not led to the creation of circumstances which themselves made removal disproportionate. It is the effects of delay to which an Adjudicator should look rather than to the fact or extent of delay itself.

In *Akaeke v SSHD*,[58] representing the high watermark of the case law for applicants, the Court of Appeal found that in the context of Article 8, delay was relevant not only to the extent of interference with family life but also to the proportionality of removal. 'Unreasonable delay' was held to be material without needing to identify any specific prejudice to the appellant. On the facts of the case, in normal circumstances the requirement for the maintenance of **4.55**

---

55 *Razgar v SSHD* (2004) UKHL 27, (2004) 2 AC 368.
56 The Court of Appeal's decision was reached despite finding that the appellant was justified in arguing that the IAT had set the Adjudicator's standard of review of the Secretary of State's decision at too low a level.
57 *MB (Huang–proportionality–Bulletins) (Croatia)* [2005] UKIAT 00092 at para 28.
58 *Akaeke v SSHD* [2005] EWCA Civ 947.

immigration control would demand the return of the appellant to Nigeria, notwithstanding that her application for entry was likely to be successful. The temporary disruption to her family life would be justified by the need to maintain public confidence in the fairness of the system overall. However, the Court of Appeal found the delay in the case to evidence such a breakdown in the system of immigration control that the Tribunal was entitled to find that confidence was unlikely to be materially improved by maintenance of a rigid policy of temporary expulsions. The Court of Appeal in *Akaeke* held that courts retained a supervisory role as final arbiters in relation to genuine issues of law. However, they should be cautious about interfering with decisions on matters within the expertise and competence of specialist tribunals, including immigration tribunals. This principle applied to the evaluation of evidence in individual claims, to questions of general principle on particular categories of claimant or particular countries, and on questions of proportionality. The tribunal, through its day-to-day experience, was found to be much better placed to justify a departure from the ordinary policy approach.

4.56   There was a return to a stricter approach to issues of delay as affecting proportionality, by the Court of Appeal in *Strbac & Anor v SSHD* [2005] EWCA Civ 848. It held that there was no rule of law that an applicant whose claim to enter or remain had been decided after unreasonable delay, and would probably have met with success if it had been decided within a reasonable time, should be treated as if it had been so decided, if he had in the meantime established a family life in the UK. When striking a balance between an applicant's rights under Article 8 and the legitimate objective of the proper maintenance of immigration control the decision maker had to have regard to delay in determining an application for asylum and its consequences. Delay was not determinative, but was merely a relevant factor. The possibility that an asylum seeker would have been granted exceptional leave to remain or asylum if his case had been decided more promptly did not entail the conclusion that he had a present right not to be removed because that would be disproportionate in terms of Article 8(2).

4.57   As an illustration of the exceptional case where delay may determine the proportionality question in the applicant's favour, practitioners may wish to refer to the facts of *Shala v Secretary of State for the Home Department*,[59] where had the asylum application been dealt with in the appropriate time period, permission to stay would probably have been granted, and thus the applicant would not have fallen into the category where policy required an application for leave to enter to be made from outside the UK. On the facts of the case, to require the applicant to go to Kosovo and apply from there for entry clearance as a spouse was clearly

---

[59] *Shala v Secretary of State for the Home Department* (2003) EWCA Civ 233.

disproportionate given the delay of over four years by the Home Office in dealing with the applicant's claim. By contrast, in the case of *Janjanin v Secretary of State for the Home Department*,[60] the Court of Appeal held that delay, whilst a relevant factor to be weighed in the balance within proportionality considerations, was not determinative. *Shala* was distinguished on the basis that it entailed the exceptional feature that, but for the delay in determining his application, the applicant would have been granted asylum or exceptional leave to remain. The delay in *Janjanin* did not have similar implications, and it was held to be relevant but not determinative of the proportionality issue.

The Court of Appeal in *HB (Ethiopia) & Ors v SSHD*[61] sought to reconcile the **4.58** different approaches and results in *Shala* and *Strbac*. It drew the distinction between claimants who had some potential right under the immigration policy to be in the UK (see *Shala*) and those who had no such potential right (see *Strbac*). In the latter case, delay was relevant to proportionality of removal, but in order to influence the outcome it would have to have very substantial effects. Arguments about the failure to apply the immigration system properly and the breakdown of consistent immigration control would usually succeed only in cases where the Secretary of State himself sought to rely on the system to justify interference with the applicant's rights.

The importance of immigration policies being consistently enforced, the lack of **4.59** candour in relation to an applicant's earlier asylum claim in a third country, and the fact that any separation between the applicant and his family would be temporary only, with family support being available in the UK, were all considered to be relevant factors in assessing proportionality, where delay was relied upon to challenge clearly unfounded certification.[62] In a recent delay case, *R (on the appln of FH and Nine Others) v SSHD*,[63] the Administrative Court held that the question for the Court was whether the delay resulted from a rational system. A system of applying resources which was not unreasonable and had been applied fairly and consistently could demonstrate that particular delays in specific cases were not to be regarded as unreasonable or unlawful. In this instance a large number of unmeritorious fresh evidence claims placed a burden on the system and resources were focused on those applicants who posed a risk to the public, were receiving support, might be granted leave, or could be more easily removed. Although a better system might be devised, this did not make the existing one unlawful

---

[60] *Janjanin v Secretary of State for the Home Department* (2004) EWCA Civ 448.
[61] *HB (Ethiopia) & Ors v SSHD* [2006] EWCA Civ 1713.
[62] *R (on the appln of Chopra) v SSHD* (20/7/2005, Admin Ct).
[63] *R (on the appln of FH and Nine Others) v SSHD* [2007] EWHC 1571 (Admin).

and the Court found that the delays had crossed neither the abuse of process threshold nor that of the lower test of unfairness.

Other examples where disproportionate interference has been found

4.60   In an entry clearance case,[64] where the applicant was in poor health, requiring her to return to Iraq, from where she would have to travel to Syria or Jordan in order to make an entry clearance application to join her husband in the UK, was found to be disproportionate.

4.61   In *GS (Article 8–public interest not a fixity) Serbia and Montenegro*[65] the AIT found that the extent of the public interest in the maintenance of immigration control as reflected by the Immigration Rules may vary in cases which fall outside the normal or the 'general run of cases'. Depending on the particular circumstances of a case it may be a relevant factor that the state has seen an individual to fall within a particular category of persons deserving of a grant of limited leave on exceptional grounds or for reasons of extra-statutory policy. In that case, the appellant had arrived in the UK in April 1999 as an orphaned unaccompanied minor from Kosovo, and had been granted limited leave to remain. Considering appeals on a 'case-by-case' basis, as mandated by *Razgar*, would be meaningless if, irrespective of particular facts relating to the past approach of the Secretary of State to a case, the interests of maintenance of effective immigration control were unfailingly a 'trump card' because it always had a fixed weight. The AIT found that this was not a case where the appellant had come to the UK without valid reasons. Nor was it a case where the appellant had stayed unlawfully or illegally. As the applicant was an orphaned unaccompanied minor aged 15 when he came, it could not easily be said he should have understood he had no secure basis for remaining. By virtue of the original grant of exceptional leave to remain and the delay in failing to make a prompt decision first on his asylum application and then on his application for further exceptional leave to remain, the respondent acquiesced in the appellant, at a particularly vulnerable and formative period of his life, developing close ties with foster parents which he has maintained. The effect of delay in his case was to encourage him to integrate with the wider community. On this basis the AIT did not interfere with the Adjudicator's assessment that the interference with the applicant's Article 8 rights would be disproportionate to the legitimate aim of upholding immigration control on the particular circumstances of the case.

---

[64] *Abbas v SSHD* [2005] EWCA Civ 992, obiter. The primary ground on which the appeal against the IAT decision was allowed was on the basis that it had no jurisdiction to hear the appeal, based on the grounds of appeal before it.

[65] *GS (Article 8–public interest not a fixity) Serbia and Montenegro* [2005] UKAIT 00121.

Another illustration of removal amounting to a disproportionate interference **4.62** with the applicant's rights under Article 8 can be derived from *R (on the appln of Jegatheeswaran) v SSHD*.[66] The Administrative Court in this case overturned the Secretary of State's 'manifestly unfounded' certification, as medical evidence indicated that a child of the family with severe learning difficulties, if removed to a safe third country, would be unable to communicate functionally in any spoken language. The removal directions in this case were made three years after the certification of the asylum claim as manifestly unfounded. Further, the medical evidence adduced by the applicant supported his contention as to the drastic effect of removal to the third country on his son, given the latter's disabilities. Thus the Administrative Court held that the Secretary of State could not reasonably reach the conclusion that the Article 8 claim was manifestly unarguable.

Finally, in *R (on the appln of S) v SSHD*,[67] the serious and possibly insurmount- **4.63** able obstacles in obtaining entry clearance following removal to Afghanistan, taken together with excessive delay in dealing with the applicant's asylum claim, made the decision to remove unlawful under Article 8. For such a decision to be reached on the grounds of delay only, the delay had to amount to conspicuous unfairness so as to constitute an abuse of power. In upholding this decision the Court of Appeal[68] held that the absence of an asylum decision in this case was due to a policy to defer consideration of older asylum applications to meet performance targets. Such a policy was unlawful as it was made without any regard for fairness and consistency. The Administrative Court was entitled to conclude that the Afghan claimant would have obtained exceptional leave to remain and thereafter indefinite leave to remain (ILR) and his failure to do so was due to an illegality.

B. Burden and Standard of Proof

The burden of proving the existence of a right protected under Article 8 and that **4.64** an immigration decision interferes with the right to respect for such a right is on the applicant. It is only in relation to the test within Article 8(2) in showing that the interference with the right arises in the pursuit of a legitimate aim that the evidential burden shifts to the decision maker, most usually the Secretary of State. On the issue of proportionality, it is doubtful whether it is useful to speak of a burden and standard of proof, as the decision maker or the appellate body would

---

[66] *R (on the appln of Jegatheeswaran) v SSHD* [2005] EWHC 1131 (Admin).
[67] *R (on the appln of S) v SSHD* [2007] EWHC 51 (Admin).
[68] [2007] EWCA Civ 546.

consider and weigh all the factors put forward by the applicant and the opposing party, if any, before a decision is reached.

4.65 In purely 'foreign' cases, however, the applicant has to show that there would be a flagrant denial or gross violation to the Article 8 right in the receiving state, such that the right would be completely denied. Lord Bingham in *R v SSHD ex p Ullah*,[69] in ruling that Articles other than Article 3 of the ECHR can be engaged in 'foreign cases' in the immigration and expulsion sphere, noted that:

> While the Strasbourg jurisprudence does not preclude reliance on Articles other than Article 3 as a ground for resisting extradition or expulsion, it makes it quite clear that successful reliance demands presentation of a very strong case. In relation to Article 3, it is necessary to show strong grounds for believing that the person, if returned, faces a real risk of being subjected to torture or to inhuman or degrading treatment or punishment: *Soering*, para 91; *Cruz Varas*, para 69; *Vilvarajah*, para 103. In *Dehwari*, para 61 . . . the Commission doubted whether a real risk was enough to resist removal under Article 2, suggesting that the loss of life must be shown to be a 'near-certainty'. Where reliance is placed on Article 6 it must be shown that a person has suffered or risks suffering a flagrant denial of a fair trial in the receiving state: *Soering*, para 113 (see para 10 above); *Drodz*, para 110; *Einhorn*, para 32; *Razaghi v Sweden*; *Tomic v United Kingdom*. Successful reliance on Article 5 would have to meet no less exacting a test. The lack of success of applicants relying on Articles 2, 5 and 6 before the Strasbourg court highlights the difficulty of meeting the stringent test which that court imposes. This difficulty will not be less where reliance is placed on Articles such as 8 or 9, which provide for the striking of a balance between the right of the individual and the wider interests of the community even in a case where a serious interference is shown. This is not a balance which the Strasbourg court ought ordinarily to strike in the first instance, nor is it a balance which that court is well placed to assess in the absence of representations by the receiving state whose laws, institutions or practices are the subject of criticism. On the other hand, the removing state will always have what will usually be strong grounds for justifying its own conduct: the great importance of operating firm and orderly immigration control in an expulsion case; the great desirability of honouring extradition treaties made with other states. The correct approach in cases involving qualified rights such as those under Articles 8 and 9 is in my opinion that indicated by the Immigration Appeal Tribunal (Mr C M G Ockelton, deputy president, Mr Allen and Mr Moulden) in *Devaseelan v Secretary of State for the Home Department* [2002] IAT 702, [2003] Imm AR 1, para 111:

> The reason why flagrant denial or gross violation is to be taken into account is that it is only in such a case—where the right will be completely denied or nullified in the destination country—that it can be said that removal will breach the treaty obligations of the signatory state however those obligations might be interpreted or whatever might be said by or on behalf of the destination state.

---

[69] *Ullah v SSHD* [2004] UKHL 26, [2004] 2 AC 323.

In his concurring opinion in *Ullah*, Lord Steyn also found that 'on principles **4.66** repeatedly affirmed by the ECtHR Article 8 may be engaged in cases of a real risk of a flagrant violation of an individual's Article 8 rights'. He added that as was apparent from the Strasbourg jurisprudence, 'where other Articles [other than Article 3] may become engaged, a high threshold test will always have to be satisfied. It will be necessary to establish at least a real risk of a flagrant violation of the very essence of the right before other Articles could become engaged'.

Therefore, whilst Article 8 is capable of being engaged in the context of 'foreign **4.67** cases', in order to show a violation of the right the applicant would have to meet a high threshold, namely that there would be a flagrant denial or gross violation to the Article 8 right by expulsion or other immigration measure. In other words, the Article 8 right will be completely denied or nullified in the destination country.

C. Appeals

Timing issues on appeal

The current statutory provisions allow for the appellate authorities to consider on **4.68** appeal not only the facts in existence at the time of the original decision but also those at the time of the hearing of the appeal itself. Section 85(4) of the Nationality, Immigration and Asylum Act 2002 (as amended by the 2004 Act) provides that:

> On an appeal under section 82(1) [immigration decisions] or 83(2) [asylum claims] against a decision [the Tribunal] may consider evidence about any matter which [it] thinks relevant to the substance of the decision, including evidence which concerns a matter arising after the date of the decision.[70]

The same approach was adopted by House of Lords in *R (on the appln of Razgar) v* **4.69** *SSHD*,[71] where Article 8 issues came before the courts not via a statutory right of appeal but through judicial review proceedings, challenging the certification of the applicant's human rights claim as manifestly unfounded, which deprived him of an in-country right of appeal.

Further, even though the old statutory regime under the 1999 Act had provided **4.70** for up-to-date evidence to be admissible at the appeal hearing in relation to

---

[70] However, see the exception in Section 85(5) in relation to appeals against refusals of entry clearance or refusals of a certificate of entitlement, where only circumstances appertaining at the time of the decision to refuse may be taken into account. See also *DR (ECO: post-decision evidence) Morocco** [2005] UKIAT 00038.

[71] *R (on the appln of Razgar) v SSHD* [2004] UKHL 27, (2004) 2 AC 3.

asylum and Article 3 appeals only, the House of Lords has considered that there is no basis for excluding such new evidence at hearings which consider other ECHR Articles. Lord Bingham in *Razgar* held:

> In the ordinary course of review, the reviewer assesses the decision under challenge on the materials available to the decision-maker at the time when the decision was made. In *Sandralingham v Secretary of State for the Home Department* [1996] Imm AR 97, 112, however, the Court of Appeal held that in asylum cases the appellate structure under the Asylum and Immigration Appeals Act 1993 was to be regarded as an extension of the decision-making process, with the result that appellate authorities were not restricted to consideration of facts in existence at the time of the original decision. This decision was given statutory effect in section 77(3) of the 1999 Act, and was also extended to human rights cases arising under Article 3. The restriction to Article 3 may well have reflected parliamentary uncertainty whether Articles other than Article 3 could be engaged in an expulsion case. But there can be no reason for distinguishing Article 3 cases from cases arising under other Articles of the Convention which (as I have held) are capable of being engaged: see *Macdonald's Immigration Law & Practice*, ed Macdonald and Webber, 5th ed (2001), para 18.150.

4.71 His Lordship also noted the statutory provisions of the 2002 Act, which were not in force vis-à-vis the particular appeal before the House.

4.72 The House of Lords in *Ullah v SSHD*[72] has also confirmed that on a human rights appeal the AIT has to decide itself whether it is unlawful to refuse leave to enter or remain, and 'it is doing so on the basis of up to date facts'.[73]

The function of the appellate authorities on issues of proportionality—review or fresh decision?

The evolution of the test

4.73 **Rejection of a differential test:** The fundamental question of the role of the appellate authorities in reviewing the original decision by the immigration authorities on proportionality is not specifically addressed in the primary or secondary legislation, governing human rights appeals in the asylum context. The tension between a narrow *Wednesbury* review and a full merits-based review together with the practical demands of the decision-making process in this sphere have led to some 'solutions', which have later been abandoned by the courts. For example, a differential test[74] was developed by the Court of Appeal on the basis

---

[72] *Ullah v SSHD* [2004] UKHL 26, [2004] 2 AC 323.

[73] *Ullah v SSHD* [2004] UKHL 26, [2004] 2 AC 323, para 13.

[74] The Court of Appeal decision in *R (Razgar) v SSHD* [2003] INLR 543 held that the test was 'whether the decision of the Secretary of State was within the range of reasonable responses' in all cases, except where this is impossible because the factual basis of the decision of the Secretary of State has been substantially undermined by the findings of the Adjudicator. In such limited category of cases a new decision had to be taken by the Adjudicator with deference to the Secretary of State's

of a distinction between cases where there were prior factual determinations by the Secretary of State which the appellate authorities could review, and other cases where no such factual determinations existed, or those which existed were displaced by other factual findings on appeal. A differently constituted Court of Appeal in the later decision of *Huang & Ors v SSHD*[75] strongly disapproved of a differential test based on such a dichotomy. It noted that under both categories of case the statutory jurisdiction on appeal was exactly the same. Moreover, the conclusion of the Court of Appeal in *Razgar* on this issue was found to be inconsistent with the House of Lords' ruling in that same case. Lord Bingham in *Razgar*[76] had held (at para 20):

> 20. The answering of question (5) [is such interference proportionate to the legitimate public end sought to be achieved?], where that question is reached, must always involve the striking of a fair balance between the rights of the individual and the interests of the community which is inherent in the whole of the Convention. The severity and consequences of the interference will call for careful assessment at this stage. The Secretary of State must exercise his judgment in the first instance. On appeal the adjudicator must exercise his or her own judgment, taking account of any material which may not have been before the Secretary of State. A reviewing court must assess the judgment which would or might be made by an adjudicator on appeal.

The Court of Appeal in *Huang*: The Court of Appeal in *Huang & Ors v SSHD*[77] **4.74** considered the question of the function of the appellate authorities in determining the issue of proportionality. Analysis of the relevant statutory provisions (in this case, section 65 of the 1999 Act and para 21 of Schedule 4 to the 1999 Act) did not determine the issue, but led to the conclusion that the adjudicator must decide *in substance* whether the action appealed against involved a violation of the appellant's Convention rights. It was noted that any other approach would constitute an abdication of the duty of the adjudicator and the Appeal Court, as public authorities, to uphold Convention rights. This part of the Court of Appeal's conclusions was upheld on appeal by the House of Lords.[78]

The conclusions reached by the Court of Appeal in *Huang* can be summarized as **4.75** follows.

(1) **The Adjudicator was required to do more than conduct a *Wednesbury* review of the Secretary of State's decision on proportionality.** This had been recognized by the House of Lords in *R (Daly) v Secretary of State* [2001]

---

decision so far as is possible. It was said to be doubtful whether, in practice, the application of the two approaches would often lead to different outcomes.

75 *Huang & Ors v SSHD* [2005] EWCA Civ 105, (2005) 3 All ER 435.
76 *Razgar* [2004] 2 AC 368.
77 *Huang & Ors v SSHD* [2005] EWCA Civ 105, (2005) 3 All ER 435.
78 *Ullah v SSHD* [2004] UKHL 26, [2004] 2 AC 323, para 11.

2 AC 532, where Lord Steyn held, in what the Committee described in *Huang* as a justly celebrated opinion:

> The starting point is that there is an overlap between the traditional grounds of review and the approach of proportionality. Most cases would be decided in the same way whichever approach is adopted. But the intensity of review is somewhat greater under the proportionality approach. Making due allowance for important structural differences between various convention rights . . . a few generalisations are perhaps permissible. We would mention three concrete differences without suggesting that my statement is exhaustive. First, the doctrine of proportionality may require the reviewing court to assess the balance which the decision maker has struck, not merely whether it is within the range of rational or reasonable decisions. Secondly, the proportionality test may go further than the traditional grounds of review inasmuch as it may require attention to be directed to the relative weight accorded to interests and considerations. Thirdly, even the heightened scrutiny test developed in *R v Ministry of Defence, Ex p Smith* [1996] QB 517, 554 is not necessarily appropriate to the protection of human rights.

(2) **Where on appeal an adjudication is required on policy matters, the Court's or Tribunal's role is closer to review than appeal.** However the degree of deference to the Secretary of State as the original decision maker does no more than respect the balance to be struck between the claims of democratic power and the claims of individual rights. Even in such 'policy cases' the correct approach was not a mere *Wednesbury* review, as was recognized in *Daly*, which itself was such 'a policy case'.

(3) **In cases where the appellate body[79] is not called upon to pass judgment on government policy, there is no basis upon which it should defer to the Secretary of State's judgment of the proportionality issue** in the individual case *unless* it were somehow an open question what weight should be given to the policy on the one hand, and what weight should be given to the Article 8 right on the other. When faced with an Article 8 case where the applicant has no claim under the Immigration Rules, the Adjudicator's task is to see whether an exceptional case has been made out such that the requirement of proportionality requires a departure from the relevant Rule in the particular circumstances.

(4) **However, in 'non-policy' cases the true restriction of the Adjudicator's role arose from the fact that in the general run of cases the Immigration Rules have themselves struck the balance between the public interest and the private right.**

4.76 Therefore, according to the Court of Appeal judgment in *Huang*, the HRA and section 65(1) of the 1999 Act require the AIT to allow an appeal against removal

---

[79] In *Huang* the analysis concerned the correct approach to be adopted by adjudicators on appeal. However, the same approach would hold for determinations by the AIT, set up under the 2004 Act.

or deportation brought on Article 8 grounds if, but only if, it concludes that the case is so exceptional on its particular facts that the imperative of proportionality demands an outcome in the appellant's favour notwithstanding that he cannot succeed under the Rules.

The House of Lords in *Huang*: The House of Lords in *Huang*[80] affirmed that   **4.77** there was no basis upon which an appellate court or tribunal should defer to the Secretary of State's judgment on proportionality in any individual case. The task of the appellate immigration authorities[81] on appeal on a Convention ground against a decision refusing leave to enter or remain was to decide whether the challenged decision is unlawful as incompatible with a Convention right. The task was 'not a secondary, reviewing, function dependent on establishing that the primary decision-maker misdirected himself or acted irrationally or was guilty of procedural impropriety'.[82] On a human rights appeal, the AIT is not reviewing the decision of the Secretary of State or other primary decision maker; it is itself deciding whether or not it is unlawful to refuse leave to enter or remain, and this is done on the up-to-date facts, as known at the time of the appellate hearing.[83]

The House of Lords set out the two steps which the AIT had to follow in its   **4.78** reasoning—to establish the relevant facts, and decide the proportionality issue, by weighing all the arguments on both sides:

> 15. The first task of the appellate immigration authority is to establish the relevant facts. These may well have changed since the original decision was made. In any event, particularly where the applicant has not been interviewed, the authority will be much better placed to investigate the facts, test the evidence, assess the sincerity of the applicant's evidence and the genuineness of his or her concerns and evaluate the nature and strength of the family bond in the particular case. It is important that the facts are explored, and summarised in the decision, with care, since they will always be important and often decisive.
>
> 16. The authority will wish to consider and weigh all that tells in favour of the refusal of leave which is challenged, with particular reference to justification under Article 8(2)....

The decision on proportionality always involves the striking of a fair balance   **4.79** between the rights of the individual and the interests of the community.[84]

---

[80] *Huang* [2007] UKHL 11, [2007] 2 WLR 581.
[81] Adjudicators, IAT, and immigration judges in the AIT.
[82] *Huang* [2007] UKHL 11, para 11.
[83] Ibid, para 13. The House of Lords recognized that the essential effect of the appellate provisions remains the same, despite the introduction of a single, unified, appellate body—the AIT (see *Huang*, para 10).
[84] As found in *R (Razgar) v SSHD* [2004] UKHL 27, [2004] 2 AC 368, para 20, and approved by *Huang v SSHD* [2007] UKHL 11, para 19.

The AIT would have to assess the severity and consequences of the interference with the Article 8 right.[85]

4.80 The ultimate question for the appellate immigration authority was whether, taking full account of all considerations weighing in favour of the refusal of leave, it prejudices the family life of the applicant in a manner so serious as to amount to a breach of the fundamental right protected by Article 8.[86] If the question is answered in the affirmative, the AIT must find that the refusal of leave is unlawful.

4.81 The House of Lords in *Huang* explained that it was not necessary to ask the additional question, whether the case meets an exceptionality test, reversing the Court of Appeal's decision on that point.[87] The House of Lords found the 'exceptionality test' as proposed by the Court of Appeal not to be a necessary legal test. It was based on an observation by Lord Bingham in *Razgar*[88] that the number of claimants not covered by the Rules and supplementary directions but entitled to succeed under Article 8 would be a very small minority. That was an expectation and did not constitute a legal test to be applied with regard to proportionality.

4.82 The House of Lords dismissed the Secretary of State's argument that the AIT should assume that the Immigration Rules and supplementary instructions had the imprimatur of democratic approval and should be taken to strike the right balance between the interests of the individual and those of the community. Thus the House of Lords did not approve that part of the Court of Appeal judgment in *Huang*. The Immigration Rules and supplementary instructions could not be said to represent considered democratic compromise in the way that domestic housing policy did. They were not a product of Parliamentary debate and those affected (non-nationals seeking leave to enter or remain) were not represented in any event. Furthermore, the premise of the statutory scheme was such that applicants may fail to qualify under the Rules and still have a valid claim under Article 8.[89] Therefore, it could not be said that the Immigration Rules have themselves struck the balance between the public interest and the private right.

Jurisdiction of the Court of Appeal on appeal of immigration/asylum decisions

4.83 The jurisdiction of the Court of Appeal to hear an appeal from the AIT, either directly, from a three-member panel, following an AIT reconsideration, or by referral of a review from the High Court, lies solely on a point of law.[90]

---

[85] Ibid.
[86] *Huang v SSHD* [2007] UKHL 11, para 20.
[87] Ibid.
[88] *R (Razgar) v SSHD* [2004] 2 AC 368, at 374F.
[89] *Huang v SSHD* [2007] UKHL 11, para 17.
[90] Nationality, Immigration and Asylum Act 2002, ss103B(1), 103C(1), 103(E)(1).

Points of law need to be in the grounds of appeal: A point of law relied upon by **4.84** an appellant must be identified in the grounds of appeal. Unless permission is given to amend the grounds, the Court of Appeal will rule (whether at the permission or find stage) only on the grounds raised. See the reasoning in *Miftari v SSHD*.[91]

Intensity of review by the Court of Appeal: Practitioners may expect that the **4.85** role of the Court of Appeal will be strictly limited to identifying and ruling on points of law. This would be in keeping with the traditional approach, as set out in *CA* [2004] EWCA Civ 1165, of deciding not whether the decision was proportionate or disproportionate but solely whether the decision was one which was not reasonably open to the appellate authority below. That is not, however, the end of the story. An appeal will not be allowed unless the error of law was material to the decision. The Court of Appeal decision in *Ram Jaha v SSHD*[92] indicated that failure by the AIT to state the correct test as set out in *Huang* would not automatically lead to an appeal against that decision being allowed.[93] The Court of Appeal would consider whether the error in applying the wrong test in relation to the intensity of review on the issue of proportionality is one which would affect the outcome of the appeal. If the Court of Appeal is satisfied that in applying the correct test the AIT would have come to the same conclusion as it did, the appeal will not be allowed.[94]

The appropriate test for the Court of Appeal was set out in *Mongoto v SSHD*[95] **4.86** as 'whether a reasonable tribunal or adjudicator could have found that the appellant's case was so exceptional as to justify a decision on the proportionality issue in his favour'. The test was clearly formulated with the Court of Appeal decision in *Huang* in mind. However, it is submitted that the same test would continue to apply, save for the omission of the reference to exceptionality. Thus, the likely test to be adopted by the Court of Appeal in human rights appeals would be whether a reasonable tribunal could have found that the appellant's case justified a decision on the proportionality issue in his favour, or against him as the case may be.

However, the role of the Administrative Court and the Court of Appeal in further **4.87** appeals and reviews has been found to be limited by different considerations.

---

[91] *Miftari v SSHD* [2005] EWCA Civ 481.
[92] *Ram Jaha v SSHD* [2005] EWCA Civ 968.
[93] The *Huang* test under consideration in *Ram Jaha* was the one set out by the Court of Appeal. See now the House of Lords judgment in *Huang* for the correct test.
[94] See *Ram Jaha v SSHD* [2005] EWCA Civ 968.
[95] *Mongoto v SSHD* [2005] EWCA Civ 751.

In *Akaeke v SSHD*[96] the Court of Appeal emphasized that whilst the Courts retained a supervisory role as final arbiters in relation to genuine issues of law, they ought to be cautious about interfering with decisions on matters within the expertise and competence of specialist tribunals. The AIT as such a tribunal, through its day-to-day experience, was much better placed to justify a departure from the ordinary policy in individual claims, on questions of general principle in particular categories of claimant or particular countries and on questions of proportionality.

D. Immigration Rules and Home Office Policies

Discretionary leave period

Periods of Discretionary Leave granted to those with marriage-based Article 8 claims (Asylum Policy Notice 3/2005, 11 April 2005)[97]

4.88 The Home Office policy for the initial grant of Discretionary Leave made to those who qualify on the basis of a marriage-based Article 8 claim has increased from two to three years. Asylum Policy Notice 3/2005 relates to both asylum and non-asylum cases, and covers cases where it is considered that removal would breach Article 8 of the ECHR on account of the person's marriage to a person settled in the UK. The notice specifies that where an application on the basis of marriage does not meet the requirements of the Rules but there are genuine Article 8 reasons that would make removal inappropriate, Discretionary Leave should be granted.

4.89 Where the person continues to qualify for Discretionary Leave at the end of the initial three-year period they should be granted a further three years. On completion of six years' Discretionary Leave they will be eligible to apply for indefinite leave to remain (ILR).

4.90 **Grants of leave made under the previous policy:** Prior to the date of this notice, individuals who qualified for Discretionary Leave on account of a marriage-based Article 8 claim were granted an initial period of two years. If they continued to qualify for Discretionary Leave they would be granted two further two-year periods until they were eligible for ILR on completion of six years.

---

[96] *Akaeke v SSHD* [2005] EWCA Civ 947.
[97] Available from <http://www.ind.homeoffice.gov.uk/documents/asylumpolicyinstructions/>— consulted on 27 August 2007.

Unmarried or same sex partners

March 06 Immigration Directorates' Instructions, Chapter 8 Section 9:
Unmarried and same sex relationships[98]

Unmarried or same sex partner of somebody present and settled in the UK: **4.91**
Under the Immigration Rules foreign nationals may seek leave to enter or remain
in the UK with a view to settlement as the unmarried or same sex partner of a
person present and settled here or being admitted on the same occasion for
settlement.

The Immigration Rules (paras 295A–295G of HC 395 as amended by HC 538 **4.92**
and 582) set out the provisions for leave to enter or remain for persons in this
category. The relationship may be same sex or heterosexual, but may not be a
consanguineous relationship, and neither the applicant nor the sponsor may be
aged under 18 on the date of arrival in the United Kingdom or (as the case may be)
on the date on which the leave to remain or variation of leave would be granted.

Practitioners will refer to the Immigration Rules for the detailed provisions which **4.93**
must be satisfied by applicants. The Home Office Immigration Directorate's
Instructions provide the following useful guidance as to how certain language
used in the rules is to be interpreted:

(1) 'Present and settled' means that the person concerned is settled in the United
    Kingdom and, at the time that an application under these Rules is made, is
    physically present here or is coming here with or to join the applicant and
    intends to make the United Kingdom their home with the applicant if the
    application is successful.
(2) 'Intention to live permanently with the other' means an intention to live
    together, evidenced by a clear commitment from both parties that they will
    live together permanently in the United Kingdom immediately following
    the outcome of the application in question or as soon as circumstances per-
    mit thereafter, and 'intends to live permanently with the other' shall be con-
    strued accordingly.

Requirements for leave to remain: The requirements to be met by a person **4.94**
seeking to remain in the United Kingdom as the unmarried or same sex partner
of a person present and settled here are:

(i) the applicant has limited leave to remain in the United Kingdom which
    was given in accordance with any of the provisions of the Immigration
    Rules; and

---

98 <http://www.ind.homeoffice.gov.uk/documents/idischapter8/section9.pdf?view=Binary>—
last consulted on 27 August 2007.

    (ii)   any previous marriage or civil partnership by either partner has permanently broken down; and

   (iii) the applicant is the unmarried or same sex partner of a person who is present and settled in the United Kingdom; and

   (iv) the applicant has not remained in breach of the immigration laws; and

    (v) the parties are not involved in a consanguineous relationship with one another; and

   (vi) the parties have been living together in a relationship akin to marriage or civil partnership which has subsisted for two years or more; and

  (vii) the parties' relationship pre-dates any decision to deport the applicant, recommend him for deportation, give him notice under section 6(2) of the Immigration Act 1971, or give directions for his removal under section 10 of the Immigration and Asylum Act 1999; and

  (viii) there will be adequate accommodation for the parties and any dependants without recourse to public funds in accommodation which they own or occupy exclusively; and

   (ix) the parties will be able to maintain themselves and any dependants adequately without recourse to public funds; and

    (x) the parties intend to live together permanently.

4.95   The key provisions require caseworkers to be satisfied that:

    (i) the applicant is here lawfully and has a relationship akin to marriage or civil partnership which has subsisted for two years or more, with a person who is present and settled here;

   (ii) the applicant's leave was granted within the Immigration Rules;

  (iii) any previous marriage or civil partnership by either partner has permanently broken down;

  (iv) the relationship is subsisting and the couple intend living together permanently.

4.96   Applicants will be expected to supply documentary evidence that their relationship with their unmarried or same sex partner has subsisted for two years or more.

4.97   Applicants will provide information on maintenance and accommodation when completing the application form. The Home Office policy provides that the whole application should be assessed according to the Rules, but refusal on maintenance and accommodation grounds is likely to be rare and must be approved at senior caseworker level or above.

4.98   **Unmarried or same sex partner of a person with limited leave to enter or remain in the UK:**   The requirements for leave to enter or remain as the unmarried or same sex partner of a person with limited leave to enter or remain in the UK are:

 (i) the applicant is the unmarried or same sex partner of a person who has limited leave to enter or remain in the United Kingdom under paragraphs 128–193, 200–239, or 263–270; and

 (ii) any previous marriage or civil partnership by either partner has permanently broken down; and

 (iii) the parties are not involved in a consanguineous relationship with one another; and

 (iv) the parties have been living together in a relationship akin to marriage or civil partnership which has subsisted for two years or more; and

 (v) each of the parties intends to live with the other as his partner during the applicant's stay; and

 (vi) there will be adequate accommodation for the parties and any dependants without recourse to public funds in accommodation which they own or occupy exclusively; and

 (vii) the parties will be able to maintain themselves and any dependants adequately without recourse to public funds; and

 (viii) the applicant does not intend to stay in the United Kingdom beyond any period of leave granted to his partner; and

 (ix) if seeking leave to enter, the applicant holds a valid United Kingdom entry clearance for entry in this capacity or, if seeking leave to remain, was admitted with a valid United Kingdom entry clearance for entry in this capacity.

Granting further leave to remain: An application for further leave to remain **4.99** in this capacity may be granted under the requirements of the Immigration Rules for unmarried or same sex partners for a period of leave not in excess of that granted to the person with limited leave to remain under HC 395 paragraphs 128–193, 200–239, or 263–270.

Where leave for less than two years was granted on entry, but the other partner **4.100** has since been granted an extension, further leave may be granted to take them up to two years in total. Where the applicant has completed a two-year period granted on this basis, further leave to remain may be granted in line with their partner.

An application for indefinite leave to remain in this category may be granted **4.101** under the requirements of the Immigration Rules for unmarried or same sex partners provided the applicant was admitted with a valid United Kingdom entry clearance for entry in this capacity and is able to satisfy the Secretary of State that each of the requirements set out in (i)–(viii) above is met and provided indefinite leave to remain is, at the same time, being granted to the person with limited leave to enter or remain under HC 395 paragraphs 128–193, 200–239, or 263–270.

4.102 **Settlement:** For the purposes of settlement, unmarried or same sex partners have to complete a two-year probationary period on limited leave. The Immigration Rules contain no specific requirement that the entire probationary period must be spent in the UK. For example, where an applicant has spent a limited period abroad in connection with his employment, this should not count against him, unless he has spent the majority of the period overseas. Each case is to be judged on its merits, taking into account reasons for travel, length of absences, and whether the applicant and sponsor travelled and lived together during the period outside the UK. These factors will need to be considered against the requirements of the Rules.

4.103 Unmarried or same sex partners who have married or formed a civil partnership during the two-year probationary period can apply for settlement under para 287 of the Immigration Rules as the spouse or civil partner of a person present and settled in the UK.

4.104 **Bereaved unmarried partners:** Paras 287(b) and 295M–295O of the Immigration Rules (HC 395 as amended by HC 582) make provision for unmarried or same sex partners who are bereaved during the probationary period to be granted indefinite leave to remain in the UK provided that the marriage or relationship was subsisting at the time of the sponsor's death.

Victims of domestic violence

4.105 In the March 2006 Immigration Directorate Instructions, Chapter 8, Section 4 (Victims of Domestic Violence),[99] domestic violence is defined as 'any incident of threatening behaviour, violence or abuse (psychological, physical, sexual, financial or emotional) between adults who are or have been intimate partners or family members, regardless of gender or sexuality'. Injury is defined as 'any harm done to a person by the acts or omissions of another'.

4.106 Indefinite leave to remain in the United Kingdom as the victim of domestic violence can be granted under para 289A of the Rules, provided the requirements under that provision are met. An applicant who has limited leave to enter or remain in the UK as the spouse, registered civil partner, or unmarried partner of a British citizen or person who is present and settled in this country and whose relationship breaks down during the probationary period as a result of domestic violence may be granted indefinite leave to remain, provided that the domestic

---

[99] <http://www.ind.homeoffice.gov.uk/documents/idischapter8/section4.pdf?view=Binary>— last consulted on 27 August 2007.

violence occurred during the probationary period whilst the marriage or relationship was subsisting and the applicant is able to provide satisfactory evidence that domestic violence has taken place. The Home Office would normally accept that the relationship was subsisting when domestic violence occurred if the couple were living at the same address when the incident took place.

The IND Instructions provide that the Rules are intended to benefit only those **4.107** who have been subjected to domestic violence during the probationary period and who make their application whilst they still have limited leave to enter or remain in the United Kingdom. The provision does not apply to a person admitted to the UK as the spouse or unmarried partner of a sponsor who has only limited leave to enter or remain in the UK, or who is a European Economic Area national exercising treaty rights, as such persons have not been admitted to the UK for the purpose of settlement.

Long residence

The 'Long Residency Concession', previously contained in Chapter 18 of the **4.108** Immigration Directorate's Instructions (September 2004), has been incorporated into the Immigration Rules on 1 April 2003 (paras 276A–276D).

Indefinite leave to remain will be granted on the basis of long residence (under **4.109** para 276C) if the requirements in IR para 276B are met, namely that the applicant:

(i) (a) has had at least ten years' continuous lawful residence in the United Kingdom; or
   (b) has had at least 14 years' continuous residence in the United Kingdom, excluding any period spent in the United Kingdom following service of notice of liability to removal or notice of a decision to remove by way of directions under paras 8–10A, or 12–14, of Schedule 2 to the Immigration Act 1971 or section 10 of the Immigration and Asylum Act 1999 Act, or of a notice of intention to deport him from the United Kingdom; and
(ii) having regard to the public interest there are no reasons why it would be undesirable for him to be given indefinite leave to remain on the ground of long residence, taking into account his:
   (a) age; and
   (b) strength of connections in the United Kingdom; and
   (c) personal history, including character, conduct, associations, and employment record; and
   (d) domestic circumstances; and
   (e) previous criminal record and the nature of any offence of which the person has been convicted; and

(f) compassionate circumstances; and

(g) any representations received on the person's behalf.

4.110 The Immigration Rules[100] define 'continuous residence' as residence in the United Kingdom for an unbroken period, where a period is not considered to have been broken where an applicant is absent for a period of six months or less at any one time, provided that the applicant has existing limited leave to enter or remain upon their departure and return. However, the continuous residence shall be considered as broken if the applicant:

(i) has been removed under Schedule 2 of the 1971 Act, section 10 of the 1999 Act, has been deported or has left the United Kingdom having been refused leave to enter or remain here; or

(ii) has left the United Kingdom and, on doing so, evidenced a clear intention not to return; or

(iii) left the United Kingdom in circumstances in which he could have had no reasonable expectation at the time of leaving that he would lawfully be able to return; or

(iv) has been convicted of an offence and was sentenced to a period of imprisonment or was directed to be detained in an institution other than a prison (including, in particular, a hospital or an institution for young offenders), provided that the sentence in question was not a suspended sentence; or

(v) has spent a total of more than 18 months absent from the United Kingdom during the period in question.[101]

4.111 'Lawful residence' is defined as residence which is continuous pursuant to:

(i) existing leave to enter or remain; or

(ii) temporary admission within section 11 of the 1971 Act where leave to enter or remain is subsequently granted; or

(iii) an exemption from immigration control, including where an exemption ceases to apply if it is immediately followed by a grant of leave to enter or remain.[102]

Families concession

One-off exercise to allow qualifying asylum-seeking families to stay in the UK

4.112 On 24 October 2003 the Home Secretary announced a concession to grant indefinite leave to remain exceptionally outside the Immigration Rules to families who have been in the UK for three or more years. The concession was promulgated as a 'one-off exercise to allow families who have been in the UK for three years or more to stay'. On 12 June 2006, it was replaced by a revised policy,

---

[100] IR, para 276A(a).
[101] IR, para 276A(a).
[102] IR, para 276A(b).

published on the IND website,[103] entitled 'One-off exercise to allow qualifying asylum seeking families to stay in the UK'. New applications from persons who have previously applied unsuccessfully under the previous notice are considered under this revised policy.

The criteria for granting leave under the concession are as follows: **4.113**

(1) The applicant applied for asylum before 2 October 2000; and
(2) The applicant had at least one dependant aged under 18 (other than a spouse) in the UK on 2 October 2000 or 24 October 2003.

Families will be eligible for the concession where the application (i) has not yet **4.114** been decided, (ii) has been refused and is subject to an appeal, (iii) has been refused and there is no further avenue of appeal but the applicant has not been removed, (iv) has been refused but limited leave has been granted, or (v) has been decided in their favour and limited leave as a refugee has been granted. Families will not be eligible if after refusal of that initial claim they have been removed or have made a voluntary departure.

For the purpose of determining whether the basic criteria of the concession are **4.115** met, a dependant is a child of the applicant, or child of the applicant's spouse or civil partner, who was or is financially and emotionally dependent on the applicant on the relevant date (ie 2 October 2000 or 24 October 2003).

Under the concession, caseworkers must be satisfied that the dependant was **4.116** living in the UK on 2 October 2000 or 24 October 2003 as part of the family unit, which will normally be the case where there is evidence on the asylum file of the dependant prior to the date of the announcement of the concession. For dependants born in the UK and not listed on the asylum file, a UK birth certificate will be required to be produced.

All dependants of the applicant who meet the basic criteria for the concession **4.117** should be granted ILR.

The Secretary of State retains discretion to grant indefinite leave even in cases **4.118** which do not meet the exact requirements of the policy. However, such discretion will be exercised 'only in the most exceptional compassionate cases'. The policy specifies that if families believe that their circumstances merit consideration on this basis, they must provide full details and supporting evidence. Where a case involves a criminal conviction for a recordable offence, discretion would not be exercised without referral to Ministers.

---

[103] <http://www.ind.homeoffice.gov.uk/documents/asylumpolicyinstructions/apunotices/one-offexercise.pdf?view=Binary>—consulted on 27 August 2007.

4.119 There have been several challenges to the policy from unaccompanied asylum-seeking children who did not qualify under its strict criteria (see *AL (Serbia) v SSHD*[104] and *Rudi and Ibrahimi v SSHD*[105]). These cases are discussed further in Chapter 5.

4.120 Additionally, in *R (on the appln of De Franco) v SSDH*[106] the families concession was challenged as irrational by a claimant who had much more established links within the UK due to having been in the country since 1996. She could not benefit from the policy, as her son was not under the age of 18 at the required date. The High Court held that the mere fact that a policy produced anomalies did not make it irrational. Simplicity and clarity for easy application were valid considerations in drafting such a policy. Whilst consistency of application among those in similar situations had to be an objective of the policy, that could not be its only objective. Administrative effectiveness and cost saving with regard to some of the most expensive asylum cases were also valid objectives, as recognized in *AL (Serbia) v SSHD*.[107] The policy was not intended to identify all those in the backlog who had a compassionate case, nor was it predicated on the aim that each individual falling within it would have a stronger case for leave than any individual outside it. The application of any particular criteria would be bound to produce anomalies. If the policy terms had excluded the applicant and left her with no means of advancing her claim, the irrationality argument would have been more persuasive. However, she had other available options.

Families where applicant has limited leave to remain or arrived under the Humanitarian Evacuation Programme

4.121 Kosovan families who arrived pursuant to the Humanitarian Evacuation Programme before 2 October 2000 but did not claim asylum until after this date are included in the scope of this exercise if they meet the necessary criteria.

Exclusions

4.122 The concession will not apply to a family where the principal applicant or any of the dependants:

(a) have a criminal conviction for a recordable offence;
(b) have been subject of an anti-social behaviour order or sex offender order;
(c) have made (or attempted to make) an application for asylum in the UK in more than one identity;

---

[104] *AL (Serbia) v SSHD* [2006] EWCA Civ 1619.
[105] *Rudi and Ibrahimi v SSHD* [2007] EWHC 60.
[106] *R (on the appln of De Franco) v SSDH* [2007] EWHC 407 (Admin).
[107] *AL (Serbia) v SSHD* (2006) EWCA Civ 1619.

(d) should have their asylum claim considered by another country (ie they are the subject of a possible third country removal). Families will be excluded where they are all subject to possible third country removal. Families where one member of the family made a claim before 2 October 2000 which has been accepted for consideration by IND and therefore is not subject to third country removal, and would otherwise fall into the concession, will not be excluded;

(e) present a risk to security;

(f) fall within the scope of Article 1F of the Refugee Convention; or

(g) whose presence in the UK is otherwise not conducive to the public good.

Marriage policy DP3/96

DP3/96 comprises Home Office Policy Guidelines for dealing with marriage **4.123** applications from illegal entrants or in cases where deportation action is being taken.

Broadly, DP3/96 states that it will normally be appropriate for the Secretary of **4.124** State to consider a grant of leave to remain, exceptionally, on the basis of a marriage if he is satisfied that:

(i) the marriage is genuine and subsisting;

(ii) it pre-dates the service of an enforcement notice by at least two years;

(iii) it is unreasonable to expect the settled spouse to accompany his/her spouse on removal.

For the purposes of the policy, 'Commencement of Enforcement Action' is to be **4.125** taken as either:

(a) a specific instruction to leave with a warning of liability to deportation if the subject fails to do so; or

(b) service of a notice of intention to deport or service of illegal entry papers (including the service of papers during the previous stay in the United Kingdom where the subject has returned illegally); or

(c) a recommendation by a Court that the person should be deported following a conviction.

Withdrawal of an adverse asylum decision does not of itself amount to with- **4.126** drawal of a consequential removal decision.[108]

---

[108] See s 77 of the 2002 Act and *AA (DP3/96–Commencement of Enforcement action) Pakistan* [2007] UKAIT 00016.

4.127 The Home Office has applied this policy also to overstayers,[109] although this immigration category is not covered on the plain reading of the policy. DP3/96 was also considered in *R v SSHD ex p Mahmood*,[110] where the Court of Appeal was critical of the way in which the policy was drafted.

Children

Age disputes

4.128 The Secretary of State's policies in relation to age disputes reflect the competing objectives of not subjecting under 18s to detention and the fact that individuals may falsely claim to be under 18 in order to benefit from the more generous asylum policies and support arrangements applicable to children. For example, unaccompanied children:

(a) will not generally be detained or be subjected to fast-track procedures;
(b) will be removed from the UK following refusal of an asylum claim only if adequate care and reception arrangements are in place in the receiving country;
(c) may benefit from being looked after by local authorities under the Children Act.

4.129 In a case concerning age disputes, *R (on the appln of I & O) v SSHD*,[111] the Administrative Court considered the applicable policies as produced by the Secretary of State, namely:

(a) a document exhibited to the statement of the Assistant Director of IND responsible for the Children and Family Asylum Policy Team, entitled 'Disputed Age Cases (2nd Edition, published January 2005)';
(b) a second exhibited document headed 'Unaccompanied Asylum Seeking Children'. This document was contended by the Secretary of State not to be a formal statement of policy but to contain a mix of policy and process information. Owen J found para 6 of the document to contain the Home Office policy, namely:

Where an applicant claims to be a child but his/her appearance strongly suggests that he/she is over 18, IND's policy is to treat the applicant as an adult and offer NASS

---

[109] See *MA (DP3/96–interpretation) Algeria* [2005] UKAIT 00127, where the AIT found that the wording of IS151A, IS151A Part 2, and IS151B made it sufficiently clear that the purport of those documents is entirely consistent with the concept of commencement of enforcement action within DP3/96. In *AA (DP3/96–Commencement of Enforcement action) Pakistan* [2007] UKAIT 00016 the AIT found that, where the notes to DP 3/96 state that commencement of enforcement action includes service of illegal entry papers, the expression 'illegal entry papers' is clearly capable of covering *IS151A*.

[110] *R v SSHD ex p Mahmood* (2001) 1 WLR 840.

[111] *R (on the appln of I & O) v SSHD* [2005] EWHC 1025.

support (if appropriate) until there is credible documentary or medical evidence to demonstrate the age claimed.[112]

(c) Further guidance was contained in Chapter 38 of the IND Operational Enforcement Manual. No ruling as to the status of this document was made in the case of *I & O*, however, the Home Office contended that it was for internal guidance to immigration enforcement staff, and although published, it was not a means of disseminating policies to the public and was in the process of being updated and revised. The Court was critical of the confusion as to the dates upon which the relevant policies or guidance to IND staff were in force, but did not consider it necessary to rule on the status of Chapter 38, as the relevant policy was sufficiently expressed in the first two documents.

In *R (on the appln of I & O) v SSHD*[113] the claimants were successful in challenging the Home Secretary's decision to continue their detention as adults for the period between the receipt of reports from a consultant paediatrician and the age assessments carried out by social services. The consultant's reports amounted to credible medical evidence to demonstrate the age claimed by the asylum seekers and consistent with the policy the claimants should have been released from detention. **4.130**

The relevant age dispute policies currently available on the IND website, include the following: **4.131**

(a) A special cases policy 'Disputed age cases'.[114] According to the wording of this policy, benefit of the doubt must be given to claimants with regard to their age, save where their physical appearance or demeanour strongly suggests that they are aged 18 or over:

> The Border and Immigration Agency will dispute the age of an applicant who claims to be a child but whose appearance and/or general demeanour strongly suggests that they are aged 18 or over, unless there is credible documentary or other persuasive evidence to demonstrate the age claimed. In borderline cases, it is Border and Immigration Agency policy to give the applicant the benefit of the doubt and treat them as a child.

> The Border and Immigration Agency will treat the applicant as a disputed age case, until age has been satisfactorily determined. The Border and Immigration Agency does not treat disputed age cases as children unless and until their age is established as being under 18. The Border and Immigration Agency does not consider that the asylum process should be delayed until the issue of age is resolved, but has put safeguards in place for disputed age cases in this instruction.

---

[112] For the full text see para 24 of the Judgment.
[113] *R (on the appln of I & O) v SSHD* [2005] EWHC 1025.
[114] <http://www.ind.homeoffice.gov.uk/documents/specialcases/guidance/>

(b) NASS policy bulletin 33, 'Age Disputes Version 1.0 Date of Issue 17 October 2000',[115] which states that benefit of the doubt should be given to the applicant's claim from the outset to be under 18 only in borderline cases:

8. ASYLUM SEEKER STATES ON ARRIVAL THAT S/HE IS A MINOR

8.1 If the applicant claims to be a minor but his/her appearance strongly suggests that s/he is over 18 the applicant will be treated as an adult until such time as credible documentary or medical evidence is produced which demonstrates that s/he is the age claimed. In borderline cases the Immigration Service will continue to give the applicant the benefit of the doubt and to deal with the applicant as a minor. In accordance with existing policy they will continue to inform the Refugee Council's Panel of Advisers of anyone who has claimed to be a minor, even when the age is disputed and the decision has been taken to treat the applicant as an adult.

Policies on unaccompanied asylum-seeking children

4.132   In relation to unaccompanied children the Immigration Rules provide:

(1) Particular priority and care is to be given to the handling of these cases due to their potential vulnerability (para 350).

(2) In assessing the claim of a child, more weight should be given to objective indications of risk than to the child's state of mind and understanding of his situation (para 351).

(3) Unaccompanied minors may be interviewed about the substance of their claim or to determine age and identity. However, when an interview is necessary it should be conducted in the presence of a parent, guardian, representative, or another adult who for the time being takes responsibility for the child (para 352).

(4) The interviewer should have particular regard to the possibility that the child will feel inhibited or alarmed. The child should be allowed to express himself in his own way and at his own speed. If he appears tired or distressed, the interview should be stopped (para 352).

(1) Asylum Policy Unit Notices
Application of Non Suspensive Appeal (NSA) Process to Unaccompanied Asylum Seeking Children (1st October 2004) (previously APU Notice 5/2004)[116]

4.133   This notice sets out the policy relating to the consideration of an asylum or human rights claim made by unaccompanied asylum-seeking children (UASC) from a country which is designated under Section 94 of the Nationality, Immigration and Asylum Act 2002. The terms of the notice also apply to a

---

[115] <http://www.ind.homeoffice.gov.uk/documents/children/pb33?view=Binary>—accessed on 27 August 2007.
[116] <http://www.ind.homeoffice.gov.uk/documents/asylumpolicyinstructions/apunotices/applicationofnsa.pdf>—last accessed on 27 August 2007.

particular category of accompanied children—namely those minors who have arrived in the UK to join a relative or other person responsible for their care where there is no prospect that should the child's claim be refused, the relative or person in question would return to the child's country of origin and continue to look after them.

Under the provisions of Section 94 of the NIA Act 2002, asylum or human rights **4.134** claims from persons who are entitled to reside in one of the States listed at Section 94(4)(as amended), if refused, are to be certified as clearly unfounded unless the Secretary of State is satisfied that they are not clearly unfounded. Asylum and human rights claims from accompanied and unaccompanied asylum-seeking children are not excluded from these provisions. However, when determining any such claims the notice demands that additional consideration should be given to the current policy not to remove any UASC, including one from a listed country, without ensuring that adequate reception and accommodation arrangements are available on return.

Period of leave to be granted

The notice specifies that until a returns programme for UASCs is in place Minis- **4.135** ters have agreed a change from the normal UASC Discretionary Leave policy, as follows:

Normal concession

> If their asylum claim is refused, any UASC from a **country listed below**, who has no family to return to and where adequate reception arrangements cannot be established, is to be granted a period of **12 months Discretionary Leave, or leave to their 18th birthday, whichever is the shorter** unless they qualify for more favourable terms of leave under other provisions of the Humanitarian Protection or Discretionary Leave polices. **This only applies to UASCs from the following countries:**
>
> **Albania, Bangladesh, Bulgaria, Jamaica, Macedonia, Moldova, Romania, Serbia and Montenegro, Sri Lanka.**

Extended concession

> UASCs from five of the countries on the designated list (**Brazil, Bolivia, Ecuador, South Africa, and Ukraine**) whose asylum claim is refused should be granted Discretionary Leave for **three years or until their 18th birthday, whichever is the shorter**, in accordance with the **normal UASC Discretionary Leave** policy unless they qualify for more favourable terms of leave under the other provisions of the Humanitarian Protection or Discretionary Leave policies.

Interviewing UASCs from NSA countries

The APU Notice draws attention to the amendment to the Immigration Rules **4.136** enabling UASCs to be interviewed in a wider set of circumstances than previously, and a pilot project with UASCs from NSA countries being set up to develop and test an effective process for substantively interviewing children. Practitioners may direct queries about this notice to the Children and Family Asylum Policy Team, AAPD, on 020 8760 8674.

(2) *Operational Enforcement Manual*

Chapter 29—Unaccompanied children[117]

4.137 The Immigration Rules define a child as a person who is under 18 or who, in the absence of documentary evidence, appears to be under 18. An unaccompanied asylum-seeking child is one who is applying for asylum in his own right and who has no adult family member or guardian to whom he can turn in this country.

4.138 Claims for asylum from unaccompanied children are dealt with by CMU 12/13, 12th Floor, Lunar House, 40 Wellesley Road, Croydon CR9 2BY. According to the *Operational Enforcement Manual*, all correspondence should be sent to ACU 1, PO Box 1234, Croydon CR9 1ZX, which sifts and allocates the cases to the appropriate Liverpool or Croydon CMU.

4.139 The *Operational Enforcement Manual* provides that unaccompanied children should not be interviewed about their asylum claim except in the most exceptional circumstances and the decision to conduct an asylum interview must be made by the relevant casework section. Additionally, unaccompanied children must only ever be detained in the most exceptional circumstances, and then only overnight, with appropriate care, whilst alternative arrangements for their safety are made. At the earliest opportunity, all cases involving unaccompanied minors must be notified by IND to the Children's Panel of the Refugee Council on 0207 582 4947 even if it is suspected that the person is over the age of 18.

4.140 The *Operational Enforcement Manual* provides that such disputed age cases comprise those where the applicant's physical appearance strongly suggests that they are aged 18 or over and there is no satisfactory documentary evidence to substantiate the claimed date of birth.

> The criteria for disputing age is: an applicant's age will only be disputed where their physical appearance strongly suggests that they aged 18 or over, and where there is no satisfactory documentary evidence to substantiate the claimed date of birth. The onus of proof is on the applicant to supply satisfactory documentary evidence or otherwise demonstrate they are in fact a child. Social Services should be asked for an age assessment in age dispute cases wherever possible and at the earliest opportunity. **The age assessment of Social Services must be accepted in all cases.**

---

[117] <http://www.ind.homeoffice.gov.uk/documents/oemsectionc/chapter29> (also at <http://www.ind.homeoffice.gov.uk/documents/oemsectionc/>)—last accessed on 27 August 2007.

Where an applicant initially claims to be an adult when they make their application for asylum, but later states that they are a child, they should be given the benefit of the doubt and treated as a child if their physical appearance strongly suggests that they are under 18. If the applicant's appearance strongly suggests that they are aged 18 or over, the onus of proof is on the applicant to supply satisfactory documentary evidence or otherwise demonstrate that they are in fact a child. This would be a 'disputed age' case.

Each unaccompanied child should be issued with an advice leaflet issued by the **4.141** Refugee Council and a Children's Statement of Evidence Form, to be returned to the Asylum Co-ordination Unit, PO Box 1234, Croydon CR9 1ZX. CMU 12/13 will not retain responsibility for the case after the child has reached the age of 18. These cases become the responsibility of the Active Review Team CMU 11, 12th Floor, Lunar House (provided that they have submitted an application for further leave to remain).

According to the *Operational Enforcement Manual*, in cases where the age of **4.142** the child is in dispute neither medical examinations nor x-rays should be commissioned. Although the relevant casework section will consider medical examinations commissioned by representatives, they should be informed that x-ray evidence will not be considered. Medical evidence in age dispute cases is seldom conclusive and can usually provide only a rough estimate of the person's age; however, it should be given due weight in considering the totality of evidence.

It is the responsibility of CMU 12/13 to establish the likelihood of removal **4.143** should the asylum claim fail. Where a case is referred to an enforcement office to effect removal, the caseworkers would have to:

(a) establish with the country to which the child is to be removed that adequate reception arrangements are in place;
(b) liaise with the social services and/or nominated guardian with responsibility for care of the child in the UK to ensure the removal is effected in the most sensitive manner possible;
(c) consider the need for escorts to accompany the child.

Further guidance on reception arrangements and other matters concerning **4.144** asylum-seeking children is contained in the Asylum Policy Instructions on Children.[118]

---

[118] <http://www.ind.homeoffice.gov.uk/documents/specialcases/guidance/>—consulted on 27 August 2007.

E. Practice and Procedure Note

Marriage applications

4.145   Sections 19 to 25 of the Asylum and Immigration (Treatment of Claimants, etc) Act 2004 provide for additional procedures where a marriage is to be solemnized in the United Kingdom and a party to the marriage is subject to immigration control. Section 19(2)(a) provides that where a marriage is to be solemnized in England and Wales, the notices under section 27 of the Marriage Act 1949 must be given to the superintendent registrar of a registration district specified in regulations. In addition, by sections 19(3), 21(3), and 23(3), the registrar to whom notice is given may not enter notice of the marriage into the marriage book unless satisfied that the party subject to immigration control either (a) has an entry clearance granted for the purpose of enabling him to marry in the United Kingdom, (b) has the written permission of the Secretary of State to marry in the United Kingdom, or (c) falls within a class specified in regulations made by the Secretary of State. Section 25 enables the Secretary of State by regulations to make provision in relation to applications for permission to marry in the United Kingdom.

4.146   Under the Immigration (Procedure for Marriage) Regulations 2005, a person seeking the permission (Certificate of Approval) of the Secretary of State to marry in the United Kingdom is required to make an application in writing, pay a fee, and provide the following information.

Information to be provided in respect of the applicant

Name, date of birth, name at birth (if different), nationality, full postal address, daytime telephone number, passport or travel document number, Home Office reference number, current immigration status, date on which current leave to enter or remain in the United Kingdom was granted, date on which that leave expires, whether he has previously been married, and if so, information showing that he is now free to marry, two passport-sized photographs, passport or travel document.

Information to be provided in respect of the other party to the intended marriage

Name, date of birth, name at birth (if different), nationality, full postal address, daytime telephone number, passport or travel document number, whether he is subject to immigration control (and if so: Home Office reference number, current immigration status, date on which current leave to enter or remain in the United Kingdom was granted, date on which that leave expires), whether he has previously been married, and if so, information showing that he is now free to marry, two passport-sized photographs, passport or travel document.

The Secretary of State adopted a policy, which was to refuse a Certificate of Approval **4.147** (COA) to anyone who did not have a valid right to enter or remain in the UK for more than six months, and with more than three months of that period outstanding. This COA regime came under challenge in *R (on the appln of Baiai & Ors) v SSHD & Anor,*[119] with the Administrative Court holding that it infringed Articles 12 and 14 of the ECHR. The Court found that as a matter of principle the Secretary of State could impose restrictions or conditions on the right to marry in the interests of an effective immigration policy without infringing Article 12. However, each restriction or condition had to comply with the requirements of proportionality. The objective of preventing sham marriages, which were entered into to avoid immigration control, was sufficiently important to justify the limitation of the right to marry. However, the new regime was not rationally connected to the legislative objective. The genuineness of a marriage was not the criterion for the decision as to whether to approve a marriage in any individual case. There was no logical connection between the length of time for which a person had leave to remain in the UK and the genuineness of a marriage. The regime also arbitrarily failed to take into account relevant factors, such as evidence of a longstanding relationship. Thus the Court found that the measures in the regime were not proportionate and constituted a substantial interference with Article 12 rights.

There was also no objective basis for presuming that all marriages conducted in *reli-* **4.148** *gious* ceremonies other than the Church of England should be automatically treated as sham marriages and requiring of Certificates of Approval. The distinction between those who wished to marry in an Anglican religious ceremony as opposed to other religious ceremonies was not justifiable. Therefore the regime discriminated on the basis the personal characteristics of religion and nationality, contrary to Articles 12 and 14.

The second round of litigation in the same case, *R (on the appln of Baiai & Ors) v SSHD* **4.149** *[No.2]*,[120] answered the more specific question as to whether there was a breach of the Claimant's Article 12 and 14 rights *as an illegal entrant*. The Court found that the scheme precluding illegal immigrants from obtaining COAs was rationally connected to the policy of immigration control, as illegal entrants had an incentive to marry EEA nationals to gain the right of residence in the UK, thus undermining immigration policy.

The Court of Appeal in *Secretary of State for the Home Department v Baiai &* **4.150** *Ors*[121] upheld the first *Baiai* judgment but reversed the second one. It ruled that

---

[119] *R (on the appln of Baiai & Ors) v SSHD & Anor* [2006] EWHC 823 (Admin), (2006) 3 All ER 608.
[120] *R (on the appln of Baiai & Ors) v SSHD [No.2]* [2006] EWHC 1454 (Admin), [2006] 4 All ER 555.
[121] *Secretary of State for the Home Department v Baiai & Ors* [2007] EWCA Civ 478, The Times, 26 June 2007.

the Home Office COA scheme was not proportionate to the legitimate aim purused. The Secretary of State was entitled to interfere with the exercise of Article 12 rights only in cases that involved, or were likely to involve, sham marriages entered into with the object of improving the immigration status of one of the parties. 'To be proportionate, a scheme to achieve that end had to either properly investigate individual cases, or at least show that it had come close to isolating cases that very likely fell into the target category. It also had to show that the marriages targeted did indeed make substantial inroads into the enforcement of immigration control.'[122] The scheme failed to satisfy this test. Further, the objection inherent in the scheme, namely that it prevents marriages on immigration status grounds, rather than on the basis of the genuineness of the marriage, applied equally to illegal entrants.

4.151 The Home Office is seeking leave to appeal to the House of Lords. In the meantime, policy updates are available on the IND website. The current policy is set out in 'Important information regarding Certificate of Approval (COA) for marriage or civil partnership applications 19 June 2007'.[123]

F. Practice and Procedure Note

Positive State obligations and damages for breach of Article 8

4.152 In *Huang v SSHD*,[124] the House of Lords held that Article 8 'imposes on member states not only a negative duty to refrain from unjustified interference with a person's right to respect for his or her family but also a positive duty to show respect for it' (para 18). For a recent ECtHR case where the respondent state was held to be under an obligation to facilitate family reunification for an unaccompanied foreign minor, practitioners are referred to *Mayeka v Belgium*,[125] para 85.

4.153 In *Ala Anufrijeva & Anor v LB Southwark, R (on the appln of N) v SSHD, R (on the appln of M) v SSHD*,[126] the Court of Appeal considered three appeals by asylum seekers where alleged failure by public authorities to provide them with timely decisions or benefits was argued to be in breach of Article 8. In *M* the claim was for delay in providing the permission that would enable his family to join him in the UK. In *Anufrijeva* the claim was for failure of the local authority to provide accommodation that met the

---

[122] *Secretary of State for the Home Department v Baiai & Ors* [2007] EWCA Civ 478, para 58.
[123] <http://www.ind.homeoffice.gov.uk/applying/generalcaseworking/coaformarriageorcivilpartnership>
[124] *Huang v SSHD* [2007] UKHL 11.
[125] *Mayeka v Belgium* (13178/03) [2006] ECHR 13178/03.
[126] *Ala Anufrijeva & Anor v LB Southwark, R (on the appln of N) v SSHD, R (on the appln of M) v SSHD* [2003] EWCA Civ 1406, (2004) QB 1124.

needs of her family, so as to enable them to enjoy a satisfactory quality of family life. In *N* the claim was for subjecting the claimant to stress resulting in psychiatric injury and also for failing to provide the support necessary to achieve a basic quality of personal life. Each case involved an allegation that the defendant was at fault in failing to take positive action, which would have averted the adverse consequences of which complaint was made.

The Court of Appeal had to consider the nature of Article 8 rights, whether and when **4.154** a duty arose under Article 8 to take positive action, the circumstances in which maladministration constituted a breach of Article 8, when damages should be awarded, and the basis of their assessment.

Positive obligations

Positive obligations on a State in the context of Article 8, as recognized by the ECtHR, **4.155** often have two aspects: (1) to require the introduction of a legislative or administrative scheme to protect the right to respect for private and family life, and (2) to require the scheme to be operated competently so as to achieve its aim. The Court of Appeal found that it is in relation to the latter aspect that maladministration can amount to a breach of Article 8.

The Court of Appeal found that Article 8 was capable of imposing a positive obliga- **4.156** tion to provide support, however, the nature and extent of that positive obligation would vary from case to case. It was hard to conceive of a situation in which the predicament of an individual will be such that Article 8 required him to be provided with welfare support, where his predicament was not sufficiently severe to engage Article 3. A positive obligation under Article 8 was most likely to arise when the welfare of children was at stake or family life was seriously inhibited.

The particular type of maladministration that had taken place in each of the **4.157** three appeals was the failure, in breach of duty, to provide the claimants with some benefit or advantage to which they were entitled under public law. The claimants had to demonstrate an element of culpability, before inaction by a public authority could amount to a lack of respect for private and family life. There had to be some ground for criticizing the failure to act. Further, no infringement of Article 8 would be found unless substantial prejudice had been caused to the applicant. Maladministration would infringe Article 8 only where the consequence to the applicant was serious.

Damages under the HRA

Damages under the Human Rights Act 1998 were not recoverable as of right and **4.158** should be awarded only when it was 'just and appropriate' and 'necessary' to achieve 'just satisfaction'.

4.159 The Court of Appeal drew attention to the following significant features distinguishing damages under the HRA from the damages in a private law contract or tort action:[127]

(a) The award of damages under the HRA is confined to the class of unlawful acts of public authorities identified by section 6(1) HRA—see sections 8(1) and (6).

(b) The Court has a discretion as to whether to make an award (it must be 'just and appropriate' to do so) by contrast to the position in relation to common law claims where there is a right to damages.

(c) The award must be necessary to achieve 'just satisfaction', as contrasted with the common law approach where a claimant is entitled to be restored to the position he would have been in if he had not suffered the injury or damage. The concept of damages being 'necessary to afford just satisfaction' provided a link with the approach to compensation by the ECtHR under Article 41.

(d) In determining whether damages are payable and the amount of damages payable, the court is required to take into account the different principles applied by the ECtHR in awarding compensation.

(e) Exemplary damages are not awarded.

4.160 In cases of maladministration, the Court of Appeal held that awards should be moderate but not minimal, as minimal awards would undermine the respect for Convention rights. In the present cases, awards of the Local Government Ombudsman on behalf of disabled persons deprived of benefits or assistance as a result of maladministration could be consulted for comparison.

4.161 However, no damages were awarded on the facts of each case, with the outcomes being as follows:

(a) In the case of *A*, the appeal was dismissed on the basis that the local authority had made reasonable efforts to meet the requirements of the claimant's mother and her family. The accommodation provided fell far short of placing the family in the type of conditions that would impose a positive obligation under Article 8 to install them in superior accommodation.

(b) In the case of *N*, the Secretary of State's appeal was allowed. If a public authority committed acts which it knew were likely to cause psychiatric harm to an individual, those acts were capable of constituting an infringement of Article 8. However, maladministration would not infringe Article 8 simply because it caused stress that caused psychiatric harm to a particularly susceptible individual in circumstances where that was could not be reasonably anticipated. The egg-shell skull

---

[127] *Ala Anufrijeva & Anor v LB Southwark, R (on the appln of N) v SSHD, R (on the appln of M) v SSHD* [2003] EWCA Civ 1406, (2004) QB 1124, para 55.

principle was found to have no application in the context of the test of breach of duty under the 1998 Act or the Convention.

(c) In the case of *M*, the Court of Appeal could find no fault with the judge's reasoning in rejecting the claim. Although there had been administrative failings that had delayed the reunion between M and his family, there had been no lack of respect for M's family life and, accordingly, no infringement of Article 8.

The Court of Appeal expressed grave concern on the disproportion of legal costs to **4.162** the amount of potential damages obtainable under the HRA. Amongst the extensive guidance it gave at para 81 of the judgment, in relation to future handling of claims, the Court of Appeal noted that before giving permission to apply for judicial review, the Administrative Court judge should require the claimant to explain why it would not be more appropriate to use any available internal complaint procedure or proceed by making a claim to the PCA or LGO at least in the first instance. The Court stressed that the complaint procedures of the PCA and the LGO were designed to deal economically (the claimant pays no costs and does not require a lawyer) and expeditiously with claims for compensation for maladministration.

5

OTHER HUMAN RIGHTS ARTICLES POTENTIALLY APPLICABLE IN THE ASYLUM AND HUMAN RIGHTS CONTEXT

A. Introduction

Can human rights enshrined in Articles other than Articles 3 and 8 be engaged in the context of removals?

5.01   As has been observed in Chapter 4, the House of Lords in *Ullah*[1] affirmed that Articles of the European Convention on Human Rights other than Article 3 could be engaged in relation to a removal of an individual where the anticipated treatment in the receiving State will be in breach of the requirements of the Convention, but such treatment does not meet the minimum requirements of Article 3. In a purely 'domestic case', where the claim is that the UK has acted within its own territory in a way which infringes the enjoyment of a Convention right by a person within that territory, it is always possible that articles other than Article 3 could be engaged. The issue in *Ullah* was whether the same applied in 'foreign' cases where it is claimed that the conduct of the UK in removing a person from its territory (whether by expulsion or extradition) to another territory will lead to a violation of the person's Convention rights in that other territory. The House of Lords found that although it was 'hard to think that a person could successfully resist expulsion in reliance on article 9 without being entitled either to asylum on the ground of a well-founded fear of being persecuted for reasons of religion or personal opinion or to resist expulsion in reliance on article 3'[2] such a possibility should not be ruled out.

The threshold test

5.02   In general, a breach of ECHR articles other than Article 3 will occur in an expulsion case only where the applicant establishes that there will be a flagrant denial or gross violation of those rights on expulsion. (Articles 2 and 4 may be exceptions to this general position.) This high threshold will be met only where the right will be completely denied or nullified in the destination country. This test was set out by the Immigration Appeals Tribunal in *Devaseelan v Secretary of State for the Home Department*[3] and was specifically approved by the House of Lords in *Ullah*. The relevant parts of Their Lordships' speeches about the threshold test in ECHR 'foreign' cases not involving Article 3 are set out in Table 5.1. It is important to note the lack

---

[1] *Ullah* [2004] 2 AC 323.
[2] Per Lord Bingham in *Ullah* at para 21.
[3] *Devaseelan v Secretary of State for the Home Department* [2002] IAT 702, [2003] Imm AR 1.

of success in applicants' reliance on ECHR Articles other than Articles 3 and 8 in the expulsion/extradition sphere. Such lack of success is clearly ascribed by Their Lordships to the difficulties attendant in meeting the stringent test of a flagrant or fundamental denial of such a right. Additionally, the House of Lords noted that in the case of qualified rights, such as Articles 8 and 9, the Convention itself provides for the striking of a balance between the right of the individual and the wider interests of the community; even in a Convention State, there would be no breach of such rights unless the interference with the protected right is disproportionate to the public interest being protected. However, the Court is not well placed to strike that balance. First, it does not have representations by the receiving State whose laws, institutions, or practices are the subject of criticism. Second, the removing State will almost always have strong grounds for justifying its conduct, such as operating firm and orderly immigration control in an expulsion case, and in an extradition case the desirability of honouring extradition treaties made with other states.

On the issue of the threshold test in non-Article 3 cases, the House of Lords said the following:

Table 5.1

Per Lord Bingham:	24. 'While the Strasbourg jurisprudence does not preclude reliance on articles other than article 3 as a ground for resisting extradition or expulsion, it makes it quite clear that successful reliance demands presentation of a very strong case. In relation to article 3, it is necessary to show strong grounds for believing that the person, if returned, faces a real risk of being subjected to torture or to inhuman or degrading treatment or punishment . . . In Dehwari, paragraph 61 . . . the Commission doubted whether a real risk was enough to resist removal under article 2, suggesting that the loss of life must be shown to be a 'near-certainty'. Where reliance is placed on article 6 it must be shown that a person has suffered or risks suffering a flagrant denial of a fair trial in the receiving state: . . . Successful reliance on article 5 would have to meet no less exacting a test. The lack of success of applicants relying on articles 2, 5 and 6 before the Strasbourg court highlights the difficulty of meeting the stringent test which that court imposes. This difficulty will not be less where reliance is placed on articles such as 8 or 9, which provide for the striking of a balance between the right of the individual and the wider interests of the community even in a case where a serious interference is shown. This is not a balance which the Strasbourg court ought ordinarily to strike in the first instance, nor is it a balance which that court is well placed to assess in the absence of representations by the receiving state whose laws, institutions or practices are the subject of criticism. On the other hand, the removing state will always have what will usually be strong grounds for justifying its own conduct: the great importance of operating firm and orderly immigration control in an expulsion case; the great desirability of honouring extradition treaties made with other states. The correct approach in cases involving qualified rights such as those under articles 8 and 9 is in my opinion that indicated by the Immigration

Appeal Tribunal (Mr C M G Ockelton, deputy president, Mr Allen and Mr Moulden) in Devaseelan v Secretary of State for the Home Department [2002] IAT 702, [2003] Imm AR 1, paragraph 111:

> The reason why flagrant denial or gross violation is to be taken into account is that it is only in such a case—where the right will be completely denied or nullified in the destination country—that it can be said that removal will breach the treaty obligations of the signatory state however those obligations might be interpreted or whatever might be said by or on behalf of the destination state.

Per Lord Steyn;[4]   It will be apparent from the review of Strasbourg jurisprudence that, where other articles may become engaged, a high threshold test will always have to be satisfied. It will be necessary to establish at least a real risk of a flagrant violation of the very essence of the right before other articles could become engaged.

Per Lord Carswell:[5]   The adjective 'flagrant' has been repeated in many statements where the Court has kept open the possibility of engagement of articles of the Convention other than article 3, a number of which are enumerated in paragraph 24 of the opinion of Lord Bingham of Cornhill in the present appeal. The concept of a flagrant breach or violation may not always be easy for domestic courts to apply—one is put in mind of the difficulties which they have had in applying that of gross negligence—but it seems to me that it was well expressed by the Immigration Appeal Tribunal in *Devaseelan v Secretary of State for the Home Department* [2003] Imm AR 1 at p 34, para 111, when it applied the criterion that the right in question would be completely denied or nullified in the destination country. This would harmonise with the concept of a fundamental breach, with which courts in this jurisdiction are familiar.

5.03   The 'flagrant breach' test derives support with regard to Article 6 from the ECtHR decision in *Soering v United Kingdom*.[6] The applicant there resisted extradition to the United States to stand trial, contending that trial in Virginia would infringe his right to a fair trial under Article 6 and that his detention on death row, if he was convicted and sentenced to death, would infringe his rights under Article 3. The ECtHR did not reject the applicant's complaint under Article 6 as ill-founded, but dismissed it on the facts:

> 113. The right to a fair trial in criminal proceedings, as embodied in Article 6, holds a prominent place in a democratic society. The Court does not exclude that an issue might exceptionally be raised under Article 6 by an extradition decision in circumstances where the fugitive has suffered or risks suffering a flagrant denial of a fair trial in the requesting country. However, the facts of the present case do not disclose such a risk.

---

4 At para 50.
5 At para 69.
6 *Soering v United Kingdom* (1989) 11 EHRR 439.

The recent case of *EM (Lebanon) v SSHD*[7] provides further guidance as to how **5.04** this threshold test is to be applied. The Court of Appeal saw a possible distinction between the complete denial of the rights guaranteed by the Convention, which was a quantitative question, and the flagrant breach or gross violation of such rights, which was a qualitative one. But the threshold which the House of Lords in *Ullah* had held that the appellant had to surmount was the complete denial of the Convention rights in the destination country. Therefore it was insufficient for the appellant to show that there would be a flagrant interference with her Article 8 and 14 rights by losing custody of her son in Lebanon. On the facts of the case such interference with these rights did not establish that these Convention rights would be completely denied or nullified.

The practical application of the test produced sophisticated and thoughtful anal- **5.05** ysis by SIAC in *Othman v Secretary of State for the Home Department*.[8] That was one of a series of cases considered by SIAC concerning decisions to deport individuals whose presence in the United Kingdom was said to be a threat to national security. In respect of a number of countries the United Kingdom government obtained assurances from the receiving State concerning treatment of the individuals on their return. Amongst the arguments advanced in his appeal was one that, applying the *Ullah* test, Articles 5 and 6 prevented removal. Recognising that in a 'foreign' expulsion case, the signatory State bears essentially indirect responsibility for the acts of a non-signatory State, SIAC considered that there ought to be a difference of approach as between the absolute, the derogable, and the qualified Articles.[9]

Thus in relation to derogable Articles, the possibility ought to be considered that **5.06** the situation in the receiving State could (if it were an ECHR signatory) have entitled it to derogate from the particular Article. Such a State might be able to demonstrate the existence of a public emergency and that any shortcomings in its systems were a proportionate response to that emergency; but by definition, it would not have had to face the need to make a derogation from a Convention to which it is not a party. SIAC considered that it could be difficult to say that any such shortcomings were outside the legitimate scope of a proportionate derogation.[10]

Separately, SIAC considered the approach to qualified Articles of the ECHR. **5.07** 'Consideration also has to be given to the scope for successful reliance by the receiving State on the qualifications to the qualified Articles, even though it is not

---

[7] *EM (Lebanon) v SSHD* [2006] EWCA Civ 1531, [2006] All ER (D) 276 (Nov).
[8] *Othman v Secretary of State for the Home Department* (SC/15/2005).
[9] At para 472.
[10] Para 461.

a party.'[11] But SIAC also considered that even if there were a total denial of a qualified right in the receiving State, the *expelling* State's interests should be distinctly considered within the qualifications. 'The further question ought to be whether the UK could justify return in these circumstances.'[12] As SIAC pointed out:

> That however would mean that indirect responsibility for a total denial of rights did not provide the complete answer to when removal would breach the returning country's obligations; it would be but the starting point.

5.08 The appeal of such on approach is particularly evident in national security cases. As SIAC put it: 'It may be that the effect of *Ullah* is that the total denial would prevent the ordinary interest of immigration control justifying removal, but it was not considered in the context of the graver matters which can arise.'[13] An alternative approach mooted by SIAC was that there should, in cases concerning the derogable and qualified rights protected by the ECHR, be a balancing exercise even when it has been shown that there is a real risk of a 'complete denial'; that would be only the starting point for consideration of the qualifications.[14]

5.09 It remains to be seen what part of SIAC's approach above, which was obiter in *Othman*, will be taken up by the AIT and higher courts in the analysis of future cases. It does demonstrate, however, that *Ullah* is unlikely to be the last word on this topic.

When is the threshold test to be applied?

5.10 Whether the threshold test has been satisfied is to be considered at the time of the relevant decision—either at first instance, when the Secretary of State makes the initial decision, or at the time of appeal, when the appellate tribunal or court determines the question.

5.11 On a human rights appeal,[15] the AIT has to decide whether removal would violate the appellant's Convention rights on the facts as they are when the appeal is heard.[16] For example, it is not open to the AIT to determine an appeal on the basis of an undertaking by the Secretary of State that he would not remove the appellant until the resolution of contact proceedings in the UK, which the appellant pursued. Where the AIT had erroneously done so, the Court of Appeal remitted the case for a decision to be made on the evidence available to the AIT at the remittal hearing as to whether removal would violate Article 8.[17]

---

[11] Para 459.
[12] Para 470.
[13] Para 468.
[14] Para 471.
[15] Under s 84(1)(g) NIAA 2002.
[16] *MS (Ivory Coast) v SSHD* [2007] EWCA Civ 133, 22 February 2007, at para 57 applying to human rights appeals the reasoning in *Ravichandran v SSHD* [1996] Imm AR 97, 114, and *Saad & Ors v SSHD* [2002] INLR 34.
[17] *MS (Ivory Coast) v SSHD* [2007] EWCA Civ 133, 22 February 2007.

Where an appeal succeeds on human rights grounds the Secretary of State must grant leave to enter or remain; he cannot simply allow the successful appellant to remain on temporary admission.[18] The effect on applicants is that successful reliance on an ECHR right, other than Article 3, to resist removal would result in discretionary leave. Thus the right would be protected, rather than allowing the applicant to remain in limbo, by virtue of being on temporary admission.[19] The Home Office policy on the appropriate grant of leave is discussed further below.

5.12

B. Article 2—The Right to Life

ECHR Article 2 provides:

5.13

1. Everyone's right to life shall be protected by law. No one shall be deprived of his life intentionally save in the execution of a sentence of a court following his conviction of a crime for which this penalty is provided by law.
2. Deprivation of life shall not be regarded as inflicted in contravention of this Article when it results from the use of force which is no more than is absolutely necessary:
   (a) in defence of any person from unlawful violence;
   (b) in order to effect a lawful arrest or prevent the escape of a person lawfully detained;
   (c) in action lawfully taken for the purpose of quelling a riot or insurrection.

The death penalty

The language of Article 2(1) sanctions the death penalty if lawfully imposed by a court. However, the UK and most other ECHR States have both signed and ratified Article 1 of Protocol 13 to the ECHR,[20] which prohibits the death penalty, both in times of peace and in times of war. The earlier Protocol 6, which prohibits the death penalty except in respect of acts committed in time of war or of imminent threat of war, has now been signed by all ECHR States and ratified by all but one (Russia). Consequently, it is now possible to argue that expulsion to face the death penalty abroad would amount to a breach of Article 2, although such an argument would remain controversial. Such an argument would be based on the proposition that universal adoption across the ECHR States of a *de jure* abolition

5.14

---

[18] *MS (Ivory Coast) v SSHD* [2007] EWCA Civ 133, 22 February 2007, para 48, and *S v SSHD* [2006] EWCA Civ 1157, para 46.

[19] *MS (Ivory Coast) v SSHD* [2007] EWCA Civ 133, 22 February 2007.

[20] 'The death penalty shall be abolished. No one shall be condemned to such penalty or executed.' Article 1 of Protocol 13 was substituted by SI 2004/1574, art 2(3) and has been in force since 22 June 2004 (see SI 2004/1574, art 1). Cf Article 2 of Protocol 6, previously in force, which allowed for the death penalty in respect of acts committed in time of war or of imminent threat of war.

of the death penalty via the Protocols would also imply an amendment to Article 2 to the effect that the death penalty is an unacceptable form of punishment in all circumstances.

5.15 The Grand Chamber of the ECtHR in *Ocalan v Turkey*[21] observed that Protocol No 13 concerning the abolition of the death penalty in all circumstances, with only three member States not having signed it, heralds the final step towards complete abolition of the death penalty. In that case the ECtHR expressed the view that in so far as Article 2 permits the death penalty in times of peace, the argument that the Article has been implicitly amended is not necessarily inconsistent with the fact that not all ECHR States have signed or ratified these Protocols.[22] However, the ECtHR declined to decide this issue or the linked issue of whether the death penalty would in itself be a breach of Article 3 of the ECHR. The ECtHR has not yet considered whether expulsion to the death penalty might be a breach of either of the Protocols if the expelling State could not itself impose the death penalty in the same circumstances because it was bound by the respective Protocol. Neither has the ECtHR considered whether expulsion to the mere imposition of the death penalty (as opposed to actual execution) might amount to a breach of the ECHR.

5.16 However, potential expulsion to face the death penalty is also likely to raise arguments under other ECHR Articles, particularly where other factors (such as an unfair trial, or prolonged detention on 'death row' between sentencing and execution) would combine with the mere fact of the death penalty, or the mere fact of its imposition. In such circumstances, claims under Articles 2, 3, and 6 have a good chance of success as the ECtHR has found that:

a. The implementation of the death penalty in respect of a person who has not had a fair trial would not be permissible.[23]

b. The manner in which the death penalty is imposed or executed, the personal circumstances of the condemned person, and a disproportionality to the gravity of the crime committed, as well as the conditions of detention awaiting execution, are examples of factors capable of bringing the treatment or punishment received by the condemned person within the proscription under Article 3.[24]

c. 'To impose a death sentence on a person after an unfair trial is to subject that person wrongfully to the fear that he will be executed. The fear and uncertainty as to the future generated by a sentence of death, in circumstances

---

[21] *Ocalan v Turkey* (Application No 46221/99) [2005] ECHR 46221/99.

[22] Para 164.

[23] *Ocalan v Turkey* (Application No 46221/99) [2005] ECHR 46221/99, para 166.

[24] *Soering v UK* [1989] ECHR 14038/88 at para 104.

where there exists a real possibility that the sentence will be enforced, must give rise to a significant degree of human anguish. Such anguish cannot be dissociated from the unfairness of the proceedings underlying the sentence which, given that human life is at stake, becomes unlawful under the Convention.'[25]

However, such claims may well be academic in the UK, because of the long-standing policy of not removing individuals to countries where they face a real risk of being executed pursuant to a sentence of death, and the amendments which have now been made to the Immigration Rules in order to implement the Qualification Directive.[26]

Obligations on the State to protect life

The right enshrined in Article 2 ranks as one of the most fundamental provisions in the Convention, from which no derogation is permissible.[27] The language of Article 2 itself sets out the circumstances when deprivation of life may be justified. These circumstances must be strictly construed, given the importance of the interests the Article protects.[28] Article 2 must be interpreted and applied so as to make its safeguards practical and effective.[29] **5.17**

Article 2 obliges States not only to refrain from the intentional and unlawful taking of life but also to take appropriate steps within their internal legal orders to safeguard the lives of those within their jurisdiction.[30] This involves a primary duty on the State to secure the right to life by putting in place an appropriate legal and administrative framework to deter the commission of offences against the person, backed up by law-enforcement machinery for the prevention, suppression, and punishment of breaches of such provisions.[31] In other words, the State is responsible for putting in place effective criminal law provisions to deter the commission of offences against the person, and to back this up with law enforcement machinery to sanction breaches.[32] **5.18**

Article 2(2) does not primarily define instances where it is permitted to intentionally *kill*, but describes situations where it is permitted to 'use force' which may result in the deprivation of life, as an unintended outcome.[33] The use of force, however, must be no more than 'absolutely necessary' for the achievement **5.19**

---

25 *Ocalan v Turkey* (Application No 46221/99) [2005] ECHR 46221/99, para 169.
26 See para 339C of the Immigration Rules.
27 *Velikova v Bulgaria* [2000] ECHR 41488/98 at para 68.
28 *Salman v Turkey* [2000] ECHR 21986/93 at para 97.
29 *McCann v UK* [1995] ECHR 18984/91 at paras 146–47.
30 *Kilic v Turkey* [2000] ECHR 22492/93 at para 62.
31 *Erdogan & Ors v Turkey* (Application No 19807/92) [2006] ECHR 19807/92, para 66.
32 *Osman v UK* (1998) 29 EHRR 245, para 115.
33 *Erdogan & Ors v Turkey* (Application No 19807/92) [2006] ECHR 19807/92, para 67.

of any of the purposes set out in sub-paragraphs (a), (b), or (c). The term 'absolutely necessary' in Article 2(2) is a stricter and more compelling test of necessity than that applicable when determining whether interference is 'necessary in a democratic society' under para 2 of Articles 8–11. In particular, the force used must be strictly proportionate to the achievement of the aims set out in the sub-paragraphs of Article 2(2).[34] Nonetheless, there is no practical distinction between the test in Article 2 and the test applied in the domestic criminal law of self defence or defence of others, namely the use of reasonable force.[35]

5.20 Courts will apply the most careful scrutiny where death results from the use of lethal force by the police or security forces.[36] The actions of the agents of the State who actually administered the force and all the surrounding circumstances including the planning and control of those actions will be taken into account.

The threshold test in foreign cases

5.21 Allegations of State involvement in a killing so as to find the *State* directly responsible for violating Article 2 requires proof of the allegations beyond reasonable doubt.[37] However, in the immigration and asylum context, the assessment of the prospective risk to the life of the applicant makes this standard inappropriate. In general, a breach will only occur in a non-Article 3 case if there will be a flagrant denial or gross violation of those rights, in the sense that the right will be completely denied or nullified in the destination country. But from Their Lordships' speeches in *Ullah* it is clear that they could discern no logical basis for drawing a distinction between Article 3 and Article 2 in the immigration context. They thought that in the context of imminent expulsion an applicant might be able to rely on Article 2, and not only Article 3. Their Lordships in *Ullah* were unable to articulate the standard of proof for establishing an Article 2 breach. However, the equivalence of the fundamental importance of two rules, set out in Articles 2 and 3, and the fact that they are both non-derogable, would tend to suggest that the applicable test for establishing a breach of Article 2 in the removals context could be the same as for Article 3—has a real risk of a violation on return been shown? However, the ECtHR case law is not clear.

---

34 *McCann v UK* [1995] ECHR 18984/91 at paras 148–9.
35 Section 3(1) Criminal Law Act 1967.
36 *McCann v UK* [1995] ECHR 18984/91 at para 150.
37 *Ayhan & Anor v Turkey* (Application No 41964/98) [2006] ECHR 41964/98, para 79. Note, however, that the Court reaffirmed that 'such proof may follow from the coexistence of sufficiently strong, clear and concordant inferences or of similar unrebutted presumptions of fact (see *Ireland v UK* [1978] ECHR 5310/71 at para 161)'. It is not altogether clear whether the ECtHR's use of the phrase 'beyond reasonable doubt' refers to the same legal concept as that in English criminal law, but this issue is beyond the scope of this work.

Lord Bingham in *Ullah* analyzed case law[38] of the ECtHR and the Commission, **5.22** including *Dehwari v Netherlands*,[39] where it was held that the standard of proving a breach of Article 2 in the context of expulsion had to be 'a near-certainty'. *Dehwari* was a 'foreign' case concerned with expulsion to Iran and the applicant's claim based on Article 2 failed on the facts. The claim was not rejected in principle, and having referred to the case law on Article 3 the Commission in *Dehwari* said:

> 61. As to the prohibition of intentional deprivation of life, including the execution of a death penalty, the Commission does not exclude that an issue might arise under Article 2 of the Convention or Article 1 of Protocol No. 6 in circumstances in which the expelling State knowingly puts the person concerned [at] such high risk of losing his life as for the outcome to be a near-certainty. The Commission considers, however, that a 'real risk'—within the meaning of the case law concerning Article 3 (see para 58 above)—of loss of life would not as such necessarily render an expulsion contrary to Article 2 of the Convention or Article 1 of Protocol No. 6, although it would amount to inhuman treatment within the meaning of Article 3 of the Convention (cf *Bahaddar v Netherlands*, op cit, para 78).

Lord Bingham in *Ullah* found that these statements in the case law must be taken to establish the possibility in principle of relying on Article 2 in a foreign case if the facts are strong enough. He considered that it would be surprising if Article 3 could be relied on and Article 2 could not.

Similarly Lord Steyn in *Ullah* expressed difficulty in understanding why Article 2 **5.23** could be excluded, where Article 3 may be engaged, particularly as cases may arise where Article 3 is not applicable whilst Article 2 does arise. At paragraph 40 of the judgment in *Ullah* he stated:

> Like article 3 this provision is absolute and not subject to derogation in time of war or public emergency under article 15. The Court of Appeal underlined the central importance of article 3 in the scheme of the ECHR. But the right to life under article 2 is also of fundamental importance. If article 3 may be engaged it is difficult to follow why, as a matter of logic, article 2 could be peremptorily excluded. There may well be cases where article 3 is not applicable but article 2 may be: see *Secretary of State for the Home Department v Kacaj* [2002] Imm AR 213 (a decision of the Immigration Appeal Tribunal), per Collins J. The positive obligation on member states to provide individuals with suitable protection against immediate threats to their lives from non-state actors abroad may be relevant, in exceptional circumstances, to an immigration decision: *Osman v United Kingdom* (1998) 29 EHRR 245. Another example could be *D v United Kingdom* (1997) 24 EHRR 423, which

---

[38] Lord Bingham considered the case of *D v United Kingdom* (1997) 24 EHRR 423, where neither the Commission nor the Court rejected the claim under Article 2 as well as 3 as untenable in principle. However, neither found it necessary to review the Article 2 complaint separately from that under Article 3. Lord Bingham also considered *Gonzalez v Spain* (Application No 43544/98, 29 June 1999, unreported), where the applicant's complaint under Article 2 (and 3) was rejected on the facts.

[39] *Dehwari v Netherlands* (2000) 29 EHRR CD 74.

was admittedly a wholly exceptional case. It concerned the proposed expulsion to St Kitts of a person suffering from AIDS in an advanced degree. The ECtHR found that his expulsion would amount to a breach of article 3. It is, however, clear that but for this decision, the applicant would have succeeded under article 2: p 450, para 59. There are principled grounds for not drawing a bright-line between articles 2 and 3.

5.24 Given the observations of Their Lordships referred to above, it is difficult to see why the test for applicability of Article 2 in the expulsion context (ie in a 'foreign case') should be different and higher than that mandated for Article 3 (at least in this type of case), notwithstanding the observations of the ECtHR to the contrary.

Procedural rights guaranteed by Article 2

5.25 The obligation to protect the right to life under Article 2 also requires by implication that there should be some form of effective official investigation when individuals have been killed as a result of the use of force.[40] The purpose of such an investigation is to secure the effective implementation of the domestic laws which protect the right to life and, in cases involving State agents, to ensure their accountability for deaths occurring under their responsibility. The form of investigation may vary in different circumstances. However, the authorities must act of their own motion once the matter has come to their attention.[41]

5.26 The investigation must also be effective in the sense that it is *capable* of leading to a determination of whether the force used in such cases was or was not justified in the circumstances and to the identification and punishment of those responsible. The obligation is not as to result (ie the offenders may not be caught), but as to means (the investigation must be bona fide and effective). The authorities must have taken the reasonable steps available to them to secure the evidence concerning the incident.[42] There must be appropriate involvement of the family of the deceased and an element of public scrutiny.

5.27 A final requirement is that of promptness and reasonable expedition by the authorities in investigating a use of lethal force as this is essential in maintaining public confidence in their adherence to the rule of law and in preventing any appearance of collusion in or tolerance of unlawful acts.[43] Thus a violation of Article 2 on the basis of inadequate investigation of a killing would be a violation of 'art 2 under its procedural limb'.[44]

---

[40] *Hugh Jordan v UK* [2001] ECHR 24746/94 para 105, *Akdeniz v Turkey* [2001] ECHR 23954/94 para 89, and *Kaya v Turkey* [1998] ECHR 22729/93 para 86.

[41] *Ayhan & Anor v Turkey* (Application No 41964/98) [2006] ECHR 41964/98, para 86.

[42] *Ayhan & Anor v Turkey* (Application No 41964/98) [2006] ECHR 41964/98, para 88.

[43] *Ayhan & Anor v Turkey* (Application No 41964/98) [2006] ECHR 41964/98, para 89. See also *Silih & Silih v Slovenia*, Application No 00071463/01, 28/6/2007, where the ECtHR found a procedural breach of Article 2 in respect of the lack of prompt examination of a death in hospital.

[44] *Ayhan & Anor v Turkey* (Application No 41964/98) [2006] ECHR 41964/98, para 99.

We are aware of no cases in which an individual facing removal has sought to rely **5.28** on the procedural obligations of Article 2. It is difficult to see how the procedural limb of Article 2 could be relied upon successfully in an expulsion case, where the authorities of the receiving country have been responsible for breaching Article 2. The removal will have no bearing on any investigation that might take place into a past killing. If the fear is that the person's own right to life would be imperilled on removal, then the procedural aspect will add nothing. It is perhaps conceivable that an individual who is the representative of someone killed under the responsibility of the British state might seek to argue that his removal from the United Kingdom during a pending Article 2 investigation would be in breach of Article 2. That would be on the basis that his removal would deprive the family of the involvement to which it is entitled.

C. Article 4—Prohibition of Slavery and Forced Labour

Article 4 provides: **5.29**

1. No one shall be held in slavery or servitude.
2. No one shall be required to perform forced or compulsory labour.
3. For the purpose of this article the term 'forced or compulsory labour' shall not include:
    a. any work required to be done in the ordinary course of detention imposed according to the provisions of Article 5 of this Convention or during conditional release from such detention;
    b. any service of a military character or, in case of conscientious objectors in countries where they are recognised, service exacted instead of compulsory military service;
    c. any service exacted in case of an emergency or calamity threatening the life or well-being of the community;
    d. any work or service which forms part of normal civic obligations.

Domestic cases

The provisions of Article 4 are also clearly applicable in domestic cases, ie where **5.30** the allegation is that the UK has breached those ECHR provisions. The ECtHR has held that Article 4(2) of the Convention, which prohibits 'forced or compulsory labour', enshrines 'one of the fundamental values of democratic societies'.[45] Unlike most of the substantive clauses of the Convention, Article 4 makes no provision for exceptions and no derogation from it is permissible under

---

[45] *Adami v Malta* (Application No 17209/02), Judgment, 20 June 2006, final 20/09/2006, para 43.

Article 15(2), even in the event of a public emergency threatening the life of the nation.

5.31 Any challenges to compulsory community service or other work imposed on asylum seekers or immigrants is likely, however, to fall within the exception within Article 4(3)(d) of 'work or service which forms part of normal civic obligations'. However, challenges to such obligations under Article 14 on discrimination grounds would be possible, as the Courts are likely to find Article 4 to be engaged.

5.32 Article 14 has effect solely in relation to 'the enjoyment of the rights and freedoms' safeguarded by the other substantive provisions of the Convention and its Protocols. Although the application of Article 14 does not presuppose a *breach* of another ECHR provision, there can be no room for its application unless 'the facts at issue fall within the ambit of' one or more of those provisions.[46]

5.33 In fact, in a recent ECHR case an applicant succeeded in claiming a breach of Article 14 in conjunction with Article 4(3)(d) on the basis that the way in which jury service had been imposed on him was discriminatory.[47] On the admissibility question the Court held that the fact that a situation corresponded to the notion of a normal civic obligation within the meaning of Article 4(3) was 'not an obstacle to the applicability of Article 4 of the Convention, read in conjunction with Article 14'.[48]

5.34 The ECtHR has recently considered several applications under Article 4, which it dismissed as manifestly ill-founded on the facts.[49] The Court noted that the applicants performed work voluntarily and their entitlement to payment had never been denied. Thus the disputes involved civil rights and obligations, but did not disclose any element of slavery or forced or compulsory labour within the meaning of Article 4.[50]

Foreign cases

5.35 An ECHR admissibility decision in *Ould Barar v Sweden*[51] considered a claim under Article 4. However, the Court found the applicant's complaint under Article 4, as well as his complaints under Articles 2 and 3, to be inadmissible on

---

[46] *Van Raalte v the Netherlands*, Judgment, 21 February 1997, *Reports of Judgments and Decisions* 1997-I, p 184, para 33, and *Petrovic v Austria*, Judgment, 27 March 1998, *Reports* 1998-II, p 585, para 22.

[47] *Adami v Malta*, (Application No 17209/02), Judgment, 20 June 2006, final 20/09/2006.

[48] Ibid, para 46. See also the concurring opinions of Judges Sir Nicolas Bratza and L Garlicki.

[49] *Ananyev v Ukraine* (Application No 32374/02), Judgment, 30 November 2006, final on 12 February 2007, *Vorona v Ukraine* (Application No 44372/02) Judgment, 9 November 2006, final on 9 February 2007, *Zafer v Slovakia*, Admissibility Decision (Application No 60228/00).

[50] *Ananyev v Ukraine*, para 11; *Vorona v Ukraine*, para 16.

[51] *Ould Barar v Sweden* (1999) 28 EHRR CD 213.

the facts. Nevertheless, the Court held 'that the expulsion of a person to a country where there is an officially recognised regime of slavery might, in certain circumstances, raise an issue under Article 3 of the Convention'. In commenting on this case, Lord Bingham in *Ullah* expressed the view that 'it would seem to be inconsistent with the humanitarian principles underpinning the Convention to accept that, if the facts were strong enough, a claim would be rejected even if it were based on article 4 alone'.

Lord Steyn in *Ullah* similarly said that: **5.36**

> Article 4(1) is absolute and not subject to derogation in time of war or public emergency. It is no doubt right that in the modern world a case alleging slavery is perhaps a little unlikely. A case asserting forced labour is less unlikely but, if it arises, would no doubt fall under article 3. But what if the applicant relied only on article 4? Is he to be turned away on the basis that article 4 cannot as a matter of legal principle be engaged? Surely that would be contrary to the spirit of a human rights convention. (paragraph 41 of the judgment in *Ullah*)

Therefore, should the facts of an expulsion or other 'foreign' case reveal that Arti-   **5.37**
cle 4 could be appropriately relied upon, a claim under that Article should be included in the initial application to the Secretary of State and in any appeal against an unfavourable decision. However, as with Article 2, outstanding questions remain about the approach that would be taken towards such claims, including whether (given the link drawn between Article 4 claims and Article 3 claims) the claimant would be required to show that he would suffer a complete denial or nullification of the rights protected by Article 4, or whether it would be sufficient to demonstrate a real risk that those rights might be infringed.

D. Article 5—Right to Liberty and Security

ECHR Article 5 provides: **5.38**

1. Everyone has the right to liberty and security of person. No one shall be deprived of his liberty save in the following cases and in accordance with a procedure prescribed by law:
   (a) the lawful detention of a person after conviction by a competent court;
   (b) the lawful arrest or detention of a person for non-compliance with the lawful order of a court or in order to secure the fulfilment of any obligation prescribed by law;
   (c) the lawful arrest or detention of a person effected for the purpose of bringing him before the competent legal authority on reasonable suspicion of having committed an offence or when it is reasonably considered necessary to prevent his committing an offence or fleeing after having done so;

(d) the detention of a minor by lawful order for the purpose of educational supervision or his lawful detention for the purpose of bringing him before the competent legal authority;

(e) the lawful detention of persons for the prevention of the spreading of infectious diseases, of persons of unsound mind, alcoholics or drug addicts or vagrants;

(f) the lawful arrest or detention of a person to prevent his effecting an unauthorised entry into the country or of a person against whom action is being taken with a view to deportation or extradition.

2. Everyone who is arrested shall be informed promptly, in a language which he understands, of the reasons for his arrest and of any charge against him.

3. Everyone arrested or detained in accordance with the provisions of paragraph 1(c) of this Article shall be brought promptly before a judge or other officer authorized by law to exercise judicial power and shall be entitled to trial within a reasonable time or to release pending trial. Release may be conditioned by guarantees to appear for trial.

4. Everyone who is deprived of his liberty by arrest or detention shall be entitled to take proceedings by which the lawfulness of his detention shall be decided speedily by a court and his release ordered if the detention is not lawful.

5. Everyone who has been the victim of arrest or detention in contravention of the provisions of this Article shall have an enforceable right to compensation.

Article 5 may be engaged in a 'foreign case' in the removals context

5.39 The possibility of Article 5 being engaged in a 'foreign' case in the removals context has been confirmed by the House of Lords in *Ullah*. Lord Steyn in *Ullah* held:

> In terms of the maintenance of the rule of law, which underlies all human rights instruments, article 5 is of great importance. Imagine a case of intended expulsion to a country in which the rule of law is flagrantly flouted, *habeas corpus* is unavailable and there is a real risk that the individual may face arbitrary detention for many years. I could, of course, make this example more realistic by citing the actualities of the world of today. It is not necessary to do so. The point is clear enough. Assuming that there is no evidence of the risk of torture or inhuman or degrading treatment, is the applicant for relief to be told that the ECHR offers in principle no possibility of protection in such extreme cases? I would doubt that such an impoverished view of the role of a human rights convention could be right.[52]

5.40 The breach of Article 5 rights in the foreign State would have to be flagrant, according to the test in *Ullah*. Having noted the above possibility of reliance on Article 5 in a foreign case, such cases are also likely to contain Article 3 grounds. Practitioners are unlikely and should not be encouraged to rely on Article 5 without

---

[52] *Ullah*, para 42.

additionally relying on Article 3, if the facts of the case allow. There is no precedent as to the circumstances where a case would fail on Article 3 but succeed in a 'foreign claim' on Article 5—ie where an infringement of Article 5 would occur in the receiving State. The greater relevance of Article 5 relates to the domestic protection it guarantees to asylum seekers and failed asylum seekers who are detained pursuant to immigration powers. This aspect of Article 5 is considered at greater length below.

Article 5 in the domestic context

As a protection from arbitrariness

The main purpose behind the protections afforded by Article 5 lies in the protection against arbitrariness in detention (see Table 5.2). This was confirmed in *Chahal v United Kingdom*,[53] where a Sikh separatist who had been detained in custody for deportation purposes as a threat to national security sought an order that his detention was not adequately reviewable under domestic law as to its lawfulness for the purposes of Article 5(4) of the Convention. The ECtHR said: **5.41**

> Where the 'lawfulness' of detention is in issue, including the question whether 'a procedure prescribed by law' has been followed, the Convention refers essentially to the obligation to conform to the substantive and procedural rules of national law, but it requires in addition that any deprivation of liberty should be in keeping with the purpose of Article 5, namely to protect the individual from arbitrariness.[54]

Table 5.2 Article 5

Purpose: To protect against arbitrary detention	
Substantive right	In the immigration context: deprivation of liberty is lawful only if: • resorted to in order to prevent unauthorized entry into the country, or • action is being taken with a view to deportation or extradition (to be read broadly to include removal).
Procedural right	In accordance with a procedure established by law.

Article 5(1)

States are entitled to control the entry and residence of non-nationals on their territory at their discretion, but this right must be exercised in conformity with   **5.42**

---

[53] *Chahal v United Kingdom* (1996) 23 EHRR 413.

[54] *Chahal v United Kingdom* (1996) 23 EHRR 413, para 118. One of the consequences of the ECtHR decision in this case was the establishment of the Special Immigration Appeals Tribunal in order (amongst other things) to enable such review.

the provisions of the Convention, including Article 5. The aim of Article 5(1) is to ensure that no one should be dispossessed of this liberty in an arbitrary fashion.[55] The list of exceptions to the right to liberty enshrined in Article 5(1) is exhaustive and is to be subject to narrow interpretation.[56]

5.43 Detention must be lawful in terms of both domestic and Convention law. The ECHR lays down an obligation to comply with the substantive and procedural rules of national law *and* requires that any deprivation of liberty should be in keeping with the purpose of Article 5, which is to protect an individual from arbitrariness. The national law authorising deprivation of liberty must be sufficiently accessible and precise, in order to avoid all risk of arbitrariness.[57]

5.44 A summary of the three aspects of Article 5(1) which must be considered by the decision maker are set out in Table 5.3.

Table 5.3 Article 5(1)

i) The detention must be lawful under domestic law.

ii) As an extra requirement, domestic law must be sufficiently accessible to the individual and sufficiently precise to enable him to foresee the consequences of the restriction on his rights.

iii) Domestic law must not be arbitrary (in the sense that it was resorted to in bad faith) or disproportionate.

See ID & Ors v Home Office [2006] 1 WLR 1003, para 96, summarizing the three aspects of Article 5(1) that have to be satisfied, as set out by the House of Lords in *R v Governor of Brockhill Prison ex p Evans (No 2)* [2001] 2 AC 19.

Detention must be lawful under domestic law

Scrutiny of the legality of immigration detention to be equally strict as in other cases

5.45 In *ID & Ors v Home Office*[58] the appellant asylum seekers appealed against an order striking out their claims relating to detention under the authority of an immigration officer. The appellants sought damages for false imprisonment and under Articles 2, 3, 5, and 8. The appellants alleged that their detention had been:

a. an unlawful exercise of power under the Immigration Act 1971;

b. unreasonable and disproportionate;

---

[55] *Amuur v France*, Judgment, 25 June 1996, *Reports* 1996-III, para 42.

[56] *K-F v Germany*, Judgment, 27 November 1997, *Reports* 1997-VII, p 2975, para 70; *Čonka v Belgium*, Judgment, 5 February 2000, ECHR 2002-I, para 42; *DG v Ireland*, Judgment, 16 May 2002, ECHR 2002-III, para 74.

[57] *Mayeka v Belgium* (13178/03) [2006] ECHR 13178/03, para 97.

[58] *ID & Ors v Home Office* [2005] EWCA Civ 1554, [2006] 1 WLR 1003.

c. unlawful due to a failure to follow applicable internal Home Office policy, and at common law; and

d. contrary to the interests of the two children involved.

The Court of Appeal held that on first principles, having been deprived of their **5.46** liberty, the appellants would have the makings of a claim against the relevant immigration officer arising out of their detention. The burden would lie on the immigration officer to establish a defence to a claim. Scrutiny of any complaints of an unlawful infringement of liberty would be just as zealous in the context of detention of foreign nationals by immigration officers under the Immigration Act 1971 Schedule 2 as they would in any other case where such a complaint was made. There was nothing in Schedule 2 to suggest a Parliamentary intention to confer immunity from suit on immigration officers who asked themselves the wrong questions, which led to their decision to detain to be a nullity and hence unlawful. The Court held that immigration officers were not entitled to immunity from an action for damages for false imprisonment.

Domestic law and policy must be accessible and precise

The requirement of accessibility of the relevant law and policy is clearly illus- **5.47** trated in the Court of Appeal case of *Nadarajah and Amirhanathan v Home Secretary*.[59] The applicant's asylums appeals had been rejected and each had noti- fied the Secretary of State of his intention to pursue legal proceedings to challenge the decisions to remove them. Each was detained on the ground that removal was imminent.

The relevant questions for the Court were summarized by Lord Phillips MR as **5.48** follows (at para 54):

> Thus the relevance of Article 5 is that the domestic law must not provide for, or per- mit, detention for reasons that are arbitrary. Our domestic law comprehends both the provisions of Schedule 2 to the Immigration Act 1971 and the Secretary of State's published policy, which, under principles of public law, he is obliged to follow. These appeals raise the following questions:
>
> (1) What is the Secretary of State's policy?
> (2) Is that policy lawful?
> (3) Is that policy accessible?
> (4) Having regard to the answers to the above questions, were N and A lawfully detained?

The Court of Appeal held that the import of Article 5 was that the domestic law, **5.49** namely Schedule 2 of the 1971 Act and the Secretary of State's published policy,

---

[59] *Nadarajah and Amirhanathan v Home Secretary* [2003] EWCA Civ 1768, [2004] INLR 139.

must not provide for arbitrary detention. When considering whether removal was imminent, the policy not to have regard to mere intimations of intention to bring proceedings challenging removal was not arbitrary or irrational. It promoted expedition in appealing or applying for judicial review, which was a legitimate end in itself. Thus the policy itself was lawful.

5.50 However, the Secretary of State's policy in that respect was not generally known and was not therefore accessible. Nor was the effect of failure to commence proceedings, of which notice had been given to the Immigration Service, foreseeable to the applicants. Thus the Secretary of State's policy was held to fail the Article 5 requirement that it be publicly accessible.

5.51 On the facts the detainees succeeded. When N was detained, his removal was not imminent. He had given notice of his intention to seek judicial review, hence his detention had been unlawful and in breach of ECHR Art 5(1)(f). Similarly A had informed the Immigration Service of his intention to pursue a human rights appeal. The reason for detaining him was to assist in procuring the documentation for removal, which did not fall within the detention policy.

Detention must be lawful under Article 5
(a) It must be for one of the purposes in Article 5(1)(f)

5.52 The purposes under Article 5 for which detention of immigrants is legitimate encompasses two scenarios—detention to prevent a person effecting an unauthorized entry into the country or detention of a person against whom action is being taken with a view to deportation or extradition (to be read broadly to include removal). These two permissible bases for detention are considered in turn below.

Article 5(1)(f)—Preventing unauthorized entry

5.53 The authoritative case which examined the first limb of the permissible grounds of immigration detention in Article 5(1)(f), the prevention of unauthorised entry, was in the context of detention of asylum seekers for the purposes of examining their applications. As the case illustrates the step-by-step analysis which the Courts would go through in an Article 5 case, it will be considered at some length. In *R (on the appln of Saadi & Ors) v SSHD*[60] the House of Lords examined the legality of the detention at the Oakington Reception Centre of four appellants, who had spent 7 to 10 days there each in the course of their asylum claims being determined. At first instance the detention at Oakington was ruled to have been unlawful. This finding was unanimously reversed by the Court of Appeal.[61] The detainees were unsuccessful before the House of Lords as well.

---

[60] *R (on the appln of Saadi & Ors) v SSHD* [2002] UKHL 41, [2002] 1 WLR 3131.
[61] [2002] 1 WLR 356.

The House of Lords examined the domestic law provisions which applied to the **5.54** detention to asylum seekers. They were as follows:

(1) Paragraph 2 of Schedule 2 of the Immigration Act 1971 provides that immigration officers may examine persons to determine inter alia whether they have leave to enter or whether they should be given or refused leave to enter. By paragraph 16 of the Schedule a person who may be required to submit to examination under paragraph 2 may be detained under the authority of an immigration officer pending his examination and pending a decision to give or refuse him leave to enter. By paragraph 18 of the Schedule, persons 'may be detained under paragraph 16 above in such places as the Secretary of State may direct' and 'a person detained under paragraph 16 is deemed to be in legal custody' (paragraph 18(4)). Detainees may be released on bail by a chief immigration officer or an adjudicator (paragraph 22(1A)) but only when seven days have elapsed since the person's arrival in the UK.

(2) Temporary admission may be granted to persons liable to be detained without their being detained or on release from detention. However, by section 11 of the 1971 Act temporary admission does not constitute entry.

(3) By section 4 of the Immigration and Asylum Act 1999 the Secretary of State 'may provide, or arrange for the provision of, facilities for the accommodation of persons' temporarily admitted under paragraph 21 of Schedule 2 to the 1971 Act or released on bail from detention.

Next the House of Lords examined the applicable immigration detention poli- **5.55** cies. The government acknowledged that there existed a presumption in favour of temporary admission or release. However, because of increased numbers of asylum seekers arriving in the country, in July 1998 the government adopted a policy[62] according to which detention was normally justified in the following circumstances:

- . . . where there is a reasonable belief that the individual will fail to keep the terms of temporary admission or temporary release;
- . . . initially, to clarify a person's identity and the basis of their claim; or
- . . . where removal is imminent.

The government's intention was that, during a period of approximately seven **5.56** days, the examination of an asylum seeker's claimed entitlement to enter or remain in the United Kingdom as a refugee should be conducted and completed, and a decision whether to grant or refuse leave to enter or remain on that basis made and communicated.

---

[62] Government paper 'Fairer, Faster And Firmer—A Modern Approach to Immigration And Asylum'.

5.57 Under the legislation there was clearly a power to detain the appellants. However, their challenges proceeded on the following three-pronged basis:

(1) Detention for administrative convenience enabling a speedy decision was 'simply not within the language of Article 5(1)(f)'.

(2) Alternatively detention was not within Article 5(1)(f) where it was not required in order to prevent unauthorized entry, as there was no risk of any of the Claimants absconding. After their claims for asylum had been refused each had been released from detention.

(3) If the detention for the purposes relied on can fall within Article 5(1)(f), this detention was argued to have been disproportionate to the reason relied on, ie to achieve a speedy determination of the case.

5.58 The appellants argued that detention where each had made a proper application for asylum and where there was no risk that each would abscond is outside Article 5(1)(f) of the Convention. Alternatively it was argued that detention was a wholly disproportionate response since concerns as to whether alternative methods of control would be effective were based merely on assumption and speculation.

5.59 The House of Lords in *Saadi* found that the power to detain was to 'prevent' unauthorized entry. Until the State has 'authorized' entry, the entry is unauthorized. The State had power to detain without violating Article 5 until the application has been considered and the entry 'authorized'. The House of Lords reasoned that if the claimants' argument was accepted, where there is no suspicion that an applicant for asylum will abscond or act contrary to the public good, he must always be granted a temporary admission or be admitted, with no power to arrest or detain even for a short period whilst arrangements were made for consideration of the request for asylum. Their Lordships found that it was not necessary to show that the applicant was seeking to enter by evading immigration control. Article 5(1)(f) covered a wider power, namely 'preventing his effecting an unauthorised entry'. As an example, the House of Lords considered that if an applicant came in and gave every indication that he would not abscond or misbehave but in the course of his interview made it clear that his claim of persecution was based on absolute lies, he *would* be seeking unauthorised entry.

5.60 Additionally, from the language of Article 5(1)(f) itself it was clear that it is not a precondition of the power to detain that detention should be 'necessary' to prevent an unauthorised entry—necessary in the sense that no other procedure would be sufficient to allow an investigation of the basis of the claim for asylum. A similar finding that 'necessity as to means' was irrelevant was made in *Chahal v UK*.[63]

---

[63] *Chahal v UK* (1996) 23 EHRR 413, para 112.

Thus, the House of Lords held that subject to any question of proportionality, **5.61** the action taken in the Oakington cases was 'to prevent [a person] effecting an unauthorised entry into the country' within the meaning of Article 5(1)(f).

Factors for the application of the proportionality test. The remaining issue was **5.62** whether 'detention was unlawful on grounds of being a disproportionate response to the reasonable requirements of immigration control'. Lord Slynn, delivering the unanimous opinion of the House in *Saadi*, held that there was nothing arbitrary or disproportionate in either:

(1) the methods of selection of these cases (are they suitable for speedy decision?); or
(2) the objective (speedy decision); or
(3) the way in which people are held for a short period (ie short in relation to the procedures to be gone through) and in reasonable physical conditions.

Procedural aspect: reasons given by the Secretary of State. On the final point, **5.63** the House of Lords in *Saadi* ruled that although the forms served on the Oakington claimants were inappropriate, the failure to give the right reason for detention and the giving of no or wrong reasons did not in the end affect the legality of the detention. It is submitted that this finding must be considered in a wider context—in this case the appellants were aware of the reasons for their detention. Where this is not the case, the Courts have reached the contrary view on the issue of reasons. For example, in *R (on the appln of Faulkner) v SSHD*,[64] continued detention following completion of criminal imprisonment was found to be unlawful as the Secretary of State had failed to give the individual reasons for the detention. Until he was told, the appellant was not in a position to have known that the reason for his detention was the Secretary of State's opinion that he posed a risk of absconding or was a risk to the public if granted bail. Similarly in *Garcia Alva v Germany*[65] the ECtHR held that the detention may be arbitrary if the applicant was given insufficient information to determine the basis of the decision to detain and in order to mount an effective challenge to that decision.[66]

In *R (on the appln of Refugee Legal Centre) v SSHD*[67] the Refugee Legal Centre **5.64** (RLC) challenged the lawfulness of the fast-track scheme at Harmondsworth Removal Centre. The scheme applied to straightforward asylum claims and was

---

[64] *R (on the appln of Faulkner) v SSHD* [2005] EWHC 2567 (Admin).
[65] *Garcia Alva v Germany* (Application No 23541/94), Judgment, 13 February 2001, para 39.
[66] The case was argued on the basis of Article 5(4) alone, and a violation of that Article was found by the ECtHR.
[67] *R (on the appln of Refugee Legal Centre) v SSHD* [2004] EWCA Civ 1481, [2005] 1 WLR 2219.

limited to single male applicants from countries where in general there was believed to be no serious risk of persecution. Substantive asylum interviews were conducted in the afternoon of the day after arrival, allowing time for the asylum seeker to consult with a solicitor that morning. The Secretary of State would then reach a decision on the third day. An expedited appeal and possibility of review by the High Court are available—the whole process lasting as little as five weeks. The RLC maintained at appeal that the scheme was unfair due to the timescale being too tight to allow asylum seekers proper opportunity to make their claim.

5.65 The Court of Appeal held that the system did provide asylum seekers with a fair opportunity to present their cases. However, in the course of the judgment the Court highlighted that:

(1) the Secretary of State's argument that there was inbuilt access to an appeal to cure any unfairness in the system was insufficient. An applicant was entitled not only to a fair appeal but to a fair initial hearing and decision. In addition, not all of the risks highlighted by the RLC would necessarily be capable of being raised on appeal.

(2) There was no test or standard for the adaptation of the three-day timetable in accordance to individual needs. A clear and accessible procedure was required, which recognised that it would be unfair not to enlarge the standard timetable in a variety of instances, such as for applicants exhausted from a long and arduous journey into the UK.

5.66 However, considered overall and at the point of entry, the judge had been right to conclude that the present system at Harmondsworth did not carry an unacceptable risk of unfairness to asylum seekers. The Harmondsworth system itself was not inherently unfair if operated in such a way so as to recognise the variety of circumstances in which an enlargement of the standard timetable would be required in the interests of fairness. A written flexibility policy to the three-day timetable was needed.

5.67 Detention as part of the Harmondsworth scheme applies to males only. However, that does not mean that the scheme did not apply to those who had family ties and who could argue that ECHR Article 8 was engaged.[68]

---

[68] See the Administrative Court decision in *R (on the appln of Zita Kpandang) v SSHD* [2004] EWHC 2130 (Admin), 17/9/2004.

Article 5(1)(f)—Deportation/Removal

In *I v Secretary of State for the Home Department*[69] the Court of Appeal considered   **5.68**
the circumstances in which detention pursuant to a power to detain for the purposes
of deportation could be challenged. The appellant in the case was an Afghan asylum seeker granted exceptional leave to remain, who was convicted of offences of
indecency and was imprisoned for three years. The Secretary of State signed a
deportation order and ordered his continued detention following his criminal
sentence. In due course *I* applied for judicial review of his detention on the basis
that removal within a reasonable time was impossible owing to the then difficulty
of removing people to Afghanistan. The appeal was allowed. The Court of Appeal
set out the applicable principles as follows:

(i) The Secretary of State must intend to deport the person and can only use the
power to detain for that purpose.

(ii) The deportee may only be detained for a period that is reasonable in all the
circumstances.

(iii) If, before the expiry of the reasonable period, it becomes apparent that the
Secretary of State will not be able to effect deportation within that reasonable
period, he should not seek to exercise the power of detention.

(iv) The Secretary of State should act with reasonable diligence and expedition to
effect removal.[70]

Principles (ii) and (iii) are conceptually distinct.

Applying the above principles in *R (on the appln of H) v SSHD*[71] Calvert-Smith J   **5.69**
found the continued detention of a failed asylum seeker pending deportation to
be unreasonable in the circumstances. The applicant had refused to accept that
he was a Kenyan national and had always done so, since arriving on a Kenyan
passport. He had maintained that he was Somali. However, his refusal to voluntarily return to Somalia where he feared torture could not reasonably be categorized as non-cooperation sufficient to justify further detention. The Court found
that there was no reasonable prospect of the detention coming to an end within
a reasonable time through *A*'s removal. The more proportionate measure was to
release the applicant subject to conditions, including electronic tagging, which
would considerably reduce the risk of absconding.

Another case where the failure to consider the option of electronic tagging   **5.70**
was taken into account in finding detention unlawful is *R (on the appln of A) v
SSHD*.[72] In that case, detention of a former prisoner for over one and a half years

---

[69] *I v Secretary of State for the Home Department* [2002] EWCA Civ 888, [2003] INLR 196.
[70] Per Dyson LJ at p 207 paragraph 46.
[71] *R (on the appln of H) v SSHD* [2005] EWHC 1702 (Admin).
[72] *R (on the appln of A) v SSHD* [2006] EWHC 3331.

was held to be unlawful due to its length, the impossibility of effecting removal to Somalia during that period, and misleading statements made by the Secretary of State in relation to the possibility of removal. However, despite the declaration of the unlawfulness of that period of detention and award of damages, the Court did not order the claimant's release, as in the meantime removals to Somalia had become possible.

5.71   Detention has been found to be unlawful and in breach of Article 5 where the decision to detain was not in accordance with the Secretary of State's policy,[73] and where the Secretary of State had failed to make a decision to deport prisoners liable to deportation by their unconditional release dates and detention had continued after these dates.[74]

5.72   However, even lengthy periods of detention could be lawful. For example, in *R (on the appln of Q) v SSHD and Governor of Long Lartin Prison*[75] the Divisional Court held that detention for 6–7 months, whilst the Algerian authorities were completing verifications of *Q*'s identity before removal, had not yet become unlawful. The Court disregarded the preceding period of detention of 8–9 months, as during this time the Claimant had an outstanding appeal against his deportation order, and the Secretary of State could not be expected to have made contingent arrangements with the Algerian authorities for the verification of *Q*'s identity. In assessing the lawfulness of the detention the Divisional Court considered the length, circumstances, and reasons for detention, which in *Q*'s case included his being a risk to national security.

(b) Detention must not be arbitrary or disproportionate

The restricted meaning of proportionality in the context of Article 5

5.73   Proportionality in the classical sense, of balancing the benefit of detention against the infringement of the right to personal liberty, does not apply to Article 5. This is clear from the absence of such reference in the language of the Article itself and from case law. In particular, this general test of proportionality was rejected by the Court of Appeal in *R (Saadi & Ors) v SSHD*.[76] In *Nadarajah and Amirhanathan v Home Secretary*[77] an argument was made that this ruling of the

---

[73] *R (on the appln of E & Ors) v SSHD* [2006] EWHC 3208. See also *S, C (by her litigation friend S) and D (by his litigation friend S) v SSHD* [2007] EWHC 1654 (Admin), where the Administrative Court found that a decision to detain a mother and her two young children after the refusal of her asylum claim under the fast-track procedure was unlawful and an infringement of Article 5. There had been no strong grounds for believing that she would not comply with temporary admission conditions.

[74] *R (on the appln of Vovk and Datta) v SSHD* [2006] EWHC 3386.

[75] *R (on the appln of Q) v SSHD and Governor of Long Lartin Prison* [2006] EWHC 2690.

[76] *R (Saadi & Ors) v SSHD* [2001] EWCA Civ 1512, [2002] 1 WLR 356, [65].

[77] *Nadarajah and Amirhanathan v Home Secretary* [2003] EWCA Civ 1768, [2004] INLR 139.

Court of Appeal in *Saadi* had been implicitly overturned by the House of Lords' judgment in the same case, *Saadi*.[78] Particular emphasis was placed on Lord Slynn's opinion in *Saadi* at paragraph 45, which refers to various aspects of the Oakington detention being neither 'arbitrary' nor 'disproportionate'. The Court of Appeal in *Nadarajah and Amirhanathan* did not accept this argument. It found that Article 5(1)(f) does not itself import the test of proportionality.[79] The Court of Appeal expressed the absence of a general proportionality requirement as follows:

> Article 5(1)(f) does not impose an obligation on States to give those whom they are in the process of removing a right to roam freely pending their removal whenever detention is not necessary to achieve ultimate removal.[80]

However, proportionality in a narrow sense remains relevant. The processes of **5.74** considering asylum seekers' applications for leave to enter, or the processes of their deportation or removal, must not be unduly prolonged. The Court of Appeal in *Saadi* held that:

> It is in relation to the duration of detention that the question of proportionality arises.[81]

Further ECHR case law requires that there must be some relationship between **5.75** the ground of permitted deprivation of liberty (eg Article 5(1)(f) in the immigration context) and the place and conditions of detention.[82] This would be of relevance to minors, victims of torture, pregnant women, and other special categories of applicants whose detention conditions have to be suitably tailored to be lawful under Article 5. For example, detention of an unaccompanied minor in a closed centre for illegal immigrants in the same conditions as adults constituted a breach of the minor's rights under Article 5(1).[83]

Summary

The principal considerations for Article 5 cases in light of the above discussion **5.76** are summarized in Table 5.3.

---

[78] *Saadi* [2002] UKHL 31, [2002] 1 WLR 3131.

[79] *Nadarajah and Amirhanathan v Home Secretary* [2003] EWCA Civ 1768, [2004] INLR 139, para 50.

[80] Ibid, para 51.

[81] *R (Saadi & Ors) v SSHD* [2001] EWCA Civ 1512, [2002] 1 WLR 356, para 65.

[82] *Aerts v Belgium*, judgment of 30 July 1998, Reports 1998-V, pp 1961–1962, para 46: 'Furthermore, there must be some relationship between the ground of permitted deprivation of liberty relied on and the place and conditions of detention. In principle, the "detention" of a person as a mental health patient will only be "lawful" for the purposes of sub-paragraph (e) of paragraph 1 if effected in a hospital, clinic or other appropriate institution. . .'

[83] *Mayeka v Belgium* (13178/03) [2006] ECHR 13178/03.

Table 5.3 **Considerations for Article 5 cases**

Is there power to detain?	(1) Is the purpose of the detention justifiable under Article 5(1)(f) • to prevent unauthorised entry into the country? • action is being taken with a view to deportation or extradition (to be read broadly to include removal)? (2) Is there compliance with the domestic law providing for detention?
Is the exercise of the power in the particular case proportionate (in the narrow sense)?	• Are there alternatives to detention available? • What are the conditions of detention? • What is the length of detention envisaged? Is it proportionate to the aim/purpose of detention? • Are there special factors such as the age, mental, and physical health of the detainee, which may make the detention disproportionate?

In certain circumstances deference is due to the Secretary of State's proportionality assessment

5.77 There are areas, however, where the Secretary of State's judgment on the factors in favour of detention is to be given greater deference. In *R (on the appln of OS) v SSHD*,[84] the Secretary of State had refused consent for a mental health patient, who was subject to a deportation order, to have unescorted community leave. *S* was appealing against the deportation order on the basis that he feared persecution in Turkey. The Court found that the Secretary of State had knowledge of matters relating to the risk of absconding above and beyond those considered by the mental health review tribunal and he was entitled to attach substantial weight to those matters. The Secretary of State was entitled to take into account the potential risk that *S* would abscond, which may have been affected by the fact that *S* was liable to be deported and that he was appealing against the deportation order on the basis that he feared persecution on return. Further, the decision had taken into account that if *S* were to abscond, there was a risk that his mental state could deteriorate, which could consequently pose a risk to the public. Unescorted community leave in the UK entailed risks, which were not the same as those of being with his family after deportation, as his reasons for absconding would have disappeared if he were in Turkey. In the circumstances the application for judicial review was refused.

Delay

5.78 Immigration officials' delay in acting on available information may in some circumstances lead to a breach of Article 5. In *R (on the appln of I and O) v SSHD*[85]

---

84 *R (on the appln of OS) v SSHD* [2006] EWHC 1903 (Admin).
85 *R (on the appln of I & O) v SSHD* [2005] EWHC 1025 (Admin).

the Home Secretary's decision to continue to detain asylum seekers as adults in a detention centre for the period between the receipt of reports from a consultant paediatrician and age assessments carried out by social services was held to be unlawful. The consultant had extensive specialist expertise, was qualified to undertake dental examinations, and gave an estimate of age accurate to within two years. That amounted to credible medical evidence to demonstrate the claim by the asylum seekers that they were minors. The decisions to continue to detain them *after* consideration of the consultant's report were irrational. Thus, the detention for the period between the Secretary of State's receipt of the consultant's reports and the age assessments carried out by the social services was unlawful.

Restriction vs deprivation of liberty

Deprivation of liberty, short of detention, which is capable of infringing Article 5 **5.79** can be established. In this regard, the control orders case of *SSHD v JJ & Ors*[86] is instructive. The case involved six Iraqi and Iranian asylum seekers, who had been detained under immigration powers and had been served with notice of intention to deport on national security grounds. Non-derogating control orders were made pursuant to the Prevention of Terrorism Act 2005, section 2, and the deportation proceedings were discontinued. The conditions of the control orders were that the defendants were to remain within their one-bedroom flat residences at all times, save for a period of six hours per day. Visitors had to provide names, addresses, dates of birth, and photo identification to the Home Office. The residences were subject to spot searches by police and, when permitted to leave their residences, the defendants were restricted to confined urban areas.

The Administrative Court determined that the obligations imposed by the con- **5.80** trol orders were so severe that they amounted to deprivation of liberty contrary to Article 5 and thus the orders were derogating control orders which the Secretary of State had no power to make. The orders were quashed, with the judge holding that he had the power to do so under s 3(12) of the Prevention of Terrorism Act 2005, as the orders were nullities, having been made without jurisdiction.

On appeal by the Secretary of State, the Court of Appeal confirmed the decision. **5.81** The Judge had properly taken the physical confinement for 18 hours a day to small flats as a starting point. Further, he had taken into account a range of other material factors that interfered with the defendants' normal lives, including the physical restraints on the defendants when allowed to leave their residences, and considered the extent to which those restrictions would prevent an individual from pursuing the life of his choice. The judge had also been right to quash the orders, as he had jurisdiction to do so.

---

[86] *SSHD v JJ & Ors* [2006] EWCA Civ 1141, [2006] 3 WLR 866.

Procedural aspects of Article 5

Legality of policies and compliance with Detention Centre Rules relevant to determination of Article 5 breach

5.82   Detention for a period longer than necessary, which resulted from an unlawful policy and a breach of the Detention Centre Rules, would amount to unlawful detention, for which compensation is payable. In *R (on the appln of D and K) v SSHD & Ors*[87] the Administrative Court held that in each case, the claimants were denied medical examination within 24 hours of their admission to the detention centre, where their asylum claims were to be subject to expedited scrutiny. This was contrary to rule 34 of the Detention Centre Rules 2001. Declaratory relief was granted against the Secretary of State and the second defendant, a private contractor running the detention centre, as the failure was the culmination of a long-standing state of affairs and rectification was necessary.

5.83   Further, the third defendant, to whom the health care services at the detention centre were sub-contracted, had a policy that medical personnel should not, when filling out an allegation of torture form, express any opinion as to the possible causes of detainees' injuries or whether the injuries were consistent with an allegation of torture. The Court found that the policy was contrary to rules 34 and 35(3) of the Detention Centre Rules. A medical practitioner compiling a report for the purposes of rule 35(3) ought not to be precluded from expressing a view that a detainee's injuries were consistent with allegations of torture made by him. Such a report was capable of constituting independent evidence suitable to be considered when the Secretary of State made the decision as to whether to release the asylum seeker.

5.84   As a result of the unlawful policy and breach of the rules on the timing of medical examination, the claimants were wrongfully detained for a period longer than was necessary. That period of detention was unlawful and in breach of Article 5 of the Convention. Compensation was payable by the Secretary of State, rather than the sub-contractors, as it was he who held the power to decide on the claimants' release.

Detainees should have access to legal advice

5.85   As Lord Bingham of Cornhill explained in *R (Daly) v Secretary of State for the Home Department*:[88]

> Any custodial order inevitably curtails the enjoyment, by the person confined, of rights enjoyed by other citizens. He cannot move freely and choose his associates as they are entitled to do. It is indeed an important objective of such an order to curtail

---

[87] *R (on the appln of D and K) v SSHD & Ors* [2006] EWHC 980 (Admin).

[88] *R (Daly) v Secretary of State for the Home Department* [2001] UKHL 26, [2001] 2 AC 532, at para 5.

such rights, whether to punish him or to protect other members of the public or both. But the order does not wholly deprive the person confined of all rights enjoyed by other citizens. Some rights, perhaps in an attenuated or qualified form, survive the making of the order. And it may well be that the importance of such surviving rights is enhanced by the loss or partial loss of other rights. Among the rights which, in part at least, survive are three important rights, closely related but free standing, each of them calling for appropriate legal protection: the right of access to a court; the right of access to legal advice; and the right to communicate confidentially with a legal adviser under the seal of legal professional privilege. Such rights may be curtailed only by clear and express words, and then only to the extent reasonably necessary to meet the ends which justify the curtailment.

In the context of the right to seek and receive legal advice, a particularly striking **5.86** illustration of the unlawful exercise of detention powers comes from the case of *R (on the appln of Karas and Miladinovic) v SSHD*.[89] The applicants, Croatians of Serbian origin, had married, whilst *K* had an outstanding application as a fresh claim under Articles 3 and 8, following the refusal of his asylum claim. About three years after the initial removal directions, which had accompanied *K*'s refusal of asylum, the applicants were detained by immigration officials and were informed that they would be removed to Croatia the following morning. The applicants were prevented from receiving legal advice until the early hours of the morning, when *M*, on advice, claimed asylum, which prevented the removal. The applicants remained in detention for two weeks.

The Administrative Court held that *K*'s claim under Articles 3 and 8 had no **5.87** prospect of success. In relation to the legality of the detention, however, the Court held that for it to be lawful, it had to be reasonable and had to satisfy the test of proportionality. The Secretary of State's failure to provide a detailed explanation in response to allegations of two weeks' unlawful detention and his seeking to deny the applicants access to legal advice was found by the Court to be extraordinary. In the circumstances of the case, the Administrative Court found that the detention was oppressive, unreasonable, and unnecessary. There was no satisfactory explanation as to why the applicants had been detained. The detention was deliberately planned with a view to a collateral and improper purpose, namely removal of the claimants from the jurisdiction before there was likely to be time for them to obtain and act upon legal advice or obtain access to the courts. Such a purpose was improper and unlawful and rendered the detention itself unlawful.

R (on the appln of E & Ors) v SSHD[90] provides a further example of detention **5.88** being rendered unlawful by its timing so as to prevent legal advice from being

---

[89] *R (on the appln of Karas and Miladinovic) v SSHD* [2006] EWHC 747 (Admin).
[90] *R (on the appln of E & Ors) v SSHD* [2006] EWHC 3208.

obtained, when there was absolutely nothing in the circumstances of the case which required urgency.

Potential application of Article 5 outside the boundaries of the UK and not in extradition/expulsion cases?

5.89 For an example of a case where consideration of potential 'extraterritorial' application of ECHR Article 5 arose in unusual circumstances, see *R (on the appln of Abdul-Razzaq Ali Al-Jedda) v SSHD*.[91] The case involved a British and Iraqi dual-national challenging the lawfulness of his continued detention by British forces in Iraq, and the refusal of the Secretary of State to return him to the UK. The Court of Appeal found that the Secretary of State was correct when he argued that UNSCR 1546 (2004) under which the appellant was detained qualified any obligations contained in human rights conventions in so far as it was in conflict with them. To the extent that UN Security Council resolution sanctioned the continued use of internment beyond the period contemplated by the Fourth Geneva Convention as a means of restoring peace to Iraq, the very essence of internment was inconsistent with the 'due process' requirements of ECHR Article 5(1) or Article 9 of the ICCPR. However, as the claimant's right to due court process under Article 5(1) of the ECHR was qualified by UNSCR 1546 (2004), the appeal was dismissed.

Article 5(4)

5.90 The purpose of Article 5(4) is to assure to persons who are arrested and detained the right to a judicial supervision of the lawfulness of the measure to which they are thereby subjected. The remedies must be made available during a person's detention with a view to that person obtaining speedy judicial review of the lawfulness of the detention capable of leading, where appropriate, to his or her release.[92] The ways of challenging immigration detention are discussed further in Chapter 8.

Article 5(5)—compensation

5.91 For detention to be lawful under Article 5, a double test is applied. The detention impugned must be lawful under domestic law, and the domestic law must be in compliance with the ECHR both substantively and procedurally. On the face of it, Article 5(5) mandates compensation for failure to comply with either test,[93] although the ECtHR sometimes concludes that the finding of a violation is

[91] *R (on the appln of Abdul-Razzaq Ali Al-Jedda) v SSHD* [2006] EWCA Civ 327, [2006] 3 WLR 954.
[92] *Slivenko v Latvia* [GC], no 48321/99, para 158, ECHR 2003-X.
[93] *R v Governor of Brockhill Prison ex p Evans* (No 2) [2001] 2 AC 19, per Lord Hobhouse of Woodborough at 47.

sufficient to constitute just satisfaction, with the consequence that it does not order compensation despite finding a breach of some other provision of Article 5.

E. Article 6—Right to a Fair Trial

Article 6 of the ECHR provides: **5.92**

1. In the determination of his civil rights and obligations or of any criminal charge against him, everyone is entitled to a fair and public hearing within a reasonable time by an independent and impartial tribunal established by law. Judgment shall be pronounced publically but the press and public may be excluded from all or part of the trial in the interests of morals, public order, or national security in a democratic society, where the interests of juveniles or the protection of the private life of the parties so require, or to the extent strictly necessary in the opinion of the court in the special circumstances where publicity would prejudice the interests of justice.
2. Everyone charged with a criminal offence shall be presumed innocent until proved guilty according to law.
3. Everyone charged with a criminal offence has the following minimum rights:
   (a) to be informed promptly, in a language which he understands and in detail, of the nature and cause of the accusation against him;
   (b) to have adequate time and facilities for the preparation of his defence;
   (c) to defend himself in person or through legal assistance of his own choosing or, if has not sufficient means to pay for legal assistance, to be given it free when the interests of justice so require;
   (d) to examine or have examined witnesses against him and to obtain the attendance and examination of witnesses on his behalf under the same conditions as witnesses against him;
   (e) to have the free assistance of an interpreter if he cannot understand or speak the language used in court.

Article 6 does not apply to domestic immigration and asylum cases, but the substance of the right is guaranteed by the common law

The Asylum and Immigration Tribunal and the Courts are public authorities for   **5.93** the purposes of the Human Rights Act 1998, and in performance of their duties they must comply with that Act. However, the Article 6 obligations, namely the right to a fair trial, do not apply to the determination of asylum or other immigration appeals, as a person's immigration status is not a civil right or obligation and does not relate to a criminal charge, which are the subject matters governed by

Article 6 (see the ECtHR decision in *Maanouia v France*,[94] followed by the IAT in *MNM**[95]). This outcome[96] is unlikely to make much, if any, practical difference, as the Tribunal and the Courts will in effect apply the same procedural fairness tests as contained in Article 6. Equivalent procedural guarantees are available under the common law, as was demonstrated by the Court of Appeal declaring procedural rules, which in effect precluded access to the immigration appellate authorities for certain categories of applicants, to be ultra vires.[97]

5.94 In *AM ('Upgrade' appeals: Art 6?) Afghanistan**[98] the IAT held that there was no basis for the application of Article 6 to the determination of the question in issue in an upgrade appeal, namely whether the claimant is entitled to the status of refugee, as that status existed only in international and public law and was not a matter of private law.

5.95 However, certain decisions relating to asylum seekers do qualify as determinations of civil rights and obligations within the meaning of Article 6. For example, the entitlement to asylum support was found to amount to a civil right, despite the relevant legislative provisions being framed in discretionary terms.[99]

Fair and public hearing, decision pronounced publicly subject to exceptions

5.96 The procedural requirements of a public hearing, including the limited exceptions for private hearings, are provided for in the Asylum and Immigration Tribunal (Procedure) Rules 2005, rule 54. These rules correspond to the exceptions as laid down in the body of Article 6(1).

Within a reasonable time

5.97 As illustrated by the cases where there has been considerable delay in immigration proceedings, discussed in Chapter 4, it is possible that the outcome of proceedings would be influenced by such delay. It is only in extreme circumstances that the substantive outcome of an immigration decision would change simply on the ground of the delay.[100] However, failure to consider a claim or relevant representations

---

[94] *Maanouia v France* (2001) 33 EHRR 1037.
[95] *MNM**[2000] INLR 576.
[96] For an in-depth critique of the correctness of the equation of civil rights with private rights and the reasoning in *Maanouia v France*, see N Blake and R Hussain, *Immigration, Asylum and Human Rights*, Oxford: Oxford University Press, 2003, pp 242–56.
[97] *R v SSHD ex p Saleem* [2000] 4 All ER 814, *FP (Iran) v SSHD, MB (Libya) v SSHD* [2007] EWCA Civ 13.
[98] *AM ('Upgrade' appeals: Art 6?) Afghanistan** [2004] UKIAT 00186.
[99] *R (on the appln of Husain) v Asylum Support Adjudicator* [2001] EWHC Admin 832, (2001) Times, November 15, 2001.
[100] See *Akaeke v SSHD* [2005] EWCA Civ 947, and *Shala v SSHD* (2003) EWCA Civ 233, as examples in the Article 8 context.

within a reasonable time is a factor to be taken into account when striking a balance on proportionality, on the way to reaching a substantive immigration decision.[101]

What constitutes a 'reasonable time' is contextually dependent. Relevant factors to consider include the complexity of the issues to be resolved, the conduct of the applicant and the authorities, and what is at stake for the applicant (in particular, whether any prejudice has been caused by the delay).[102] **5.98**

By an independent and impartial tribunal established by law

The *independence* of a tribunal can in large part be ascertained from the security of tenure of its members.[103] Lack of bias and the appearance of bias[104] are of equal importance with regard to the *impartiality* of the tribunal. **5.99**

Right of access to the Court

Compatibility with Article 6 is also to a large degree dependent on effective access to a court or tribunal. Although there is no such express right on the face of Article 6(1), the right to access to a court has been found to be implicit in the Article.[105] **5.100**

Successful challenges have been mounted to the vires of procedural rules, which result in unfair denial of access to the courts. Thus in *FP (Iran) v SSHD, MB (Libya) v SSHD*[106] the Court of Appeal found Rules 19(1) and 56 of the Asylum and Immigration Tribunal (Procedure) Rules 2005 to be unlawful, as their combined effect was to deny the appellants the opportunity to be heard where through no fault of their own but purely through the fault of their representatives they had not been aware of the hearing dates of their asylum appeals. The appeals had been determined against the appellants in their absence. The procedure rules were **5.101**

---

101 When striking a balance between an applicant's rights under Article 8 and the legitimate objective of the proper maintenance of immigration control, the decision maker had to have regard to delay in determining an application for asylum and its consequences. Delay was not determinative, but was merely a relevant factor: *Strbac & Anor v SSHD* [2005] EWCA Civ 848.

102 *Zimmerman v Switzerland* (1983) 6 EHRR 17. See also *Vayic v Turkey* (App no 18078/02) [2006] ECHR 18078/02, where a violation of Article 6(1) was found on the basis that the complexity of the proceedings did not suffice to justify their substantial duration and the authorities had not conducted the criminal proceedings with the special diligence required (including lengthy intervals between hearings, following the applicant's release pending trial).

103 *R (on the appln of Husain) v Asylum Support Adjudicator* [2001] EWHC Admin 832, (2001) Times, November 15, 2001.

104 The test of apparent bias is whether all relevant circumstances 'would lead a fair-minded and informed observer to conclude that there was a real possibility, or a real danger, the two being the same, that the Tribunal was biased'. Per Lord Phillips MR in *Director-General of Fair Trading v Proprietary Association of Great Britain* [2001] 1 WLR 700, at 721.

105 *Golder v UK* (1975) 1 EHRR 524, paras 34–36.

106 *FP (Iran) v SSHD, MB (Libya) v SSHD* [2007] EWCA Civ 13.

found to have denied the very essence of the right to be heard, and to have sacrificed fairness to speed, denying the AIT the ability to balance each of these considerations. Rules 19(1) and 56 were thus ultra vires the empowering statute, namely section 106 NIAA 2002.

5.102 Similarly, the impossibility of challenging or mitigating sanctions imposed on carriers according to the Immigration and Asylum Act 1999 (ss 32–37) was a factor which contributed to the whole sanctions regime being found by the Court of Appeal to be incompatible with Article 6.[107]

5.103 However, access to the courts need not be via a statutory appeal. A fair administrative decision-making process, combined with the possibility of judicial review, would satisfy the requirements of Article 6. This was the effect of the Court of Appeal decision in *R (on the appln Q & Ors) v SSHD*,[108] where the absence of any right to appeal against the refusal of asylum support under s 55 was found not to be incompatible with Article 6 if the deficiencies in the procedures were remedied.

Resisting removal so as to maintain access to the UK courts

5.104 In a number of cases applicants who have outstanding court cases in the UK may seek to resist removal on the basis that following expulsion they will not have access to the court where their case is to be heard. The likelihood of succeeding in such a claim is context-and fact-dependent. However, in the vast majority of cases the likely finding is that access to the courts would not be completely barred, as the court cases could be pursued from abroad. For example, in *R (on the appln of Obasi) v SSHD*,[109] Sullivan J held that the claimant could advance his assault case from Nigeria, and while he may need to attend court for any hearing, it was open to him to seek leave to enter on that basis. Should leave be refused at that stage, the claimant could rely on Article 6.

5.105 The exceptional case (although not founded on Article 6), where an out-of-country access to the UK courts may not be sufficient, can be illustrated by the case of *R (on the appln of Yee Kiong Lim and Yet Kiow Sew) v SSHD*.[110] There the High Court held that an out-of-country right of appeal against the Secretary of State's removal decision would not provide the particular claimant with a fair hearing, as he would not be able to participate by giving evidence. Thus the claimant was found to have the right to challenge the removal decision by way of judicial review. The Court, however, stressed that the case was exceptional.

---

[107] *International Transport Roth GmbH & Ors v SSHD* [2002] EWCA Civ 158, [2002] 3 WLR 344.
[108] *R (on appln Q & Ors) v SSHD* [2003] 3 WLR 365.
[109] *R (on the appln of Obasi) v SSHD* [2007] All ER (D) 214 (Feb).
[110] *R (on the appln of Yee Kiong Lim and Yet Kiow Sew) v SSHD* [2006] EWHC 3004.

The power to issue removal directions depended on the existence of a precedent fact, namely the claimant's failure to observe a condition of his leave. In these particular circumstances, an out-of-country appeal was found not to afford fair, adequate, and proportionate protection against the risk that the decision had been taken without jurisdiction.

Damages for breach of Article 6

With regard to damages for established breaches of Article 6, the House of Lords **5.106** in *R (on the appln of Greenfield) v SSHD*[111] set out quite a narrow framework for their availability and amount. Their Lordships found that a domestic court could not award damages under section 8 of the HRA:

a. unless it was satisfied that it was necessary to do so, and
b. further, it had to take into account the principles applied by the European Court of Human Rights in awarding compensation under ECHR Article 41, as to whether compensation should be awarded, and the amount.

With regard to the latter criterion, the practice of the ECtHR was generally to **5.107** hold that a finding of a violation of Article 6 was in itself just satisfaction under Article 41. It was only where the ECtHR found a causal connection between the violation and the loss for which an applicant sought to be compensated that a departure from this practice was warranted. In cases of structural bias, the practice of the ECtHR was not to make an award for physical and mental suffering.

Finally, the House of Lords held that it was not appropriate for awards under **5.108** section 8 to be comparable to tortious awards in domestic courts. On the facts of the case, no award of damages was made.

Application in foreign cases

In *Soering v UK*[112] the European Court of Human Rights considered that the risk **5.109** of a 'flagrant violation' of the right to a fair trial in the receiving country might 'exceptionally' engage the responsibility of an expelling State. However, the gravity of the violation must pass a very high threshold.

> The right to a fair trial in criminal proceedings, as embodied in Article 6 (art 6), holds a prominent place in a democratic society (see, inter alia, the Colozza judgment of 12 February 1985, Series A no 89, p 16, § 32). The Court does not exclude that an issue might exceptionally be raised under Article 6 (art 6) by an extradition decision in circumstances where the fugitive has suffered or risks suffering a flagrant denial of a fair trial in the requesting country. However, the facts of the present case do

---

[111] *R (on the appln of Greenfield) v SSHD* [2005] UKHL 14, (2005) 1 WLR 673.
[112] *Soering v UK*, 7 July 1989, no 25803/94, at para 113.

not disclose such a risk. Accordingly, no issue arises under Article 6 § 3 (c) (art 6-3-c) in this respect. (para 113)

5.110 Lord Steyn in *Ullah* held:

Article 6(1) provides:

In the determination of his civil rights and obligations or of any criminal charge against him, everyone is entitled to a fair and public hearing within a reasonable time by an independent and impartial tribunal established by law.

This is a qualified right and it is subject to derogation in time of war or public emergency. Moreover, in deciding what amounts to a fair trial the triangulation of interests of the accused, the victim, and the public interest may require compromises, eg to protect children in abuse cases, women in rape cases, and national security. On the other hand, there are universal minimum standards. It is important to bear in mind the status of the right to a fair trial. It is a universal norm. It requires that we do not allow any individual to be condemned unless he has been fairly tried in accordance with law and the rule of law. The guarantee of a fair trial is a core value under the ECHR. In *Einhorn v France* (decided by the ECtHR (Application No 71555/01) (unreported) 16 October 2001), which was not cited in the Court of Appeal, the Strasbourg court summarized the position. It observed (para 32):

... the Court reiterates that it cannot be ruled out that an issue might exceptionally be raised under article 6 of the Convention by an extradition decision in circumstances where the fugitive has suffered or risks suffering a flagrant denial of justice in the requesting country (see the *Soering* judgment cited above, p 45, § 113, and, *mutatis mutandis*, the *Drozd and Janousek v France and Spain* judgment of 26 June 1992, Series A no 240, p 34, para 110).

This was said in the context of extradition but, on the principles laid down by the ECtHR, the same would apply in an expulsion case. In *Einhorn*, as in the earlier cases, no violation was found established. That cannot, however, affect the binding force of the Strasbourg jurisprudence on the point. '*It can be regarded as settled law that where there is a real risk of a flagrant denial of justice in the country to which an individual is to be deported article 6 may be engaged.*' (emphasis added)

5.111 As with Article 5 in the context of a foreign case, although the possibility exists of successfully relying on a flagrant breach of Article 6 by the State of proposed return, such cases are unlikely to be common in practice. Where the denial of Article 6 rights in the State to where return is contemplated would be so overwhelming as to reach the heightened threshold of 'flagrant breach' or 'gross violation', as mandated by the House of Lords decision in *Ullah*, the factual matrix is likely to satisfy the requirements of Article 3. Thus in practice reliance and success solely on Article 6 in the purely 'foreign' case would be an extremely rare event.

The Strasbourg case law gives a fairly clear indication of where the threshold for **5.112** a 'flagrant denial of justice' lies.

(a) In *Einhorn v France*[113] the ECtHR, having referred to the *Soering* test, stated (at paragraph 33) that:

> a denial of justice[114] undoubtedly occurs where a person convicted *in absentia* is unable subsequently to obtain from a court which has heard him a fresh determination of the merits of the charge, in respect of both law and fact, where it has not been unequivocally established that he has waived his right to appear and to defend himself.

The indication that such circumstances would meet the *Soering* test of a flagrant denial of justice is consistent with the ECtHR's earlier decision (on very similar facts) in *Drozd and Janousek v France and Spain*.[115]

(b) The case of *Bader v Sweden*[116] concerned the potential deportation from Sweden to Syria of a man who had been tried in his absence for murder and sentenced to death. Although Article 6 was not expressly raised as an issue preventing deportation, the ECtHR stated (at paragraph 47):

> Furthermore, in the instant case, it transpires from the Syrian judgment that no oral evidence was taken at the hearing, that all the evidence examined was submitted by the prosecutor and that neither the accused nor even his defence lawyer was present at the hearing. The Court finds that, because of their summary nature and the total disregard of the rights of the defence, the proceedings must be regarded as a flagrant denial of a fair trial (see *mutatis mutandis*, *Mamatkulov and Askarov v Turkey*, para 88).

(c) The case of *Mamatkulov*, referred to in *Bader*, was a case in which the ECtHR concluded that the threshold of a flagrant denial of justice had *not* been reached. The case concerned the extradition of two political dissidents from Turkey to Uzbekistan. There was an issue as to whether their extradition (which had already taken place by the time of the hearings in Strasbourg) had been in breach of Article 6. The Court held that the issue had to be considered primarily by reference to facts that were known, or ought to have been known, to Turkey at the time of the extradition. In this regard, the Court referred to an Amnesty International report that was contemporaneous with the extradition (see paragraph 54 of the judgment). That report included the following relevant paragraph:

> In the majority of these cases, if not all, that have come to the attention of Amnesty International, those detained were denied prompt access to a lawyer of their choice, to their families and to medical assistance. The responsible authorities, from procurators to courts at all levels and the parliamentary ombudsman, persistently failed to launch timely, full and independent investigations into

---

[113] *Einhorn v France, Reports of Judgments and Decisions* 2001-XI, p 275.
[114] From the context, a *flagrant* denial of justice.
[115] *Drozd and Janousek v France and Spain* (1992) 14 EHRR 745.
[116] *Bader & Ors v Sweden* (Application No 13284/04).

widespread allegations of torture and ill-treatment. According to independent and credible sources, self-incriminating evidence reportedly extracted by torture was routinely included in trial proceedings and served in many of the cases reviewed by Amnesty International as the basis for a guilty verdict.

Notwithstanding this evidence, the conclusion of the ECtHR was (at paragraph 91) to the following effect:

> The applicants were extradited to Uzbekistan on 27 March 1999. Although, in the light of the information available, there may have been reasons for doubting at the time that they would receive a fair trial in the State of destination, there is not sufficient evidence to show that any possible irregularities in the trial were liable to constitute a flagrant denial of justice within the meaning of paragraph 113 of the aforementioned *Soering* judgment.

The following broad conclusions can be drawn from the Strasbourg cases.

(a) A flagrant denial of justice (or, in the instructive words of Lord Bingham in *Ullah*, a complete nullification of that right) will be found where an individual has not been granted a trial at all, or has not been entitled to play any part in his trial. 'A total disregard for the rights of the defence.'

(b) However, a flagrant denial of justice is unlikely be found where a trial of some sort has taken place, even if safeguards necessary for compliance with Article 6 within an ECHR state were absent.

5.113 The practical application of this flagrant denial test has been considered in SIAC in cases involving proposed deportation in national security cases where the deportee would face a trial in his home country. In *Othman v Secretary of State for the Home Department*[117] between paragraphs 391 and 430 SIAC recited the deficiencies that his trial, on return to Jordan, would have by reference to Article 6, but concluded that such deficiencies did not amount to a complete denial of the right. In a very thoughtful analysis of the Strasbourg jurisprudence and the domestic cases, SIAC explored the underlying reasoning and concluded that the ECtHR has not enunciated any general theory of indirect responsibility for those acts of a receiving State which amount to a complete denial of a right. The jurisprudence is developing. In the case of articles from which derogation is permitted (which includes Article 6), SIAC considered that the potential acts complained of in the receiving State had to be incapable of justification, including by reference to the possibility that the receiving State might be able to demonstrate circumstances which would, had it been a signatory state to the ECHR, have justified a derogation—see paragraphs 452–470.

5.114 Furthermore, SIAC drew a distinction between the approach in Article 3 removal cases, where no balance is allowed once the relevant risk of ill-treatment is established, and qualified rights and those from which derogation is permitted,

---

[117] *Othman v Secretary of State for the Home Department* (SC/15/2005).

where they may be a balance. In national security cases the effect of the Strasbourg jurisprudence is that if Article 3 is in play, no account is taken of the risks posed to others of the continued presence in the United Kingdom of the prospective deportee. SIAC concluded that a similar approach was not dictated when Article 5 and 6 were in play—see paragraphs 471–473. This conclusion was not part of the ratio of the case, the earlier conclusion being that there was no risk of a complete denial of the right, but at least at first instance it is likely that this approach will be followed.

F. Article 7—No Punishment without Law

Lord Steyn in *Ullah* held: **5.115**

45. Article 7 provides:

(1) No one shall be held guilty of any criminal offence on account of any act or omission which did not constitute a criminal offence under national or international law at the time when it was committed. Nor shall a heavier penalty be imposed than the one that was applicable at the time the criminal offence was committed.

(2) This article shall not prejudice the trial and punishment of any person for any act or omission which, at the time when it was committed, was criminal according to the general principles of law recognised by civilised nations.

This is among the first tier of core obligations under the ECtHR. It is absolute and non derogable. It is not likely to arise often in the context of immigration decisions to expel aliens. It could, however, arise. Bearing in mind the principles laid down by the ECtHR in respect of extradition and expulsion involving a real risk of a flagrant violation of fair trial rights, the same must be the case in respect of this obligation.

In the circumstances, Article 7 is unlikely to be applicable in the immigration **5.116** context. If it does arise on the facts of a case, however, the flagrant breach test for 'foreign' cases would apply to it. For an example where this Article arose in the domestic context see *Kenneth Togher v Revenue & Customs & Ors*.[118]

G. Article 9—Freedom of Thought, Conscience, and Religion

Article 9 of the Convention provides: **5.117**

(1) Everyone has the right to freedom of thought, conscience and religion; this right includes freedom to change his religion or belief and freedom, either alone or in community with others and in public or private, to manifest his religion or belief, in worship, teaching, practice and observance.

(2) Freedom to manifest one's religion shall be subject only to such limitations as are prescribed by law and are necessary in a democratic society in the interests of

---

[118] *Kenneth Togher v Revenue & Customs & Ors* (5 July 2007), CA (Civ Div) (Chadwick LJ, Dyson LJ, Thomas LJ).

public safety, for the protection of public order, health or morals, or for the protection of the rights and freedoms of others.

5.118 This was the Article which arose for consideration in *Ullah*. Although no breach was found on the facts of the case, the House of Lords confirmed that it was possible to rely on a feared breach of Article 9 in the destination country if there was a real risk of a flagrant denial or gross violation of the rights protected under that Article. The breach in the country of return would have to nullify or completely deny the very essence of the right before the risk of a breach of Article 9 by another State would be sufficient to halt removal. Further, it ought to be emphasized that the right to manifest one's religion is a qualified right, which may be restricted in accordance with Article 9(2), provided that the restriction is proportionate to the legitimate aims set out therein.

5.119 The European case law provides examples of infringements of Article 9. Restrictions on the freedom of movement so as to prevent people from being able to observe their religious beliefs and to access places of worship was found to amount to an infringement of Article 9,[119] as was the refusal to register the amendments to the statute of a religious organisation for irrelevant and insufficient reasons.[120]

5.120 The right to conscientious objection to military service, however, has not gained such wide recognition. In *Sepet and Bulbul* the Court of Appeal found,[121] and the House of Lords agreed,[122] that the right to conscientious objection was not so well established that its denial would constitute persecution. Developments in the case law under Article 9 may in the future provide the basis of a different decision on this point.

H. Article 10—Freedom of Expression

5.121 Article 10 of ECHR provides:

1. Everyone has the right to freedom of expression. This right shall include the freedom to hold opinions and to receive and impart information and ideas without interference by public authority and regardless of frontiers. This article shall not prevent States from requiring the licensing of broadcasting, television or cinema enterprises.
2. The exercise of these freedoms, since it carries with it duties and responsibilities, may be subject to such formalities, conditions, restrictions or penalties as are prescribed by law and are necessary in a democratic society, in the interests of national security, territorial integrity or public safety, for the prevention of disorder or

---

[119] *Cyprus v Turkey* (Appln no 25781/94) (2001) 11 BHRC 45.
[120] *Svyato-Mykhaylivska Parafiya v Ukraine*, Application No 00077703/01, 14 June 2007.
[121] *Sepet and Bulbul v SSHD* [2001] EWCA Civ 681.
[122] [2003] UKHL 15, [2003] 3 All ER 304.

crime, for the protection of health or morals, for the protection for the reputation or rights of others, for preventing the disclosure of information received in confidence, or for maintaining the authority and impartiality of the judiciary.

Domestic cases

In *R v SSHD ex p Farrakhan*[123] the Secretary of State had refused admission to the **5.122** UK to Louis Farrakhan, a US citizen and the leader of the Nation of Islam group. The Administrative Court had quashed that decision and the Secretary of State appealed. In allowing the appeal the Court of Appeal held as follows.

Is Article 10 engaged?

(1) The State had the right under international law to control the entry of non-nationals into its territory. Where entry is refused or an alien is expelled for reasons which are wholly independent of the exercise by the alien of Convention rights, the fact that this has the consequence that he cannot exercise those rights in the territory from which he is excluded will not constitute a violation of the Convention.

(2) In exceptional circumstances the obligation to protect Convention rights can override the right of a State to control the entry into its territory or presence within its territory of aliens.

(3) Where the State authorities refuse entry or expel an alien exclusively for the purpose of preventing him from exercising an ECHR right within the territory, or by way of sanction for the exercise of such right, the Convention will be directly engaged.

(4) Where Article 10 is engaged, Article 10(2) will be applied to determine whether or not the interference with the alien's freedom of expression is justified.

On the facts of the case the Secretary of State did not exclude Farrakhan simply **5.123** because he held views that would be offensive. The exclusion was based on the effect that his admission would have on community relations and the risk that meetings attended by him would be occasions for disorder. However, Article 10 was found to be engaged, as one object of Farrakhan's exclusion could be said to have been to prevent him exercising the right of freedom of expression in this country.

Justification and proportionality

With regard to the justification and proportionality tests inherent in Article **5.124** 10(2), the Court of Appeal held:

(1) The Secretary of State was correct to balance freedom of speech against the risk of disorder. Prevention of disorder was a legitimate justification under Article 10(2) for restricting freedom of expression.

---

[123] *R v SSHD ex p Farrakhan* [2002] EWCA Civ 606, (2002) 3 WLR 481, CA (Civ Div).

(2) The proportionality test as applicable at the judicial review stage was as outlined in *R v Secretary of State for the Home Department, ex parte Daly*[124] with a margin of discretion being accorded to the Secretary of State.

(3) The Court did not apply Article 16 of the Convention, which provides that nothing in Articles 10, 11, and 14 shall be regarded as preventing the States from imposing restrictions on the political activity of aliens. This provision appeared to be something of an anachronism.

5.125 There were several factors in the *Farrakhan* case that made it appropriate to accord a particularly wide margin of discretion to the Secretary of State.

(1) The Secretary of State was far better placed to reach an informed decision about the likely consequences of admitting Farrakhan to the UK than the court.

(2) The decision was made personally by the Secretary of State, after detailed consideration involving wide consultation.

(3) The Secretary of State was democratically accountable for this decision. There was no right of appeal where he had certified that he had personally directed the exclusion of a person on the ground that this was conducive to the public good. Therefore the effect of the legislation was to require the court to confer a wide margin of discretion on the Secretary of State.

(4) In immigration decisions the ECtHR attached considerable weight to the right under international law of a State to control immigration into its territory.

(5) Finally, Farrakhan's freedom of expression was restricted only to a very limited extent, namely as to forum. He was free to disseminate his views and information within the UK by other means of communication.

5.126 The Court of Appeal found that the judge had replaced his own evaluation of the relevant facts for that of the Secretary of State. The merits of the appeal were finely balanced, but the Secretary of State had provided sufficient explanation for a decision that turned on his personal, informed assessment of risk. He had demonstrated that his decision did not involve a disproportionate interference with freedom of expression. His decision struck a proportionate balance between the legitimate aim of the prevention of disorder and freedom of expression. Leave to appeal was refused by the House of Lords.[125]

Foreign cases

5.127 As with other qualified Articles, it is possible to rely on a feared breach of Article 10 in the destination country if there was a real risk of a flagrant denial or gross

---

[124] *R v Secretary of State for the Home Department, ex parte Daly* (2001) 2 WLR 1622.
[125] On 10 July 2002.

violation of the rights protected under that Article. The breach in the country of return would have to nullify or completely deny the very essence of the right for a claimant to successfully resist removal on the basis of this Article. The principles applied would be the same as those discussed earlier in the chapter concerning, in particular, Articles 5 and 6.

I. Article 12 and Article 14—Right to Marry and Prohibition of Discrimination

Article 12

ECHR Article 12 provides: **5.128**

> Men and women of marriageable age have the right to marry and to found a family, according to the national laws governing the exercise of this right.

The ECtHR interpretation of the right to marry being conferred on 'men and **5.129** women' has been held not to refer to the strictly biological interpretation of those terms.[126]

The right to marry is recognized as an important and fundamental right, not to be **5.130** lightly interfered with, although the right is not 'absolute' in nature in the way Article 3 is.[127]

The concluding words of Article 12, referring to 'national laws governing the **5.131** exercise of [the Article 12] right', do not allow State interference in marriages in the pursuit of other social goals. They simply relate to national laws promoting the institution of marriage, such as rules relating to bigamy or consanguinity.[128] The terms of the article itself, and the ECHR jurisprudence, recognize and support national laws that ensure that 'marriages' are proper and properly engaged in.[129]

Article 12 does not confer any right to marry in a particular country, even if the **5.132** parties are currently present in the country in which they wish to marry.[130] Immigration control, as an end, and the prohibition of marriages of convenience, as a means, have been regarded as legitimate.[131]

---

[126] *Goodwin v United Kingdom* (Application No 28957/95), 11 July 2002.
[127] *Hamer v United Kingdom* (1979) 4 EHRR 139, *F v Switzerland* (1987) 10 EHRR 411, and *Secretary of State for the Home Department v Baiai & Ors* [2007] EWCA Civ 478, para 29(i).
[128] *Secretary of State for the Home Department v Baiai & Ors* [2007] EWCA Civ 478, para 21.
[129] Ibid, para 29(ii).
[130] Ibid, para 29(iv).
[131] Ibid, para 29(iii).

5.133 However, a State is entitled to interfere only with marriages which are marriages of convenience and thus not genuine marriages. Inhibition of marriages of convenience can be seen as reinforcing, and not as undermining, Article 12's support for 'marriage'.[132] If a State did institute a policy of inhibiting genuine marriage, that would raise serious issues both under Article 12 and under immigration law.[133]

5.134 In *Secretary of State for the Home Department v Baiai & Ors*[134] the Court of Appeal found the Certificate of Approval scheme, set up by the Secretary of State to tackle abuse of the immigration system by marriages of convenience, to infringe Article 12. The Secretary of State was permitted to interfere with the exercise of Article 12 rights only in cases that involve, or very likely involve, sham marriages entered into with the object of improving the immigration status of one of the parties. To be proportionate, a scheme had to either properly investigate individual cases, or at least show that it had come close to isolating cases that very likely fall into the sham marriage category.

5.135 The criteria used, however, were not to be based on the assessment of the genuineness of a marriage, as the length of time for which a person has leave to remain in the UK does not necessarily or logically relate to the genuineness of the proposed marriage. Such a criterion was effectively a statutory presumption that a marriage involving a person with less than six months leave to stay was not a genuine marriage. The Administrative Court found, and the Court of Appeal agreed, that such blanket interference with Article 12 rights was disproportionate.

5.136 In 'foreign' cases, as with other qualified Articles, it is possible to rely on a feared breach of Article 12 in the destination country if there was a real risk of a flagrant denial or gross violation of the rights protected under that Article. The breach in the country of return would have to nullify or completely deny the very essence of the right for a claimant to successfully resist removal on the basis of this Article. The principles applied would be the same as those discussed earlier in the chapter concerning, in particular, Articles 5 and 6.

Article 14

5.137 ECHR Article 14 provides:

> The enjoyment of the rights and freedoms set forth in this Convention shall be secured without discrimination on any ground such as sex, race, colour, language, religion, political or other opinion, national or social origin, association with a national minority, property, birth or other status.

---

132 *Secretary of State for the Home Department v Baiai & Ors* [2007] EWCA Civ 478, para 29(vi).
133 Ibid, para 29(vi).
134 *Secretary of State for the Home Department v Baiai & Ors* [2007] EWCA Civ 478.

In the context of Article 14 discrimination means treating differently, without an **5.138** objective and reasonable justification, persons in relevantly similar situations.[135] However, not every difference in treatment will amount to a violation of Article 14. The applicant must establish that other persons in an analogous or relevantly similar situation enjoy preferential treatment and that this distinction is discriminatory.[136] It is only discrimination in connection with rights guaranteed under the Convention with which Article 14 is concerned, rather than a free standing and general right not to be discriminated against.

A difference of treatment is discriminatory for the purposes of Article 14 if it **5.139** has no objective and reasonable justification. A difference of treatment in the exercise of a right laid down by the Convention must not only pursue a legitimate aim, it must also satisfy the requirements of proportionality. Thus Article 14 will be violated when it is clearly established that there is no 'reasonable relationship of proportionality between the means employed and the aim sought to be realized'.[137]

Article 14 does not prohibit distinctions in treatment which are founded on an **5.140** objective assessment of essentially different factual circumstances and which, being based on the public interest, strike a fair balance between the protection of the interests of the community and respect for the rights and freedoms safeguarded by the Convention.[138]

As already indicated, the non-discrimination provisions of Article 14 relate only **5.141** to the enjoyment of Convention rights. Therefore any challenge based on Article 14 has to establish discrimination on one of the prohibited grounds in the exercise of another right enshrined in the ECHR. In dealing with an Article 14 claim, in conjunction with another ECHR article, the Court of Appeal in *Wandsworth LBC v Michalak*[139] has set the following guidelines as to the issues to be determined:

(i) Do the facts fall within the ambit of one or more of the substantive Convention provisions (for the relevant Convention rights see Human Rights Act 1998, section 1(1))?

(ii) If so, was there different treatment as respects that right between the complainant on the one hand and other persons put forward for comparison ('the chosen comparators') on the other?

---

135 *Willis v the United Kingdom*, no 36042/97, para 48, ECHR 2002-IV.
136 *Unal Tekeli v Turkey*, no 29865/96, para 49, 16 November 2004.
137 *Adami v Malta* (Application No 17209/02), Judgment, 20 June 2006, final on 20/09/2006.
138 Ibid.
139 *Wandsworth LBC v Michalak* [2002] EWCA Civ 271, [2003] 1 WLR 617.

(iii) Were the chosen comparators in an analogous situation to the complainant's situation?

(iv) If so, did the difference in treatment have an objective and reasonable justification: in other words, did it pursue a legitimate aim and did the differential treatment bear a reasonable relationship of proportionality to the aim sought to be achieved?[140]

5.142 The apparent overlap between questions (iii) and (iv) has come under criticism. For example, Lord Hoffmann in *R (Carson) v Secretary of State for Work and Pensions*[141] preferred to ask the single question: 'Is there enough of a relevant difference between X and Y to justify different treatment?'

5.143 In the European case law, discrimination contrary to Article 14 taken together with Article 8 was found in *Abdulaziz, Cabales and Balkandali v UK*.[142] The Immigration Rules applicable at the time unfairly discriminated against males wishing to join their female spouses in the UK, as compared with the reverse situation—females joining their male spouses in the UK.

5.144 A more recent example in the domestic context, involving discrimination in the exercise of the right to marry (Articles 12 and 14), related to the introduction of a new regime in relation to those who were subject to immigration control being able to enter into civil marriage.[143] The regime was introduced by the Asylum and Immigration (Treatment of Claimants, etc) Act 2004, sections 19 to 25, together with the Immigration (Procedure for Marriage) Regulations 2005[144] and the Immigration Directorate's Instructions. The aim of the regime was to prevent the abuse of immigration rights by sham marriages, ie marriages entered into solely in order to obtain leave or status under the immigration rules. The regime required that marriages involving a party subject to immigration control, as

---

[140] *Wandsworth LBC v Michalak* [2002] EWCA Civ 271, [2003] 1 WLR 617, para 20.

[141] *R (Carson) v Secretary of State for Work and Pensions* [2005] 2 WLR 1369, para 31.

[142] *Abdulaziz, Cabales and Balkandali v UK* (1985) 7 EHRR 471.

[143] Sections 19–25 of the Asylum and Immigration (Treatment of Claimants, etc) Act 2004 provide for additional procedures where a marriage is to be solemnized in the United Kingdom and a party to the marriage is subject to immigration control. Section 19(2)(a) provides that where a marriage is to be solemnized in England and Wales, the notices under section 27 of the Marriage Act 1949 must be given to the superintendent registrar of a registration district specified in regulations. In addition, by sections 19(3), 21(3), and 23(3), the registrar to whom notice is given may not enter notice of the marriage into the marriage book unless satisfied that the party subject to immigration control either (a) has an entry clearance granted for the purpose of enabling him to marry in the United Kingdom, (b) has the written permission of the Secretary of State to marry in the United Kingdom, or (c) falls within a class specified in regulations made by the Secretary of State. Section 25 enables the Secretary of State by regulations to make provision in relation to applications for permission to marry in the United Kingdom.

[144] Under the Immigration (Procedure for Marriage) Regulations 2005, a person seeking the permission of the Secretary of State to marry in the United Kingdom is required to make an application in writing, pay a fee, and provide extensive information.

defined by section 19(4)(a) of the 2004 Act, could not take place without a Certificate of Approval from the Secretary of State. The only marriages that fell outside the new regime were those according to the rites of the Church of England.

5.145 This regime came under challenge in *R (on the appln of Baiai & Ors) v SSHD & Anor*.[145] The claimants argued that the new regime disproportionately interfered with the right to marry under Article 12 and was discriminatory as it treated people in analogous positions differently, on the basis of their religion or nationality. The policy was defended by the SSHD on the basis that the maintenance of a system of immigration control was one of the recognised considerations of public interest, which could justify restricting the exercise of the right to marry.

5.146 The Administrative Court held that the regime introduced by the SSHD infringed Articles 12 and 14 of the ECHR. The Court of Appeal has confirmed the Article 12 finding (see *Secretary of State for the Home Department v Baiai & Ors*[146] and discussion under Article 12 above). The conclusion that the scheme infringed Article 14, taken together with Article 12, was not subject to appeal.

5.147 With regard to Article 14, the Administrative Court found as follows. There was also no objective basis for presuming that all marriages conducted in *religious* ceremonies other than the Church of England should be automatically treated as sham marriages and requiring of Certificates of Approval. The distinction between those who wished to marry in an Anglican religious ceremony as opposed to other religious ceremonies was not justifiable. No evidence was adduced to show that those who married in non-Anglican ceremonies were any more likely to engage in sham marriages than those who married in Anglican ceremonies. The new regime unfairly and unjustifiably discriminated on the basis of the personal characteristics of religion and nationality, contrary to Articles 12 and 14.

J. Article 8 and Article 14—Right to Respect for Family and Private Life and Prohibition of Discrimination

5.148 A challenge to the Home Office 'Family Indefinite Leave to Remain Exercise' on the basis of Article 8 and Article 14 was unsuccessful in *AL (Serbia) v SSHD*[147]

---

[145] *R (on the appln of Baiai & Ors) v SSHD & Anor* [2006] EWHC 823 (Admin), (2007) 1 WLR 693, (2006) 3 All ER 608.

[146] *Secretary of State for the Home Department v Baiai & Ors* [2007] EWCA Civ 478.

[147] *AL (Serbia) v SSHD* [2006] EWCA Civ 1619.

and in *Rudi and Ibrahimi v SSHD.*[148] The claimants challenged the policy on the basis that it discriminated unlawfully against unaccompanied minors.

5.149 In *AL (Serbia)* the Court of Appeal held that according benefits to a person because he was a member of a family and refusing similar benefits to someone who was not would fall within the ambit of Article 14. However, the discrimination had been justified, as the family amnesty policy had been implemented to cut costs and reduce the burden on the system. The practical and economic reasons underpinning the policy did not apply to single asylum seekers. That rationale of the policy was specifically in relation to families, as they had an incentive to delay removal with sequential applications, and resulted in large support costs. The policy had not been designed to exclude unaccompanied minors.

5.150 In *Rudi and Ibrahimi* a slightly different aspect of the policy came under challenge. The applicants, unaccompanied minors on arrival but who had turned 18, could not benefit from the policy, whereas had they been a part of a family unit in October 2003 they would have been eligible for indefinite leave to remain. The High Court accepted the Secretary of State's assertion that most of the persons benefiting under the policy comprised individuals living as a family unit in the same household. Therefore there was a rationale for the difference in treatment between young adults who had arrived as accompanied minors and those who had not. The latter category, which included the claimants, was more easily removable as there were no family connections, and employment was less likely to remove a family from dependency on public resources.

K. Practice and Procedure Note

Home Office policies on leave to be granted following a successful human rights claim

5.151 Since the abolition of exceptional leave to remain from 1 April 2003, there have been two possible types of leave granted following a successful human rights claim—Humanitarian Protection and Discretionary Leave. The residual category of Leave Outside the Rules has also remained. Finally, there is a further category of Temporary Protection, for which limited leave to enter or remain will be granted.

---

[148] *Rudi and Ibrahimi v SSHD* [2007] EWHC 60.

Humanitarian Protection

Humanitarian Protection (HP) has been consolidated into the Immigration Rules. **5.152**
Granting HP is governed by paragraphs 339C and E of the Immigration Rules (IR). The
conditions for the grant of HP[149] are that the Secretary of State is satisfied that:

(i) a person is in the United Kingdom or has arrived at a port of entry in the United
Kingdom;

(ii) he does not qualify as a refugee as defined in regulation 2 of The Refugee or
Person in Need of International Protection (Qualification) Regulations 2006;[150]

(iii) substantial grounds have been shown for believing that the person concerned, if
he returned to the country of return, would face a real risk of suffering serious
harm and is unable or, owing to such risk, unwilling to avail himself of the protection
of that country; and

(iv) he is not excluded from a grant of humanitarian protection.

Serious harm is defined in IR para 339C as consisting of: **5.153**

(i) the death penalty or execution;

(ii) unlawful killing;

(iii) torture or inhuman or degrading treatment or punishment of a person in the
country of return; or

(iv) serious and individual threat to a civilian's life or person by reason of indiscriminate violence in situations of international or internal armed conflict.

Therefore Humanitarian Protection would be granted in the majority of cases where **5.154**
an Article 2 or an Article 3 claim succeeds. There are, however, some important exceptions to this. The current Home Office policy should be consulted for the details of
such exceptions. At the time of writing the Home Office Asylum Policy Instructions on
Humanitarian Protection (API/October 2006, Version 4101006—see appendix) provides for the following Article 2 and 3 cases where HP would not be granted:

a. Cases where despite a successful Article 2 or Article 3 claim, Humanitarian
Protection is excluded under Rule 339D (see 'Exclusion criteria' section below).

b. Article 3 claims based on prison conditions where there is a real risk of imprisonment in conditions which reach the threshold for Article 3, but the reason for the
imprisonment falls within the Exclusion Criteria. In such a case the appropriate
leave to grant would be Discretionary Leave.

c. Article 3 claims based on the applicant's medical condition. Such cases may qualify
for Discretionary Leave.

---

[149] IR, para 339C.
[150] Broadly, 'a refugee' is a person who falls within Article 1(A) of the Geneva Convention and is
not excluded by Articles 1D, 1E, or 1F of that Convention.

d. 'Other severe humanitarian conditions meeting the Article 3 threshold.' The examples given in the API relate to the general conditions in the country of return, such as the absence of water, food or basic shelter. Such cases would only fall for consideration of Discretionary Leave.

5.155 Eligibility for HP should be considered only after any application for asylum has been considered.[151] HP is granted for a period of five years.[152] Those granted HP on or after 30 August 2005 have the right to family reunion immediately.[153] By comparison, those granted HP before 30 August 2005 will normally become entitled to family reunion once the sponsor has obtained indefinite leave to remain, which for those cases would usually occur after three years of HP leave.[154]

Settlement

5.156 Persons who have completed five years' Humanitarian Protection leave will be eligible for indefinite leave to remain (ie settlement). Where a person has held leave on grounds other than HP, the qualifying periods are as follows:

a. leave on HP grounds and Refugee Leave in any combination: five years;
b. leave on HP grounds and Discretionary Leave in any combination: six years (save where exclusion from HP results in Discretionary Leave—then the minimum period is ten years).[155]

It is important that the application for settlement is made in time, ie before the HP leave expires. Should the application be made out of time, a full review will be conducted to determine whether the person still qualifies for HP, whereas no such review is done for in-time applications.[156]

Exclusion criteria

5.157 A person will not be eligible for Humanitarian Protection if:[157]

(i) there are serious reasons for considering that he has committed a crime against peace, a war crime, a crime against humanity, or *any other serious crime*, or instigated or otherwise participated in such crimes;
(ii) there are serious reasons for considering that he is guilty of acts contrary to the purposes and principles of the United Nations or has committed, prepared,

---

[151] See Home Office Asylum Policy Instructions on Humanitarian Protection (API/October 2006, Version 4101006), Part 3, p 7.
[152] Paragraph 339E of the Immigration Rules.
[153] See Home Office Asylum Policy Instructions on Humanitarian Protection (API/October 2006, Version 4101006), p 5.
[154] Ibid.
[155] See Home Office Asylum Policy Instructions on Humanitarian Protection (API/October 2006, Version 4101006), Part 9, p 21.
[156] Ibid.
[157] IR para 339D.

or instigated such acts or encouraged or induced others to commit, prepare, or instigate such acts;

(iii) there are serious reasons for considering that he constitutes *a danger to the community or to the security of the United Kingdom*; and

(iv) prior to his admission to the United Kingdom the person committed a crime outside the scope of (i) and (ii) that would be punishable by imprisonment were it committed in the United Kingdom and the person left his country of origin solely in order to avoid sanctions resulting from the crime. (See further discussion below of italicised terms.)

A serious crime. The Home Office Policy Instructions[158] define a 'serious crime' as:

(a) one for which a custodial sentence of at least 12 months has been imposed in the UK; or **5.158**

(b) a crime serious enough to exclude the person from being a refugee in accordance with Article 1F(b) of the Refugee Convention; or

(c) conviction for an offence listed in an order made under section 72 NIAA 2002 ('particularly serious crimes').

A danger to the community or to the security of the United Kingdom. The **5.159** Home Office Asylum Policy Instructions on Humanitarian Protection (API/October 2006, Version 4101006) give an indicative but non-exhaustive list of who may be considered to present 'a danger to the community or to the security of the United Kingdom':

(a) Those included on the Sex Offenders Register.

(b) Those whose presence in the UK is deemed not conducive to the public good by the Secretary of State (for example, on national security grounds, because of their character, conduct or associations).

(c) Those who engage in one or more 'unacceptable behaviours' whether in the UK or abroad. The policy states that:'The list of unacceptable behaviours includes using any means or medium . . . to express views which:

- foment, justify or glorify terrorist violence in furtherance of particular beliefs;
- seek to provoke others to terrorist acts;
- foment other serious criminal activity or seek to provoke others to serious criminal acts; or
- foster hatred which may lead to inter-community violence in the UK.'

---

[158] See Home Office Asylum Policy Instructions on Humanitarian Protection (API/October 2006, Version 4101006—see appendix).

Revocation of humanitarian protection

5.160   Under paragraph 339G of the Immigration Rules HP will be revoked or not renewed if:

- *paragraph 339G (i):* the circumstances which led to the grant of HP have ceased to exist or have changed to such a degree that such protection is no longer required. The change of circumstances has to be of such a significant and non-temporary nature that the person no longer faces a real risk of serious harm;
- *paragraph 339G (ii)–(iv) and (vi):* the person granted HP should have been or is excluded from Humanitarian Protection (see the 'Exclusion criteria section' above);
- *paragraph 339G (v):* the person granted HP misrepresented or omitted facts, including the use of false documents, which were decisive to the grant of HP.

Discretionary leave

5.161   Discretionary leave is currently governed by the Home Office Asylum Policy Instruction on Discretionary Leave (see appendix). Discretionary Leave may be granted:

(a) in cases where the return of an individual would involve a breach of Article 8 of the ECHR (right to respect for private and family life) on the basis of family life established in the UK. This category applies to both asylum and non-asylum cases;

(b) in cases where return would breach Article 3 of the ECHR but where Humanitarian Protection is not applicable;

(c) in other cases where the Article 3 breach does not arise from a need for protection, eg where a person's medical condition or severe humanitarian conditions in the country of return would make return contrary to Article 3;

(d) in other cases where return would breach the ECHR. This category applies to asylum and non-asylum cases where the breach would not give rise to a grant of Humanitarian Protection and is not covered by the categories above. For example, where return would result in a flagrant denial of an ECHR right in the person's country of origin;

(e) for unaccompanied asylum-seeking children (UASCs). If they do not qualify for asylum or Humanitarian Protection, they will qualify for Discretionary Leave if there are inadequate reception arrangements available in their own country. Where an unaccompanied child qualifies for Discretionary Leave on more than one ground (ie on the ground of inadequate reception arrangements and also on another ground), they should be granted leave on the basis of the ground that provides the longer period of stay;

(f) in a residual category of 'other cases'.

Discretionary Leave will normally be given for three years. This policy is subject to several exceptions: **5.162**

(a) *UASCs*: Where leave is granted to a UASC on the basis of inadequate reception arrangements in their home country, the UASC should be granted DL. For decisions made before 1 April 2007 this grant of DL will be for three years or leave until age 18, whichever is the shorter.[159] For all decisions made on or after 1 April 2007, where asylum/HP is being refused, DL must be granted only to the age of 17.5 years or 3 years (or 12 months for certain countries), whichever is the shorter period of time.

(b) *Those excluded from Humanitarian Protection* will be granted six months' Discretionary Leave. The same six-month time period applies to any subsequent grants following an active review.

(c) *Case-specific short Discretionary Leave*. Cases where it is *clear* from the particular circumstances that the factors leading to Discretionary Leave being granted are going to be short lived.[160] A shorter period of leave will be appropriate in such cases, with the reasons for granting such shorter period to be included in the letter to the applicant.

Finally, the policy contemplates that where return would be possible within six months **5.163** of the date of decision 'it will normally be appropriate to refuse the claim outright, not to grant a period of Discretionary Leave, and to defer any removal until such time as it is possible'. The practical implementation of this policy contemplates as an alternative to granting discretionary leave the giving of an undertaking 'not to remove the individual or expect them to return until the circumstances preventing their return have changed'.[161] However, in appellate proceedings the Court of Appeal has ruled that the AIT cannot rely on such an undertaking, and must decide on the evidence at the date of the hearing on the substantive question of the infringement of an ECHR right on return and the appropriate discretionary leave.[162] As cases decided under this part of the policy cannot succeed on appeal, the lawfulness of this part of the policy may also be subject to challenge.

Exclusion from Discretionary Leave?

The Discretionary Leave API policy speaks of the grounds for exclusion from **5.164** Humanitarian Protection applying also to Discretionary Leave. However, it is difficult

---

[159] Or the shorter of 12 months or leave until age 18 in certain specified countries.

[160] Eg an Article 8 case where a person is permitted to stay because of the presence of a family member in the UK, where it is known that the family member will be able to leave the UK within, say, 12 months; or a case where a grant of leave is appropriate to enable a person to stay in the UK to participate in a court case.

[161] Home Office Asylum Policy Instructions on Humanitarian Protection.

[162] *MS (Ivory Coast) v SSHD* [2007] EWCA Civ 133, 22 February 2007.

to see how it could be said that those excluded from HP are also excluded from Discretionary Leave, when the latter is the specific remedy which is to be applied to avoid a breach of the UK's ECHR obligations in those excluded cases and the API specifically provides for a usual period of Discretionary Leave to be given in such cases (six months). The API attempts to resolve this friction as follows:

> The grounds for exclusion from Humanitarian Protection will apply to Discretionary Leave. . . . A person who is excluded from Discretionary Leave will be expected to leave the UK. Where neither enforced nor voluntary return is possible without material prejudice to the rights protected under this instruction, Discretionary Leave will usually be granted for six months.

5.165 It is perhaps more appropriate to describe Discretionary Leave as applying to cases excluded from Humanitarian Protection. However, as the leave is discretionary, not only is the usual three-year leave period not applicable but in certain exceptional cases Discretionary Leave may not be granted.

5.166 The Secretary of State is expected to follow the terms of the Discretionary Leave policy, and departures from it can be subject to legal challenge. For example, in *R (on the appln of S & Ors) v SSHD*[163] ('the Afghan hijackers case'), the Court of Appeal held that the statutory scheme of immigration control postulated that someone who successfully maintained that his removal would amount to a violation of his ECHR rights should be entitled to leave to remain for however limited a period. Hence it was not open to the Secretary of State to place the appellants on temporary admission, a status inappropriate to their position. He had to grant them Discretionary Leave.

Settlement

5.167 Before being eligible to apply for indefinite leave to remain/settlement, persons granted Discretionary Leave will need to complete at least six years' leave in total. In cases excluded from refugee and/or humanitarian protection, this period is at least ten years.

5.168 However, settlement may be denied in the excluded cases, where Ministers decide in the light of all the circumstances of the case that the person's presence in the United Kingdom is not conducive to the public good. Where it is not possible to remove the person, a further period of Discretionary Leave would be granted. In such a case, for so long as the individual remains in the UK, a fresh decision will be taken at least every three years on whether settlement should continue to be denied.

5.169 Any period spent in prison in connection with a criminal conviction will not count towards the qualifying period for settlement of six (or ten) years.

---

[163] *R (on the appln of S & Ors) v SSHD* [2006] EWCA Cov 1157, 9 October 2006, The Times.

Temporary protection

Temporary Protection is a further category of leave which has been incorporated into **5.170** the Immigration Rules (Part 11A). It stems from the Temporary Protection Directive,[164] a European-wide measure to afford protection by Member States in the event of a mass influx of displaced persons. In accordance with Rule 355C the Secretary of State would grant limited leave to enter or remain, allowing employment, for a period not exceeding 12 months. Applicants can request six-monthly extensions thereafter. To be granted temporary protection the Secretary of State has to be satisfied that:[165]

(i) the applicant is in the United Kingdom or has arrived at a port of entry in the United Kingdom; and

(ii) the applicant is a person entitled to temporary protection as defined by, and in accordance with, the Temporary Protection Directive; and

(iii) the applicant does not hold an extant grant of temporary protection entitling him to reside in another Member State of the European Union. This requirement is subject to the provisions relating to dependants set out in paragraphs 356 to 356B and to any agreement to the contrary with the Member State in question; and

(iv) the applicant is not excluded from temporary protection under the provisions in paragraph 355A.

If a person makes an asylum claim, the asylum claim has to be considered before the **5.171** question of granting Humanitarian Protection or Discretionary Leave arises. However, in contrast, if the applicant is also eligible for temporary protection, the Secretary of State may decide not to consider the asylum application until the applicant ceases to be entitled to temporary protection.[166]

Leave outside the rules

This category of Leave Outside the Rules (LOTR) is applied outside asylum or protection **5.172** cases. The Immigration Directorate's Instructions (April 2006), Chapter 1, Section 14,[167] give only two circumstances where it will be necessary to consider granting LOTR, namely:

(a) where someone qualifies under one of the immigration policy concessions;[168] or

(b) for reasons that are particularly compelling in circumstance.

---

[164] Council Directive 2001/55/EC of 20 July 2001.

[165] Rule 355.

[166] Rule 355G.

[167] Cited in *MS (Ivory Coast) v SSHD* [2007] EWCA Civ 133, 22 February 2007, at paras 44–45, see <http://www.ind.homeoffice.gov.uk/documents/idischapter1/section14.pdf?view=Binary>.

[168] Listed in Annex A to The Immigration Directorate's Instructions (April 2006), Chapter 1, Section 14—IMMIGRATION POLICY CONCESSIONS.

Documentation

5.173 A UK Residence Permit (UKRP) is a secure vignette, based on a common EU format, which is issued in the claimant's passport or status document and must be accompanied by a photograph. UKRP is issued to those granted refugee status, humanitarian protection, and discretionary leave. In the case of refugees, it is held in the Immigration Status Document. For applicants granted Humanitarian Protection or Discretionary Leave, the UKRP is to be held in the national passport if available, and otherwise in the Immigration Status Document. For further guidance on the documentation processing, including requests for National Insurance number, practitioners are referred to the Home Office Asylum Policy Notice (APN) 08/2006—'Guidance for issuing status documentation for grants of leave including further guidance for cases where no photographs have been provided'.[169]

Please note: It is planned to incorporate these immigration policy concessions into the proposed Points Based System, as outlined in the Five-Year Strategy for Asylum and Immigration. In the interim, advice on each concession should be obtained from the relevant policy lead.

- Airline staff
- BUNAC students
- Carers of seriously ill or disabled relatives
- Civilian personnel in foreign armed forces based in UK
- Employees of firms under contract to NATO
- Entertainers
- EU Leonardo da Vinci programme
- Film crew on location
- Japan Youth Exchange Scheme
- Jewish Agency employees
- Knowledge exchange category
- Medical treatment under the NHS—bilateral healthcare arrangements
- Medical treatment under the NHS—specific treatment arrangements
- Off-shore workers
- Over-age dependants of intra-company transfer work permit holders
- Overseas lawyers
- Pestalozzi Children's Trust
- Research assistants to MPs
- Representatives of overseas insurance companies
- St George's University School of Medicine
- Sportspersons

[169] <http://www.ind.homeoffice.gov.uk/documents/implementingandservingdecision/guidance/guidanceforissuingstatusdocs.pdf?view=Binary>.

6

RIGHTS OF APPEAL

A. Old Rights of Appeal

6.01 The first system for adjudicating immigration appeals was introduced by the Immigration Appeals Act 1969. This brought in a two-tier system of appeals which survived, albeit in a considerably altered form, until the introduction of a one-tier system by the Asylum and Immigration (Treatment of Claimants Act) 2004. Only Commonwealth citizens had the right of appeal under the 1969 Act. The Immigration Act 1971 was the first piece of legislation to provide a right of appeal to aliens and repealed almost all previous immigration legislation. The 1971 Act did not, however, deal with asylum. Rules made under the 1971 Act provided that when a person made a claim for asylum, full account should be taken of the United Kingdom's obligations under the Refugee Convention 1951.

6.02 The next major piece of legislation to be enacted in this area was the Asylum and Immigration Appeals Act 1993 which established, as the name suggests, a system for asylum appeals. The 1993 Act provided an in-country appeal for all asylum seekers and an accelerated appeals procedure for those asylum seekers who had travelled through a safe third country.

The Asylum and Immigration Act 1996 provided for further categories of asylum   **6.03**
seeker to be subject to the accelerated appeals procedure. Regulations introduced
a 'white-list' of countries which were deemed to be safe, although some countries
were subsequently held by the courts to be unlawfully designated.

The Immigration and Asylum Act 1999 introduced the 'one-stop' appeal system,   **6.04**
the purpose of which was to ensure that all issues relating to a person's (and their
family's) entitlement to stay in the United Kingdom be dealt with in one appeal.
It also introduced a free-standing appeal to an adjudicator where a person alleged
that a decision under the Immigration Acts relating to his entitlement to enter or
remain in the United Kingdom breached his human rights or racially discriminated against him.[1] The bringing of an appeal based on these grounds suspended
removal in all cases save where the asylum claimant was to be removed to a safe
third country or another EU member state and the Secretary of State certified as
manifestly unfounded a claim that removal would breach the claimant's human
rights.[2]

The Nationality, Immigration and Asylum Act 2002 re-structured the appeals   **6.05**
system to define and group together specific immigration decisions which attract
a right of appeal and the grounds of appeal which lie against them. The 2002 Act
also introduced a certification regime which removed suspensive appeal rights
from those whose claims were certified as manifestly unfounded.[3] It also listed a
series of countries, added to by statutory instrument, which were deemed safe for
returns. Prior to the 2002 Act, if the Immigration Appeal Tribunal refused permission to appeal the remedy was judicial review. The 2002 Act introduced 'statutory
review' which was a review on the papers only and subject to more restrictive time
limits than judicial review.[4] Prior to the 2002 Act, the jurisdiction of the Tribunal
allowed for appeals on the basis of an error of fact or law. The 2002 Act curtailed
the jurisdiction of the Tribunal to a point of law only.[5]

B. The Current Appeals System

The Asylum and Immigration (Treatment of Claimant's Act) 2004 (the 2004   **6.06**
Act) introduced a single-tier appellate system. From 4 April 2005 all appeals, save
for those caught by transitional provisions and those involving national security,
go to the Asylum and Immigration Tribunal (AIT). The 2004 Act provides that

---

[1] IAA 1999 s 65 as amended by the Race Relations (Amendment) Act 2000.
[2] Sections 11 and 12, Immigration and Asylum Act 1999 (IAA 1999).
[3] Section 94, Nationality, Immigration and Asylum Act 2002 (NIAA 2002).
[4] Section 101(2) NIAA 2002.
[5] Section 101 (1) NIAA 2002.

appeals may be heard either by a single member or by a panel of members depending on the complexity and other circumstances of the case.[6]

6.07 If a person is the subject of an 'immigration decision' as defined by section 82 of the 2002 Act they have a right of appeal to the AIT. A right of appeal also exists under sections 83 and 83 A of the 2002 Act on asylum grounds only. The Immigration (European Economic Area) Regulations 2006 also provide for a right of appeal to the AIT.[7]

6.08 Some appeal rights are exercisable only whilst the appellant is in the United Kingdom and some only from abroad. These are referred to as suspensive (or in-country) and non-suspensive appeal rights, as the effect of reliance on certain grounds of appeal is to suspend any action to remove the appellant from the United Kingdom.

6.09 The grounds of appeal on which the appellant may rely are contained in section 84 of the 2002 Act. The appellant may rely on one or a number of these grounds depending on the nature of his application. The grounds of appeal that may be relied on are, however, limited by sections 88–92 of the 2002 Act.

6.10 The powers of the AIT in determining an appeal are contained in section 86 of the 2002 Act. The matters which the AIT must consider in determining an appeal are set out at section 85 of the 2002 Act. Where the AIT allows an appeal, section 87 gives the power to make a direction for the purpose of giving effect to its decision. We deal with the jurisdiction of the AIT at paragraph 6.113 below.

6.11 Thereafter, in all cases save for where the decision was made by three or more qualified members, a party may apply for a review of the Tribunal's decision to the High Court on the grounds that the Tribunal made an error of law (s 103 A of the 2004 Act). If the Tribunal that made the decision consisted of three or more legally qualified members, the appeal lies to the Court of Appeal on a point of law (s 103E of the 2004 Act). On an appeal under section 103A, the High Court may order the Tribunal to reconsider its decision if it thinks the Tribunal has made an error of law, or if it thinks the appeal raises a question of law of such importance that it should be decided by the Court of Appeal, may refer the appeal to that Court (s 103C). An appeal from the Tribunal following reconsideration under section 103A(1) or after remittal to the Tribunal under sections 103C, 103B, or 103 E lies on the application of a party to the Court of Appeal on a point of law (s 103B).

6.12 The rules which govern the procedure to be followed by the Tribunal are to be found in the Asylum and Immigration Tribunal (Procedure) Rules 2005

---

[6] NIAA 2002, Sch 4, para 7 (substituted by the Asylum and Immigration (Treatment of claimants, etc) Act 2004 (AIA 2004), s 26 from 4 April 2005 (SI 2005/565)).

[7] The Immigration (European Economic Area) Regulations 2006, regs 26, 27.

(as amended)[8] and the Asylum and Immigration Tribunal (Fast Track Procedure) Rules 2005 (as amended).[9] Rules governing the service of notices are contained in the Immigration (Notices Regulations) 2003.[10]

C. Rights of Appeal

The decisions which attract a right of appeal are set out at sections 82 and 83 and **6.13** 83A of the Nationality, Immigration and Asylum Act 2002 (as amended by the 2004 and 2006 Acts). In short, subject to the limitations and exceptions set out below, the following decisions attract a right of appeal:

(1) an immigration decision as defined under section 82 of the 2002 Act;
(2) a refusal of asylum under section 83 of the 2002 Act where a person has been granted leave to enter or remain for a period exceeding one year or for periods exceeding one year in aggregate;
(3) a decision to curtail or refuse to extend limited leave granted to a refugee where a decision has been taken that he is no longer a refugee and he has limited leave to enter or remain otherwise than as a refugee (s 83A of the 2002 Act as inserted by the 2006 Act[11]);
(4) a decision by the Secretary of State to make an order depriving a person of his citizenship;[12]
(5) an EEA decision.[13]

Appeals against all of the decisions listed in the above paragraph are usually made **6.14** to the AIT. There are a number of people for whom an appeal lies instead to the Special Immigration Appeals Commission because of the political or national security grounds of their decision.

Nationality, Immigration and Asylum Act 2002

It is only an 'immigration' decision, as defined under section 82, that gives rise to **6.15** a right of appeal. The decisions in Table 6.1 are immigration decisions for the purposes of section 82 of the 2002 Act.

---

[8] SI 2005, No 230 from 4 April 2005 (as amended by SI 2005/569 from 4 April 2005, SI 2006/2788 from 13 November 2006 and SI 2007/835 from 10 April 2007).

[9] SI 2005, No 560 as amended by SI 2006/2789 from 13 November 2006 and SI 2006/2898 from 27 November 2006.

[10] SI 2003, No 658 as amended by SI 2006/2168.

[11] Section 1 from 31 August 2006 (SI 2006/2226) in respect of decisions made on after that date (by virtue of Article 4 of SI 2006/2226).

[12] Section 40A British Nationality Act 1981 (inserted by NIAA 2002, s 4).

[13] As defined in s 2 Immigration (European Economic Area) Regulations 2006.

Table 6.1 Immigration decisions that give rise to a right of appeal

- Refusal of leave to enter the United Kingdom (s 82(2)(a)).
- Refusal of entry clearance (s 82 (2)(b)).
- Refusal of a certificate of entitlement to the right to abode under section 10 of the 2002 Act (s 82 (2)(c)).
- Refusal to vary a person's leave to enter or remain in the United Kingdom if the result of the refusal is that the person has no leave to enter or remain (s 82(2)(d)).
- Variation of a person's leave to enter or remain in the United Kingdom if when the variation takes effect the person has no leave to enter or remain (s 82(2)(e)).
- Revocation under section 76 of the 2002 Act of indefinite leave to enter or remain in the United Kingdom (s 82(2)(f)).
- A decision that a person is to be removed from the United Kingdom by way of directions under [section 10(1)(a), (b) (ba) or (c)] of the Immigration and Asylum Act 1999 (s 82(2)(g)) (ie as a person who has breached the conditions of his leave to enter or remain or is an overstayer; as a person who has obtained or sought to obtain leave to remain by deception; as a person who has had his indefinite leave to enter or remain revoked under section 76 (3) of the 2002 Act (person ceasing to be a refugee) or as the family member of someone being removed on these grounds) (s 82(2)(g)), *words in square brackets substituted by Immigration, Asylum and Nationality Act 2006, section 2 from 31 August 2006 (SI 2006/2226) in respect of decisions made on or after that date.*
- A decision that an illegal entrant is to be removed from the United Kingdom by way of directions under paragraphs 8 to 10 of Schedule 2 to the Immigration Act 1971 (s 82(2)(h)).
- A decision that an illegal entrant is to be removed from the United Kingdom by way of directions under section 47 of the Immigration, Asylum and Nationality Act 2006 (removal: persons with statutorily extended leave) (s 82(2)(ha), *inserted by section 47 of that Act from a date to be appointed.*
- A decision that a person is to be removed from the United Kingdom by way of directions given by virtue of paragraph 10A of Schedule 2 to the Immigration Act 1971 ((ie as a family member of a person removed as an illegal entrant or after refusal of leave to enter) (s 82(2)(i)).
- A decision that a person is to be removed from the United Kingdom by way of directions given under paragraph 12 (2) of Schedule 2 to the Immigration Act 1971 (c77) (seamen and aircrews) (s 82(2)(ia)), *inserted by the Asylum and Immigration (Treatment of Claimants, etc) Act 2004, section 26 from 4 April 2005 (SI 2005/565).*

Table 6.1   *Cont.*

- A decision to make an order depriving someone of the right of abode under section 2A of the 1971 Act (s 82(2)(ib)), *inserted by section 57 of the 2006 Act from 16 June 2006 (SI 2006/1497).*

- A decision to make a deportation order under section 5(1) of the 1971 Act (s 82(2)(j)).

- Refusal to revoke a deportation order under section 5(2) of the 1971 Act (s 82(2)(k)).

Asylum appeals
Under Section 82

6.16   The refusal of asylum is not an 'immigration decision' for the purposes of section 82 and hence is not an appealable decision per se under this section. An asylum applicant will have a right of appeal under this section only if the refusal of asylum is accompanied by a relevant 'immigration decision' or when an 'immigration decision' is made at a later date. He may then bring his appeal under section 84(g) on the basis that his removal from the United Kingdom in consequence of the immigration decision would breach the United Kingdom's obligations under the Refugee Convention.

6.17   There is, however, a free-standing right of appeal against the refusal of asylum under sections 83 and 83A of the 2002 Act (as amended). An appeal lies under section 83 where the Secretary of State has rejected a person's asylum claim, but has granted him leave to enter or remain for a period exceeding one year, or for periods exceeding one year in aggregate. Section 83A applies where a person is no longer recognised as a refugee but is allowed to stay in the United Kingdom on another, limited, basis. We deal with appeals under these sections below.

6.18   The nature of the decision on the applicant's claim for asylum will depend on the nature of the applicant's status. Applications for asylum at port where the applicant has not legally entered the United Kingdom are treated as applications for leave to enter and hence the decision accompanying the refusal would be a refusal of leave to enter. Applications for asylum in country where the applicant has existing leave are treated as applications to vary leave and hence the decision accompanying the refusal would be a refusal to vary leave or a decision to curtail limited leave (see below). Where a person has entered illegally or has overstayed their existing leave then the decision will be the decision to remove by way of removal directions.

6.19   Not all of these decisions will be immigration decisions for the purpose of section 82 giving rise to a right of appeal. The following are examples of decisions accompanying a refusal of asylum which do not give rise to a right of appeal: a refusal to vary leave where a person still has leave to enter or remain after the refusal (but an appeal may lie under section 83 if the period or periods of leave exceed one year); a decision to refuse an overstayer or illegal entrant asylum where no accompanying decision to remove is made.

Under Section 83

6.20 This section reads:

> (1) This section applies where a person has made an asylum claim and:
>
> (a) his claim has been rejected by the Secretary of State, but
>
> (b) he has been granted leave to enter or remain in the United Kingdom for a period exceeding one year (or for periods exceeding one year in aggregate).
>
> (2) The person may appeal to the Tribunal against the rejection of his asylum claim.

6.21 In other words, where the Secretary of State has rejected a person's asylum claim but has granted him leave to enter or remain for a period exceeding one year, or for periods exceeding one year in aggregate, he may appeal to the Tribunal on asylum grounds.

6.22 The purpose of this section is to allow a person refused asylum but granted some form of leave of the appropriate length to contend that they should be recognised as a refugee. These appeals have come to be known as 'upgrade' appeals.

6.23 It is important to note that 'leave' for the purposes of section 83 means any kind of leave that has been granted.[14] Hence a person granted a period or periods of limited leave exceeding one year as a student, spouse, or visitor as well as someone granted indefinite leave to remain may appeal under this section. The trigger for the appeal is the period of leave granted. Since the grant of leave must exceed one year, a person granted leave to enter for a period of 12 twelve months or two periods of six months would qualify only after a further extension of leave.[15]

6.24 It is also important to note that the leave must be 'granted' to qualify under this section. Therefore an extension of leave under sections 3C and 3D of the 1971 Act (as amended) does not count towards the period of leave required. These sections of the 1971 Act allow for leave to continue pending a decision on or an appeal against an application to vary leave, and an appeal against a curtailment or revocation of leave respectively. Since leave under these sections is extended rather than granted it does not count towards the required period.

6.25 Some commentators have suggested that it is unclear from the wording of section 83 whether leave granted before the refusal of asylum counts towards the

---

[14] Asylum Policy Instructions (APIs) Appeals—Rights of Appeal in asylum cases (July 2006), para 2.

[15] APIs Appeals—Rights of Appeal in asylum cases, para 2.2.

period required to trigger an appeal or whether it is only leave granted after the refusal that triggers the appeal. Any ambiguity in the wording of the section is unlikely to cause litigation due to the interpretation given to the section in the Immigration and Nationality Directorate's Asylum Policy Instructions. The Asylum Policy Instruction (API/July 2006) states:

> An appeal under section 83 arises in two main cases:
> - When a decision to grant leave to someone who has been (or is being) refused asylum will take the total period of leave granted to over a year, and
> - When a decision is made to refuse asylum to a person who has already been granted leave for over a year.[16]

It is clear, therefore, that periods of leave granted before the refusal of asylum will be counted towards the requirement. **6.26**

An appeal under section 83 is on asylum grounds only. This is because section 84 (3) states that an appeal under section 83 must be brought on the grounds that the removal of the appellant from the United Kingdom would breach the United Kingdom's obligations under the Refugee Convention.[17] **6.27**

Under section 83A

This section was inserted into the 2002 Act by the 2006 Act and applies only to decisions made on or after 31 August 2006. It reads: **6.28**

(1) This section applies where –
    (a) a person has made an asylum claim,
    (b) he was granted limited leave to enter or remain in the United Kingdom as a refugee within the meaning of the Refugee Convention,
    (c) a decision is made that he is not a refugee, and
    (d) following the decision specified in paragraph (c) he has limited leave to enter or remain in the United Kingdom otherwise than as a refugee.
(2) The person may appeal to the Tribunal against the decision to curtail or to refuse to extend his leave.

From 30 August 2005 the Secretary of State changed his policy on the type of leave granted to refugees. Whilst the recognition of a refugee had previously been followed by a grant of indefinite leave to remain, all grants of leave after the above date are of five years leave to enter or remain. It is only after five years that a refugee becomes eligible for settlement.[18] This leave is reviewed in certain circumstances.[19] **6.29**

---

16 API Appeals, as above, para 2.1.

17 *LA (Section 83(2) appeals–human rights) Eritrea* [2004] UK IAT 00113, reported.

18 API on Refugee Leave (October 2006)—refugees will normally be granted five years leave to enter under paragraphs 330 and 335 of the Immigration Rules (para 2.5 API).

19 API on Refugee Leave—triggers for review are on the basis of actions or alleged actions of individual refugees, where there has been a significant and non-temporary change in the conditions in a

6.30 Where a decision is made that someone is no longer a refugee it would normally be accompanied by an immigration decision giving rise to a right of appeal under section 82 (2).[20] This purpose of section 83A is to give a right of appeal on asylum grounds to someone who is no longer recognised as a refugee but granted limited leave to enter or remain on another basis.

6.31 The 'limited leave' for the purposes of this section is any kind of limited leave granted and includes limited discretionary leave granted outside the Immigration Rules.[21]

6.32 An appeal under section 83A can be brought on asylum grounds only (section 84 (4) as inserted by the 2006 Act). As with section 83, this section applies only in respect of decisions made on or after 31 August 2006.

Human rights and race discrimination

6.33 There is no free-standing right of appeal under the 2002 Act against a decision which is incompatible with a person's human rights or racially discriminatory. This contrasts with the position under the 1999 Act where a person could appeal a decision 'relating' to his 'entitlement to enter or remain in the UK'(section 65) on the grounds that it breached his human rights or racially discriminated against him. Subject to the limitations and exclusions discussed below, an 'immigration decision' as defined in section 82(2) or EEA decision attracts a right of appeal on human rights grounds and/or grounds of race discrimination.

Appeals against immigration decisions

6.34 Before we move on to consider the grounds of appeal under the 2002 Act, we briefly comment on each of the immigration decisions in section 82(2) in relation to issues which may arise on appeal and relevant Home Office Policy.

Refusal of leave to enter—section 82(2)(a)

6.35 Leave to enter may be refused at port where an immigration officer is not satisfied that an applicant qualifies for entry under the immigration rules or on the basis of human rights or asylum. No further immigration decision is required in order for the Secretary of State to enforce removal. The question of whether or not the applicant may appeal from within the United Kingdom depends on the nature of the claim. The section on exclusions below details which appeals may be conducted in-country. On an appeal against a decision to refuse leave to enter the

---

particular country and where a refugee applies for ILR or reaches the five-year point. The review should take place when the trigger occurs and not at the end of the five-year period (para 4.1 API).

[20] API Rights of Appeal in asylum cases, para 3.
[21] API Rights of Appeal, para 3.

Tribunal may consider evidence about any matter which it thinks relevant to the substance of the decision, including evidence which concerns a matter arising after the date of the decision.[22] An appeal will always be available against refusal of leave to enter on asylum, human rights, or race discrimination grounds unless certified as clearly unfounded.

As we discuss below,[23] section 6 of the IAN Act 2006 has restricted the availability **6.36** of an appeal against refusal of leave to enter to those persons who had entry clearance on arrival and who seek leave to enter for the same purpose as that specified in the entry clearance unless the appeal is brought on race discrimination, human rights, or asylum grounds.[24]

Refusal of entry clearance—section 82(2)(b)

As we shall see below, a right of appeal against entry clearance can only be exer- **6.37** cised from abroad. On determining an entry clearance appeal, the Tribunal is restricted to considering only those circumstances which pertained at the date of the decision to refuse.[25] We discuss matters of jurisdiction below.

When section 88A[26] of the NIA Act comes into force a person will not be able to **6.38** appeal against the refusal of entry clearance unless their application was made for the purpose of visiting a class of person prescribed by regulations[27] or entering as the dependant of persons prescribed by regulations[28] unless the appeal is brought on race discrimination or human rights grounds.[29] The regulations made under this section may make provision by reference to whether the applicant is a member of the family of the person he seeks to visit,[30] provide for the determination of whether one person is dependent on the other,[31] and make provisions by reference to the circumstances of the applicant and of the person whom he intends to visit or on whom he depends[32] in relation to the person's immigration status in the UK[33] and the duration of the two individuals' residence together[34] and the applicant's purpose in entering as a dependant.[35]

---

[22] Section 85(4) NIAA 2002—see paragraph 6.115 below on jurisdiction.
[23] Para 6.67.
[24] Section 6 of IAN Act 2006 substitutes s 89 NIA Act 2002.
[25] Section 85(5) NIAA 2002. See para 6.115 and 6.137 below on jurisdiction.
[26] Inserted by s 4 of the IAN Act 2006, from a date to be appointed, see para 6.66.
[27] Section 88A(1)(a).
[28] Section 88A(1)(b).
[29] Section 88A(3)(a).
[30] Section 88A (2)(a).
[31] Section 88A(2)(b).
[32] Section 88A(2)(c).
[33] Section 88A(2)(c)(i).
[34] Section 88A(2)(c)(ii).
[35] Section 88A(2)(d).

6.39 The effect of these provisions will be that persons refused entry clearance for other purposes such as students and persons who want to work in the UK will have a right of appeal only on human rights and race discrimination grounds. The Secretary of State must appoint a person to monitor refusals of entry clearance where there is only an appeal on human rights or race discrimination grounds.[36] Within three years from the commencement of section 88A the Secretary of State must report to Parliament on its effect.[37]

Refusal of a certificate of entitlement under section 10—section 82(2)(c)

6.40 An appeal against the refusal of a certificate of entitlement to the right of abode may normally be brought in the United Kingdom. The exceptions and limitations are set out below. As with an appeal against a refusal of entry clearance, the Tribunal may consider only those circumstances that pertained at the date of the decision to refuse.[38]

Refusal to vary a person's leave to enter or remain in the United Kingdom if the result of the refusal is that there is no leave—section 82(d)

6.41 The right of appeal arises when, as a result of the decision to refuse to vary existing leave to enter or remain, the applicant has no leave. Therefore, for a right of appeal to accrue, the applicant must have existing leave at the date of the application and when he is notified of the refusal of further leave, *his leave must have expired*. It is clear from the wording of the section that no appeal lies against an out-of-time application. This is because it is not possible to 'vary' non-extant leave and further because the section requires that it is as a *result of the refusal* that there is no leave. If leave had expired for failure to apply during the currency of existing leave, the absence of further leave would not be as a result of the refusal.

6.42 Since the right of appeal accrues only when as a result of the refusal there is no leave, if the applicant still has leave at the date of notification of the decision there is no right of appeal. There may, however, be a right of appeal on asylum grounds under section 83 (see paragraph 6.20 above).

6.43 The Tribunal may consider evidence about any matter which it thinks is relevant to the substance of the decision, including evidence which concerns a matter arising after the date of the decision.[39] Subject to the exclusions and limitations set out below, appeals against this decision can generally be brought from within the UK.

---

[36] Section 4(2) IAN Act 2006 substituting a new s 23(1) into the Immigration and Asylum Act 1999.

[37] Section 4(3) IAN Act 2006.

[38] Section 85(5) NIAA 2002. See paras 6.115 and 6.137 below on jurisdiction.

[39] Section 85(4) NIAA 2002. See paras 6.115 and 6.133 below on jurisdiction.

Variation of a person's leave if when the variation takes effect there is no leave—section 82(2)(e)

This decision is commonly referred to as the 'curtailment of leave'. The power to **6.44** curtail leave is to be found in section 3 (3)(a) of the Immigration Act 1971. The grounds under which this power may be used are set out at paragraph 323 of the Immigration Rules. The circumstances in which the Home Office curtail leave are set out at in the APIs.[40] On an appeal against the curtailment of leave the Tribunal may consider evidence about any matter which it thinks relevant to the substance of the decision, including evidence which concerns a matter arising after the date of the decision.[41] Appeals against this decision can generally be brought in the United Kingdom, subject to the exclusions and limitations set out below.

Revocation of indefinite leave to remain under section 76 of the 2002 Act—section 82(2)(f)

The decision to revoke a person's indefinite leave to enter or remain in the **6.45** UK gives rise to an in-country right of appeal, subject to the exclusions and limitations set out below. The 2006 Act also inserts a new right of appeal under section 82(2)(g) against a decision to remove following the revocation of ILR under section 10(1)(ba) of the 1999 Act (see below). This means that a person has a separate right of appeal at each of the stages of decision making, the first at the revocation stage and the second at the stage the decision to remove is made. On an appeal against the revocation of indefinite leave to remain the Tribunal may consider evidence about any matter which it thinks relevant to the substance of the decision, including evidence which concerns a matter arising after the date of the decision.[42]

A decision that a person is to be removed from the United Kingdom by way of directions under section 10(1)(a), (b), (ba), or (c) of the Immigration and Asylum Act 1999—section 82(2)(g)

A decision to remove under all four of the above sub-sections carries a right of **6.46** appeal. These decisions are to remove by way of directions:

• a person who has breached the conditions of his leave to enter or remain or is an overstayer;

---

[40] The Chapter in the APIs entitled 'Curtailment of Limited Leave in cases where an asylum/ Human rights application has been refused' deals with situations where a person is in the UK with limited leave and the application for asylum/human rights claim indicates that they do not have the intention to leave at the end of their stay and the person has leave in a category for which intention to leave at the end of the stay is required (ie, visitor, student, au-pair etc). Hence the making of the asylum/human rights claim indicates that they no longer have the intention to leave.
[41] Section 85(4) NIAA 2002. See paras 6.115 and 6.133 below on jurisdiction.
[42] Section 85(4) NIAA 2002. See paras 6.115 and 6.133 below on jurisdiction.

- a person who has obtained or sought to obtain leave to remain by deception;
- a person who has had his indefinite leave to enter or remain revoked under section 76 (3) of the 2002 Act (person ceasing to be a refugee);
- the family member of someone being removed on these grounds.

6.47 The IAN 2006 inserted section 82 (2)(ba) into the 2002 Act, allowing a right of appeal against removal after the revocation of indefinite leave to remain of a person who ceases to be a refugee in addition to the right of appeal at the revocation stage.[43] This separation of appeal rights was considered necessary in the light of the importance of refugee status. No decision to remove will be taken while an appeal against revocation is pending.[44]

6.48 It is important to note that it is not the setting of removal directions but the decision to remove which gives rise to a right of appeal. Removal directions do not give rise to a right of appeal under the 2002 Act. An appeal under this section does not generally lie from within the United Kingdom unless a claim which suspends removal has been made (see below). On an appeal against a decision to remove under this section the Tribunal may consider evidence about any matter which it thinks relevant to the substance of the decision, including evidence which concerns a matter arising after the date of the decision.[45]

A decision that an illegal entrant is to be removed from the United Kingdom by way of directions under paragraphs 8 to 10 of Schedule 2 to the Immigration Act 1971— section 82 (2) (h)

6.49 As above, it is the decision to remove and not the setting of removal directions which gives rise to a right of appeal. An appeal will lie in the United Kingdom only if a claim suspending removal has been made (see below).

A decision that an person is to be removed from the United Kingdom by way of directions under section 47 of the Immigration, Asylum and Nationality Act 2006—section 82 (2)(ha)

6.50 This section provides a new immigration decision which allows the Secretary of State to make a decision to give removal directions to a person whose leave to enter or remain has been extended by statute pending an appeal.[46] An appeal against a decision to give removal directions under this section may be brought from within the UK[47] unless an asylum or human rights claim has been made and

---

[43] Section 2 NIAA, from 31 August 2006 (SI 2006/2226).

[44] Explanatory Notes to IAN 2006, para 16.

[45] Section 85(4) NIAA 2002—see paras 6.115 and 6.133 below on jurisdiction.

[46] Inserted by s 47 (6) IAN 2006 from a date to be appointed. Leave pending appeal extended by IA 1971 s 3C(2)(b) and 3D(2)(a) as inserted by s 11 NIA from 31 Aug 2006 (SI 2006/2226).

[47] s 47(7) amends s 92 NIA 2002.

certified as manifestly unfounded.[48] This section is not yet in force at the time of writing.

A decision that a person is to be removed from the United Kingdom by way of directions given by virtue of paragraph 10A of that Schedule ((ie as a family member of a person removed as an illegal entrant or after refusal of leave to enter)— section 82 (2) (i)

The points made in paragraph 6.48 with regard to removal directions above apply equally here. **6.51**

A decision that a person is to be removed from the United Kingdom by way of directions given under paragraph 12 (2) of Schedule 2 to the Immigration Act 1971 (c77) (seamen and aircrews)—section 82 (ia)

The points made in paragraph 6.48 with regard to removal directions above apply equally here. **6.52**

A decision to made an order under section 2A of the 1971 Act (deprivation of right of abode)—section 82 (2) (ib)

This new immigration decision allows a person to appeal where the Secretary of State has made a decision to make an order removing his right of abode on the grounds that his removal or exclusion from the UK would be conducive to public good.[49] On an appeal against this decision the Tribunal may consider evidence about any matter which it thinks relevant to the substance of the decision, including evidence which concerns a matter arising after the date of the decision.[50] **6.53**

A decision to make a deportation order under section 5(1) of the 1971 Act— section 82(2)(j)

Since the enactment of section 10 of the Immigration and Asylum Act 1999 which rendered overstayers and those in breach of conditions of leave liable to administrative removal rather than deportation, the list of those liable to deportation has decreased. The following categories of people are liable to be deported and hence have a right of appeal before removal: **6.54**
- persons recommended for deportation by a criminal court;
- persons whose deportation is deemed by the Secretary of State to be conducive to the public good and his family members;[51]

---

[48] s 47(8) amends s 94 (1A) NIA 2002.
[49] Inserted by s 57 IAN 2006 from 16 June 2006 (SI 2006/1497).
[50] Section 85(4) NIAA 2002—see paras 6.115 and 6.133 below on jurisdiction.
[51] Section 3(5)(6) IA 1971.

- persons who overstayed their stay before October 2000 and applied to regularize their stay before this date and those subject to transitional provisions.[52]

6.55 Section 79 of the 2002 Act provides that a deportation order may not be made where an appeal against the decision to make the order could be brought or is pending.[53] An appeal against a refusal of leave to enter, refusal of a certificate of a right to abode, a refusal to vary a person's leave to enter or remain, and a revocation of indefinite leave to remain under section 82 of the 2002 Act is to be treated as finally determined if a deportation order is made against an appellant.[54] On an appeal against a decision to make a deportation order the Tribunal can consider evidence about any matter which it thinks relevant to the substance of the decision, including evidence which concerns a mater arising after the date of the decision.[55]

*A refusal to revoke a deportation order under section 5(2) of the 1971 Act—
section 82(2)(k)*

6.56 An appeal against a refusal to revoke a deportation order may not be brought from within the UK unless the appellant has made an asylum claim or a human rights claim whilst within the UK and that claim has not been certified as clearly unfounded[56] or is an EEA national or a member of the family of an EEA national and claims that the decision breaches his Community Treaty rights.[57] On an appeal against a refusal to revoke a deportation order the Tribunal can consider evidence about any matter which it thinks relevant to the substance of the decision, including evidence which concerns a matter arising after the date of the decision.[58]

Appeals against EEA decisions

Refusal to issue, renew, and revocation of residence documents

6.57 There is an appeal to the AIT against a decision by the Secretary of State to refuse to issue, or to revoke or refuse to renew a residence certificate, a residence card, or document certifying permanent residence. The refusal to issue a residence card or certificate to an EEA national or family member may be on grounds of public policy, public security, or public health, on the grounds that the holder has ceased to have the right to reside under the Regulations.[59]

---

[52] Section 9 of the IAA 1999, Sch 12, paras 11 and 12 of the Immigration (Regularisation Period for Overstayers) Regulations 2000, SI 2000/265.

[53] 'Pending' is defined in s 104 of the 2002 Act as beginning when it is instituted and ending when it is finally determined, withdrawn, or abandoned (or when it lapses under s 99).

[54] Section 104 (5) 2002 Act.

[55] Section 85(4) 2002 Act.

[56] Section 92(4)(a), s 94 (2) 2002 Act.

[57] Section 92(4)(b) 2002 Act.

[58] Section 85(4) 2002 Act see paragraphs 6.115 and 6.133 on jurisdiction.

[59] Regulation 20 The Immigration (Economic Area) Regulations 2006.

Decisions to remove on public policy grounds

Where removal is on the grounds of public policy, public security, or public **6.58** health[60] the person is to be treated as if he were liable to deportation under section 3(5)(a) of the 1971 Act (conducive to public good grounds) and section 5 and Schedule 3 apply.[61] Where the Secretary of State certifies that the decision to remove was taken on the grounds of the interests of national security or in the interests of the relationship between the UK and another country or otherwise in the public interest, the appeal lies to the Special Appeals Commission.[62] In all other cases an appeal against an EEA decision is to the Tribunal.[63]

Decisions to remove on grounds of non-qualification

Where a decision is taken to remove a person if he ceases to have a right to reside **6.59** under the Regulations,[64] he is to be treated as an overstayer.[65] If the person claims to be an EEA national, there is no right of appeal unless the person produces a valid national identity card or passport issued by an EEA State.[66] If the person claims to be a family member or relative of an EEA national he may not appeal under the Regulations unless he produces an EEA family permit or other proof that he is related as claimed to the EEA national.[67] The grounds of appeal on which an appellant may rely are race discrimination, human rights, breach of Community Treaties rights, that the decision is not in accordance with the law, and that removal would breach the UK's obligations under the Refugee Convention and ECHR.[68]

D. Grounds of Appeal

An appeal against an immigration decision must be brought on one or more of **6.60** the following grounds under section 84(1) of the 2002 Act:

(a) that the decision is not in accordance with immigration rules;

(b) that the decision is unlawful by virtue of section 19B of the Race Relations Act 1976 (discrimination by public authorities);

---

[60] Regulation 19 (3)(b) The Immigration (Economic Area) Regulations 2006.
[61] Regulation 24(3).
[62] Regulation 28.
[63] Regulation 26 (6).
[64] Regulation 19 (3)(a).
[65] Regulation 24 (2) and s 10 of the 1999 Act applies to him.
[66] Regulation 26(2).
[67] Regulation 26(3).
[68] Regulation 26(7) and Schedule 1 (applying s 84(1), except paragraphs (a) and (f), s 85 to 87, s 103A to 103E, s 105 and any regulations made under that section; and s 106 and any rules made under that section to appeals under the Regulations).

(c) that the decision is unlawful under section 6 of the Human Rights Act 1998 (public authority not to act contrary to Human Rights Convention) as being incompatible with the appellant's Convention Rights;

(d) the appellant is an EEA national or a member of the family of an EEA national and the decision breaches the appellant's rights under Community Treaties in respect of entry or residence in the United Kingdom;

(e) that the decision is otherwise not in accordance with the law;

(f) that the person taking the decision should have exercised differently a discretion conferred by immigration rules;

(g) that removal of the appellant from the United Kingdom in consequence of the immigration decision would breach the United Kingdom's obligations under the Refugee Convention or would be unlawful under section 6 of the Human Rights Act 1998 as being incompatible with the appellant's Convention rights.

6.61 As stated at paragraphs 6.27 and 6.32 above, appeals under sections 83 and 83 A are limited to asylum grounds by sections 84 (3) and (4).

6.62 Save for the exceptions and limitations set out below, an appeal may be brought against an immigration decision on more than one of the grounds listed. Therefore, an appellant may rely on grounds not previously before the Secretary of State when appealing an existing immigration decision. For example, a non-asylum decision may be appealed on asylum grounds.

E. Exceptions and Limitations

6.63 In general, where an immigration decision is made in respect of a person he may appeal on any of the grounds in section 84. However, there are exceptions and limitations to this principle, as set out below.

Ineligibility—section 88

6.64 This section limits the grounds on which an appeal may be brought where a refusal is based on a failure to meet a non-discretionary requirement of the Immigration Rules. Section 88 applies to the following immigration decisions:

- refusal of leave to enter (s 82(2)(a));
- refusal of entry clearance (s 82(b));
- refusal to vary leave to enter or remain where the result is that there is no leave to enter or remain (s 82(d));
- variation of a person's leave to enter or remain in the United Kingdom if when the variation takes effect the person has no leave to enter or remain (s 82(e))

A person in respect of whom the above decisions have been taken may only **6.65** appeal on race discrimination, human rights, or asylum grounds if the decision was taken on the grounds that he (or a person on whom he is dependent):

- does not satisfy a requirement as to age, nationality, or citizenship specified in immigration rules (s 88(2)(a);
- does not have an immigration document of a particular kind or any immigration document (s 88(2)(b);[69]
- has failed to supply a medical report or a medical certificate in accordance with a requirement of the immigration rules (s 88(2)(ba));[70]
- is seeking to be in the United Kingdom for a period greater than that permitted in his case by immigration rules(s 88(2)(c)); or
- is seeking leave to enter or remain in the United Kingdom for a purpose other than one permitted in accordance with the immigration rules (s 88(2)(d)).

Ineligibility—section 88A

This section provides power to enact secondary legislation to limit entry clear- **6.66** ance appeals to race discrimination and human rights grounds. The power has never been invoked. The 2006 Act provides for the substitution of section 88 A, 90, and 91 of the 2002 Act by a new section 88A which restricts full appeal rights against refusal of entry clearance to those seeking entry clearance as a dependant or family visitor. The categories of people will be defined in regulations. At the time of writing this section is not in force.

Refusal of leave to enter—section 89

The 2006 Act replaces section 89 of the 2002 Act with a provision that restricts **6.67** full rights of appeal against a refusal of leave to enter to those who have entry clearance and are seeking leave to enter for the same purpose as that specified in the entry clearance. If these requirements are not satisfied then the appeal is limited to race discrimination, human rights, and asylum grounds. This section has effect only in relation to decisions made on or after 31 August 2006.[71]

---

[69] 'Immigration document' is defined by s 88(3) of the 2002 Act to mean entry clearance, a passport, a work permit, or other immigration employment document within the meaning of s 122 of the 2002 Act (namely, any document which relates to employment and is issued for a purpose of immigration rules or in connection with leave to enter or remain in the UK. NB s 122 is repealed, subject to the saving that sub-section (2) continues to have effect so far as is necessary for the purposes of s 88(3)(c)), and a document which relates to a national of a country other than the UK and which is designed to serve the same purpose as a passport.

[70] Inserted by s 5 of the IAN Act 2006, from 31 August 2006 (SI 2006/2226).

[71] Section 89 substituted by IAN Act 2006, s 6 from 31 August 2006 (SI 2006/2226).

6.68 Decisions made before 31 August 2006 are governed by section 89 of the 2002 Act. This provides that there is no right of appeal against refusal of leave to enter as a visitor, a short or prospective student, or a dependant of the same unless the person holds entry clearance at the time of the refusal. There is an appeal on race discrimination, asylum, or human rights grounds.

Non-family visitor—section 90

6.69 There is no right of appeal against refusal of entry clearance as a visitor save for on race discrimination or human rights grounds. The only exception to this is if the application was made to visit family members, in which case there are full rights of appeal against refusal of entry clearance.

6.70 The term 'family member' is defined by the Immigration Appeals (Family Visitor) Regulations 2003[72] as:

- the applicant's spouse, parent, child, sibling, grandparent, grandchild, uncle, aunt, nephew, niece, first cousin;
- the applicant's spouse's parent, sibling, or child;
- the applicant's stepfather, stepmother, stepson, stepdaughter, stepbrother, or stepsister; or
- a person with whom the applicant has lived as a member of an unmarried couple for at least two of the three years before the date of the application for entry clearance.

6.71 For the purposes of the Regulations, 'first cousin' means the son or daughter of his aunt or uncle.[73] This section will be replaced by the new section 88A[74] when it comes into force.

Applications for entry clearance from short-term or prospective students—section 91

6.72 An appeal may be brought against a refusal of entry clearance on race discrimination and human rights grounds only if entry clearance was sought:

- to follow a course of study for which the applicant has been accepted and which will not last longer than six months;
- in order to study but without having been accepted on a course;
- as a dependant of one of the above.

6.73 This section will be replaced by the new section 88A[75] when it comes into force.

---

[72] SI 2003 No. 518.
[73] Paragraph 2(2) The Immigration Appeals (Family Visitor) Regulations 2003 (SI 2003, No 518).
[74] See para 6.66 above
[75] See para 6.66 above.

Earlier right of appeal—section 96

This section must be read with section 120 of the 2002 Act. These sections set **6.74** out the 'one-stop' arrangements which exclude a further right of appeal where a person seeks to rely on matters which he has already had the opportunity to argue in a previous appeal. We deal fully with these provisions below.[76] In brief, this section allows the Secretary of State or an immigration officer to 'certify' an appeal which has the effect of precluding an appeal against a second immigration decision. The 'one-stop' system applies only to cases where there is or may be an appeal from within the UK.[77]

National security—section 97

Section 97 excludes the right of appeal to the AIT in respect of decisions taken **6.75** under sections 82(1), 83 (2), 83A(2) NIA Act 2002[78] and provides that an appeal already lodged will lapse where the Secretary of State in person[79] certifies that a person's exclusion or removal is:

- in the interests of national security;[80] or
- in the interests of a relationship between the United Kingdom and another country.[81]

Or if the Secretary of State in person[82] certifies that the decision was taken in reli- **6.76** ance on information which should not be made public:

- for reasons of national security;[83]
- in the interests of the relationship between the United Kingdom and another country;[84] or
- otherwise in the public interest.[85]

In all such cases the appeal route is to the Special Immigration Appeals **6.77** Commission—see also paragraph 6.95 below.

---

[76] See Chapter 7, and Practice Notes and below para 6.96.
[77] IDIs Section 1—Rights of Appeal, para 2.
[78] Reference to ss 83(2) and 83A inserted by s 14 and Schedule 1 of the NIA 2006 from 31 August 2006 SI 2006/2226.
[79] Section 97 (4) NIA Act 2002.
[80] Section 97(2)(a) NIA Act 2002.
[81] Section 97(2)(b) NIA 2002.
[82] Section 97(3)(4) NIA Act 2002.
[83] Section 97(3)(a) NIA Act 2002.
[84] Section 97(3)(b) NIA Act 2002.
[85] Section 97 (3)(c) NIA Act 2002.

Grounds of public good—section 98

6.78 This section excludes a right of appeal against refusal of leave to enter and entry clearance where the Secretary of State acting in person certifies that the decision was taken on the grounds of public good. There is a right of appeal on human rights, race discrimination, and, in the case of a refusal of leave to enter only, on asylum grounds.

Third country cases—Schedule 3 of 2004 Act

6.79 Schedule 3 to the 2004 Act creates a presumption of safety with regard to return to specified countries of destination. All EU countries, Norway, Iceland, Bulgaria and Romania (and other countries as may be provided by order) are deemed safe.[86] The statutory presumption is that there is no threat in these countries to a claimant's life or liberty on grounds of race, religion, nationality, membership of a particular social group, or political opinion.[87] Further, these countries are deemed not to return a person to a place where his life and liberty are at risk for a Convention reason or in breach of his human rights.[88] In the case of *R (on the appln of Javad Nasseri) v SSHD*[89] McCombe J held that this deeming provision, in creating an irrebuttable statutory presumption that an asylum applicant would not be subject to unlawful *refoulement* by a specified State in contravention of the ECHR, was incompatible with the ECHR. His Lordship made a declaration of incompatibility under section 4 of the Human Rights Act to that effect.

6.80 Other States are deemed to be safe with regard to the Refugee Convention but there is no statutory presumption that they will not remove a person in breach of his human rights.[90] Other States are deemed to be safe for particular individuals in respect of the Refugee Convention.[91] Where a certificate has been issued under Schedule 3 of the 2004 Act and any human rights claim has been certified as

---

[86] Asylum and Immigration (Treatment of Claimants, etc)Act, Schedule 3, Part 2 'First List of Safe Countries (Refugee Convention and Human Rights)', Part 3 'Second List of Safe Countries (Refugee Convention and Human Rights)'. Bulgaria and Romania were added from 1 January 2007 by Asylum (List of Safe Countries) (Amendment) Order 2006 SI 2006/339 to take effect on or after 1 January 2007 in relation to an asylum or human rights claim made before that date provided that no decision to refuse the claimant leave to enter or remove him from the UK following that claim has been made before that date.

[87] Schedule 3, para 3 (2)(a) Asylum and Immigration (Treatment of Claimants, etc) Act 2004.

[88] Schedule 3, para 3 (2)(b)(c) Asylum and Immigration (Treatment of Claimants, etc) Act 2004.

[89] [2007] EWHC 1548 (Admin)—see Chapter 7.

[90] Schedule 3, Part 4 'Third List of Safe Countries (Refugee Convention Only)'; no orders have as yet been made under this section specifying countries.

[91] Schedule 3, Part 5 'Countries Certified as Safe for Individuals'; this Part does not contain a presumption of safety, but prevents an appeal where the claim has been certified.

clearly unfounded, no appeal can be brought in the United Kingdom.[92] No appeal can be brought on a ground which is inconsistent with the statutory presumptions in the certificate.[93]

F. In-Country and Out of Country Appeal Rights

Some immigration appeals may only be brought from within the United Kingdom and others from outside it. These are commonly referred to as suspensive and non-suspensive appeal rights. Appellants may appeal from within the United Kingdom only in the following circumstances.   **6.81**

Appeals from within the United Kingdom—section 92

Section 92 of the 2002 Act sets out the immigration decisions which can be appealed from within the United Kingdom, suspending any removal which might follow from the decision: **6.82**

- Refusal of leave to enter (s 82 (2)(a)) if at the time of the refusal the appellant is in the United Kingdom and on his arrival had entry clearance[94] (but not if his leave to enter has been cancelled by an immigration officer on arrival because the person's purpose in arriving in the UK is different from the purpose specified in his entry clearance[95] or the refusal of leave to enter which specifies that the grounds for refusal are that the leave is sought for a purpose other than that specified in the entry clearance[96]) or is a British national within the meaning of the British Nationality Act 1981 who holds a work permit and is in the UK.[97] NB there are no in country appeal rights if the leave is cancelled or refused and the grounds for this are that the passenger's purpose in coming to the UK is not that specified in the entry clearance or leave.[98]
- Refusal of a certificate of entitlement (s 82(2)(c)).
- Refusal to vary existing leave to enter or remain where as a result the applicant has no leave (s 82(2)(d)).
- Variation of leave to enter or remain so that the person has no leave (s 82(2)(e)).
- Revocation of indefinite leave to enter (s 82(2)(f)).

---

[92] Schedule 3, paras 5, 10, 15 and 19.
[93] Schedule 3, paras 6, 11, 16 and 19 (d).
[94] Section 92(3).
[95] Section 92 (3A) and (3B).
[96] Section 92(3C).
[97] Section 92(3D).
[98] Sections 92(3B) and (3C).

- A decision that a person is to be removed from the UK by way of directions under section 47 of the Immigration, Asylum and Nationality Act 2006 (removal: persons with statutorily extended leave) (s 82(2)(ha));[99]
- A decision to make a deportation order under section 5(1) of the Act (s 82(2)(j)).

6.83 There are, therefore, a number of immigration decisions that cannot be appealed from within the United Kingdom. However, section 92 (4) provides an in-country right of appeal against any immigration decision if the appellant:

- has made an asylum claim, or a human rights claim, while in the United Kingdom;[100] or
- is an EEA national or member of the family of an EEA national and makes a claim that the decision breaches his Treaty rights.[101]

6.84 Race discrimination grounds are not amongst the grounds which suspend removal.

Appeals from outside the United Kingdom

6.85 Therefore, under section 92, unless an appellant has made an asylum or human rights claim (which has not been certified as 'clearly unfounded'), or a claim that removal breaches Treaty rights, the following immigration decisions cannot be appealed whilst the appellant is in the United Kingdom:

- refusal of leave to enter (save for in the circumstances set out at paragraph 6.82 above) (s 82(2)(a));
- a decision that a person is to be removed from the United Kingdom by way of directions under section 10(1)(a),(b) (ba) or (c) of the Immigration and Asylum Act 1999 (ie as a person who has breached the conditions of his leave to enter or remain or is an overstayer; as a person who has obtained or sought to obtain leave to remain by deception; as a person who has had his indefinite leave to enter or remain revoked under section 76 (3) of the 2002 Act (person ceasing to be a refugee) or as the family member of someone being removed on these grounds) (s 82 (2) (g));
- a decision that an illegal entrant is to be removed from the United Kingdom by way of directions under paragraphs 8 to 10 of Schedule 2 to the Immigration Act 1971 (s 82 (2)(h));
- a decision that a person is to be removed from the United Kingdom by way of directions given by virtue of paragraph 10A of that Schedule (family) (s 82 (2)

---

[99] Substituted by IAN 2006, s 47 from a date to be appointed.
[100] Section 94(4)(a).
[101] Section 94(4)(b).

(i)) (ie as a family member of a person removed as an illegal entrant or after refusal of leave to enter);

- a decision that a person is to be removed from the United Kingdom by way of directions given under paragraph 12 (2) of Schedule 2 to the Immigration Act 1971 (c77) (seamen and aircrews) (s 82(2)(ia));
- a decision to make an order under section 2A 1971 Act (deprivation of right of abode) (s 82(2)(ib));
- refusal to revoke a deportation order under section 5(2) of the 1971 Act (s82(2)(k)).

Entry clearance

A refusal of entry clearance (s 82)(2)(b)) may only be appealed from outside the **6.86** UK unless the applicant is an EEA national or a family national of an EEA member and claims that the decision breaches his Treaty rights.[102] Applications for entry clearance are necessarily made from outside the United Kingdom. Therefore the issue which arises is whether the appellant is entitled to travel to the United Kingdom to attend his appeal. Only EEA nationals may do so (s 92 (4)). An entry clearance appeal may not be brought on asylum grounds as no appeal from outside the UK can be brought on asylum grounds.[103]

Appeals may also only be brought from outside the United Kingdom in the fol- **6.87** lowing circumstances.

Third country cases—Schedule 3 of 2004 Act

A person may not bring an appeal from within the United Kingdom where the **6.88** Secretary of State certifies after 1 October 2004 that an asylum or human rights claimant is to be removed to a safe third country and certifies that the human rights claim is clearly unfounded.[104]

A person may not bring an appeal from within the United Kingdom where the **6.89** Secretary of State certified before 1 October 2004 that the asylum applicant was to be removed to a safe third country under sections 11(2) or 12(2) of the Immigration and Asylum Act 1999 unless he makes a human rights claim which is not certified as clearly unfounded.[105]

---

[102] Section 92(4)(b).
[103] Section 95 NIA Act 2002 (except in a case to which s 94(9) applies).
[104] Asylum and Immigration (Treatment of Claimants, etc) Act 2004, Sch 3, paras 5, 10, 15, 19.
[105] Section 93 (2) of the NIA Act 2002, repealed by 2004 Act, transitional provisions contained in SI 2004/2523, Art 3.

Clearly unfounded human rights claims—section 94

6.90 Under section 94(1A) a person may not rely on section 92 (2), and hence there is no in-country appeal against the following immigration decisions where an asylum or human rights claim has been certified as clearly unfounded:

- refusal of a certificate of entitlement (s 82(2)(c));
- refusal to vary existing leave to enter or remain where as a result the applicant has no leave (s 82(2)(d));
- variation of leave to enter or remain so that the person has no leave (s 82(2)(e));
- a decision that a person is to be removed from the United Kingdom by way of directions under section 47 of the Immigration, Asylum and Nationality Act 2006 (removal: persons with statutorily extended leave) (s 82(2)(ha)).[106]

6.91 Section 94 (1A) does not exclude reliance on section 92 (2) and hence there is an in-country right of appeal even where the asylum or human rights claim has been certified as clearly unfounded against the following immigration decisions:

- revocation of indefinite leave to enter (s 82(2)(f));
- a decision to make a deportation order (s 82(2)(j)).

6.92 If an applicant would have an in country right of appeal only on the basis that they have made an asylum or human rights claim,[107] the certificate removes that right of appeal.[108] We deal in detail with certification in Chapter 7.

Against an EEA decision

6.93 There is no in-country appeal against an EEA decision to refuse to admit a person to the UK unless:[109]

- the person held an EEA family permit, a registration certificate, a residence card, a document certifying permanent residence, or a permanent residence card on his arrival in the UK or can otherwise prove that he is resident in the UK;[110]
- the person has been in the UK on temporary admission or in detention for at least three months from the date on which notice of decision to refuse to admit him is given but is deemed not to have been admitted to the UK under the Regulations;[111]

---

[106] Substituted by IAN Act 2006, s 47 from a date to be appointed.
[107] ie under s 92 (4)(a).
[108] Section 94 (2).
[109] Regulation 27(1)(a) The Immigration (European Economic Area) Regulations 2006 SI 2006, No 1003.
[110] Regulation 27(2)(a).
[111] Regulation 27(2)(b).

- the person is in the UK and a ground of appeal is that, in taking the decision, the decision maker acted in breach of his rights under the Human Rights Convention or the Refugee Convention, unless the Secretary of State certifies that the ground of appeal is clearly unfounded.[112]

There is no in-country appeal against removal from the UK after a person has **6.94** entered or sought to enter the UK in breach of a deportation order unless a ground of appeal is that the decision maker acted in breach of the appellant's human rights or the Refugee Convention in taking the decision, unless the Secretary of State certifies that ground of appeal is clearly unfounded.[113] There is no in-country right of appeal against the refusal to revoke a deportation order[114] and the refusal to issue an EEA family permit.[115]

National security: deportation—section 97A

This section is inserted into the 2002 Act by section 7 of the 2006 Act.[116] **6.95** Where the Secretary of State certifies under section 97 A(1) that the decision to make a deportation order has been made on national security grounds, a deportation order may be made before any appeal is disposed of. This section disapplies section 79 of the NIA Act 2002,[117] which precludes the making of a deportation order where an appeal can be brought or is pending. Appeals against a decision to make a deportation order on national security grounds can normally only be made from outside the United Kingdom unless the appellant makes a human rights claim which is not certified under section 97A(2)(iii). Under this section the Secretary of State may certify that removal would not breach the UK's obligations under the ECHR. There is, however, an in-country appeal against this certificate to the Special Immigration Appeals Commission.[118]

G. The One-Stop Procedure

The one-stop procedure applies to all cases where there is or may be an appeal **6.96** from within the United Kingdom. The procedure is designed to ensure that all the grounds that an appellant has for remaining in the United Kingdom are considered under the umbrella of a single appeal. Essentially, the Secretary

---

[112] Regulation 27(2)(c).
[113] Section 27(3).
[114] Regulation 27(1)(b).
[115] Regulation 27(1)(c).
[116] From 31 August 2006 (SI 2006/2226).
[117] Section 97A(2)(a).
[118] Section 97A(3).

of State may serve a 'one-stop' notice requiring the recipient to state his 'additional' reasons or grounds relating to his entitlement to enter or remain. The consequences of non-compliance with the notice may be that a further appeal is precluded.

6.97   Section 120 of the NIA Act 2002 gives the Secretary of State the power to serve a 'one-stop' notice on a person who has made an application to enter or remain in the UK or in respect of whom an immigration decision within the meaning of section 82 has been or may be taken (s 120 (a) and (b)). The Secretary of State may therefore serve a notice where a person has not actually made an application, but where he wants to compel someone (eg an illegal entrant or an overstayer) to state any grounds they may have for remaining in the UK.

6.98   There is no statutory obligation to serve a one-stop notice, but failure to do so may mean that the Secretary of State is unable to certify a further appeal. The Immigration Directorate Instructions (IDIs) (Ch 12 section 3, Nov 06) state when a notice should be served in different types of cases:

- in asylum and human rights cases the notice should be served at an early stage;
- where an application has been made in time under the immigration rules, it will not normally be necessary to serve a one-stop notice at this point;
- unsuccessful applicants who have a right of appeal in the UK should usually be given a one-stop notice with the refusal notice and appeal form.

6.99   The notice must be in writing and requires a person to state:

- his reasons for wishing to enter or remain in the United Kingdom;
- any grounds on which he should be permitted to enter or remain in the United Kingdom; and
- any grounds on which he should not be removed from or required to leave the United Kingdom (s 120(2)).

6.100 The recipient of the one-stop notice states any additional reasons required above in the 'Statement of Additional Grounds'. There is no requirement to repeat the grounds set out in an earlier application (s 120(3)(a)) or the grounds relied on to resist the original decision (s 120(3)(b)) in the Statement of Additional Grounds.

6.101 There is no statutory time limit for the return of the Statement of Additional Grounds and no obligation on the Secretary of State to await its return before making a decision. The IDIs (see above) state that in each case the caseworker should tell the applicant how long it will be before a decision is taken. Further, the caseworker is free to set an appropriate time limit that is reasonable in the circumstances of the case, but care should be taken to treat applicants equitably, and standard periods should be given. The IDIs also state that the statement should be considered even if it arrives late even if an appeal has been lodged.

There is also no statutory requirement for the Secretary of State to respond to the **6.102** Statement of Additional Grounds. Where the one-stop notice is served with the refusal notice and appeal form, the current IDIs state that there is normally no need for a response where the grounds of appeal relate to existing issues or the appellant has simply put grounds of appeal into the additional grounds box on the form. Where there is no response from the Secretary of State, the Tribunal is obliged to consider any matter raised in the statement of additional grounds which constitutes a ground of appeal within section 84 (1) against the decision appealed against.

The wording for the one-stop notice is not defined in any legislation. IDIs state **6.103** that the unsuccessful applicants who have a right of appeal in the UK should usually be given a one-stop notice with the refusal notice and appeal form. The one-stop notice should usually be served as a paragraph within the notice of decision or the reasons for refusal letter. There will be a box in the appeal form in which the appellant can enter any additional grounds. Caseworkers are advised to use standard wording for one-stop notices.

H. Suspensory Effect of Pending Appeals

We have seen that some appeals may only be brought from within the UK and **6.104** others only from outside its borders. When an appeal against an immigration decision under section 82(1) is pending,[119] an appellant may not be removed or required to leave the UK.[120] However the following actions may be taken whilst an appeal is pending:

- the giving of a direction for the appellant's removal from the UK;[121]
- the making of a deportation order in respect of the appellant[122] (but a deportation order may not be made while an appeal against the decision to make the order could be brought, ignoring the possibility of an appeal out of time

---

[119] Under s 104 NIA Act 2002.
[120] Section 78(1) NIA Act 2002.
[121] Section 78(3)(a).
[122] Section 78(3)(b).

with permission, or is pending,[123] unless the case is certified on the grounds of national security[124]);

- the taking of any other interim or preparatory action.[125]

6.105 An appeal is pending until it is finally determined, withdrawn, abandoned, or lapses.[126] An appeal is not finally determined while:

- an application for reconsideration under section 103A(1) (other than an application out of time with permission) could be made or is awaiting determination;
- reconsideration of an appeal has been ordered and has not been completed;
- an appeal has been remitted to the Tribunal and is awaiting determination;
- an application for permission to appeal to the Court of Appeal could be made or is awaiting determination (other than an application out of time with permission);
- an appeal to the Court of Appeal is awaiting determination; or
- a reference by the Tribunal to the Court of Appeal is awaiting determination.

6.106 In *YD (Turkey) v SSHD*[127] the Court of Appeal held that once permission to appeal an out of time application had been granted, the appeal would be pending and hence the appellant could not be removed by virtue of section 78 of the 2002 Act.

6.107 Where a person has applied for a variation of limited leave to remain during the currency of their existing leave and the leave expires without the application being decided, their leave is extended during the period in which the appeal could be brought (ignoring the possibility of an appeal out of time with permission) or is pending. The appeal must be brought whilst the appellant is in the UK.[128] This extended leave lapses when the person leaves the UK.[129]

6.108 Similarly, where a person's leave to enter or remain is varied with the result that they have no leave or leave is revoked, leave is extended during the period where an appeal could be brought while the person is in the UK against the variation or

---

123 Section 79 NIA Act 2002.

124 Section 97A NIA Act 2002 inserted by the IAN Act 2006, s 7 from 31 August 2006 (SI 2006/2226)

125 Section 78(3)(c).

126 Section 104(1). An appeal lapses by virtue of s 99 of the 2002 Act when a certificate is issued under s 96(1),(2) (certified on basis of earlier right of appeal), s 97 (national security) or s 98 (public good).

127 [2006] EWCA Civ 52, [2006] WLR 1646.

128 Section 3C of the 1971 Act as substituted by the NIA Act 2002, s 118 from 1 April 2002 (SI 2003/754) and amended by the INA Act 2006, s 11 from 31 August 2006 (SI 2006/2226), applying to applications made before that date in respect of which no decision has been made, as it applies to applications made on or after that date.

129 Section 3C (3) 1971 Act.

revocation (ignoring the possibility of an out of time appeal with permission) or is pending.[130] This extended leave lapses when the person leaves the UK.[131]

An appeal will be treated as abandoned: **6.109**

- if the appellant leaves the UK;[132]
- if the appellant is granted leave to enter or remain in the UK unless he:
  - (i) appeals on asylum grounds and is granted leave to enter or remain in the UK for a period exceeding 12 months and gives notice under the Procedure Rules that he wishes to pursue the appeal on that ground;[133] or
  - (ii) appeals on race discrimination grounds where he gives notice under the Procedure Rules that he wants to pursue the appeal on that ground.[134]

An appeal against a refusal of leave to enter, a refusal of a certificate of entitlement, **6.110** a refusal to vary leave where as a result the person has no leave, the curtailment of leave, and a revocation of indefinite leave are to be treated as finally determined if a deportation order is made against the appellant.[135]

Section 47 of the Immigration, Asylum and Nationality Act, when it comes into **6.111** force, will give the Secretary of State a new power to decide to remove an appellant by way of removal directions whose leave is extended pending appeal. The decision may be taken in respect of a person:

- who has applied for a variation of leave during the period of their limited leave and whose leave is extending by statute for the period during which an appeal could be brought while the appellant is in the UK against the decision on the application for variation (ignoring the possibility of an appeal out of time with permission);[136]
- who has had their leave to enter or remain in the UK varied with the result that they have no leave to remain or whose leave to remain has been revoked and has had their leave extended by statute for the period during which an appeal could be brought, while the person is in the UK, against the variation or revocation (ignoring any possibility of an appeal out of time with permission).[137]

---

[130] Section 3D (2) 1971 Act.
[131] Section 3D (3) 1971 Act.
[132] Section 104 (4) substituted by IAN 2006, s 9 from 13 November 2006 (SI 2006/2838).
[133] Section 104 (4B) as inserted by IAN Act 2006, s 9 from 13 November 2006 (SI 2006/2838).
[134] Section 104 (4C) as inserted by IAN Act 2006, s 9 from 13 November 2006 (SI 2006/2838).
[135] Section 104 (5).
[136] ie a person whose leave is extended by s 3C(2)(b) of the 1971 Act, as substituted by the NIA Act 2002, s 118 from 1 April 2002 (SI 2003/754) and amended by the IAN Act 2006, s 11 from 31 August 2006 (SI 2006/2226), applying to applications made before that date in respect of which no decision has been made, as it applies to applications made on or after that date.
[137] ie a person whose leave is extended by s 3D(2)(a) of the 1971 Act, as inserted by IAN Act 2006, s11 from 31 August 2006 (SI 2006/2226) only in relation to a decision made on or after that date.

6.112 The removal decision can be made during the period of statutorily extended leave, but removal directions cannot be given until the period of leave ends.[138]

I. Jurisdiction—Powers of the Tribunal

6.113 The power of the Tribunal to determine an appeal is found in section 86(3) of the 2002 Act. The Tribunal must allow the appeal in so far as it thinks that:

- the decision against which the appeal is brought or is treated as being brought was not in accordance with the law (including the immigration rules) (s 86(3)(a)); or
- a discretion exercised in making a decision against which the appeal is brought or is treated as being brought should have been exercised differently (s 86(3)(b)).

6.114 Otherwise, the Tribunal must dismiss the appeal (s 86(5)). A decision to remove a person from the United Kingdom under one provision is not to be regarded as unlawful if it could lawfully be made by reference to removal under another provision.[139] Therefore if an illegal entrant is incorrectly categorized as an over-stayer, the decision to remove is still lawful. Refusal to depart from or authorise departure from the immigration rules is not the exercise of a discretion for the purposes of section 86 (3)(b).[140]

Matters to be considered

6.115 An appeal under section 82(1) can only be brought on the grounds set out in section 84 of the 2002 Act (paragraph 6.60 above). The matters which the Tribunal must consider when determining an appeal are listed in section 85. This section must be read in conjunction with section 120 of the NIA Act 2002 which defines the 'one-stop' procedure (see paragraph 6.96). An appeal under section 82 (1) against a decision shall be treated by the Tribunal as including an appeal against any decision in respect of which the appellant has a right of appeal under section 82(1).[141] This means that if more than one decision relating to the appellant has been made under this section it must be dealt with in the same appeal. If an appellant makes a statement of additional grounds under section 120 in response to a one-stop notice, the Tribunal must consider any matter raised in the statement which constitutes a ground of appeal.[142] This duty applies whether

---

[138] Section 47 (1) IAN Act 2006.
[139] Section 86(4) NIA Act 2002.
[140] Section 86(6) NIA Act 2002.
[141] Section 85(1) NIA Act 2002.
[142] Section 85(2) NIA Act 2002.

the statement was made before or after the appeal was commenced.[143] Section 86(3)(b) obliges the Tribunal to consider additional grounds when deciding whether to allow an appeal by the wording 'a decision against which the appeal is bought or *is treated as being brought*'.

On an appeal under section 82(1), 83(2) (asylum), or section 83A(2) the Tribunal **6.116** may consider evidence on any matter which it thinks is relevant to the substance of the decision, including evidence of post-decision facts.[144] The only exception to this is appeals in relation to a refusal of entry clearance or a certificate of entitlement where the Tribunal is confined to hearing evidence pertaining to the circumstances as at the date of the decision to refuse.[145]

In determining an appeal under sections 82(1), 83, or 83A the Tribunal must **6.117** determine any matter raised as a ground of appeal and any matter which section 85 obliges them to consider.[146]

Not in accordance with the law

The Tribunal must allow an appeal if the decision against which it is brought was **6.118** not in accordance with the law. What 'the law' is, for the purposes of this limb of section 86(3), has caused the courts much vexation. The 'law', for these purposes, includes the immigration rules and statutes, the Human Rights Act, and EU law regarding free movement, but also includes general principles of administrative and public law, as we discuss below.

In *Abdi* [1996] Imm AR 148 the Court of Appeal held that 'the law' under which **6.119** the Appellate Authorities operated included the general principles of administrative and public law and that failure by the Secretary of State to follow his own published policy would be 'not in accordance with the law'. Miss Abdi had applied for entry clearance under the Somali Family Reunion Policy under which dependent relatives of the refugee's household in Somalia were allowed to join the sponsor in the UK. The Adjudicator found that she was, contrary to the Respondent's view, a dependent member of the household and therefore came within the terms of the policy. The Court of Appeal held that the Respondent's decision was not in accordance with the law and her application for entry clearance would have to be reconsidered under the policy, in the light of the Adjudicator's findings of fact.[147] However, the Adjudicator's jurisdiction was

---

[143] Section 85(3) NIA Act 2002.
[144] Section 85(4) NIA Act 2002—see para 6.133.
[145] Section 85(5) NIA Act 2002—see para 6.137.
[146] Section 86(2) NIA Act 2002.
[147] It has been held that the Secretary of State should not go behind an Adjudicator's findings of fact, unless fresh evidence shows that the Adjudicator was wrong or circumstances have changed (*ex p Danaie* [1998] ImmAR 84).

limited in that he could not allow the appeal outright if he found the appellant to come within the terms of the policy but could allow the appeal only to the limited extent that the application remained outstanding before the Respondent, for him to reconsider it under the policy.

6.120 Until recently, the limits of the *Abdi* jurisdiction were confined to allowing the appeal to the limited extent described in paragraph 6.119. However, recent case law appears to have extended the jurisdiction of the Tribunal to allowing certain appeals outright where the Secretary of State has failed to follow his published policy.

The *Abdi* jurisdiction clearly allows the Tribunal to decide the facts which determine whether a policy is applicable in principle in any particular case and to decide those facts which concern the appellant's situation in relation to the subject matter of the policy. There is recent authority which also contemplates the Tribunal moving into the realm of applying policy.

6.121 The Court of Appeal in *Fouzia Baig v SSHD* [2005] EWCA Civ 1246 approved of an argument asserting that following *Huang*[148] that the question of the application of a policy to an individual case was a matter for the Tribunal and not simply a matter for review of the decision of the Secretary of State. In *IA ('applying policies') Mauritius* [2006] UKIAT 00082 the Tribunal considered the comments in *Baig* and whilst noting that they were strictly obiter, held that they should be given appropriate weight. The Tribunal in *IA* held that where there is a clear and obvious breach of a policy an immigration judge can find that the decision is not in accordance with the law. However, the Tribunal stressed that it will only be in very unusual circumstances that such a finding can be made properly. Usually the immigration judge cannot decide if an appellant satisfies the requirements of a policy because he cannot make the necessary findings either about the scope and operation of the policy or the appellant's circumstances.

6.122 It appears therefore on the authorities of *Baig* and *IA* that in the case of a clear and obvious breach the Tribunal can decide whether the facts found by it mean that the appellant satisfies the requirement of the policy. Whether the Tribunal can exercise a discretion, if there is one under the policy, in favour or against the appellant has been the subject of conflicting decisions. In *Baig* the Court of Appeal seems to contemplate the Tribunal engaging with the discretion under the policy if the exercise of discretion was perverse.[149] However, in *SS (Jurisdiction–Rule*

---

[148] *Huang v Secretary of State for the Home Department* (2005) EWCA Civ 105.
[149] See paragraph 34, per Buxton LJ, see also *SB (Bangladesh) v Secretary of State for the Home Department* [2007] EWC Civ 28.

62(7); Refugee's family; Policy) Somalia [2005] UKIAT 00167, the Tribunal held that if the policy includes a discretion (ie by use of words such as 'consider' or 'normally'), that is a discretion which involves the exercise of the royal prerogative and it is not for members of the Tribunal to exercise this prerogative.

The existence of a policy is capable of affecting the balancing exercise under Article 8 (2) (see *IA (applying policies) Mauritius* [2006] UKAIT 00082 and *R (on the appln of Mehmet Tozlukaya) v SSHD* 920060 EWCA 379). **6.123**

In *CP (Section 86(3) and (5); wrong immigration rule) Dominica* [2006] UKAIT 00040[150] the Tribunal held that where the Secretary of State (or Entry Clearance Officer) applies the wrong immigration rule, the resulting immigration decision is technically unlawful. The immigration judge should apply the correct rule when deciding an appeal. If, in applying the correct rule, any (or all) of the requirements are not satisfied, the appeal will be dismissed in substance under section 86(5), but allowed in part under section 86(3) to the limited (and inconsequential) extent that the decision was 'not in accordance with the law'. **6.124**

'Including the immigration rules'

The Tribunal may allow an appeal where the immigration authorities have decided that the appellant does not satisfy the Immigration Rules and the Tribunal finds that they are satisfied. The Tribunal may find that the immigration authorities misunderstood the relevant rule, applied the wrong rule to the facts or made incorrect findings of fact. **6.125**

The Immigration Rules deal both with asylum and humanitarian protection. As a result of the enactment of the Refugee or Person in Need of International Protection (Qualification) Regulations[151] ('the Protection Regulations') and the Statement of Changes in Immigration Rules,[152] all asylum-related appeals require a decision to be made by the Tribunal as to eligibility for 'humanitarian protection'. Whilst there is a specific provision for an asylum and human rights ground of appeal,[153] there is no specific provision for a humanitarian protection ground of appeal and hence the appeal has to be framed in terms of the decision granting or refusing humanitarian protection being 'not in accordance with the immigration rules', or possibly that the decision is 'not in accordance with the law' if it is said **6.126**

---

[150] Reported.

[151] SI 2006/2525 implementing Council Directive 1004/83/EC of 29 April 2004 on minimum standards for the qualification and status of third country nationals or stateless persons as refugees or as persons who otherwise need international protection.

[152] Cm6918.

[153] Section 84(g) NIA Act 2002.

that a policy should have been applied recognising the appellant's eligibility for humanitarian protection.

6.127 In *RM (Kwok On Tong: HC395 para 320) India* [2006] UKAIT 00039[154] the Tribunal held that an immigration judge cannot allow an appeal outright on the ground that the decision was not in accordance with the Immigration Rules unless satisfied that all the relevant the requirements of the Immigration Rules were (or are, as appropriate) met. An appeal is not limited to the issues raised in the notice of refusal. If new elements of the Immigration Rules come into play they are to be dealt with on the appeal, and the parties must be allowed any appropriate adjournment in order to avoid the injustice of being taken by surprise. If the position before the immigration judge is that only some of the requirements of the Rules are or can be dealt with, it may well be right for him to look at only those requirements and to make findings on them: if his findings are all in favour of the appellant, he will allow the appeal to that extent, and the Entry Clearance Officer, Immigration Officer, or Secretary of State as appropriate should be directed to continue his consideration of the application or case in accordance with the findings made by the immigration judge.

6.128 In *CP (Section 86(3) and (5); wrong immigration rule) Dominica* [2006] the Tribunal held that where the Secretary of State or immigration officer applies the wrong immigration rule, then subject to the interests of fairness,[155] the immigration judge should apply the correct rule when deciding the appeal. Where the appellant satisfies all the requirements of the rule, the appeal will be allowed in full; where he does not, the appeal will be dismissed in substance under section 86(5) but allowed in part and to the limited and inconsequential extent that the decision was 'not in accordance with the law'. Also, if an application (as presented) could be considered under alternative parts of a relevant rule it will be the decision maker's duty to do so.[156]

6.129 However, in *SZ (Applicable immigration rules) Bangladesh* [2007] UKAIT 00037 the Tribunal held that there is no general duty on the Tribunal to consider whether a claimant's case if differently presented or if made the subject of a different application might have succeeded on a different basis from that on which the application or claim was made. The duty to consider the applicable rules is not an all-embracing obligation to seek out and find any (or every) potentially

---

[154] Reported—the Tribunal found that *Kwok On Tong*, a case decided under s 19 of the 1971 Act, was still good law and there was no material difference between the formulation of s 86 of the 2002 Act and s 19 of the 1971 Act.

[155] ie, allowing an adjournment.

[156] See *IAT v Tohur Ali* [1988] Imm AR 237 (CA) and *Mohammed Fazor Ali v SSHD* [1988] Imm AR 274 (CA).

applicable rule. In *Mohammed Fazor Ali v SSHD*[157] Mann LJ pointed out (at p 282) it was not 'any part of an immigration officer's duty to conduct a roving expedition through all the paragraphs to see whether a person before him is eligible under any of them'. As a result of the fact that the Tribunal is not the primary decision maker, the focus of the Tribunal's inquiry must always be the basis on which the application was made. However, there will occasionally be situations where the basis of the application, or the scope of the decision, or the grounds themselves, do require the Tribunal to consider more than the self-evidently applicable rule. Where there is an obvious link or connection between another rule and the primary way in which the application or grounds are put, it may be the obligation of the Tribunal to consider and apply another rule subject always to the requirements of fairness. In particular, if there is reason to suppose that the appellant may want to challenge the decision on grounds other than those set out in the notice of appeal, there may in certain circumstances be an obligation to consider whether the grounds of appeal should be amended.

Discretion

The Tribunal must allow an appeal in so far as it thinks that a discretion exercised **6.130** in making a decision against which the appeal is brought or is treated as being brought should have been exercised differently.[158] Refusal to depart from or authorize departure from the immigration rules is not the exercise of a discretion for these purposes.[159] Therefore the Tribunal only has jurisdiction to exercise a fresh discretion in cases within the immigration rules.

In asylum and human rights appeals the question of the exercise of a discretion **6.131** does not arise. A person either is or is not a refugee, and is or is not entitled to humanitarian protection, or the recognition that his human rights will be breached on the basis of the risk he faces on return. The Immigration Rules concerning asylum and humanitarian reflect this by use of the wording 'will' or 'shall' grant leave.[160]

Under the Immigration Rules, most of the Rules state that leave may be granted **6.132** if the applicant fulfills the given criteria. The word 'may' imports a discretion, which means that despite fulfilling the substantive requirements of a Rule, an applicant may be refused entry clearance or leave under the general grounds of refusal under paragraph 320 (1)–(7) of the Immigration Rules. There is a further discretion under paragraphs 320(8)–(21) which define when entry clearance or

---

[157] *Mohammed Fazor Ali v SSHD* [1988] Imm AR 274 (CA).
[158] Section 86(3)(b) NIA 2002.
[159] Section 86(6) NIA 2002.
[160] Paragraphs 327–339.

leave to enter the UK should normally be refused. The Tribunal has the power to review all of these exercises of discretion.[161]

Admissible evidence
Section 85(4)

6.133 Save for on appeals against entry clearance or the refusal of a certificate of entitlement to the right of abode, the Tribunal may consider evidence about any matter which it thinks relevant to the substance of the decision, including evidence which concerns a matter arising after the date of the decision.

6.134 In *LS (Gambia)* UKIAT 00085 the Tribunal found that it is only in appeals against the refusal of entry clearance and a certificate of entitlement that the 'clock stops' so that evidence of circumstances appertaining after the date of the decision cannot be taken into account. In all other cases if an Appellant claims that the decision 'is not in accordance with immigration rules', he is entitled to adduce evidence as to the present position, even if it is clear that the requirements of the Immigration Rules were not met at the date of the decision itself. The Tribunal considered that this interpretation accords with the 'one-stop' approach to in-country appeals, since, if the Tribunal is limited to circumstances appertaining at the date of the decision, it is at risk of producing a determination which, however correct, is of no practical interest, because the Appellant's circumstances may have changed since that date.

6.135 In *EA (Section 85 (4) explained) Nigeria* [2007] UKAIT 00013 the Tribunal held that as evidence is admissible only in so far as the Tribunal thinks it 'relevant to the substance of the decision', it is not the relevance of the evidence to the appellant's claim or his application that is in question: it is its relevance to the decision that was actually made. Therefore, it is not open to an appellant to argue simply that, on the date of the hearing, he meets the requirements of the Immigration Rules. He can succeed only if he shows that the decision that was made was one which was not in accordance with the Immigration Rules. Section 85(4) allows him to show that by reference to evidence of matters postdating the decision itself but that does not mean that the Tribunal is the primary decision maker. The Tribunal's task remains that of hearing appeals against decisions actually made.

---

[161] See *JC (Part 9 HC395–burden of proof) China* [2007] UKIAT 00027—in relation to all the general grounds contained in Part 9 of the Immigration Rules, including 320(15), the burden of proof rests on the decision maker to establish any contested precedent fact. If an appellant has failed to meet the requirements of the Immigration Rules set out in Parts 2–8, then he cannot succeed, even if it transpires that paragraph 320(15) grounds have been wrongly applied against him. However, where there is an overlap in the reasons given for finding the requirements of the substantive immigration rules not to be met and those given for finding that paragraph 320(15) applies, an error in the latter may (depending on the facts of the individual case) infect the former.

The correct interpretation of section 85(4) is that the appellant cannot succeed by showing that he would be granted leave if he made an application on the date of the hearing: he can succeed only by showing that he would be granted leave if he made, on the date of the hearing, the same application as that which resulted in the decision under appeal. The subsection does not permit an appellant to change his case under the Immigration Rules for being allowed to remain in the United Kingdom.

In *TB (Student application–variation of course–effect) Jamaica* [2006] UKAIT **6.136**
00034[162] the Tribunal held that where an appellant had changed her course from that specified in her application prior to the Secretary of State's decision and without notifying him, the immigration judge had erred in law in allowing post-decision evidence under section 85(4) of her changed course of study, as the nature of the change was such that she could not comply with the course for which she initially applied.

Section 85(5)—admissible evidence on appeals against the refusal of entry clearance or a certificate of entitlement

In an appeal relating to the refusal of entry clearance or a certification of entitle- **6.137**
ment the Tribunal may consider only the circumstances appertaining at the time of the decision to refuse. Section 85(5) specifically disapplies section 85(4), excluding 'evidence which concerns a matter arising' after the date of the decision.

In *DR (ECO: post-decision evidence) Morocco** [2005] UKIAT 00038 held that **6.138**
'evidence arising' after the date of the decision is not excluded provided it relates to circumstances appertaining at the time of the decision to refuse. For example, if there was an issue about whether at the time of the decision a couple intended to live together as man and wife, evidence of that intention can be provided by subsequent actions which cast light upon what the position then was (ie evidence of phone calls and letters which postdate the decision). However, evidence about a subsequent change in intention is clearly excluded.

Jurisdiction in asylum and human rights appeals

The applicable ground of appeal in asylum and human rights cases is section **6.139**
84(1) (g), that the removal of the appellant from the UK would breach the UK's obligations under the Refugee Convention or would be unlawful under section 6 of the HRA as being incompatible with his Convention rights.

---

[162] Reported.

6.140   The Court of Appeal held in the landmark case of *Ravichandran*[163] that in an asylum appeal, the Tribunal has to look at the position at the date of the appeal. In *Razgar*[164] this approach was extended to all human rights cases involving removal. It is clear from the wording of section 84(1)(g), that the statute looks to the future.[165] In *JM v Secretary of State for the Home Department*[166] the Court of Appeal held that even where removal is not imminent, human rights should be considered under section 84(1)(g).[167] Once a human rights point is properly before the Tribunal, it is obliged to deal with it. In *MS (Ivory Coast) v SSHD*[168] the Court of Appeal considered that a survey of the authorities showed that in both asylum and human rights cases the Tribunal was required to hypothesize a removal and not proceed on the basis that there was not going to be a removal.

6.141   Hence, in an asylum appeal or human rights appeal involving removal, the Tribunal is an extension of the decision-making process. This has a number of ramifications for the Tribunal's jurisdiction. The Tribunal may, in certain cases, become the first instance decision maker in an asylum or human rights appeal. If the Secretary of State has refused an application for asylum on non-compliance grounds[169] and hence made no substantive decision on the claim, for example because the claimant has failed to attend an interview or return a statement of evidence form, the Tribunal must determine the substantive appeal.

6.142   On an appeal under section 84(1)(g) the Tribunal must consider the position that would exist *within* an appellant's home country or place of former habitual residence if he were removed in consequence of the immigration decision despite the fact that no removal directions have been set. The Courts have dealt in a number of recent cases with the issue of jurisdiction under section 84(1)(g) where no removal directions have been set and the appellant asserts that he would be at risk due to the route or method of return or would be refused entry at the border.

---

[163] [1996] Imm AR 97, CA, *Saad & Ors v Secretary of State for the Home Department* [2002] INLR.

[164] [2004] UKHL 27, para 15.

[165] Laws LJ pointed out in *JM* [2006] EWCA Civ 1402 that s 84(1)(g) was to all intents and purposes identical to s 8 of the 1993 Act, in respect of which it had been held that all asylum appeals are hypothetical in the sense that they involve the consideration of a hypothesis or assumption.

[166] [2006] EWCA Civ 1402.

[167] On a variation of leave appeal where removal was not imminent because removal directions had not been set, the immigration decision was nevertheless a decision 'in consequence of which' (s 84(1)(g)) the appellant would be removed as removal was an indirect consequence of the decision.

[168] [2007] EWCA Civ133.

[169] *Ali Haddad* [2000] INLR 117.

In *GH v Secretary of State for the Home Department*,[170] the appellant, GH, was an Iraqi Kurd from the Kurdish Autonomous area in Northern Iraq who claimed asylum in the UK. It was found that following the toppling of Saddam Hussein's regime he could live safely in his former home area. The appellant contended, however, that he would be at risk when travelling within Iraq from the point of arrival to his home area and the Tribunal should consider the safety of the route and method of return. The Court of Appeal had to determine the question of whether the Tribunal has jurisdiction to take account of what may happen in the course of travelling to his safe home area. The Court of Appeal held that, because no removal directions had been set,[171] there was no jurisdiction to consider what might happen to the appellant on route because the method and route of return to the appellant's home area were wholly unknown. In such circumstances the appellant was in no position to establish either a well-founded fear of persecution or a risk amounting to a breach of Articles 2 and 3 ECHR arising solely as a consequence of the method or route of return to his home area. The remedy in such cases is therefore to judicially review the removal directions when they are set.

6.143

However, the Court of Appeal in *GH* was of the view that there would be cases where the Tribunal could properly consider the route and method of return even in the absence of removal directions, because the Secretary of State has committed himself through a policy statement or otherwise to a particular route of return. Where it is implicit in the decision to remove from the UK that a particular method or route of return would be adopted, the safety of that method or route could be considered by the Tribunal as part and parcel of the 'immigration decision' under section 82(1). The wording of section 84(1)(g) was wide enough to give the Tribunal jurisdiction to take into account 'en route' risks in such cases.

6.144

In *AK v Secretary of State for the Home Department*[172] the Court of Appeal distinguished *GH* in a case where the appellant asserted that he would be refused re-entry at the border of his place of former habitual residence. The appellant in *AK* claimed that he would be refused re-entry whatever method or route of return the Secretary of State chose. The Court of Appeal held that there was no difference in principle between consideration of the position *within* the territory and consideration of the position *at the border* of the territory. If an appellant claims to fear persecution at the border, there is no reason why that claim should not be examined by the Tribunal in the same way as a claim to fear persecution or ill-treatment by reason of the conduct of the State authorities within the territory. As his case

6.145

---

170 [2005] EWCA Civ 1182; [2006] Imm AR 19; [2006] INLR 26.

171 And there is no right of appeal against the giving of removal directions as such action is not within the definition of an 'immigration decision' within s 82(1) of the NIA 2002.

172 [2006] EWCA Civ 1117.

was that he would be refused re-entry whatever route or method was chosen by the Secretary of State, the issue did not depend on some future contingency or variable and hence was distinguishable from the position in *GH*.

6.146   In *Gedow*[173] the Court of Appeal again dealt with the issue of the Tribunal's jurisdiction to consider risk relating to the 'mechanics' of return. The appellant acknowledged that after his arrival at his home there was not a real risk of suffering inhuman and degrading treatment. He claimed that there was a real risk that he would suffer that treatment upon arrival at an airport in Mogadishu or upon his journey from that airport to his home. The Court of Appeal held that it is impossible for immigration judges in cases of this kind (involving the safety of arrival at an airport and of a journey into Mogadishu) to deal with all the eventualities at the time of the hearing. The judge may have to make it clear what has to be done by the Secretary of State so that an enforced returnee does not face a real risk of Article 3 ill-treatment at the point of his return. The judge is then entitled to assume, for the purposes of the hearing before him, that what is required will be done. Undertakings were not appropriate from the Secretary of State to the Court as to the method of return.

Directions where an appeal is allowed

6.147   Under section 87(1) of the 2002 Act, if the Tribunal allows an appeal under sections 82, 83, or 83A it may give a direction for the purpose of giving effect to its decision. A person responsible for making an immigration decision shall act in accordance with any such relevant direction.[174] A direction will not have effect where the allowed appeal in respect of which the direction was given is under challenge.[175] A direction is to be treated as part of the Tribunal's decision on the appeal for the purposes of an application for reconsideration under section 103A.[176]

6.148   The Tribunal may therefore direct that the immigration authorities grant leave to enter, entry clearance, or a certificate of entitlement. It is normally the case that the immigration authorities would in any event take such action without the need for a direction from the Tribunal. There may, however, be occasions when a direction to grant entry clearance is not appropriate, because circumstances have changed since the date of the original decision or there are aspects of a rule that the Tribunal has been unable to consider. In *RM (India)* [2006] UKAIT 00039 the Tribunal stated that if the position before the immigration judge is that only

---

[173]   *Gedow v SSHD* [2006] EWCA Civ 1342.
[174]   Section 87(2) NIA 2002.
[175]   Section 87(3) NIA 2002.
[176]   Section 87(4) NIA 2002.

some of the requirements of the Rules are or can be dealt with, it may well be right for him to look at only those requirements and to make findings on them: if his findings are all in favour of the appellant, he will allow the appeal to that extent, and the Entry Clearance Officer, Immigration Officer, or Secretary of State as appropriate should be directed to continue his consideration of the application or case in accordance with the findings made by the immigration judge.

In *MS (Ivory Coast) v SSHD*[177] the Court of Appeal appears to have extended the **6.149** jurisdiction of the Tribunal to have the power to direct the type of leave which should be granted on an allowed appeal. On the basis of past authorities, it appeared that the Tribunal did not have this power. In *Omeed Sharif*[178] an Adjudicator had allowed an appeal under Article 3 and directed that the appellant be granted indefinite leave to remain. The IAT held that he should have made no such direction. However, in *MS* the Court of Appeal stated that the Tribunal could decide for itself under section 87(1) what period of discretionary leave would be appropriate.

Recommendations where an appeal is dismissed

There is no statutory power which provides for the Tribunal to make a 'recom- **6.150** mendation' to the Secretary of State to exercise a discretion in the appellant's favour where the appeal falls to be dismissed. A 'recommendation' is therefore a discretionary extra-statutory indication of what the Tribunal considers to be an appropriate action for the Secretary of State to take. A recommendation is not part of the determination and a failure to make one cannot be challenged on judicial review.[179]

Since the enactment of the HRA 1998, the use of recommendations has declined **6.151** and the Tribunal has discouraged immigration judges from making them. In *AM (Extra statutory recommendations generally undesirable) Angola*[180] the Tribunal stated that adjudicators are rarely in a position to know all the facts that would be relevant to an exercise by the Secretary of State of his discretion to allow a person to stay: therefore it is wrong to seek to bind the Secretary of State to act on find-ings based on incomplete evidence. Further, such recommendations can be seen as a vehicle for applying their own subjective standards as to what is or is not a compassionate circumstance. There is often no clear set of objective legal princi-ples, such as those which govern assessment under the Refugee Convention and the Human Rights Act, which an adjudicator can be seen to be drawing upon.

---

[177] [2007] EWCA Civ 133.
[178] [2002] UKIAT 953.
[179] *R v Immigration Tribunal, ex parte Chavrimootoo* [1995] Imm AR 267, QBD.
[180] [2004] UKIAT 00146.

6.152 However, in *Shilova*[181] the High Court considered that recommendations were useful in situations where human rights issues are not engaged but the Secretary of State should be made aware of an appellant's contribution to society and relations with family in the UK.

J. Appeals from the Asylum and Immigration Tribunal

6.153 As stated in paragraph 6.06 above, since 4 April 2005, since the AIT is a one-tier structure, applications for reconsideration and review no longer go to the appellate authority but to the High Court or Court of Appeal. The avenue for appeal depends on the manner in which the Tribunal being appealed was constituted and whether the application is for reconsideration or renewal. However, for an unspecified period beginning on 4 April 2005, a filter provision has been introduced by Schedule 2 to the 2004 Act. Due to fear that the High Court would be inundated by applications, an application for an order requiring the Tribunal to review its decision is initially considered by the Tribunal itself, with a right to apply to the High Court where the immigration judge decides not to order reconsideration. We deal in detail with applications for reconsideration and renewal below.

Applications for reconsideration—section 103A

6.154 A party to an appeal under sections 82, 83, or 83A of the 2002 Act may apply to the High Court, on the grounds that the Tribunal made an error of law, for an order requiring the Tribunal to reconsider its decision on the appeal.[182] Where the jurisdiction of the Tribunal was exercised by three or more legally qualified members an appeal lies directly to the Court of Appeal and not the High Court.[183] The High Court may make an order for reconsideration only if it thinks that the Tribunal may have made an error of law and only once in relation to an appeal.[184] Therefore, after the Tribunal has reconsidered its decision, any further appeal is to the Court of Appeal on a point of law.[185]

6.155 The relevant statutory provisions concerning the reconsideration of appeals are to be found in:

- section 103A of the 2002 Act;
- paragraph 30 of Schedule 2 to the 2004 Act ('the filter provision');

---

[181] *R (on the appln of Shilova) v Secretary of State for the Home Department* [2002] INLR 611.
[182] Section 103A NIA Act 2002 (as inserted by s 26(6) of the 2004 Act).
[183] Section 103E NIA Act 2002.
[184] Section 103A (2) NIA 2002.
[185] Section 103(B) NIA 2002.

- Rules 24 to 33 of the Procedure Rules;
- Rules 16 to 23 of the Fast Track Rules;
- Rules 53.28 to 54.36 of the Civil Procedure Rules 1998 (CPR).[186]

An application for reconsideration is determined on the papers.[187] It is deter- **6.156**
mined by reference only to the written submissions of the applicant and where
the rules of court permit, other written submissions.[188] Whilst the decision of
the High Court on an application for reconsideration is expressed to be final,[189]
an application for judicial review of the original decision is available where there
are appropriate grounds. In *R (on the appln of AM) (Cameroon)*[190] the Court of
Appeal reviewed the case law and held that it would only be in exceptional cases
that the court would exercise its discretion to move for judicial review.[191] The
Court of Appeal in *AM* cited *G & M* where it was held that the 'statutory regime,
including statutory review of a refusal of permission to appeal, provides adequate
and proportionate protection of the asylum seeker's rights. It is accordingly a proper
exercise of the court's discretion to decline to entertain an application for judicial
review of issues which have been, or could have been, the subject of statutory
review'.[192] An application for reconsideration may be made after a decision following remittal from the Court of Appeal under sections 103B, 103C, or 103E.[193]

It is only substantive decisions which may be the subject of reconsideration under **6.157**
section 103(A). No procedural, ancillary, or preliminary decision may be
appealed.[194] This means that the only remedy for challenging the procedural,
ancillary, or preliminary decisions is by way of judicial review. However, the
Court of Appeal in *AM*[195] held, relying on case law under the previous statutory
regime, that if the alleged error in an interlocutory decision 'persists in the final
determination' to which section 103A applies, and will be the subject of review
under section 103A, the court will still be as reluctant as previously to grant

---

[186] As inserted by rule 7 of the Civil Procedure (Amendment) Rules 2005).
[187] Section 103A (5) NIA 2002.
[188] Section 103A(5)(a)(b) NIA Act 2002.
[189] Section 103A(6) NIA 2002.
[190] [2007] EWCA Civ 131.
[191] Applying *R(G & M) v Immigration Tribunal* [2005] 1 WLR 1445.
[192] *R(G & M) v Immigration Tribunal* [2005] 1 WLR 1445, paragraph 26. The Court of Appeal
added: 'We would add two observations. First, the applicability of the well-established principle that
judicial review is a remedy of last resort is tested objectively by the court. Thus our conclusion has
had regard to the legislative purpose and effect of section 101 but not to any wider policy —if there
is one—of excluding recourse to the courts. Secondly, our decision concerns only cases, such as the
two before us, in which the application for judicial review is co-extensive with the available statutory
review Judicial review remains open in principle in cases of justiciable errors not susceptible of statutory review' (at paragraph 27).
[193] Section 103A(7)(b) NIA 2002.
[194] Section 103A(7)(a) NIA 2002.
[195] *R (on the appln of AM) (Cameroon)* [2007] EWCA Civ 131.

permission to judicially review an interlocutory decision. In such circumstances an application for judicial review of an interlocutory decision is premature because the appellant has not exhausted his remedies in that he may apply for reconsideration of the substantive determination on the basis that the interlocutory decision gave rise to an error of law.

6.158 However, the Court of Appeal held in *AM* that there will be exceptional circumstances where an application for judicial review may be available notwithstanding the outstanding remedy under section 103A. Whilst Their Lordships eschewed an exhaustive definition of the exceptional, Lord Justice Rix opined that the logic of the situation is such that a case must (a) go beyond the complaint that the interlocutory decision impugned was unfair in itself, (b) demonstrate such a challenge to the fairness of the final hearing as to amount to a denial of justice, and do so (c) in circumstances where the statutory review is not well adjusted to give relief.[196]

Procedure and time limits on applications under section 103A

6.159 The time limit for appealing depends on whether the appellant is in the United Kingdom. An application made by an appellant while he is in the United Kingdom must be made within five days from the date which he is treated as receiving the Tribunal's decision.[197] The five-day time limit also applies to an application made by a party to the appeal who is not the appellant (ie the Secretary of State).[198] If the appellant is outside the United Kingdom the application must be made within 28 days beginning on the date on which he is treated as receiving notice of the Tribunal's decision.[199] Separate rules apply to applications in the fast track where the application notice must be filed not later than two days after deemed service.[200]

6.160 Rule 55 of the Procedure Rules 2005 provides that where a document is sent by post or DX, deemed service (ie the date someone is treated as having received a decision) takes place:

- where a document is sent from and to a place is the United Kingdom the second day after it was sent;[201]

---

[196] At para 128. Lord Justice Waller gave an example of such a circumstance if a decision was that a particular witness should be called where there was a strongly arguable case that the calling of the witness would endanger that witness. Such a decision could not be challenged by the section 103A procedure and because by the time a section 103A review came about, it would be too late to protect the witness, judicial review must be available to challenge such a decision (at para 153).

[197] Section 103A(3)(a).

[198] Section 103A(c).

[199] Section 103A(3)(b).

[200] The Asylum and Immigration (Fast Track Time Limits) Order 2005 (SI 2005, No 561) Article 3(2).

[201] Rule 55(5)(a).

- where a document is sent from or to a place outside the United Kingdom on the 28th day after it was sent.[202]

In any other case deemed service takes place on the day that the document was sent, delivered to, or left with the person.[203] Time is to be calculated according to Rule 2.8 of the CPR.[204] **6.161**

An application for reconsideration may be made outside the time limits set out above if the High Court thinks that the application could not reasonably practicably have been made within that period.[205] **6.162**

If an application is made for permission to proceed out of time it is prudent also to apply for a stay on removal pending reconsideration. This is because an out of time application for reconsideration, even with permission (ie allowed to proceed despite being out of time), is not treated as a pending appeal pursuant to section 104(2)(a) of the 2002 Act and hence an appellant is liable to removal until reconsideration is ordered. **6.163**

The filter provision

Until the Lord Chancellor decides otherwise, all applications for reconsideration are dealt with by a member of the Tribunal under the transitional provisions contained in Part 2 of Schedule 2 of the 2004 Act. For the transitional period references in section 103A to the High Court are to be taken as references to the member of the Tribunal considering the application.[206] An application for an order for reconsideration must be made by filing an application notice with the Tribunal at the address specified in the relevant practice direction.[207] The applicant must file with the application notice the notice of immigration decision, any document giving reasons for the decision, the grounds of appeal to the Tribunal, the Tribunal's determination, and any other documents material to the application which were before the Tribunal, in addition to the grounds of appeal.[208] The immigration judge may order reconsideration under section 103A(1) or grant permission for an out of time application to proceed under section 103A(4)(b).[209] **6.164**

---

[202] Rule 55(5)(b).
[203] Rule 55(5)(c), ie where it is faxed, emailed, or personally served.
[204] Part 54.28(4) CPR.
[205] Section 103A(4)(b) NIA Act 2002.
[206] Schedule 2, Part 2, para 30(3)(a), Asylum and Immigration (Treatment of Claimants, etc) Act 2004.
[207] Part 54.29 CPR, unless the appeal is in detention when the applicant may serve the documents on his custodian.
[208] Part 54.29 (2).
[209] Schedule 2, Part 2, para 30(4)(a), Asylum and Immigration (Treatment of Claimants, etc) Act 2004.

He must decide the application not later than ten days after the Tribunal receives the application notice.[210]

6.165 The fast track procedure differs from the procedure outlined above. Where an application under section 103A is filed with the Tribunal in a fast track case the Tribunal must serve copies of the application notice and any documents which were attached to it on the other party to the appeal as soon as practicable and the other party to the appeal may file submissions in response to the application not later than one day after the day on which it is served with the application.[211]

6.166 If the immigration judge does not propose to make an order for reconsideration or grant permission to proceed with the application out of time, he must notify the High Court and the applicant.[212]

6.167 The Procedure Rules apply to applications to the Tribunal under the filter provision. Part 3 of the Procedure Rules deals with applications considered by a member or members of the Tribunal. The application is decided without a hearing and by reference only to the applicant's written submissions and the documents filed with the application notice.[213] In fast track cases the immigration judge also considers any submissions served in response to the application.[214]

What grounds can the Tribunal consider in deciding whether to make an order for reconsideration?

6.168 The Procedure Rules provide that the immigration judge is not required to consider any grounds for ordering the Tribunal to reconsider its decision other than those set out in the application notice.[215] There is a requirement established in *R v SSHD ex p Robinson*[216] to consider an obvious point of Convention law even if it is not included in the grounds of appeal. In *Miftari v SSHD*[217] Maurice Kay LJ observed that *Robinson* remained good law even though the jurisdiction of the IAT was now restricted to an error of law, stating that the decision in *Robinson*:

> enabled, indeed required, the immigration appellate authorities to consider an obvious point of Convention jurisprudence which may avail an appellant, even if it is not pleaded or otherwise advanced on his behalf. The rationale was that, if such a point were ignored on technical grounds, there will be a danger that this country will be in

---

[210] Rule 26(4) Procedure Rules 2005.
[211] Rule 17, Fast Track Procedure Rules 2005.
[212] Schedule 2, Part 2, para 30(4)(b), Asylum and Immigration (Treatment of Claimants, etc) Act 2004.
[213] Rule 26(2) Procedure Rules.
[214] Rule 18, The Asylum and Immigration (Fast Track Procedure) Rules 2005.
[215] Rule 26(3) Procedure Rules.
[216] [1998] QB 929.
[217] [2005] EWCA Civ 481.

breach of its obligations under the Convention (per Lord Woolf MR, giving the judgment of the Court of Appeal, at p 946C).

In *Miftari* Maurice Kay LJ stated that he was not convinced that the decision in *Robinson* could ever avail the Secretary of State. In *A(Iraq)*[218] the Court of Appeal held that in an appeal by the Secretary of State the IAT had jurisdiction to correct a clear error of law in the application of the statutory definition of 'refugee'. Lord Justice Carnwath stated however that, in relation to an appeal by the Secretary of State, even if an 'obvious' point has been missed, it would be wrong to allow it to be taken for the first time on appeal if it depends on the finding of further facts which are left uncertain by the decision. If the facts are clear, however, then it is the duty of the Tribunal to ensure that the correct legal test is applied. The issue as to whether the *Robinson* principle (or any variant of it) can be invoked by the Secretary of State in other circumstances has not arisen for decision. In *AM (Serbia)*[219] it was held that the *Robinson* principle also applied to the ECHR. **6.169**

When will the Tribunal order reconsideration?

The immigration judge may order reconsideration only if he thinks that the Tribunal may have made an error of law and there is a real possibility that the Tribunal would decide the appeal differently on reconsideration.[220] This means that if the Tribunal considers that there was or may have been an error of law but that it was not material to the determination, it cannot order reconsideration. **6.170**

Error of law

What constitutes an error of law? This question was addressed by the Court of Appeal in *E & R v Secretary of State for the Home Department* [2004] EWCA Civ 49. The Court of Appeal concluded that the various procedures had evolved to the point where it has become a generally safe working rule that the substantive grounds for intervention are identical in an appeal to the Court of Appeal (ie on a point of law) and on judicial review. Appeals (or review procedures) confined to law are treated as encompassing the traditional judicial review grounds of excess of power, irrationality, and procedural irregularity. **6.171**

The Court also comprehensively reviewed the case law on the issue of whether, and in what circumstances, a mistake of fact can constitute an error of law. The Court concluded that 'a mistake of fact giving rise to unfairness is a separate head of challenge in an appeal on a point of law, at least in those statutory contexts **6.172**

---

[218] [2005] EWCA Civ 1438.
[219] *AM (Serbia & Ors) v SSHD* [2007] EWCA Civ 16.
[220] Rule 26(6) Procedure Rules.

where the parties share an interest in cooperating to achieve the correct result. Asylum law is undoubtedly such an area'. Whilst making clear that it was not laying down a precise code, the Court stated that the ordinary requirements for a finding of unfairness arising from a mistake of fact are:

- first, there must have been a mistake as to an existing fact, including a mistake as to the availability of evidence on a particular matter;
- second, the fact or evidence must have been 'established', in the sense that it was uncontentious and objectively verifiable;
- third, the appellant (or his advisers) must not been have been responsible for the mistake;
- fourth, the mistake must have played a material (not necessarily decisive) part in the Tribunal's reasoning.

6.173 In order to establish this unfairness, fresh evidence is clearly required. The court acknowledged the intrinsic difficulty in many asylum cases of obtaining reliable evidence of the facts that gave rise to the fear of persecution and the need for some flexibility in the application of *Ladd v Marshall* principles. In *Ladd v Marshall* [1954] 1 WLR 1489 Lord Denning held that the decision of the judge could be overturned by the use of further evidence only if it could be shown that:

(1) the new evidence could not with reasonable diligence have been obtained for use at the trial (or hearing);
(2) the new evidence must be such that, if given, it would probably have had an important influence on the result of the case (though it need not be decisive);
(3) the new evidence was apparently credible although it need not be incontrovertible.

6.174 In conclusion in *E & R* Carnwarth LJ said at para 91 that on an appeal on the basis of unfairness resulting from 'misunderstanding or ignorance of an established and relevant fact' the admission of new evidence was subject to *Ladd v Marshall* principles, which might be departed from in exceptional circumstances where the interests of justice required.

6.175 In *R (Iran)* [2005] EWCA Civ 982 the Court of Appeal considered the jurisdiction of the IAT to correct errors of law. Whilst the case was concerned with the IAT's powers under the transitional provisions, those parts of the judgment addressing the jurisdiction to correct an error of law are equally relevant to the current statutory regime. The Court gave examples of errors of law commonly encountered in practice:

- making perverse or irrational findings on a matter or matters that were material to the outcome ('material matters');
- failing to give reasons or any adequate reasons for findings on material matters;

- failing to take into account and/or resolve conflicts of fact or opinion on material matters;
- giving weight to immaterial matters;
- making a material misdirection of law on any material matter;
- committing or permitting a procedural or other irregularity capable of making a material difference to the outcome or the fairness of the proceedings;
- making a mistake as to a material fact which could be established by objective and uncontentious evidence, where the appellant and/or his advisers were not responsible for the mistake, and where unfairness resulted from the fact that a mistake was made.

The Court emphasized that each of these grounds for detecting an error of law **6.176** contain the word 'material' (or 'immaterial'). Errors of law of which it can be said that they would have made no difference to the outcome do not matter. Under the current statutory regime this need to identify an error of law which would have made a material difference to the outcome is underscored by Rule 31 (2)(b), which states that in carrying out the reconsideration the Tribunal must first decide whether the original Tribunal made a material error of law. This is defined in Rule 31(5) as 'an error of law which affected the Tribunal's decision upon the appeal'.

The principles emerging from the judgment as they apply to the jurisdiction of **6.177** the AIT to correct an error of law are as follows:

- Before the Tribunal (or High Court on the cessation of the transitional provisions) can set aside a decision of the original Tribunal on the grounds of error of law, it has to be satisfied that the correction of the error would have made a material difference to the outcome, or to the fairness of the proceedings. This principle applies equally to decisions of the Tribunal on proportionality in connection with human rights issues.
- A finding might be set aside for error of law on the grounds of perversity only if it was irrational or unreasonable in the Wednesbury sense, or one that was wholly unsupported by the evidence.
- A decision should not be set aside for inadequacy of reasons unless the original Tribunal failed to identify and record the matters that were critical to its decision on material issues, in such a way that the Tribunal was unable to understand why he reached that decision.
- A failure without good reason to apply a relevant country guidance decision might constitute an error of law.

In the course of the judgment the Court made a number of comments in respect **6.178** of the above annunciated principles directed at the tendency of some practitioners to bring cases on unarguable grounds. The Court criticized the use of the words 'irrational' or 'perverse' when these epithets are completely inappropriate. The Court further stated that unjustified complaints by practitioners that are based on an alleged failure to give reasons, or adequate reasons, are seen far too often. The Court emphasized that the practice of bringing appeals because the adjudicator or immigration judge has not made reasoned findings on matters of peripheral importance must now come to an end. These comments must clearly be borne in mind when considering whether to make an application for reconsideration, particularly in view of the restrictive funding regime.

The admission of fresh evidence on an application for reconsideration

6.179 The Procedure Rules do not contain an express provision for the admission of fresh evidence on an application for reconsideration. However, the applicable Practice Direction[221] states at paragraph 13.8 that a party seeking to adduce evidence that was not before the original Tribunal must explain in the application the significance of that evidence with regard to *both* of the requirements of Rule 26 (6) (ie with regard to both why it is alleged that the Tribunal made an error of law and why there is a real possibility that the Tribunal would decide the appeal differently on reconsideration) and refers the reader to *E & R*.[222]

6.180 Where an immigration judge decides an application for permission under section 103A(4)(b) or application for an order under section 103A(1) he must give written reasons for his decision which may be in summary form.[223] These reasons must be adequate in the public law sense. If the immigration judge makes an order for reconsideration, the notice must state the grounds on which the Tribunal is ordered to reconsider its decision on the appeal[224] and may give directions for the reconsideration hearing of the appeal.[225] These directions may specify the number or class of members of the Tribunal who will hear the reconsideration (see Practice Note) and provide for further appropriate directions under rule 45(4).[226] The Practice Direction states at paragraph 13.9 that the immigration judge who has decided to make an order for reconsideration will decide under rule 27(2)(b) whether to direct that a CMR hearing be held before the reconsideration hearing takes place and whether to make a direction as to the evidence to be adduced at the hearing initially fixed for the reconsideration.

6.181 In *DK (Serbia) & Ors v Secretary of State for the Home Department* [2006] EWCA Civ 1747 the Court of Appeal gave guidance both as to the scope of and

---

221 Consolidated version as at 30 April 2007.
222 See para 6.171 above.
223 Rule 27(1).
224 Rule 27 (2)(a).
225 Rule 27 (2)(b).
226 Rule 27 (2) (b)(i) and (ii).

procedure on reconsideration. In relation to directions at the stage where reconsideration is ordered, the Court of Appeal stated that the parties should expect a direction restricting argument to the points of law identified by the immigration judge. The immigration judge can also give directions under Rule 27(2)(b), which can include directions as to how the reconsideration should be dealt with in the event the Tribunal agrees with him as to the error of law which he had identified. This provides an opportunity for the structure of the reconsideration to be put into place.[227]

Form and service of the decision

The procedure with regard to the service of the decision varies depending on the nature of the appeal. In fast track cases if submissions were filed in response to the application the Tribunal must serve a copy of the notice of decision and any directions on every party to the appeal not later than one day after they were filed.[228] If no submissions were filed the notice of decision must be served not later than one day after the Respondent filed submissions.[229] **6.182**

Where the review is of an appeal under section 82 where the appeal relates wholly or partly to an asylum claim and the appellant is in the United Kingdom, the Tribunal must serve on the Secretary of State the notice of decision, any directions, and (unless the Secretary of State made the application for reconsideration) the application notice and any attached documents.[230] The Secretary of State then must serve the documentation on the appellant no later than 28 days after receiving it from the Tribunal.[231] When the Secretary of State has served the documentation he must notify the Tribunal as soon as practicable on what date and by what means it was served.[232] If the Secretary of State does not notify the Tribunal within 29 days after the Tribunal serves the notice of decision on it, the Tribunal must then serve the documents on the appellant as soon as reasonably practicable thereafter.[233] **6.183**

In all other cases the Tribunal must serve a copy of the notice of decision and any directions on every party to the appeal and where the immigration judge orders reconsideration serve on the party who did not make the application a copy of the application notice and any attached documents.[234] **6.184**

---

[227] *DK (Serbia)* paragraph 28.
[228] Rule 19 (a) Fast Track Procedure Rules.
[229] Rule 19(b) Fast Track Procedure Rules.
[230] Rule 27(5) Procedure Rules.
[231] Unless the appellant made the application for reconsideration, Rule 27 (5)(b) Procedure Rules.
[232] Rule 27(5)(c).
[233] Rule 27(5)(d).
[234] Rule 27(3).

Renewal of the application to the High Court

6.185 Where the Tribunal gives notice that it does not intend to make an order for reconsideration or grant permission to apply out of time, the applicant may notify the High Court that he wishes to renew his application.[235] He must notify the High Court within five days from deemed service[236] unless the case is on the fast track, in which case the time limit is two days of deemed service.[237] The High Court then will consider the application if it was given notice within the prescribed period.[238] If the notice was given out of time the High Court will consider the application only if it concludes that the notice could not reasonably practicably have been given within the five-day time period.[239] The Civil Procedure Rules and Practice Directions apply.[240] The application is determined by reference only to the written submissions of the applicant.[241] If the High Court thinks that the application raises a question of law of such importance that it should be decided by the Court of Appeal, it may refer the appeal to that court. The Court of Appeal has all the normal powers, but in addition it may restore the application under section 103A to the High Court. The procedure for continuing an application in circumstances in which it would otherwise be treated as abandoned is also prescribed.[242]

The reconsideration hearing

6.186 The immigration judge who made the order for reconsideration will have stated the grounds on which the Tribunal is ordered to reconsider the decision (Rule 27(2)(a)) and will have decided whether to direct a CMR hearing (Rule 27(2)(b)) to be held before the reconsideration hearing takes place. Directions may have been made as to the evidence to be adduced at the hearing fixed for the reconsideration.

6.187 The Rules applying to the initial determination of an appeal also apply to reconsideration appeals. Specifically, Rules 15 to 23, except for Rule 23 (2) and (3)

---

[235] Paragraph 30(5)(a) Schedule 2, Asylum and Immigration (Treatment of Claimants) Act 2004.

[236] Paragraph 30(5)(b) Schedule 2, Asylum and Immigration (Treatment of Claimants) Act 2004—Rule 2.8 CPR applies to the calculation of time periods under this paragraph by virtue of Part 54.28 (4)(b) CPR.

[237] Article 4 (2) The Asylum and Immigration (Fast Track Time Limits) Order 2005, SI 2005/561.

[238] Paragraph 30(5)(c)(i) Schedule 2, Asylum and Immigration (Treatment of Claimants) Act 2004.

[239] Paragraph 30(5)(c)(ii) Schedule 2, Asylum and Immigration (Treatment of Claimants) Act 2004.

[240] CPR Part 54.28–54.36.

[241] CPR Part 54.33.

[242] CPR Part 54.36—appeals which would otherwise be treated as abandoned under section 104(4A) of the 2002 Act.

(relating to special procedures and time limits in asylum appeals), and Part 5 (general provisions) apply to the reconsideration of an appeal.[243] There are also specific rules relating to the procedure on reconsideration of appeals which provide for the service of a reply,[244] the admission of further evidence,[245] and orders for funding on reconsideration.[246]

If the respondent to an application for reconsideration contends that the Tribunal **6.188** should uphold the initial determination for different reasons or additional reasons to those in the determination, he must serve on the Tribunal and the applicant a reply setting out his case.[247] This must be done not later than five days before the earliest appointed date for any hearing of or in relation to the reconsideration of the appeal.[248]

Where an order for reconsideration has been made, the Tribunal must reconsider **6.189** an appeal as soon as reasonably practicable after that order has been served on both parties to the appeal.[249] In fast track cases this will be not later than 2 days after the day on which that order has been served on both parties to the appeal or as soon as practicable thereafter.[250]

Where the reconsideration is pursuant to an order under section 103A the **6.190** Tribunal must first decide whether the original Tribunal made a material error of law[251] and if it decides that the original Tribunal did not make a material error of law[252] must order that the original determination of the appeal shall stand.[253] Subject to this the Tribunal must substitute a fresh decision to allow or dismiss the appeal.[254] In carrying out the reconsideration the Tribunal may limit submissions or evidence to one or more specified issues[255] and must have regard to

---

[243] Rule 29 Procedure Rules, ie the rules relating to where an appeal lapses, is abandoned, treated as finally determined, the rules for determining an appeal without a hearing, withdrawal, hearing in the absence of a party, combined hearings, adjournments, and the giving of determinations and the general rules relating to the conduct of appeals and applications, the constitution of the Tribunal, directions, notification of hearings and representation, summoning of witnesses etc.
[244] Rule 30 Procedure Rules.
[245] Rule 32 Procedure Rules.
[246] Rule 33 Procedure Rules, section 103D NIA Act 2002.
[247] Rule 30 Procedure Rules.
[248] Rule 30(2) Procedure Rules.
[249] Rule 31(1) Procedure Rules.
[250] Rule 21(1) Fast Track Procedure Rules.
[251] Rule 31(2)(a) Procedure Rules.
[252] Material error of law means an error of law which affected the Tribunal's decision upon the appeal (Rule 31(5)).
[253] Rule 31(2)(b) Procedure Rules.
[254] Rule 31(3) Procedure Rules.
[255] Rule 31(4)(a) Procedure Rules.

any directions given by the immigration judge or court which ordered the reconsideration.[256]

6.191 The Practice Direction (Consolidated Version 30 April 2007) provides that reconsideration of appeals will be heard by a legally qualified member or two or more members, at least one of whom is legally qualified.[257]

Scope of reconsideration

6.192 Case law under the previous statutory regime consistently reiterated that the IAT had jurisdiction to consider the appeal to them only if a point of law could be found within the formulated grounds.[258] In *Ismet Jasarevic v Secretary of State for the Home Department*,[259] Buxton LJ stated that it is necessary for a point of law to be reasonably discernible in the grounds of appeal on the basis on which permission to appeal has been given.[260]

6.193 This question has been addressed under the current statutory regime in the case of *DK (Serbia)*[261] in which the Court of Appeal gave guidance on the scope of reconsideration under section 103A and what procedures should be adopted by the Tribunal in dealing with the reconsideration. The Court of Appeal considered that the reasoning of the Tribunal in *AH (Scope of s103A reconsideration) Sudan*[262] was essentially sound. The Court approved the determination of the Tribunal in *AH* concluding that there was no justification to be found in the 2004 Act or the Rules for restricting the scope of a reconsideration, either in relation to the question as to what, if any, errors of law could be identified in the original decision, or as to the scope of the reconsideration if such an error of law has been found. The only constraint implicit in the structure is that reconsideration is restricted to the grounds of the original appeal, subject to the caveat that there might be an obvious point of Convention law so far overlooked. Rule 31(4) did not empower the Tribunal to restrict the scope of a reconsideration to the grounds upon which the reconsideration had been ordered, but only to 'have regard' to the directions given by the immigration judge ordering the reconsideration, and limiting submissions or evidence to specific issues. Rule 31(3) required the Tribunal, having

---

[256] Rule 31(4)(b) Procedure Rules.

[257] Paragraph 2.2(3).

[258] *Emrush Miftari v Secretary of State for the Home Department* [2005] EWCA Civ 481; *B v Secretary of State* [2005] EWCA Civ 61.

[259] [2005] EWCA Civ 1784.

[260] Citing *B v Secretary of State for the Home Department* [2005] EWCA Civ 61; *Miftari v Secretary of State for the Home Department* [2005] EWCA Civ 481 at paragraphs 21 to 24; *R (Iran) v Secretary of State for the Home Department* [2005]EWCA Civ 982; *ZT v Secretary of State for the Home Department* [2005] EWCA Civ 142.

[261] *DK (Serbia) & Ors v Secretary of State for the Home Department* [2006] EWCA Civ 1747.

[262] [2006] UKAIT 00038.

identified a material error of law, to 'substitute a fresh decision'. The Court of Appeal approved the Tribunal's reasoning that 'in general the Tribunal should always adopt those parts of a previous decision which are not shown to be unsound'.

The scope in practice of any particular reconsideration

- The identification of any error or errors of law should normally be restricted to those grounds upon which the immigration judge ordered reconsideration, and any point which properly falls within the category of an obvious or manifest point of Convention jurisprudence, as described in *Robinson*.[263]
- Therefore parties should expect a direction either from the immigration judge ordering reconsideration or the Tribunal on reconsideration restricting argument to the points of law identified by the immigration judge when ordering the reconsideration.
- Nothing in either the 2004 Act or the Rules, however, expressly precludes an applicant from raising points of law in respect of which he was not successful at the application stage itself. And there is no appellate machinery which would enable an applicant who is successful in obtaining an order for reconsideration to challenge the grounds upon which the immigration judge ordered such reconsideration.
- It must, however, be very much the exception, rather than the rule, that a Tribunal will permit other grounds to be argued. But clearly the Tribunal needs to be alert to the possibility of an error of law other than that identified by the immigration judge, otherwise its own decision may be unlawful.

With regard to the second stage of a reconsideration, the Court of Appeal opined **6.194** that since it is a reconsideration by the same body which made the original decision, there were a number of consequences:

- The most important consequence is that any body asked to reconsider a decision on the grounds of an identified error of law will approach its reconsideration on the basis that any factual findings and conclusions or judgments arising from those findings which are unaffected by the error of law need not be revisited. It is not a rehearing.
- The general principle of the 2004 Act is that the process of reconsideration is carried out by the same body as made the original decision even if it is in fact carried out by a differently constituted Tribunal.
- The right approach to the directions which should be considered by the immigration judge ordering reconsideration or the Tribunal carrying out the

---

[263] *R v SSHD ex p Robinson* [1998] QB 929—see para 6.168.

reconsideration is to assume, notionally, that the reconsideration will be, or is being, carried out by the original decision maker.

- It follows that if there is to be any challenge to the factual findings, or the judgments or conclusions reached on the facts which are unaffected by the errors of law that have been identified, that will only be other than in the most exceptional cases on the basis of new evidence or new material as to which the usual principles as to the reception of such evidence will apply, as envisaged in Rule 32(2) of the Rules.
- Rule 32(2) imposes the obligation on the parties to identify the new material well before the reconsideration hearing. This requirement is underlined in the new Practice Direction 14A.
- Rule 32(2) does not require the party in question to produce the evidence, but to identify the nature of the evidence. The Tribunal and the other party are entitled to be given a clear indication before the reconsideration commences as to the nature of any new evidence or material upon which either party intends to rely which is capable of affecting the scope of the reconsideration. Such a notice, together with any reply under Rule 30 (2) are necessary documents for ensuring that a reconsideration is carried out economically, effectively, and fairly.
- Therefore, in conclusion, as far as the scope of reconsideration is concerned, 'the Tribunal is entitled to approach it, and to give directions accordingly, on the basis that the reconsideration will first determine whether or not there are any identifiable errors of law and will then consider the effect of any such error or errors on the original decision. That assessment should prima facie take place on the basis of the findings of fact and the conclusions of the original Tribunal, save and in so far as they have been infected by the identified error or errors of law. If they have not been infected by any error or errors of law, the Tribunal should only re-visit them if there is new evidence or material which should be received in the interest of justice and which could affect those findings and conclusions or if there are other exceptional circumstances which justify reopening them.'(paragraph 25)

Procedure on reconsideration

6.195 The Court of Appeal in *DK* then gave guidance on the procedure to be adopted in a reconsideration. The Court considered it preferable that both stages of reconsideration should be dealt with at one hearing, but stated that the test in any case is 'has the reconsideration been conducted fairly?'. In some cases a single hearing should suffice, in other cases this might be wholly inappropriate because it fails to give either party a fair opportunity to deal with the substance of the reconsideration: the error or errors of law identified by the Tribunal, if any, may result in the need to consider evidence or material not available in the initial hearing. The Court considered the following comments to be helpful:

- By Rule 27(2)(b) the immigration judge can give directions for the reconsideration which can include directions as to how the reconsideration should be dealt with in the event that the Tribunal agrees with him as to the error of law which he had identified.
- At the initial hearing the Tribunal should have been provided with any reply from the party other than the one on whose application the order for reconsideration was made, as well as any notices under Rule 32(2). Between them, together with the notice of application and the order for reconsideration and directions (if any), the issues to be determined at the initial hearing should be clearly identifiable.
- On the assumption that there has not been a previous directions hearing, which could conceivably be appropriate in a particularly complex case, the procedure for the reconsideration should sensibly form the first part of the hearing. Both parties can then make submissions as to whether they consider that the reconsideration can be disposed of at the initial hearing or whether it will be either necessary or desirable for the initial hearing to be restricted to the identification of any error or errors of law, with the second stage being adjourned until that had been determined.
- At the same time the Tribunal can determine finally what, if any, limitations should be imposed upon submissions or evidence pursuant to Rule 31(4).
- The Practice Direction rightly starts from the assumption that the reconsideration should be dealt with at one hearing unless good reason is shown to the contrary. The requirements for notice under Rule 32(2) and the reply under Rule 31(2) play a critical part in enabling the Tribunal to come to a sensible decision as to the procedure to be adopted. If a party has not filed a Rule 32(2) notice, the Tribunal is entitled to assume that there is no further evidence or material it wishes to put before the Tribunal for the purposes of the reconsideration. And if he has not filed a reply, the Tribunal is entitled to assume that the other party does not wish to rely on any arguments or material other than those upon which the original decision was based.
- If the Tribunal adjourns or transfers the second stage in accordance with the Practice Direction, it is imperative that the written reasons for its finding should be sufficiently full and clear for the parties to be able to understand how the Tribunal's conclusion will impact upon the scope of the second stage of the reconsideration. It may be sensible for the Tribunal when giving its reasons, to consider what directions, if any, it considers appropriate at the beginning of the initial hearing. The Tribunal should be prepared to give the parties an

opportunity to make submissions in relation to any such directions either in writing or at the commencement of the second hearing.

6.196   In *(Wani) v Secretary of State for the Home Department*[264] and the decision of the AIT in *JA (Practice on Reconsideration–Wani Applied) Ecuador*[265] it was established that the practice required to be followed in this two-stage reconsideration procedure is that all matters relating to the existence of a material error of law are to be conclusively determined at the first stage and that decision is to be incorporated into the second-stage determination. At the second stage it is not open to the parties (save in exceptional circumstances) to reargue issues going to the existence or otherwise of a material error of law. The correct avenue for arguing that a first-stage conclusion that there was such an error was wrong is on appeal to the Court of Appeal. Such an appeal lies under section 103B with permission after the end of the AIT process. If the reasons given at the first stage are too exiguous to be sensibly incorporated into the second-stage determination, then the author or authors of the first-stage decision should be asked to expand them into a form in which they can properly appear in the final determination.

6.197   In *NM (Iraq) v SSHD*[266] the Court of Appeal emphasized that it is essential that members of the AIT involved at various stages of the complex reconsideration process ask themselves the right questions. At the leave stage, where a review is sought, the question is whether there has been an *arguable* error of law. At the first stage of the reconsideration proper, the question is whether there has been an *actual* error. The decision maker at each stage must focus on the critical question.

6.198   In *OB (Iraq) v SSHD*[267] the Court of Appeal held that, having detected a material error of law in the Adjudicator's reasoning, it was open to the AIT at the first stage of reconsideration to direct that the second stage be 'de novo'. It was not unreasonable for the panel to regard the Adjudicator's error as sufficiently serious not to be a 'discrete element' capable of being hived off.

6.199   In *AA (Pakistan) v SSHD*[268] the Court of Appeal held that because the AIT erred in law at the 'second stage' of its reconsideration, that did not mean that the Adjudicator's determination, which had been found to err in law at the 'first stage', now revived. Both decisions were flawed and the appeal would have to be heard afresh.

---

[264] [2005] EWHC 2815 (Admin).
[265] [2006] UKAIT 00013.
[266] [2007] EWCA Civ 359.
[267] [2007] EWCA Civ 585.
[268] [2007] EWCA Civ 45.

In *Rafiq Swash v SSHD*[269] the Tribunal held that, as a general rule, a judge to **6.200** whom proceedings are transferred in the course of the reconsideration of an appeal should receive the original decision. Special circumstances may arise where the interests of justice require that proceedings be transferred to a judge who is not aware of the terms of the original determination, but they will be rare. In such circumstances, the panel of the Tribunal which identifies the error of law can direct that the proceedings be transferred to a judge who is not to be provided with the original determination. In the absence of such an order, the parties should proceed on the premise that the judge to whom the matter is transferred will have received the original decision.

Funding of reconsideration hearings

An appellant may recover the costs of an application for reconsideration, the **6.201** preparation for reconsideration, and the hearing of the reconsideration only if the Tribunal or High Court makes an order for payment out of the Community Legal Services Fund. The relevant statutory provisions are to be found in:

- section 103 D (inserted by 2004 Act and amended by 2006 Act);
- Rule 28 A (inserted by Asylum and Immigration Tribunal (Procedure) (Amendment) Rules 2005) and Rule 33 as amended by the 2006 Rules;
- the Community Legal Service (Asylum and Immigration Appeals) Regulations 2005, as amended by the Community Legal Service (Asylum and Immigration Appeals) (Amendment) Regulations 2007.

The Tribunal or High Court can make a costs order in immigration review **6.202** proceedings[270] only where an appellant is represented by a supplier (as defined in the CLS Regulations) acting pursuant to a grant of Legal Representation or by counsel instructed by a supplier.[271] No costs order can be made in fast track proceedings.[272]

The Tribunal (under the filter provision) or the High Court may only make **6.203** an order under section 103(D)(1) for the appellant's costs of an application for reconsideration where:

- if it dismisses or makes no order on the application for reconsideration, where there has been a change in any relevant circumstances or a change in the law

---

[269] [2006] EWCA Civ 1093.

[270] Defined under reg 3 of the CLS Regs 2005 as (i) applications to the High Court under s 103A of the 2002 Act (including applications which are considered by a member of the Tribunal pursuant to para 30 of Schedule 2 to the 2004 Act); and (ii) proceedings for the reconsideration of an appeal by the Tribunal pursuant to an order under s 103A of the 2002 Act.

[271] Reg 4(1) CLS Regs.

[272] Reg 4(2) CLS Regs.

since the application was made; and at the time when the application was made, there was a significant prospect that the appeal would be allowed upon reconsideration (reg 5(4)).

6.204   If the High Court decides to refer the appeal to the Court of Appeal under section 103C of the 2002 Act, it must make an order for costs under section 103D(1) (reg 5(3)).

6.205   Where an order for reconsideration is made, on the application of the appellant the Tribunal may order that the appellant's costs for the application for reconsideration, preparation for reconsideration, and the reconsideration hearing should be paid out of the CLS Fund.[273] The Tribunal may make an order under section 103D(3) only where:

- it has reconsidered its decision on an appeal; or
- an order for reconsideration has been made but the reconsideration does not take place or is not completed because (i) the appeal lapses, or is treated as abandoned or finally determined, by operation of an enactment; or (ii) the appeal is withdrawn by the appellant, or is treated as withdrawn because the respondent withdraws the decision or decisions to which the appeal relates.[274]

6.206   If the Tribunal allows an appeal on reconsideration it must make a costs order.[275] If the Tribunal dismisses an appeal on reconsideration, it must not make a costs order unless it is satisfied that, at the time when the appellant made the application for reconsideration, there was a significant prospect that the appeal would be allowed upon reconsideration.[276] If an order for reconsideration is made but the reconsideration does not take place or is not completed, the Tribunal must not make an order under section 103D(3) unless it is satisfied that, at the time when the appellant made the section 103A application, there was a significant prospect that the appeal would be allowed upon reconsideration.[277] If the Tribunal decides not to make a costs order following reconsideration of an appeal it must give reasons for its decision.[278]

6.207   Under Rule 33 of the Procedure Rules, following a reconsideration where the appellant's representative has specified that he seeks an order for his costs, the Tribunal must make a separate determination (the funding determination) stating whether it orders that the appellant's costs in respect of the application for reconsideration, in respect of the preparation for reconsideration, and in respect

---

273   Section 103D(2)(3) as amended by s 8 2006 Act.
274   Reg 6(1A) CLS Regs as inserted by the 2007 Amendment Regs.
275   Reg 6(2) CLS Regs.
276   Reg 6(3) CLS Regs.
277   Reg 6(3A) CLS Regs as inserted by the 2007 Amendment Regs.
278   Reg 6(4) CLS Regs.

of the reconsideration should be paid out of the CLS Fund. The Tribunal must send the funding determination to the appellant's representative and, if a funding order is made, to the CLS Fund. Where the reconsideration determination is served by the Respondent, the funding determination must not be sent to the appellant's representative until the respondent has notified the Tribunal that the substantive determination has been served or the Tribunal has served the substantive determination itself (Rule 33(4)).

The Practice Direction (Consolidated Version April 2007) provides that unless it **6.208** directs otherwise the Tribunal shall hear any submissions as to costs at the conclusions of the proceedings on the reconsideration. However, in *DM (timing of funding application)*[279] the Tribunal held that no time limit is prescribed in the legislative framework of the 2002 Act within which a request must be made for a Funding Order. It does not have to be made in the application form seeking review, or at the reconsideration hearing. The Tribunal stated that it would be convenient if such a request were made before the conclusion of the reconsideration hearing.

A supplier, or counsel instructed by a supplier, may apply to the Tribunal in writ- **6.209** ing for a review of a decision by the Tribunal not to make an order under section 103D(3) or to make a section 103D order under regulation 8(2).[280] An application under this regulation must be filed within ten business days after the supplier is served with the Tribunal's decision, or such longer period as the Tribunal may allow.[281]

The review is carried out by a senior immigration judge who was not a member of **6.210** the Tribunal, or a member of the constitution of the Tribunal, which made the original decision.[282] The senior immigration judge may carry out the review without a hearing or hold an oral hearing, if one is requested by the supplier or counsel.[283] The senior immigration judge may make a funding order or confirm the Tribunal's original decision[284] and must give reasons for his decision on a review.[285]

The CLS Regulations (reg 9) modify the Legal Services Commission's Funding **6.211** Code by disapplying the Commission's usual criteria for granting of legal aid for representation in immigration proceedings (other than criteria relating to financial eligibility) in respect of proceedings within the scope of this scheme.

---

[279] [2006] UKIAT 88.
[280] Reg 7(1) CLS Regs.
[281] Reg 7(2) CLS Regs.
[282] Reg 7(3) CLS Regs.
[283] Reg 7(4) CLS Regs.
[284] Reg 7(5) CLS Regs.
[285] Reg 7(6) CLS Regs.

Appeals to the Court of Appeal

6.212 An order for reconsideration can be made only once in relation to an appeal (s 103A(2)(b)). When an appeal to the Tribunal has been reconsidered a party to the appeal may bring a further appeal to the Court of Appeal (s 103(B)). An appeal also lies directly to the Court of Appeal where the original decision of the Tribunal was exercised by three or more qualified members (s 103E). Where on an application for reconsideration the High Court thinks that the appeal raises a question of law of such importance that it should be decided by the Court of Appeal it may refer the appeal to that Court (s103(C)). In each of these cases, the appeal to the Court of Appeal is on a point of law only. We deal with errors of law in paragraph 6.171 above.

Appeal from the Tribunal following reconsideration—section 103(B)

6.213 An appeal to the Court of Appeal following reconsideration by the Tribunal or from a legally qualified panel may be brought only with the permission of the Tribunal or if the Tribunal refuses permission with the permission of the Court of Appeal (s103B(3)). The Court of Appeal may:

- affirm the Tribunal's decision;
- make any decision which the Tribunal could have made;
- remit the case to the Tribunal;
- affirm a direction under section 87;
- vary a direction under section 87;
- give a direction which the Tribunal could have given under section 87.

6.214 An application is made by filing with the Tribunal an application notice for permission to appeal (Rule 34(1) Procedure Rules 2005). The application notice must be made on a form approved for the purpose by the President, state the grounds of appeal, and be signed by the applicant or his representative and dated (r 34(2)). If it is completed by a representative, the representative must certify in the notice that he has completed the application notice in accordance with the applicant's instructions (r 34(3)). The Tribunal must notify the other party to the appeal as soon as practicable that the appeal has been filed (r 34(4)).

6.215 The application notice must be filed in accordance with the procedure in Rule 34 not later than ten days after service of the Tribunal determination unless the applicant is in detention under the Immigration Acts where it must be filed not later than five days after service (r 35).

6.216 The application for permission to appeal must be determined by a senior immigration judge without a hearing who may either grant or refuse permission to appeal (r 36(1)(2)). Where the immigration judge intends to grant permission to appeal he may, if he thinks that the Tribunal made an administrative error in relation to the proceedings, instead set aside the Tribunal's determination and direct that the proceedings be reheard by the Tribunal (r 36(3)). The Tribunal must serve on every party written notice of its decision including reasons, which may be in a summary form.

Requests for permission from the Court of Appeal

If the Tribunal refuses permission the applicant may seek permission directly from the Court of Appeal. The procedure for appeals to the Court of Appeal is governed by CPR Part 52 and the accompanying Practice Direction. Paragraph 21.7 of the Practice Direction deals with Asylum and Immigration Appeals. **6.217**

Time limits

Permission must be requested in the appellant's notice which must be filed at the Court of Appeal within 14 days after the appellant is served with written notice of the Tribunal's decision to grant or refuse permission to appeal.[286] The appellant's notice must be served on the respondent and the AIT as soon as practicable and not later than seven days after it is filed.[287] On being served with the appellant's notice, the AIT must send to the Court of Appeal copies of the documents which were before the relevant Tribunal when considering the appeal.[288] The Practice Direction also sets out the procedure on a referral under section 103C.[289] **6.218**

Time starts to run on the day the judge below makes his decision, not when the order is drawn up. If the appellant requires an extension of time beyond the statutory 14-day period he should apply to the appeal court (r 52.6, paragraph 5.2 Practice Direction). Rule 3.1 (2)(a) provides that the court may extend time for compliance with any rule, practice direction, or court order even if the time for compliance has expired. The application must be made in the appellant's notice. It should state the reasons for the delay and the steps taken before the application was made. The Respondent has the right to be heard on this application (paragraph 5.3 Practice Direction). **6.219**

In *YD Turkey*[290] the Court of Appeal gave guidance in general terms about extension of time. *YD* was a case in which it was sought to stay removal directions when not only had no permission to appeal been granted by the AIT, but the AIT had not even been applied to within the time limit. That meant that under the **6.220**

Para 21.7(3) Part 52 Practice Direction.
[287] Rule 52.4(3) and para 21.7(4) Part 52 Practice Direction.
[288] Para 21.7(5) Part 52 Practice Direction.
[289] Para 21.7A.
[290] *YD (Turkey) v SSHD* [2006] EWCA Civ 52.

legislation the AIT could not consider the application, which had to be made to the Court of Appeal. The Court stated that 'in any case in which an extension of time for appealing in excess of say two months' is sought the court would have strongly in mind the fundamental common law principle that the outcome of litigation should be final, and would not grant an extension of time except in an exceptional case where it is satisfied that a significant injustice has probably occurred.

6.221   In *BR (Iran)*[291] Buxton LJ expressed concern about some aspects of *YD*. Since inquiries under the Refugee Convention are not private litigation, a different perspective from the finality of litigation should apply. Where the question is whether the UK will fulfil its obligations under the Refugee Convention, any rule of thumb based simply on length of delay would seem to be misplaced. In *BR* a senior immigration judge had granted permission to appeal to the Court of Appeal and the time limit was exceeded due to the fault of the appellant's representatives. In that limited category of cases the following principles are to be followed:

- There should be a presumption that where the AIT has granted permission to appeal to the Court of Appeal the appeal ought to be heard.
- If a procedural fault causes the Court to have to consider whether the appeal should proceed, the presumption may be displaced if it can be shown that the decision of the SIJ was plainly wrong, in the sense that it is clear that failure to pursue the appeal would not lead to the United Kingdom being in breach of its international obligations.
- Length of delay, when caused by legal representatives, should not be relevant.
- Where delay has been caused by the applicant, the Court is likely to look carefully at the light that that sheds on the credibility of the assertion that the applicant has a good claim for international protection. At the same time, the Court will remind itself that if after that scrutiny such a claim is established, then the claimant is indeed entitled to international protection despite the domestic Court's disapproval of his conduct or his way of promoting his case.

Contents of appellant's notice

6.222   The grounds in the notice of appeal should set out clearly why it is said that the decision of the lower court is wrong or that the decision of the lower court is unjust because of a serious procedural or other irregularity. The appellant must specify in respect of each ground whether it raises an appeal on a point of law or against a finding of fact. Where the appellant seeks to rely on the Human Rights Act he must comply with paragraph 5.1A of the Practice Direction.

---

[291]   *BR (Iran) v SSHD* [2007] EWCA Civ 198.

Documents to be filed

The appellant is not required to file an appeal bundle in accordance with paragraph 5.6A of the Practice Direction but must file the documents specified in paragraphs 5.6(2)(a) to (f) together with a copy of the Tribunal's determination.[292] **6.223**

Permission stage

The appeal court can and in many cases will deal with applications for permission on paper (see paragraph 4.11 of the Practice Direction). Particularly difficult cases are generally referred by the Appeal Court for oral hearing. If the Appeal Court refuses permission on the paper, the appellant is entitled to have the have the matter reconsidered at an oral hearing (r 52.3(4) and paragraph 4.13 of the Practice Direction). The request for such an oral hearing must be filed within seven days after service of the notice that permission has been refused (r 52.3(5) and paragraph 4.14 of the Practice Direction). The procedure to be followed after the appellant has applied for an oral hearing can be found in paragraphs 4.14A–4.17 of the Practice Direction. **6.224**

Permission to appeal may be given only where the appeal appears to have real prospects of success or there is some other compelling reason why the appeal should be heard (r 52.3(6)). An order giving permission to appeal may limit the issues to be heard (r 52.3(7)(a)) or may be made subject to conditions (r 52.3(7)(b)). The purpose of the power to limit is to exclude points that are entirely without merit at an early stage. **6.225**

The appeal operates as a stay of the decision or order of the Tribunal and hence whilst an appeal is pending an appellant may not be removed (r 52.7(b)). An out of time application for permission does not prevent removal until permission is granted and in those circumstances it is necessary to apply for a stay under Rule 52.7 CPR. **6.226**

K. Transitional Appeal Provisions

From 4 April 2005 the Immigration Appeal Tribunal ceased to exist and the appeal provisions of the Asylum and Immigration (Treatment of Claimants etc) Act applied. The appeals which were not finally determined by that date, namely appeals pending before adjudicators and the IAT, applications for statutory review pending before the Administrative Court, and appeals to the Court of Appeal, all fell to be considered under the transitional provisions of Articles 3–9 **6.227**

---

[292] Paragraph 21.7(2) Practice Direction.

of the Asylum and Immigration (Treatment of Claimants, etc) Act 2004 (Commencement No 5 and Transitional Provisions) Order 2005.

6.228 The following is a summary of the relevant provisions:

1. Where an Adjudicator or the IAT completed the hearing of the appeal but had not produced the written determination, or the written determination has not been served on all the parties before 4 April 2005, the appeal continues as an appeal to an adjudicator or the IAT until the determination has been served.[293]

2. A member of the AIT who was an adjudicator or member of the IAT before 4 April 2005 will be deemed to remain so to the extent necessary for completing the determination as described in (1) above.[294]

3. Subject to (1) and (2) above, an appeal or application to an adjudicator which is pending immediately before 4 April 2005 shall continue after that date as an appeal or application to the AIT and any appeal to the IAT which is pending before 4 April 2005 continues after that date as an appeal to the AIT.[295]

4. Where an appeal which before 4 April 2005 was pending before an Adjudicator having been remitted by a court or the AIT or pending before the AIT, subject to (1) and (2) above, the AIT will deal after the 4 April 2005 with the appeal in the same way as if it had originally decided the appeal and it was reconsidering its decision. Following the determination of the appeal by the AIT a party may not apply to the High Court under section 103A for an order for reconsideration but may, subject to section 103B(3) bring a further appeal on a point of law to the Court of Appeal under section 103B(1).[296]

5. Where an application for permission to appeal to the IAT against an adjudicator's decision is pending immediately before 4 April 2005 it will be treated after this date as an application under section 103A(1) for an order to require the AIT to reconsider the Adjudicator's decision on appeal.[297]

6. Where an adjudicator has determined an appeal and no application for permission to appeal to the IAT is pending immediately before 4 April 2005 a party to the appeal may apply after that date under section 103A(1) for an order requiring the AIT to reconsider the adjudicator's decision on the appeal.[298] In these circumstances, where a time period specified in the rules under section 106 for applying for permission to appeal to the IAT has started

---

[293] Article 3 (1) The Asylum and Immigration Act Order 2005, SI No. 565.
[294] Article 3 (2).
[295] Article 4(a)(b).
[296] Article 5.
[297] Article 6(1).
[298] Article 6(2).

to run before 4 April 2005 an application under section 103A may be made at any time before the expiry of that time period, notwithstanding the time period specified in section 103A(3).[299]

7. An application to a court under section 101(2) (review of the IAT's decision upon an application for permission to appeal) which is pending immediately before 4 April 2005 will continue after that date as if the section had not been repealed.[300] A party who before 4 April 2005 was entitled to make an application under section 101(2) may make the application as if the section had not been repealed.[301] Where by virtue of these provisions an application under section 101(2) is made or continues after 4 April 2005 paragraphs (a) and (c) of section 101(3) apply as if they had not been repealed and the judge determining the application may affirm the IAT's decision to refuse permission to appeal, reverse the IAT's decision to grant permission to appeal, or order the AIT to reconsider the Adjudicator's decision on the appeal.[302]

8. An appeal to the Court of Appeal or Court of Session under section 103 (appeal from IAT) or an application to the Court of Appeal or Court of Session for permission to appeal under section 103 which is pending immediately before the 4 April 2005 continues after this date as if that section had not been repealed.[303] Where an application for permission to appeal under section 103 is pending before 4 April 2005 it will be determined by the AIT after this date and section 103 will continue to apply to the application as if it had not been appealed.[304] A party who is granted permission to appeal under section 103 or was entitled before 4 April 2005 to apply to the Court of Appeal or Court of Session for permission to appeal under section 103 may appeal or apply for permission to appeal under section 103 as if the section had not been repealed.[305] A party who immediately before 4 April 2005 was entitled to apply to the AIT for permission to appeal under section 103 may apply to the AIT for permission to appeal under that section which shall continue to apply as if not repealed.[306] Where the Court of Appeal or Court of Session determines an appeal under section 103 after 4 April 2005, section 103B(4) will apply in relation to the appeal as it would in relation to an appeal under section 103B(1) but references to the Tribunal are to be interpreted as references to the IAT.[307]

---

[299] Article 6(4).
[300] Article 7(1).
[301] Article 7(2).
[302] Article 7(3).
[303] Article 8(1).
[304] Article 8(2).
[305] Article 8(3).
[306] Article 8(4).
[307] Article 8(6).

L. Practice and Procedure Note

6.229 These Practice Notes guide the reader through the practice and procedure relating to appeals from the notice of decision through to end of the first instance hearing before the Asylum and Immigration Tribunal. We deal with reconsiderations hearings and onward appeals and the procedure relating to them in the body of the appeals chapter above.

6.230 The procedure on appeals is governed by the Immigration (Notices) Regulations,[308] the Asylum and Immigration Tribunal (Procedure) Rules 2005 (the Procedure Rules)[309] and the Asylum and Immigration (Fast Track Procedure) Rules 2005 (Fast Track Rules).[310] We deal with Fast Track Procedure at paragraph 6.371 below.

6.231 The AIT also has the power to make 'practice directions' which set out the practice to be followed in appeals. In April 2007 the President of the Tribunal issued a consolidated Practice Direction with an annex containing a number of Guidance Notes. This Practice Direction and the accompanying Guidance Notes can be obtained from the AIT website at <www.ait.gov.uk>. The AIT came into being on 4 April 2005 and all Practice Directions made by the Chief Adjudicator and the President before that date cease to have effect save in so far as they are necessary for giving effect to any transitional provisions under the Asylum and Immigration (Treatment of Claimants, etc) Act 2004.

6.232 The transitional provisions relating to appeals are summarized at 6.227 above. The Procedure Rules contain their own transitional provisions at Rule 62.[311] The Procedure Rules apply to any appeal or application to an Adjudicator or to the IAT which was pending before 4 April 2005 and which continues on or after that date as if it had been made after that date by virtue of a transitional provisions order.[312]

6.233 The 'overriding objective' of the Procedure Rules is to secure that proceedings before the Tribunal are handled as fairly, quickly, and efficiently as possible.[313] The European Court of Human Rights has held that Article 6 of the ECHR does not apply to proceedings

---

[308] SI 2003, No 658 (as amended by SI 2006/2168).

[309] SI 2005/230, from 4 April 2005 (as amended by SI 2005/569 from 4 April 2005, SI 2006/2788 from 13 November 2006 and SI 2007/835 from 10 April 2007).

[310] SI 2005/560 (as amended by SI 2006/2789 from 13 November 2006 and SI 2006/2898 from 27 November 2006).

[311] In *AM (Serbia & Ors) v SSHD*, AIT and *the Lord Chancellor* [2007] EWCA Civ 16 the Court of Appeal held that Rule 62(7) of the Procedure Rules 2005 which restricts the grounds upon which an appeal can be considered in 'transitional' cases to those on which the IAT granted leave to appeal, is perverse and irrational in *Wednesbury* terms.

[312] Subject to the remainder of the Rule.

[313] Rule 4 Procedure Rules.

concerning the right of an alien to reside in a country.[314] The Tribunal is, however, under a common law duty to behave fairly.[315]

Constitution of the Tribunal

The constitution of the AIT is governed by Schedule 4 of the 2002 Act. Members of the AIT are appointed by the Lord Chancellor. They are required to be solicitors or barristers with seven years' experience or have legal or non-legal experience which, in the opinion of the Lord Chancellor, makes them suitable for appointment. Those members who have legal experience are known as 'legally qualified' members of the Tribunal. A member holds office until the age of 70 unless he resigns by notice in writing to the Lord Chancellor or the terms of his appointment provide that he shall vacate office. **6.234**

The President of the AIT is appointed by the Lord Chancellor and is a member of the Tribunal who holds or has held high judicial office. One or more members of the Tribunal are appointed by the Lord Chancellor to be Deputy President and may act for the President if he is unable to act or unavailable and shall perform such functions as the President may delegate or assign. **6.235**

The jurisdiction of the Tribunal is exercised by one or a number of members as the President directs, having regard to the complexity and other circumstances of the case or cases. Directions given by the President may relate to the whole or part of proceedings, enable jurisdiction to be exercised by a single member, and may require or permit the transfer of whole or part of proceedings from one member to another, one group of members to another, from one member to a group of members, or from a group of members to one member. The directions may be revoked or varied by another direction and are subject to Rules made under section 106 of the 2002 Act. **6.236**

The President may make arrangements for the allocation of proceedings to members of the Tribunal. In the Practice Direction (Consolidated version, 30 April 2007) the President has made directions regarding how the Tribunal should be constituted when dealing with specified matters.[316] **6.237**

Representation and parties to an appeal

Appellants may only be represented by people permitted to represent them under the Immigration and Asylum Act 1999.[317] When a representative attends court, he will be **6.238**

---

[314] *Maaouia v France* (Application No 39652/98, 5 October 2000, unreported).

[315] *R (on the appln of the Refugee Legal Centre) v SSHD* [2004] EWCA Civ 1481, [2004] All ER (D) 201 (Nov), *R (on the appln of Anufrijeva) v SSHD* [2003] UKHL 36, [2003] Imm AR 570, [2003] INLR 521.

[316] At paragraph 2.2.

[317] Rule 48(1). See Part V—Immigration Advisors and Immigration Service Providers. However, a sponsor as an ordinary family member, as a person acting other than in the course of a business, is not caught by the prohibitions of section 82(2) and 84 of this Act and can be the appellant's

asked to complete a 'section 84 form'.[318] Representatives are under a duty to inform the AIT and the immigration authorities when they begin acting for an appellant.[319] Where a notice of appeal is signed by a representative, the representative will be deemed to have notified the Tribunal and the other party that he is acting for a party.[320] Where a notice of appeal is not signed by a representative, the representative must file a separate notice with the Tribunal and serve it on the other party.[321]

6.239 Every party and his representative is under a duty to notify the Tribunal in writing of a postal address at which documents may be served on him and of any changes to that address.[322] Until a party or representative notifies the Tribunal of a change of address any document served on him at the most recent address notified to the Tribunal shall be deemed to have been properly served on him.[323]

6.240 Where a representative is acting for an appellant, the appellant is under a duty to maintain contact with the representative until the appeal is finally determined and notify the representative of any change of address.[324] Where the representative ceases to act for a party, the representative and the party must immediately notify the Tribunal and the other party in writing of that fact and of the name and address of any new representative (if known).[325] Notification may be given orally at a hearing to the Tribunal and to any other party present at the hearing but otherwise must be in writing.[326] Until the Tribunal is notified that a representative has ceased to act for a party, any document served on that representative shall be deemed to be properly served on the party he was representing.[327]

6.241 It is of extreme importance that these procedures are observed as failure to do so leads to appellants losing their appeals. In *FP (Iran)*[328] the Court of Appeal held that in asylum cases, there is no general principle which imputed parties with the procedural errors of their representatives. Hence, in asylum cases, where it is the fault of the

---

representative—notification of acting as a representative should have been given by the sponsor if that was the intention under the procedure rules 48(4) and (7) (*HH (Sponsor as representative) Serbia* [2006] UKIAT 00063).

[318] Section 84 Immigration and Asylum Act 1999.
[319] Rule 48(4).
[320] Rule 48(4A) as inserted by SI 2006/2788.
[321] Rule 48 (4B) as inserted by SI 2006/2788.
[322] Rule 56(1).
[323] Rule 56(2).
[324] Rule 48(6).
[325] Rule 48 (7) as amended by SI 2006/2788.
[326] Rule 48(8).
[327] Rule 48(9).
[328] *FP (Iran); MB (Libya) v SSHD* [2007] EWCA Civ, 23 Jan 2007—*Al Mehdawi v SSHD* [1990] Imm AR 140 distinguished.

representative to notify the Tribunal of a change of address, with result that the hearing is determined in the appellant's absence, there will be a remedy.

The parties to an appeal are the appellant[329] and the respondent.[330] In asylum claims the Tribunal must allow the UK representative of the UNHCR to attend and make representations, provided notice has been given that they wish to participate in proceedings.[331] **6.242**

In *HK (interview as advocate: unfair?)*[332] the Tribunal held that although, with some exceptions, their codes of practice forbid barristers and solicitors from giving evidence in cases where they are acting as representatives, there is no general prohibitions on other representatives doing so. It is not intrinsically unfair for the same official who conducted the asylum interview to appear as the Home Office Presenting Officer on a subsequent appeal. If, however, it is the interviewing officer's conduct which is criticized, it would be better for that officer not to present the case at the hearing, especially if he is to give evidence about what happened. **6.243**

Notice of decision

The appeal procedure commences when the immigration authority[333] serves notice of the decision. Under the Notices Regulations[334] the immigration authority must give written notice of: **6.244**

- any immigration decision or EEA decision which is appealable;[335]
- the grant of leave to enter or remain for a period of leave exceeding one year in aggregate where an asylum claim has been rejected giving rise a right of appeal under section 83(2) of the 2002 Act;[336]
- the decision that a person is no longer a refugee as a result of the revocation of refugee leave where the person still has limited leave and hence has a right of appeal under section 83(2)(A) of the 2002 Act.[337]

---

[329] 'A person who has given notice of appeal to the Tribunal against a relevant decision' (Rule 2); 'relevant decision' is 'a decision against which there is an exercisable right of appeal to the Tribunal' (Rule 2).

[330] 'The decision maker specified in the notice of decision against which a notice of appeal has been given' (Rule 2).

[331] Rule 49.

[332] [2006] UKIAT 81.

[333] ie the Home Office or Entry Clearance Officer.

[334] The Immigration (Notices) Regulations 2003 (as amended).

[335] Reg 4(1).

[336] Reg 4(2).

[337] Reg 4(2A) inserted from 31 August 2006 (SI 2006/2168).

Contents of notice

6.245   The notice must include the following information:

- a statement of the reasons for the decision to which it relates;[338]
- if it relates to an immigration decision specified in section 82(2)(a), (g), (h), (i), (ia), or (j) of the 2002 Act, the notice shall state the country or territory to which it is proposed to remove the person, or if it appears to the decision maker that the person to whom the notice is to be given may be removable to more than one territory or country, state such countries or territories;[339]
- if the notice is given informing a person that they have a right of appeal under section 83(2),[340] it must include or be accompanied by a statement of the reasons for the rejection of the claim for asylum;[341]
- the right of appeal and the statutory provision on which the right of appeal is based;[342]
- whether or not such an appeal may be brought while in the United Kingdom;[343]
- the grounds on which the appeal may be brought;[344]
- the facilities available for advice and assistance in connection with an appeal;[345]
- a statement referring to a provision limiting or restricting the right of appeal under Part 5 of the Nationality, Immigration and Asylum Act 2002.

6.246   The notice of decision must also be accompanied by notice of appeal indicating the time limit for bringing the appeal, the address to which it should be sent or may be taken by hand, and a fax number for service by fax.[346] If the right of appeal is excluded save on grounds of race discrimination, asylum, or human rights, the notice of decision is not required to include information about appeal rights or enclose a notice of appeal.[347] Where a person is served with notice of such a decision and then makes a race discrimination, asylum or human rights claim, the decision maker must as soon as practicable re-serve the notice of decision which includes information about appeal rights and a notice of appeal.[348] The time limit for an appeal is then calculated from the date on which the decision was re-served.[349]

---

[338] Reg 5(1)(a).
[339] Reg 5(1)(a)(b) substituted from 31 August 2006 (SI 2006/2168).
[340] Under Reg 4(2).
[341] Reg 5(2).
[342] Reg 5(3)(a).
[343] Reg 5(3)(b).
[344] Reg 5(3)(c).
[345] Reg 5(3)(d).
[346] Reg 5(4).
[347] Reg 4(6).
[348] Reg 5(7).
[349] Reg 5(8).

Invalid notice

In *R v SSHD ex parte Jeyeanthan*[350] the Court of Appeal drew a distinction between **6.247** mandatory and directive requirements of the Procedure Rules in relation to notices of appeal. It held that a notice of appeal was not bad for failure to comply with all the requirements of the Procedure Rules, provided that there had been substantial compliance. In *Jeyeanthan* the Master of the Rolls suggested that the right approach is to regard the question of whether a requirement is directory or mandatory as only at most a first step. In the majority of cases there are other questions which have to be asked which are more likely to be of greater assistance than the application of the mandatory/directory test. The questions which are likely to arise are as follows:

- Is the statutory requirement fulfilled if there has been substantial compliance with the requirement and, if so, has there been substantial compliance in the case in issue even though there has not been strict compliance? (The substantial compliance question.)
- Is the non-compliance capable of being waived, and if so, has it, or can it and should it be waived in this particular case? (The discretionary question.)
- If it is not capable of being waived or is not waived then what is the consequence of the non-compliance? (The consequences question.)

These questions apply to procedural requirements for both parties and at all stages of **6.248** the appeal process. In *AH (Notices required) Bangladesh*[351] the Tribunal held that although some of the requirements of the Notices Regulations can be waived and not all of the requirements for giving notice of appeal are mandatory, there can be no appeal without a notice of decision and a notice of appeal.

Service of notice

A notice of decision may be given by hand, sent by fax, or sent by post in which deliv- **6.249** ery or receipt is recorded to an address provided for correspondence by the person or his representative or, where no address has been provided, his last-known or usual address or place of business or that of his representative.[352] Where a person's whereabouts are not known and *either* no address has been provided and the decision maker does not know the address of the person, *or* the address which has been provided is wrong or no longer in use and no representative is acting, then the notice is deemed to be served when a signed notice is placed on the file at the Home Office.[353] Where the person in respect of whom a notice has been served on the file is located, he must be given a copy of the notice and details of when and how it was given as soon as

---

[350] [2000] 1 WLR 354.
[351] [2006] UKAIT 00029.
[352] Reg 7(1).
[353] Reg 7 (2) (this procedure is generally known as 'service on the file').

practicable.[354] Where the notice is sent by a method not prescribed by the Notice Regulations (for example, by post but not recorded delivery) then it will not be treated as lawfully served and time will not start to run against an intending appellant.[355]

6.250   Unless the contrary is proved, a notice which is sent by post is deemed have been served on the second day after it was posted if sent to a place within the UK or on the 28th day after it was posted if sent to a place outside the UK.[356] In both cases the day on which the notice is posted is not included in calculating the period, and where the notice was posted in the UK any day which is not a business day[357] is excluded.[358]

6.251   If a notice is validly served, time starts to run even if it was not in fact received by the intended recipient. There is a discretion to extend the time limit for appealing under the Procedure Rules[359] and in cases of non-receipt a request for an extension should be made.

Notice of appeal

6.252   The notice of appeal must be made on a form approved for the purpose by the President.[360] Paragraph 2A of the Practice Direction states that the form of notice approved for the purpose of Rule 8 (notice of appeal), Rule 34 (application for permission to appeal to appropriate appellate court), or Rule 38 (application for bail) is the appropriate form as displayed on the Tribunal's website at the time when the notice is given, or that form with any variations that the circumstances may require. The appeal form must also be served in time. We deal with the time limits for appeals below. The forms currently displayed on the AIT website are:

- Form AIT 1 – for in-country appeals;
- Form AIT 2 – for out of country appeals against an entry clearance decision; and
- Form AIT 3 – for appeals which can be exercised only after having left the UK or where the appellant has chosen to leave the UK before exercising the right of appeal (but not entry clearance appeals which must be appealed on an AIT 2).

6.253   The notice of appeal must:

- state the name and address of the appellant;
- state whether the appellant has authorised a representative to act for him in the appeal and, if so, give the representative's name and address;

---

[354] Reg 7(3).

[355] *OI (Nigeria)* [2006] UKIAT 00042.

[356] Reg 7(4).

[357] 'Business day' means any day other than Saturday or Sunday, a day which is a bank holiday under the Banking and Financial Dealings Act 1971 in the part of the UK to which the notice is sent, Christmas Day, or Good Friday (Reg 7(6)).

[358] Reg 7(5).

[359] Rule 10 Procedure Rules.

[360] Rule 8(1) Procedure Rules (as amended by SI 2006 No 2788 from 13 November 2006).

- set out the grounds for the appeal;
- give reasons in support of those grounds; and
- so far as reasonably practicable, list any documents which the appellant intends to rely upon as evidence in support of the appeal;[361]
- if reasonably practicable be accompanied by the notice of decision against which the appellant is appealing or a copy of it;[362]
- be signed by the appellant or his representative and dated;[363]
- if signed by the appellant's representative, must be certified by the representative in the notice of appeal that he has completed it in accordance with the appellant's instructions.[364]

These provisions also apply to cases on the fast track.[365] The notice of appeal must be completed in English or if the proceedings have a connection with Wales, a document may be filed with the Tribunal in Welsh.[366] **6.254**

The forms also require other details from the appellant, such as age, sex, nationality, whether the appellant has appealed previously, and whether any member has a pending appeal before the Tribunal or intends to appeal against an immigration decision. The forms also include a box for the appellant to indicate whether he wishes to have an oral hearing and whether the appellant or any witness will need an interpreter. It is the duty of the AIT to provide interpreters for the hearing, and should any particular dialect be required this should be indicated in the relevant box. **6.255**

The requirements of Rule 8 with regard to the completion of the notice of appeal are strict and representatives and applicants should be careful to ensure that they comply with the requirements. In *HH (Sponsor as representative) Serbia*[367] the Tribunal considered that a failure to comply with the requirements of Rule 8 would not cause a notice of appeal to be invalid. This was because Rule 9, which was at the time of the appeal headed 'rejection of invalid notice of appeal' contained provisions only for the rejection of a notice of appeal where there is no 'relevant decision', that is to say no decision carrying a right of appeal to the Tribunal. The Tribunal in *HH* also held that the validity or otherwise of a notice of appeal is an issue to be determined between the parties. If the respondent has not sought to take an issue of compliance with Rule 8 at an early stage in the proceedings, he ought to be treated as having waived the issue in the appellant's favour. Generally speaking, therefore, if the matter is not raised in direct response to service of the notice (or purported notice) of appeal, it is **6.256**

---

361 Rule 8(1)(a)–(e).
362 Rule 8(2).
363 Rule 8(3).
364 Rule 8(4).
365 Rule 6(b) Fast Track Procedure Rules.
366 Rule 52(1)(2) Procedure Rules.
367 [2006] UKAIT 00063.

unlikely that the respondent would be successful in excluding an appeal on this ground at a later stage.

6.257 In *RS and FD (Appeals without grounds) Jamaica*[368] the Tribunal held that whilst a breach of the requirements of Rule 8 will in many cases not prevent an appeal being valid, that does not mean that the breach has no effect at all. It has the effect that the appeal may be determined without a hearing in accordance with Rule 15(2)(c).

6.258 The general law requires only that there be 'substantial' compliance with even mandatory procedural requirements.[369] Whether the Tribunal will determine the appeal without a hearing under Rule 15(2)(c) in the event of a failure to comply with the requirements of Rule 8 is a matter to be assessed on the facts of the individual case. The law gives no encouragement to those who would seek to exclude an appellant for procedural reasons that are purely matters of form.[370]

6.259 In *HH*, although the form itself was incorrectly completed, the notice of decision was included and, as a result, there was no doubt about who the appellant was to be or what was the subject of the appeal. Further, full grounds accompanied the form. Whilst the appellant had not signed the form, the sponsor had signed the declaration appropriate to the appellant. The Tribunal found in these circumstances there were ample grounds for finding that there had been substantial compliance with the requirements of Rule 8.

6.260 In *RS* the Tribunal dealt with the question of the failure to comply with the requirement of Rule 8 to provide grounds of appeal. Where the appellant fails to provide any grounds for the appeal the first question for the immigration judge is likely to be whether the appeal should be determined without a hearing under sub-paragraphs (a), (b), or (c) of Rule 15(2). The Tribunal considered that it is likely that in the vast majority of cases, appeals to which any of these provisions apply will be determined without a hearing. The Tribunal observed that the fact that the appellant has sought (or apparently sought) a hearing of the appeal is unlikely to have any impact on the issue in these circumstances. This did not mean necessarily dismissing the appeal. The immigration judge is bound to consider all the material before him. It may be that some documents sent in with the notice of appeal imply a submission by the appellant supported by evidence. If the respondent's bundle has not yet arrived, it may be necessary to await it or seek it, in order to assess the effect of the implication, if it is material to the outcome of the appeal. In appeals without grounds, the Tribunal's decision is likely to be made without a hearing, without further delay.

---

[368] [2006] UKAIT 00064 AIT Reported.
[369] *R v IAT ex parte Jeyanthan* [2000] 1 WLR 354; [2000] Imm AR 10, CA.
[370] *HH (Sponsor as Representative) Serbia* [2006] UKIAT 00063.

Grounds of appeal

The Procedure Rules require that the grounds of appeal are set out in the notice of **6.261** appeal.[371] This is a reference to the statutory grounds of appeal in section 84 of the 2002 Act (see paragraph 6.60 above) and the relevant statutory grounds relied on by the appellant should be included in the notice. The Procedure Rules also require reasons to be given in support of those grounds[372] and the appeal forms ask for as much detail as possible and boxes are provided for this purpose.

The AIT 1 and AIT 3 ask for the following information in relation to asylum decisions **6.262** in response to the Home Office decision: the situation in the country of origin, internal relocation, credibility, Convention reason, and human rights grounds. If a one-stop notice has been served with the refusal decision,[373] any additional grounds should be set out in the notice of appeal. The one-stop procedure applies to in-country appeals only and hence it is only the AIT 1 which provides a box for this information.

The grounds do not have to be exhaustive but should relate the facts of the appellant's **6.263** case to the statutory grounds of appeal. Any Immigration Rule or Home Office Policy which is relied on should be stated, as should the basis on which an appellant claims asylum and any relevant Articles of the ECHR should be cited along with the reasons why it is said they would be breached. If it is said that the decision was not in accordance with the law or that a discretion should have been exercised, or exercised differently, reasons should be given.

Due to the strict time limits for submitting the grounds of appeal, representatives may **6.264** find it difficult to submit full grounds of appeal due to difficulties obtaining instructions. Representatives must certify in the notice of appeal that it has been completed in accordance with the client's instructions[374] and should exercise caution in ensuring the grounds accurately reflect the factual basis of any claim since a subsequent change of account could lead to an adverse credibility finding. If an important ground of appeal is not stated in the notice there will be an opportunity to amend the grounds of appeal either at the CMR hearing[375] or at the substantive hearing of the appeal. However, the grounds of appeal may be varied only with the permission of the Tribunal.[376] The Tribunal is unlikely to deny an appellant permission to vary his grounds of appeal, particularly where the one-stop provisions apply.

The consequence of a failure to raise an available ground of appeal in a hearing before **6.265** the AIT is that an appellant may be precluded from relying on this ground of appeal in

---

[371] Rule 8(1)(c).
[372] Rule 8(1)(d).
[373] Section 120 of the NIA Act 2002.
[374] Rule 8(4).
[375] See Practice Note.
[376] Rule 14 Procedure Rules.

an appeal against a subsequent immigration decision if the Home Office issue a certificate under section 96 of the 2002 Act.[377]

6.266 The consequence of a failure to provide any grounds of appeal is likely to be that the appeal is determined without a hearing.[378] The Procedural Rules require the grounds to be sent with the notice of appeal.[379] However, there will be occasions where it will be impossible for a representative to send the grounds of appeal with the notice. In *RS* the Tribunal stated that sometimes a properly completed notice of appeal will give some good reason why the grounds, or some of the grounds, cannot accompany it. In those circumstances, an immigration judge, probably the Duty Judge at the registry, may authorise time to be extended for submitting the grounds, and a letter can be sent out by the AIT accordingly.

Service of notice of appeal

6.267 The notice of appeal must be filed with the Tribunal in accordance with Rule 55 (1) of the Procedure Rules.[380] The notice of appeal which is sent to the appellant with the notice of decision indicates the address to which it should be sent or may be taken by hand and a fax number for service by fax.[381] Rule 55(1) provides that a document (here the notice of appeal) may be:

- delivered, or sent by post, to an address;
- sent via a document exchange to a document exchange number or address;
- sent by fax to a fax number; or
- sent by email to an email address, specified for that purpose by the Tribunal or a person to whom the document is directed.

6.268 There are two situations where the appellant has a choice as to whether to serve the notice of appeal on the Tribunal:

- Where a person is in detention under the Immigration Acts he may instead give notice of appeal by serving it on the person having custody of him.[382] Where this is done the custodian must endorse on the notice the date that it is served on him and forward it to the Tribunal within two days.[383]
- Where a person who is outside the UK wishes to appeal against the decision of the entry clearance officer he may give notice of appeal by serving it on the entry

---

[377] See Certification and Removal—Chapter 7.
[378] See paras 6.257–6.260 above.
[379] *RS and FD (Appeals without grounds) Jamaica* [2006] UKAIT 00064 AIT Reported.
[380] Rule 6 Procedure Rules.
[381] Reg 5(4) Immigration (Notices) Regulations 2003.
[382] Rule 6(3)(b).
[383] Rule 6(5)(a)(b).

clearance officer.[384] Where notice is served on an entry clearance officer he must endorse on the notice the date that it is served on him, forward it to the Tribunal as soon as reasonably practicable and in any event within ten days and if it is practicable to do so within this time limit send to the Tribunal with the notice of appeal a copy of the documents required by Rule 13(1).[385]

These provisions also apply to the Fast Track Procedure with some small modifications.[386]   **6.269**

Time limit for appealing to the AIT

The time limits for appealing against a decision of the immigration authority depends on whether the appellant was in the UK when the decision was made and whether the appellant is detained in the UK under the Fast Track Procedure.   **6.270**

If the appellant is in detention under the Immigration Acts when he is served with the notice of decision against which he is appealing he must give notice of appeal not later than five working days after he is served with that notice.[387] If the case is in the fast track the appellant must give notice of appeal not later than two days after the day on which he was served with the notice.[388] In any other case the appellant must give notice of appeal not later than ten working days after he is served with the notice of decision.[389]   **6.271**

Where the appellant was in the UK when the decision against which he is appealing was made but the appeal is out of country the notice of appeal must be given no later than 28 days after his departure from the UK.[390] In any other case where the appellant is outside the UK the notice of appeal must be given not later than 28 days after he was served with the notice of decision.[391]   **6.272**

Where a person is served with a notice of a decision to reject an asylum claim and does not on the date that he is served with the notice have a period of leave to enter or remain exceeding one year in aggregate, but later is granted such leave, then the time limits for giving notice of appeal apply from the date on which the appellant is served with the notice of the decision to grant leave to enter or remain in the UK.[392]   **6.273**

---

384 Rule 6(4)(b).
385 See paragraph 6.282 below for the rules as to the filing of documents by the Respondent.
386 Rule 6 Fast Track Procedure Rules.
387 Rule 7(1)(a) Procedure Rules.
388 Rule 8(1) Fast Track Procedure Rules.
389 Rule 7(1)(b).
390 Rule 7(2)(a).
391 Rule 7(2)(b).
392 Rule 7(3).

6.274 In *OI (Notice of decision: time calculations) Nigeria*[393] the Tribunal held that the deemed times in the Notices Regulations are of importance in calculating the time for appealing. The time for appealing itself is as set out in the Tribunal's Procedure Rules even if there is other or misleading information in the Notice of Decision. If the officer making the decision chooses not to date it or to indicate the method of service, the Appellant's statements on those issues may well be unchallengeable.

6.275 Where notice of appeal is given by serving it on a custodian or entry clearance officer[394] it is deemed to be served on the day which it is received.[395] There are no provisions in the Procedure Rules dealing with deemed service of the notice of appeal on the Tribunal. It is therefore advisable to send notices of appeal by recorded delivery in order to be able to prove service.

6.276 The effect of the provision in the Procedure Rules[396] with regard to the calculation of time is that for all appeals the day on which the notice of decision is served is excluded.[397] With in-country appeals, any day which is not a business day is excluded from the calculation of time.[398] For all appeals, if the time period for lodging the appeal falls on a day which is not a business day, the appeal can be lodged on the next business day.[399]

Notice of appeal where there is no relevant decision

6.277 Where a person has given notice of appeal to the Tribunal and there is no relevant decision[400] the Tribunal will not accept the notice of appeal.[401] In these circumstances the Tribunal must notify the person who gave notice of appeal and the respondent and take no further action.[402] This provision enables the Tribunal to weed out cases where there is in fact no right of appeal because the decision was not one against which a right of appeal lies.

6.278 The Practice Direction[403] states that the Tribunal will scrutinise a notice of appeal as soon as practicable after it has been given and notes that Rule 9 makes no provision

---

[393] [2006] UKAIT 00042.
[394] In accordance with Rule 6(3)(b) or 6(4)(b).
[395] Rule 55(6), Fast Track Rule 27.
[396] Rule 57(1) Calculation of time.
[397] Rule 57(1)(a).
[398] Rule 57(1)(b) provides that where the period is 10 days or less any day which is not a business day is excluded from the calculation of time, unless the period is expressed as a period of calendar days. 'Business day' is defined by Rule 2 of the Procedure Rules as 'any day other than a Saturday or Sunday, a bank holiday, 25th to 31st December or Good Friday.
[399] Rule 57(2).
[400] 'Relevant decision' is defined by Rule 2 of the Procedure Rules as a decision against which there is an exercisable right of appeal to the Tribunal.
[401] Rule 9 (1) Procedure Rules as amended by SI 2006 No 2788 from 31 November 2006.
[402] Rule 9(2) (a)(b).
[403] April 2007, paragraph 3.

for the issue of validity to be determined by means of a hearing or by reference to any representations of the parties. The Practice Direction also states that the fact that a hearing date may have been given to the parties does not mean that the appeal must be treated as valid. The Tribunal will therefore act accordingly if at a hearing (including a CMR hearing) it transpires that the notice of appeal does not relate to a decision against which there is an exercisable right of appeal. Rule 9 does not apply in the case of a fast track appeal and any issue as to the validity of any such appeal will be dealt with at the hearing.

Late notice of appeal

Where a notice of appeal is given to the AIT outside the time limit it must include an application for an extension of time for appealing.[404] A box is provided in the AIT forms 1 to 3 for applying for an extension of time. The appellant must: **6.279**

- include a statement of reasons for failing to give the notice within the time limit; and
- provide any written evidence relied on in support of those reasons.[405]

If it appears to the Tribunal that the notice of appeal is out of time but there is no application for an extension of time, it may extend time of its own initiative, or must notify the person giving notice of appeal in writing that it proposes to treat the appeal as being out of time.[406] The Practice Direction stresses that parties must *not* assume that the existence of this power means that the limits specified in Rule 7 (time limit for appeal) can in practice be ignored. The power is intended to be used where, for instance, a disruption of the postal service delays notices that would otherwise have been received in time.[407]   **6.280**

Where the appellant is given notice that the Tribunal proposes to treat the notice as being out of time, the appellant can contend that: **6.281**

- the notice of appeal was given in time; or
- there were special circumstances for failing to give the notice of appeal in time which could not reasonably have been stated in the notice of appeal.[408]

If the appellant contends that either of the above circumstances apply then he may file written evidence in support of that contention.[409] The written evidence must be filed not later than three business days after the appellant was notified by the Tribunal   **6.282**

---

[404] Rule 10.
[405] Rule 10(1)(a)(b).
[406] Rule 10(2).
[407] Practice Direction, April 2007, paragraph 4.4.
[408] Rule 10(3)(a)(b).
[409] Rule 10(3).

that it proposes to treat the appeal as out of time if the appellant is in the UK and ten business days if the appellant is outside the UK.[410]

6.283 Where the notice of appeal was given out of time, the Tribunal may extend the time for appealing if satisfied that by reason of special circumstances it would be unjust not to do so.[411] The Tribunal must decide whether or not the notice of appeal was given in time and consider whether to extend time for appealing by way of a preliminary decision without a hearing.[412] In coming to its decision it may only take account of:

- the matters stated in the notice of appeal;
- any written evidence filed by the person giving notice of appeal as described above;
- and other relevant matters of fact within the knowledge of the Tribunal.[413]

6.284 Generally, it is the 'Duty Judge' based in Loughborough who makes a decision on whether time for appealing should be extended. In *BO & Ors*[414] the Tribunal gave guidance to Duty Judges and others on the principles to be employed by the Tribunal in deciding whether to extend time for notices of appeal. The explanation given by the appellant for the lateness should be the Immigration Judge's starting point. If there is no explanation at all, or no satisfactory explanation, or an explanation which is not supported by evidence that ought to have been readily available, the Tribunal considered that it is very unlikely indeed that time should be extended. In the absence of an explanation, it would only be where there were obvious and quite exceptional reasons for extending time and where the issue is one of wider public importance or where (despite the lack of information provided by the appellant) it is clear that there has been a serious denial of justice, that time would be extended in circumstances in which no, or no properly supported, explanation for the lateness is given. Where the delay in lodging the appeal was said to be the fault of the representatives, this could be a satisfactory explanation.

6.285 Whilst emphasizing that each case must be determined on its merits, the Tribunal in *BO* held that other likely factors to be taken into account in considering whether there are special circumstances are likely to be the strength of the grounds of appeal, the consequences of the decision, the length of the delay, the prejudice to the respondent, and the mistakes, delays, and breaches of the Rules by the respondent. The stronger the grounds of appeal, the more likely justice will demand that they be heard. If the decision, which is likely to be final as it is not appealable, has as a consequence the

---

[410] Rule 10 (4)(a)(b).
[411] Rule 10(5).
[412] Rule 10(6).
[413] Rule 10(6)(a)–(c).
[414] *(Extension of time for appealing) Nigeria* [2006] UKAIT.

removal of the appellant, this is more likely to militate in favour of extending time than an entry clearance decision where an appellant may simply reapply.

The Tribunal's decision on the timeliness of an appeal is not amendable to an applica- **6.286** tion for reconsideration.[415] The only challenge to the decision that an appeal is out of time is therefore by way of judicial review. However, in *EA (Ghana)*[416] the Tribunal held that if a member of the Tribunal is persuaded that a notice of appeal to the Tribunal which has been treated out of time was in fact clearly given in time, he should ignore the decision that it was out of time and give parties notice that despite the Tribunal's previous indication there is an appeal pending before it which will proceed to determination.

Where the Tribunal makes a preliminary decision on timeliness it must give written **6.287** notice of its decision including reasons which may be in summary form.[417] Save for in the circumstances detailed below, it must serve the written notice on the parties.[418]

Where the notice of appeal that was given out of time relates in whole or in part to an **6.288** asylum claim and the appellant is in the UK and the Tribunal refuses to extend time for appealing then the Tribunal must serve the written notice on the respondent.[419] The respondent must then serve the notice of decision on the appellant not later than 28 days after receiving it from the Tribunal, and as soon as practicable after serving the notice of decision notify the Tribunal on what date and by what means it was served.[420] If the respondent does not notify the Tribunal of the date and means of service within 29 days the Tribunal must serve the notice on the appellant as soon as practicable thereafter.[421]

Imminent removal cases

Where the Home Office notifies the Tribunal that removal directions have been issued **6.289** against a person who has given notice of appeal and it is proposed to remove him from the UK within five calendar days of the date on which the notice of appeal was given, the Tribunal must, if reasonably practicable, make its decision on the timeliness of the appeal before the date and time proposed for his removal.[422] In these circumstances the Tribunal may give its decision that it proposes to treat the notice of appeal as out of time orally,[423] shorten the time for the appellant to provide evidence in

---

[415] Section 103A(7)(a) NIA Act 2002.
[416] [2006] UKIAT 00036.
[417] Rule 6A as inserted by SI 2006 No 2788 from 13 November 2006.
[418] Rule 10(7).
[419] Rule 10(8)(a)–(c).
[420] Rule 10 (8)(c).
[421] Rule 10 (9).
[422] Rule 11(1).
[423] Rule 11 (3)(a).

support of his contention that his appeal is in time or that there were special circumstances,[424] and direct that that evidence be given orally, which may include requiring the evidence to be given by telephone hearing.[425] Apart from these modifications, Rule 10 applies in full and the Tribunal must given written notice of its decision.

6.290 The Practice Direction states that imminent removal cases under Rule 11 will normally be dealt with by senior immigration judges on a 'rota' basis. The senior immigration judge concerned will decide whether to exercise all or any of the powers conferred by Rule 11(3), having regard to the circumstances of the particular case. These may include whether the person concerned is able to give evidence by telephone, in particular where that person's language is not English, and, where that person is represented, the practicability of receiving submissions from the representative. The judge may decide to hold a hearing or a telephone hearing for the purpose of receiving evidence.

Filing of documents by the respondent

6.291 When the notice of appeal is received by the Tribunal it must serve a copy on the respondent as soon as reasonably practicable (unless the notice of appeal was served on an entry clearance officer).[426] When the respondent is served with a notice of appeal it must, unless it has already done so, file with the Tribunal a copy of:

- the notice of decision to which the notice of appeal relates, and any other document served on the appellant giving reasons for the decision;[427]
- any statement of evidence form completed by the appellant and interview record in relation to the decision being appealed;[428]
- any other unpublished document which is referred to in a document giving reasons for the decision or relied on by the respondent;[429] and
- the notice of any other immigration decision made in relation to the appellant in respect of which he has a right of appeal under section 82 of the 2002 Act.[430]

6.292 The documents referred to above are traditionally known as 'the respondent's bundle' or 'Home Office Bundle'. In any asylum appeal this will usually contain the Statement of Evidence Form (SEF), the Asylum Interview Record (AIR) and the 'reasons for refusal letter' (RFRL).

6.293 The respondent must file the above documents in accordance with any directions given by the Tribunal and if no such directions are given, as soon as reasonably

---

[424] Rule 11 (3)(b).
[425] Rule 11(3)(c).
[426] Rule 12(1).
[427] Rule 13(1)(a).
[428] Rule 13 (1)(b).
[429] Rule 13 (1)(c).
[430] Rule 13(1)(d).

practicable, and in any event no later than 2pm on the business day before the earliest date appointed for any hearing of or in relation to the appeal.[431] If the Tribunal considers timeliness of a notice of appeal as a preliminary issue under Rule 10 then the respondent must file the documents listed above as soon as reasonably practicable after being served with a decision of the Tribunal allowing the appeal to proceed, and in any event no later than 2pm on the business day before the earliest date appointed for any hearing of or in relation to the appeal following that decision.[432]

The consequence of the failure to serve the documentation required by the Procedure Rules was dealt with in the case of *OE & NK (no hearing; compliance with the Rules)*.[433] The Tribunal held that where a direction of the AIT has not been complied with (eg for the Respondent to file the documents required by Rule 13 by a certain date) the immigration judge must still determine the appeal on the available evidence, rather than regarding the failure to comply as fatal to one side or the other. Where a document needs to be scrutinized but has not been provided because the respondent's bundle has not been provided after a further direction to the respondent, the Tribunal may simply assume that the contents of the document are what the appellant says they are. This does not necessarily mean that the appellant will win the appeal. Even where there is a paucity of evidence, the burden remains on the appellant to show that he fulfils the requirements of the Immigration Rules. **6.294**

The respondent must also serve on the appellant all of the documents which it is required to file with the Tribunal unless they have already been sent by the respondent.[434] **6.295**

Certification of pending appeal

The Secretary of State or an immigration officer may issue a certificate under sections 97 or 98 (on national security and public good grounds) whilst an appeal is pending to the Tribunal. If an appeal is certified on these grounds he must file a notice of certification with the Tribunal.[435] Where a notice of certification is filed the Tribunal must notify the parties and take no further action in relation to the appeal.[436] This is because the effect of the certificate is to end proceedings before the Tribunal. **6.296**

---

[431] Rule 13(2).
[432] Rule 13 (3).
[433] [2006] UKIAT 51.
[434] Rule 13(4).
[435] Rule 16(1).
[436] Rule 16(2).

Withdrawal of appeals

6.297 An appeal is pending from when it is instituted until it is fully determined, withdrawn or abandoned, or lapses.[437] Withdrawal of an appeal implies a positive act whereas abandonment implies an absence of action. Under the Procedure Rules, an appellant may withdraw an appeal orally, at a hearing or at any time, by filing written notice with the Tribunal.[438] The appeal is also deemed to be withdrawn if the respondent notifies the Tribunal that the decision (or where the appeal relates to more than one decision, all of the decisions) to which the appeal relates has been withdrawn.[439] Where an appellant dies before his appeal has been determined by the Tribunal, the Tribunal may direct that the appeal shall be treated as withdrawn or where the Tribunal considers it necessary, the personal representative of the appellant may continue the proceedings in the place of the appellant.[440] If an appeal is withdrawn or treated as withdrawn, the Tribunal must serve on the parties a notice that the appeal has been recorded as having been withdrawn.[441]

6.298 In *AP (Withdrawals–nullity assessment) Pakistan*[442] the Tribunal reviewed the previous case law and summarized the position with regard to withdrawals:

- If a notice of withdrawal has been given, either orally at a hearing, or by written notice prior to the hearing, the appeal then ceases to exist and is at an end.
- The clear guidelines on withdrawal/abandonment given in the criminal jurisdiction both by the Court of Appeal in *Reg v Medway* [1976] 2 WLR[443] and in the Archbold commentary on the Criminal Procedure Rules 2005[444] should be adopted as the correct and consistent approach to be taken by the Tribunal.
- When an application is made to challenge a notice of withdrawal as invalid the Tribunal will then proceed to hear the application. Based on all of the evidence placed before it, the Tribunal must be satisfied, on the balance of probabilities, that the withdrawal was not the result of a deliberate and informed decision; 'in other words, that the mind of the applicant did not go with his act of abandonment

---

[437] Section 104 NIAA 2002.
[438] Rule 17(1).
[439] Rule 17(2).
[440] Rule 17(2)(A) as inserted by SI 2006 No.2788.
[441] Rule 17(3).
[442] [2007] UKAIT 00022.
[443] Whilst the Court has jurisdiction to permit the withdrawal of an abandonment of an appeal where it is shown that the circumstances are present to treat the abandonment as a nullity, there is no jurisdiction to permit such a withdrawal where the abandonment was as a result of a deliberate decision. At paragraph 545.
[444] 'The Crown Court cannot entertain an appeal once it has been validly abandoned, unless the abandonment is a nullity by reason of mistake or fraudulent inducement . . . Nor can the Court reinstate abandoned appeals, unless it is satisfied that the notice of abandonment is a nullity.' *Archbold* (2007) at para 2-176.

[withdrawal]' before concluding that the be purported withdrawal was in fact a nullity and the appeal is extant.

The Tribunal gave non-exhaustive guidelines as to why a withdrawal could be found to lack validity: **6.299**

- The appellant has had an almost immediate change of mind, which is promptly communicated to a representative, prior to the matter coming for hearing before the Tribunal.
- A letter or notice purporting to withdraw an appeal has been sent to the respondent, rather than to the Tribunal itself (NB a notice of withdrawal should have no legal validity until the actual notice of appeal is communicated to the Tribunal, either in writing or at a hearing before the Tribunal).
- A withdrawal has been communicated to the Tribunal by a representative without there being clear understanding, or meeting of the minds, between an appellant and the representative.
- A withdrawal has been communicated to the Tribunal by a representative on the instructions of a Sponsor (who has completed section 5 of the appeal form) rather than on the actual instructions of the appellant.
- A representative has communicated a withdrawal to the Tribunal in error, through either lack of due care or a simple mistake.

Abandonment of appeal

As we saw in the body of the appeals chapter, an appeal is deemed to be abandoned in the following circumstances: **6.300**

- If the appellant leaves the UK.[445]
- If the appellant is granted leave to enter or remain in the UK unless he:
    - (i) appeals on asylum grounds and is granted leave to enter or remain in the UK for a period exceeding 12 months and gives notice under the Procedure Rules that he wishes to pursue the appeal on that ground;[446] or
    - (ii) appeals on race discrimination grounds where he gives notice under the Procedure Rules that he wants to pursue the appeal on that ground.[447]

Rule 18 (1)(a) of the Procedure Rules provides that a party to an appeal which is pending before the Tribunal must notify the Tribunal if they are aware that the appeal has been abandoned because the appellant leaves the UK,[448] is granted leave to enter **6.301**

---

[445] Section 104 (4) substituted by IAN Act 2006, s 9 from 13 November 2006 (SI 2006/2838).
[446] Section 104 (4B) as inserted by IAN Act 2006, s 9 from 13 November 2006 (SI 2006/2838).
[447] Section 104 (4C) as inserted by IAN Act 2006, s 9 from 13 November 2006 (SI 2006/2838).
[448] Section 104 (4).

or remain,[449] or the appeal is treated as finally determined because a deportation order is made against the appellant.[450] The parties to a pending appeal must also notify the Tribunal if, in an EEA appeal, they are aware that the appeal has been abandoned because a person has been issued with a residence permit or other document,[451] registration certificate, residence card, a document certifying permanent residence or a permanent residence card under the Immigration (European Economic Area) Regulations 2006, or a registration certification under the Accession (Immigration and Worker Registration) Regulations 2004.[452]

6.302 Where an appellant has been granted leave to remain for a period exceeding 12 months and wishes to pursue an asylum appeal, or is granted leave to enter or remain and wishes to pursue an appeal on race discrimination grounds, he must file a notice with the Tribunal within 28 days of the date on which he received notice of the grant of leave to enter or remain.[453] Where the appellant does not comply with these time limits the appeal will be treated as abandoned.[454] The appellant must also serve a copy of the notice on the respondent.[455] Where an appeal is pursued on these grounds the notice must state:[456]

- the appellant's full name and date of birth;
- the Tribunal's reference number;
- the Home Office reference number, if applicable;
- the Foreign and Commonwealth Office reference number, if applicable;
- the date on which the appellant was granted leave to enter or remain in the United Kingdom for a period exceeding 12 months; and
- that the appellant wishes to pursue the appeal in so far as it is brought on the ground specified in section 84(1)(g) of the 2002 Act which relates to the Refugee Convention or section 84(1)(b) of the 2002 Act which relates to section 19B of the Race Relations Act 1976.

6.303 Where a party files a notice under Rule 18 (1A) that they wish to pursue an appeal on asylum or race discrimination grounds the Tribunal will notify the appellant of the date on which it received the notice[457] and send this notice to the respondent.[458]

---

[449] Section 104 (4A).
[450] Section 104 (5).
[451] Immigration (European Economic Area) Regulations 2000, Reg 33(1A).
[452] Paragraph 4(2) of Schedule 2 to the Immigration (European Economic Area) Regulations 2006.
[453] Rule 18 (1A) as inserted by SI 2006 No 2788 from 13 November 2006.
[454] Rule 18 (1B) as inserted by SI 2006 No 2788 from 13 November 2006.
[455] Rule 18 (1C) as inserted by SI 2006 No 2788 from 13 November 2006.
[456] Rule 18 (1D) and (1E) as inserted by SI 2006 No 2788 from 13 November 2006.
[457] Rule 18 (1F) as inserted by SI 2006 No 2788 from 13 November 2006.
[458] Rule 18 (1G) as inserted by SI 2006 No 2788 from 13 November 2006.

Where an appeal is treated as abandoned or finally determined the Tribunal must **6.304** serve a notice on the parties informing them that the appeal is being treated as abandoned or finally determined and take no further action in relation to the appeal.[459] There is no case law on the question of whether the Tribunal's decision to treat an appeal as abandoned is a 'determination' for the purposes of Rule 2 of the Procedure Rules, and therefore amenable to an application for reconsideration or onward appeal. Under Rule 2, if the decision is one that is 'procedural, ancillary, or prelimi- nary', it is only amenable to judicial review; if it is a decision to allow or dismiss an appeal, it is a 'determination' and may be reviewed or appealed. From the wording of Rule 2, it seems more likely that the decision to treat an appeal as abandoned is a pre- liminary decision. However, in a case under earlier procedure rules,[460] the Tribunal considered that an Adjudicator's decision to treat an appeal as abandoned when the appellant failed to prosecute it amounted to a determination, hence it is certainly arguable that the situation is the same under the current rules.

Notice of hearing

When the Tribunal fixes a hearing it must serve notice of the date, time, and place **6.305** of the hearing on every party.[461] The Tribunal may vary the date of the hearing, but must serve notice of the new date, time, and place of the hearing on every party.[462]

In an appeal where the appellant is in the UK and which relates in whole or in part to **6.306** an asylum claim, the Tribunal must fix a date for the hearing not later than 35 days after the date on which it receives the notice of appeal, or where it has made a prelimi- nary decision on the timeliness of an appeal, the date on which notice of that decision is served on the appellant.[463]

However, if the respondent does not file the appeal documents in accordance within **6.307** the time limits specified or directions given under Rule 13(1) the Tribunal may vary the hearing date if it is satisfied that it would be unfair to the appellant to proceed with the hearing on the date fixed.[464]

Standard directions

In most cases the Tribunal will issue 'standard directions' including those cases where a **6.308** Case Management Review Hearing (CMR) is held. The following directions are normally

---

[459] Rule 18(2).
[460] *Gremesty* [2001] INLR 132.
[461] Rule 46(1).
[462] Rule 46(2).
[463] Rule 23(1)(2) as amended by SI 2006 No 2788 from 13 November 2006.
[464] Rule 23(3).

given to the parties with the Notice of Hearing sent out before any CMR is held (paragraph 6.5 Practice Direction):

- not later than five working days before the full hearing (or ten days in the case of an out of country appeal) the appellant shall serve on the Tribunal and the respondent:
  - (i) witness statements of the evidence to be called at the hearing, such statements to stand as evidence in chief at the hearing;
  - (ii) a paginated and indexed bundle of all the documents to be relied upon at the hearing with a schedule identifying the essential passages;
  - (iii) a skeleton argument, identifying all relevant issues including human rights claims and citing all the authorities relied upon; and
  - (iv) a chronology of events;
- not later than five working days before the full hearing the respondent shall serve on the Tribunal and the appellant a paginated and indexed bundle of all the documents to be relied on at the hearing, with a schedule identifying the relevant passages, and a list of any authorities relied upon.

Case Management Review hearings and directions

6.309 Except where the Tribunal otherwise directs, a CMR hearing is to be held in respect of every asylum appeal[465] (other than a fast track appeal and an appeal in respect of which the determination of the Tribunal is ordered to be reconsidered) where the appellant is present in the United Kingdom and has a right of appeal whilst in the United Kingdom (Practice Direction 6.1).

6.310 The purpose of the CMR is to define the issues prior to the full hearing and to give any necessary directions for the conduct of the case. The CMR is usually heard by a single immigration judge.[466] Both parties should be represented at the CMR as it is a hearing in the appeal and the appeal may be determined by the Tribunal under Rule 15(2) (determination of an appeal without a hearing) or Rule 19 (hearing of appeal in the absence of a party) if a party does not appear and is not represented at that hearing.[467]

Matters to be dealt with by the appellant

6.311 The appellant will, by the time of the CMR, have completed the notice of appeal with accompanying reasons. At the CMR the appellant must provide the Tribunal and the respondent with:[468]

- particulars of any application for permission to vary the grounds of appeal;
- particulars of any amendments to the reasons in support of the grounds of appeal;

---

[465] Defined by para 6.10 as an appeal that relates in whole or in part to an asylum claim.
[466] Para 2.2 Practice Direction.
[467] Practice Direction 6.2.
[468] Practice Direction para 6.3.

- particulars of any witnesses to be called or whose written statement or report is proposed to be relied upon at the full hearing; and
- a draft of any directions that the appellant is requesting the Tribunal to make at the CMR hearing.

Matters to be dealt with by the respondent

The respondent should have already served on the AIT and the appellant the docu- **6.312** ments in Rule 13.[469] If they have not done so, this matter should be raised at the CMR. In addition, the respondent must provide the Tribunal and the appellant at the CMR hearing with:[470]

- any amendment that has been made or that is proposed to be made to the notice of decision to which the appeal relates or to any other document served on the appellant giving reasons for that decision; and
- a draft of any directions that the respondent is requesting the Tribunal to make at the CMR hearing.

Directions given by the Tribunal

At the end of the CMR hearing, the Tribunal will give to the parties any further written **6.313** directions relating to the conduct of the appeal.[471] The Tribunal may also direct that the jurisdiction of the Tribunal at the full hearing should be exercised by a group of members the Tribunal.[472] At the end of the CMR hearing the Tribunal shall also give to the parties written confirmation of:[473]

- any issues that have been agreed at the CMR hearing as being relevant to the determination of the appeal; and
- any concessions made at the CMR hearing by a party.

Issues that may be dealt by way of directions before the substantive hearing

We have dealt above with standard directions and the matters the Practice Direction **6.314** states must or should be dealt with at the CMR. The Tribunal also has the power to give directions, which may be given orally or in writing, to the parties 'relating to the conduct of any appeal or application'.[474] These directions may be made at the CMR, if one is held, or may be applied for by the parties, in which case an application for a case management hearing should be made in order that the application may be heard.[475] The Tribunal has the power to give directions on procedural matters only

---

[469] See para 6.282 above.
[470] Practice Direction para 6.4.
[471] Practice Direction para 6.5.
[472] Paragraph 6.8.
[473] Paragraph 6.9.
[474] Rule 45(1).
[475] Rule 45(4)(d)(ii).

and may not direct that the respondent take substantive steps. For example, the Tribunal has no power to direct that the respondent reconsider the case or interview the appellant.[476]

6.315   In addition to the standard directions listed above, the Tribunal may give directions to:[477]

- specify the length of time allowed for anything to be done;
- vary any time limit in the Procedure Rules or in directions previously given by the Tribunal for anything to be done by a party;
- provide for any matter to be dealt with as a preliminary issue, a case management hearing to be held, a party to provide further details of his case or any other information necessary for determining the appeal, the witnesses to be heard, and the manner in which evidence is to be given (for example by directing that witness statements are to stand as evidence in chief);[478]
- file and serve details of whether an interpreter will be required at the hearing and in respect of what language and dialect;
- limit the number or length of documents upon which a party may rely at the hearing, the length of oral submissions, the time allowed for examination and cross-examination of witnesses and the issues which are to be addressed at the hearing;
- require the parties to take steps to enable hearings to be combined;
- provide for a hearing to be conducted or evidence given or representations to be made by video link or other electronic means; and
- make provision to secure the anonymity of a party or a witness.

6.316   The Tribunal must not direct an unrepresented party to do something unless it is satisfied that he is able to comply with the direction.[479]

Variation of grounds of appeal

6.317   We have seen that an appellant is obliged to give particulars of any application to amend the grounds of appeal at the CMR. An appellant may vary his grounds of appeal only with the permission of the Tribunal.[480] Permission to vary the grounds of appeal is not required where the appellant raises a fresh ground of appeal in response to a one-stop notice under section 120 of the 2002 Act.[481]

---

[476]   *TK* [2004] UKIAT 00149; *Mwanza* [2001] Imm AR 557; *KK* [2005] UKIAT 54.

[477]   Rule 45 (4).

[478]   The Tribunal recognises that there may be cases where it will be appropriate for appellants or witnesses to have the opportunity of adding to or supplementing their witness statements. Parties are referred to the judgment of the Court of Appeal in *R v Secretary of State for the Home Department ex p Singh* [1998] INLR 608 (Practice Direction 6.7).

[479]   Rule 45(5).

[480]   Rule 14.

[481]   Rule 14 with reference to s 85(2).

In asylum and human rights cases the discretion to permit an amendment to the **6.318** grounds of appeal is a wide one. In such cases the appellant is subject to the 'one-stop' procedure which obliges him to raise any grounds on which he should be permitted to enter or remain in the UK and on which he should not be removed from the UK.[482] In the circumstances if the Tribunal refused permission to amend to include a new ground of appeal, the Secretary of State would be likely to be precluded from certifying the case under section 96 of the 2002 Act. The Tribunal is responsible for ensuring that proceedings are handled fairly, quickly, and efficiently in the interests of the parties and the wider public interest.[483] Given the fundamental nature of the rights at stake in a case concerning asylum and human rights and the fact that strict time limits mean the potential grounds may come to light only late in the day, the Tribunal is unlikely to refuse permission to amend.

Applications and further directions

We deal now with specific applications and directions that may be sought in order to **6.319** ensure the just disposal of an appeal. The Procedure Rules give the Tribunal power to grant adjournments, summon witnesses, order combined hearings, exclude the public from a hearing, give a direction as to the constitution of the Tribunal, and direct that a party furnishes further details of his case. We deal with these procedural powers in turn.

Adjournments

Asylum and human rights appeals often raise matters which are difficult for repre- **6.320** sentatives to deal with inside the strict timetable prescribed by the Procedure Rules for listing a hearing. As we saw above, in asylum appeals where the appeal is to be considered by the Tribunal at a hearing, the hearing must be fixed for a date not more than 35 days after receipt of the notice of appeal or the decision on timeliness.[484] Where an expert needs to be instructed or medical evidence obtained, it may simply not be possible to comply with this timetable. In such circumstances an application for an adjournment may have to be made.

The Tribunal must not adjourn a hearing of an appeal on the application of a party **6.321** unless satisfied that the appeal cannot otherwise be justly determined.[485] Where a party applies for an adjournment of a hearing of an appeal he must, if practicable, notify all other parties of the application, show good reason why an adjournment is necessary, and produce evidence of any fact or matter relied on in support of

---

[482] Section 120 NIA Act 2002.
[483] Rule 4 'overriding objective'.
[484] Rule 23 (2), as amended by SI No 2788/2006.
[485] Rule 21(2).

the application.[486] Further, the Tribunal must not adjourn a hearing on the application of a party to allow more time to produce evidence unless it is satisfied that the evidence relates to a matter in dispute in the appeal; it would be unjust to determine the appeal without permitting the party a further opportunity to produce the evidence, and where the party has failed to comply with directions for the production of the evidence, he has provided a satisfactory explanation for that failure.[487]

6.322 As stated above, the Procedure Rules require a party to show good reason why an adjournment is necessary and produce evidence in support of the application. So, if an appellant or vital witness cannot attend due to illness, medical evidence will need to be produced. If an adjournment is being sought for the purposes of obtaining medical, expert, or other evidence, evidence of what steps have been taken to obtain the evidence and when such evidence will be available is likely to be required. The Tribunal must also be satisfied that the evidence is relevant to the matters in dispute in the appeal.

6.323 The Practice Direction[488] states that applications for the adjournment of appeals (other than fast track appeals) listed for hearing before the Tribunal must be made not later than 4pm one clear working day before the date of the hearing. Any application made later than the end of this period must be made to the Tribunal at the hearing and will require the attendance of the party or the representative of the party seeking the adjournment.[489] It will be only in the most exceptional circumstances that late applications for adjournment will be considered without the attendance of a party or representative.[490] Parties must not assume that an application, even if made in accordance with time limit specified above, will be successful and they must always check with the Tribunal as to the outcome of the application.[491] This is because if an adjournment is not granted and a party fails to attend the hearing, the Tribunal may proceed to hear the appeal in their absence.[492]

6.324 There are three main reasons for an application for an adjournment: on medical grounds, on the grounds that time is required to obtain legal representation, and on the grounds that further evidence is required.

6.325 In medical cases the grant or refusal of an adjournment will depend on the facts of the case. Where it is unclear when an appellant may be able to give evidence due to mental illness, an adjournment is likely to be refused. In *Ramirez v SSHD*[493] Sedley LJ considered

---

[486] Rule 21(1).
[487] Rule 21(3).
[488] At para 9.1.
[489] Paragraph 9.3.
[490] Paragraph 9.5.
[491] Paragraph 9.6.
[492] Under Rule 19 (1).
[493] [2001] EWCA Civ 1365, [2002] Imm AR 240.

that it was unarguable that justice will demand indefinite adjournments in any case where an applicant wishes to exercise his right to be present and give evidence but is prevented by mental illness from doing so. In each case the nature of the condition, its prognosis, the nature of the applicant's case, and the scope of the evidence which both will and will not be available if he is absent will all be relevant to the conscientious judgment the immigration judge must make as to whether justice calls for an adjournment. In particular the immigration judge must consider when, if ever, the applicant is likely to be able to attend if an adjournment is granted.

In *R (on the appln of Bogou) v SSHD*[494] Maurice Kay took issue with a line of **6.326** Tribunal decisions which held that representation in asylum appeals was a matter of presumption and axiomatic. He stated that there would be cases where it will be necessary to adjourn an appeal because the just disposal of the case requires representation. There will be other cases where it did not. The Guidance Note to Immigration Judges on Unrepresented Appellants[495] states that the decision to adjourn should always be made with regard to the overriding objective in the Procedure Rules. The request of an unrepresented appellant for more time to instruct another representative should generally be resisted. If he has failed the CLR merits test with one firm he is likely to fail it with another. If the appellant is seeking more time to instruct a lawyer privately the Guidance Note states that before agreeing to an adjournment in those circumstances the immigration judge should consider how realistic such a prospect is, what efforts have already been made and whether the appellant's case has already been set out. The SEF, interview, and witness statement may mean that a lawyer would not add much to the appellant's case.

We have dealt with the requirements of the Procedural Rules where a party seeks an **6.327** adjournment to produce further evidence above. It is clear that where a party is permitted to produce new evidence which was not sent to the other party, an adjournment may be necessary to avoid prejudice.[496]

Where the hearing of an appeal is adjourned, the Tribunal will fix a new hearing date **6.328** which will not be more than 28 days after the original hearing date unless the Tribunal is satisfied that because of exceptional circumstances the appeal cannot justly be heard within that time.[497]

The refusal of an adjournment is a preliminary decision which is not amenable to **6.329** review or appeal.[498]

---

[494] [2000] Imm AR 494.
[495] Issued in 2003 but still relevant guidance as it is in the annex to the Consolidated Practice Direction.
[496] *Macharia v IAT* [2000] INLR 156, CA.
[497] Rule 21(4).
[498] But see the discussion at para 6.157 above.

Combined hearings

6.330 Where two or more appeals are pending at the same time, the Tribunal may direct them to be heard together if it appears that:

- some common question of law or fact arises in each of them;
- they relate to decisions or action taken in respect of persons who are members of the same family;
- for some other reason it is desirable for the appeals to be heard together.[499]

6.331 The Tribunal has made use of this power with regard to common questions of fact in Country Guidance (CG) cases. Often, members of the same family have appeals pending before the Tribunal at the same time. It frequently makes good sense to have them heard together as the factual basis of the accounts interrelate. It is also is an unsatisfactory judicial outcome if contradictory findings of fact and credibility are made in appeals relating to family members. Whilst the existence of concurrent applications by members of the family is a relevant consideration and it may, in an appropriate case, point to an adjournment, it does not mean an adjournment must be granted.[500] Appellants who have their appeals heard together should not be excluded from the hearing room during the combined appeal and their appeals should not fail just because their evidence differs.[501]

Summoning of witnesses

6.332 The Tribunal may issue a witness summons to require any person in the UK to attend as a witness at a hearing of an appeal and to answer any question or produce any documents in his custody or which relate to a matter in issue.[502] A person is not required to attend unless the summons is served upon him and he is paid the necessary expenses of his attendance.[503] If the witness summons is issued at the request of a party, that party must pay or tender the expenses of his attendance.[504]

6.333 Witness summonses are infrequent in proceedings before the AIT but may be of use, for example, to compel the attendance of a Home Office official who has failed to provide documentation which is of central importance in an appeal.

---

[499] Rule 20.

[500] *Rajan (starred appeal)* Appeal No: 01TH00244.

[501] *Tabores and Munoz* (17819) (24 July 1998, unreported).

[502] Rule 50(1)—a person can only be compelled to give evidence or produce any document which he would could be compelled to give or produce at a trial of a civil claim in the part of the UK in which the hearing is taking place (Rule 51(2)).

[503] Rule 50(2).

[504] Rule 50(3).

Exclusion of the public from the hearing

Every hearing must be held in public unless:[505]   **6.334**

- the Tribunal is hearing an allegation that a document relied on to a party to an appeal under section 82, 83, or 83A is a forgery and that the disclosure to that party of a matter relating to the detection of the forgery would be contrary to the public interest.[506] Where the Tribunal is considering an allegation of forgery, all members of the public must be excluded from the hearing and any party or representative of a party may be excluded from the hearing;[507]
- it is necessary in the interests of public order or national security or to protect the private life of a party or the interests of a minor to exclude any or all the members of the public from part or all of a hearing;[508]
- in exceptional circumstances, to ensure that publicity does not prejudice the interests of justice, but only if and to the extent that it is strictly necessary to do so.[509]

Where an asylum or human rights appeal concerns sensitive issues such as rape or   **6.335** sexual transmitted diseases the Tribunal may exclude members of the public to protect the appellant's private life. There will also be occasions where an appellant may feel inhibited in giving evidence due to the fact that their case is going to be given publicity. Publicity could also cause an appellant to be at risk in their home country.[510] In such circumstances it can be argued that publicity would prejudice the interests of justice.

Constitution of the Tribunal

The Tribunal is under no duty to consider any representations by a party about the   **6.336** number or class of members of the Tribunal which should exercise the jurisdiction of the Tribunal.[511] Representatives may nevertheless make representations about the appropriate constitution of the Tribunal. In cases involving allegations of rape it is not uncommon for an appellant to request a female Tribunal.

---

505 Rule 54.

506 Under section 108 of the 2002 Act—in *RP (proof of forgery) Nigeria* [2006] UKIAT 00086 the Tribunal held that an allegation of forgery needs to be proved by evidence and by the person making it. A bare allegation of forgery, or an assertion by an ECO that he believed the document to be forged can in these circumstances carry no weight. The Tribunal treats a document as forged only on the basis of clear evidence before it.

507 Rule 54(2).

508 Rule 54(3).

509 Rule 54(4).

510 The Tribunal also has the power to give directions to make provision to secure the anonymity of a witness or party (Rule 45 (4)(i)).

511 Rule 44 (1).

Further details of the respondent's case

6.337 As we noted above, the Tribunal may give directions for a party to provide further details of their case.[512] The respondent is obliged by the Notice Regulations[513] to provide a statement of reasons for the decision.[514] In an asylum appeal this will be the Reasons for Refusal Letter. The respondent is also obliged to file with the Tribunal and serve on the appellant any unpublished document referred to in the notice of decision or reasons for the decision.[515]

6.338 It is not uncommon for the respondent not to provide clear reasons for the decision and not to provide a document referred to in the Reasons for Refusal Letter or Notice of Decision. In such circumstances it may be appropriate to request a direction for further detail of the respondent's case.[516]

The Tribunal hearing

6.339 In general, all asylum appeals and human rights appeals are considered by the Tribunal at an oral hearing with both parties in attendance. However, an appeal may be dealt with in the absence of a party and may be determined without a hearing. We deal with these situations in turn.

Determining an appeal in the absence of a party

6.340 The Tribunal may hear an appeal in the absence of a party or his representative if satisfied that:[517]

- the party or his representative has been given notice of the date, time, and place of the hearing; and
- there is no good reason for his absence.

6.341 Where the above does not apply, the Tribunal may hear an appeal in the absence of a party if satisfied that:[518]

- a representative of the party is present at the hearing;
- the party is outside the UK;
- the party is suffering from a communicable disease or there is a risk of him behaving in a violent or disorderly manner;

---

[512] Rule 45 (d)(iii).
[513] See paragraph above.
[514] Regulation 5 (1)(a).
[515] Rule 13.
[516] Under Rule 45 (d)(iii).
[517] Rule 19(1) as amended by SI 2007 No 835. The previous Rule 19 (1) was held to be ultra vires in *FP (Iran) MB (Libya) v Secretary of State for the Home Department* [2007] EWCA Civ 13. Under the old Rule 19(1), the Tribunal was under a duty to determine the hearing in the absence of the party or his representative where rule 19 (1) applied.
[518] Rule 19(2).

- the party is unable to attend the hearing because of illness, accident, or some other good reason;
- the party is unrepresented and it is impracticable to give him notice of the hearing; or
- the party has notified the Tribunal that he does not wish to attend the hearing.

The requirements of the Rule are discretionary. Hence the Tribunal is not obliged to hear the appeal in the absence of a party if satisfied that any of the criteria apply. It may also adjourn the appeal, subject to the requirements of Rule 21. **6.342**

The Home Office does not always provide a representative to attend the hearing. The Tribunal has set out guidelines as to how the hearing should proceed and particularly the role of the immigration judge in the absence of the respondent.[519] It is the practice of some representatives to ask for the case to be determined 'on the papers' when the appellant will not be attending. However, the Tribunal cannot determine the appeal without a hearing unless 'all parties consent to this course'.[520] If the respondent is represented therefore, the hearing will proceed by way of submissions unless the respondent decides not to make any, in which case the appeal may be determined without a hearing because all parties consent. **6.343**

The most frequent cause of hearings taking place in the absence of appellants is the non-receipt of notices. It is therefore vital importance for appellants and representatives to notify the Tribunal of any change of address. We addressed the obligations on parties and representatives at paragraph 6.238 above. **6.344**

Where an appeal is determined in the absence of a party it can reviewed or appealed in the normal way. **6.345**

Determining an appeal without a hearing

Every appeal must be considered by the Tribunal at a hearing except where the appeal:[521] **6.346**

- lapses pursuant to section 99 of the 2002 Act (ie where a pending appeal is certified under section 96 (earlier right of appeal) section 97 (national security) or section 98 (public good grounds));[522]
- is treated as abandoned pursuant to section 104(4) of the 2002 Act (ie if a person leaves the UK);[523]

---

[519] See Practice Notes to Asylum Chapter – 'the Surendran Guidelines' attached to the starred case of *MNM* (00TH02423) 1 November 2000.
[520] Rule 15(2). See paragraph 6.327 below on determining an appeal without a hearing.
[521] Rule 15.
[522] Rule 15(1)(a)(i).
[523] Rule 15(1)(a)(ii).

- is treated as finally determined pursuant to section 104(5) of the 2002 Act (ie if a deportation order has been made against the appellant on an appeal against a decision to refuse leave to enter, refuse a certificate of entitlement to the right of abode, refuse to vary leave, curtail leave, and revoke indefinite leave);[524]
- is withdrawn by the appellant or treated as withdrawn in accordance with Rule 17.[525]

6.347 Where an appeal is abandoned, treated as finally determined, or withdrawn, the Tribunal will make no decision on the substance of the appeal and will issue a notice to the parties informing them of such.[526] It is only a 'decision on an appeal' which can be reviewed under section 103A which does not include 'a procedural, ancillary, or preliminary decision'. If the Tribunal was misinformed and the appeal should not have been treated as abandoned or withdrawn it is arguable that this should be treated as a determination for the purposes of applying for a section 103A review.

6.348 The Tribunal has a discretion to determine an appeal without a hearing if:

- all the parties to the appeal consent;[527]
- the appellant is outside the UK or it is impracticable to give him notice of a hearing and, in either case, he is unrepresented;[528]
- a party has failed to comply with a provision of the Procedure Rules or a direction of the Tribunal and the Tribunal is satisfied in all the circumstances including the extent of the failure and any reasons for it that it is appropriate to determine the appeal without a hearing;[529]
- the Tribunal is satisfied having regard to the material before it and the nature of the issues raised that the appeal can be justly determined without a hearing. The Tribunal may take this course of action only after first giving the parties notice of its intention to do so and an opportunity to make written representations as to whether there should be a hearing.[530]

6.349 In *OE and NK (Nigeria)*[531] the Tribunal gave guidance as to when it is appropriate to exercise the discretionary power to proceed with a hearing:

- The appellant's failure to enclose the notice of decision with the notice of appeal is a failure to comply with the Rules but it does not make the appeal invalid.

---

524 Rule 15(1)(a)(iii).
525 Rule 15(a)(iv). See para 6.288 above.
526 Rule 17(3), 18(2).
527 Rule 15(2)(a).
528 Rule 15(2)(b).
529 Rule 15(2)(c).
530 Rule 15(2)(d) and (3).
531 [2006] UKAIT 00055.

- The respondent's failure to send the appeal bundle (with or without a direction to do so) is a failure to comply with the Rules or a direction but it does not amount to conceding the appeal or reversing the burden of proof.
- It may be possible to deal with the fact that a document is missing by issuing a further direction to send it stating precisely what the consequence will be if this direction is not complied with.

In an in-country asylum appeal, where the appeal is determined without a hearing, **6.350** the appeal must be determined not more than 35 days after the date on which the Tribunal receives the notice of appeal or makes a preliminary decision on a late notice of appeal.[532] Where an appeal is determined without a hearing in the circumstances described above it may be reviewed or appealed in the normal way.

Procedure at the hearing

Subject to the Procedure Rules, the Tribunal has a discretion to decide the procedure **6.351** to be followed in relation to any appeal or application.[533] It is clear from the case law that in asylum and human rights appeals only the highest standards of fairness will suffice. The overriding objective of the Procedure Rules is to ensure that proceedings are handled as fairly, quickly, and efficiently as possible in the interests of the parties to the proceedings and in the wider public interest. [534]

Asylum appeals are conducted in an informal fashion. Hearings normally commence **6.352** at 10am. The immigration judge will check with the usher which cases are ready to proceed and decide on an order. Legal representatives must complete a 'section 84' form[535] which the usher will give to the immigration judge prior to the hearing. Any applications for adjournments will be dealt with first.[536]

The immigration judge will check with the representatives that he has all the papers **6.353** he should have. If there is evidence that he has not seen, or fresh evidence submitted on the day, if the evidence is admitted, the case may need to be put back for everyone to read the papers.

Once the immigration judge has established that the case is ready to proceed, he must **6.354** ensure that the appellant and the interpreter understand each other. The appellant should have requested an interpreter in the appeal form, specifying any particular dialect required. The interpreter must inform the immigration judge of the language and any dialect. The interpreter will inform the immigration judge of any difficulties he is encountering. If the difficulties are due to the appellant and interpreter not

---

[532] Rule 23 (2)(b) as amended by SI 2006 No2788.
[533] Rule 43(1).
[534] Rule 4.
[535] Section 84 Immigration and Asylum Act 1999.
[536] See above on adjournments.

speaking the same dialect, the hearing will have to be adjourned unless another interpreter is available. The Tribunal is under no duty to consider untranslated documents,[537] but, where fairly short documents have been brought to the hearing in an untranslated form, the interpreter may be willing to translate on the spot.

6.355 Once the immigration judge has established that the appellant and interpreter understand each other, he will explain to the appellant how the appeal will proceed. The 'Adjudicator Guidance Note No.3', which is annexed to the Practice Direction, gives a suggested form of words to be used by immigration judges. Essentially, the immigration judge should explain that the hearing will take the form of the appellant being asked questions, first by their own representative and then by the Home Office. The Guidance suggests that the immigration judge should then inform the appellant that they should listen to the questions carefully, answer the questions asked, and break up answers into small parts for interpretation purposes. The appellant should be asked to say if they do not understand something and informed that they will not be expected to give a full account of what happened in their own country because the immigration judge already has that information in the papers. It should be explained that at the end of the evidence the representatives will make their submissions.

6.356 Once these formalities are completed, the immigration judge may discuss with the parties whether the issues can be narrowed, whether there is any application to vary the grounds of appeal, or whether there are any jurisdictional issues. Any concession by the Home Office should be carefully noted, as the immigration judge may not go behind a concession.

Evidence in chief

6.357 Before the appellant or any other witness gives his evidence he may be asked to take an oath or affirm that his evidence will be the truth.[538] It is the practice of most immigration judges not to ask for evidence to be given on oath or affirmation.

6.358 A standard direction will normally have been given prior to the hearing that the witness statement should stand as evidence in chief. The Practice Directions state, however, that although in normal circumstances a witness statement should stand as evidence in chief, there may be cases where it will be appropriate for appellants or witnesses to have the opportunity of adding to or supplementing their witness statements. Parties are referred by the Practice Direction to the judgment of the Court of Appeal in *R v Secretary of State for the Home Department ex p Singh* [1998] INLR 608.

---

537 Rule 52(3).
538 Rule 53(1).

An unrepresented appellant must be given every assistance in putting his case. The **6.359** 'Guidance Note' for dealing with unrepresented appellants[539] states that the appellant should be asked to confirm that the contents of his previous statements and interview record are true. If he disputes the contents it may be necessary for the court interpreter to read back what was recorded for comment. When he has agreed with the version of events he is now putting forward he should be asked if there is anything else he wants to add.

Cross-examination

The purpose of cross-examination is to test the appellant's credibility and expose any **6.360** inconsistencies in his account. Generally, immigration judges allow Presenting Officers latitude in their questioning. However, cross-examination should be confined to issues which are of relevance to the appeal. The immigration judge should curb any cross-examination which is not relevant or appears to be a fishing expedition. If he does not, it is open to a representative to object to a line of questioning which covers fresh matters not raised in the appeal before or that is vague or confusing.

The cross-examination of unrepresented appellants must not be hostile or aggres- **6.361** sive.[540] Where the Home Office is not represented, the immigration judge must never cross-examine the appellant.[541]

Re-examination

Re-examination should be confined to issues arising out of cross-examination which **6.362** the appellant's representative needs to address. If a representative has forgotten to ask a question in examination in chief, the immigration judge's permission should be sought. The Presenting Officer should then also be allowed to ask questions arising out of the fresh evidence.

The immigration judge usually waits for re-examination to conclude before asking **6.363** any questions of a witness. If the judge asks a number of questions, at the end of re-examination both representatives should be given an opportunity to ask questions of the witness arising out of those questions.[542]

Other witnesses

Where further witnesses are called the process described above applies. It is the con- **6.364** vention for witnesses who have not given their evidence to wait outside the hearing room until they are called. After giving evidence they may remain in the hearing room. Generally, the appellant gives evidence first and any other witnesses follow, particularly

---

539 Guidance Note No 5 annexed to the Practice Direction at <www.ait.gov.uk>.
540 Guidance Note on Unrepresented Appellants.
541 'Surendran Guidelines' attached to the starred determination in *MNM* [2000] INLR 576.
542 *Oyono* [2002] UKIAT 02034.

when credibility is in issue. However, the conduct of the hearing is a matter for the immigration judge and the normal order may be reversed, for example due to the presence of an expert witness.

Submissions

6.365 When all the witnesses have given their evidence, both parties may make submissions to the immigration judge. The Presenting Officer goes first, followed by the appellant's representative. Appellants' submissions should set out the statutory ground or grounds of appeal, the issues between the parties, specify what findings of fact the judge is asked to make, take the judge to the relevant evidence in respect of those facts, deal with all credibility points taken by the respondent, both in the RFRL and in submissions, deal with any country guidance cases, and take the judge to the relevant background material. The judge should be asked to allow the appeal and to make any relevant directions.

6.366 Immigration judges are strongly discouraged from agreeing to the submission of post-hearing submissions or documents or evidence prior to the determination being written.[543] It is only in exceptional cases that this will be allowed and if it is unavoidable a direction must be made in writing detailing what steps are to be taken by the representatives in relation to the submissions. Representatives must be directed to highlight the urgency of the documentation and the need to ensure that it gets to the named immigration judge promptly.[544]

The record of proceedings

6.367 The Procedure Rules do not require the Tribunal to keep a record of proceedings, but the Practice Direction states that the Tribunal shall keep a proper record of proceedings of any hearing.[545] The record should be signed and dated by the member of the Tribunal responsible for taking the record and be attached to the Tribunal's case file. Where an application for a reconsideration is based on an assertion of fact which differs from the record of proceedings, it should be supported by evidence.[546]

The determination

6.368 The determination is a 'decision by the Tribunal in writing to allow or dismiss the appeal, and does not include a procedural, ancillary or preliminary decision'.[547] In all cases save for in-country asylum appeals the Tribunal must serve on every party a written

---

[543] Adjudicator Guidance Note No 4.
[544] Paragraph 5 Adjudicator Guidance Note No 4.
[545] At para 11.
[546] *R (on the appln of Bosombanguwa) v IAT and SSHD* [2004] EWHC 1656 (Admin), [2004] All ER (D) 260.
[547] Rule 2.

determination containing its decision and reasons for it.[548] If the appeal was considered at a hearing, the Tribunal must send its determination not later than ten days after the hearing finishes.[549] If the appeal is determined without a hearing it must be sent no later than ten days after it is determined.[550]

In an in-country asylum appeal the Tribunal must serve its determination on the respondent not later than ten days after the hearing finishes, if the appeal is considered at a hearing.[551] If the appeal is determined without a hearing the Tribunal must serve it on the Respondent not later than ten days after it is determined.[552] The respondent then serves the determination on the appellant not later than 28 days after receiving it from the Tribunal unless the respondent applies for permission to appeal or for a review, in which case the appellant must be served not later than the date of the application.[553] **6.369**

The Practice Direction states that where the jurisdiction of the Tribunal is exercised by more than one member, the determination is that reached by the majority of those members. It goes on to state that it is accordingly inappropriate that a dissenting view should be expressed or that the determination should indicate that it is that of a majority.[554] **6.370**

The determination must make clear the decision appealed against and the legislation under which the appeal is brought. The burden and standard of proof must be stated, although there is no requirement for the citation of authorities such as *Sivakumaran* and *Kaja*.[555] The immigration judge must deal with all the issues, including all points raised in the explanatory statement or refusal letter and relied on by the Presenting Officer.[556] There is a statutory obligation to determine any matter raised as a ground of appeal.[557] The Tribunal may not because it decides to allow an appeal on one ground, refuse to determine the other grounds of appeal.[558] **6.371**

---

[548] Rule 22(1).

[549] Rule 22(2)(a).

[550] Rule 22(2)(b).

[551] Rule 23(4)(a)—Rule 23 applies to all (and only) appeals in relation to *asylum* claims. It does not apply to all (or only) determinations on asylum *grounds (HH (Rule 23: meaning and extent) Iraq* [2007] UKIAT 00036).

[552] Rule 23(4)(b).

[553] Rule 23(5)(a)(i)(ii)—compliance with Rule 23 (a)(i) is a precondition for a valid section 103A application by the respondent (*HH (Rule 23: meaning and extent) Iraq* [2007] UKIAT 00036).

[554] At para 10.

[555] *SR (Iran) v SSHD* [2007] EWCA Civ 460—although it is customary for determinations to refer to the familiar guidelines in these cases, a failure to do so is not an error of law. To require the Tribunal to recite such cases 'would be to substitute formulaic for substantive justice'.

[556] *DC* [2005] UKIAT 11.

[557] Section 86 (2)(a) 2002 Act.

[558] *Emunefe v Secretary of State for the Home Department* [2005] EWCA Civ 1002; *CS (Jamaica)* UKIAT 00004.

6.372 The determination also must be adequately reasoned. We deal at paragraph 6.171 above with what amounts to a material error of law. In *R & Ors*[559] the Court of Appeal adapted what was said in a number of leading authorities to demonstrate what is required from a sustainable determination:

> [An adjudicator] should give his reasons in sufficient detail to show the [IAT] the principles on which he has acted and the reasons that have led him to his decision. They need not be elaborate. I cannot stress too strongly that there is no duty on [an adjudicator], in giving his reasons, to deal with every argument presented by [an advocate] in support of his case. It is sufficient if what he says shows the parties and, if need be, the [IAT], the basis on which he has acted, and if it be that the [adjudicator] has not dealt with some particular argument but it can be seen that there are grounds on which he would have been entitled to reject it, [the IAT] should assume that he acted on those grounds unless the appellant can point to convincing reasons leading to a contrary conclusion.

> [I]f the appellate process is to work satisfactorily, the judgment must enable the [IAT] to understand why the [adjudicator] reached his decision. This does not mean that every factor which weighed with the [adjudicator] in his appraisal of the evidence has to be identified and explained. But the issues the resolution of which were vital to the [adjudicator]'s conclusion should be identified and the manner in which he resolved them explained. It is not possible to provide a template for this process. It need not involve a lengthy judgment. It does require the [adjudicator] to identify and record those matters which were critical to his decision. If the critical issue was one of fact, it may be enough to say that one witness was preferred to another because the one manifestly had a clearer recollection of the material facts or the other gave answers which demonstrated that his recollection could not be relied upon.

6.373 A determination is not invalid because it is not served within the time limits set out above.[560] The Tribunal has stated that where credibility is in issue a period of more than three months between the date of the hearing and promulgation is unacceptable. Where credibility is not in issue, the question of whether the delay renders the determination unsafe is likely to be a question of what prejudice has been caused.

Errors of procedure and correction of orders

6.374 Where there has been an error of procedure such as a failure to comply with a rule, the error does not invalidate any step taken in the proceedings unless the Tribunal so orders. Before determining the appeal the Tribunal may make any order or take any other step to remedy the error.[561] A determination made in an appeal or application is valid notwithstanding that a hearing did not place or the determination was not made or served within a time period specified in the Procedure Rules.[562]

---

559 [2005] EWCA Civ 982.
560 Rule 59(2)(b).
561 Rule 59(1).
562 Rule 59(2).

The Tribunal also has the power to correct clerical errors, slips, or omissions in orders, **6.375** notices of decision, or determinations.[563] The President may, either of his own motion or on application, review any order, notice of decision, or determination made by the Tribunal and, after consulting all the parties to the appeal, may set it aside and direct that the relevant proceedings be dealt with again by the Tribunal, on the ground that it was wrongly made as the result of an administrative error on the part of the Tribunal or its staff.[564] An application under this Rule must be filed, if the party making the application is in the United Kingdom, within ten days; or if the party making the application is outside the United Kingdom, within 28 days, of the date on which the party is served with the order, notice of decision, or determination.[565] At the same time as filing the application, the party making the application must serve a copy on the other party to the appeal.[566] The President may delegate this power to a Deputy President or a senior immigration judge.[567]

The Tribunal must serve the amended documents on the parties on whom it served **6.376** the originals and if the error was contained in the determination of the appeal time for appealing or applying for a reconsideration runs from the date on which the party is served with the amended determination. [568]

Evidence

We have dealt with the substantive provisions on the admissibility of evidence in the **6.377** body of the appeals chapter. We have dealt with the burden and standard of proof and the approach to evidence generally in Chapter 2. We also deal with evidence relating to credibility, expert evidence, and medical evidence elsewhere. Here we deal with the procedure relating to the admission of evidence and some particular evidential issues that arise in asylum and human rights appeals.

There are no strict rules of evidence in hearings before the AIT. Any oral or documen- **6.378** tary evidence which appears to the Tribunal to be relevant to an appeal may be admitted even if it would be inadmissible in a court of law.[569] This means that 'hearsay' evidence may be admitted. The Tribunal may not compel a party or a witness to give any evidence or produce any document that he could not be compelled to give or produce in a civil claim.[570] This situation would only ever arise in the rare event of a witness summons being issued.

---

[563] Rule 60(1).
[564] Rule 60(1A) as inserted by SI 2006 No 2788.
[565] Rule 60 (1B)(a)(b) as inserted by SI 2006 No 2788.
[566] Rule 60(1C) as inserted by SI 2006 No 2788.
[567] Rule 60(1D) as inserted by SI 2006 No 2788.
[568] Rule 60(3).
[569] Rule 51(1).
[570] Rule 51(2).

Exclusion of evidence for failure to comply with directions

6.379 Where the Tribunal has given directions for the filing and serving of written evidence, it must not consider any written evidence which is not filed or served in accordance with those directions unless satisfied that there are good reasons for doing so.[571] The prohibition extends to written evidence only and therefore the Tribunal has no power to exclude oral evidence under this rule.

6.380 In *MD (Good Reasons to Consider) Pakistan*[572] the Tribunal identified as 'good reasons' for not excluding evidence that the evidence was highly pertinent and would cause no unfair difficulty to the other side. Although an exhaustive list of 'good reasons' could not be compiled, it was incumbent on an immigration judge to consider whether there were any good reasons and explain if there were none. In asylum and human rights appeals different considerations apply regarding the exclusion of evidence to those that apply in immigration appeals due to the requirement of 'anxious scrutiny' in asylum appeals.[573] In *AK (Admission of Evidence–Time Limits)*[574] the Tribunal observed that in asylum cases, the requirement that justice is done in appeals requiring 'most anxious scrutiny' will in most cases outweigh the understandable desire on the part of the AIT to ensure that its directions and the provisions of the Procedure Rules are not flouted with impunity. In *BY (A good reason to exclude) Nigeria*[575] the Tribunal held that in the case of an unrepresented appellant there was all the more reason to admit relevant evidence.

6.381 Subject to a hearing on the allegation of forgery,[576] the Tribunal must not take account of any evidence which has not been made available to all the parties.[577]

6.382 In *A (Somalia)*[578] the IAT held that an Adjudicator had been wrong not to allow oral evidence from a witness on the basis that a witness statement had not been served in accordance with directions. The Tribunal considered that the evidence was plainly material to the case and might have persuaded the Adjudicator to take a different view. Further, save in the case of 'persistent or contumelious' refusal to comply with directions, the Tribunal found it difficult to conceive of a situation where a witness should be stopped from giving relevant evidence because of a non-compliance with directions.

---

[571] Rule 51(4).
[572] [2004] UKIAT 00197.
[573] *EA (Immigration–Rule 48(5) Ghana* [2004] UKIAT 00227—decided under the previous procedural rules.
[574] *(Iran)* [2004] UKIAT 00103.
[575] [2004] UKIAT 00319.
[576] Under s 108 of the 2002 Act.
[577] Rule 51(7).
[578] [2004] UKIAT 00065.

Previous appeals concerning the same appellant

Since the introduction of the one-stop procedure, cases where there have been previ- **6.383**
ous findings of fact in relation to the same appellant have become less frequent.
Guidelines for the approach to be taken towards such findings were given by the IAT
in the case of *Devaseelan*[579] and approved by the Court of Appeal in *Djebbar*.[580] The
relevant guidelines are that:

- the first determination stands as an assessment of the claim the appellant was then
  making at the time of that determination. It is not binding on the second immigration judge, but it is the starting point;
- facts personal to the appellant that were not brought to the attention of the first
  immigration judge, although they were relevant to the issues before him, should
  be treated with the greatest of circumspection. However, considerations of credibility will not be relevant in cases where the existence of additional factors is beyond
  dispute;
- evidence of other facts, for example country guidance, may not suffer from the
  same concerns as to credibility but should be treated with caution. The situation in
  the appellant's own country at the time of the first determination is very unlikely to
  be relevant in deciding whether his removal at the time of the second determination would breach his human rights.

As a general rule, a judge who hears the second appeal should receive the original **6.384**
decision, even if the first appeal contains findings that are vitiated by an error of law.
Special circumstances may arise where the interests of justice require that proceedings be transferred to a judge who is not aware of the contents of the original determination, but they will be rare.[581]

Appeals concerning findings of fact in respect of members of the same family

It is frequently the case that an appellant will call a family member as a witness to give **6.385**
evidence where the facts of their cases overlap. Where the appeal of the family member has been determined the Tribunal may take the determination into account.

In *AS and AA (Effect of previous linked determination) Somalia* [2006] UKIAT 00052 **6.386**
it was held that the rule that a judicial determination stands as the determination of
the issue between the parties does not govern later litigation between different parties. When it is said that a previous determination of the claim or appeal of another
claimant is relevant in assessing a later claim by a different person: (1) the previous
determination has no evidential value as such, but (2) its narrative content is
to be taken as evidence of what was said and done leading up to that determination;

---

[579] [2003] Imm AR 1.
[580] *Djebbar v SSHD* [2004] EWCA Civ 804.
[581] *Swash v SSHD* [2006] EWCA Civ 1093.

(3) the Tribunal determining the later case is required to make its own decision on the evidence before it; (4) no rule of general law or practice supports the argument that the decision in an earlier claim should bind or be regarded as part of the evidence in an appeal by a different person, and therefore (5) the later Tribunal should not regard itself as bound to follow a previous decision in respect of another claimant or to make a decision consistent with such a previous decision; (6) on the other hand, principles of good administration require that decisions should not be needlessly divergent, so (7) the earlier decision should be treated as a starting point, but (8) the Tribunal will not hesitate to depart from the starting point in every case where the evidence requires it.

6.387   In *Gustavo Suvarez Ocampo* the Court of Appeal confirmed this approach to be correct, holding that the *Deveseelan* guidelines are relevant to cases such as these where the parties involved are not the same but there is a material overlap of evidence.[582] The Court of Appeal stated that the guidance may need adaptation according to the nature of the new evidence, the circumstances in which it was given or not given in the earlier proceedings, and its materiality to securing a just outcome in the second appeal along with the consistency in the maintenance of firm immigration control.[583]

Starred decisions

6.388   In 2001 Mr Justice Collins, who was at that point President of the Tribunal, introduced a system of 'starred' decisions, decided by legal members of the Tribunal, and intended to be binding on other Tribunals. The purpose of this system was and is to prevent inconsistent and conflicting decisions by different Tribunals.

6.389   The Practice Directions states at paragraph 18 that reported directions of the Tribunal and IAT which are 'starred' shall be treated as authoritative in respect of the matter to which the 'starring' relates, unless inconsistent with other authority that is binding on the Tribunal.

Fast track appeals

6.390   An appeal will be on the 'fast track' where the appellant is detained in a specified removal centre, has been served with the immigration decision against which they are appealing, and has continued to be detained in a specified removal centre.[584] The specified removal centres are Harmondsworth Immigration Removal Centre, Campsfield House, Colnbrook House, and Yarls Wood Immigration Removal Centre.

6.391   Appeals on the fast track have their own procedural rules, the Asylum and Immigration Tribunal (Fast Track Procedure) Rules 2005. Here we deal only with the procedure

---

[582] *Ocampo v SSHD* [2006] EWCA Civ 1276, [2006] All ER (D) 59 (Oct).
[583] At para 25.
[584] Rules 3, 5, 15 and Sch 2 to the Asylum and Immigration (Fast Track Procedure) Rules 2005.

relating to fast track appeals, which apply considerably more restrictive time limits than the principal Procedure Rules. Some of the principal Procedural Rules apply to the Fast Track Procedural Rules.[585] All references below are to the Fast Track Procedure Rules, unless the contrary is stated.

In fast track appeals, standard directions apply[586] but the parties must serve the documents on the date of the hearing or, if practicable, on the business day immediately proceeding the date of the hearing.[587] Witness statements stand as evidence in chief, but there may be cases where it will be appropriate for appellants or witnesses to have the opportunity of adding to or supplementing their witness statements. Parties are referred to the judgment of the Court of Appeal in *R v Secretary of State for the Home Department ex p Singh* [1998] INLR 608.[588] **6.392**

Procedure and timetable relating to fast track appeals

- Notice of appeal must be given not later than two days after the day on which the notice of the immigration decision has been served.[589] Where a notice of appeal is given outside this time limit, the Tribunal must not extend time for appealing unless satisfied that, because of circumstances outside the control of the person giving notice of appeal or his representative, it was not practicable for the notice of appeal to be given within that time limit.[590]
- Any issue of timeliness is dealt with as a preliminary issue at the substantive hearing.[591] If a notice of appeal is given outside the time limit an appellant should apply for an extension of time including a statement of the reasons for failing to give notice within the time period and accompanied by any written evidence relied upon in support of those reasons.[592] Where the notice of appeal was given outside the applicable time limit and the Tribunal does not grant an extension of time, the Tribunal must take no further action in relation to the notice of appeal, except that it must serve on every party written notice of its decision, including its reasons which may be in summary form, not later than one day after the day on which the decision is made.[593]
- If notice of appeal is served on a custodian (ie the officer at the detention centre) the officer must endorse on the notice the date that it is served on him and forward

---

585 Rule 6(1) to (3) omitting the reference to Rule 6(4) in Rule 6(2), Rule 8, Rule 10(1), Rule 13(1) and (4), Rule 14, and Rules 17 and 19— applied to the Fast Track by Rule 6.
586 For which see para 6.299 above.
587 Paragraph 7, Practice Direction.
588 Paragraph 6.7 Practice Direction.
589 Rule 8 (1).
590 Rule 8 (2).
591 Rule 12(1).
592 Rule 10 (1) applied to the Fast Track Procedure Rules by Rule 6(c).
593 Rule 12 (3) as amended by SI 2006/2789.

it to the Tribunal immediately.[594] The notice of appeal may also be served on the Tribunal.[595] When the Tribunal receives a notice of appeal it shall immediately serve a copy on the respondent.[596]

- The respondent must file the appeal documents (ie notice of decisions, any other document containing reasons for the decision, interview record and any unpublished document referred to[597]) not later than two days after the day on which the Tribunal serves the respondent with the notice of appeal.

- The AIT will fix a hearing date which is no later than two days after the date on which the respondent files the relevant documents or if the Tribunal is unable to arrange a hearing within that time, as soon as practicable thereafter.[598] The Tribunal must serve notice of the date, time, and place of the hearing on every party as soon as practicable, and in any event not later than noon on the business day before the hearing.[599] This will be the substantive hearing of the appeal as there are no CMR hearings in fast track appeals.[600]

- The AIT must serve its written determination containing its decisions and reasons on the parties not later than two days after the day on which the hearing of the appeal finishes, if there was a hearing, or if the appeal is determined without a hearing, not later than two days after the day on which it is determined.[601]

- The time limit for an application for a review of the Tribunal's decision under section 103 A(1) on the fast track is two days beginning on the date of deemed receipt of the Tribunal's decision.[602]

- When an application for review is filed with the Tribunal, the Tribunal must serve copies of the application notice and any documents attached to it on the other party to the appeal as soon as practicable.[603] The party who is not applying for the review may file submissions in response to the application not later than one day after the day on which it is served with the application.[604]

- The Tribunal must serve a copy of the notice of decision and any directions on every party if the other party filed submissions in response, not later than one day after they were filed, and if they did not, not later than one day after the time limit for filing those submissions ran out.[605]

---

594 Rule 9.
595 Rule 6(1)–(3) applied to the Fast Track by Rule 6(a).
596 Rule 9.
597 ie all documents referred to in Rule 13(1) of the principal rules.
598 Rule 11(1).
599 Rule 11 (2).
600 Paragraph 6.1 Practice Direction.
601 Rule 14(2).
602 Article 3, The Asylum and Immigration (Fast Track Time Limits) Order 2005 SI 2005/561.
603 Rule 17(a).
604 Rule 17 (b).
605 Rule 19 (a)(b).

- The time limit for applying to the High Court for a review of the Tribunal's decision is two days from the date of deemed receipt of the Tribunal's decision.[606]
- Where an order for reconsideration is made, the Tribunal must fix a hearing date for the reconsideration of its decision on the appeal which is not later than two days after the day on which that order has been served on both parties to the appeal; or if the Tribunal has been unable to arrange a hearing within that time, as soon as practicable thereafter.[607] The Tribunal must serve notice of the date, time, and place of the reconsideration on every party not later than noon on the business day before the hearing.[608]
- An application for permission to appeal to the Court of Appeal must be filed not later than two days after the day on which the appellant is served with the Tribunal's determination.[609] The Tribunal may not extend the time limit for appealing and must notify the other party to the appeal that it has been filed.[610]
- The Tribunal must determine the application for permission to appeal and serve its determination on every party not later than one day after the day on which the Tribunal receives the application notice.[611]

Calculating time

The rules with regard to the calculation of time in the principal Rules are applied to the Fast Track Rules[612] with the modification that 'business day' means any day other than a Saturday or Sunday, a bank holiday, 24 to 31 December, Maundy Thursday, Good Friday, or the Tuesday after the last Monday in May.[613]   **6.393**

Adjournments

The Tribunal may adjourn a hearing only where there is insufficient time to hear it, a party has not been served with notice of hearing, or the Tribunal is satisfied by evidence filed or given by or on behalf of a party that: **6.394**

- the appeal or application cannot be justly determined on the date on which it is listed for hearing; and
- there is an identifiable future date, not more than ten days after the date on which the appeal is listed for hearing, by which it can be justly determined or the Tribunal makes an order transferring the appeal out of the fast track.

---

[606] Article 4 (2) The Asylum and Immigration (Fast Track Time Limits) Order 2005 SI 2005/561.
[607] Rule 21(1).
[608] Rule 21 (2).
[609] Rule 25.
[610] Rule 25(2).
[611] Rule 26.
[612] By Rule 3(4).
[613] Rule 2(3).

Transfer out of the fast track

6.395   The Tribunal must transfer an appeal out of the fast track where:[614]

- all the parties consent;
- it is satisfied by evidence filed or given by or on behalf of a party that there are exceptional circumstances which mean that the appeal or application cannot otherwise be justly determined; or
- the respondent has failed to comply with a provision of the Fast Track Rules or the principal rules or a direction of the Tribunal; and
- the Tribunal is satisfied that the appellant would be prejudiced by that failure if the appeal or application were determined in accordance with the Fast Track Rules.

6.396   Where an appeal is taken out of the fast track, it may be adjourned and directions given for the further conduct of the appeal or application.[615] When the Tribunal adjourns a hearing it must fix a new date, time, and place for the hearing and must not adjourn for more than 28 days after the original hearing date unless satisfied that because of exceptional circumstances the appeal cannot justly be heard within that time.[616]

6.397   When the appeal has been taken out of the fast track the principal rules apply.[617] When a period of time for doing something has started to run under the Fast Track Rules and the provision ceases to apply because the appeal has been taken out of the fast track, if the principal rules contain a time limit for doing the same thing, that time limit shall apply and the relevant period of time will be treated as running from the date on which the period of time under the fast track rules started to run.[618]

---

[614] Rule 30(1).
[615] Rule 30 (2).
[616] Rule 30 (3).
[617] Rule 31 (1).
[618] Rule 31 (2)(3).

7

CERTIFICATION AND REMOVAL

A. Third Country Certification—Dublin Convention and Safe Third Country Certification

7.01 Where an asylum seeker has passed through a country which is deemed to be safe, his claim for asylum will not be decided in the United Kingdom but he will be removed to the safe 'third country'. That country will then decide their claim for asylum. Under the 2004 Act, the Home Office will issue a certificate under section 33(1) and parts 2, 3, 4, or 5 of Schedule 3 to the 2004 Act which enables an asylum seeker to be removed the a safe 'third country'. This system has been in force since 1 October 2004. We deal below with the four categories of third country cases created by the 2004 Act and we deal with the procedures which enable applicants to challenge certificates issued under the Act. There are transitional provisions[1] for cases where a certificate was issued before 1 October 2004 and the system under the 1999 and 2002 Acts applies to such cases.

7.02 We then deal with Dublin Convention certification. The Dublin Convention came into force on 1 September 1997. Its purpose was to define the criteria by which responsibility could be allocated amongst the member states for dealing with asylum seekers who had passed through their territories. The Dublin Convention was replaced from 2 September 2003 by the 'Dublin II Regulation'[2] which does not differ a great deal from the original Convention save for the fact that the time limits for transfers are now shorter. We deal with the criteria for allocating responsibility, the time limits for removals, and Home Office discretion to consider asylum claims substantively despite the formal criteria being fulfilled below.

B. Third Country Certification

7.03 There are four categories of third country cases under the 2004 Act. With the first three categories, a certificate may be issued on the basis that the particular third country is safe and there are therefore three lists of countries. With the fourth category, the Home Office may return an applicant to any country when return is considered to be safe for the particular applicant.

7.04 The protection against removal in the 2004 Act differs for each of the categories reflecting how safe each of the categories of countries is deemed to be. The provisions for third country certification under the 2004 Act only apply to removals to third countries of which the applicant is not a national.

---

[1] Art 3 Asylum and Immigration (Treatment of Claimants) Act 2004 (Commencement No 1) Order 2004.

[2] European Commission Regulation (EC No 343/2003) implemented by EC Regulation No 1560/2003.

The first list of safe countries—Part 2, Schedule 3, 2004 Act

The countries in the first category are the members of the European Union and   **7.05**
Norway, Iceland, Bulgaria, and Romania and are part of the arrangements under
the Dublin Convention (see below).[3] All of these countries are deemed to be
places:[4]

- where an applicant will not be at risk of persecution under the Refugee
  Convention;
- from which an applicant will not be sent to another State in contravention of
  his rights under the Refugee Convention;
- from which he will not be sent to another State in contravention of his rights
  under the ECHR.

In the case of *R (on the appln of Javad Nasseri) v SSHD*[5] McCombe J held that this   **7.06**
deeming provision, in creating an irrebuttable statutory presumption that an
asylum applicant would not be subject to unlawful *refoulement* by a specified state
in contravention of the ECHR, was incompatible with the ECHR. His Lordship
made a declaration of incompatibility under section 4 of the Human Rights Act
to that effect. The defendant had certified the case under this Part, as the claimant
had previously claimed asylum in Greece, a safe third country under the deeming
provisions. The claimant's representatives had contended that his removal would
breach his rights under Article 3, because there was evidence that he would not
have access to a fair asylum determination process in Greece. The defendant
adduced evidence that Greece had changed its procedures and therefore was safe.

His Lordship considered that the deeming provisions could not be in clearer   **7.07**
terms as they required 'any person, tribunal or court' that had to determine
whether a claimant for asylum or human rights protection might be removed
from this country to treat Greece as a place from which 'a person will not be sent
in contravention of his Convention rights'. Parliament had therefore precluded
both the Secretary of State and the High Court from considering the law and
practice on *refoulement* in any of the listed countries and the exercise the defendant
was urging the court to undertake, namely to look at the current situation in Greece,
was an impermissible one. The deeming provision impeded an investigation into

---

[3] Austria, Belgium, Republic of Cyprus, Czech Republic, Denmark, Estonia, Finland, Estonia,
Finland, France, Germany, Greece, Hungary, Iceland, Ireland, Italy, Latvia, Lithuania, Luxembourg,
Malta, Netherland, Norway, Poland, Portugal, Slovak Republic, Slovenia, Spain, Sweden, Iceland,
and Norway. Bulgaria and Romania were added on 1st January 2007 by Asylum (List of Safe
Countries) (Amendment) Order 2006 SI 2006/339 to take effect on or after 1 January 2007 in relation to an asylum or human rights claim made before that date provided that no decision to refuse
the claimant leave to enter or remove him from the UK following that claim has been made before
that date.

[4] Paragraph 3(2).

[5] [2007] EWHC 1548 (Admin).

a risk of loss or life, torture, or inhuman or degrading treatment and therefore directed the defendant not to comply with the substantive obligation of investigation arising under Article 3.

7.08 Since a declaration of incompatibility empowers rather than obliges Parliament to remedy the incompatibility,[6] and this Part is still in force, and the declaration is currently under appeal, we set out the full provisions of this Part of the Schedule.

7.09 In order remove a national of these countries under the safe third country procedure the Secretary of State must certify that:

- it is proposed to remove the applicant to one of these countries;[7]
- in his opinion the applicant is not a national of any of these countries.[8]

7.10 The effect of the certificate is that:

- the Home Office does not determine the asylum or human rights claim substantively;
- the applicant may not bring an in-country asylum or human rights appeal against removal on the basis that removal to the safe third country would breach the UK's obligation under the Refugee Convention or ECHR;[9]
- the applicant may bring an ECHR claim on other grounds than that his removal to a safe third country would breach his rights under the Refugee Convention or ECHR unless the Secretary of State certifies that his claim is clearly unfounded. The Secretary of State will certify that the claim is clearly unfounded unless satisfied that it is not clearly unfounded.[10] Therefore, if the human rights claim is certified, the only way the applicant will have an in-country right of appeal is if he successfully challenges the certificate by way of judicial review. Otherwise the applicant can appeal from outside the UK on human rights grounds that do not challenge his removal from the safe third country;
- there is no appeal from outside the UK on the grounds that the provisions in this Part which deem the countries in the list to be safe are wrong.[11]

---

[6] Since Parliament is not a 'public authority' for the purposes of the HRA 1998 it has no obligation to act compatibly with the ECHR, save under international law—see ECHR Chapter 3.

[7] Paragraph 5(1)(a).

[8] Paragraph 5(1)(b).

[9] Paragraph 5(2).

[10] Paragraph 5 (4)(5).

[11] Paragraph 6.

The second list of safe countries—Part 3, Schedule 3, 2004 Act

The countries deemed to be safe in this Part of the Act are not specified in the **7.11**
Act itself but will be specified by order of the Secretary of the Secretary of
State. No order has yet been made. All of these countries will be deemed to be
places:

- where the applicant is not at risk on Refugee Convention grounds;[12]
- from which an applicant will not be sent to another country otherwise in accordance with the Refugee Convention.[13]

In order to remove nationals of these countries under the safe third country pro- **7.12**
cedure the Secretary of State must certify that:

- it is proposed to remove the applicant to one of these countries;[14]
- in his opinion the applicant is not a citizen or national of that country.[15]

The effect of the certificate is that: **7.13**

- the Secretary of State does not have to determine the asylum claim
  substantively;
- there is no in country right of appeal on the grounds that the applicant is at risk
  on Refugee Convention grounds in the safe third country or on the grounds
  that the third country would remove the applicant to a country where he would
  be at risk on Refugee Convention grounds;[16]
- the countries to be specified under this Part of the Act are *not* deemed to be safe
  on ECHR grounds;
- the applicant may bring an ECHR claim on any grounds unless the Secretary
  of State certifies that his claim is clearly unfounded. The Secretary of State will
  certify that the claim is clearly unfounded unless satisfied that it is not clearly
  unfounded.[17] Therefore, if the human rights claim is certified, the only way the
  applicant will have an in-country right of appeal is if he successfully challenges
  the certificate by way of judicial review. Otherwise the applicant can appeal
  from outside the UK on human rights grounds;
- there is no appeal from outside the UK on the grounds that the provisions in
  this Part which deem the countries in the list to be safe are wrong.[18]

---

12 Paragraph 8(2)(a).
13 Paragraph 8(2)(b).
14 Paragraph 10(1)(a).
15 Paragraph 9(b).
16 Paragraph 10(3).
17 Paragraph 10(4).
18 Paragraph 11.

The third list of safe countries—Part 4, Schedule 3, 2004 Act

7.14 The countries deemed to be safe in this Part of the Act are not specified in the Act itself but will be specified by order of the Secretary of State. No order has yet been made. All of these countries will be deemed to be places:

- where the applicant is not at risk on Refugee Convention grounds;[19]
- from which an applicant will not be sent to another country otherwise in accordance with the Refugee Convention.[20]

7.15 In order to remove nationals of these countries under the safe third country procedure the Secretary of State must certify that:

- it is proposed to remove the applicant to one of these countries;[21]
- in his opinion the applicant is not a citizen or national of that country.[22]

7.16 The effect of the certificate is that:

- the Secretary of State does not have to determine the asylum claim substantively;
- there is no in-country right of appeal on the grounds that the applicant is at risk on Refugee Convention grounds in the safe third country or on the grounds that the third country would remove the applicant to a country where he would be at risk on Refugee Convention grounds;[23]
- the countries to be specified under this Part of the Act are *not* deemed to be safe on ECHR grounds;
- there is an in-country right of appeal in relation to any ECHR claim unless the Secretary of State certifies that the claim is clearly unfounded.[24] There is no *presumption* under this Part that that the Secretary of State will certify the claim as clearly unfounded;
- if the claim is certified then the applicant will have to successfully challenge the certificate by way of judicial review in order to retain an in-country right of appeal on human rights grounds. If unsuccessful, the applicant can appeal from outside the UK on human rights grounds;
- there is no appeal from outside the UK on the grounds that the provisions in this Part which deem the countries in the list to be safe are wrong.[25]

---

[19] Paragraph 12(2)(a).
[20] Paragraph 12 (2)(b).
[21] Paragraph 15(1)(a).
[22] Paragraph 15(1)(b).
[23] Paragraph 15(3).
[24] Paragraph 15(4).
[25] Paragraph 16.

Countries certified as safe for individuals—Part 5

This Part of the Schedule does not contain a list of countries as its purpose is to **7.17** certify any country as safe for a particular individual for the purposes of the Refugee Convention enabling them to be removed there.

In order to use the third country procedure under this Part the Secretary of State **7.18** must certify that:

- it is proposed to remove the applicant to the specified country;[26] and
- in the Secretary of State's opinion, the person is not a national or citizen of the specified country;[27] and
- in the Secretary of State's opinion the specified country is a place where the person is not at risk for the purposes of the Refugee Convention and from which the applicant will not be sent to another country otherwise than in accordance with the Refugee Convention.[28]

The effect of the certificate is that: **7.19**

- the applicant may not bring an in-country appeal on Refugee Convention grounds which asserts that the specified country would breach the UK's obligations under the Refugee Convention or on the grounds that the specified country will return the applicant to a country which would breach his rights under the Refugee Convention;[29]
- the certificate can be challenged by judicial review;
- the applicant may bring an in-country appeal on any human rights grounds unless the Secretary of State certifies that the claim is clearly unfounded.[30] There is no *presumption* under this Part that the Secretary of State will certify the claim as clearly unfounded. If the claim is certified then the applicant will have to successfully challenge the certificate by way of judicial review in order to retain an in-country right of appeal on human rights grounds. If unsuccessful, the applicant can appeal from outside the UK on human rights grounds.

Amendments of lists of countries under Schedule 3, 2004 Act

The Secretary of State may add a country to the first three categories of safe **7.20** third countries by statutory instrument. The Secretary of State may remove a country from the second and third categories of safe third countries by statutory

---

[26] Paragraph 17(a).
[27] Paragraph 17(b).
[28] Paragraph 17(c).
[29] Paragraph 19(b).
[30] Paragraph 19(c).

instrument but may only remove a country from the first category of countries by an Act of Parliament.

Immigration Rules

7.21 The Immigration Rules[31] state that the Secretary of State will not issue a certificate under the 2004 Act unless either:

- the asylum seeker has not arrived in the UK directly from the country in which he claims to fear persecution but arrived from another 'third' country or territory and has had an opportunity at the border or within the third country or territory to make contact with authorities of that third country in order to seek their protection; or
- there is other clear evidence of the applicant's admissibility to a third country or territory.

7.22 In *Kandasmy*[32] the High Court held that in order to have had an 'opportunity' to claim asylum in a safe third country, the question was whether the applicant was physically able to approach the authorities at the border or within the third country and could have had an asylum claim accepted by the authorities. In *Dursan*[33] the Court of Appeal held that the fact that an agent has arranged the journey and is responsible for the applicant's movements does not preclude the applicant from claiming in the safe third country.

7.23 In the case of removals to other Dublin Regulation countries, 'clear evidence of admissibility' is not an issue since the terms of the Regulation provide sufficient evidence of admissibility to other Member States. Evidence of admissibility remains an issue in respect of non-designated countries. In these cases, other re-admission agreements or documentation such as visas or permits showing a right of entry could be evidence of admissibility.

Discretion under the Immigration Rules

7.24 The Immigration Rules also state that where the Secretary of State is satisfied that the statutory conditions for third country removal are fulfilled under the 2004 Act, he will 'normally' decline to examine the asylum application substantively and issue a certificate. This imports a discretion into the Rule. We deal at paragraph 7.38 below with challenges to third country certification on the basis that the Secretary of State should exercise his discretion in an applicant's favour.

---

31 Paragraph 345(2) Immigration Rules (HC 395).
32 *R v Special Adjudicator, ex p Kandasamy* [1994] Imm AR 333, QBD.
33 *Dursun v SSHD* [1993] Imm AR 169.

C. Dublin Convention Certification

As stated above, Council Regulation (EC) No 343/2003 (the 'Dublin II Regulation') **7.25** lays down the criteria and mechanisms for determining the Member States responsible for examining an application for asylum lodged in one of the Member States by a third country national. Even if the Member State is not responsible according to the criteria of the Regulation, it may examine an asylum application by a third country national, in which case it will become the responsible State within the meaning of the Regulation.[34] The process of determining the Member State responsible starts as soon as an application for asylum is lodged.[35]

The Regulation is a detailed document, and what follows is a summary of the provi- **7.26** sions only. The hierarchy of criteria for responsibility must be applied in the order set out below.[36] Article 5 (2) states that 'the Member States responsible in accordance with the criteria shall be determined on the basis of the situation obtaining when the asylum seeker first lodged his application with a Member State'.

This Article was recently interpreted by the Court of Appeal in *AA (Somalia) v* **7.27** *SSHD*[37] as meaning that an asylum claim should be processed by the Member State which conducted an enquiry, and in which State the application for asylum was first lodged and at the time it was lodged. The Court of Appeal agreed with the judgment in *R (on the appln of G)*[38] that consideration of the hierarchy of criteria should only be conducted once, and that a claimant could not demand a further consideration of it. Where a Member State had already conducted the process of considering the 'hierarchy of criteria' (or 'screening process'), it was also responsible for the substantive examination of a claimant's asylum claim. It offended against the policy of the Dublin Regulation to allow a claimant who was not satisfied with the result of the screening process to move to another Member State and reveal further or different facts and demand that the process be undertaken again.

The hierarchy of criteria is as follows: **7.28**

• **Unaccompanied minor**—Where the applicant for asylum is an unaccompanied minor and the family member is legally present, the State where the family member[39] is legally present will have responsibility only providing it is in the

---

[34] Article 3(2).
[35] Article 4—see the Regulation for full details of when an application is deemed to be lodged.
[36] Article 5 (1).
[37] [2006] EWCA Civ 1540.
[38] [2004] EWHC 2848 (Admin).
[39] Family member is defined in Article 2 of the Regulations as a spouse or unmarried partner in a stable relationship, a minor child of such couples, and the father, mother, or guardian when the

best interests of the minor. In the absence of a family member, the Member State responsible for examining the application will be the one in which the minor has lodged his or her application for asylum.[40]

- **Family member**—A state in which the asylum seeker has a family member who is a refugee or a family member whose application is being considered, provided the persons concerned desire.[41]

- **Valid visa or residence document**—Where the asylum seeker is in possession of a valid residence document or visa, the Member State which has issued the document, unless the visa was issued when acting for or on the written authorization of another Member State when the latter Member State shall be responsible. Where the asylum seeker is in possession of more than one valid residence document or visa issued by different Member States, the responsibility is assumed in the following order: the Member State which issued the residence document conferring the right to the longest period of residency or, where the periods of validity are identical, the Member State which issued the residence document having the latest expiry date; the Member State which issued the visa having the latest expiry date where various visas are of the same type; where visas are of different kinds, the Member State which issued the visa having the longest period of validity, or where the periods of validity are identical, the Member state which issued the visa having the latest expiry date. Where the asylum seeker is in possession of one or more residence documents which have expired less than two years previously or one or more visas which have expired less than six months previously and which enabled him actually to enter the territory of a Member State the provisions apply for such time as the applicant has not left the territories of the Member States. Where over two years or six months have elapsed since the expiry of the residence documents or visas, the responsible Member State is the one in which the application is lodged.[42]

- **Asylum seekers irregularly crossing borders**—Where an asylum seeker has irregularly crossed the border into a Member State from a safe third country, the Member State so entered will be responsible. Responsibility will cease

---

applicant is a minor and unmarried. In *AA (Somalia) v SSHD* [2006] (see above) the Court of Appeal held that there was considerable support in the Dublin Regulation for the view that a guardian should have concrete formal status and was more than a person who had no more nor less than de facto care of a minor (paras 42 and 43).

[40] Article 6.
[41] Articles 7 and 8.
[42] Article 9—where the residence document or visa was issued on the basis of a false or assumed identity or on the basis of forged documents the Member State which issued it is still responsible unless it can be established by the Member State that a fraud was committed after the visa or document had been issued (Article 9(4)).

12 months after the date of the entry and the responsibility transfers to a State where the applicant has been previously living for a period of at least five months. If the applicant has lived in several Member States for this period the Member State where the applicant has lived most recently for this period will be responsible.[43]

- **Waiver of visa requirement**—A Member State which has waived the need for a visa unless the applicant lodges their application for asylum in another Member State in which the need for a visa is also waived, in which case that Member State is responsible.

- **International transit area**—A Member State in which the asylum seeker makes the application in an international transit area.[44]

- **No Member State responsible**—Where no Member State responsible for examining the application for asylum can be designated on the basis of these criteria, the first Member State with which the application for asylum was lodged shall be responsible for examining it.[45]

- **Family unity**—Where several members of a family submit applications for asylum in the same Member State at the same time, or close enough in time for the procedures for determining responsibility to be conducted together, and where the application of the criteria could cause them to be separated, responsibility will lie with the State which the criteria indicate is responsible for taking charge of the largest number of family members, and failing this, which the criteria indicate is responsible for examining the application of the oldest of them.[46]

The Humanitarian Clause

This clause reflects the emphasis in the Dublin Regulation on family unity. Even where a Member State is not responsible under the criteria set out above, it may bring together family members, as well as other dependent relatives, on humanitarian grounds based in particular on family or cultural considerations. The Member State must, at the request of another Member State, examine the application for asylum of the person concerned provided the family members consent.[47] Where the person concerned is dependent on the assistance of the other due to pregnancy, a recent birth, serious illness, severe handicap, or old age, Member States should normally keep or bring the asylum seeker together with

7.29

---

[43] Article 10—see Article 18(3) as to how such entry is established.
[44] Article 12.
[45] Article 13.
[46] Article 14.
[47] Article 15(1).

another relative, provided that ties existed in the country of origin.[48] Where the asylum seeker is an unaccompanied minor with relatives in a Member State who can take care of him or her, Member States should if possible reunite them, provided this is in the best interests of the minor.[49]

Taking charge and taking back

7.30 Where a Member State with which an application for asylum has been lodged considers that another Member State is responsible for determining the application it must call upon the other Member State to take charge of the application within three months. If it fails to do so, it will assume responsibility. [50] The Member State to whom the request is made must give a decision on the request to take charge of the applicant within two months.[51] The requesting Member State may ask for an urgent reply in specified cases and state the time period in which a reply is expected.[52] Where urgency is pleaded, the reply must come within one month.[53] Failure to act within the two-month period and one-month period mentioned above is tantamount to accepting the request.[54]

7.31 Where the Member State to whom the request is made accepts that it should take charge of the applicant for asylum, the Member State with whom the application was lodged will notify the applicant of this fact and of the obligation to transfer the applicant to the responsible Member State.[55] The decision may be subject to an appeal or review, but this will not have the effect of suspending the transfer unless the courts in the Member State so decide.[56]

7.32 The transfer must take place as soon as practicably possible and at the latest within six months of acceptance of the request that charge be taken or of the decision on appeal or review where there is a suspensive effect.[57] Where the transfer does not take place within the six-month time period, the effect is that responsibility will lie with the Member State in which the application for asylum was lodged.[58]

---

[48] Article 15 (2).
[49] Article 15 (3).
[50] Article 17(1).
[51] Article 18 (1).
[52] Article 17 (2).
[53] Article 17(6).
[54] Article 17 (7).
[55] Article 19(1).
[56] Article 19 (2).
[57] Article 19 (3).
[58] Article 19 (4)—this time limit may be extended up to a maximum of one year if the transfer could not be carried out due to imprisonment of the asylum seeker or up to 18 months if the prisoner absconds.

An asylum seeker will be 'taken back' in the following circumstances:[59] **7.33**

- when his application is under examination and he is in the territory of another Member State without permission;
- when he has withdrawn his application which was under examination and made an application in another Member State;
- when his application has been rejected and he goes to the territory of another Member State without permission.

The procedure for taking back in these circumstances is subject to strict time limits, **7.34** and where the requested Member State does not comply, it will be considered to have agreed to take back the asylum seeker.

The Court of Appeal held in *Omar*[60] that a breach of procedures under the **7.35** Dublin Regulation does not give rise to a right on the part of an asylum seeker to have their asylum claim dealt with in the UK. In *R (on the appln of AA) (Afghanistan)*[61], a case under the Dublin Convention, the Court of Appeal overturned the Administrative Court's decision that a two-year delay in returning the claimant to Austria after Austria had accepted responsibility was unreasonable. The Court of Appeal held that whilst the delay was deplorable and unexplained, the removal directions could not be quashed in order to punish the Home Office, particularly as Austria had consistently accepted responsibility. However, in *AA (Somalia) v SSHD*[62] where removal directions had been set some ten months after the six-month time limit for taking back under Article 20.1d of the Dublin Regulation, the Court of Appeal held that there were grounds for the Claimant to challenge removal directions on the basis that the UK had a responsibility to deal with his asylum claim by virtue of the expiry of the time limit.

Administrative cooperation

In the Articles in this Chapter of the Dublin Regulation the Member States agree **7.36** to communicate and exchange personal data relating to the asylum seeker as is 'appropriate, relevant and non-excessive' for the purposes of determining the Member State responsible, examining the application for asylum, and implementing any obligation arising under the Regulation.[63] The nature of the information that may be requested is set out, as are the procedures and time limits for requesting the information.[64] The asylum seeker has the right to be informed of

---

[59] Article 20.
[60] *Omar (Mohammed Abdi) v SSHD* [20005] EWCA 285.
[61] *R (on the appln of AA) (Afghanistan) v SSHD*) [2006] EWCA Civ 1550.
[62] [2006] EWCA Civ 1540.
[63] Article 21 (1).
[64] Article 21 (2)–(11).

any data that is processed concerning him, and if it is incorrect or inaccurate is entitled to have it corrected, erased, or blocked.[65] Member States may also, on a bilateral basis, establish administrative arrangements between themselves concerning the practical details of the implementation of the Regulation.[66]

7.37   The Dublin Regulation has direct effect, which means that an individual is able to rely on its provisions in a national court when these come into conflict with national law. Whether an individual can rely on the direct effect appears to depend on the Article in question. In *Mota v SSHD*[67] the Court of Appeal reviewed the case law on whether an Article has direct effect. In *Omar v Secretary of State*[68] Chadwick LJ had held that Article 11 (5) read together with Article 29 of the Dublin Convention may well have direct effect. However, in *G*[69] Maurice Kay LJ held that 'the effect of Article 15 is not to confer a freestanding substantive right on individual applicants. Rather, it is to regulate the relationship between two or more Member States'. The Court of Appeal in *Mota* held that a private law right may arise upon a breach of duty by the United Kingdom.

Discretion in third country cases

7.38   As we have already seen, the Dublin Regulation allows Member States a discretion to determine applications for asylum substantively even if the examination is not its responsibility according to the criteria.[70] The Immigration Rules (see paragraph 7.26 above) also import a discretion into third country removal cases. The Secretary of State's policy on when a discretion should be exercised in third country cases was restated by Beverley Hughes MP on 22 July 2002.[71] According to this policy, a claimant will not normally be removed to a third country if:

- an applicant has a spouse in the UK (provided that the marriage took place before the applicant's arrival in the UK);
- an applicant has unmarried minor children in the UK;
- an applicant is an unmarried minor with a parent in the UK.

7.39   Discretion may also be exercised if the minor is married, or where the applicant is an elderly or otherwise dependent parent, or where there was clear evidence that the applicant was wholly or mainly dependent on the relative in the UK and there was an absence of similar support elsewhere.

---

[65] Article 21 (9).
[66] Article 23.
[67] [2006] EWCA Civ 1380.
[68] [2005] EWCA Civ 28.
[69] *R (on the appln of G) v SSHD* [2005] EWCA Civ 546.
[70] Articles 3 (2) and 15.
[71] Parliamentary Answer, Hansard, Column 860W.

In *Djassebi & Mosayebi v SSHD*[72] the court considered that this policy involves **7.40**
an assessment no different from that involved under Article 8.

D. Clearly Unfounded Certification—Section 94, 2002 Act

This section, which has been the subject of numerous amendments, allows the **7.41**
Home Office to exclude in-country appeal rights to those who have made an asylum or human rights claim by certifying them as 'clearly unfounded'. Certificates
under this section may be issued to applicants of any nationality, but in the case
of nationals from States listed in the section, there is a presumption that the claim
will be clearly unfounded.

The certificate may only be challenged by judicial review. In most cases, the **7.42**
applicant will be able to remain in the UK whilst the challenge takes place, and if
the challenge is successful, the Home Office is likely to withdraw the certificate
with the effect that there is an in-country appeal against the decision on the original
claim. If the challenge to the certificate fails, then the applicant can only appeal
from outside the UK. The time limit for appealing is 28 days from the date of
the applicant's departure. Where the appeal is brought from outside the UK the
appeal will be considered as if the applicant had not been removed from the UK.[73]
This means that an applicant may conduct their appeal on the grounds that their
removal is in breach of the Refugee Convention and their human rights from their
home country.

The in-country appeal rights excluded by a section 94 certificate

Not all in country appeal rights are excluded when a certificate is issued under **7.43**
section 94. Whether or not an appeal can be brought from within the UK depends
on the nature of the immigration decision. The section applies only to immigration decisions under section 82. It does not apply to in-country 'status' appeals
under sections 83 and 83A.[74]

If an applicant would have an in-country right of appeal only on the basis that **7.44**
they have made an asylum or human rights claim,[75] the certificate removes that
right of appeal.[76] A 'clearly unfounded' certificate will also exclude an in-country
right of appeal against a decision to refuse a certificate of entitlement, refuse to

---

72 [2005] EWHC 2298 (Admin).
73 Section 94 (9).
74 See Chapter 6.
75 ie under section 92 (4)(a).
76 Section 94 (2).

extend leave, and to curtail leave.[77] A certificate will also exclude an in-country right of appeal against a decision that a person to be removed is a person with statutorily extended leave, when section 47 of the 2006 Act comes into force.[78] However, a clearly unfounded certificate will not preclude an in-country right of appeal against a decision to revoke indefinite leave to enter or to make a deportation order.[79]

7.45 There is also a discrete provision in section 94(7) excluding an in-country appeal under section 92 (4) if the Secretary of State certifies that it is proposed to remove the person to a country of which he is not a national or citizen and there is no reason to believe that his rights under the ECHR will be breached. There is a statutory presumption of safety in respect of the country specified in section 94(7).[80] This provision conflicts with other provisions and has never been used by the Home Office.

7.46 The 2006 Act inserts a new provision[81] into section 94, which will allow the Secretary of State to exempt certain people, by order, from certification of their asylum or human rights claims as clearly unfounded. It will apply to people who have had their leave to remain varied or a variation of leave refused so that they have no leave in circumstances which will be specified in the order.

When will a clearly unfounded certificate be issued?

7.47 As stated above, a clearly unfounded certificate may be issued in respect of claims from any country, but where the Secretary of State is satisfied that an asylum or human rights claimant is entitled to reside in one of the States listed in the section he 'shall' certify the claim unless 'satisfied that it is not clearly unfounded'.[82] The Secretary of State may by order add a State or part of a State to the list if satisfied that there is in general in that State or in part no serious risk of persecution and that removal will not in general breach the UK's obligations under the ECHR.[83] The Secretary of State also has the power to add to the list countries which are safe in respect of certain descriptions of persons, namely on the basis of gender, language,

---

[77] Section 94 (1A).
[78] Reference to s 82(ha) to be substituted by s 47 2006 Act from a date to be appointed.
[79] Section 94 (1A).
[80] Section 94(8).
[81] Section 94 (6B) inserted by s 13 of the 2006 Act, from a date to be appointed.
[82] Section 94(3)—this section does not apply in relation to an asylum claimant or human rights claimant who is subject to extradition proceedings (s 94(6A) inserted by s 27(7) 2004 Act from 1 October SI 2004/2523).
[83] Section 94 (5).

race, religion, nationality, membership of a social or other group, political opinion, or other attribute, as appropriate.[84] The current list of countries is:[85]

The Republic of Albania	Gambia (in respect of men)
Serbia	Ghana (in respect of men)
Montenegro	Nigeria (in respect of men)
Jamaica	Kenya (in respect of men)
Macedonia	Liberia (in respect of men)
The Republic of Moldovia	Malwai (in respect of men)
Bolivia	Mali (in respect of men)
Brazil	Mauritius
Ecuador	Peru
South Africa	Sierra Leone (in respect of men)
Ukraine	
India	
Mongolia	

The test for certifying a claim as clearly unfounded

We consider the Home Office Policy on clearly unfounded certification and how **7.48**
to challenge a clearly unfounded certificate in the Practice Note below. Here we
consider the test applied by the Courts for determining whether a claim should
be certified. The test for certifying a human rights claim as clearly unfounded
under the 2002 Act is the same as certifying a claim as 'manifestly unfounded'
under the provisions in the 1999 Act. In *Thangarasa v Secretary of State for the
Home Department*, [86] a case under the previous provisions, Lord Bingham stated
at paragraph 14:

> . . . the Home Secretary must carefully consider the allegation, the grounds on which
> it is made and any material relied on to support it. But his consideration does not
> involve a full-blown merits review. It is a screening process to decide whether the
> deportee should be sent to another country for a full review to be carried out there
> or whether there appear to be human rights arguments which merit full considera-
> tion in this country before any removal order is implemented. No matter what the
> volume of material submitted or the sophistication of the argument deployed to
> support the allegation, the Home Secretary is entitled to certify if, after reviewing

---

[84] Section 94(5A)–5(C).
[85] Bangladesh was removed from the list by SI 2005/1016, Bulgaria and Romania were removed
by SI 2006/3215.
[86] [2002] UKHL 36.

this material, he is reasonably and conscientiously satisfied that the allegation must clearly fail.

7.49 In *ZL and DL v SSHD*[87] the Court of Appeal set out the steps a decision maker must take:

- consider the factual substance and detail of each claim;
- consider how it stands with the known background data;
- consider whether, in the round, it is capable of belief;
- if not, consider whether some part of it is capable of belief;
- consider whether, if believed, it is capable of coming within the Convention.

7.50 If the answers are such that the claim cannot on any legitimate view succeed, then the claim is clearly unfounded; if not, it is not. In *Y v SSHD*,[88] Charles J summarized the law as follows:

(a) A certificate can only be lawfully issued if the claim would be bound to fail in the sense that there is no prospect that an appeal would succeed. Bound to fail is not the same as likely to fail.

(b) The court is required to subject the decision of the Secretary of State to anxious scrutiny. That essentially requires the court to determine whether the claim is clearly unfounded.

(c) The court can consider all the evidence that has been submitted and not merely the evidence at the date of decision.

7.51 With regard to certification on the basis of the credibility of the claimant, the Court in *ZL and VL* said: 'Only where the interviewing officer is satisfied that nobody could believe the claimant's story will it be appropriate to certify the claim as clearly unfounded on the ground of lack of credibility alone.'

7.52 Where a person produces medical evidence, it is to be taken as correct[89] but the Court is not precluded from considering the nature and quality of the medical evidence and the precise grounds upon which any diagnosis was made.[90]

E. Earlier Right of Appeal Certification—Section 96 2002 Act

7.53 The 2004 Act substituted a new section 96 from 1 October 2004.[91] This section must be read with section 120 of the 2002 Act. These sections set out the 'one-stop'

---

[87] [2003] 1 WLR 1230.

[88] (2004) EWHC 3199 Admin.

[89] *R (on the appln of Razgar) v SSHD* [2004] UKHL 27, paragraph 70.

[90] *R (on the appln of Mehmeti) v SSHD* [2004] EWHC 2999 Admin per Beatson J at paragraph 37.

[91] Section 30 of the 2004 Act, SI 2004/2523.

arrangements which exclude a further right of appeal where a person seeks to rely on matters which he has already had the opportunity to argue in a previous appeal. In brief, this section allows the Secretary of State or an immigration officer to 'certify' an appeal which has the effect of precluding an appeal against a second immigration decision.

Failure to comply with a one-stop notice—section 96—the one-stop certificate

The effect of a certificate under section 96 is that an appeal cannot be brought **7.54** against a second immigration decision in the following two situations:

- where the Secretary of State or an immigration officer certifies that the person was notified of a right of appeal under section 82(1) against an earlier decision (whether or not an appeal was brought and whether or not any appeal brought has been determined), that the claim or application to which the new decision relates relies on a matter that could have been raised in appeal against the old decision, and that in the opinion of the Secretary of State or the immigration officer, there is no satisfactory reason for that matter not having been raised in an appeal against the old decision;[92]
- where the Secretary of State or an immigration officer certifies that the person received a notice under section 120 by virtue of an earlier application or decision, that the new decision relates to an application or claim which relies on a matter that should have been, but has not been, raised in a statement made in response to that notice, and that in the opinion of the Secretary of State or the immigration officer, there is no satisfactory reason for that matter not to have been raised in a statement made in response to that notice.[93]

Therefore an appeal is precluded if a ground of appeal could have been relied on **7.55** in an earlier appeal or in additional grounds in response to a one-stop notice. The one-stop procedure precludes a further appeal only where a further immigration decision under section 82 is taken in respect of someone who has made a previous application or been the subject of previous immigration decision. So, for example, if a person appealed against a decision to refuse to vary leave and was then subject to a further immigration decision to remove them as an overstayer and raised asylum grounds for the first time against this second decision, the Secretary of State could issue a certificate.

Section 96(5) provides that a person's right of appeal can be certified where he has **7.56** left the UK since an earlier right of appeal arose or an earlier one-stop notice was

---

[92] Section 96 (1).
[93] Section 96 (2).

served. This provision serves to prevent failed asylum seekers who return to the UK from being able to appeal against a new decision where there is no satisfactory reason for not having raised the new grounds before.

F. National Security—Section 97 2002 Act

7.57   As we saw in Chapter 6, section 97 excludes the right of appeal to the AIT in respect of decisions taken under sections 82(1), 83(2), and 83A(2) NIA Act 2002 and provides that an appeal already lodged will lapse where the Secretary of State in person[94] certifies that a person's exclusion or removal is:

- in the interests of national security;[95] or
- in the interests of a relationship between the United Kingdom and another country.[96]

7.58   Or if the Secretary of State in person[97] certifies that the decision was taken in reliance on information which should not be made public:

- for reasons of national security;[98]
- in the interests of the relationship between the United Kingdom and another country;[99] or
- otherwise in the public interest.[100]

G. National Security: Deportation—Section 97A

7.59   This section was inserted in to the 2002 Act by section 7 of the 2006 Act.[101] Where the Secretary of State certifies under section 97A(1) that the decision to make a deportation order has been made on national security grounds, a deportation order may be made before any appeal is disposed of. This section disapplies section 79 of the NIA Act 2002[102] which precludes the making of a deportation order where an appeal can be brought or is pending. Appeals against a decision to make a deportation order on national security grounds can normally only be made from outside the United Kingdom unless the appellant makes a human

---

[94]   Section 97 (4) NIA Act 2002.
[95]   Section 97(2)(a) NIA Act 2002.
[96]   Section 97(2)(b) NIA 2002.
[97]   Section 97(3)(4) NIA Act 2002.
[98]   Section 97(3)(a) NIA Act 2002.
[99]   Section 97(3)(b) NIA Act 2002.
[100]   Section 97 (3)(c) NIA Act 2002.
[101]   From 31 August 2006 (SI 2006/2226).
[102]   Section 97A(2)(a).

rights claim which is not certified under section 97A(2)(iii). Under this section the Secretary of State may certify that removal would not breach to UK's obligations under the ECHR. There is, however, an in-country appeal against this certificate to the Special Immigration Appeals Commission.[103]

H. Grounds of Public Good—Section 98 2002 Act

This section excludes a right of appeal against refusal of leave to enter and entry clearance where the Secretary of State acting in person[104] certifies that the decision was taken wholly or partly on the grounds of public good.[105] There is a right of appeal on human rights, race discrimination,[106] and, in the case of a refusal of leave to enter only, asylum grounds.[107]   **7.60**

I. Certification Under the 2006 Act—Refugee Convention Certification—Section 55

This section came into force on 31 August 2006[108] and applies to any appeal before the AIT from that date. This section applies to an asylum appeal where the Secretary of State issues a certificate that the appellant is not entitled to the protection of Article 33 (1) of the Refugee Convention because: **7.61**

- Article 1 (F) applies to him (whether or not he would otherwise be entitled to protection);[109] or
- Article 33 (2) applies to him on grounds of national security (whether or not he would otherwise be entitled to protection).[110]

For the purposes of the section, asylum appeal means an appeal under sections 82, 83, or 101 of the 2002 Act or section 2 of the Special Immigration Appeals Commission Act 1997 and in which the appellant claims that to remove him or require him to leave the UK would breach his rights under the Refugee Convention.[111]   **7.62**

---

103 Section 97A(3).
104 Section 98 (3).
105 Section 98 (1)(2).
106 Section 98 (4).
107 Section 98 (5).
108 SI 2006/2226.
109 See section on exclusion clauses in Asylum Chapter.
110 Section 55 (1)(a)(b).
111 Section 55 (2)(a)(b).

7.63   Where the Secretary of State has issued a certificate under this section the Tribunal must consider whether Article 1F applies first.[112] If the Tribunal agrees that it applies it must 'dismiss such part of the asylum appeal as amounts to an asylum claim (before considering any aspect of the case)'.[113]

7.64   The section does not require that the Tribunal hear the evidence in relation to Article 1F in isolation. Indeed, there may be many cases where the Article 1F issue is inextricably interlinked with the factual circumstances of the claim for persecution. The AIT is not prohibited from considering all the evidence but required to make a decision in respect of Article 1F only, if it applies.

J. Fresh Claims and Further Representations

7.65   A claim for asylum based on human rights grounds after an earlier claim has been refused will not give rise to an appeal unless a fresh immigration decision is taken which generates a further right of appeal. Where representations are made that circumstances have come into being which constitute a fresh claim for asylum, the Secretary of State will decide whether to treat the representations as a fresh claim or further representations.

The task of the Secretary of State

7.66   A fresh immigration decision will be taken only if the Secretary of State considers that the grounds advanced constitute a fresh claim for the purposes of paragraph 353 of the Immigration Rules. This paragraph of the Immigration Rules states that further representations will amount to a fresh claim if they are significantly different from the material that has previously been considered. The submissions will only be significantly different if the content:

- had not already been considered; and
- taken together with the previously considered material, created a realistic prospect of success, notwithstanding its rejection.

7.67   In *WM (DRC) v SSHD*[114] the Court of Appeal considered the task of the Secretary of State in assessing whether further representations constitute a fresh claim. Buxton LJ stated that the consideration of whether there is a realistic prospect of success will involve not only judging the reliability of the new material, but also judging the outcome of tribunal proceedings based on that material. The Secretary of State, in assessing the reliability of new material, can have in mind

---

[112]   Section 55 (3).
[113]   Section 55 (4).
[114]   [2006] EWCA Civ 1495.

both how the material relates to other material already found by an immigration judge to be reliable, and also have in mind, where that is relevantly probative, any finding as to the honesty or reliability of the applicant that was made by the previous immigration judge. However, he must also bear in mind that the latter may be of little relevance when the new material does not emanate from the applicant himself, and thus cannot be said to be automatically suspect because it comes from a tainted source.

The Court of Appeal in *WM* further stated that the Rule only imposes a modest **7.68** test that the application has to meet before it becomes a fresh claim. First, the question is whether there is a realistic prospect of success in an application before an immigration judge, but not more than that. Second, the immigration judge himself does not have to achieve certainty, but only to think that there is a real risk of the applicant being persecuted on return. Third, the Secretary of State, the immigration judge, and the Court must be informed by the anxious scrutiny of the material that is axiomatic in decisions that if made incorrectly may lead to the applicant's exposure to persecution.

The task of the Court

There is no provision for appeal from a decision of the Secretary of State as to the **7.69** existence of a fresh claim. The only means of challenge is therefore through the medium of judicial review. In *R v SSHD ex p Onibiyo*[115] Sir Thomas Bingham MR, giving the judgment of the Court, concluded 'with some misgivings' that the decisions of the Secretary of State were challengeable only on *Wednesbury* grounds. In *Cakabay v SSHD*[116] the Court held that in any asylum case anxious scrutiny must enter the equation. Therefore the test is one of irrationality and a decision will be irrational if it is not taken on the basis of anxious scrutiny. In *WM (DRC) v SSHD*[117] the Court of Appeal held that the task of the Court when reviewing a decision of the Secretary of State as to whether a fresh claim exists must address the following matters:[118]

- First, has the Secretary of State asked himself the correct question? The question is not whether the Secretary of State himself thinks that the new claim is a good one or should succeed, but whether there is a realistic prospect of an immigration judge, applying the rule of anxious scrutiny, thinking that the applicant will be exposed to a real risk of persecution on return. The Secretary of State can, and should, treat his own view of the merits as a starting point for

---

[115] [1996] QB 768.
[116] [1999] Imm AR 176.
[117] [2006] EWCA Civ 1495.
[118] At para 11.

that inquiry, but it is only a starting point in the consideration of a question that is distinctly different from the exercise of the Secretary of State making up his own mind.

- Second, in addressing that question, both in respect of the evaluation of the facts and in respect of the legal conclusions to be drawn from those facts, has the Secretary of State satisfied the requirement of anxious scrutiny? If the court cannot be satisfied that the answer to both of those questions is in the affirmative, it will have to grant an application for review of the Secretary of State's decision.

7.70 Even if further representations are accepted as a fresh claim, the Secretary of State may prevent a further appeal by issuing a certificate under section 96 of the 2002 Act.[119] The IDIs state that if a decision is made to treat the application as a fresh claim section 96 certification should be considered. Caseworkers should only consider certification under section 96 if they have first considered the application, reached a conclusion on the matters advanced by the applicant, and decided to refuse to grant leave.[120]

K. Removal Cases—Injunctions and Emergency Injunctions

7.71 We deal in this section of the chapter with obtaining injunctions through the judicial review procedure where a person has been served with removal directions. It is beyond the scope of this work to deal with the various means by which removal is enforced against failed asylum seekers and illegal entrants, and readers are referred to the *Operational Enforcement Manual* on the Borders and Immigration Agency website at <www.ind.homeoffice.gov.uk> for the Home Office practice and procedures relating to enforcement.[121]

7.72 The Procedure Rules and Practice Directions for judicial review applications are set out in Part 54 of the Civil Procedure Rules (CPR). The CPR and Practice Directions can be found at <www.dca.gov.uk> and the 'Administrative Court Notes for Guidance on Applying for Judicial Review' are available at <www.courtservice. gov.uk>. The court forms are to be found at <www.dca.gov.uk> on the CPR link.

7.73 It is beyond the scope of this work to deal with the law and procedures relating to judicial review. What follows is a summary of the practice and procedure in removal cases. In removal cases the remedy sought by the claimant will be an injunction to prevent removal under CPR 54.2(d). This is an interim order,

---

[119] See para 7.50 above.
[120] Immigration Directorate Instructions, Chapter 12, Section 3—The One Stop Procedure.
[121] *OEM*—Section A, Chapter 9 deals with removal of illegal entrants, Section B deals with deportation and administrative removal.

preventing removal while the claim is outstanding. Evidently the claimant must be able to found the claim for judicial review on the grounds that the decision is illegal, irrational, or procedurally unfair. The claim should be filed promptly and in any event not later than three months after the grounds to make the claim first arose.[122] There are two stages, namely the permissions stage and the substantive hearing. An application for an injunction to prevent removal will be made before the permission stage as the Home Office defers removal once permission is granted. An application for an injunction may be included as interim relief in the claim for seeking permission to apply for judicial review. In very urgent cases an application for an injunction may be made in advance of the preparation and lodging of the claim form and exceptionally can be made over the telephone to the duty judge.

The application for judicial review is initiated by completing a form N461. **7.74** In urgent cases a form N463 must additionally be completed. The N463 requires details of the reasons for urgency, the proposed timetable for application for interim relief and the application for permission and the substantive hearing, if permission is granted. A draft order must also be attached.

The claim form must include full details of the claimant, the defendant, and any **7.75** interested parties, and must include or be accompanied by a detailed statement of the grounds for judicial review, a statement of the facts relied on, and any application for extending time or directions. The form must also be accompanied by written evidence in support of the claim or application to extend time, a copy of any order the claimant seeks to have quashed, where the claim for judicial review relates to a decision of a Court or Tribunal, an approved copy of the reasons for reaching that decision, copies of any documents on which the claimant proposes to rely, copies of any relevant statutory material, and a list of essential documents for advance reading by the Court.[123] The claimant must file two copies of a paginated and indexed bundle containing the above documents with the Court. Readers are referred to Part 54 and the accompanying Practice Directions for full details of the procedures to be adhered to.

In deciding whether to grant an injunction, the Court will consider the underly- **7.76** ing merits of the case. If it is clear that permission to apply for judicial review will not be given then the Court would not grant an injunction. In many cases, where the application for permission would be before the Court, it would also refuse permission at that stage. In general, however, the Court will be astute to ensure that the usually irrevocable step of removal does not occur before the merits

122 CPR Part 54.5.
123 Practice Direction Rule 54.6.

of the underlying legal complaint can be determined, even if that determination may follow very shortly thereafter. Save in cases of extreme urgency (which should not in practice arise), the Home Office must be notified of any application to seek an injunction.

7.77 The Home Office has changed its practice on deferring removal pending judicial review challenges following the notification of removal directions. We append the policy below. From March 2007, the Home Office gives 72 hours' notice of removal, including two full working days. The last 24 hours will include a working day. When the Home Office notifies the individual of the removal directions, it will inform him that the case is one to which paragraph 18 of the Practice Direction supplementing Part 54 of the Civil Procedure Rules applies, and of the address to which any claim must be copied to IND in accordance with paragraph 18.2(2) of the Practice Direction. The Home Office will also try to provide a short, factual summary of the case with the notice of removal including a brief immigration history and other relevant information (including the name of a responsible officer to contact in the event of an injunction).

7.78 In cases where a person has been served with a copy of directions for his removal by the Home Office and notified by the Home Office that it applies, section II of the Practice Direction applies.[124] We append a copy of this section of the Practice Direction in the Practice Notes below. This section of the Practice Direction applies where a person makes an application for permission to apply for judicial review before his removal takes effect.

7.79 The requirements in this Part of the Practice direction are additional to other requirements. The claim form must indicate on its face that this Section of the Practice Direction applies and be accompanied by a copy of the removal directions and the decision to which the application relates, and any document served with the removal directions including any document which contains the Immigration and Nationality Directorate's factual summary of the case; and contain or be accompanied by the detailed statement of the claimant's grounds for bringing the claim for judicial review. If the claimant is unable to comply with these requirements as to documentation, the claim form must contain or be accompanied by a statement of the reasons why. The claimant must send copies of the claim and accompanying documents to the IND at the addressed supplied by them.

7.80 Where the claimant has not filed the relevant documentation and has provided reasons why he is unable to comply, and the Court has issued the claim form,

---

[124] Section II—Applications for Permission to apply for Judicial Review in Immigration and Asylum Cases—Challenging removal.

the Administrative Court will refer the matter to a Judge for consideration as soon as practicable; and will notify the parties that it has done so.

It can be seen from the policy statement that the Home Office will defer removal **7.81** only where an application for judicial review is made prior to removal and a copy of the claim form is issued by the Court, and a copy of the detailed statement of grounds are received by them. Where the claimant has not filed the relevant documentation and the matter is to be placed before a judge as described above, the Home Office will defer removal only if the Court decides that good reason has been provided for failure to comply (and gives a direction, eg that detailed grounds be submitted by a specified date), or permission to proceed to judicial review is granted or the court has not yet considered the matter by the time/date of removal, in which case it will be necessary to defer until the Court has reached a decision. However, the Home Office will not normally defer removal pending any challenge concerning compliance.

Where it is not possible to file a claim due to the Administrative Court office **7.82** being closed, the Home Office may defer removal if provided with a copy of detailed grounds. The onus remains on the claimant to file the claim form as soon as possible on the next day the Administrative Court Office is open and to notify IND that the claim form has been issued.

Given the restrictive nature of the Home Office policy on deferring removal, it is **7.83** crucial that representatives do their utmost to comply with the requirements of the Practice Direction.

L. Practice and Procedure Note

Home Office guidance to caseworkers and policy

Safe third country cases—Dublin Regulation

The Home Office policy on safe third country cases is set out in the APIs. In Dublin **7.84** Regulation cases the APIs give the following guidance to caseworkers:

> 7.2 In all safe third country cases Third Country Unit caseworkers must be satisfied that:
> - the applicant is not a national or citizen of the country of destination;
> - the applicant's life and liberty would not be threatened in that country by reason of race, religion, nationality, membership of a particular social group or political opinion; and the government of that country would not send the applicant to another country other than in accordance with the 1951 Convention (the concept of 'non-refoulement').
>
> 7.3 As with other types of removal, the removal to a safe third country must not breach the United Kingdom obligations under the ECHR. Consideration should be given to any human rights challenge against removal from the UK including whether it is 'clearly unfounded' in accordance with the relevant legislation (see Section 8 'Safe Third Country Legislation').

7.4 In non-Dublin cases TCU caseworkers must also be satisfied in each case that an applicant:
- had an opportunity at the border or within the territory of a safe third country to make contact with that country's authorities in order to seek protection; or
- that there is other clear evidence of the applicant's admissibility to a safe third country.

Safe Third Country cases—Schedule 3, 2004 Act
The first list of safe countries (at Part 2)

7.85 The APIs give the following guidance to caseworkers for cases in the first list of cases:

> When considering any ECHR challenge made on Article 3 or Article 8 grounds Third Country Unit caseworkers should consider recent court rulings. Third Country Unit caseworkers should also bear in mind when assessing whether the human rights claim is not clearly unfounded that Article 8 is a qualified right. Even if such a right is established, paragraph 8(2) ECHR permits a state to interfere with this right in defined circumstances, for example where the action is proportionate, is necessary in a democratic society and is in pursuit of a legitimate aim, such as the maintenance of immigration control. In the majority of new cases being considered for the first time by TCU caseworkers the applicant will have only remained in the UK for a relatively short time and so the likelihood of engaging Article 8 will be reduced.

The second list of safe countries (at Part 3)

7.86 The APIs give the following guidance to caseworkers for cases in the second list of countries:

> All human rights challenges to removal from the UK will be certified as clearly unfounded unless the Secretary of State was satisfied they are not clearly unfounded in line with the guidance for the first list of countries. Third Country Unit caseworkers should consider the human rights claim with reference to recent court rulings. If relevant to the basis of the claim against removal, TCU caseworkers should also consider information about the third country. If in doubt TCU caseworkers should seek advice from senior management.

The third list of safe countries (at Part 4)

7.87 The APIs give the following guidance to caseworkers for cases in the third list of countries:

> Any ECHR challenge to removal is to be considered to determine whether it is appropriate to certify as 'clearly unfounded' for this particular applicant. TCU caseworkers should consider the human rights claim with reference to recent court rulings. If relevant to the basis of the claim TCU caseworkers should also consider information about the third country. If in doubt TCU caseworkers should seek advice from senior management.

The fourth list of safe countries (at Part 5)

7.88 The APIs give the following guidance to caseworkers for cases in the third list of countries:

> Any ECHR challenge to removal is considered to determine whether it is appropriate to certify as 'clearly unfounded' in the individual case. If a case is referred to TCU for possible certification under this provision TCU caseworkers should seek advice from senior management in the first instance.

Home Office Guidance to Caseworkers on 'clearly unfounded certification'—section 94 of the 2002 Act

The Guidance to caseworkers is set out in the APIs under 'Certification' and makes the **7.89**
following general points:

- An asylum or human rights claim made by a claimant from one of the listed States should be considered on its individual merits. It is only if a claim falls to be refused that the question of certification arises.
- It is crucial that each claim be considered with reference to the relevant country information and in particular with reference to the relevant Operational Guidance Note.
- All decisions to certify a claim under section 94 will be subject to a second pair of eyes.
- If a claimant does not make an explicit human rights claim but their asylum claim raises a fear of mistreatment in their country that claim should be treated as an implied human rights claim (Article 3 ECHR), even the caseworker considers the fear of mistreatment to be objectively unfounded.
- Where both an asylum and a human rights claim (whether explicit or implied) have been made, they should be considered separately for certification.
- It will be a rare case which will be certified on the basis of credibility alone. In the majority of cases, caseworkers will need to be able to certify on the basis that, even accepting the claimant's account as credible and taking that account at its highest, the claim is bound to fail.

The APIs also set out the following categories of 'clearly unfounded' claims: **7.90**

- A claim which raises nothing that could be construed as amounting to an expression of a fear of mistreatment upon return. For example, a person says they are seeking asylum but gives as their reason that they are fleeing poverty or unemployment.
- The claim expresses a fear of mistreatment but based on an objective assessment there is no arguable case that the feared mistreatment will arise.
- The claim expresses a fear of mistreatment, but from the objective evidence it is not arguable that the mistreatment, even if it occurred, would amount to persecution or treatment contrary to Article 3.
- The claim expresses a fear of persecution or Article 3 treatment by non-State actors but the State provides a sufficiency of protection against such actions.
- Where internal relocation is obviously available.
- Where there is no Convention.
- Where the claimant says they are making a human rights claim and perhaps mentions some of the ECHR Articles, but the claim contains nothing which could be construed as raising an issue under the European Convention on Human Rights. For example, a person says removal would breach their human rights, but their

claim is based solely on the general lack of job prospects in the claimant's country of origin.

- Where the feared mistreatment does not arguably amount to a flagrant breach of a non-Article 3 right.
- Article 8 claims where:
  (i) the claimant claims close family ties in the UK but those ties do not exist (eg there is no evidence of the existence of the claimed family members or no evidence that there is a longstanding bond between them and the claimant);
  (ii) there are no insurmountable obstacles to the family member(s) in question living with the claimant outside the UK;
  (iii) there are no strong reasons why the claimant could not return to their country of origin and seek entry clearance under the Immigration Rules to return to the UK.

Challenging certification

Challenging third country removals under the 2004 Act

7.91 As stated above (see paragraph 7.06), a declaration of incompatibility has been made in respect of Part 2 of Schedule 3 to the 2004 Act. The government is appealing the declaration, but the domestic courts must continue to apply this provision as the declaration of incompatibility does not affect its validity. Clearly, if the government loses the appeal it will take steps to amend the legislation to ensure compliance. Given the current uncertainty, we set out the means of challenging certificates under this Part.

7.92 As we saw above, the first three lists of countries are deemed to be safe under the Refugee Convention, both in respect of a risk of persecution within the third country and being sent on by the third country. There is no right of appeal at all on Refugee Convention grounds. However, an in-country right of appeal exists on ECHR grounds. In the first list of cases an in-country right of appeal exists on the grounds that removal to the third country could breach the applicant's rights under the ECHR. In the second and third lists of countries an in-country right of appeal exists against the refusal of any ECHR claim. Therefore, in order to overcome the 'deeming provision' which prevents the in-country right of appeal, claims should, if they can, be framed in ECHR terms. Generally, if a person has a claim under the Refugee Convention, a claim also exists under the ECHR. Representatives can therefore argue that the ECHR claim has the effect of freeing the applicant from the 'deemed' safety provisions. However, as we saw above, the Home Office will certify claims in the first and second list of countries as clearly unfounded unless satisfied that they are not clearly unfounded. The certificate will then have to be challenged by way of judicial review.

7.93 As we saw above, the successful challenge in *Nasseri* was due to the fact that the provisions which deem that the third country will not send an applicant on to a country where they are at risk were held to create an irrebuttable presumption of safety which was inconsistent with the ECHR.

There is no deeming provision in respect of safety for the fourth list of countries. **7.94**
Hence if the Home Office issue a certificate this can be challenged by judicial review.
Since an in-country right of appeal exists on ECHR grounds, a human rights claim may
be pursued unless certified.

Therefore, save for in the circumstances successfully challenged in *Nasseri*, a chal- **7.95**
lenge to removal may be made on the following ECHR grounds:

- that there is a risk of a breach of the applicant's human rights in the third country;
- that removal to the third country would amount to a breach of the applicant's private and/or family life under Article 8—with regard to private life, the applicant can
  also argue that the removal would breach his 'physical and moral integrity'—see
  Chapter 4;
- that the removal from the third country would breach the applicant's human rights.

Challenging clearly unfounded certificates

We considered the test for certifying a claim as 'clearly unfounded' in paragraph 7.48 **7.96**
above and the Home Office Policy on clearly unfounded certification at 7.89 above. It
should be remembered that a claim is properly certified only when it is bound to fail.
Where certification on this basis has taken place, the Home Office may take steps to
remove the person concerned quickly. It is therefore necessary to act quickly if the certificate is to be challenged by judicial review or further representations are to be made.

When considering whether to mount a challenge by way of judicial review, represent- **7.97**
atives should bear in mind the approach that will be adopted by the High Court when
considering a challenge to a clearly unfounded certificate. It is a predictive approach.
The reviewing Court must consider how an appeal would be likely to fair before an
immigration judge as the tribunal responsible for deciding the appeal if there were an
appeal. This means that the reviewing Court must ask itself essentially the questions
which would have to be answered by an immigration judge.[125]

The first step is to establish the basis for the asylum or human rights claim. The ele- **7.98**
ments of the claim should be examined. Is there a Convention reason? Does the person fear persecution or serious harm? Is that fear objectively well founded? Is there a
sufficiency of protection? Does an internal flight alternative exist? Is there an arguable
Article 8 claim?

In assessing whether the certificate can be challenged, a representative should exam- **7.99**
ine the facts of the claim and the evidence in support of the claim much in the same
way as Secretary of State is enjoined to do in *ZL and DL v SSHD*,[126] namely: consider

---

[125] *R (on the appln of Razgar) v SSHD* [2004] UKHL 27, [2004] 3 WLR 58.
[126] [2003] 1 WLR 1230.

the factual substance and detail of each claim; consider how it stands with the known background data; consider whether, in the round, it is capable of belief; if not, consider whether some part of it is capable of belief; consider whether, if believed, it is capable of coming within the Convention. It should be remembered, however, that it is a rare case that should be certified on the basis of credibility alone. Generally, a case should not be certified unless, even if taken as credible and at its highest, it is bound to fail.

7.100 Representatives should examine the grounds relied on by the Secretary of State for concluding that the claim is bound to fail before an immigration judge. Can these grounds be challenged on the basis of objective evidence or case law? Clearly the objective material should be examined to ascertain whether the persecution the claimant asserts he fears is supported by evidence. Any country guidance cases should be considered against up-to-date country material.

7.101 The RFRL should be scrutinized to establish whether the Secretary of State has had proper regard to all relevant documentation submitted by the claimant. Consideration should also be given as to whether further supportive documentation can be obtained in support of the claim. Could a medical or country expert's report be obtained? Are their supporting documents in the claimant's possession that could be authenticated? If so, further representations can be made to the Secretary of State.

7.102 On the basis of the above considerations a decision can be made whether to mount a challenge to the certificate by way of judicial review.

Home Office policy on removal

Change of policy

Relating to the circumstances in which removal will be deferred following challenge by judicial review.

7.103 From 12 March 2007 the Home Office has been operating a revised policy for handling judicial review challenges made after removal directions have been served. The reason given for the change of policy is that it is designed to ensure prompt lodging of detailed grounds and swift disposal of weak claims as part of the strategy to streamline the removals process. A new Practice Direction has been issued by the courts in response to this policy, which we include below.

> **IND STATEMENT OF POLICY: Judicial review challenges following notification of removal directions**
>
> **Notice of removal**
>
> 1. From 12 March 2007 IND will give at least 72 hours' notice of removal, including two full working days. The last 24 hours of the 72 hours will include a working day (to allow proceedings to be filed during this period).

2. When notifying an individual of directions for removal, IND will indicate to the individual:
   - that the case is one to which paragraph 18 of the Practice Direction supplementing Part 54 of the Civil Procedure Rules applies, and
   - the address to which any claim must be copied to IND in accordance with paragraph 18.2(2) of the Practice Direction.
3. IND will aim to provide a short, factual summary of the case with the notice of removal including a brief immigration history and other relevant information (including the name of a responsible officer to contact in the event of an injunction).
4. At the time of being notified of the removal, the individual will be advised by IND to seek legal advice and, if detained, provided with the means to contact a legal adviser or representative.

Deferral of removal

Claim form issued with detailed grounds

5. IND will defer removal if an application for judicial review is made prior to removal, and
   - a copy of the claim form as issued by the court, and
   - a copy of the detailed statement of grounds,
   are received by IND.

Claim form issued with statement of reasons for non-compliance with the Practice Direction

6. In cases where the claim form has been issued and the claimant has provided a statement of reasons for non-compliance with the practice direction, the court will notify IND and the matter will be placed before a judge for consideration as soon as practicable. In these circumstances IND will defer removal if—
   - The court decides that good reason has been provided for failure to comply (and gives a direction, e.g. that detailed grounds be submitted by a specified date),
   OR
   - Permission to proceed to judicial review is granted,
   OR
   - The court has not yet considered the matter by the time/date of removal. In such circumstances it will be necessary to defer until the court has reached a decision.
7. Where it is not possible to file a claim due to the Administrative Court office being closed, IND may defer removal if provided with a copy of detailed grounds. The onus remains on the claimant to file the claim form as soon as possible on the next day the Administrative Court Office is open and to notify IND that the claim form has been issued.

Notification that removal directions will not be deferred

8. IND will not normally defer removal pending any challenge to the court's decision concerning compliance made under paragraph 18.3 of the Practice Direction (see paragraph 6 above).
9. If on refusal of permission the Administrative Court has indicated that the case is clearly without merit IND will notify the individual that removal will not be deferred pending any application for oral renewal.

DATE: 2 March 2007

PRACTICE DIRECTION SUPPLEMENTING PART 54

SECTION II—APPLICATIONS FOR PERMISSION TO APPLY FOR JUDICIAL REVIEW IN IMMIGRATION AND ASYLUM CASES—CHALLENGING REMOVAL

18.1 (1) This Section applies where—

   (a) a person has been served with a copy of directions for his removal from the United Kingdom by the Immigration and Nationality Directorate of the Home Office and notified that this Section applies; and

    (b) that person makes an application for permission to apply for judicial review before his removal takes effect.

  (2) This Section does not prevent a person from applying for judicial review after he has been removed.

  (3) The requirements contained in this Section of this Practice Direction are additional to those contained elsewhere in the Practice Direction.

18.2 (1) A person who makes an application for permission to apply for judicial review must file a claim form and a copy at court, and the claim form must—

  (a) indicate on its face that this Section of the Practice Direction applies; and

  (b) be accompanied by—

    (i) a copy of the removal directions and the decision to which the application relates; and

    (ii) any document served with the removal directions including any document which contains the Immigration and Nationality Directorate's factual summary of the case; and

  (c) contain or be accompanied by the detailed statement of the claimant's grounds for bringing the claim for judicial review; or

  (d) if the claimant is unable to comply with paragraph (b) or (c), contain or be accompanied by a statement of the reasons why.

  (2) The claimant must, immediately upon issue of the claim, send copies of the issued claim form and accompanying documents to the address specified by the Immigration and Nationality Directorate.

(Rule 54.7 also requires the defendant to be served with the claim form within 7 days of the date of issue. Rule 6.5(8) provides that service on a Government Department must be effected on the solicitor acting for that Department, which in the case of the Immigration and Nationality Directorate is the Treasury Solicitor. The address for the Treasury Solicitor may be found in the Annex to Part 66 of these Rules.)

18.3 Where the claimant has not complied with paragraph 18.2(1)(b) or (c) and has provided reasons why he is unable to comply, and the court has issued the claim form, the Administrative Court—

  (a) will refer the matter to a Judge for consideration as soon as practicable; and

  (b) will notify the parties that it has done so.

18.4 If, upon a refusal to grant permission to apply for judicial review, the Court indicates that the application is clearly without merit, that indication will be included in the order refusing permission.

8

DETENTION AND BAIL

A. Introduction

8.01 As we shall see, the powers to detail immigrants are drafted in wide terms. There is no statutory presumption in favour of bail in the immigration legislation, nor are there express statutory time limits on the period of detention. However, limits to the powers to detain are implied by statute and have been construed narrowly by the courts. The powers to detain are also limited by Home Office policy and human rights law. The courts have recognised the fundamental right to liberty and have set down clear markers on the limits of the power to detain.

8.02 Before the introduction of the Nationality, Immigration and Asylum Act 2002, the powers to detain were ancillary to examination, removal, and decision making on a claim. As a result of the enactment of this legislation the Secretary of State may now detain pending a decision and where he has a reasonable belief that he has to power to detain under the Act. Detention may also be authorised where there is a breach of conditions attached to the grant of leave.

8.03 The immigration legislation also does not specify the factors which should be considered when the decision to detain is made. The factors influencing the decision to detain are therefore a matter of Home Office policy. The legality of detention, as we explore below, is often a question of whether or not the Home Office has followed its stated policy. The current Home Office policy on detention is contained in the *Operational Enforcement Manual* (OEM) at Chapter 38. The relevant parts of this policy and other policy statements on detention are contained in the Practice Notes at the end of this chapter.

8.04 Chapter 38 of the OEM consolidates the government policy towards detention as set out in the 1998 White Paper 'Fairer, Faster and Firmer—A Modern Approach to Immigration and Asylum' and the 2002 White Paper 'Secure Borders, Safe Haven'. In the 1998 White Paper the government stated that there was a presumption in favour of temporary admission or release and that, wherever possible, it would use alternatives to detention. The White Paper went on to say that detention would most usually be appropriate to effect removal, initially to establish a person's identity or basis of claim, or where there is reason to believe that the person will fail to comply with any conditions attached to the grant of temporary admission or release.

8.05 The Home Office has used detention as a means of expediting claims from asylum applicants whose claim appears to be straightforward and capable of being decided quickly. Since March 2000 such applicants have been detained at Oakington Reception Centre. The Nationality, Immigration and Asylum Act 2002 introduced legislative machinery for detaining such 'fast track' cases by means of the use of reception, accommodation, and removal centres. The policy for fast track processes was updated in February 2006 and is contained in the

OEM. We deal with the policy and procedure peculiar to the fast track regime at para 8.136 below.

There is always an alternative to detention in any of the circumstances where the **8.06** power may be exercised under Schedule 2 to the Immigration Act 1971, namely the grant of temporary admission to the UK. The power to grant temporary admission may be exercised by an immigration officer or the Secretary of State. We deal with temporary admission and the conditions which may be attached to it at 8.120 below.

B. Powers to Detain

The powers to detain immigrants and asylum seekers are contained in the follow- **8.07** ing legislation:

- paragraph 16 of Schedule 2 and paragraph 2 of Schedule 3 of the Immigration Act 1971;
- section 10 (7) of the Immigration and Asylum Act 1999;
- section 62 of the Nationality, Immigration and Asylum Act 2002;
- section 71(3) of the Nationality, Immigration and Asylum Act 2002.

Some of these powers may be exercised by an immigration officer and some by **8.08** the Secretary of State. The 2002 Act introduced a wider range of powers for the Secretary of State to detain people. Now, officers in the Home Office have the ability to authorise detention in circumstances where the power previously lay with an immigration officer only. The purpose of this change was to enable the officer in the Home Office with conduct of a case to make the detention decision. There is therefore now a considerable overlap between the powers of immigration officers to detain and those of the Secretary of State. For the sake of clarity we set out their discrete powers in Tables 8.1 and 8.2.

Immigration officers' powers to detain

Under Schedule 2 to the 1971 Act immigration officers may examine persons **8.09** arriving in the United Kingdom for the purpose of determining their status. To facilitate this task the immigration legislation also gives them power to detain pending the completion of the examination and a decision to give or refuse leave to enter. The powers to detain immigrants under the 1971 Act have been frequently amended and we include full references to changes in Table 8.1.

Where the examination is of a port case or illegal entrant who claims asylum, the **8.10** examination in Schedule 2 refers to the whole asylum procedure and the only limitation implied on the detention is that the period should be reasonably necessary for the examination and necessary decision.

361

Table 8.1 Persons who may be detained by immigration officers

Port cases

- A person who has arrived in the UK may be detained pending examination for the purposes of deciding whether or not they should be granted leave to enter.
  Power to detain—Immigration Act 1971, Schedule 2 para 16(1)
- A person who arrived in the UK with leave to enter but whose leave to enter has been suspended may be detained pending completion of an examination by an immigration officer and pending a decision on whether that leave to enter should be cancelled.
  Power to detain—Immigration Act 1971, Schedule 2, Para 16 (1A) inserted by Immigration and Nationality Act 1999 from 14 February 2000
- A person who is embarking or seeking to embark in the UK may be examined by an immigration officer to establish whether he is a British citizen and if not a British citizen, his identity and the legality of his status, and may be detained for a period not exceeding 12 hours pending the completion of such examination.
  Power to detail—Immigration Act 1971, Schedule 2, Para 16 (1B) inserted by the Immigration, Asylum and Nationality Act 2006, s 42 from 31 August 2006 (SI 2006/2226)
- A person who is refused leave to enter and a person who is reasonably suspected of having been refused leave to enter may be detained by an immigration officer pending a decision on whether or not to give directions for his removal and pending his removal in pursuance of those directions.
  Power to detain—Immigration Act 1971, Schedule 2, Paras 8, 16(2) as amended by NIAA 2002, s 73(5) from 10 February 2003 (SI 2003/1)

Illegal entrants

- A person who is an illegal entrant or reasonably suspected of being an illegal entrant may be detained pending a decision on whether or not to give directions for his removal and pending his removal in pursuance of those directions.
  Power to detain—Immigration Act 1971, Schedule 2, Paras 9, 16(2) as amended by NIAA 2002 s 73 (5) from 10 February 2003 (SI 2003/1)

Persons subject to administrative removal

- Persons who overstay their leave to remain, do not observe a condition attached to their leave, use deception (whether successfully or not) in seeking leave to remain, have their indefinite leave to remain revoked because they cease to be a refugee, and any family members of people in the above categories in respect of whom removal directions have been given or anyone who is reasonably suspected of being in any of the above categories may be detained pending a decision to remove them or pending removal.
  Power to detain—Immigration and Asylum Act 1999, s 10(1)(a)(b)(ba)(c) and (7) as amended by the Nationality, Immigration and Asylum Act 2002 ss 74 and 76 from 10 February 2003 (SI 2003/1)

Seamen and aircrews

- Members of crews of ships or aircrafts who remain beyond the period of their leave to enter or who abscond having lawfully entered without leave, or whom an immigration officer reasonably expects intends to do so, may be detained.
  Power to detain—Immigration Act 1971, Schedule 2, paras 12–14, 16(2)

EEA nationals

An immigration officer may detain EEA nationals under para 16 of Schedule 2 to the Immigration Act 1971:

- a person who claims a right of admission as a family member of an EEA national or a family member who has retained the right of residence or person who has a permanent right of residence pending examination of the claim (Immigration (European Economic Area) Regulations 2006 reg 22 (1)(a));

Table 8.1 Persons who may be detained by immigration officers *(Cont)*

- an EEA national where there is reason to believe that he may be excluded from the UK on the grounds of public policy, public security, or public health, pending examination of the claim (reg 22(1)(b));
- a person who has been refused admission to the UK because he does not qualify for admission under the EEA Regulations, pending removal from the UK (reg 23(1)(a));
- a person who has been refused admission to the UK by an immigration officer on arrival because his EEA family permit, residence card, or permanent residence card has been revoked on the grounds of public policy, public security, or public health or on the grounds that he or his family cease to have a right to reside or right of permanent residence under the EEA Regulations pending removal from the UK (reg 23(1)(a));
- a person who has been refused admission to the UK who is an EEA national, a family member of an EEA national, or a family member of an EEA national, who has retained a right of residence or person with a permanent right of residence under the EEA regulations if his exclusion is justified on the grounds of public policy, public security, or public health pending removal from the UK (reg 23(1)(b));
- a person who does not have or ceases to have the right to reside under the EEA regulations (reg 24(2));
- a person who enters or seeks to enter in breach of a deportation order (reg 24 (4)).

Persons with statutorily extended leave
- When section 47 of the Immigration, Asylum and Nationality Act 2006 comes into force the Secretary of State may decide that a person with statutorily extended leave (leave to enter is extended pending an appeal by section 3C(2)(b) and 3D(2)(a) of the 1971 Act) is to be removed from the UK in accordance with directions given by an immigration officer if and when the leave ends. A person may be detained under para 16 to Schedule 2 of the 1971 Act when the directions are issued (and the administrative provisions of Schedule 2 to the 1971 Act apply in relation to directions under s 47 by virtue of s 47(3)). It is clear that there is no power to give removal directions, and hence no ancillary power to detain, whilst an appeal may be brought or is pending.

Immigration, Asylum and Nationality Act 2006, s 47

Secretary of State's powers to detain

Until the enactment of the Nationality Immigration and Asylum Act 2002, the **8.11** Secretary of State's powers to detain were restricted to those persons liable to deportation specified in Schedule 3 to the Immigration Act 1971. Under the 2002 Act, the Secretary of State may now detain illegal entrants, port entrants, and asylum seekers in the circumstances set out in Table 8.2. There is now also an additional power to detain EEA nationals under the EEA Regulations 2006.

Table 8.2 Persons who may be detained by the Secretary of State

Illegal entrants
- Persons refused leave to enter, illegal entrants, and members of their families and overstaying crew members in accordance with paras 10, 10A and 14 of Schedule 2 to the 1971 Act pending a decision whether to give removal directions and pending removal.
  Power to detain—s 62(1)(a)(b) Nationality Immigration and Asylum Act 2002

Table 8.2 Persons who may be detained by the Secretary of State *(Cont.)*

- Persons in respect of whom the Secretary of State has reasonable grounds to suspect he may make one of the decisions above.
  Power to detain—s 62(7) Nationality Immigration and Asylum Act 2002

Port cases

- Persons seeking leave to enter the UK, pending the Secretary of State's examination, decision to give or refuse leave to enter, decision to give directions for removal, or removal in pursuance of directions.
  Power to detain—s 62(2)(a)(b)(c)(d)Nationality, Immigration and Asylum Act 2002
- Persons in respect of whom the Secretary of State has reasonable grounds to suspect he may make one of the decisions above.
  Power to detain—s 62(7) Nationality Immigration and Asylum Act 2002

Asylum seekers

- Persons who make a claim for asylum (including an Article 3 ECHR claim) when they have leave to enter and their dependants may be detained if they breach a restriction placed on them as to residence, reporting, and occupation.
  Power to detain—s 71 Nationality Immigration and Asylum Act 2002 and Schedule 2 of the 1971 Act

Deportation

Recommendation for deportation

- Where a recommendation for deportation made by a court is in force and a person is not detained in pursuance of the sentence or order of the Court he must be detained pending the making of a deportation order in pursuance of the recommendation unless the Court by which the order is made or the appeal court otherwise directs or the Secretary of State orders him to be released pending further consideration of his case or he is released on bail.
  Power to detain—para 2 (1), 1 (A) Schedule 3 Immigration Act 1971 as amended by s 34 (1) of the 2004 Act from October 2004 (SI 2004/2523), para 2, 1 (A) inserted by the Criminal Justice Act 1982 Sch 10

Decision to deport

- Where a person has been given notice of intention to make a deportation order, or when there is such notice ready to be given, and he is not detained in pursuance of the sentence or order of a court, he may be detained pending the making of a deportation order;
  Power to detain—para 2(2) Schedule 3 Immigration Act 1971 as amended by s 34 (2) of the 2004 Act from 1 October 2004 and para 2 (4) of the 1971 Act as inserted by s 53 of the 2006 Act from 31 August 2006 (SI/2226)

Deportation order

- Where a deportation order is in force against a person, or such order is ready to be made, he may be detained pending his removal or departure from the UK. If he is already detained under either of the above two provisions he shall continue to be detained unless he is released on bail or the Secretary of State directs otherwise.
  Power to detain—para 2(3) Schedule 3 Immigration Act 1971 as substituted by Sch 7 of the 2002 Act from 1 April 2003 (SI 2003/754) and para 2 (4) of the 1971 Act as inserted by s 53 of the 2006 Act from 31 August 2006

EEA nationals

- Where a decision has been taken that a person who would otherwise be entitled to remain under the EEA Regulations should be removed on the grounds of public policy, public security, or public health he may be detained under the powers contained in Schedule 3 to the 1971 Act.
  Power to detain—Regulation 24 (3) EEA Regulations 2006

Home Office policy

The fact that a person may be detained because they fall into one of the categories **8.12** liable to detention set out above does not mean that they will be detained. The decision whether to detain is a matter of discretion and the Home Office have issued detailed policy guidance to their operatives on when a decision in favour of detention should be made. Where these policies are not followed, the detention will be unlawful. We set out all the relevant policies on detention with commentary in the Practice Notes on Home Office Policy at the end of this chapter. The following are the main policies relevant to detention:

• General detention policy—Chapter 38 of the *Operation Enforcement Manual.*

• Reasons for detention—Form IS 91R—lists the reasons for detention and is given to detainees on their detention and was held in *Amirthanathan*[1] to be an important part of published policy on detention.

• Vulnerable detainees—Chapter 38 of the OEM—categories of people who are either never to be detained or may be detained only in specified circumstances.

• Fast track detainees—Chapter 38 of the OEM.

• International materials—UNHCR Guidelines for the detention of asylum seekers; UNHCR Guidelines for the detention of refugee children.

• Policy on removal where judicial review proceedings have been commenced— as of 12 March 2007 the Home Office has changed its policy on removal. The Home Office will defer removal if an application for judicial review is made prior to removal, and a copy of the claim form as issued by the Court, and a copy of the detailed statement of grounds, are received by the Home Office— the full details of the policy and accompanying Practice Direction are to be found in the Practice Notes at the end of Chapter 7.

• Other sources of policy—Home Office letters and other documents containing statements of policy.

The lawfulness of detention

Although the powers to detain immigrants are drafted in wide terms there are **8.13** clear limits to these powers. In *R v Governor of Durham Prison, ex parte Singh*[2] Woolf J (as he then was) held that whilst the power given to the Secretary of State

---

[1] *R (on the appln of Amirthanathan) v Secretary of State for the Home Department* [2003] EWCA Civ 1768 para 37.
[2] [1984] 1 All ER 983.

under Schedule 3 to the 1971 Act was not subject to any express limitation of time, it was subject to the following limitations:

- the power can only be used pursuant to the statutory purpose;

- the detention is impliedly limited to a period which is reasonably necessary for that purpose;

- the period which is reasonably necessary depends on the circumstances of the particular case;

- if the Secretary of State is unable to operate the machinery provided in the Act to remove persons within a reasonable period, it would be wrong for the Secretary of State to exercise his powers of detention;

- it is implicit that the Secretary of State should exercise all reasonable expedition to ensure that the steps are taken which will be necessary to ensure the removal of the individual within a reasonable time.

8.14 The right to liberty is scrupulously protected by the courts. In *Tam Te Lam & Ors*[3] Lord Browne-Wilkinson expressed the view of the Court in stating that 'the courts should construe strictly any statutory provision purporting to allow the deprivation of individual liberty by administrative detention and should be slow to hold that statutory provisions authorise administrative detention for unreasonable periods or in unreasonable circumstances'.

8.15 *Tam Te Lam* also established that the burden of proving that the detainee is detained 'pending removal' is on the Secretary of State on the balance of probabilities.[4]

8.16 In summary, and as we explore below, the limits to the power to detain can be classified as follows:

- Detention must be and must continue to be pursuant to a statutory purpose.

- The detention will be lawful only if the statutory requirements are satisfied in each particular case.

- Detention must not continue for a period beyond which is reasonable in all of the circumstances of the case.

- The exercise of the discretion to detain must be consistent with Home Office Policy,[5] reasonable, and proportionate, the decision to detain should have

---

[3] *Tan Te Lam & Ors v Superintendent of Tai A Chau Detention Centre & Anor* [1996].
[4] Para 115E.
[5] *R (on the appln of Amirthanathan) v SSHD* [2003] EWCA Civ 1768.

taken into account all relevant considerations, and fair procedures should have been used.

- The decision to detain must be for a lawful purpose and proportionate to a legitimate aim under Article 5 ECHR.

The purpose of the detention

The powers to detain under the immigration legislation are set out in tables 8.1 **8.17** and 8.2 above. Under the 1971 Act, detention is only lawful if it is used pursuant to a statutory purpose *ex parte Singh* (above). Generally speaking, under the 1971 Act detention may be pending examination, pending a decision on whether to grant, refuse, or cancel leave, pending the giving of removal directions, pending the making of a deportation order, and pending removal or departure from the UK. If a person is detained for a reason other than provided by statute, the detention will be unlawful.

In *Tam Te Lam*, a case decided under Hong Kong law but where detention had **8.18** been authorised on similar powers 'pending removal' to the 1971 Act, detention was held to be unlawful because removal was not pending as it was a practical impossibility. The case concerned the Vietnamese boat people who had arrived in Hong Kong and who the Vietnamese government refuse to repatriate. The applicants successfully contended that since there was no possibility that they would be repatriated their detention was not 'pending removal' and was therefore unlawful as there was no power to detain.

In *Khadir*[6] the House of Lords opined that as long as the Secretary of State **8.19** remains intent upon removing the person and there is some prospect of achieving this, the 1971 Act authorises detention meanwhile. However, it may become unreasonable actually to detain the person pending a long delayed removal (ie throughout the whole period until removal is finally achieved).

In *Saadi v United Kingdom*[7] the European Court of Human Rights upheld the **8.20** judgment of the House of Lords that there is no requirement in Article 5 § 1 (f) that the detention of a person to prevent his effecting an unauthorised entry into the country be reasonably considered necessary. Therefore, provided that the statutory basis for detention is satisfied, the Home Office are not obliged to show additionally that there is a risk of committing an offence or absconding: 'All that is required is that the detention should be a genuine part of the process to determine whether the individual should be granted immigration clearance

---

[6] *R v Secretary of State for the Home Department ex parte Khadir* [2005] UKHL 39.
[7] *Saadi v United Kingdom* (Application No 13229/03) (2006) The Times, 3 August, [2006] All ER (D) 125 (Jul), ECrt HR.

and/or asylum, and that it should not otherwise be arbitrary, for example on account of its length.'[8]

8.21 Where detention is pursuant to an improper purpose it will be unlawful. A stark example of this arose in *R (on the appln of Karas & Anor)*[9] where the Court discerned a practice operated by the Secretary of State of detaining an individual close to or after the close of business hours with a view to removing them before business hours the following morning. The Court found that the purpose of this practice was i) to give both the claimants and their solicitors the minimum possible time to react to the decision letter; ii) not to alert the solicitors to the fact that their clients' removal was imminent; iii) to minimize the chance of the claimants being able to contact their solicitors before they were removed; iv) to minimize the chance of the solicitors being able to do anything effective before their clients were removed; and v) to minimize the chance of the claimants being able to apply to a judge. In short, in order to deny them access to legal advice and access to the court.

8.22 Expressing the censure of the Court, Mr Justice Munby said:

> I am driven to conclude that the claimants' detention was deliberately planned with a view to what in my judgment was a collateral and improper purpose—the spiriting away of the claimants from the jurisdiction before there was likely to be time for them to obtain and act upon legal advice or apply to the court. That purpose was improper. It was unlawful. And in my judgment it renders the detention itself unlawful. (para 84)

Statutory requirements for detention must be satisfied

8.23 Clearly, detention will be unlawful if the relevant statutory requirements for detention are not satisfied. So, for example, if detention of any asylum seeker is authorised under section 71 of the 2002 Act on the basis that a condition of residence has been breached, and no such breach has taken place, detention will be unlawful.

Detention must be for a reasonable period

8.24 We set out the principles set out in *ex parte Singh* at para 8.13 above. Detention is lawful only for a period which is reasonably necessary to carry out the immigration action. The period which is reasonably necessary depends on the circumstances of the particular case. If the Secretary of State cannot remove persons within a reasonable period, it would be wrong to exercise the powers of

---

[8] *Saadi v UK* above at para 44.

[9] *R (on the appln of Karas & Anor) v Secretary of State for the Home Department* [2006] EWHC 747 (Admin).

detention. The Secretary of State should exercise all reasonable expedition to ensure that the steps are taken which will be necessary to ensure the removal of the individual within a reasonable time. The principles applied in *Singh* were approved in *Tam Te Lam* and *R (I) v Secretary of State for the Home Department*.[10]

The case law reveals that there are a number of factors to be taken in to account **8.25** in determining whether the period of detention is reasonable. In *Singh* the applicant, Mr Hardial Singh, entered the country lawfully but committed two offences as a result of which the Secretary of State deemed his deportation to be conducive to the public good. Mr Singh did not argue with that conclusion. On the completion of his sentence he was detained under immigration powers pending removal to India. Mr Singh had fully cooperated with the authorities. The Home Office, however, were found by the judge to have been dilatory in their efforts obtain the travel documentation necessary to remove him. At the time of the hearing he had been detained for a five-month period. The judge took into account the following factors in assessing the reasonableness of the period of detention:

• the lawfulness of the applicant's presence in the UK;
• whether the Home Office had taken all the necessary action;
• whether it had taken that action promptly;
• the applicant's compliance with the action to remove him;
• the fact that the applicant had become distressed by the detention and tried to take his own life.

In the case of *R (I) v Secretary of State for the Home Department*[11] Simon Brown LJ **8.26** reviewed the case law concerning the reasonableness of the period of detention, extrapolated the relevant principles, and applied them to the facts of the case. He cited with approval the principles outlined in *Singh* and the dictum of Law J (as he then was) in *Re Wasfi Suleman Mahmod:*[12]

> While, of course, Parliament is entitled to confer powers of administrative detention without trial, the courts will see to it that where such a power is conferred the statute that confers it will be strictly and narrowly construed and its operation and effect will be supervised by the court according to high standards. In this case I regard it as entirely unacceptable that this man should have been detained for the length of time he has while nothing but fruitless negotiations have been carried on.

The approach of the Court of Appeal in *R (I)* is an instructive illustration of how **8.27** the principles of *Singh* are applied in practice. The applicant was an Afghani asylum seeker who had his application for asylum refused but had been granted

---

10 [2002] EWCA Civ 888.
11 [2002] EWCA Civ 888.
12 [1995] Imm AR 311.

indefinite leave to remain. He was convicted of indecent assault and recommended for deportation. On completion of his sentence a deportation order was made against him and he was detained for over 15 months before his release on an application for habeas corpus was ordered by the Court of Appeal. During the period of his detention he had made a further asylum claim, his claim refused, and his appeal dismissed by an Adjudicator. At the time of the order for release he still had extant rights of appeal to the Immigration Appeal Tribunal. At the time of the hearing before the Court of Appeal, the Home Office were unable to enforce returns as there were no direct flights to Afghanistan although voluntary returns via neighbouring countries were possible. The appellant was in his cell for 19 hours a day, was unable to undertake education or work due to lack of availability, and needed medication to help him sleep.

8.28   The Court of Appeal considered that the following factors were relevant to the 'reasonableness of the period of detention':

- the reference to 'a reasonable time' in *Singh* is to a reasonable further period of time having regard to the period already spent in detention (para 20);

- the likelihood or otherwise of the detainee absconding and/or re-offending is an obviously relevant circumstance. If it was highly probable that, upon release, the detainee would commit a serious offence, that would justify allowing the Secretary of State a substantially longer period of time within which to arrange the detainee's removal abroad (para 29);

- however, the relevance of the likelihood of absconding, if proved, should not be overstated. It is not a trump card to be relied on by the Secretary of State in every case where such a risk was made out regardless of all other considerations, not least the length of the period of detention, as this would be a wholly unacceptable outcome where human liberty is at stake (para 53);[13]

- the applicant's ability to end his detention by voluntary repatriation is a relevant circumstance (para 33), although the refusal of an offer of voluntary repatriation cannot make reasonable a period of detention which would otherwise be unreasonable (para 51). It is for the Secretary of State to satisfy the court that it is right to infer from the refusal by a detained person of an offer of voluntary repatriation that, if released, he or she will abscond (para 58);

- the detained asylum seeker cannot invoke the delay necessarily occasioned by his own asylum claim (and any subsequent appeal(s)) to contend that his

---

[13] But see para 77 of *R (on the appln of A) v SSHD* [2007] EWCA Civ 804 per Keene LJ 'I respectfully disagree with that part of the judgment of Dyson LJ in *R (I)* at para 53, where he stressed the need not to overstate the importance of the risk of absconding. It is, in my judgment, a factor which in most cases will be of great importance.'

removal is clearly 'not going to be possible within a reasonable time', so that he must be released (para 35);

- however, where there has been no lengthening whatever of the detention period as a result of the asylum claim, the relevant and substantial cause of the detainee's non-removal should be regarded as the political impossibility of returning him, rather than his claim for asylum (para 36);

- the burden lay on the Secretary of State to prove on the balance of probabilities that the appellant was being properly detained 'pending removal' (applying *Tam Te Lam* para 115E);

- if, before the expiry of the reasonable period, it becomes apparent that the Secretary of State will not be able to effect deportation within that reasonable period, he should not seek to exercise the power of detention (para 46);

- the conditions in which the detained person is being kept and the effect of detention on him and his family (para 48).

Applying those principles to the facts of the case Their Lordships (Mummery LJ **8.29** dissenting) held that detention of a period of 16 months was too long. The Secretary of State could establish no more than a hope of being able to remove the appellant forcibly within a few months. In those circumstances, Browne-Wilkinson LJ held that substantially more in the way of a risk of re-offending (and not merely a risk of absconding) than existed would in his judgment be necessary to have justified continuing his detention for an indeterminate further period. Whilst the appellant could, by the date of the appeal hearing, have agreed to return voluntarily to Afghanistan, that possibility arose only on the day before the hearing and it would not have been right, given his unwillingness to go (and his asylum claim), to subject him to an indeterminate period of further detention merely on that account.

In the case of *R (on the appln of A) v SSHD*,[14] the applicant refused to accept **8.30** voluntary repatriation because the situation in Somalia was volatile and chaotic. Toulson LJ held that this factor was not relevant to the assessment whether his continuing detention was lawful. It was understandable that the applicant did not wish to return to Somalia, but his legal position was that he had no right to remain in the United Kingdom and was the subject of a deportation order requiring him to leave.

It is evident from the case law discussed above that the Secretary of State frequently **8.31** encounters practical difficulties in returning applicants to their home countries.

---

[14] [2007] EWCA Civ 804.

Where removal becomes a practical impossibility or the negotiations pending their removal become are overly protracted detention will be unlawful.

8.32 Some countries will not accept the return of nationals on documents issued by the United Kingdom, and insist instead on carrying out their own inquiries before issuing their own travel documentation. Such inquiries may be protracted and the period they take is not within the control of the Home Office. Under section 34 of the Asylum and Immigration (Treatment of Claimants) Act 2004 the Secretary of State may now require a person to cooperate with the Home Office in order to obtain travel documentation. Failure to do so without reasonable excuse is an offence punishable with a prison term of up to two years.

8.33 There may also, as in the case of *R (I)*, be practical impediments to return and ongoing negotiations with receiving countries. In *Re Mahmod*[15] the High Court considered a ten-month detention to obtain travel documents excessive where nothing but fruitless negotiations had been carried on. In such cases in order to assess the legality of the continuing detention it will be necessary to attempt to establish from the Home Office when return is likely to take place.

The role of the Court

8.34 In *Karas*[16] the High Court applied *Youseff*[17] in holding that the reasonableness of the Home Secretary's view that there was a real prospect of removal is to be judged by the court as the primary decision maker. The Court is also the primary decision maker in judging the reasonableness of the length of the detention. In *R (on the appln of A) v SSHD*,[18] Toulson LJ considered the role of the Court and held that it must be for the Court to determine the legal boundaries of administrative detention. There may be incidental questions of fact which the Court may recognise that the Home Secretary is better placed to decide, and the Court will take such account of the Home Secretary's views as may seem proper. Ultimately, however, it is for the Court to decide what is the scope of the power of detention and whether it was lawfully exercised. Those two questions are often inextricably interlinked.

8.35 In *R (on the appln of A)* Toulson LJ considered that the responsibility of the Court lies at common law and does not depend on the Human Rights Act, although he stated that Human Rights Act jurisprudence would tend in the same direction. Keene LJ considered that the Court is required by section 6(1) of the

---

[15] *Re Mahmod (Wasfi)* [1995] Imm AR 311.

[16] *R (on the appln of Karas & Anor) v Secretary of State for the Home Department* [2006] EWHC 747 (Admin).

[17] *Youssef v The Home Office* [2004] EWHC 1884 (QB).

[18] [2007] EWCA Civ 804.

HRA to decide whether or not the detention of the individual is compatible or not with his rights under Article 5, because only by so doing can the Court ensure that it is acting lawfully. The Court could not do that merely by asking whether it was open to the Home Secretary to decide that the length of detention was reasonable, as opposed to whether it was actually reasonable in the eyes of the Court.

Detention in breach of Home Office policy

It was conceded on behalf of the Secretary of State in the case of *Amirthanathan*[19] that a failure to follow his own published policy constitutes an error of law entitling the Court to interfere with his decision.[20] Therefore, if a detainee falls into one of the categories of persons in respect of whom the Secretary of State operates a policy not to detain, the detention will be unlawful absent the giving of full reasons for departure from the policy. The detention of the elderly, those suffering from serious medical conditions, or the mentally ill, those where there is independent evidence that they have been tortured, and people with serious disabilities would normally be unlawful as it is the Home Office's published policy in Chapter 38.10 of the OEM not to detain these categories of people. **8.36**

An example of a case where the Secretary of State failed to follow his published policy is *R (Johnson) v SSHD*.[21] It was Home Office policy that detention in Oakington Reception Centre under the fast track would be kept under review and if the claim could not be decided within one week the detainee would be released. Mr Johnson was detained for over five weeks before the decision was made on his asylum and human rights claim and a few more weeks thereafter. The High Court held that his detention became unlawful after the sixth day in detention.[22] **8.37**

Where the policy itself is unlawful any detention pursuant to the policy will also be unlawful.[23] In *Amirthanathan* the Secretary of State had detained the applicant pursuant to a policy which was unpublished. The applicant's representatives had **8.38**

---

[19] *R (on the appln of Amirthanathan) v Secretary of State for the Home Department* [2003] EWCA Civ 1768 para 37, citing the concession made in *R (on the appln of Amirthanathan) v Secretary of State for the Home Department* [2003] EWHC 1107 (Admin).

[20] Followed in *R (on the appln of Konan) v Secretary of State for the Home Department* [2004] EWHC 22 (Admin), *R (on the appln of Johnson) v Secretary of State for the Home Department* [2004] EWHC 1550 (Admin).

[21] *R (on the appln of Johnson) v Secretary of State for the Home Department* [2004] EWHC 1550 (Admin).

[22] See also *S & Ors v SSHD* [2007] EWHC 1654 (Admin) where Williams J held that the SSHD's policy that all reasonable alternatives to detention should be considered before detention was authorised had not been followed. Since the detention of S's children had been inherent in the decision to detain S, the policy should have, and had not, been applied with full vigour.

[23] *R (on the appln of Amirthanathan) v Secretary of State for the Home Department* [2003] EWCA Civ 1768 paras 64–67.

informed the Secretary of State that they were about to commence judicial review proceedings. The applicant's representatives were unaware, because it was not known, that the policy of the immigration service, when considering the imminence of removal, was to disregard information from those acting for asylum seekers that proceedings were about to be initiated, however credible that information might be. In the circumstances the Court of Appeal found that the policy was not accessible as required by law, nor were the consequences of failing to commence proceedings foreseeable.[24]

8.39 In *Amirthanathan* the Court also held that in order to be lawful, a policy must not be arbitrary or irrational.[25] A policy that is arbitrary will also be in breach of Article 5(1)(f) ECHR. The Court of Appeal held that it was neither arbitrary nor irrational to have a policy not to have regard to mere intimations of intention to bring proceedings challenging removal, when considering whether removal is imminent. However, the policy had to be accessible in order to be lawful, which in this instance it was not.

Fairness, reasonableness, and rationality

8.40 The decision to detain or to continue detention must be in accordance with the public law requirements of fairness, reasonableness, and rationality. These issues often arise in policy cases. In *R (on the appln of I)*[26] the applicant asylum seekers claimed to be under 18 and to be entitled to benefit from the policies in force in respect of unaccompanied minors, including the presumption that, save for exceptional cases, they would not be detained. The Secretary of State disputed that they were minors. The applicants' solicitors relied on a report by a consultant paediatrician confirming that the applicants were under 18, but the Secretary of State continued detention, relying on reports prepared by social workers which came to a contrary conclusion. Detention was held to be irrational once the Secretary of State had considered the consultant's report. There was no rational basis for preferring the reports of social workers over those of a consultant paediatrician with his specialist expertise.

8.41 Detention may be unfair because it is based on a misapprehension of material facts. There is also a continuing duty to review the circumstances of the detention to ensure that continuing detention is lawful. In *R (Mohamed)*[27] the applicant sought judicial review of his continuing detention. Bail had been refused by an

---

[24] Applying *The Sunday Times v The United Kingdom* (1979) 2 EHRR 245.
[25] *Amirthanathan* para 60.
[26] *R (on the appln of I) v Secretary of State of the Home Department* [2005] EWHC 1025 (Admin).
[27] *R (Mohamed) v Secretary of State for the Home Department* [2003] EWHC 1530 (Admin).

Adjudicator on the basis of a bail summary which was prepared by the Home Office and which contained two factual inaccuracies. First, the applicant was said to have claimed asylum after the completion of his prison sentence, which the High Court considered might have given an impression of opportunism. Second, the bail summary stated that the applicant had committed a further offence after release from prison, which was simply incorrect. The Secretary of State also failed to consider properly the fact that the applicant's asylum appeal had been allowed. It was held that it was incumbent on the Secretary of State to consider the continuing detention with the utmost care and in the circumstances he had failed to do so. The detention was unlawful.

A further example of a case where the failure to review detention was unlawful is **8.42** *ex parte B*.[28] In that case the Secretary of State was found not to have considered new circumstances relating to the availability of sureties and the strength of the asylum claim. The continuing detention was held be unlawful.

Reasons for detention

Whilst there is no requirement under primary legislation to give reasons for **8.43** detention, this is done as a matter of policy. Reasons are required to be given for detention under Article 5(2) of the ECHR and the OEM acknowledges this.[29] It is Home Office policy to serve written reasons in a notice called IS 91 on detainees at the moment of their initial detention.[30] The detainee must be informed of the power under which he is detained, the reasons for the detention, the basis on which the decision was made, and his bail rights. If he cannot understand English, the reasons must be interpreted.[31] The OEM also requires regular reviews of the detention, initially after 24 hours by an inspector, and thereafter as directed, weekly and then monthly.[32]

In *R (on the appln of Faulkner)*[33] the Court held that a detainee must be told the **8.44** essential legal and the essential factual grounds for the detention and a failure to give such reasons rendered the detention unlawful.[34]

---

[28] *R v Special Adjudicator and Secretary of State for the Home Department, ex parte B* [1998] INLR 315, QBD.

[29] OEM Chapter 38.6.3.

[30] OEM Chapter 38.6.3.

[31] OEM Chapter 38.6.3.

[32] OEM, Chapter 38.8.

[33] *R (on the appln of Faulkner) v Secretary of State for the Home Department* [2005] EWHC 2567 (Admin).

[34] Applying *Taylor v Chief Constable of Thames Valley Police* [2004] 1 WLR 315.

8.45 In *Saadi v United Kingdom*[35] the ECtHR held unanimously that there was a breach of Article 5 (2) of the ECHR where the applicant had not been informed of the essential legal and factual grounds for his detention within 76 hours. A delay of this length in providing reasons for detention was not compatible with the requirement of the provision that such reasons should be given 'promptly'.

Article 5 of the European Convention on Human Rights

8.46 This Article is dealt with in detail in Chapter 5. Article 5(1)(f) states:

> 5(1) Everyone has the right to liberty and security of person. No one shall be deprived of his liberty save in the following cases and in accordance with a procedure prescribed by law:
>
> (f) the lawful arrest or detention of a person to prevent his effecting an unauthorised entry into the country or of a person against whom action is being taken with a view to deportation or extradition.

8.47 Article 5 (1) (f) therefore permits detention in two circumstances, first, to prevent unauthorised entry into the country, and second, where action is being taken with a view to deportation or extradition. In *Saadi v United Kingdom*[36] the ECtHR agreed with the House of Lords that the detention of an asylum seeker for the purposes of deciding whether to grant leave to enter on the basis of asylum was not in breach of Article 5(f). The Court did not accept the applicant's argument that, as soon as a potential immigrant has surrendered himself to the immigration authorities, he is seeking to effect an 'authorised' entry, with the result that detention could not be justified under the first limb of Article 5(1)(f). The Court agreed with the Secretary of State that, until a potential immigrant had been granted leave to remain in the country, he has not effected a lawful entry, and detention can reasonably be considered to be aimed at preventing unlawful entry.[37]

8.48 The ECtHR also agreed with the House of Lords that there was no requirement under Article 5(1)(f) that the detention of a person to prevent his effecting an unauthorised entry into the country be reasonably considered necessary in order to prevent his committing an offence or fleeing:

> All that is required is that the detention should be a genuine part of the process to determine whether the individual should be granted immigration clearance and/or asylum, and that it should not otherwise be arbitrary, for example on account of its length.[38]

---

[35] *Saadi v United Kingdom* (Application No 13229/03) (2006) All ER (D) 125 (Jul) ECtHR.
[36] *Saadi v United Kingdom* (Application No 13229/03) (2006) All ER (D) 125 (Jul) ECtHR.
[37] *Saadi* para 40.
[38] *Saadi* para 44.

In the circumstances, the government policy of detaining asylum seekers at **8.49** Oakington Detention Centre with a view to making a rapid decision on their claims was lawful.

Where action is taken with a view to deportation or extradition under the second **8.50** limb of Article 5(f) the deprivation of liberty will be justified under Article 5(1)(f) only for as long as deportation proceedings are in progress.[39] As with the first limb, there is no requirement to prove that detention be reasonably considered *necessary* in order to effect deportation or extradition.[40]

Under Article 5, detention must not be 'arbitrary'. The detention of the applicant **8.51** in *Amirthanathan*[41] was held to be arbitrary because it relied on an unpublished policy which the applicant's advisors were not aware of. Detention under Article 5 must not be disproportionate. In *Saadi*[42] the ECtHR considered that pro- portionality required that 'reasonable balance' is struck between the requirements of society and the individual's freedom. In the immigration context the Court accepted that the State has a broader discretion to decide whether to detain potential immigrants than is the case for other interferences with the right to liberty.

C. Bail

The powers to detain have been set out in Tables 8.1 and 8.2 above. In all circum- **8.52** stances where there is a power to detain, there is also a power to grant bail. Bail may be granted by the immigration authorities, by the Secretary of State, in some cases by the police, and by the Asylum and Immigration Tribunal. The powers to grant bail largely overlap.

Bail from the immigration authorities

The powers of the immigration officers to grant bail are contained in paragraphs 22, **8.53** 29(1)(2), and 34 of Schedule 2 to the 1971 Act, paragraph 2(4A), Schedule 3 of the 1971 Act and section 10(7) of the 1999 Act. Where it is an immigration officer who grants bail, he must be of the rank of a chief immigration officer;[43] where a police officer grants bail he must not be below the rank of a police inspector.[44]

---

[39] *Chahal v the United Kingdom* (1996) 23 EHRR 413.
[40] *Chahal* para 112.
[41] *Amirthanathan* [2003] EWCA Civ 1768.
[42] *Saadi* para 44.
[43] Para 22 1(A) Schedule 2, 1971 Act.
[44] Para 29(2) Schedule 2, 1971 Act.

8.54   Paragraph 22 of Schedule 2 of the 1971 and paragraph 4A of Schedule 3 of the 1971 Act deals with the grant of bail pending examination and removal. Bail may be granted by the immigration authorities to those liable to detention pending examination or pending a decision on whether to cancel leave to enter and pending the giving of removal directions.[45] A person who is, or is a suspected illegal entrant or overstayer, may also be granted bail pending the giving of directions.[46] Bail may also be granted to persons detained pending the making of a deportation order in pursuance of a court recommendation, pending a decision to make an order for deportation and where a deportation order is in force.[47] All these bail provisions also apply to those detained by the Secretary of State but only after the applicant has been detained for more than eight days.[48]

8.55   These powers to grant bail also apply to the AIT. Essentially, therefore, these paragraphs deal with the circumstances when new arrivals and those detained pending removal may be granted bail. New arrivals are not eligible for bail unless seven days have elapsed since the date of their arrival in the UK.[49] Bail may be granted by a chief immigration officer on entering into a recognizance with a condition to appear at a place and time notified in writing by an immigration officer.[50] The immigration officer may also impose further conditions in order to secure the attendance of the person bailed at the required place and time.[51] Bail may also be granted under paragraph 22 to persons against whom removal directions are in force.[52]

8.56   Paragraph 29 deals with the power to grant bail pending appeal. The immigration authorities, as well as the AIT, have power to grant bail pending appeal. As with bail under paragraph 22, bail must be granted by a chief immigration officer but may also be granted by police officer of the rank of inspector or above.[53] The same provisions with regard to recognizances apply.[54]

8.57   If, therefore, the immigration authorities have refused to grant temporary admission, an application can be made to them for a grant of bail. If a surety is available, bail may be granted where temporary admission was not. Chapter 39 of the OEM contains the Home Office policy on the grant of bail. It is recommended that advisors read Chapter 39 before making an application for bail from the

---

45 Para 22 (1)(a)(aa)(b), Schedule 2, 1971 Act.
46 Para 22 (1)(b), ibid.
47 Para 4A, Schedule 3, 1971 Act.
48 Section 62(3) NIAA 2002, s 68(1)(2) NIAA 2002.
49 Para 22 (1B), Schedule 2, 1971 Act.
50 Para 22(1A) Schedule 2, 1971 Act.
51 Para 22(2), Schedule 2, 1971 Act.
52 Para 34, Schedule 2, 1971 Act.
53 Para 29 (2) ibid.
54 Paras 29(2)(3)(4) ibid.

immigration authorities as it sets out the factors taken into account in determining whether to grant bail. With regard to sureties, it states the following at 39.6.1.

39.6 Recognizances and sureties
39.6.1 Fixing the amount of bail

> The amount of bail should be viewed in relation to the means of the applicant and his sureties, and should give a substantial incentive to appear at the time and place required. Each case should be assessed on its individual merits but a figure of between £2,000 and £5,000 per surety will normally be appropriate. Where there is a strong financial incentive to remain here, it is justifiable to fix bail (or suggesting to the adjudicator that it be fixed) at a larger sum. Property such as houses or businesses, or cars, may be offered but they are difficult to seize and should be rejected unless there are wholly exceptional circumstances in view of the potential hardship this could cause to others who have no part in the bail application.

39.6.3 Acceptable sureties

In order to be acceptable, a surety should:

- have enough money or disposable assets (clear of existing liabilities) to be able to pay the sum due if bail is forfeited;
- be aged 18 or over and settled in the United Kingdom. A person on temporary admission or with limited leave will rarely be acceptable as his own stay may be limited/curtailed;
- be a householder or at least well established in the place where he lives;
- be free of any criminal record. The gravity with which a particular offence is viewed and the consequent effect upon the bail application will be a matter for the discretion of the CIO or Secretary of State. Officers are reminded of the need to ensure that a conviction is not spent by virtue of the 1974 Rehabilitation of Offenders Act (see IDIs Chapter 32 Section 2);
- not have come to adverse notice in other immigration matters, particularly previous bail cases or applications for temporary admission;
- have a personal connection with the applicant, or be acting on behalf of a reputable organisation which has an interest in his welfare.

There must be some credible reason why a person should be prepared to act as a surety. Unsubstantiated claims to be a friend of the applicant should be treated with caution. Professional sureties suspected of acting for financial gain or with a view to aiding evasion should be rejected.

Bail from the Asylum and Immigration Tribunal

8.58 The AIT has the same powers to grant bail under paragraphs 22, 29, and 34 of Schedule 2 to the 1971 Act, paragraphs 2(4A), Schedule 3 of the 1971 Act, and section 10(7) of the 1999 Act as the immigration authorities. There is a power to grant bail in almost all circumstances where a person is administratively detained under the Immigration Acts. The only instance where there is no power to grant bail appears to be in the case of a new arrival to the UK who is detained whilst examined by an immigration officer pending a decision whether to grant or refuse leave. Such a person has no entitlement to apply for bail unless seven days has elapsed since their arrival.[55] In the circumstances, the issue of whether an immigration judge has the power to grant bail will rarely arise.

Bail pending appeal

8.59 Where a detainee has an appeal pending under Part 5 of the Nationality, Immigration and Asylum Act 2002 he may apply for bail to the AIT.[56] The decisions giving rise to a right of appeal under Part 5 are the general right of appeal under section 82, the 'upgrade' asylum appeal under section 83, and the appeal against a variation of limited leave under section 83A. The definition of a 'pending appeal' is set out at section 104 of the NIAA 2002. An appeal is pending during the period beginning when it is instituted and ending when it is finally determined, withdrawn, abandoned, or it lapses. Therefore, any person who has a live appeal against the above mentioned immigration decisions may be granted bail by the AIT.

8.60 It also appears that a detainee may apply for bail to the AIT in circumstances where he is applying to the High Court or appealing to the Court of Appeal against a decision of the AIT. This is because section 104 includes within the definition of a 'pending appeal' the following applications and appeals:

- an in-time application to the High Court for an order for reconsideration under section 103A of the 2002 Act which has either been made, could still be made, or is awaiting determination;

- where reconsideration of an appeal has been ordered under section 103(A) and has not been completed;

- where an appeal has been remitted to the Tribunal and is awaiting determination;

- where an in-time application under section 103B or 103E (to the Court of Appeal) for permission to appeal has been made, could be made, or is waiting determination;

- where an appeal under section 103B or 103E (in the Court of Appeal) is awaiting determination;

---

[55] Para 22 (1B) ibid.
[56] Para 29 (1) ibid.

- where a reference to the Court of Appeal under section 103C has been made by the High Court and is awaiting determination.

It can be seen therefore that the power to grant bail pending appeal exists through- **8.61**
out the appellate process. However, even if no appeal is outstanding, the power to grant bail is still likely to exist where a person's immigration status means that they are 'liable to detention' under the Immigration Acts.

Paragraph 30 of Schedule 2 to the 1971 requires the consent of the Secretary of **8.62**
State to the grant of bail if removal directions are in force or if the power to give removal directions may be exercised. This would appear to oblige the AIT to obtain the consent of the Secretary of State to grant bail in these circumstances. The provision is in fact not relied on by the Secretary of State, and if it were, would be likely to breach Article 5(4) of the ECHR.

Procedure on bail before the Asylum and Immigration Tribunal

The procedure for applications for bail before the AIT is governed by Part 4 **8.63**
of the Asylum and Immigration Tribunal (Procedure) Rules 2005.[57] The approach to grant of bail taken by the AIT is to be found in 'Guidance Notes for Adjudicators' (May 2003) (Third Edition). The Guidance Notes have 11 appendices, including an extract from Chapter 38 of the OEM, the UNHCR's Guidelines on the Detention of Asylum Seekers, various notices, and a surety checklist. There is a further 'Guidance Note for Adjudicators on deposit of recognizances' (June 2003).[58]

In general, Practice Directions and Guidance Notes which predated the creation **8.64**
of the AIT on 4 April 2005 ceased to have effect on this date. However, the President has confirmed[59] that members of the Tribunal are to have regard to the Guidance Notes covering bail proceedings, subject to any qualifications or modifications necessary as a result of the creation of the Tribunal and of any changes in the relevant legislation.

The application for bail should be heard within three working days of receipt of **8.65**
the application by the Tribunal unless it is received after 3.30pm in which case it will be treated as received on the next business day.[60] Controlled Legal Representation is available at bail hearings and we deal with this at 8.143 below.

---

[57] (SI 2005, No 230).
[58] All Guidance Notes can be found on the AIT website at <www.ait.gov.uk>.
[59] Introduction to consolidated Practice Direction dated 30 April 2007.
[60] Para 19.1 Practice Direction 30 April 2007.

The Application

8.66   The bail application form must be made by filing with the Tribunal the application notice on the form approved for the purpose by the President of the
Tribunal.[61] The prescribed form is the 'B1'. It can be found on the AIT website.[62]
The application must contain the applicant's full name, date of birth, date of
arrival in the UK, the address of the place where the applicant is detained, whether
an appeal to the Tribunal is pending, the address where the applicant will reside
if his application for bail is granted, or, if he is unable to give such an address, the
reason why an address is not given.[63]

8.67   The application must also state the amount of any recogizance offered by the
applicant, the full names, addresses, occupations, and dates of birth of any sureties, and the amount of the surety offered, the grounds on which the application
is made and where a previous application has been refused, the details in any
change of circumstances since the refusal. Where the applicant is aged 18 or over
the application must state whether he will, if required, agree as a condition of bail
to cooperate with electronic monitoring under section 36 of the 2004 Act. The
application must state whether an interpreter will be required at the hearing and
if so what language or dialect will be required.[64] The application must be signed
by the applicant or his representative or, in the case of an applicant who is a child
or is incapable of acting for any other reason, by a person on his behalf. [65]

8.68   The bail application should be sent to the Hearing Centre nearest to the Detention Centre where the applicant is held.[66] If the correct form is not used, one will
be faxed by the AIT to the applicant's representatives by the AIT for completion
and return.[67]

The bail hearing

8.69   Where an application for bail is filed the Tribunal must as soon as reasonably
practicable serve a copy of the application on the Secretary of State and fix a hearing.[68] As stated above, if practicable, bail hearings are listed within three working
days of receipt of the application.[69]

---

[61] Rule 38(1) Procedure Rules 2005.
[62] <www.ait.gov.uk>.
[63] Rule 38 (2) Procedure Rules 2005.
[64] Rule 38 (2) ibid.
[65] Rule 38 (3) ibid.
[66] Guidance Note on Bail (Third Edition) para 2.1.3.
[67] Ibid—a list of hearing centres can be found at Appendix 11 of the Guidance Notes on Bail.
[68] Rule 39(1) Procedure Rules 2005.
[69] Para 19.1 Practice Direction 30 April 2007.

If the Secretary of State wishes to contest the application, he must file with the **8.70**
Tribunal and serve on the applicant a written statement of his reasons for doing
so no later than 2pm on the business day before the hearing or if he was served
with notice of hearing less than 24 hours before that time, as soon as reasonably
practicable.[70] The document containing the Secretary of State's objections to bail
is called the 'bail summary'. Bail summaries can be factually incorrect and therefore applicants will need to read them to be able to deal with any errors.

The Guidance Notes state that there is a common law presumption in favour **8.71**
of bail, subject to the restrictions on the granting of bail under paragraph 30 of
Schedule 2 of the 1971 Act. Paragraph 30 (2) states that the Tribunal shall not be
obliged to release an appellant if it appears to the Tribunal that:

- the appellant, if released on bail on a previous occasion, failed to comply with
  the bail conditions;

- the appellant is likely to commit an offence unless he is retained in detention;

- the release of the appellant is likely to cause danger to public health;

- the appellant is suffering from mental disorder and his continued detention is
  necessary in his own interests or for the protection of any other person;

- the appellant is under the age of 17, arrangements ought to be made for his care
  in the event of his release, and that no satisfactory arrangements have been
  made for his care.

The burden and standard of proof in bail hearings

Given the common law presumption in favour of bail, the burden on proving the **8.72**
need for detention is on the Secretary of State. The Guidance Notes states at 2.5:

> The burden of proving that the presumption in favour of liberty does not apply lies
> on the Secretary of State. As detention is an infringement of the applicant's human
> right to liberty, you have to be satisfied to a high standard that any infringement of
> that right is essential.

With regard to the standard of proof the Guidance Notes state: **8.73**

> 2.5.3 There is no precise test laid down as to the standard of proof in bail cases.
> Useful guidance is available in the Bail Act 1976. A defendant need not be granted
> bail if the Court is satisfied 'there are substantial grounds for believing that the
> defendant, if released on bail (whether subject to conditions or not), would fail to
> surrender to custody'. It is suggested you adopt the 'substantial grounds for believ-
> ing' test which would be higher than the balance of probabilities but less than the
> criminal standard of proof.

---

[70] Rule 39 (2) Procedure Rules 2005.

Procedure at the hearing

8.74 The Guidance Notes deal with procedure at the hearing at 2.7. If the appropriate prescribed form (B1) has not been used, the Guidance notes state that the correct form should be supplied to the representatives for completion as use of this form is mandatory. Minor failures to comply with Rule 38 if they do not prejudice the Secretary of State should not prevent the hearing proceeding if the correct information as required by the Rule is then supplied.

8.75 The Guidance note then advocates a three stage approach to the application.[71] First, is this a case where bail is right in principle, subject to suitable conditions if necessary? Second, are sureties necessary? Third, are the sureties and recognizances offered satisfactory? If the immigration judge indicates that bail is right in principle, he must make it clear that this decision is subject to there being suitable and satisfactory conditions and sureties, if required.[72]

Bail in principle

8.76 What does the immigration judge look at when determining whether bail is right in principle? First, he will look at the Secretary of State's reasons for opposing bail in the bail summary. The burden of proving the need for detention and of proving the facts asserted in the bail summary is on the Secretary of State. If allegations in the bail summary are contested in evidence, the Guidance Notes state that the Secretary of State should adduce evidence, including any documents relevant to the decision to detain, in support of such allegations.[73]

8.77 If there is a dispute of fact concerning the content of the bail summary, it is prudent to put the Secretary of State on notice so that he may adduce evidence, if it exists, to prove the assertions. If the bail summary has been served in accordance with the Rules by 2pm on the day prior to the hearing,[74] there should be sufficient time for the Secretary of State to be put on notice.

8.78 If no bail summary is served in compliance with the Rules, or the bail summary is served late what effect does this have on proceedings? The Guidance Notes state at paragraph 2.7.2:

> If no bail summary is available, then you should proceed without it. This implies that bail would have to be granted. If it is provided late, then you can consider it. However if the allegations contained in it are disputed, its late submission and the lack of time given to the applicant to prepare his response to it must affect the evidential weight you can attach to it and any evidence submitted in its support.

---

[71] Para 2.7.4 Guidance Notes.
[72] Ibid.
[73] Para 2.5.3 Guidance Notes.
[74] Rule 39(2) Procedure Rules.

If the immigration judge considers the bail summary to be inadequate, the **8.79** Guidance Notes state that the Presenting Officer should be informed at the beginning of the hearing and he may be allowed a short adjournment to obtain additional information.

The applicant should respond to all the reasons given in the bail summary for **8.80** the detention. The response may be by way of written or oral evidence and submissions.

Factors to be considered

The purpose of the bail hearing is not to challenge the legality of the detention. **8.81** If the applicant contends that the detention itself is unlawful, then his remedy will be judicial review or habeas corpus (see paragraph 8.108 below). The purpose of the bail hearing is to deal with the reasons given by the Secretary of State for detaining the applicant. These reasons should have been set out firstly in the Form IS 91R (see Practice Note) and then in the bail summary.

Home Office Policy on detention is a relevant factor on a bail application as are **8.82** the UNHCR Guidelines on the detention of asylum seekers. The Guidance Notes on Bail state that immigration judges should be familiar with the Immigration Service's Policy on Detention and Temporary Release set out in Chapter 38 of the OEM and the UNHCR Guidelines and both are appended to the Guidance Notes.[75] Whilst the Policy and the Guidelines are not binding on the Tribunal, they may take them into account.

In the Guidance Notes, the factors to be considered on an application for bail are **8.83** set out at 2.6. Whilst the risk of absconding is said to be the principal factor, it is just one of the factors to take into account on the application for bail and must be balanced against other factors. The risk of absconding should not be overstated. The Court of Appeal held in *R (I)* that the risk of absconding is not a trump card to be relied on by the Secretary of State in every case where such a risk was made out regardless of all other considerations.

Immigration judges are referred in the Guidance notes to the case of *R (I) v* **8.84** *Secretary of State for the Home Department*[76] as providing guidance for cases relating to detention pending decision or appeal. We set out the list of circumstances relevant to a decision to detain taken from this case at paragraph 8.28 above.

The decision of the Tribunal on bail must be compatible with the applicant's **8.85** human rights. On a bail hearing, Articles 3 and 8 may be of relevance. If the

---

[75] Guidance Notes on Bail (3rd Edition).
[76] [2002] EWCA Civ 888.

conditions of detention are such that the threshold of a 'minimum level of severity' of harm is reached, the detention may be in breach of Article 3. This will be a matter of evidence, and it is unlikely that an applicant would make out such an allegation if the matter had not been taken up with the Home Office first. For conditions in detention to amount to a violation of Article 3 they would have to be very poor indeed.[77] Where detention separates families or the conditions of detention amount to an interference with the physical and moral integrity aspect of private life, reliance may be placed on Article 8.

8.86 An application for bail presupposes that the detention itself is lawful, and if it is alleged that the detention is unlawful under Article 5 ECHR then the appropriate course is to commence proceedings for habeas corpus or judicial review.

Bail conditions

8.87 If the Tribunal considers that bail should be granted in principle it will then move on to stage two, namely whether sureties or other conditions are necessary. Conditions as to residence, reporting, sureties, and electronic monitoring may be imposed.

8.88 The Guidance Notes deal with conditions at paragraph 2.4. The primary condition imposed on granting bail is to appear before the Tribunal or an immigration officer at a specified place and on a specified date. The Tribunal then needs to decide whether it is necessary to impose further conditions to ensure compliance with the primary condition.

8.89 The Guidance states that if it is decided that secondary conditions are necessary, it is usually appropriate to require conditions of residence and reporting to the local Police Station or Immigration Reporting Centre. The Home Office Presenting Officer will be able to supply information about the nearest place to report. The frequency of reporting is a matter for the immigration judge but the Guidance states that initially at least once a week is appropriate and this can subsequently be varied at a later hearing.[78]

8.90 The Guidance further states that the immigration judge is at liberty to impose such secondary conditions as may be considered necessary to ensure that the applicant answers his bail. However, there is no jurisdiction to impose conditions which are not necessary to ensure the applicant answers to bail, such as a condition prohibiting employment.[79]

---

[77] See, for example *Kalashnikov v Russia*, App No 47095/99.
[78] Para 2.4.5 Guidance Notes.
[79] Para 2.4.6 ibid.

Sureties

Immigration judges are instructed in the Guidance Notes that sureties are only **8.91** required where they cannot otherwise be satisfied that the applicant will observe the conditions they may wish to impose. Where there is no prospect of an applicant being able to obtain sureties, but in principle there is a case for granting bail, they should consider if more stringent conditions might meet the particular needs of the case.[80]

If the details of the surety were included in the application form, as required by **8.92** the Rules, the Secretary of State should have checked them prior to the hearing. If the details of the surety are advanced for the first time at the hearing the immigration judge may ask to check the details and the immigration judge is likely to allow them time to do so.[81]

The surety must be suitable. The immigration judge must be satisfied that the **8.93** sureties have the means to enter into the recognizances they have offered, that they understand the obligations which they will be undertaking, and that they are suitable people to undertake such obligations. The reference to suitability includes family and social ties as well as residence and financial considerations. If there is no attendance from surety and the immigration judge considers that attendance is necessary in order to carry out an assessment of suitability, the bail application may be refused.[82] In such circumstances it may be better to withdraw the bail application, as a fresh application may be made when the surety is available.

It will be in a rare case only that bail will be granted without the attendance of the **8.94** applicant and/or the sureties.[83] If bail is granted in these circumstances the immigration judge will complete a form giving authority to the Governor of the Detention Centre at which the applicant is detained and/or the Inspector of Police for the area in which the surety resides to take recognizances.

Appendix 4 to the Guidance Notes contains a notice to applicants, their repre- **8.95** sentatives, and sureties. Representatives are reminded that it is their responsibility to ensure that the proposed sureties bring with them suitable evidence to prove their identity, income, and assets. They are particularly requested to bring the following documents:

- passport or other means of establishing identity;
- if right to reside in the UK is limited, evidence of when that right expires;

---

[80] Para 2.2.3 Guidance Notes.
[81] Para 2.7.1 ibid.
[82] Para 2.2.3 ibid.
[83] Para 2.7.9 ibid.

- recent wage slips or, if self-employed, a copy of their latest set of accounts as submitted to the Inland Revenue or a letter from their accountants certifying their personal taxable income;

- bank statements and building society passbooks, preferably covering the last three months, with evidence of current balances;

- rent books or mortgage statements, together with documentation showing the address of the surety, eg current driving licence or NHS medical card;

- any documentary evidence showing the value of any property or other assets belonging to the surety.

8.96 Appendix 6 to the Guidance Notes contains a surety checklist for immigration judges. The Notes state that questions should be asked of the proposed surety on the following matters, subject to their relevance:

Identification

- The proposed surety should bring his/her passport or other means of identification.

- If his right to reside in the UK is limited, evidence of when that right expires.

- He should have proof of address, eg rent book, mortgage statement, current driving licence, or recent council tax, gas, or electricity bills.

- Obtain a telephone number for future reference.

Relationship to the applicant

- Is the surety a blood relative by marriage, or not related at all?

- How long has the surety know the applicant?

- How much contact has there been between the surety and the applicant in the UK?

- Will the applicant feel a sense of moral responsibility towards the surety?

- Will the applicant live with the surety, and what arrangements have been made?

Occupation and income of surety

- Details of employment. These will include length, position, nature of work, and hours.

- Evidence of income by way of the pay slips or bank/building society statements/passbooks. These should cover a sufficient period of time to satisfy you that the income is regular.

- If self-employed, the latest set of accounts submitted to the Inland Revenue or a statement from accountants.

Immigration judges are also advised to ask questions concerning the surety's **8.97** assets and liabilities, documentary evidence, criminal convictions, stability, and awareness of obligations.

With regard to the amount of the recognizance, the Guidance Notes state that it **8.98** must be fixed with regard to the surety's means, but must be an adequate and sufficient sum to secure attendance. The amount of the recognizance should be assessed bearing in mind the following:

- It must be realistic in the sense that it must be well within the resources of the surety, and not so high as to be prohibitive.
- It must be assessed in relation to the means of the surety alone.
- It must be sufficient to satisfy the immigration judge that the applicant and the surety will meet their obligations.
- It must be realizable in the event of forfeiture.[84]

Recognizances

Under the 1971 the immigration judge is required to take a recognizance from **8.99** the applicant before he is released on bail. If the applicant has no assets, the Guidance suggests this may be a nominal sum of £10.[85]

Where bail is granted

The Tribunal must serve written notice of its decision on the parties and the per- **8.100** son having custody of the applicant.[86] Where bail is granted, the notice must include the conditions of bail and the amount in which the applicant and any sureties are to be bound.[87] A person having custody of the applicant must release him upon being served with a copy of the decision to grant bail and being satisfied that any recognizance required as a condition of that decision has been entered into.[88]

If bail is granted pending a decision or removal it will be to an Immigration **8.101** Officer and if it is pending an appeal it will be to the Tribunal.[89] If it is granted pending a decision or removal it will be to a date when the decision or removal is expected. The Presenting Officer at the hearing will advise the immigration judge of when this is likely to be. If it is granted pending appeal, and the date of the

---

84 Para 2.2.3 Guidance Notes.
85 Para 2.42.1 Guidance Notes.
86 Rule 39(3) Procedure Rules 2005.
87 Rule 39(4) Procedure Rules 2005.
88 Rule 41 Procedure Rules 2005.
89 Para 2.7.8 Guidance Notes.

appeal hearing is known it should be to this date at the hearing centre where the appeal will be heard. It is suggested in the Guidance Notes that bail should not be granted or renewed for a period of more than three months.[90]

Where bail is refused

8.102   Where bail is refused, the notice must include reasons for the refusal.[91] If bail has been refused, the applicant has the right to make a fresh application on the same grounds and on any further grounds that may arise. Renewed applications are not a review of the previous bail decision. The immigration judge who hears the renewed application will have the reasons given by the previous immigration judge before them. Immigration judges are instructed that they should have regard to the reasons for the decision given by the previous judge and should expect to see fresh additional grounds and/or a change in circumstances.[92] The bail form (B1) requires full details of any change in circumstances since bail was refused.

Continuation of bail

8.103   If the immigration judge grants bail it will continue until the applicant is removed, he succeeds in his appeal, or he is re-detained for a breach or likely breach of his conditions of bail. An immigration judge has no power to revoke bail after it has been granted. Where bail has been granted pending an appeal, the applicant should attend as bail will have been granted on condition of this attendance. Only in exceptional circumstances will his attendance be excused such as illness or unavoidable circumstances.[93] The Tribunal has no power to require the attendance of the sureties, but the Guidance Notes say that they should be advised to attend to see that the applicant has done so.[94]

8.104   Where bail has been granted pending a decision or removal it will have been to an Immigration Officer. Provided the conditions of bail have been adhered to, the applicant will be granted temporary admission.

Variation of bail conditions

8.105   Where bail has been granted to a specified date before the Tribunal and the applicant has complied with his bail conditions in the interim, bail may be varied.

---

90   Para 2.7.8.
91   Rule 39(5) Procedure Rules 2005.
92   Para 3.1 Guidance Notes.
93   Para 4.2 Guidance Notes.
94   Para 4.2 ibid.

Conditions such as the frequency of reporting may be varied in the light of compliance.

Forfeiture

If the applicant fails to appear before the Tribunal or an immigration officer on the specified date forfeiture proceedings may be commenced.[95] The Tribunal only has jurisdiction to hear forfeiture proceedings if the applicant fails to attend. A breach of secondary conditions such as reporting to a police station or residence does not give rise to proceedings. In assessing whether and in what sum the recognizances should be forfeit, the Guidance Notes state that the following matters should be taken into account: **8.106**

- the level of their responsibility for the applicant's failure and the steps taken by them to ensure compliance;
- any steps taken by them to report any concerns to the immigration authorities;
- whether the applicant failed to comply with any secondary conditions;
- any steps taken by the sureties to ensure compliance; and
- any other explanations offered by the sureties.[96]

If the applicant and sureties fail to appear without explanation, the whole of the recognizance is likely to be forfeit. **8.107**

High Court remedies

Habeas corpus

There are two remedies available for challenging detention in the High Court, namely habeas corpus and judicial review. Habeas corpus is an ancient remedy dating back to the 13th century which lies both at common law and statute where a person is illegally imprisoned or detained without legal justification.[97] The distinction between habeas corpus and judicial review was set out by Lord Donaldson of Lymington MR in *R v Home Secretary ex p, Cheblak* [1991] 1 WLR 890 at 894: **8.108**

> A writ of habeas corpus will issue where someone is detained without any authority or the purported authority is beyond the powers of the person authorising the detention and so is unlawful. The remedy of judicial review is available where the decision or action sought to be impugned is within the powers of the person taking it but, due to procedural error, a misapprehension of the law, a failure to take account of relevant

---

[95] Para 31 Schedule 3 1971 Act.
[96] Guidance Notes, para 6.4.
[97] The right to a writ of habeas corpus exists at common law (*Ex parte Besset* (1844) 6 QB 481) independently of any statute although the right has been confirmed and regulated by statute.

matters, or taking account of irrelevant matters or the fundamental unreasonableness of the decision or action, it should never have been taken.

8.109 It is frequently the case that the challenge to the decision to detain raises issues concerning both the lawfulness of the power and the exercise of the power to detain. In such cases both procedures should be used.

8.110 The principles which the Court will apply will be the same whether the application is for habeas corpus or judicial review.[98] If the applicant makes out a prima facie case that he has been unlawfully detained[99] the burden of proof rests with the immigration authorities to show that he has been lawfully detained.[100] The standard of proof on the immigration authorities is the civil standard, but given that issues of personal liberty are at stake, the degree of probability required is high.[101] However, where the order for detention and removal of a person as an illegal entrant is completely in order, it is prima facie good and the burden is on the applicant to show that he is being unlawfully detained, for example by showing that his passport had been stamped with lawful authority.[102]

8.111 An application for a writ of habeas corpus is entitled to be treated as urgent business by the High Court because it concerns the liberty of the subject. It is given precedence over all other proceedings before the Court or judge on the day which it is made.[103] It will be unusual for an application for habeas corpus to be made in isolation as the statutory powers to detain are so wide. There will be instances however, where there is no power to detain because, for example, it is impossible to remove someone and therefore the detention is not 'pending removal'. In such circumstances the issue of a writ will be appropriate.

8.112 The procedure for an application for a writ of habeas corpus is set out at RSC Order 54. The application is made without notice in the first instance. Unless the application is made on behalf of a child, upon the hearing, if the Court gives leave, the application is usually adjourned for notice to be served on the persons directed by the Court. If the application succeeds at the adjourned hearing the writ is ordered to issue. The application is made to a judge in the High Court unless the Court directs it must be made to the Divisional Court of the QBD.

---

98 *Khawaja v Secretary of State for the Home Department* [1984] AC 74 at 124.

99 Because, for example the applicant's leave to enter is valid, see *Khawaja v Secretary of State for the Home Department* [1984] AC 74 at 124.

100 Ibid at para 101, [1983] 1 All ER 765 at 774–775, HL per Lord Wilberforce, at 112 and 782-783 per Lord Scarman.

101 Ibid.

102 *R v Secretary of State ex parte Choudhary* [1978] 1 WLR 1177.

103 CPR Sch 1 RSC Ord 54 1 (1).

In an application for habeas corpus the Court will adopt the 'most anxious scru-
tiny' test that was found to apply to asylum cases in *R v Secretary of State ex parte
Bugdaycay* [1987] 1 AC 514; *R v Secretary of State ex parte Osman* [1993] COD 39
(Woolf LJ and Pill J).

8.113

Judicial review

In judicial review proceedings, as with habeas corpus, the burden of proving that
the power to detain exists and that it is exercised pursuant to a statutory purpose
is on the Secretary of State.[104] As with habeas corpus, the standard of proof on the
immigration authorities is the civil standard, but given that issues of personal liberty are at stake, the degree of probability required is high.[105] Where the immigration authorities' power to detain depends on the precedent establishment of an
objective fact (for example that an immigrant's leave to enter was fraudulently
obtained), the Courts will decide whether the fact exists. They will not limit
themselves to deciding whether the immigration authorities had reasonable
grounds for believing the fact to exist.[106]

8.114

Judicial review proceedings are therefore appropriate to challenge decisions to
detain which are alleged to be in breach of, or an improper application of Home
Office Policy; where the policy itself is alleged to be unlawful; where the policy
has been exercised unreasonably or arbitrarily and where the length of the detention is unreasonable. In the case of *Khadir*[107] the House of Lords held that the
power to detain exists as long as the Secretary intends to remove a person and
there is some prospect of doing so. The length of the detention does not go to the
question of the existence of power to detain but to reasonableness of the detention. Hence, the appropriate remedy where the length of detention is reasonable
is judicial review rather than habeas corpus.

8.115

Compensation for unlawful detention

If a person has been unlawfully detained under the immigration acts he may
bring a claim for damages for false imprisonment, an action under the Human
Rights Act, or a claim for misfeasance in public office. These are private law
causes of action which may be brought in the county court.

8.116

A claim for damages may also be included in a claim for judicial review.[108] The
claim must, however, be included in addition to a claim for one of the judicial

8.117

---

[104] *Khawaja v SSHD* at para 101, [1983] 1 All ER 765 at 774–775, HL per Lord Wilberforce, at
112 and 782–783 per Lord Scarman.
[105] *Khawaja* see above.
[106] *Khawaja* at paras 104-105 and 776-777.
[107] *R v Secretary of State for the Home Department ex parte Khadir* [2005] UKHL 39.
[108] Supreme Court Act s 31(4).

review remedies. Damages will be awarded only if the claimant can establish a private law cause of action or a claim under the Human Rights Act 1998.[109] The judicial review procedure does not therefore create a remedy in damages, but means that a claim for damages may be made ancillary to a claim for judicial review.

8.118 In *ID v Home Office*[110] the claimants, who were Czech Roma, were found by the Court of Appeal to have been unlawfully detained causing post-traumatic stress disorder and depression. The Court held that it was established law that aliens had the same civil rights as British citizens and that it had been established in *Khawaja*[111] that the rule of law extended to aliens subject to administrative detention. Further, immigration officers were not immune from suit and could be sued for false imprisonment on a strict liability basis.

8.119 The case law does not give any particular guidance on the assessment of damages for unlawful detention in immigration cases. The largest body of case law in respect of damages for false imprisonment relates to civil actions against the police and courts have followed the same approach in immigration cases.

D. Temporary Admission

8.120 A person who is liable to detention under Schedule 2 to the 1971 Act may also be temporarily admitted to the United Kingdom on the written authority of an immigration officer or the Secretary of State.[112] A person who is detained under the same powers may be granted 'temporary release' under the same provisions.[113] There is a presumption under Home Office policy[114] in favour of temporary admission or release. Temporary admission and temporary release are generally both referred to as temporary admission and we use this term to mean both throughout this chapter.

8.121 Temporary admission may be subject to restrictions as to residence, employment, or occupation and reporting to a police station or an immigration officer or the Secretary of State.[115] These restrictions may be varied and both the Secretary of

---

[109] *R (Bernard) v Enfield BC* [2002] EWHC 2282; *Anufrijeva v Southward LBC* [2003] EWCA 1406, [2004] QB 1124; and *R (Greenfield) v Secretary of State for the Home Department* [2005] 1 WLR 673.

[110] [2005] EWCA Civ 38.

[111] *Khawaja v SSHD* [1983] 1 All ER 765.

[112] Immigration Act 1971 Schedule 2, para 21 (1)(immigration officers); Nationality and Immigration Act 2002 section 62(3)(b) Secretary of State.

[113] See 112 above.

[114] Chapter 38 Operational Enforcement Manual.

[115] Immigration Act 1971 Schedule 2, para 21 (2); Nationality, Immigration and Asylum Act 2002, s 63 (3)(b).

State and an immigration officer have the power to vary restrictions imposed by the other.[116] A failure to observe a restriction without reasonable excuse constitutes an offence under section 24(1)(e) of the 1971 Act and may lead to detention or re-detention.

Release on temporary admission is without prejudice to the power to detain at a later time,[117] although such detention may be unlawful if there is no change of circumstances. Equally, a person who is detained may subsequently be granted temporary admission. A person who has been granted temporary admission is deemed not to have 'entered' the UK.[118] They will not 'enter' the UK unless and until granted leave to enter.   **8.122**

The first step to gaining temporary admission is to approach the official in the Home Office with conduct of the case. Clearly the availability of a residential address is an issue as are the effects on the applicant of the detention. When a person is released on temporary admission, he should be served with an IS 96 informing him of his release and the restrictions imposed on him.[119]   **8.123**

Restrictions on temporary admission

As stated at 8.121 above, temporary admission may be subject of conditions. In addition to the above restrictions section 36 of the AITC Act 2004 allows electronic monitoring to be made part of the residence and reporting conditions.   **8.124**

Residence

Obtaining the grant of temporary admission is problematic if the applicant has no residential address. Asylum seekers may be entitled to accommodation through NASS. A residence restriction may also be imposed on an asylum-seeker under section 70 of the NIAA 2002 requiring him or his dependants to reside at an induction centre for a period of 14 days.   **8.125**

Reporting

Persons subject to reporting restrictions may be required to report to a police station, a reporting centre, or a port. The policy on reporting is set out at Chapter 38.20.2 of the OEM. It states that persons subject to reporting restrictions should not be required to report to police stations if they could report to an immigration reporting centre instead. Where reporting to a police station is considered essential, this should not be more frequently than monthly (unless authorised by an   **8.126**

---

[116] Nationality, Immigration and Asylum Act s 62 (4)(a)(b).
[117] Immigration Act 1971 Schedule 2, para 21 (1).
[118] Immigration Act 1971, s 11(1).
[119] Chapter 38.20.4 OEM.

inspector in exceptional circumstances). If the case remains unresolved after three years and the offender has abided by the terms of his temporary admission or release on restrictions reporting restrictions should be lifted (unless removal is imminent).

Employment

8.127 Under paragraph 360 of the Immigration Rules an asylum applicant may seek permission from the Secretary of State to take up employment if his asylum application has not been determined within one year of making the application. Under paragraph 360A if he is granted such permission it shall only be until such time as his application has been determined.

Electronic monitoring

8.128 Under section 36 of the AITC Act 2004, where a residence restriction is imposed as a condition of temporary admission the person may be required to cooperate with electronic monitoring.[120] Failure to comply with the requirement to cooperate is treated as failure to observe the residence restriction.[121] Where a reporting restriction could be imposed as a condition of temporary admission, a person may be required to cooperate with electronic monitoring instead.[122] This requirement is treated as a reporting restriction.

8.129 Electronic monitoring can take the form of tagging, which involves wearing an electronic bracelet that sends a signal to a receiver at their home address, reporting by voice recognition technology, and tracking which involves the use of global satellite technology (GPS) to establish the individual's whereabouts. The tracking by GPS, whilst technically feasible, is not yet available.

8.130 When person makes an asylum claim when he already has leave to enter or remain in the United Kingdom he may be subject to the same restrictions as a person with temporary admission, namely residence, reporting, and employment.[123] His dependants may also be subject to the same restrictions. If the asylum seeker or his dependant fails to comply with a restriction, he is liable to detention in the same way as a person with temporary admission.[124] The purpose of this section is to ensure that all asylum seekers are subject to the same process.[125]

---

[120] Section 36(2)(a) AITC Act 2004.
[121] Section 36(2)(b) AITC Act 2004.
[122] Section 36(3)(a) AITC Act 2004.
[123] Section 71 NIA Act 2002.
[124] Section 71(3)(a) NIA 2002.
[125] Explanatory Notes to 2002 Act.

Temporary admission is generally granted for a certain period, after which it will **8.131** either be renewed, if the immigration action is still pending, or the person may be detained if departure is about to be enforced. It may also end if a period of leave is granted. Temporary admission may be renewed in writing and does not necessarily involve the attendance of the person.

The issue of whether leave to enter should be granted instead of temporary admis- **8.132** sion where removal of a person is not possible was determined in the House of Lords in the case of *Khadir*.[126] The appellant argued that due to the impossibility of removing him to his home country, Iraq, he should be granted leave to enter rather than temporary admission. He contended principally that because of the continuing inability to find a safe route for his return to the Kurdish Autonomous Area, there was no longer power to authorise his temporary admission under Schedule 2 so that the Secretary of State had no alternative but to grant him exceptional leave to enter. In summary the appellants argued that the power to detain under Schedule 2 exists only when removal is 'pending'; removal cannot be said to be 'pending' unless it will be possible to effect it within a reasonable time; since removal was not 'pending', they were not liable to be detained. The limitation was upon the existence and not merely the exercise of the detention power.

The House of Lords disagreed, holding that the true position is that 'pending' **8.133** means no more than 'until'. So long as the Secretary of State remains intent upon removing the person and there is some prospect of achieving this, paragraph 16 of Schedule 2 authorises detention meanwhile. Whilst it may become unreasonable actually to detain the person pending a long delayed removal, that does not mean that the power has lapsed. He remains 'liable to detention' and the possibility of his temporary admission in lieu of detention arises under paragraph 21.

The House of Lords did however consider that: **8.134**

> There may come a time when the prospects of the person ever being able safely to return, whether voluntarily or compulsorily, are so remote that it would irrational to deny him the status which would enable him to make a proper contribution to the community here, but that is another question. It certainly did not arise on the facts of this case.[127]

In *SSHD v S & Ors*[128] the Court of Appeal held that temporary admission is avail- **8.135** able, as an alternative to detention, for people who have arrived in the UK, pending their examination by an immigration officer and pending a decision to grant or refuse them leave to enter. It is not intended for those who have been already

---

[126] *R (on the appln of Khadir) v Secretary of State for the Home Department* [2005] UKHL 39, [2006] 1 AC 207, [2005] 4 All ER 114
[127] Per Baroness Hale, para 4.
[128] [2006] EWCA Civ 1157

examined by an immigration officer and refused leave to enter, but who have been found on appeal not to be removable, because removal would breach their human rights. Leave to enter must be granted to such people. The Secretary of State's policy of keeping them on temporary admission was not lawful as it was ultra vires the 1971 Act.

E. Fast Tracking

8.136 The policy on 'fast track' cases is contained in Chapter 38.4 of the OEM. The list of people considered suitable by the Home Office for fast tracking is contained in the 'Detained Fast Track Processes Suitability List' (see below). Fast track cases are cases that are considered capable of being decided quickly and where detention is used as a means of speeding up the decision-making and appeals process. The Home Office also operates a policy on where the strict timetable should be enlarged, 'Detained fast track flexibility', which can be found on the Home Office website under Law and Policy. The fast track process was first operated for asylum seekers in March 2000 at Oakington Reception Centre. Detention for a short period of time to enable a rapid decision to be taken on an asylum/human rights claim has been upheld as lawful by the ECtHR.[129]

8.137 From 7 November 2002 a separate procedure was introduced for dealing with cases which were considered capable of being certified as clearly unfounded under section 94 of the Nationality, Immigration and Asylum Act 2002 ('non-suspensive cases', see Chapter 6). In April 2003 a 'Detained Fast Track' process was set up at Harmondsworth which includes an expedited in-country appeals procedure for male claimants. In May 2005, the Detained Fast Track was expanded to include the processing of female claimants at Yarls Wood.

8.138 The OEM instructs officers to consider whether asylum seekers meet the Detained Fast Track Suitability List criteria. All potentially suitable applicants must be referred to the National Intake Unit (NIU) Oakington coordinator who will confirm whether they are accepted into either the process at Oakington, Harmondsworth, or Yarl's Wood.

8.139 The OEM states that any claim may be referred to the Detained Fast Track, whatever the nationality or country of origin of the applicant, where it appears after screening to be one that may be decided quickly. If an asylum seeker is a national of the countries listed on the Detained Fast Track Suitability List he is likely be referred to the NIU unless he falls within one of the excluded categories. The following

---

[129] *Saadi v United Kingdom* (Application No 13229/03) (2006) All ER (D) 125 (Jul) ECtHR.

categories of people set out at 38.4 of the OEM are considered by the Home Office to be usually unsuitable for the Detained Fast Track:

- unaccompanied minors (always unsuitable, see 38.9 Young Persons);
- age dispute cases—the policy of detaining age dispute cases for the purposes of Fast Tracking was updated in February 2006;
- disabled applicants, except the most easily manageable;
- pregnant females of 24 weeks and above;
- any person with a medical condition which requires 24-hour nursing or medical intervention;
- anybody identified as having an infectious/contagious disease;
- anybody presenting with acute psychosis, eg schizophrenia, and requiring hospitalization;
- anybody presenting with physical and/or learning disabilities requiring 24-hour nursing care;
- violent or uncooperative cases, for non-suspensive appeal nationalities;
- those with criminal convictions, except where specifically authorised;
- where detention would be contrary to published criteria.

Where there is a dispute over age, the policy states that applicants claiming to be **8.140** under 18 should be accepted into Detained Fast Track processes only if one or more of the following criteria apply:

- there is credible and clear documentary evidence that they are 18 years of age or over;
- a full 'Merton-compliant' age assessment by Social Services is available stating that they are 18 years of age or over. Assessments completed by Social Services' Emergency Duty Teams are not acceptable evidence of age;
- their physical appearance/demeanour very strongly indicates that they are significantly 18 years of age or over and no other credible evidence exists to the contrary.

Age dispute cases that do not fall within at least *one* of the criteria above are not **8.141** considered suitable for Detained Fast Track. Officials are instructed that if there is any room for doubt as to whether a person is under 18 they should not be referred to the National Intake Unit.

Fast track cases have their own procedure rules, the Asylum and Immigration **8.142** Tribunal (Fast Track Procedure) Rules 2005. A successful application for bail will take a case out of the fast track.

F. Controlled legal representation (CLR)

8.143 Funding is available for bail applications to the AIT through the Legal Services Commission. In general, CLR may be available for appeals before the AIT, and applications under section 104A to the High Court provided that the funding criteria are met. CLR for bail applications and immigration appeals is in the form of 'Full Representation', which means it will cover advocacy at the bail hearing.

8.144 The 'General Funding Code' applies to applications for legal funding for bail applications and immigration appeals.[130] This involves a 'means and a merits test'. The General Funding Code states that CLR is not available if alternative funding is available to an applicant.

8.145 The first test is the 'merits test'. CLR will be refused if the chances of achieving a successful outcome for the client are unclear or borderline, save where the case has a significant wider public interest, is of overwhelming importance to the client, or raises significant human rights issues. CLR will always be refused if the prospects of success are poor.

8.146 The definitions of these terms are provided in the Funding Code.[131] In this context, 'borderline' means that the prospects are not poor, but because there are difficult disputes of fact, law, or expert evidence it is not possible to say that the prospects of success are better than 50 per cent. 'Poor' means clearly less than 50 per cent so that the claim is likely to fail. 'Unclear' means that the case cannot be put into a particular category because further investigation is needed. The expression 'overwhelming importance to the client' means a case which has exceptional importance to the client beyond the monetary value, because the case concerns life, liberty, or personal safety of the client, his or her family, or a roof over their heads. 'Wider public interest' means the potential of the proceedings to produce real benefits for individuals other than the client.

8.147 The second test is the cost-benefit test. Unless the case has a significant wider public interest, CLR will be refused unless the likely benefits to be gained from the proceedings justify the likely costs. The test is based on an analysis of what the hypothetical privately paying client would be prepared to do; so if the reasonable privately paying client would be prepared to take the proceedings, having regard to the prospects of success and all the other circumstances, CLR will be granted.

8.148 CLR is only available from those suppliers who have a contract with the Legal Services Commission, details of which may be founds on their website. Most

---

[130] 'Legal Funding Code' Legal Services Commission Manual—<www.legalservices.gov.uk>.
[131] At 2.3 'Merits, Costs and Damages'

suppliers are able to take decisions on eligibility for CLR through 'devolved powers'. Others, however, need to make an application on a case by case basis to the Legal Services Commission before they are granted CLR.

G. Practice and Procedure Note

Home Office policies

Operation Enforcement Manual—Chapter 38

This chapter of the OEM sets out the general policy on detention and the current version was published in the Autumn of 2005. Readers should be aware that Home Office policy is subject to frequent alteration and the Home Office website should be checked regularly (<www.ind.gov.uk>). The relevant extracts of Chapter 38 are set out below. **8.149**

Form IS 91R

The Home Office uses various forms in connection with detention. The policy on the use of these forms is to be found in Chapter 38 of the OEM (IS 91RA 'Risk Assessment' (see 38.6.1), IS 91 'Detention Authority' (see 38.6.2), IS 91R 'Reasons for detention' (see 38.6.3), and IS 91M 'Movement notification' (see 38.6.4)). We set out the details of Form IS 91R which is the form that is given to detainees on their detention and informs them of the reasons for detention. This form was held to be an important part of published policy in *Amirthanathan* [2003] EWCA Civ 1768 and failure to serve this document within 76 hours was held to be unlawful under Article 5 (2) ECHR in *Saadi v United Kingdom* (Application No 13229/03) (2006) All ER (D) 125 (Jul) ECtHR. **8.150**

Home Office policy on removal

The Home Office policy on removal where judicial review proceedings have been implemented was revised and published in March 2007. That policy and the accompanying Practice Direction are also set out in the Practice Note accompanying the Certification and Removal Chapter. **8.151**

Chapter 38—Detention and temporary release

38.1 Policy

General   In the 1998 White Paper 'Fairer, Faster and Firmer—A Modern Approach to Immigration and Asylum',the Government made it clear the power to detain must be retained in the interests of maintaining effective immigration control. However, the White Paper confirmed that there was a presumption in favour of temporary admission or release and that, wherever possible, we would use alternatives to detention (see 38.20 and Chapter 39). The White Paper went on to say that detention would most usually be appropriate:

- to effect removal;
- initially to establish a person's identity or basis of claim; or
- where there is reason to believe that the person will fail to comply with any conditions attached to the grant of temporary admission or release.

Use of detention   In all cases detention must be used sparingly, and for the shortest period necessary. It is not an effective use of detention space to detain people for lengthy periods if it would be practical to effect detention later in the process once any rights of appeal have been exhausted. A person who has an appeal pending or representations outstanding might have more incentive to comply with any restrictions imposed, if released, than one who is removable. The routine use of prison accommodation to hold detainees ended in January 2002 in line with the Government's strategy of detaining in dedicated removal centres. Nevertheless, the Government also made clear that it will always be necessary to hold small numbers of individual detainees in prison for reasons of security and control. There is a presumption in such cases of transfer to a removal centre in Britain unless the person concerned expresses a desire to remain in Northern Ireland.

38.1.1.2 Article 8 of the ECHR

Article 8(1) of the ECHR provides:

Everyone has the right to respect for private and family life . . ..

It may be necessary on occasion to detain the head of the household only, thus separating a family. Article 8 is a qualified right. Interference with the right to family life is permissible under Article 8(2) if it is (i) in accordance with the law; (ii) for a legitimate aim and (iii) proportionate. It is well established that the interests of the State in maintaining an effective immigration policy for the economic well-being of the country and for the prevention of crime and disorder, justifies interference with rights under Article 8(1). It is therefore arguable that a decision to detain which interferes with a person's right to family life in order to enforce immigration control and maintain an effective immigration policy pursues a legitimate aim and is in accordance with the law. But it would have to be shown to a court that the decision to detain (and thereby interfere with family life) was proportionate to the legitimate aim pursued. Assessing whether the interference is proportionate involves balancing the legitimate aim in Article 8(2) against the seriousness of the interference with the person's right to respect for their family life. The conclusion reached will depend on the specific facts of each case and will therefore differ in every case.

38.3 Factors influencing a decision to detain (excluding pre-decision fast track cases)

1. There is a presumption in favour of temporary admission or temporary release.
2. There must be strong grounds for believing that a person will not comply with conditions of temporary admission or temporary release for detention to be justified.
3. All reasonable alternatives to detention must be considered before detention is authorised.
4. Once detention has been authorised, it must be kept under close review to ensure that it continues to be justified.
5. Each case must be considered on its individual merits.

The following factors must be taken into account when considering the need for initial or continued detention.

For detention:

- What is the likelihood of the person being removed and, if so, after what timescale?
- Is there any evidence of previous absconding?
- Is there any evidence of a previous failure to comply with conditions of temporary release or bail?
- Has the subject taken part in a determined attempt to breach the immigration laws (eg entry in breach of a deportation order, attempted or actual clandestine entry)?
- Is there a history of complying with the requirements of immigration control (eg by applying for a visa, further leave, etc)?
- what are the person's ties with the United Kingdom? Are there close relatives (including dependants) here? Does anyone rely on the person for support? Does the person have a settled address/employment?
- What are the individual's expectations about the outcome of the case? Are there factors such as an outstanding appeal, an application for judicial review, or representations which afford incentive to keep in touch?

Against detention:

- Is the subject under 18?
- Has the subject a history of torture?
- Has the subject a history of physical or mental ill health?

(See also sections 38.6—Detention Forms, 38.7—Detention Procedures, and 38.9—Special Case.)

38.9 Special cases
38.9.1 Detention of women

Pregnant women should not normally be detained. The exceptions to this general rule are where removal is imminent and medical advice does not suggest confinement before then, or, for pregnant women of less than 24 weeks, at Oakington and Yarl's Wood as part of a fast-track process.

38.9.2   Spouses of British citizens or EEA nationals

Immigration offenders who are living with their settled British spouses may only be detained with the authority of an inspector/senior caseworker in the relevant case-working section. Where strong representations for temporary release continue to be received, the decision to detain must be reviewed by an Assistant Director as soon as is practicable. If an offender is married to an EEA national, detention should not be considered unless there is strong evidence available that the EEA national spouse is no longer exercising treaty rights in the UK, or if it can be proved that the marriage was one of convenience and the parties had no intention of living together as man and wife *from the outset of the marriage*. For further guidance, refer to Chapter 36.5 and 36.5.1.

38.9.3   Young Persons

Unaccompanied minors (ie persons under the age of 18) must only ever be detained in the most exceptional circumstances and then *only normally overnight*, with appropriate care, whilst alternative arrangements for their care and safety are made. This includes age dispute cases where we are treating the person concerned as a minor. This exceptional measure is intended to deal with unexpected situations where it is necessary to detain unaccompanied minors very briefly for their care and safety. In circumstances where responsible family or friends in the community cannot care for children they should be placed in the care of the local authority as soon as practicable. In all cases, unaccompanied young persons may only be detained with the authority of an inspector/senior caseworker in the relevant caseworking section. An Assistant Director must review detention at the earliest opportunity and in every case of an unaccompanied child as soon as detention has exceeded 24 hours.

Juveniles may only be detained in a place of safety as defined in the Children and Young Persons Act 1933 (for England and Wales), the Social Work (Scotland) Act 1968 (for Scotland) or the Children and Young Persons Act (Northern Ireland) 1968 (for Northern Ireland). The Children and Young Persons Act 1933 defines a place of safety as 'any home provided by a local authority under Part 11 of the Children Act 1948, any remand home or police station or any hospital, surgery or any other suitable place, the occupier of which is willing temporarily to receive a child or young person'. The Social Work (Scotland) Act 1968 defines a place of safety as 'any residential or other establishment provided by a local authority, a police station, or any hospital, surgery or other suitable place, the occupier of which is willing temporarily to receive a child'. The Children and Young Persons Act (Northern Ireland) 1968 defines a place of safety as 'any remand home, any home provided by [the Ministry of Home Affairs] under Part VII, any constabulary station, any hospital or surgery, or any other suitable place, the occupier of which is willing temporarily to receive a child or young person'. If detention accommodation is required exceptionally for a young person, the request must be made via the DEPMU CIO (see 38.12).

38.9.3.1 *Persons claiming to be under 18*

Sometimes people over the age of 18 claim to be minors in order to prevent their detention or effect their release once detained. In all such cases people claiming to be under the age of 18 must be referred to the Refugee Council's Children's Panel. The Panel can be contacted at:

The Refugee Council Panel of Advisers for Unaccompanied Refugee Children, 240-250 Ferndale Road,
London SW9 8BB
Tel: 020 7582 4947
Fax: 020 7820 3005

IND will accept an individual as under 18 (including those who have previously claimed to be an adult) unless one or more of the following criteria apply:

- there is credible and clear documentary evidence that they are 18 years of age or over;
- a full 'Merton-compliant' age assessment by Social Services is available stating that they are 18 years of age or over (note that assessments completed by social services emergency duty teams are not acceptable evidence of age);
- their physical appearance/demeanour very strongly indicates that they are significantly 18 years of age or over and no other credible evidence exists to the contrary.

IND does not commission medical age assessments. However, the claimant may submit medical age assessment independently. This must be considered and due weight must be attached to it when considering an age dispute case. It should be noted though that the margin for error in these cases can be as large as five years either way. This is a complex area and, if in doubt, caseworkers should seek the advice of the Children and Family Asylum Policy Team in the Asylum Appeals Policy Directorate. Once treated as a minor the applicant must be released as soon as suitable alternative arrangements have been made for their care. Where an applicant claims to be a minor but their appearance very *strongly* suggests that they are significantly 18 years of age, or over the applicant should be treated as an adult until such time as credible documentary or other persuasive evidence such as a full 'Merton-compliant' age assessments by Social Services is produced which demonstrates that they are the age claimed, and the appropriate entry made in section 1 of the IS 91. In borderline cases it will be appropriate to give the applicant the benefit of the doubt and to deal with the applicant as a minor. It is IND policy not to detain minors other than in the most exceptional circumstances. However, where the applicant's appearance very *strongly* suggests that they are an adult and the decision is taken to detain it should be made clear to the applicant and their representative that:

- we do not accept that the applicant is a minor and the reason for this (for example, visual assessment suggests the applicant is18 years of age or over); and
- in the absence of acceptable documentation or other persuasive evidence the applicant is to be treated as an adult.

38.9.4 Families

The decision to detain an entire family should always be taken with due regard to Article 8 of the ECHR (see 38.1.1.2). Families, including those with children, can be detained on the same footing as all other persons liable to detention. This means that families may be detained in line with the general detention criteria (see 38.3). Form IS 91 must be issued for each person detained including for each minor.

Detention of an entire family must be justified in all circumstances and, as in any case, there will continue to be a presumption in favour of granting temporary release. Detention must be authorised by an inspector at whatever stage of the process it is considered necessary and, although it should last only for as long as is necessary, it is not subject to a particular time limit. Family detention accommodation should be pre-booked by arrangement with MODCU. Full details of all family members to be detained must be provided to MODCU. As a matter of policy we should aim to keep the family as a single unit. However, it will be appropriate to separate a child from its parents if there is evidence that separation is in the best interests of the child. The local authority's social services department will make this decision. In such cases, prior arrangement and authority will be required from MODCU and the child's parents should provide agreement in writing. As long as the child is taken into care in accordance with the law, and following a decision of a competent authority, Article 8 of the ECHR will not be breached (see 38.1.1.2). No families should be detained simply because suitable accommodation is available.

38.10 Persons considered unsuitable for detention

Certain persons are normally considered suitable for detention in only very exceptional circumstances, whether in dedicated IS accommodation or elsewhere. Others are unsuitable for IS detention accommodation because their detention requires particular security, care and control.

The following are normally considered suitable for detention in only very exceptional circumstances, whether in dedicated IS detention accommodation or elsewhere:

- unaccompanied children and persons under the age of 18 (but see 38.9.3 above);
- the elderly, especially where supervision is required;
- pregnant women, unless there is the clear prospect of early removal and medical advice suggests no question of confinement prior to this (but see 38.4 above for the detention of women in the early stages of pregnancy at Oakington or Yarl's Wood);
- those suffering from serious medical conditions or the mentally ill;
- those where there is independent evidence that they have been tortured;
- people with serious disabilities.

38.10.1 Criteria for detention in prison

Immigration detainees should only be held in prison establishments when they present specific risk factors that indicate they are unsuitable for immigration removal centres, for reasons of security or control. Immigration detainees will only normally be held in prison accommodation in the following circumstances:

- national security—where there is specific (verified) information that a person is a member of a terrorist group or has been engaged in terrorist activities;
- criminality—those detainees who have completed prison sentences of four years or more, have been involved in the importation of Class A drugs, committed serious offences involving violence, or committed a serious sexual offence requiring registration on the sex offenders' register;
- security—where the detainee has escaped or attempted to escape from police, prison, or immigration custody, or planned or assisted others to do so;
- control—engagement in serious disorder, arson, violence, or damage, or planning or assisting others to so engage.

When a detainee meets the above criteria DEPMU will refer them to the Population Management Unit (PMU) of the National Offender Management Service (NOMS) who will consider their allocation to a prison.

Where it is agreed with the DEPMU CIO that a person normally considered unsuitable may, exceptionally, be detained in a dedicated IS removal centre, full details must initially be detailed on the IS 91RA part A and entered on the 'risk factors' section of form IS 91 served on the detaining agent (see 38.6).

All cases who have completed a prison sentence will be assessed by DEPMU on an individual basis as to whether they should remain in prison or be transferred to an IS removal centre. Any individual may request a transfer from prison to an IS removal centre and, if rejected by DEPMU, will be given reasons for this decision.

38.11 Dual detention

38.11.1 Detention of illegal entrants and those subject to administrative removal who are facing or have been convicted of criminal offences

Whilst detention on criminal charges does not affect a person's liability to removal as an illegal entrant or a person liable to administrative removal, it is not practice to remove the person where criminal charges are extant. Officers must not seek to influence police decisions about whether or not to pursue criminal matters.

Where an illegal entrant or person subject to administrative removal is convicted of a criminal offence and recommended for deportation, this should be considered by CCT before removal is enforced. In the event of an illegal entrant/person subject to administrative removal being convicted of a serious offence but not recommended for deportation by the Court, CCT may wish to consider non-conducive deportation under section 3(5)(a) of the 1971 Act (as amended by the 1999 Act).

It is unclear whether there is an immigration power to detain where a person is already detained under an order or sentence of a court, or is remanded in custody. Therefore the sensible course is for any immigration decision to detain to be expressed as taking effect once any existing detention ends. Such a person is not exempt from the arrangements for release on temporary licence (home leave) (see 38.19).

38.11.2 Detention pending criminal proceedings

Where an illegal entrant or person served with notice of administrative removal is granted bail by the Court pending trial, there is no bar to continued detention under the 1971 Act, but full account must be taken of the circumstances in which bail was granted and an Inspector must authorise such detention. Where an illegal entrant or person served with notice of administrative removal is remanded in custody awaiting trial but it is not necessary to detain him under IS powers, serve IS 96 granting him temporary release to the place of detention.

38.11.3 Immigration detention in deportation cases

Para 2(1) of Schedule 3 to the 1971 Act concerns the detention of a person who has been court recommended for deportation in the period following the end of his sentence pending the decision by the Secretary of State whether to make a deportation order. Para 2(2) of Schedule 3 defines the scope of the power to detain a person who has not been recommended for deportation by a court but who has been served with a notice of intention to deport (an appealable decision) in accordance with section 105 of the Nationality, Immigration and Asylum Act 2002, pending the making of a deportation order.

There is no immigration power to detain where a person is already detained under an order or sentence of a court. Therefore the sensible course is for any immigration decision to detain to be expressed as taking effect once any existing detention ends.

A person who is detained under the sentence or order of a court may not be detained under Schedule 3 to the 1971 Act pending the making of a deportation order. This means that detention orders may not be made or enforced against prisoners who are serving sentences or persons remanded in custody awaiting trial. It is important, therefore, in criminal cases, to monitor the offender's release date for service of the detention/restriction forms at the appropriate time. A person served with a deportation order can be detained in such circumstances (para 2(3) of Schedule 3 to the 1971 Act refers).

There is no bar to detaining a person under Immigration Act powers, pending the making of a deportation order, who is on police bail pending enquiries and who has not yet been charged. It is unlikely such a person will be detained under Immigration Act powers in practice, however, as he will no longer be eligible for such detention once charged.

38.12.2 Detention after an appeal has been allowed

If a detainee wins an appeal, but IS wish to challenge the immigration judge's decision, it is sometimes considered necessary to maintain detention until the challenge is heard. While it may be justifiable to continue detention in the short term pending such a challenge, especially if there is considered to be a risk of the person absconding, care should be taken to ensure detention on this basis does not continue beyond a reasonable time period. Detention after an appeal has been allowed is not automatic and temporary release should always be considered. Any decision on what constitutes a reasonable period of time should be on a case by case basis. As with any case, detention and associated risk factors should be reviewed regularly to decide whether the detainee's circumstances have changed, and whether the person still presents a risk of absconding.

38.14 Detention for the purpose of removal

In cases where a person is being detained because their removal is imminent the lodging of a suspensive appeal or other legal proceedings that need to be resolved before removal can proceed will need to be taken into account in deciding whether continued detention is appropriate. Release from detention will not be automatic in such circumstances: there may be other grounds justifying a person's continued detention, eg a risk of absconding, or the person's removal may still legitimately be considered imminent if the appeal or other proceedings are likely to be resolved reasonably quickly. An intimation that such an appeal or proceedings may or will be brought would not, of itself, call into question the appropriateness of continued detention. (See chapter 44 for separate guidance on Judicial Review).

Following the death in 1993 of Joy Gardner while being detained for deportation, the then Home Secretary instituted a review of procedures in cases where the police are involved in assisting the IS with the removal of people under Immigration Act powers (the Joint Review of Procedures in Immigration Removal Cases). One of the provisions introduced immediately after the report of the Joint Review was issued was that there should be a period of at least one to two days between detention and the proposed removal of an offender. Only in exceptional cases will removal proceed on the day of arrest and this must be authorised by an Assistant Director.

Form IS 91R Reasons for detention

8.152 The details of this form and the instructions on how it is to be completed are contained in Chapter 38.6.3 of the OEM. It must be served on every detained person at the time of their initial detention. The immigration officer must complete all three sections of the form. The immigration officer must specify the power under which a person has been detained, the reasons for detention and the basis on which the decision to detain was made. The detainee must also be informed of his bail rights and the immigration officer must sign, both at the bottom of the form and overleaf, to confirm the notice has been explained to the detainee (using an interpreter where necessary) and that he has been informed of his bail rights.

8.153 If the detainee does not understand English, officers should ensure that the form's contents are interpreted. The six possible reasons for detention are set out on form IS 91R and are listed below. The immigration officer must tick all the reasons that apply to the particular case:

- You are likely to abscond if given temporary admission or release.
- There is insufficient reliable information to decide on whether to grant you temporary admission or release.
- Your removal from the United Kingdom is imminent.
- You need to be detained whilst alternative arrangements are made for your care.
- Your release is not considered conducive to the public good.
- I am satisfied that your application may be decided quickly using the fast track procedures.

  Fourteen factors are listed, which will form the basis of the reasons for the decision to detain. The IO must tick all those that apply to the particular case:

  - You do not have enough close ties (eg family or friends) to make it likely that you will stay in one place.
  - You have previously failed to comply with conditions of your stay, temporary admission, or release.

- You have previously absconded or escaped.
- On initial consideration, it appears that your application may be one which can be decided quickly.
- You have used or attempted to use deception in a way that leads us to consider that you may continue to deceive.
- You have failed to give satisfactory or reliable answers to an Immigration Officer's inquiries.
- You have not produced satisfactory evidence of your identity, nationality, or lawful basis to be in the United Kingdom.
- You have previously failed or refused to leave the United Kingdom when required to do so.
- You are a young person without the care of a parent or guardian.
- Your health gives serious cause for concern on grounds of your own wellbeing and/or public health or safety.
- You are excluded from the United Kingdom at the personal direction of the Secretary of State.
- You are detained for reasons of national security, the reasons are/will be set out in another letter.
- Your previous unacceptable character, conduct, or associations.
- I consider this reasonably necessary in order to take your fingerprints because you have failed to provide them voluntarily.

H. Practice and Procedure Note

Vulnerable detainees

The UNHCR considers that the detention of asylum seekers is inherently undesirable, **8.154** particularly in the case of single women, children, unaccompanied minors, and those with special needs. Under Home Office Policy on detention (Chapter 38, see Practice Note above), children, unaccompanied minors, pregnant women, and those with special needs are considered to be generally unsuitable for detention; single women may be detained.

The UNHCR Guidelines are not part of our law and hence are not binding on the **8.155** courts. They are however appended to the Guidance Note on Bail for Adjudicators (3rd Edition, May 2003) and hence are clearly intended to be taken into account by the Tribunal when considering whether to grant bail. We were reproduce them in full below.

The UN Convention on the Rights of the Child has not been incorporated into national **8.156** law. It is clear, however, that since the incorporation of the ECHR there is a requirement to interpret its provisions consistently with other human rights instruments (*Golder v United Kingdom* (1975) 1 EHRR 524). The UN Convention on the Rights of the Child states that parties to the Convention shall ensure that:

> No child shall be deprived of his or her liberty unlawfully or arbitrarily. The arrest, detention and imprisonment of a child shall be in conformity with the law and shall be used only as a measure of last resort and for the shortest appropriate period of time.

UNHCR Guidelines on Detention of Asylum Seekers

1. The use of detention against asylum seekers is, in the view of UNHCR, inherently undesirable. This is even more so in the case of vulnerable groups such as single women children unaccompanied minors and those with special medical or psychological needs.

2. Of key significance to the issue of detention is **Article 31 of the 1951 Convention**. Article 31 exempts refugees coming directly from a country of persecution from being punished on account of their illegal entry or presence, provided they present themselves without delay to the authorities and show good cause for their illegal entry or presence. The Article also provides that Contracting States shall not apply to the movements of such refugees restrictions other than those which are necessary and that any restrictions shall only be applied until their status is regularized or they obtain admission into another country.

3. It follows from this Article that detention should only be resorted to in cases of necessity. The detention of asylum seekers who come 'directly' in an irregular manner should, therefore, not be automatic, nor should it be unduly prolonged. The reason for this is that once their claims have been examined they may prove to be refugees entitled to benefit from Article 3 1. Conclusion No. 44 (XDDCVH) of the Executive Committee on the Detention of Refugees and Asylum Seekers sets the standard in more concrete terms of what is meant by the term **'necessary'**. It also provides guidelines to States on the use of detention, and recommendations as to certain procedural guarantees to which detainees should be entitled.

4. The term **'coming directly'** covers the situation of a person who enters the country in which asylum is sought directly from the country of origin, or from another country where his protection could not be assured. It is clear from the travaux préparatoires, however, that the term also covers a person who transits an intermediate country for a short time without having applied for or received asylum there. The drafters of the Convention introduced the term 'coming directly' not to exclude those who had transited another country, but rather to exclude those who 'had settled temporarily' in one country, from freely entering another (travaux préparatoires A/CONF.2/SR 14 p. 10). No strict time limit can be applied to the concept 'coming directly', and each case will have to be judged on its merits.

The issue of 'coming directly' is also related to the problem of identifying the country responsible for examining an asylum request and granting adequate and effective protection.

5. Given the special situation of a refugee, in particular the frequent fear of auth other problems, lack of information and general insecurity, and the fact that these and circumstances may vary enormously from one refugee to another, there is no time limit which can be mechanically applied associated with the term **'without delay'** [a condition foreseen in Article 3 1 (I)]. Along with the term **'good cause'** [another condition foreseen in Article 31 (I)], it must take into account all of the circumstances under which the asylum seeker fled (e.g. having no time for immigration formalities).

S. The term 'asylum seeker' throughout the survey and these guidelines also includes individuals who have been rejected from the refugee status determination procedure on purely formal grounds (for example pursuant to the application of the safe third country concept) or on substantive grounds with which UNHCR would not concur (such as in case of persecution by non-State agents). In the absence of an examination of the merits of the case in a fair and efficient asylum procedure or when the rejection after substantive examination of the claim is not in conformity with UNHCR doctrine, such rejected asylum seekers continue to be of concern to UNHCI;L These guidelines do not, however, relate to 'rejected asylum seekers stricto sensu', that is, persons who, after due consideration of their claims to asylum in fair procedures (satisfactory procedural safeguards as well as an interpretation of the refugee definition in conformity with UNHCR standards), are found not to qualify for refugee status on the basis of the criteria laid down in the 1951 Convention, nor to be in need of international protection on other grounds, and who are not authorized to stay in the country concerned for other compelling humanitarian reasons.

Guideline 1: Scope of the Guidelines

These Guidelines apply to all asylum seekers who are in detention or in detention-like situations. They apply to all persons who are confines within a narrowly bounded or restricted location, including prisons, closed camps, detention facilities or airport transit zones, where the only opportunity to leave this limited area is to leave the territory.[132][1]

---

[132][1] This definition is based on the Note of the Sub-Committee of the Whole on International Protection of 1986 (37th Session EC/SCP/44 Para 25) which defined detention to mean 'confinement in prison, closed camp or other restricted area, on the assumption that there is a qualitative difference between detention and other restrictions on freedom of movement'.

Although the concept of 'detention' is not defined in EXCOM Conclusion No 44, it is stated in the 1988 Note on International Protection (39th. Session A/AC.96/713) that the Conclusion is of direct relevance to situations other than detention in prisions.

413

Persons who are subject to limitations on domicile and residency are not general considered to be in detention.

When considering whether an asylum seeker is in detention, the cumulative impact of the restrictions as well as the degree and intensity of each one should also be assessed.

Guideline 2: General Rule

The right to liberty is a fundamental right, recognized in all the major human rights instruments both at global and regional levels. The right to seek asylum is, equally, recognized as a basic human right. The act of seeking asylum can therefore not be considered an offence or a crime. Consideration should be given to the fact that asylum seekers may already have suffered some form of persecution or other hardship in their country of origin and should be protected against any form of harsh treatment.

As a general rule, asylum seekers should not be detained.

The position of asylum seekers differs fundamentally from that of the ordinary alien and this element should be taken into account in determining any measures of punishment or detention based on illegal presence or entry. Reference is made to the provisions of Article 14 of the Universal Declaration of Human Rights, which grants all individuals the right to seek and enjoy asylum and Article 31 of the 1951 Convention which exempts refugees from penalties for illegal presence or entry when 'coming directly' from a territory where their life or freedom was threatened. There is consensus that Article 31 should not be applied restrictively.[133][2]

Guideline 3: Exceptional Grounds of Detention

Detention of asylum seekers may exceptionally be resorted to, if it is clearly prescribes by a national law which is in conformity-with general norms and principles of international human rights law.[134][3]

---

[133][2] Article 31 of the 1951 Convention; for further reference and interpretation see above introductory notes to the UNHCR Guidelines.

EXCOM Conclusion No 22 (XXXII) Para II B 2(a).

EXCOM Conclusion No 44 (XXXVII) Para (d).

Note on International Protection 1987 Para 16.

Sub-Committee of the Whole on International Protection EC/SCP 4 and EC/SCP 44 1986 Para 31.

[134][3] Article 9(I) International Convenant on Civil and Political Rights ('ICCPR').

Article 37(b) UN Convention on the Rights of the Child ('CRC').

Article 5(1)(f) European Convention for the Protection of Human Rights ('ECHR').

Article 7(3) American Convention on Human Rights 1969 ('American Convention').

Article 6 African Charter on Human and People's Rights ('African Center').

EXCOM Conclusion No 44 (XXXVII).

The permissible exceptions to the general rule that detention should normally be avoided must be prescribes by law. In such cases, detention of asylum seekers may only be resorted to, if necessary, in order:

(i) to verify identity;
(ii) (ii)to determine the elements on which the claim for refugee status or asylum is based;
(iii) (iii) to deal with cases where refugees or asylum seekers have destroyed their travel and/or identity documents or have used fraudulent documents in order to mislead the authorities of the State, in which they intend to claim asylum; [135][4] or
(iv) (iv) to protect national security or public order.

Where detention of asylum seekers is considered necessary it should only be imposed where it is reasonable to do so and without discrimination. It should be proportional to the ends to be achieved (i.e. to ensure one of the above purposes) and for a minimal period. [136][5]

Where there are monitoring mechanisms which can be employed as viable alternatives to detention (such as reporting obligations or guarantor requirements), these should be applied first unless there is evidence to suggest that such an alternative will not be effective.

Detention of asylum seekers which is applied for any other purpose, for example, as part of a policy to deter future asylum seekers, is contrary to the principles of international protection. [137][6]

Under no circumstances should detention be used as a punitive or disciplinary measure for failure to comply with administrative requirements or breach of reception centre, refugee camp or other institutional restrictions.

---

[135][4] EXCOM Conclusion No 44 (XXXVII).

Detention for the purpose of a preliminary interview to determine the elements of the refugee status or asylum claim is not the same as detention of a person for the entire duration of a prolonged asylum procedure, which the Conclusion does not endorse. As regards asylum seekers using fraudulent documents or traveling with to mislead the authorities. Thus, asylum seekers who arrive without documentation because they were unable to obtain any in their country or origin, should not be detained solely for that reason (see Note on International Protection, A/AC.96/713 para 19, 15 August 1988).

[136][5] Article 9(1) ICCPR.
Article 37(b) CRC.
Article 5(1)(f) ECHR.
Article 7(3) American Convention.
Article 6 African Charter.
EXCOM Conclusion No 44 (XXXVII).
[137][6] Sub-Committee of the Whole on International Protection Note EC/ECP/44 Para51 (c).

415

Escape from detention should not lead to automatic discontinuance of the asylum procedure, nor to return to the country of origin, having regard to the principle of non-refoulement.[138][7]

Guideline 4. Procedural Safeguards[139][8]

Upon detention, asylum seekers should be entitled to the following minimum procedural guarantees:

(i) (i) the right to be informed of the reasons for detention and of the rights in connection thereto, in a language and in terms which they understand;

(ii) (ii) the right to challenge the lawfulness of the deprivation of liberty promptly before a competent, independent and impartial authority, where the individual may present his arguments either personally or through a representative. Such a right should extend to all aspects of the legality of the case and act simply to the lawful exercise by the executive of the discretion to detain. To this end, he should receive legal assistance. Moreover, there should be a possibility of a periodic review.

(iii) (iii) the right to contact the local UNHCR Office, available national refugee or other agencies and a lawyer. The means to make such contact should be made available.

Guideline 5: Detention of Persons under the Age of 18[140][9]

In accordance with the General Rule stated at Guideline 2 and the UNHCR Guidelines on Refugee Children, minors who are asylum seekers should not be detained.

However if States do detain children, this should, in accordance with Article 37 of the Convention on the Rights of the Child be as a measure of last resort, for the shortest appropriate period of time and in accordance with the exceptions stated at Guideline 3.

138[7] Sub-Committee of the Whole on International Protection Note EC/SCP/44 Para 41.
139[8] Article 9(2) and (4) ICCPR.
Article 37(d) CRC.
Article 5(2) and (4) ECHR.
Article 7(1) African Charter.
Article 7(4) and (5) American Convention.
EXCOM Conclusion No 44 (XXXVII).
UN Standard Minimum Rules for the Treatment of Prisoners 1955.
UN Body of Principles for the Protection of All Persons under Any Form of Detention or Imprisonment 1990.
140[9] CRC Articles 3, 9, 20, 22 and 37.
UN Rules for Juveniles Deprived of their Liberty.
UNHCR Guidelines on Refugee Children 1994.

Particular reference is made to:

- Article 3 of the Convention on the Rights of the Child, which provides that in any action taken by States Parties concerning minors, the best interests of the child shall be a primary consideration;
- Article 9 which grants children the right not to be separated from their parents against their will; and
- Article 22 according to which States Parties are obliged to provide special measures of protection to refugee children and asylum seekers who are minors, whether accompanied or not.

If children who are asylum seekers are detained in airports, immigration-holding centres or prisons, they must not be held under prison-like conditions. M efforts must be made to have them released from detention and placed in other accommodation. If this proves impossible, special arrangements must be made for living quarters which are suitable for children and their families.

During detention, children have the right to education which should optimally take place outside the detention premises in order to facilitate the continuance of their education upon release. Under the UN Rules for Juveniles Deprived of their Liberty, States are required to provide special education programmes to children of foreign origin with particular cultural or ethnic needs.

Children who are detained benefit from the same minimum procedural guarantees (listed at Guideline 4) as adults. In addition, unaccompanied minors should be appointed a legal guardian.

Guideline 6: Conditions of Detention[141][10]

Conditions of detention for asylum seekers should be humane with respect for the inherent dignity of the person. They should be prescribed by law.

Reference is made to the applicable norms and principles of international law and standards on the treatment of such persons. Of particular relevance are the UN Standard Minimum Rules for the Treatment of Prisoners of 1955, the UN Body of Principles for the Protection of All Persons under any form of Detention or Imprisonment of 1990, the UN Rules for the Protection of Juveniles Deprived of their Liberty and the European Prison Rules.

---

[141][10] Article 10(1) ICCPR.
UN Standard Minimum Rules for the Treatment of Prisoners 1955.
UN Body of Principles for the Protection of All Persons under Any Form of Detention or Imprisonment 1990.
UN Rules for Juveniles Deprived of their Liberty 1990.
European Prison Rules 1987.

The following points in particular should be emphasized:

(i) (i) the segregation within facilities of;
   men and women, and
   children from adults (*unless these adults are relatives*);
   and asylum seekers from convicted criminals;
(ii) (ii) the possibility regularly to contact and receive visits from friends, relatives and legal counsel;
(iii) (iii) the possibility to receive appropriate medical treatment and to conduct some form of physical exercise; and
(iv) (iv) the possibility to continue further education or vocational training.

It is also recommended that certain vulnerable categories such as pregnant women, nursing mothers, children, the aged, the sick and handicapped should benefit from special measures which take into account their particular needs whilst in detention.

9

FUTURE REFORMS

On 1 April 2007 the Immigration and Nationality Directorate of the Home   **9.01**
Office became an independent agency—the Border and Immigration Agency.
The changes in the immigration and asylum field which this heralds are unlikely
to be cosmetic. The reform will be far reaching and the public commitments
already made are very ambitious.

As we look ahead to the future, the government is likely to continue to pursue its   **9.02**
commitment to fast track asylum decisions and remove failed asylum seekers.
The Border and Immigration Agency is responsible for fulfilling target 4 of the
Home Office's Public Services Agreement, which is to 'reduce unfounded asylum
claims as part of a wider strategy to tackle abuse of the immigration laws and pro-
mote controlled legal migration'.

Currently, the Home Office is succeeding in removing more failed asylum seekers   **9.03**
than new anticipated unfounded applications for 2006, and it is also managing
to make 35 per cent of asylum decisions within six months.[1] The trend is likely to
continue, with the commitment to increase the efficiency of the decision-making
process becoming much more ambitious. Whereas currently the initial decision
in 35 per cent of cases occurs within six months, by the end of 2011 the aim is to
grant or remove (hence, following exhaustion of all rights of appeal) 90 per cent

---

[1] Home Office, Immigration Reform Progress April 2007, published at <http://www.homeof-
fice.gov.uk/about-us/organisation/home-office-reform/ind-reform-details/ind-review-milestone-
3-progress/?view=Standard>—accessed on 16 July 2007.

of new asylum cases within the same time period of six months.[2] To achieve this target, the Border and Immigration Agency would seek to grant or remove within six months 40 per cent by December 2007, 60 per cent by December 2008, and 75 per cent by December 2009.[3] To do so, the Border and Immigration Agency has committed to operational reform in asylum decision-making procedures.

The operational reforms

9.04   In February 2005, the government published a five-year strategy for immigration and asylum.[4] The strategy contained the New Asylum Model (NAM), which seeks to introduce a faster, more tightly managed asylum process with an emphasis on rapid integration or removal. All new asylum cases as of 5th March 2007 are dealt with within the new model, with a significant number of cases (an estimated 450,000), known as 'Case Resolution' (formerly 'Legacy') cases, falling outside it. The Case Resolution cases include those not fully determined as at 5 March 2007, those where applications for further leave have been made, cases awaiting appeal, or cases where the rights of appeal have been exhausted but the applicants remain in the UK. These Case Resolution claims are to be resolved by June 2011.

9.05   Despite the many criticisms levied against different aspects of the NAM,[5] it has significant advantages in terms of segmentation (so that specialist caseworkers deal with particular categories of case, for example minors) and the assignment of a dedicated case owner to each NAM case. The NAM case owners deal with all aspects of an asylum case, from setting reporting conditions to the interview and decision on the asylum claim itself, and, save in the more difficult cases, with any subsequent appeals. The introduction of a case owner as the direct point of contact for the claimant, his legal representatives, and the courts is a key achievement in the reformed system.

---

2   <http://www.ind.homeoffice.gov.uk/aboutus/ourtargets>—accessed on 16 July 2007—to achieve the Home Office's Public Service Agreement target 5.

3   'Fair, effective and transparent and trusted: rebuilding confidence in our immigration system', Home Office report published on 25 July 2006 ('2006 Immigration Report'), available at <www.ind.homeoffice.gov.uk/6353/aboutus/indrev.pdf>, para 2.10, Chapter 2, though the annex introduces a certain ambiguity by referring to the same targets not for 'granting or removal' but for 'concluding asylum decisions'.

4   'Controlling our borders: Making migration work for Britain'—the Home Office five-year strategy for asylum and immigration, published in February 2005.

5   See Refugee Council's NAM briefing (<http://www.refugeecouncil.org.uk/policy/briefings/2007/nam.htm>), expressing concern over the short timescales for submitting applications and evidence; the discontinuation of the Statement of Evidence Forms (SEFs); the difficulty in challenging segmentation, which can be arbitrary; absence of clear guidance on flexible application of timescales; and the rapid pace of implementation.

Substantive reforms

Substantively, the five-year strategy has given rise to legislation and planned legal **9.06** reform. A central theme in the planned legislative developments and a means to achieving ambitious removals targets is the restriction of rights of appeal.

The Immigration, Asylum and Nationality Act 2006,[6] when brought fully into **9.07** force, will place significant restrictions on rights of appeal, as discussed in Chapter 6. In particular, the Act restricts full appeal rights against refusal of entry clearance to those seeking entry clearance as a dependant or a family visitor,[7] restricts full appeal rights against a refusal of entry at port in certain cases,[8] limits appeal rights if an applicant fails to provide a medical report or medical certificate where to do so is a requirement of the immigration rules,[9] and mandates that an appeal against a decision to make a deportation order on national security grounds could normally only be brought from outside the UK, save for uncertified human rights claims where an appeal lies in-country to SIAC.[10]

Further restriction of rights of appeal is likely to continue in future legislation. **9.08** Under the Borders Bill, for example, foreign national prisoners will face 'automatic' deportation[11] if convicted in the United Kingdom of a qualifying offence. The level of severity of the qualifying offence is yet to be finally determined—the government's revised proposal of offences carrying 12 months' imprisonment has been increased by the Lords to two years at the time of writing. Importantly, the Bill reduces the scope for challenging the 'automatic' deportation decisions through the appeals system.

Consolidation and simplification of all immigration and asylum law

The government has announced four objectives in its immigration policy, under- **9.09** pinning future reform:[12]

(1) **Strengthen our borders; use tougher checks abroad** so that only those with permission can travel to the UK; and ensure that we know who leaves so that we can take action against those who break the rules.

---

6 Which follows two government proposals: 'Controlling our borders: Making migration work for Britain', the Home Office five-year strategy for asylum and immigration, published in February 2005; and 'Confident Communities in a Secure Britain', the Home Office Strategic Plan, 2004–2008, published in July 2004.

7 Replacing ss 88A, 90, and 91 of the Nationality, Immigration and Asylum Act 2002.

8 Replacing s 89 of the INAA 2002.

9 By amending s 88 (2) of the INAA 2002.

10 By inserting s 97A into the NIAA 2002.

11 The Secretary of State will be required to make a deportation order unless he thinks that removal would breach a person's ECHR or Refugee Convention rights, or one of the other exceptions in clause 32 applies.

12 The 2006 Immigration Report.

(2) **Fast-track asylum decisions**, remove those whose claims fail and integrate those who need our protection.

(3) **Ensure and enforce compliance with our immigration laws**, removing the most harmful people first and denying the privileges of Britain to those here illegally.

(4) **Boost Britain's economy** by bringing the right skills here from around the world, and ensuring that this country is easy to visit legally.

To implement these objectives the government has committed to providing 'a stronger and simpler legal framework for immigration', as the current one, dating back to 1971, is 'now complex and unwieldy'.[13]

9.10 On 6 June 2007, the Minister for Immigration, Citizenship and Nationality brought out a consultation paper on Simplifying the Current Immigration and Citizenship Law.[14] The government plans a fundamental overhaul of the legal framework. The law currently contained in many immigration statutes, statutory instruments, the Immigration Rules, and policy and procedures will be consolidated at each level. In addition the legal framework will be simplified.

9.11 These two goals—consolidation and simplification—are, however, quite distinct. It is clear that there is a pressing need to consolidate the primary and secondary legislation as well as Home Office guidance, policy, practice, and procedure notes. Navigating the present maze of provisions and amendments is often bewildering for practitioners and Home Office employees alike. However, simplifying the law, in particular primary legislation, is quite a distinct challenge, which should be approached with caution. The main reason for this is that considerable case law has grown around the interpretation of particular provisions, be they statutory, in the Immigration Rules, or even in policy documents (such as DP3/96, for example). When these are amended, in however simplified terms, the courts would have to rule on the interpretation of the new provisions. Some might say, the more simplified and general the legislative or other provision, the more room for disagreement there might be as to how it is to be applied in practice. In the short term this may result in legal challenges and create uncertainty as to how to apply the legal provisions. Settling contentious points can often take years, if the appellate process proceeds all the way up to the House of Lords. Therefore, as some have urged the government in response to the consultation process,[15] the consolidation exercise should come first, and should not be undertaken together with the simplification one.

---

[13] Ibid.

[14] <http://www.ind.homeoffice.gov.uk/lawandpolicy/consultationdocuments/currentconsultations>—accessed on 16 July 2007.

[15] Migration Watch UK, Briefing paper 8.16, 29 June 2007.

Whilst the consolidation and simplification exercises are open for consultation at **9.12** the conceptual level, with the regard to whether and how they are to be realized, the government has published specific details regarding simplification of work and study immigration provisions. From 2008, a points-based system, similar to that in Australia, will be introduced in the UK. The aim is to control migration more effectively, tackle abuse, and identify the most talented workers. The system will consolidate more than 80 existing work and study application routes into five tiers as follows:

- tier 1—highly skilled, eg scientists or entrepreneurs;
- tier 2—skilled workers with a job offer, eg nurses, teachers, engineers;
- tier 3—low-skilled workers filling specific temporary labour shortages, eg construction workers for a particular project;
- tier 4—students; and
- tier 5—youth mobility and temporary workers, eg working holiday-makers or musicians coming to play a concert.[16]

This rationalization of the present system is a welcome development.

The new phase of immigration and asylum reform will herald new legal challenges. **9.13** For example, the government has committed to increase removal and deportation effectiveness by tagging or monitoring *all* asylum claimants.[17] Any such system when implemented is likely to be challenged under the Human Rights Act.

The legal reform will also concentrate on integration of legal migrants and refu- **9.14** gees. A July 2007 green paper, 'The Governance of Britain' notes:

> The Government will consider how to ensure that new arrivals are well integrated into their local communities, helping local authorities to create positive strategies for building cohesive communities where rights and responsibilities are clearly understood and protected and where positive relations between new arrivals and long-term residents are supported.

Good community relations with asylum seekers, refugees, and migrants are per- **9.15** haps the key to the success of immigration reform.

---

[16] <http://www.ind.homeoffice.gov.uk/aboutus/ourplans/apointsbasedsystem>—accessed 16 July 2007.

[17] The 2006 Immigration Report.

Appendices

APPENDIX 1

Model JR Grounds

IN THE HIGH COURT OF JUSTICE   CASE NO:
BETWEEN:

THE QUEEN
On the Application of SUNSHINE GOLD

<u>Claimant</u>

V

ASYLUM AND IMMIGRATION TRIBUNAL

<u>Defendant</u>

SECRETARY OF STATE FOR THE HOME DEPARTMENT

<u>Interested Party</u>

DETAILED GROUNDS OF CHALLENGE

---

1. <u>Summary of the Claimant's case</u>
2. The Claimant is a national of Zimbabwe. The appeal of her late husband (in which the Claimant and her seven year old child were dependents) was allowed by an Immigration Judge on the ground that his removal to Zimbabwe as an unsuccessful asylum seeker would infringe Article 3 of the ECHR.
3. The Secretary of State for the Home Department (SSHD) applied to the Tribunal for reconsideration of that decision. Before the application was heard, the Claimant's husband died. Pursuant to a new rule (paragraph 17(a) of the Asylum and Immigration Tribunal Procedure Rules), the Tribunal has a discretion to allow an appeal to be continued by a deceased's personal representatives. The Claimant, as the deceased's dependent spouse, had a clear interest in that happening here, as did her child. In the event that the SSHD's application for reconsideration had been unsuccessful (a very real possibility), she and her seven year old child would have been entitled to leave to remain in the UK.
4. The Tribunal refused to permit the deceased's representatives to assume conduct of the appeal for the purpose of defeating the Respondent's application for reconsideration. Instead the Tribunal treated the original appeal as withdrawn without regard to the merits of the application for reconsideration. The Tribunal gave wholly inadequate reasons for adopting this course and/or reached a decision that was Wednesbury unreasonable.
5. <u>Factual background</u>
6. The Claimant is a national of Zimbabwe. She entered the United Kingdom with her husband on 2 January 2003, in possession of a valid visitor's visa. The husband (who had

contracted the AIDS virus) sought asylum on two alternative grounds, recorded in paragraph 3(a) of the Immigration Judge's (IJ) determination. These were as follows:

    (a) That if returned to Zimbabwe involuntarily he would be perceived by the Zimbabwean authorities as an opponent of the regime and subjected to persecution/treatment in breach of Article 3.

    (b) His condition as an AIDs sufferer would render his removal unlawful under Article 3.

7. The Claimant's late husband never asserted that he was politically active in Zimbabwe or that he had been mistreated by the regime in the past [see paragraph 12 of the IJ's determination]. His claim (in terms of mistreatment upon return) was based exclusively on the risk to any unsuccessful asylum seeker upon return to Zimbabwe due to the perception that they were opponents of the Mugabe regime.

8. The IJ rejected the suggestion that returning her late husband as an AIDs sufferer would constitute a breach of his rights under Article 3. He found, however, that the rights of the Claimant's husband under Article 3 of the ECHR would be breached were he to be returned as an unsuccessful asylum seeker. There was (and is) no country guidance case which prevented the IJ from forming this view. The most recent CG case at the time of the hearing before the IJ (AA UKAIT 00144) had concluded that involuntary returnees in the Appellant's position would be at risk of treatment in breach of Article 3. Whilst that determination had been the subject of a remittal by the Court of Appeal, the remitted hearing remained outstanding.[1]

9. The Home Office applied for reconsideration (see bundle). The first ground of challenge was (as recognised by the AIT) misconceived, since credibility had never been an issue in the appeal. Reconsideration was ordered on 24.8.06 in relation to the second ground of challenge, namely the allegedly erroneous reliance by the IJ on the country guidance decision of AA AA UKAIT 00144. The Tribunal stated that the issue was of 'general importance'.

10. The Claimant's husband died on 2.1.07. The Tribunal was notified of this fact and, on 24.2.07 (see bundle), invited the deceased's representatives to make submissions at the reconsideration hearing on 24.6.07 as to the application of the new rule 17(2A), which reads as follows:

Where an Appellant dies before his appeal has been determined by the Tribunal, the Tribunal may direct that

    (a) the appeal should be treated as withdrawn; or

    (b) where the Tribunal considers it necessary, the personal representative of the appellant may continue the proceedings in the place of the appellant.

11. <u>The hearing on 24.6.07</u>

12. The following oral submissions were made at the said hearing on behalf of the Appellant:

    (a) If the Home Office had not applied for reconsideration of the IJ's decision the appeal would have been finally determined prior to the death of the Appellant and accordingly the Claimant would have been entitled to leave in line as his dependant.

    (b) The reasoning which led the IJ to allow the Appellant's appeal applies equally to the Claimant. Indeed there is nothing to distinguish her case from that of her husband. Both would be involuntary returnees. Both would be perceived as opponents of the Mugabe regime.

---

[1] The issue of whether returnees without a political profile or history of past treatment are at risk remains outstanding to this day. Whilst, upon remittal, the AIT found that there was no real risk, the Court of Appeal has since overturned that decision (and remitted the case again) on the basis that relevant evidence was not taken into account [see AA [2007] EWCA Civ 149].

(c) These are precisely the circumstances where the Tribunal should exercise its discretion to permit the Claimant's personal representatives to continue proceedings, at the very least until it has decided whether there was a material error of law in the determination of the Immigration Judge. There was no necessity for the Tribunal to hear evidence in order to determine whether the original determination should stand.

13. The decision of the Tribunal

14. Rule 17(2A) is a new rule which has not been the subject of any previous reported decision by the Tribunal. Despite that fact, the totality of the Tribunal's reasoning in this case is contained in two, short paragraphs. They read as follows:

> *I find that even if the immigration judge's decision discloses no error of law is immaterial because the Immigration Judge's decision was about the risk to the appellant's husband, Michael Golden, only [sic]. It was only the appellant, who the Immigration Judge found that on return to Zimbabwe as a failed asylum seeker, he ran a real risk of inhuman or degrading treatment during interrogation [sic]. Therefore the outcome of this reconsideration cannot make any difference to his wife.*

> *Therefore, applying rule 17(2A)(a), there is no conceivable reason to 'consider it necessary' to continue with this appeal.*

15. No right to reconsideration or appeal was given in relation to the above determination. Accordingly the only remedy open to the Claimant is judicial review.[2]

16. Grounds of challenge

17. The Tribunal's reasoning as set out in the determination is flawed and/or inadequate because:

(a) There is no consideration at all of the purpose behind paragraph 17(2)(A) or indeed the criteria which would have to be met in order for an appeal to be continued by an individual's personal representatives. This was a new rule in respect of which there was no reported guidance and which merited full consideration by the Tribunal. There was, at the very least, a strong argument for suggesting that a central purpose behind the rule was to safeguard the interests of dependants in precisely the position of the Claimant and her son.

(b) There was no attempt to engage with submission (b) above, namely that the finding of risk in relation to the deceased Appellant (who had no political profile) applied equally to the Claimant. There is nothing to distinguish them.

(c) The assertion that 'the outcome of this consideration cannot make any difference to the wife' is wrong. The Claimant plainly had an interest in the outcome of proceedings given that, if the application for reconsideration was unsuccessful, she would be entitled to leave to remain in the UK. The Tribunal recorded this submission but failed to engage with it.

(d) The exercise of discretion was exercised without regard to the merits of the application for reconsideration despite the submission, recorded by the Tribunal in paragraph 5, that the IJ's determination revealed no error of law and should stand. It is further the case that the Tribunal had itself concluded (when ordering reconsideration) the question was one of 'general importance'.

18. In the circumstances, the Court is respectfully asked to grant the relief claimed in the Claim Form.

---

[2] The Claimant has written separately to the Home Office asking it to grant leave on the basis of the original IJ's determination. A response to that application is awaited. Nothing in these grounds should be taken as an indication that the Home Office is not obliged to grant the Claimant leave in any event given the findings of the original IJ which have not been successfully challenged.

APPENDIX 2

Model JR Permission Grounds

In the matter of an application for permission for Judicial Review

BETWEEN:

THE QUEEN (On the Application of
Mr NASSIR RATURGUCHAN)

Claimant

-V-

THE SECRETARY OF STATE FOR THE HOME
DEPARTMENT

Defendant

GROUNDS OF CHALLENGE

INTRODUCTION

1. The Claimant seeks permission to challenge the Defendant's continuing failure to:
   i) give effect to the Immigration Judge's determination of 14 February 2006, which held that the Immigration Officer's decision to curtail the Claimant's leave to remain ('the Decision') was unlawful;
   ii) abide by its concession before the IJ that the Decision was unlawful;
   iii) return the Claimant his passport so as to enable the Claimant to continue with his studies and employment.

RELEVANT FACTUAL BACKGROUND

2. The Claimant, a national of Thailand, born on 2 March 1976, first arrived the United Kingdom ('UK') on 25 February 2004 with leave to enter as a student until 20 April 2005.
3. On 27 April 2005 the Claimant was granted a Residence Permit giving him non-lapsing leave to remain in the UK until 31 May 2006. The only conditions applicable to the Claimant's leave to remain in the UK were that:
   i) he was not permitted to have recourse to public funds, and
   ii) he was only able to carry on work authorised by the Secretary of State.
4. Between 30 November 2005 and 16 January 2006 the Claimant went back to Thailand for a holiday. On the Claimant's return to the UK an Immigration Officer decided to interview the Claimant. Since the Claimant was in possession of a valid Residence Permit, the legal basis for the decision to interview is unclear.

5. The Immigration Officer subsequently purported to curtail the Claimant's leave to remain in the UK on the grounds that the Immigration Officer was not satisfied that the Claimant had been studying due to:
   a) information supplied by the Claimant's college indicating that he had only attended 50% of his classes, which was less than the required minimum 15 hours per week;
   b) the fact that the Claimant had admitted that he had not studied since November 2005 (when he travelled back to Thailand) and was considering enrolling in a new course in February 2006;
   c) the fact that the Claimant was unable to provide telephone numbers/address of his place of employment.

6. The Immigration Officer formed the view that the Claimant had used false representations and/or made omissions of material facts to obtain leave to enter and/or that his leave should be cancelled because of the significant change in his circumstances ('the Decision'). None of these conclusions is explained. No account was taken of the fact that the Claimant, being in possession of a Residence Permit, would have had no reason to think that he would have to prove his entitlement to remain in the UK on re-entry.

7. Following this decision the Claimant was given temporary admission to the UK. The notice of temporary admission made it clear that the Claimant was liable for detention and was prohibited from entering into any employment.

8. On 17 January 2006 the Claimant exercised his statutory right to appeal under s82 Nationality, Immigration and Asylum Act 2002, against this Decision. In support of his appeal he produced evidence from his College confirming that had attended 71% of his classes.

9. On 14 February 2006 the Claimant's appeal came before an Immigration Judge. The Defendant's representative, after taking instructions, conceded that:
   i) the decision to cancel the Claimant's leave to remain had taken place outside the UK; and
   ii) an Immigration Officer had no power to make such a decision.

10. In a determination promulgated on 14 February 2006 the Immigration Judge provided a reasoned determination explaining his decision as to why, pursuant to Article 13(7) of the Immigration (Leave to Enter and Remain) Order 2000, an immigration officer had no power to cancel the Claimant's leave to remain ('the Determination').

11. The Asylum Immigration Tribunal has confirmed that there has been no application by the Defendant for reconsideration of the Determination. The time limit for making such an application has expired.

12. Despite the Defendant's concession and the binding Determination the Defendant continues to refuse to return the Claimant's passport. Instead, the Defendant provides the Claimant with temporary admission. This does not equate to leave to enter the UK and prevents the Claimant studying, enrolling in a new course and continuing his employment.

THE LEGAL FRAMEWORK

13. The UK is a signatory to the Residence Permit Scheme (Council Regulation (EC) No. 1030/2002). Pursuant to this scheme, from November 2003, eligible third country nationals are to be granted a Residence Permit by the UK, allowing them to stay legally in the UK for the duration of the Permit. A person, such as the Claimant, who has a Residence Permit, therefore has non-lapsing leave to remain in the UK for the duration of the permit.

14. Article 13(7) of the Immigration (Leave to Enter and Remain) Order 2000 provides that, where the holder of non-lapsing leave to remain in the UK is outside the UK, his leave to remain may *only* be cancelled by the Secretary of State.

15. Pursuant to Sch 2, paragraph 2A(2) and (8) of the Immigration Act 1971 ('1971 Act') a person's leave to remain may only be cancelled on the grounds of false representations or non-disclosure of material facts where:

    i) the false information and/or material non-disclosure was *material to the obtaining* of the leave: namely the leave must have been obtained by reason of the misleading information;

    ii) the said information was provided by the applicant in person as opposed to his advisor or other third party.

16. Pursuant to Sch 2, paragraph 2A (2) (a) of the 1971 Act a person's leave to remain may only be cancelled where the change in circumstances effectively removes the basis of the holder's claim for admission.

17. Pursuant to s87 (2) NIAA 2002 the Defendant is compelled (subject to his right to challenge the determination by applying for a reconsideration) to give effect and/or act in accordance with directions given by the AIT in determining the appeal.

18. In *SSHD v Bakhtear Rashid* [2005] EWCA Civ 744 the Court of Appeal confirmed that a failure to abide by a policy or public undertaking could amount to an abuse of power and thus be unlawful:

    Where the court considers that a lawful promise was made or practice has given rise to a substantive legitimate expectation, the court will in a proper case consider whether 'to frustrate the expectation is so unfair that to take a new and different course will amount to an abuse of power [p48]'.

Grounds for judicial review

Failure by the Defendant to give effect to the Determination

19. The effect of the Determination and/or the Defendant's concession is that the Claimant's leave to remain in the UK has not been lawfully cancelled. It therefore remains extant. Pursuant to this leave to remain, which is endorsed in the Claimant's passport in the form of a Residence Permit, the Claimant is entitled to study and work.

20. In order to give effect to the Immigration Judge's determination the Defendant is required to return the Claimant his passport. The Defendant's continuing refusal to return the passport, whilst only granting the Claimant temporary admission, wholly frustrates the effect of the Determination. The grant of temporary admission does not amount to leave to enter or remain, a fact reflected by the Claimant's liability to detention.

21. Further or alternatively, the Claimant had a legitimate expectation that the Defendant would honour the concession that it made before the Immigration Judge. The Defendant's subsequent failure to abide by its undertaking is 'so unfair' so as to amount to an abuse of power.

22. In practical terms the Defendant's unlawful refusal to return his passport prevents the Claimant from either studying or working in the UK. As such it plainly has a significant detrimental impact on his Article 8 ECHR private life rights. The Claimant is effectively being kept in 'limbo' in the UK; unlawfully denied the right to pursue the studies, which were the very reason he elected to come to the UK.

23. Furthermore, the Defendant's wholly unreasonable (and unexplained) continuing refusal to return the Claimant his passport inevitably impacts on the Claimant's ability to renew

his leave to remain in the UK in May 2006. The Claimant (as he indicated during his interview in January 2006) wishes to enrol in a course with a different college. The Claimant needs to enrol in the new course before 31 May 2006 and requires his passport in order to do so.

CONCLUSION

24. By reason of the Immigration Officer's unlawful purported cancellation of the Claimant's leave to remain, the Claimant has been denied the opportunity to study and work since 16 January 2006. Despite having successfully exercised his statutory right of appeal, the Claimant is still prevented from exercising these rights by virtue of the Defendant's wholly unreasonable refusal to return his passport and/or give effect to the Determination.

25. The Claimant reserves the right to claim damages and compensation from the Defendant in so far as the Defendant's unlawful actions give rise to financial loss (in particular past loss of earnings and/or if it transpires that the Claimant loses his employment).

26. It is submitted that, in all the circumstances, permission to apply for judicial review of the Defendant's continuing refusal to return the Claimant's passport and/or otherwise give effect to the Immigration Judge's determination should be granted.

APPENDIX 3

Model Grounds of Appeal

IN THE IMMIGRATION APPEALS TRIBUNAL   Hx/44444/2004

BETWEEN:

Mr HASSAN

Appellant

-and-

THE SECRETARY OF STATE FOR THE
HOME DEPARTMENT

Respondent

GROUNDS OF APPEAL

1. The Appellant, a 40 year old national of Turkey, seeks permission to appeal against the determination of the Tribunal, promulgated on 20.12.06, upholding (upon reconsideration) the decision of Mr Hollingworth of 21.2.06 to dismiss the Appellant's asylum and human rights appeal.

2. The Appellant's grounds of appeal should be viewed in the context of the fact that this was an appeal which the Home Office agreed at the outset of the hearing should proceed to a second stage reconsideration where the evidence would be heard de novo. Despite that agreement, the Tribunal refused to accept that there was any material error of law in the Immigration Judge's determination.

3. **Grounds of appeal**

4. <u>Ground one</u>

5. <u>The Tribunal erred in law in concluding that there was no material error of law in the Immigration Judge's treatment of a newspaper article (published in a reputable Turkish newspaper) which recorded the possible murder of the Claimant's brother at the hands of the Turkish security forces. The Immigration Judge's treatment of this article was plainly perverse.</u>

6. The Appellant relied on two newspaper articles: the first confirmed that there were strong suspicions that the Turkish authorities were involved in the recent killing of his brother ('the Article'), the second confirmed that the Appellant's village had been razed to the ground by the Turkish authorities due to perceived PKK involvement of the inhabitants ('the Second Article').

7. The Article [page 25 Appellant's bundle]—published in a reputable national newpaper—stated:

> Mustafa Hassan (47) was gunned down by unknown attackers in the Mazgirt district of Bikram. Mr Hassan's house had been raided by the special security forces one week ago . . . he was travelling in his tractor from Mazgirt when he was attacked . . . it is believed that the attackers tried to set fire to the tractor but the tractor did not catch fire.

Mr Hassan was shot 3 times . . . Special security forces had raided his house. According to local sources, Mr Hassan's house had been raided frequently by special security forces and had been taken to the police station for questioning regarding his alleged connection to the PKK. It has been reported that 3 M-16 bullets have been recovered from the scene. M-16 type of rifle is usually used by the special security forces.

8. In the Appellant's SEF (completed four years prior to the Article) the following details are provided concerning his brother: *Mustafa Hassan, born and living in Mazgirt* [B.10].

9. The Adjudicator did not suggest that the article was a forgery (as it plainly is not). Neither did he take issue with the fact that it related to the Appellant. The Adjudicator instead reached a conclusion in relation to the article which was simply not open to him. He stated in paragraph [ ] that:

The most that can be said about this article is that it was 'criminal activity'.

10. In fact the article expressly suggested that:
    a. the deceased's house had been raided by security forces a week before his death;
    b. the M-16 bullets found near the body were commonly used by the special security forces;
    c. the home of the deceased had been regularly raided by the security forces and he had been routinely questioned by the authorities concerning his alleged involvement with the PKK;
    d. attempts had been made to burn the tractor—thus discounting crime/robbery as a motive.

11. The Adjudicator, by concluding that *the most that* can be said is that 'it was criminal activity', reached a conclusion which was plainly perverse and contrary to the entire thrust of the Article. In the Article there is no suggestion of criminal activity, whilst there is clear reference to evidence that the authorities had recently and regularly targeted the deceased and that the bullets found near the body were of a make used by the security forces. Conclusive evidence of security forces' involvement in a killing is notoriously difficult for any asylum seeker to obtain. The Courts have on numerous occasions stressed that it may well be unreasonable to expect an asylum seeker to obtain independent evidence in support of his claim. In this case, the Claimant had obtained such evidence.

12. The Tribunal's treatment of this issue was itself irrational and perverse. Firstly, the Tribunal stated that:

It is evident that the Adjudicator did not accept that the Mustafa Hassan named in the newspaper report was the appellant's brother.

13. There is no conclusion to that effect in the Adjudicator's determination and the finding of the Tribunal was accordingly perverse. The Adjudicator treated the newspaper report as 'authentic' [paragraph 41]. He noted that it 'appears to show an individual with same name as the Appellant' [ibid]. He then goes on to state that 'even giving the Appellant the maximum benefit of the doubt that this individual may have been his brother the most that can be said about it is that it was criminal activity only'. There is nothing in the Adjudicator's determination which entitled the Tribunal to conclude that he did not accept that the article referred to the Appellant's brother. On a proper construction of the Adjudicator's determination, he was accepting on the lower standard that the article *did* relate to the Appellant's brother but at most it was evidence of criminal activity. The Tribunal then states that 'we do not than on the evidence before him (sic), it can properly be argued that his conclusion that the attack was due to criminal activity was an error of law'. This was not, in fact, what the Adjudicator said—he had instead concluded that the

most which the article was capable of demonstrating was that the attack constituted criminal activity. This was an entirely perverse conclusion and the Tribunal failed to address it. It would not have been open to the Adjudicator, in any event, to conclude that the brother was killed as a result of criminal activity in the light of the contents of the newspaper article and the lower standard of proof.

14. The Tribunal go on to state that any error was immaterial. In reaching this conclusion, the Tribunal compounded an error committed by the Adjudicator (and complained of in the grounds of appeal), who failed to have to regard to any of the objective evidence as to risk *at the point of return* caused by the anti-state activities of family members. The objective evidence and indeed numerous Tribunal decisions identify this as a highly relevant risk factor. Indeed it is little more than common sense that the murder by Turkish security forces of the Appellant's brother just months before the appeal before the Adjudicator was heard was plainly a significant and relevant risk factor which cannot be written off as immaterial.

15. The Tribunal, in concluding that any error was immaterial, relied upon the fact that the Appellant had four brothers and four sisters in Turkey. It stated that 'it was not his evidence that any of his brothers or family members have suffered adversely as a consequence of Mustafa's death'. It was not open to the Tribunal to rely upon this factor as rendering the Adjudicator's error immaterial. There was only a period of six months between the murder of the Appellant's brother and the hearing of the appeal before the Adjudicator. The fact that no acts against family members took place within this six-month period is no basis upon which to dismiss risk upon return. Secondly, for the Tribunal to assert that 'it was not his evidence that any of his brothers or family members have suffered adversely as a consequence of Mustafa's death' simply does not do justice to the Appellant's case. The general targeting of the Appellant and family members was a central part of his case. Indeed paragraph 5 of the grounds of appeal before the Tribunal stated:

Insofar as relevant, the Appellant's fear of persecution arose from his perceived political involvement due to family association: in particular he and his family began to be targeted after his cousin joined the PKK: see SEF: B13/18/19/29, interview C10 and C17, p.6 of statement and the skeleton argument. The fact that the Appellant and his family were Alevi Kurds and lived in Mazgirt, a village in southern Turkey burnt down by the authorities, provides the context within which to assess his account of past detentions and ill-treatment by the authorities.

16. Ground two:

17. The Tribunal erred in law by failing to conclude that the Adjudicator had given an impression of bias and/or irrationality and/or unfairness by:
    i) stating in open court that he never attached weight to newspaper articles and did not believe what he read in newspapers;
    ii) refusing permission to recall the Appellant after having indicated for the first time, during submissions, and despite an implied concession by the Respondent, that he was considering whether the Appellant's past detentions had in fact occurred.

18. The Adjudicator stated prior to looking at the newspaper report that he never attached weight to newspaper articles. This was verified by a statement (see AB4). The Appellant's interpreter, John Smith, recalls that the Adjudicator had said that he 'always had a great deal of suspicion of newspaper articles' (see AB5). The Tribunal dealt with this issue in the following manner:

We note that the Immigration Judge was not asked for his comment. Nevertheless, we find that even if the Immigration Judge had made that comment, it is apparent from the determination that his comment did not affect his treatment of the newspaper report. He evaluated the newspaper report and found that it was authentic. We find that any appearance of bias created at the hearing was not reflected in his evaluation of the newspaper report.

19. The Appellant submits that the Tribunal committed a clear error of law. Firstly, the appearance of bias is enough. There is no requirement upon an Appellant to prove that this affected proceedings in a specific way. In any event, there is clear evidence that the Adjudicator's attitude to newspaper articles *did* affect his treatment of the article relied upon by the Appellant. It is hard to see any other reason why he could have concluded that the most the article showed was criminal activity. The article in question was central to the Appellant's case. The Adjudicator's flawed and unfair treatment of this article inevitably serves to undermine the reliability of his remaining factual findings.

20. As to paragraph 18(ii) there was no challenge in the course of cross-examination to any of the Appellant's evidence by the Home Office. No such challenge was made in the course of submissions by the Home Office at the hearing. It is a fundamental and elementary feature of any adversarial system that a challenge should be put in the course of cross-examination if the credibility of evidence is disputed. When the Appellant's counsel was making submissions the Adjudicator indicated, for the first time, that he was minded to reject the Appellant's assertion that he had been the subject of previous arrests. As a consequence the Appellant's counsel made an application for the Appellant to be recalled so that he could answer in his evidence any concerns which the Adjudicator had. The Adjudicator refused that application. The Tribunal dealt with this point in the following manner:

We find that the Immigration Judge's refusal to give permission for the Appellant to be recalled, following his doubts about the appellant's past detentions, does not raise an error of law. It was clear from the Secretary of State's reasons for refusal letter that the Secretary of State did not believe any of the Appellant's evidence. The Immigration Judge's determination did not reveal that the HOPO who appeared before him had conceded that the detentions had in fact occurred. A concession has to be clear and unambiguous. The fact that the HOPO did not question the Appellant on his detentions did not mean that he had impliedly accepted that the detentions occurred.

21. Whether or not the failure of the HOPO to take credibility points in the course of cross-examination or submissions amounted to an implied concession of credibility, the Tribunal failed to deal with the point that it is incumbent upon a party to challenge during the course of cross-examination those parts of the evidence which they do not consider to be credible. Given that such a challenge had not taken place, asking for the Appellant to be recalled to answer any doubts the Adjudicator had was a perfectly reasonable request. Failing to accede to that request was a breach of natural justice. The Appellant's case before the Tribunal (maintained in these grounds) is that the Adjudicator attached excessive weight to what he regarded as discrepancies and inconsistencies in the Claimant's evidence. Failing to put those matters to him served to compound the unfairness which the Appellant suffered.

APPENDIX 4

Model Skeleton Argument 1

IN THE MATTER OF A RECONSIDERATION UNDER S.103A OF THE
NATIONALITY IMMIGRATION AND ASYLUM ACT 2002

BETWEEN:

THE SECRETARY OF STATE FOR THE
HOME DEPARTMENT

Respondent

-and-

Ms SHAHEEN ABDULLAH

Claimant

SKELETON ARGUMENT
ON BEHALF OF THE CLAIMANT

INTRODUCTION

1. By decision dated 31.02.06 the Respondent was given permission to challenge the Immigration Judge's ('IJ') determination promulgated on 19.11.05. The reasons given for the grant of permission were that:

    i) the IJ 'has failed to make findings of fact and draw conclusions, to give reasons therefore in relation to her finding that the Claimant was a member of a social group' ('the reasons challenge');

    ii) whilst the IJ refers to documents and page references in respect of evidence she relies on to support her findings, 'she does not summarize the evidence, nor reveal any reasoning or the application of any methodology, and its results, to the exercise of the fact finding. . .';

    iii) it is arguable that the IJ failed to take into account the personal factual evidence of the Claimant when considering risk on return to Kabul.

2. The Respondent's grounds of appeal:

    i) do *not* contain a challenge to the adequacy of the IJ's reasons—they simply mistakenly assert that 'a dispute or blood feud cannot be considered as a social group' [g.2];

    ii) do *not* contain a challenge to the IJ's summary of evidence, reasoning or failure to apply a methodology;

    iii) assert that the IJ did not consider internal flight [g.5], before conceding that IJ did make a finding that there was no sufficiency of protection in Kabul and attacking the rationality of this conclusion [g.5/6].

PRELIMINARY ISSUES

3. The scope of the AIT's statutory jurisdiction was considered in *Miftari v. SSHD* [2005] EWCA Civ 481 (where the Court of Appeal confirmed that the grounds of appeal are the only basis upon which permission to appeal is granted) and in *R & Ors v SSHD* [2005] EWCA Civ 982, where the Court of Appeal provided the following additional guidance:
   * examples of errors of law commonly encountered [para 9]—in so far as relevant to this case the examples include making a material misdirection of law;
   * perversity 'a very high hurdle' requiring irrationality in the *Wednesbury* sense [para 11]
4. In *GH (Afghanistan) v SSHD* [2005] EWCA Civ 1603 the Court of Appeal confirmed that an otherwise unexplained assertion that the IJ had failed to provide reasons for his conclusion that a return to the 'grim' circumstances of Afghanistan breached Article 3 [p.7/9], did not identify an error of law which gave the AIT jurisdiction to consider the appeal. The Court of Appeal noted in particular that a loose challenge to the Article 3 finding did not entitle the SSHD to argue that the wrong legal threshold had been applied. [p.19].
5. It is submitted that the grounds of appeal manifestly fail to identify an error of law for the reasons set out below:
   i) Ground 2: the IJ found that the Claimant belonged to a social group comprising of 'women of the Pushtun Tribe who reside in Afghanistan and adheres to the Pashtunwali code' [p 38]. The Respondent's challenge (referring to 'a dispute or blood dispute') neither engages with the actual finding made by the IJ, nor identifies an arguable error of law in the IJs's finding. Furthermore, there is not even a suggestion that the Respondent considers that the IJ's reasons are inadequate;
   ii) Grounds 3 and 4 are mere disagreements with the IJ's findings: they plainly fail to identify an error of law, and indeed fail to indicate where the IJ:
      i. held (whether expressly or implicitly) that a local Jirga had authority over every Pashtun [ground 4];
      ii. held that the Islamic Government support practices such as forced divorce/marriages [ground 5].
   iii) Ground 5: is inherently inconsistent and fails to identify any error of law. Contrary to what is asserted in the grounds:
      i. the IJ clearly considered internal flight and found that there was no effective protection (see paragraph 46 and the IJ's express reliance on pages 6–9 of Part 2 of Dr Cherry's report which stated that internal flight was unduly harsh since the Claimant was at risk of being located and there was no effective protection);
      ii. such a finding is wholly consistent with the *NS Afghanistan (Social Group) CG* [2004] UKIAT00328 and/or the Respondent has failed to identify the grounds on which it is suggested that the objective evidence renders irrational the IJ's conclusion.
   iv) Ground 6: is irrational. The Claimant was held to be credible. Her evidence is that she is separated from her husband and her family are in hiding for their safety [p 4] and that she would have to live in Kabul alone with her daughter [p 10]. There is no challenge to the IJ's findings on credibility. There is therefore no basis (whether in fact or law) for suggesting that the IJ erred in failing to consider that the Claimant will be being returned to her husband and family.

THE GRANT OF PERMISSION

6. Save for the issue of internal flight to Kabul (which although referred to in the grounds of appeal, is not formulated in such a way so to disclose an error of law), it is submitted that the AIT has no jurisdiction to consider the matters raised in the grant of permission, since these issues cannot be found in the Respondent's grounds of appeal.
7. If, contrary to the Claimant's primary case, the AIT accepts jurisdiction, the arguments raised in the grant of permission are misconceived.

RELEVANT CASE LAW CONCERNING AFGHANISTAN

8. In *NS Afghanistan (Social Group) CG* [2004] UKIAT00328 the IAT held that:
    i) the Appellant, who was separated from her husband (with whom she had lost contact and/or was in detention), was a member of a particular social group comprising of 'women in Afghanistan' [74–81];
    ii) the Appellant was at risk of persecution from men who might consider her to be available for marriage [p 82]
    iii) it would be unduly harsh to expect the Appellant (who whilst she may have a home in Kabul [p 94] was suffering from PTSD) and her daughters [p 96] to relocate to Kabul [100–102].

PROCEEDINGS BEFORE THE IJ

9. The evidence before the IJ disclosed that the Claimant's sister (who was heavily involved in the situation which culminated in the Claimant fleeing from Afghanistan) had had her appeal allowed by an IJ [pp 20–24].
10. The IJ noted the Claimant's assertion that Kabul was not safe because Sabeeran Khan (the non-state agent of persecution) was a relative of the Commander of Hazjat Ali [p 16]. The IJ accepted that the Claimant was a credible witness, and having regard to her account of events faced a very high risk of persecution, if returned, on account of her membership of a social group comprising of 'women of the Pushtun Tribe who reside in Afghanistan and adhere to the Pashtunwali code' [p 38]. The IJ went on to:
    i) expressly remind herself that the Claimant's sister's asylum status was not determinative of the Claimant's appeal [p 39];
    ii) provide cogent and compelling reasons for why she found the Claimant to be a credible witness [p 40], noting that the Claimant's evidence was consistent with the particular pages (124 and 129) of the objective evidence [p 42] and accepting the documentary evidence of the Jirga supplied by the Claimant [p 44/45 applying *Tanveer Ahmed*];
    iii) provide reasons as to why she found particular paragraphs of Dr Cherry's expert evidence concerning the Jirga to be reliable, referring to the fact that the report was well sourced and reached reasonable conclusions [p 41];
    iv) rely on a United Nations Special Report (p 111) in concluding that there was no effective protection for those who fall foul of Jirgas;
    v) rely on paragraphs 6.122 and 6.177 of CIPU 2004 and pages 6–9 of Dr Cherry's report in holding that there was no effective protection from any source (this was a direct response to the Respondent's assertion, recorded at paragraph 24, that the authorities in Kabul could provide the Claimant with protection). In this regard it is noteworthy that the Adjudicator was expressly endorsing Dr Cherry's conclusions and reasons contained on page 9 of the report as to why Kabul is not a viable option.

SUBMISSIONS

11. There is no challenge to the IJ's finding that the Claimant's removal to Afghanistan gives rise to a real risk of breach of her human rights.

12. The Respondent's challenge to the IJ's conclusion that the Claimant faces a real risk of persecution due to her membership of a particular social group is wholly misconceived. The Respondent has failed to:
    i) appreciate the nature of the defining characteristics of the social group identified by the IJ;
    ii) appreciate that the social group identified by the IJ is fully consistent with *NS Afghanistan;*
    iii) identify any error of law in the actual social group identified by the IJ.

13. The issues identified in the grant of permission (which are not discernible in the Respondent's grounds) are equally misconceived. The IJ has made clear findings of fact (unequivocally accepting the Claimant's account of events in Afghanistan [p 38], for reasons both of consistency in her account and between the witnesses [p 40], the lack of exaggeration by the Claimant [p 40] and the fact that her version of events is consistent with the objective evidence [p 42]). There is no basis for asserting that these reasons are irrational.

14. The IJ's methodology is readily apparent from the determination: namely she has assessed the credibility of the Claimant's account in the context of consistency (both in relation to her account and the evidence of her sister) and the objective evidence. It cannot be faulted.

15. Furthermore, there is simply no requirement in law to summarize evidence. The IJ expressly refers to aspects of the objective evidence she relies on in reaching her conclusions. This is plainly sufficient for the parties to discern the reasons why she concluded that the Claimant's fear of ill-treatment (including forcible marriage to her brother-in-law in a country where there is no effective protection for women) was by reason of her membership of a social group comprising of Pushtun women.

16. In relation to internal flight, it is clear that at the hearing the Respondent asserted that there was sufficiency of protection in Kabul [p 24]. It is equally clear that the IJ, whilst noting this submission, preferred the evidence of the United Nations Special Report on the situation facing women in Afghanistan (2003) [p 42], Dr Cherry and CIPU [p 46]. It is simply unarguable that the IJ's decision that the Claimant, as a lone woman, would be unable to avail herself of sufficient protection, is irrational.

17. Furthermore, the IJ's conclusion (bearing in mind that the Claimant has a young daughter) is entirely consistent with *NS Afghanistan.*

CONCLUSION

18. In conclusion, the grant of permission refers to matters not identified in the Respondent grounds and/or which fail to identify any error of law. Further, the Respondent's grounds of appeal do not identify any error of law and should be dismissed.

19. Further or alternatively, having regard to the IJ's findings of fact, the objective evidence and the current AIT case law, it was plainly open to her to conclude that the Claimant faced a real risk of persecution by reason of her membership of a social group (namely women in Afghanistan) and that, having lost touch with her husband, and with a young daughter, internal flight would be unduly harsh.

APPENDIX 5

Model Skeleton Argument 2

IN THE IMMIGRATION APPEALS AUTHORITY   HX/98765/2004

IN THE MATTER OF AN APPEAL UNDER S.101 (1) OF THE NATIONALITY IMMIGRATION AND ASYLUM ACT 2002

BETWEEN:

PENELOPE GRUZAMBA

Appellant

-and-

THE SECRETARY OF STATE FOR THE
HOME DEPARTMENT

Respondent

SKELETON ARGUMENT
ON BEHALF OF THE APPELLANT

References to [p.] are to paragraphs in the determination. References to
[page*] are to pages in the Appellant's bundle*

INTRODUCTION

1. In a decision, dated 18 January 2005, Davis J allowed the Appellant's application for statutory review. Davis J was particularly concerned by the IJ's failure to have regard to the evidence of the Claimant's sister ('Gabrielle'), whose credibility had been accepted and whose evidence corroborated the Claimant's account.

ISSUES

2. It is the Appellant's case that the IJ erred in:
   i) failing to consider the Appellant's primary case: namely the risk of persecution that she faced by reference to Gabrielle's past experiences and/her relationship/perceived association with Gabrielle: a recognised refugee who the IJ recognised was 'clearly' at risk of persecution [p.45];
   ii) failing to consider adequately or at all the corroborative evidence of Gabrielle whose credibility was unchallenged at the hearing and who the Home Office Presenting Officer (HOPO) recognised needed international protection [p.28];
   iii) making material findings of fact which were inconsistent with the evidence [p.16] and/or irrational given his acceptance of the Gabrielle's account/claim for international protection [p.38/39];

iv) purporting to distinguish Gabrielle's situation from the Appellant's for a reason which was wholly irrational or irrelevant [p.45];

v) failing to consider the Appellant's credibility/risk on return in the context of the facts that he accepted and/or the objective evidence; and

vi) failing to make any or any adequate findings in relation to Article 8 and family life, and in particular failing to consider the fact that Gabrielle cannot be expected to return to Zimbabwe, leaving her parents in an impossible quandary.

3. Insofar as an error of law is established that Appellant will seek to rely on the evidence from the CAB which establishes that, contrary to the views expressed by the IJ and Davis J, the Appellant did in fact refer to her fear of being returned to Zimbabwe in 2003 when she applied to remain with her parents [p.46]. The fact that she did not make the correct application, with reference to the fear that she was expressing, should not detract from the credibility of her factual assertion.

Factual Background

4. Since 1999 the Appellant, a citizen of Zimbabwe, born on 11th October 1980, studied in a boarding college in South Africa, returning to her home in Zimbabwe for short periods during her holidays [p.11]. She first came to the UK in December 2002, and subsequently returned briefly to South Africa to complete her studies. Her parents (her mother works as nurse) and (other) younger sister all have permission to remain in the UK.

5. On 13 May 2003 the Appellant and Gabrielle applied to remain in the UK with their parents. In her application the Appellant made express reference to the harassment that she had suffered in Zimbabwe and her fear of being returned to Zimbabwe [p.46]. By decision dated 27 August 2003 the Secretary of State refused both their applications [p.36].

6. Thereafter, the Appellant and Gabrielle claimed asylum in April 2004. Their SEFs were almost identical. As is clear from the Appellant's witness statement the factual basis upon which she asserted that she had a well-founded fear of persecution was heavily dependant on Gabrielle's evidence [p.55–58]. This was because it was the Appellant's case that she spent most of her time in South Africa and, consequently she relied:

i) events which she and Gabrielle had witnessed together;

ii) events/attacks on their family home which Gabrielle had witnessed in her absence;

iii) the likelihood that, if returned, she would face a real risk of:

a) similar ill-treatment treatment to that meted out to Gabrielle, and/or

b) persecution from those who wished to locate or harm Gabrielle or her family.

7. The Appellant and Gabrielle were interviewed over a 2 day period by different caseworkers in mid 2004. Within a few days of interview, Gabrielle was granted asylum (on 7 June 2004), whereas the Appellant's entire claim (which was based on the same facts and incidents which had resulted in Gabrielle being recognised as a refugee) was rejected (on 14 June 2004).

The IJ's determination

8. In a determination promulgated on 7 September 2004 [page 31] the IJ, having heard evidence from both sisters, dismissed the Appellant's appeal. In so far as material the IJ:

i) concluded that there was no evidence of any incidents in September/December 2004 [p.16], despite the evidence of both sisters concerning the break ins/harassment/poisoning of the guard dogs [page 32].

ii) noted that the HOPO accepted that Gabrielle had a well-founded fear of persecution [p. 28] and accepted the facts of Gabrielle's claim [p. 41].

iii) dismissed the claim that the Appellant's/Gabrielle's home had been attacked after their father left in July 2002, on the grounds that it was not plausible that their father would have left them at risk [p. 28]: this finding is wholly inconsistent with Gabrielle's evidence (who was the main witness to these events since the Appellant was in South Africa) [page 35].

iv) held that the Appellant had not sought international protection in 2003 [p 37]: this finding is plainly inconsistent with the evidence (which was not before the IJ) of the Appellant's application in 2003 [page 38].

v) distinguished Gabrielle's case on the basis that in March 2002, 9 months before she left Zimbabwe, she was forced to attend a Zanu-PF rally [p. 40]: the finding that the fact of attending a rally organised by the ruling party/the perpetrators of the persecution places Gabrielle at greater risk of persecution than the Appellant is simply irrational.

vi) held that the Appellant had no emotional dependency on her parents: despite the abundance of evidence that she lived with her parents, was entirely dependant on them financially and emotionally, no reason is provided for this finding.

Submissions

i) Failure to engage with and/or address the Appellant's primary case

9. The two sisters relied on the same past incidents of harassment in support of a claim for asylum. Broadly speaking, it was their case that, after the departure of their father in July 2002, they and their home were subjected to an escalating wave of violence by Zanu-PF youths. Whilst neither sister actually suffered significant bodily harm, they became increasingly afraid as to their vulnerability to these continuing attacks, and therefore decided to leave Zimbabwe in December 2002 and travel to the UK to join their parents. Due to the fact that the Appellant was mostly in South Africa, it was Gabrielle who witnessed must of the harassment attacks on the family home.

10. It is plain from the determination that the IJ fundamentally misunderstood the Appellant's case. Whilst the IJ recognised that the Appellant did not allege that she had ever been attacked or beaten (a stance which is hardly consistent with someone fabricating a claim for asylum) and accepted that she had spent most of the time in South Africa, the IJ failed to recognise that the Appellant's claim was based principally on what had happened/been witnessed by her sister. In effect the Appellant feared that she too would fall victim to the dangers/harassment/burglaries witnessed by her sister (and the Appellant when she was at home) if she returned. The IJ, in failing to consider or make any findings as to the principle reason why the Appellant feared persecution, erred in law.

11. Whilst it is accepted that separate claims fall to be determined individually, in a case where two sisters, both of whom give evidence and rely on the same allegations of past persecution which affect them both (attacks on their home etc), it is simply irrational for an IJ to accept the evidence in relation to one sister and to reject the other's claim as an 'utter abuse of the asylum process' [p. 33]. These mutually contradictory findings demonstrate the extent to which the IJ failed to comprehend or engage with the basis of the Appellant's claim for asylum.

ii)–iv) Failure to consider/adequately or at all Gabrielle's evidence

12. It is clear from the determination that both the IJ and the HOPO accepted that Gabrielle was deserving of international protection and accepted her credibility. It is equally clear that:

    i) the IJ erred in dismissing important aspects of the Appellant's account, which were either corroborated or based on Gabrielle's evidence, either without realising that Gabrielle had witnessed these incidents or without providing any or any adequate explanation for her findings [p. 40]; and

    ii) neither the IJ nor the HOPO considered whether, in light of their acceptance that Gabrielle faced a real risk of persecution, the Claimant (who was Gabrielle's sister and who would be returning as a single young girl to the family home, which according to Gabrielle had been repeatedly attacked) faced a similar risk if returned to Zimbabwe.

13. The sole justification identified by the IJ for distinguishing the Gabrielle's claim from the Appellant's is manifestly irrelevant: the IJ states that Gabrielle was a minor when she was forced to attend a Zanu-PF rally and chant slogans [p. 37]. It is inconceivable that the fact that Gabrielle attended a Zanu-PF rally in March 2002 (i.e. a pro-government rally) places her at any greater risk than the Appellant. This evidence is, however, relevant to a proper assessment of what awaits the Appellant on return to Zimbabwe, and was plainly not considered in this context.

14. Furthermore, this incident in fact occurred in March 2002, 9 months before the sisters left for the UK. Neither the Appellant nor Gabrielle indicated stated that this incident caused them to leave Zimbabwe: their case was that they left Zimbabwe due to the attacks of their home by the Zanu-PF which had started after their father's departure in 2002.

v) The Appellant's credibility in light of facts that were accepted

15. The IJ accepted the incident in July 2002 where *both* sisters were threatened by Zanu-PF for putting up MDC posters [page. 36]. This incident plainly occurred after their father left Zimbabwe. It provides a clear reason both for a) why the attacks on their house started shortly thereafter and b) why when their father departed he would have not have been aware of the risk that his daughter were facing, since the incident had not yet taken place. The IJ's failure to consider or address the possibility that it was the act of putting up the MDC posters which triggered the subsequent harassment amounted to clear error of law.

16. Furthermore, the absence of past persecution is not determinative of future risk of persecution. Having regard to the fact that Gabrielle, as a young single female, was at risk of persecution if returned to Zimbabwe, it was clearly incumbent on the IJ to consider and make findings as to whether, in the context of the objective evidence, the Appellant, as a young single female and sister of a person who had been targeted for persecution would be at risk on return. The IJ made no such assessment.

vi) Article 8

17. The IAT erred in failing to find that IJ's consideration of Article 8 was flawed. As is plain from their evidence the Appellant and her sister endured harassment together in Zimbabwe and fled to the UK together. Whilst in the UK the Appellant has lived with her parents and two younger sisters (other than when was at boarding school) for nearly two years. At all times she has been financially supported by her parents. In the context of this factual background the generic and formulaic finding at paragraph 52 is wholly inadequate and

contrary to the approach set out by the Court of Appeal in *Nadarajah Senthuran v Secretary of State for the Home Department* [2004] EWCA Civ 950.

18. Furthermore, the finding on proportionality is plainly wrong in so far as it fails to take into account the fact that Gabrielle, as a refugee who lives with her parents, cannot be expected to return to Zimbabwe. In addition the IJ's conclusions concerning the alleged abuse by the Appellant of the immigration rules are unsustainable bearing in mind the grant of asylum to Gabrielle, who adopted an identical approach to claiming asylum.

CONCLUSION

19. This is one of the truly rare cases where justice requires the grant of status to one sister be determinative of the claim of the other. This is because *from the outset* the claims of both sisters were dependant principally on the account of events witnessed by the sister who has been granted refugee status. This is not a case where one applicant changes her account to benefit from the fact that another member of her family has been granted status. In these circumstances, where it is accepted that, although neither sister actually suffered harm, but that escalating level of violence directed at their home created a real risk of persecution, consistency in decision making requires both sisters to be treated in the same manner.

20. On a proper analysis the grounds upon which the IJ rejects the Appellant's credibility relate almost exclusively to events which took place outside of Zimbabwe. It is trite law that such incidents are not determinative of risk of persecution in the country of origin.

21. On a fair reading of the current objective evidence the situation in Zimbabwe (both on return and after return) is dire. Whilst it is accepted that in *SSHD v. AA & LK* [2005] EWCA Civ 401, the Court of Appeal held that mere fact that enforced returnees were at risk did not entitle asylum seekers to refugee status, it is also true that in *Januzi v SSHD* UKHL5 15.02.06, para 55, held that the:

> The fact that the same conditions apply throughout the country of the claimant's nationality is not irrelevant to the question whether the conditions in the country generally, as regards the most basic of human rights that are universally recognised—the right to life and the right not to be subjected to cruel or inhuman treatment—are so bad that it would be unduly harsh for the claimant to seek a place of relocation there.

22. Having regard to current objective evidence and Gabrielle's account, even if the Appellant could safely negotiate the point of return (which is denied), relocation for a young single unaccompanied female would clearly be unduly harsh.

23. The AIT are therefore invited to substitute a finding that the Appellant is entitled to refugee status in line with that granted to her sister, or alternatively HP. Further or alternatively, the matter should be adjourned for re-consideration.

APPENDIX 6

The Asylum and Immigration Tribunal Procedure Rules (2005), Effective from 10.04.07

2005 No 230

(L 1)

IMMIGRATION

ASYLUM AND IMMIGRATION TRIBUNAL (PROCEDURE)
RULES 2005

Made	6th February 2005
Laid before Parliament	8th February 2005
Coming into force	4th April 2005

The Lord Chancellor, in exercise of the powers conferred by sections 106(1)–(3) and 112(3) of the Nationality, Immigration and Asylum Act 2002 and section 40A(3) of the British Nationality Act 1981, after consulting with the Council on Tribunals in accordance with section 8 of the Tribunals and Inquiries Act 1992, makes the following Rules:

PART 1 INTRODUCTION

1. Citation and commencement

These Rules may be cited as the Asylum and Immigration Tribunal (Procedure) Rules 2005 and shall come into force on 4th April 2005.

2. Interpretation

In these Rules—

'the 2002 Act' means the Nationality, Immigration and Asylum Act 2002;
'the 2004 Act' means the Asylum and Immigration (Treatment of Claimants, etc) Act 2004;
'appellant' means a person who has given a notice of appeal to the Tribunal against a relevant decision in accordance with these Rules;
'appropriate appellate court' has the meaning given in sections 103B(5) and 103E(5) of the 2002 Act;
'apropriate court' has the meaning given in section 103A(9) of the 2002 Act;. . .
'asylum claim' has the meaning given in section 113(1) of the 2002 Act;'business day' means any day other than a Saturday or Sunday, a bank holiday, 25th to 31st December or Good Friday;
'determination', in relation to an appeal, means a decision by the Tribunal in writing to allow or dismiss the appeal, and does not include a procedural, ancillary or preliminary decision;
'the Immigration Acts' means the Acts referred to in section 44(1) of the 2004 Act;
'immigration decision' means a decision of a kind listed in section 82(2) of the 2002 Act;

'immigration rules' means the rules referred to in <u>section 1(4)</u> of the Immigration Act 1971;

'order for reconsideration' means an order under section 103A(1) or any other statutory provision requiring the Tribunal to reconsider its decision on an appeal;

'President' means the President of the Tribunal;

'relevant decision' means a decision against which there is an exercisable right of appeal to the Tribunal;

'respondent' means the decision maker specified in the notice of decision against which a notice of appeal has been given;

'section 103A' means section 103A of the 2002 Act (Review of Tribunal's decision) and

'section 103A application' means an application under section 103A;

'Tribunal' means the Asylum and Immigration Tribunal;

'United Kingdom Representative' means the United Kingdom Representative of the United Nations High Commissioner for Refugees.

3. Scope of these Rules

(1) These Rules apply to the following proceedings—
  (a) appeals to the Tribunal;
  (b) section 103A applications which are considered by a member of the Tribunal in accordance with paragraph 30 of Schedule 2 to the 2004 Act;
  (c) reconsideration of appeals by the Tribunal;
  (d) applications to the Tribunal for permission to appeal to the Court of Appeal, the Court of Session, or the Court of Appeal in Northern Ireland; . . .
  (e) applications to the Tribunal for bail[; and
  (f) proceedings incidental to any of the above proceedings, including in particular applications relating to the Tribunal's exercise of its powers under section 103D of the 2002 Act (Reconsideration: legal aid)].

(2) These Rules apply subject to any other Rules made under section 106 of the 2002 Act which apply to specific classes of proceedings.

4. Overriding objective

The overriding objective of these Rules is to secure that proceedings before the Tribunal are handled as fairly, quickly and efficiently as possible; and, where appropriate, that members of the Tribunal have responsibility for ensuring this, in the interests of the parties to the proceedings and in the wider public interest.

PART 2 APPEALS TO THE TRIBUNAL

5. Scope of this Part

This Part applies to appeals to the Tribunal.

6. Giving notice of appeal

(1) An appeal to the Tribunal may only be instituted by giving notice of appeal against a relevant decision in accordance with these Rules.

(2) Subject to paragraphs (3) and (4), notice of appeal must be given by filing it with the Tribunal in accordance with rule 55(1).

(3) A person who is in detention under the Immigration Acts may give notice of appeal either—
  (a) in accordance with paragraph (2); or
  (b) by serving it on the person having custody of him.

(4) A person who is outside the United Kingdom and wishes to appeal against a decision of an entry clearance officer may give notice of appeal either—
  (a) in accordance with paragraph (2); or
  (b) by serving it on the entry clearance officer.
(5) Where a notice of appeal is served on a custodian under paragraph (3)(b), that person must—
  (a) endorse on the notice the date that it is served on him; and
  (b) forward it to the Tribunal within 2 days.
(6) Where a notice of appeal is served on an entry clearance officer under paragraph (4)(b), the officer must—
  (a) endorse on the notice the date that it is served on him;
  (b) forward it to the Tribunal as soon as reasonably practicable, and in any event within 10 days; and
  (c) if it is practicable to do so within the time limit in sub-paragraph (b)
   send to the Tribunal with the notice of appeal a copy of the documents listed in rule 13(1).

7. Time limit for appeal

(1) A notice of appeal by a person who is in the United Kingdom must be given—
  (a) if the person is in detention under the Immigration Acts when he is served with notice of the decision against which he is appealing, not later than 5 days after he is served with that notice; and
  (b) in any other case, not later than 10 days after he is served with notice of the decision.
(2) A notice of appeal by a person who is outside the United Kingdom must be given—
  (a) if the person—
   (i) was in the United Kingdom when the decision against which he is appealing was made; and
   (ii) may not appeal while he is the United Kingdom by reason of a provision of the 2002 Act, not later than 28 days after his departure from the United Kingdom; or
  (b) in any other case, not later than 28 days after he is served with notice of the decision.
(3) Where a person—
  (a) is served with notice of a decision to reject an asylum claim; and
  (b) on the date of being served with that notice does not satisfy the condition in section 83(1)(b) of the 2002 Act, but later satisfies that condition, paragraphs (1) and (2)(b) apply with the modification that the time for giving notice of appeal under section 83(2) runs from the date on which the person is served with notice of the decision to grant him leave to enter or remain in the United Kingdom by which he satisfies the condition in section 83(1)(b).

8. Form and contents of notice of appeal

(1) The notice of appeal must be [made on a form approved for the purpose by the President] and must—
  (a) state the name and address of the appellant; and
  (b) state whether the appellant has authorised a representative to act for him in the appeal and, if so, give the representative's name and address;
  (c) set out the grounds for the appeal;
  (d) give reasons in support of those grounds; and
  (e) so far as reasonably practicable, list any documents which the appellant intends to rely upon as evidence in support of the appeal.

(2) The notice of appeal must if reasonably practicable be accompanied by the notice of decision against which the appellant is appealing, or a copy of it.

(3) The notice of appeal must be signed by the appellant or his representative, and dated.

(4) If a notice of appeal is signed by the appellant's representative, the representative must certify in the notice of appeal that he has completed it in accordance with the appellant's instructions.

9. Notice of appeal where there is no relevant decision

(1) Where—

    (a) a person has given a notice of appeal to the Tribunal; and

    (b) there is no relevant decision, the Tribunal shall not accept the notice of appeal.

(2) Where the Tribunal does not accept a notice of appeal, it must—

    (a) notify the person giving the notice of appeal and the respondent; and

    (b) take no further action.

10. Late notice of appeal

(1) If a notice of appeal is given outside the applicable time limit, it must include an application for an extension of time for appealing, which must—

    (a) include a statement of the reasons for failing to give the notice within that period; and

    (b) be accompanied by any written evidence relied upon in support of those reasons.

(2) If a notice of appeal appears to the Tribunal to have been given outside the applicable time limit but does not include an application for an extension of time, unless the Tribunal extends the time for appealing of its own initiative, it must notify the person giving notice of appeal in writing that it proposes to treat the notice of appeal as being out of time.

(3) Where the Tribunal gives notification under paragraph (2), if the person giving notice of appeal contends that—

    (a) the notice of appeal was given in time, or

    (b) there were special circumstances for failing to give the notice of appeal in time which could not reasonably have been stated in the notice of appeal,he may file with the Tribunal written evidence in support of that contention.

(4) Written evidence under paragraph (3) must be filed—

    (a) if the person giving notice of appeal is in the United Kingdom, not later than 3 days; or

    (b) if the person giving notice of appeal is outside the United Kingdom, not later than 10 days, after notification is given under paragraph (2).

(5) Where the notice of appeal was given out of time, the Tribunal may extend the time for appealing if satisfied that by reason of special circumstances it would be unjust not to do so.

(6) The Tribunal must decide any issue as to whether a notice of appeal was given in time, or whether to extend the time for appealing, as a preliminary decision without a hearing, and in doing so may only take account of—

    (a) the matters stated in the notice of appeal;

    (b) any evidence filed by the person giving notice of appeal in accordance with paragraph (1) or (3); and

    (c) any other relevant matters of fact within the knowledge of the Tribunal.

(6A) Where the Tribunal makes a decision under this rule it must give written notice of its decision, including its reasons which may be in summary form.

(7) Subject to paragraphs (8) and (9), the Tribunal must serve [the] written notice [given under paragraph (6A)] . . . on the parties.

(8) Where—
    (a) a notice of appeal under section 82 of the 2002 Act which relates in whole or in part to an asylum claim was given out of time;
    (b) the person giving notice of appeal is in the United Kingdom; and
    (c) the Tribunal refuses to extend the time for appealing, the Tribunal must serve written notice of its decision on the respondent, which must—
        (i) serve the notice of decision on the person giving notice of appeal not later than 28 days after receiving it from the Tribunal; and
        (ii) as soon as practicable after serving the notice of decision, notify the Tribunal on what date and by what means it was served.

(9) Where paragraph (8) applies, if the respondent does not give the Tribunal notification under sub-paragraph (ii) within 29 days after the Tribunal serves the notice of decision on it, the Tribunal must serve the notice of decision on the person giving notice of appeal as soon as reasonably practicable thereafter.

11. Special provisions for imminent removal cases

(1) This rule applies in any case in which the respondent notifies the Tribunal that removal directions have been issued against a person who has given notice of appeal, pursuant to which it is proposed to remove him from the United Kingdom within 5 calendar days of the date on which the notice of appeal was given.

(2) The Tribunal must, if reasonably practicable, make any preliminary decision under rule 10 before the date and time proposed for his removal.

(3) Rule 10 shall apply subject to the modifications that the Tribunal may—
    (a) give notification under rule 10(2) orally, which may include giving it by telephone;
    (b) shorten the time for giving evidence under rule 10(3); and
    (c) direct that any evidence under rule 10(3) is to be given orally, which may include requiring the evidence to be given by telephone, and hold a hearing or telephone hearing for the purpose of receiving such evidence.

12. Service of notice of appeal on respondent

(1) Subject to paragraph (2), when the Tribunal receives a notice of appeal it shall serve a copy upon the respondent as soon as reasonably practicable.

(2) Paragraph (1) does not apply where the notice of appeal was served on an entry clearance officer under rule 6(4)(b).

13. Filing of documents by respondent

(1) When the respondent is served with a copy of a notice of appeal, it must (unless it has already done so) file with the Tribunal a copy of—
    (a) the notice of the decision to which the notice of appeal relates, and any other document served on the appellant giving reasons for that decision;
    (b) any—
        (i) statement of evidence form completed by the appellant; and
        (ii) record of an interview with the appellant, in relation to the decision being appealed;
    (c) any other unpublished document which is referred to in a document mentioned in sub-paragraph (a) or relied upon by the respondent; and
    (d) the notice of any other immigration decision made in relation to the appellant in respect of which he has a right of appeal under section 82 of the 2002 Act.

(2) Subject to paragraph (3), the respondent must file the documents listed in paragraph (1)—

    (a) in accordance with any directions given by the Tribunal; and

    (b) if no such directions are given, as soon as reasonably practicable and in any event not later than 2.00 pm on the business day before the earliest date appointed for any hearing of or in relation to the appeal.

(3) If the Tribunal considers the timeliness of a notice of appeal as a preliminary issue under rule 10, the respondent must file the documents listed in paragraph (1) as soon as reasonably practicable after being served with a decision of the Tribunal allowing the appeal to proceed, and in any event not later than 2.00 pm on the business day before the earliest date appointed for any hearing of or in relation to the appeal following that decision.

(4) The respondent must, at the same time as filing them, serve on the appellant a copy of all the documents listed in paragraph (1), except for documents which the respondent has already sent to the appellant.

14. Variation of grounds of appeal

Subject to section 85(2) of the 2002 Act, the appellant may vary his grounds of appeal only with the permission of the Tribunal.

15. Method of determining appeal

(1) Every appeal must be considered by the Tribunal at a hearing, except where—

    (a) the appeal—

        (i) lapses pursuant to section 99 of the 2002 Act;

        (ii) is treated as abandoned pursuant to section 104(4) of the 2002 Act;

        (iii) is treated as finally determined pursuant to section 104(5) of the 2002 Act; or

        (iv) is withdrawn by the appellant or treated as withdrawn in accordance with rule 17;

    (b) paragraph (2) of this rule applies; or

    (c) any other provision of these Rules or of any other enactment permits or requires the Tribunal to dispose of an appeal without a hearing.

(2) The Tribunal may determine an appeal without a hearing if—

    (a) all the parties to the appeal consent;

    (b) the appellant is outside the United Kingdom or it is impracticable to give him notice of a hearing and, in either case, he is unrepresented;

    (c) a party has failed to comply with a provision of these Rules or a direction of the Tribunal, and the Tribunal is satisfied that in all the circumstances, including the extent of the failure and any reasons for it, it is appropriate to determine the appeal without a hearing; or

    (d) subject to paragraph (3), the Tribunal is satisfied, having regard to the material before it and the nature of the issues raised, that the appeal can be justly determined without a hearing.

(3) Where paragraph (2)(d) applies, the Tribunal must not determine the appeal without a hearing without first giving the parties notice of its intention to do so, and an opportunity to make written representations as to whether there should be a hearing.

16. Certification of pending appeal

(1) If the Secretary of State or an immigration officer issues a certificate under section 97 or 98 of the 2002 Act which relates to a pending appeal, he must file notice of the certification with the Tribunal.

(2) Where a notice of certification is filed under paragraph (1), the Tribunal must—
- (a) notify the parties; and
- (b) take no further action in relation to the appeal.

17. Withdrawal of appeal

(1) An appellant may withdraw an appeal—
- (a) orally, at a hearing; or
- (b) at any time, by filing written notice with the Tribunal.

(2) An appeal shall be treated as withdrawn if the respondent notifies the Tribunal that the decision (or, where the appeal relates to more than one decision, all of the decisions) to which the appeal relates has been withdrawn.

[(2A) Where an appellant dies before his appeal has been determined by the Tribunal, the Tribunal may direct that—
- (a) the appeal shall be treated as withdrawn; or
- (b) where the Tribunal considers it necessary, the personal representative of the appellant may continue the proceedings in the place of the appellant.]

(3) If an appeal is withdrawn or treated as withdrawn, the Tribunal must serve on the parties a notice that the appeal has been recorded as having been withdrawn.

18. Abandonment of appeal

(1) Any party to a pending appeal must notify the Tribunal if they are aware that an event specified in—
- (a) section 104(4)[, (4A)] or (5) of the 2002 Act; or
- (b) regulation 33(1A) of the Immigration (European Economic Area) Regulations 2000 ('the 2000 Regulations') [or, on or after 30th April 2006, paragraph 4(2) of Schedule 2 to the Immigration (European Economic Area) Regulations 2006 ('the 2006 Regulations')], has taken place.

(1A) Where section 104(4A) of the 2002 Act applies and the appellant wishes to pursue his appeal, the appellant must file a notice with the Tribunal—
- (a) where section 104(4B) of the 2002 Act applies, within 28 days of the date on which the appellant received notice of the grant of leave to enter or remain in the United Kingdom for a period exceeding 12 months; or
- (b) where section 104(4C) of the 2002 Act applies, within 28 days of the date on which the appellant received notice of the grant of leave to enter or remain in the United Kingdom.

(1B) Where the appellant does not comply with the time limits specified in paragraph (1A) the appeal will be treated as abandoned in accordance with section 104(4) of the 2002 Act.

(1C) At the same time as filing the notice under paragraph (1A), the appellant must serve a copy of the notice on the respondent.

(1D) Where section 104(4B) of the 2002 Act applies, the notice filed under paragraph (1A) must state—
- (a) the appellant's full name and date of birth;
- (b) the Tribunal's reference number;
- (c) the Home Office reference number, if applicable;
- (d) the Foreign and Commonwealth Office reference number, if applicable;

(e) the date on which the appellant was granted leave to enter or remain in the United Kingdom for a period exceeding 12 months; and

(f) that the appellant wishes to pursue the appeal in so far as it is brought on the ground specified in section 84(1);

(g) of the 2002 Act which relates to the Refugee Convention.

(1E) Where section 104(4C) of the 2002 Act applies, the notice filed under paragraph (1A) must state—

(a) the appellant's full name and date of birth;

(b) the Tribunal's reference number;

(c) the Home Office reference number, if applicable;

(d) the Foreign and Commonwealth Office reference number, if applicable;

(e) the date on which the appellant was granted leave to enter or remain in the United Kingdom; and

(f) that the appellant wishes to pursue the appeal in so far as it is brought on the ground specified in section 84(1)(b) of the 2002 Act which relates to <u>section 19B</u> of the Race Relations Act 1976.

(1F) Where an appellant has filed a notice under paragraph (1A) the Tribunal will notify the appellant of the date on which it received the notice.

(1G) The Tribunal will send a copy of the notice issued under paragraph (1F) to the respondent.](2) Where an appeal is treated as abandoned pursuant to section 104(4) [or (4A)] of the 2002 Act or regulation 33(1A) of the 2000 Regulations [or paragraph 4(2) of Schedule 2 to the 2006 Regulations], or finally determined pursuant to section 104(5) of the 2002 Act, the Tribunal must—

(a) serve on the parties a notice informing them that the appeal is being treated as abandoned or finally determined; and

(b) take no further action in relation to the appeal.

19. Hearing appeal in absence of a party

(1) The Tribunal may hear an appeal in the absence of a party or his representative, if satisfied that—

(a) the party or his representative has been given notice of the date, time and place of the hearing, and

(b) there is no good reason for such absence.

(2) Where paragraph (1) does not apply, the Tribunal may hear an appeal in the absence of a party if satisfied that—

(a) a representative of the party is present at the hearing;

(b) the party is outside the United Kingdom;

(c) the party is suffering from a communicable disease or there is a risk of him behaving in a violent or disorderly manner;

(d) the party is unable to attend the hearing because of illness, accident or some other good reason;

(e) the party is unrepresented and it is impracticable to give him notice of the hearing; or

(f) the party has notified the Tribunal that he does not wish to attend the hearing.

20. Hearing two or more appeals together

Where two or more appeals are pending at the same time, the Tribunal may direct them to be heard together if it appears that—

(a) some common question of law or fact arises in each of them;

(b) they relate to decisions or action taken in respect of persons who are members of the same family; or

(c) for some other reason it is desirable for the appeals to be heard together.

21. Adjournment of appeals

(1) Where a party applies for an adjournment of a hearing of an appeal, he must—
   (a) if practicable, notify all other parties of the application;
   (b) show good reason why an adjournment is necessary; and
   (c) produce evidence of any fact or matter relied upon in support of the application.

(2) The Tribunal must not adjourn a hearing of an appeal on the application of a party, unless satisfied that the appeal cannot otherwise be justly determined.

(3) The Tribunal must not, in particular, adjourn a hearing on the application of a party in order to allow the party more time to produce evidence, unless satisfied that—
   (a) the evidence relates to a matter in dispute in the appeal;
   (b) it would be unjust to determine the appeal without permitting the party a further opportunity to produce the evidence; and
   (c) where the party has failed to comply with directions for the production of the evidence, he has provided a satisfactory explanation for that failure.

(4) Where the hearing of an appeal is adjourned, the Tribunal will fix a new hearing date which—
   (a) shall be not more than 28 days after the original hearing date, unless the Tribunal is satisfied that because of exceptional circumstances the appeal cannot justly be heard within that time; and
   (b) shall in any event be not later than is strictly required by the circumstances necessitating the adjournment.

22. Giving of determination

(1) Except in cases to which rule 23 applies, where the Tribunal determines an appeal it must serve on every party a written determination containing its decision and the reasons for it.

(2) The Tribunal must send its determination—
   (a) if the appeal is considered at a hearing, not later than 10 days after the hearing finishes; or
   (b) if the appeal is determined without a hearing, not later than 10 days after it is determined.

23. Special procedures and time limits in asylum appeals

(1) This rule applies to appeals under section 82 of the 2002 Act where—
   (a) the appellant is in the United Kingdom; and
   (b) the appeal relates, in whole or in part, to an asylum claim.

(2) Subject to paragraph (3)—
   (a) where an appeal is to be considered by the Tribunal at a hearing, the hearing must be fixed for a date not more than [35] days after the later of—
      (i) the date on which the Tribunal receives the notice of appeal; or
      (ii) if the Tribunal makes a preliminary decision under rule 10 (late notice of appeal), the date on which notice of that decision is served on the appellant; and
   (b) where an appeal is to be determined without a hearing, the Tribunal must determine it not more than [35] days after the later of those dates.

(3) If the respondent does not file the documents specified in rule 13(1) within the time specified in rule 13 or directions given under that rule—

    (a) paragraph (2) does not apply; and

    (b) the Tribunal may vary any hearing date that it has already fixed in accordance with paragraph (2)(a), if it is satisfied that it would be unfair to the appellant to proceed with the hearing on the date fixed.

(4) The Tribunal must serve its determination on the respondent—

    (a) if the appeal is considered at a hearing, by sending it not later than 10 days after the hearing finishes; or

    (b) if the appeal is determined without a hearing, by sending it not later than 10 days after it is determined.

(5) The respondent must—

    (a) serve the determination on the appellant—

        (i) if the respondent makes a section 103A application or applies for permission to appeal under section 103B or 103E of the 2002 Act, by sending, delivering or personally serving the determination not later than the date on which it makes that application; and

        (ii) otherwise, not later than 28 days after receiving the determination from the Tribunal; and

    (b) as soon as practicable after serving the determination, notify the Tribunal on what date and by what means it was served.

(6) If the respondent does not give the Tribunal notification under paragraph (5)(b) within 29 days after the Tribunal serves the determination on it, the Tribunal must serve the determination on the appellant as soon as reasonably practicable thereafter.

(7) In paragraph (2) of this rule, references to a hearing do not include a case management review hearing or other preliminary hearing.

Part 3 Reconsideration of Appeals etc

24. Scope of this Part

(1) Section 1 of this Part applies to section 103A applications made during any period in which paragraph 30 of Schedule 2 to the 2004 Act has effect, which are considered by an immigration judge in accordance with that paragraph.

(2) Section 2 of this Part applies to reconsideration of appeals by the Tribunal pursuant to—

    (a) an order under section 103A(1) made by—

        (i) the appropriate court; or

        (ii) an immigration judge in accordance with paragraph 30 of Schedule 2 to the 2004 Act; and

    (b) remittal by the appropriate appellate court under section 103B(4)(c), 103C(2)(c) or 103E(4)(c) of the 2002 Act.

(3) Section 3 of this Part applies to applications for permission to appeal to the appropriate appellate court.

Section 1
Section 103A Applications Considered by Members of the Tribunal

25. Procedure for applying for review

Where paragraph 30 of Schedule 2 to the 2004 Act has effect in relation to a section 103A application, the application must be made in accordance with relevant rules of court (including any practice directions supplementing those rules).

26. Deciding applications for review

(1) A section 103A application shall be decided by an immigration judge authorised by the President to deal with such applications.

(2) The immigration judge shall decide the application without a hearing, and by reference only to the applicant's written submissions and the documents filed with the application notice.

(3) The immigration judge is not required to consider any grounds for ordering the Tribunal to reconsider its decision other than those set out in the application notice.

(4) The application must be decided not later than 10 days after the Tribunal receives the application notice.

(5) In deciding a section 103A application, the immigration judge may—

  (a) in relation to an application for permission under section 103A(4)(b), either—

    (i) permit the application to be made outside the period specified in section 103A(3); or

    (ii) record that he does not propose to grant permission; and

  (b) in relation to an application for an order under section 103A(1), either—

    (i) make an order for reconsideration; or

    (ii) record that he does not propose to make such an order.

(6) The immigration judge may make an order for reconsideration only if he thinks that—

  (a) the Tribunal may have made an error of law; and

  (b) there is a real possibility that the Tribunal would decide the appeal differently on reconsideration.

27. Form and service of decision

(1) Where an immigration judge decides[—

  (a) an application for permission under section 103A(4)(b); or

  (b) an application for an order under section 103A(1)], he must give written notice of his decision, including his reasons which may be in summary form.

(2) Where an immigration judge makes an order for reconsideration—

  (a) his notice of decision must state the grounds on which the Tribunal is ordered to reconsider its decision on the appeal; and

  (b) he may give directions for the reconsideration of the decision on the appeal which may—

    (i) provide for any of the matters set out in rule 45(4) which he considers appropriate to such reconsideration; and

    (ii) specify the number or class of members of the Tribunal to whom the reconsideration shall be allocated.

(3) The Tribunal must, except in cases to which paragraph (5) applies—

  (a) serve a copy of the notice of decision and any directions on every party to the appeal to the Tribunal; and

(b) where the immigration judge makes an order for reconsideration, serve on the party to the appeal other than the party who made the section 103A application a copy of the application notice and any documents which were attached to it.

(4) Paragraph (5) applies to reviews of appeals under section 82 of the 2002 Act where—

    (a) the appellant is in the United Kingdom; and

    (b) the appeal relates, in whole or in part, to an asylum claim.

(5) In cases to which this paragraph applies—

    (a) the Tribunal must send to the respondent to the appeal—

        (i) the notice of decision,

        (ii) any directions, and

        (iii) the application notice and any documents which were attached to it (unless the respondent to the appeal made the application for reconsideration);

    (b) the respondent must serve on the appellant—

        (i) the notice of decision and any directions; and

        (ii) the application notice and any documents which were attached to it (unless the appellant made the application for reconsideration),not later than 28 days after receiving them from the Tribunal;

    (c) the respondent must, as soon as practicable after serving the documents mentioned in sub-paragraph (b), notify the Tribunal on what date and by what means they were served; and

    (d) if the respondent does not give the Tribunal notification under sub-paragraph (c) within 29 days after the Tribunal serves the notice of decision on it, the Tribunal must serve the documents mentioned in sub-paragraph (b) on the appellant as soon as reasonably practicable thereafter.

28. Sending notice of decision to the appropriate court

The Tribunal must send to the appropriate court copies of—

    (a) the notice of decision; and

    (b) the application notice and any documents which were attached to it, upon being requested to do so by the appropriate court.

28A. Orders for funding on section 103A applications

(1) This rule applies where a section 103A application has been made by an appellant in relation to an appeal decided in England, Wales or Northern Ireland.

(2) If an immigration judge, when he considers a section 103A application, makes an order under section 103D(1) of the 2002 Act, the Tribunal must send a copy of that order to—

    (a) the appellant's representative; and

    (b) the relevant funding body.

(3) If, pursuant to regulations under section 103D of the 2002 Act, the appellant's representative applies for an order under section 103D(1) of the 2002 Act where an immigration judge has made an order for reconsideration of an appeal but the reconsideration does not proceed—

    (a) the immigration judge may decide that application without a hearing; and

    (b) the Tribunal must send notice of his decision to—

        (i) the appellant's representative; and

        (ii) if he makes an order under section *103D(1)* [103D(3)], the relevant funding body.

(4) In a case to which rule 27(5) applies, the Tribunal must not send an order or decision under this rule to the appellant's representative until either—

    (a) the respondent has notified the Tribunal under rule 27(5)(c) that it has served the documents mentioned in rule 27(5)(b) on the appellant; or

    (b) the Tribunal has served those documents on the appellant under rule 27(5)(d).

(5) In this rule, 'relevant funding body' has the same meaning as in rule 33.]

SECTION 2
RECONSIDERATION OF APPEALS

29. Rules applicable on reconsideration of appeal

Rules 15 to 23, except for rule 23(2) and (3), and Part 5 of these Rules apply to the reconsideration of an appeal as they do to the initial determination of an appeal, and references in those rules to an appeal shall be interpreted as including proceedings for the reconsideration of an appeal.

30. Reply

(1) When the other party to the appeal is served with an order for reconsideration, he must, if he contends that the Tribunal should uphold the initial determination for reasons different from or additional to those given in the determination, file with the Tribunal and serve on the applicant a reply setting out his case.

(2) The other party to the appeal must file and serve any reply not later than 5 days before the earliest date appointed for any hearing of or in relation to the reconsideration of the appeal.

(3) In this rule, 'other party to the appeal' means the party other than the party on whose application the order for reconsideration was made.

31. Procedure for reconsideration of appeal

(1) Where an order for reconsideration has been made, the Tribunal must reconsider an appeal as soon as reasonably practicable after that order has been served on both parties to the appeal.

(2) Where the reconsideration is pursuant to an order under section 103A—

    (a) the Tribunal carrying out the reconsideration must first decide whether the original Tribunal made a material error of law; and

    (b) if it decides that the original Tribunal did not make a material error of law, the Tribunal must order that the original determination of the appeal shall stand.

(3) Subject to paragraph (2), the Tribunal must substitute a fresh decision to allow or dismiss the appeal.

(4) In carrying out the reconsideration, the Tribunal—

    (a) may limit submissions or evidence to one or more specified issues; and

    (b) must have regard to any directions given by the immigration judge or court which ordered the reconsideration.

(5) In this rule, a 'material error of law' means an error of law which affected the Tribunal's decision upon the appeal.

32. Evidence on reconsideration of appeal

(1) The Tribunal may consider as evidence any note or record made by the Tribunal of any previous hearing at which the appeal was considered.

(2) If a party wishes to ask the Tribunal to consider evidence which was not submitted on any previous occasion when the appeal was considered, he must file with the Tribunal and serve on the other party written notice to that effect, which must—

(a) indicate the nature of the evidence; and

(b) explain why it was not submitted on any previous occasion.

(3) A notice under paragraph (2) must be filed and served as soon as practicable after the parties have been served with the order for reconsideration.(4) If the Tribunal decides to admit additional evidence, it may give directions as to—

(a) the manner in which; and

(b) the time by which, the evidence is to be given or filed.

33. Orders for funding on reconsideration

(1) This rule applies where—

(a) the Tribunal has reconsidered an appeal following a section 103A application made by the appellant in relation to an appeal decided in England, Wales or Northern Ireland; and

(b) the appellant's representative has specified that he seeks an order under section 103D of the 2002 Act for his costs to be paid out of the relevant fund.

(2) The Tribunal must make a separate determination ('the funding determination') stating whether it orders payment out of the relevant fund of the appellant's costs—

(a) in respect of the application for reconsideration;

(b) in respect of the preparation for reconsideration; and

(c) in respect of the reconsideration.

(3) The Tribunal must send the funding determination to—

(a) the appellant's representative; and

(b) if the Tribunal has made an order under section 103D, the relevant funding body.

(4) Where the determination of the reconsidered appeal ('the principal determination') is served in accordance with rule 23, the Tribunal must not send the funding determination to the appellant's representative until—

(a) the respondent has notified the Tribunal under rule 23(5)(b) that it has served the principal determination on the appellant; or

(b) the Tribunal has served the principal determination on the appellant under rule 23(6).

(4A) Where, in accordance with regulations under section 103D of the 2002 Act, a senior immigration judge reviews a decision by the Tribunal not to make an order under section 103D(3), the Tribunal must send notice of the decision upon that review to—

(a) the appellant's representative; and

(b) if the senior immigration judge makes an order under section 103D(3), the relevant funding body.]

(5) In this Rule—

(a) 'relevant fund' means—

(i) in relation to an appeal decided in England or Wales, the Community Legal Service Fund established under <u>section 5</u> of the Access to Justice Act 1999;

(ii) in relation to an appeal decided in Northern Ireland, the fund established under paragraph 4(2)(a) of Schedule 3 to the Access to Justice (Northern Ireland) Order 2003; and

(b) 'relevant funding body' means—

(i) in relation to an appeal decided in England or Wales, the Legal Services Commission;

(ii) in relation to an appeal decided in Northern Ireland, the Northern Ireland Legal Services Commission.

SECTION 3
APPLICATIONS FOR PERMISSION TO APPEAL TO THE APPROPRIATE APPELLATE COURT

34. Applying for permission to appeal

(1) An application to the Tribunal under this Section must be made by filing with the Tribunal an application notice for permission to appeal.

(2) The application notice for permission to appeal must—

(a) be [made on a form approved for the purpose by the President];

(b) state the grounds of appeal; and

(c) be signed by the applicant or his representative, and dated.

(3) If the application notice is signed by the applicant's representative, the representative must certify in the application notice that he has completed the application notice in accordance with the applicant's instructions.

(4) As soon as practicable after an application notice for permission to appeal is filed, the Tribunal must notify the other party to the appeal to the Tribunal that it has been filed.

35. Time limit for application

(1) In application notice for permission to appeal must be filed in accordance with rule 34—

(a) if the applicant is in detention under the Immigration Acts when he is served with the Tribunal's determination, not later than 5 days after he is served with that determination;

(b) in any other case, not later than 10 days after he is served with the Tribunal's determination.

(2) The Tribunal may not extend the time limits in paragraph (1).

36. Determining the application

(1) An application for permission to appeal must be determined by a senior immigration judge without a hearing.

(2) The Tribunal may either grant or refuse permission to appeal.

(3) Where the Tribunal intends to grant permission to appeal it may, if it thinks that the Tribunal has made an administrative error in relation to the proceedings, instead set aside the Tribunal's determination and direct that the proceedings be reheard by the Tribunal.

(4) The Tribunal must serve on every party written notice of its decision, including its reasons, which may be in summary form.

PART 4 BAIL

37. Scope of this Part and interpretation

(1) This Part applies to applications under the Immigration Acts to the Tribunal, by persons detained under those Acts, to be released on bail.

(2) In this Part, 'applicant' means a person applying to the Tribunal to be released on bail.

(3) The parties to a bail application are the applicant and the Secretary of State.

38. Applications for bail

(1) An application to be released on bail must be made by filing with the Tribunal an application notice in [a form approved for the purpose by the President].

(2) The application notice must contain the following details—
    (a) the applicant's—
        (i) full name;
        (ii) date of birth; and
        (iii) date of arrival in the United Kingdom;
    (b) the address of the place where the applicant is detained;
    (c) whether an appeal by the applicant to the Tribunal is pending;
    (d) the address where the applicant will reside if his application for bail is granted, or, if he is unable to give such an address, the reason why an address is not given;
    (e) where the applicant is aged 18 or over, whether he will, if required, agree as a condition of bail to co-operate with electronic monitoring under section 36 of the 2004 Act;
    (f) the amount of the recognizance in which he will agree to be bound;
    (g) the full names, addresses, occupations and dates of birth of any persons who have agreed to act as sureties for the applicant if bail is granted, and the amounts of the recognizances in which they will agree to be bound;
    (h) the grounds on which the application is made and, where a previous application has been refused, full details of any change in circumstances which has occurred since the refusal; and
    (i) whether an interpreter will be required at the hearing, and in respect of what language or dialect.

(3) The application must be signed by the applicant or his representative or, in the case of an applicant who is a child or is for any other reason incapable of acting, by a person acting on his behalf.

39. Bail hearing

(1) Where an application for bail is filed, the Tribunal must—
    (a) as soon as reasonably practicable, serve a copy of the application on the Secretary of State; and
    (b) fix a hearing.

(2) If the Secretary of State wishes to contest the application, he must file with the Tribunal and serve on the applicant a written statement of his reasons for doing so—
    (a) not later than 2.00 pm on the business day before the hearing; or
    (b) if he was served with notice of the hearing less than 24 hours before that time, as soon as reasonably practicable.

(3) The Tribunal must serve written notice of its decision on—
    (a) the parties; and
    (b) the person having custody of the applicant.

(4) Where bail is granted, the notice must include—
   (a) the conditions of bail; and
   (b) the amount in which the applicant and any sureties are to be bound.
(5) Where bail is refused, the notice must include reasons for the refusal.

40. Recognizances

(1) The recognizance of an applicant or a surety must be in writing and must state—
   (a) the amount in which he agrees to be bound; and
   (b) that he has read and understood the bail decision and that he agrees to pay that amount of money if the applicant fails to comply with the conditions set out in the bail decision.
(2) The recognizance must be—
   (a) signed by the applicant or surety; and
   (b) filed with the Tribunal.

41. Release of applicant

The person having custody of the applicant must release him upon—
   (a) being served with a copy of the decision to grant bail; and
   (b) being satisfied that any recognizances required as a condition of that decision have been entered into.

42. Application of this Part to Scotland

This Part applies to Scotland with the following modifications—
   (a) in rule 38, for paragraph (2)(f) and (g) substitute—'(f) the amount, if any, to be deposited if bail is granted;(g) the full names, addresses and occupations of any persons offering to act as cautioners if the application for bail is granted;';
   (b) in rule 39, for paragraph (4)(b) substitute—'(b) the amount (if any) to be deposited by the applicant and any cautioners.';
   (c) rule 40 does not apply; and(d) in rule 41, for sub-paragraph (b) substitute—'(b) being satisfied that the amount to be deposited, if any, has been deposited.'.

Part 5 General Provisions

43. Conduct of appeals and applications

(1) The Tribunal may, subject to these Rules, decide the procedure to be followed in relation to any appeal or application.
(2) Anything of a formal or administrative nature which is required or permitted to be done by the Tribunal under these Rules may be done by a member of the Tribunal's staff.

44. Constitution of the Tribunal

(1) The Tribunal shall be under no duty to consider any representations by a party about the number or class of members of the Tribunal which should exercise the jurisdiction of the Tribunal.
(2) Where the President directs that the Tribunal's jurisdiction shall be exercised by more than one member, unless the President's direction specifies otherwise a single immigration judge may—
   (a) conduct a case management review hearing;

   (b) give directions to the parties; and

   (c) deal with any other matter preliminary or incidental to the hearing of an appeal or application.

45. Directions

(1) The Tribunal may give directions to the parties relating to the conduct of any appeal or application.

(2) The power to give directions is to be exercised subject to any specific provision of these Rules.

(3) Directions must be given orally or in writing to every party.

(4) Directions of the Tribunal may, in particular—

   (a) relate to any matter concerning the preparation for a hearing;

   (b) specify the length of time allowed for anything to be done;

   (c) vary any time limit in these Rules or in directions previously given by the Tribunal for anything to be done by a party;

   (d) provide for—

      (i) a particular matter to be dealt with as a preliminary issue;

      (ii) a case management review hearing to be held;

      (iii) a party to provide further details of his case, or any other information which appears to be necessary for the determination of the appeal;

      (iv) the witnesses, if any, to be heard;

      (v) the manner in which any evidence is to be given (for example, by directing that witness statements are to stand as evidence in chief);

   (e) require any party to file and serve—

      (i) statements of the evidence which will be called at the hearing;

      (ii) a paginated and indexed bundle of all the documents which will be relied on at the hearing;

      (iii) a skeleton argument which summarises succinctly the submissions which will be made at the hearing and cites all the authorities which will be relied on, identifying any particular passages to be relied on;

      (iv) a time estimate for the hearing;

      (v) a list of witnesses whom any party wishes to call to give evidence;

      (vi) a chronology of events; and

      (vii) details of whether an interpreter will be required at the hearing, and in respect of what language and dialect;

   (f) limit—

      (i) the number or length of documents upon which a party may rely at a hearing;

      (ii) the length of oral submissions;

      (iii) the time allowed for the examination and cross-examination of witnesses; and

      (iv) the issues which are to be addressed at a hearing; and

   (g) require the parties to take any steps to enable two or more appeals to be heard together under rule 20.

   (h) provide for a hearing to be conducted or evidence given or representations made by video link or by other electronic means; and

      (i) make provision to secure the anonymity of a party or a witness.

(5) The Tribunal must not direct an unrepresented party to do something unless it is satisfied that he is able to comply with the direction.

(6) The President may direct that, in individual cases or in such classes of case as he shall specify, any time period in these Rules for the Tribunal to do anything shall be extended by such period as he shall specify.

46. Notification of hearings

(1) When the Tribunal fixes a hearing it must serve notice of the date, time and place of the hearing on every party.

(2) The Tribunal may vary the date of a hearing, but must serve notice of the new date, time and place of the hearing on every party.

47. Adjournment

Subject to any provision of these Rules, the Tribunal may adjourn any hearing.

48. Representation

(1) An appellant or applicant for bail may act in person or be represented by any person not prohibited from representing him by section 84 of the Immigration and Asylum Act 1999.

(2) A respondent to an appeal, the Secretary of State or the United Kingdom Representative may be represented by any person authorised to act on his behalf.

(3) If a party to whom paragraph (1) applies is represented by a person not permitted by that paragraph to represent him, any determination given or other step taken by the Tribunal in the proceedings shall nevertheless be valid.

(4) Where a representative begins to act for a party, he must immediately notify the Tribunal and the other party of that fact.

(4A) Where a notice of appeal, or an application for bail under rule 38, is signed by a representative, the representative will be deemed to have notified the Tribunal and the other party that he is acting for a party in accordance with paragraph (4).

(4B) Where a notice of appeal, or an application for bail under rule 38, is not signed by a representative, the representative must file a separate notice with the Tribunal and serve it on the other party to comply with his obligations under paragraph (4).]

(5) Where a representative is acting for a party, he may on behalf of that party do anything that these Rules require or permit that party to do.

(6) Where a representative is acting for an appellant, the appellant is under a duty—
    (a) to maintain contact with his representative until the appeal is finally determined; and
    (b) to notify the representative of any change of address.

(7) Where a representative ceases to act for a party, the representative and the party must immediately notify the Tribunal and the other party [in writing] of that fact, and of the name and address of any new representative (if known).

(8) Notification under paragraph (4) . . .—
    (a) where a representative is appointed to act for a party on the day of a hearing, may be given orally at [that] hearing to the Tribunal and to any other party present at that hearing; but
    (b) must otherwise be given in writing.

(9) Until the Tribunal is notified that a representative has ceased to act for a party, any document served on that representative shall be deemed to be properly served on the party he was representing.

49. United Kingdom Representative

(1) The United Kingdom Representative may give notice to the Tribunal that he wishes to participate in any proceedings where the appellant has made an asylum claim.

(2) Where the United Kingdom Representative has given notice under paragraph (1)—

    (a) rules 54(6) and 55(7) shall apply; and

    (b) the Tribunal must permit him to make representations in the proceedings if he wishes to do so, and may give directions for that purpose.

50. Summoning of witnesses

(1) The Tribunal may, by issuing a summons ('a witness summons'), require any person in the United Kingdom—

    (a) to attend as a witness at the hearing of an appeal; and

    (b) subject to rule 51(2), at the hearing to answer any questions or produce any documents in his custody or under his control which relate to any matter in issue in the appeal.

(2) A person is not required to attend a hearing in obedience to a witness summons unless—

    (a) the summons is served on him; and

    (b) the necessary expenses of his attendance are paid or tendered to him.

(3) If a witness summons is issued at the request of a party, that party must pay or tender the expenses referred to in paragraph (2)(b).

51. Evidence

(1) The Tribunal may allow oral, documentary or other evidence to be given of any fact which appears to be relevant to an appeal or an application for bail, even if that evidence would be inadmissible in a court of law.

(2) The Tribunal may not compel a party or witness to give any evidence or produce any document which he could not be compelled to give or produce at the trial of a civil claim in the part of the United Kingdom in which the hearing is taking place.

(3) The Tribunal may require the oral evidence of a witness to be given on oath or affirmation.

(4) Where the Tribunal has given directions setting time limits for the filing and serving of written evidence, it must not consider any written evidence which is not filed or served in accordance with those directions unless satisfied that there are good reasons to do so.

(5) Where a party seeks to rely upon a copy of a document as evidence, the Tribunal may require the original document to be produced.

(6) In an appeal to which section 85(5) of the 2002 Act applies, the Tribunal must only consider evidence relating to matters which it is not prevented by that section from considering.

(7) Subject to section 108 of the 2002 Act, the Tribunal must not take account of any evidence that has not been made available to all the parties.

52. Language of documents

(1) Subject to paragraph (2)—

    (a) any notice of appeal or application notice filed with the Tribunal must be completed in English; and

    (b) any other document filed with the Tribunal must be in English, or accompanied by a translation into English signed by the translator to certify that the translation is accurate.

(2) In proceedings in or having a connection with Wales, a document may be filed with the Tribunal in Welsh.

(3) The Tribunal shall be under no duty to consider a document which is not in English (or, where paragraph (2) applies, in Welsh), or accompanied by a certified translation.

53. Burden of proof

(1) If an appellant asserts that a relevant decision ought not to have been taken against him on the ground that the statutory provision under which that decision was taken does not apply to him, it is for that party to prove that the provision does not apply to him.

(2) If—

    (a) an appellant asserts any fact; and

    (b) by virtue of an Act, statutory instrument or immigration rules, if he had made such an assertion to the Secretary of State, an immigration officer or an entry clearance officer, it would have been for him to satisfy the Secretary of State or officer that the assertion was true, it is for the appellant to prove that the fact asserted is true.

54. Admission of public to hearings

(1) Subject to the following provisions of this rule, every hearing before the Tribunal must be held in public.

(2) Where the Tribunal is considering an allegation referred to in section 108 of the 2002 Act—

    (a) all members of the public must be excluded from the hearing, and

    (b) any party or representative of a party may be excluded from the hearing.

(3) The Tribunal may exclude any or all members of the public from any hearing or part of a hearing if it is necessary—

    (a) in the interests of public order or national security; or

    (b) to protect the private life of a party or the interests of a minor.

(4) The Tribunal may also, in exceptional circumstances, exclude any or all members of the public from any hearing or part of a hearing to ensure that publicity does not prejudice the interests of justice, but only if and to the extent that it is strictly necessary to do so.

(5) A member of the Council on Tribunals or of its Scottish Committee acting in that capacity is entitled to attend any hearing and may not be excluded pursuant to paragraph (2), (3) or (4) of this rule.

(6) The United Kingdom Representative, where he has given notice to the Tribunal under rule 49, is entitled to attend any hearing except where paragraph (2) applies, and may not be excluded pursuant to paragraph (3) or (4) of this rule.

55. Filing and service of documents

(1) Any document which is required or permitted by these Rules or by a direction of the Tribunal to be filed with the Tribunal, or served on any person may be—

    (a) delivered, or sent by post, to an address;

    (b) sent via a document exchange to a document exchange number or address;

    (c) sent by fax to a fax number; or

    (d) sent by e-mail to an e-mail address, specified for that purpose by the Tribunal or person to whom the document is directed.

(2) A document to be served on an individual may be served personally by leaving it with that individual.

(3) Where a person has notified the Tribunal that he is acting as the representative of an appellant and has given an address for service, if a document is served on the appellant, a copy must also at the same time be sent to the appellant's representative.

(4) If any document is served on a person who has notified the Tribunal that he is acting as the representative of a party, it shall be deemed to have been served on that party.

(5) Subject to paragraph (6), any document that is served on a person in accordance with this rule shall, unless the contrary is proved, be deemed to be served—

    (a) where the document is sent by post or document exchange from and to a place within the United Kingdom, on the second day after it was sent;

    (b) where the document is sent by post or document exchange from or to a place outside the United Kingdom, on the twenty-eighth day after it was sent; and

    (c) in any other case, on the day on which the document was sent or delivered to, or left with, that person.

(6) Any notice of appeal which is served on a person under rule 6(3)(b) or 6(4)(b) shall be treated as being served on the day on which it is received by that person.

(7) Where the United Kingdom Representative has given notice to the Tribunal under rule 49 in relation to any proceedings, any document which is required by these Rules or by a direction of the Tribunal to be served on a party in those proceedings must also be served on the United Kingdom Representative.

56. Address for service

(1) Every party, and any person representing a party, must notify the Tribunal in writing of a postal address at which documents may be served on him and of any changes to that address.

(2) Until a party or representative notifies the Tribunal of a change of address, any document served on him at the most recent address which he has notified to the Tribunal shall be deemed to have been properly served on him.

57. Calculation of time

(1) Where a period of time for doing any act is specified by these Rules or by a direction of the Tribunal, that period is to be calculated—

    (a) excluding the day on which the period begins; and

    (b) where the period is 10 days or less, excluding any day which is not a business day (unless the period is expressed as a period of calendar days).

(2) Where the time specified by these Rules or by a direction of the Tribunal for doing any act ends on a day which is not a business day, that act is done in time if it is done on the next business day.

58. Signature of documents

Any requirement in these Rules for a document to be signed by a party or his representative shall be satisfied, in the case of a document which is filed or served electronically in accordance with these rules, by the person who is required to sign the document typing his name or producing it by computer or other mechanical means.

59. Errors of procedure

(1) Where, before the Tribunal has determined an appeal or application, there has been an error of procedure such as a failure to comply with a rule—

    (a) subject to these Rules, the error does not invalidate any step taken in the proceedings, unless the Tribunal so orders; and

(b) the Tribunal may make any order, or take any other step, that it considers appropriate to remedy the error.

(2) In particular, any determination made in an appeal or application under these Rules shall be valid notwithstanding that—

    (a) a hearing did not take place; or

    (b) the determination was not made or served, within a time period specified in these Rules.

60. Correction of orders and determinations

(1) The Tribunal may at any time amend an order, notice of decision or determination to correct a clerical error or other accidental slip or omission.

(1A) The President may, either of his own motion or on application, review any order, notice of decision or determination made by the Tribunal and, after consulting all the parties to the appeal, may set it aside and direct that the relevant proceedings be dealt with again by the Tribunal, on the ground that it was wrongly made as the result of an administrative error on the part of the Tribunal or its staff.

(1B) An application under paragraph (1A) must be filed—

    (a) if the party making the application is in the United Kingdom, within 10 days; or

    (b) if the party making the application is outside the United Kingdom, within 28 days, of the date on which the party is served with the order, notice of decision or determination.

(1C) At the same time as filing an application under paragraph (1A), the party making the application must serve a copy on the other party to the appeal.

(1D) The President may delegate his power under paragraph (1A) to a Deputy President or a senior immigration judge.

(2) Where an order, notice of decision or determination is amended under this rule—

    (a) the Tribunal must serve an amended version on the party or parties on whom it served the original; and

    (b) if rule 10(8) and (9), rule 23(5) and (6) or rule 27(5)(b)–(d) applied in relation to the service of the original, it shall also apply in relation to the service of the amended version.

(3) The time within which a party may apply for permission to appeal against, or for a review of, an amended determination runs from the date on which the party is served with the amended determination.

Part 6 Revocation and Transitional Provisions

61. Revocation

The Immigration and Asylum Appeals (Procedure) Rules 2003 are revoked.

62. Transitional provisions

(1) Subject to the following paragraphs of this rule, these Rules apply to any appeal or application to an adjudicator or the Immigration Appeal Tribunal which was pending immediately before 4th April 2005, and which continues on or after that date as if it had been made to the Tribunal by virtue of a transitional provisions order.

(2) Where a notice of a relevant decision has been served before 4th April 2005 and the recipient gives notice of appeal against the decision on or after 4th April 2005—

    (a) rules 6–8, 12 and 13 of these Rules shall not apply; and

    (b) rules 6–9 of the 2003 Rules shall continue to apply as if those Rules had not been revoked, but subject to the modifications in paragraph (4).

(3) Where a notice of appeal to an adjudicator has been given before 4th April 2005, but the respondent has not filed the notice of appeal with the appellate authority in accordance with rule 9 of the 2003 Rules—

    (a) rules 12 and 13 of these Rules shall not apply; and

    (b) rule 9 of the 2003 Rules shall continue to apply as if it had not been revoked, but subject to the modifications in paragraph (4).

(4) The modifications referred to in paragraphs (2)(b) and (3)(b) are that—

    (a) references to an adjudicator or the appellate authority shall be treated as referring to the Tribunal;

    (b) in rule 9(1) of the 2003 Rules—

        (i) the words 'Subject to rule 10' shall be omitted; and

        (ii) for 'together with' there shall be substituted 'and must also when directed by the Asylum and Immigration Tribunal file'; and

    (c) for rule 9(2) of the 2003 Rules there shall be substituted—

        '(2) The respondent must, as soon as practicable after filing the notice of appeal, serve on the appellant—

            (a) a copy of all the documents listed in paragraph (1), except for documents which the respondent has already sent to the appellant; and

            (b) notice of the date on which the notice of appeal was filed.'.

(5) Where, pursuant to a transitional provisions order, the Tribunal considers a section 103A application for a review of an adjudicator's determination of an appeal, Section 1 of Part 3 of these Rules shall apply subject to the modifications that—

    (a) in rules 26(3) and 27(2), the references to 'its decision' shall be interpreted as referring to the adjudicator's decision; and

    (b) in rules 26(6)(a) and 27(3)(a), the references to 'the Tribunal' shall be interpreted as referring to the adjudicator.

(6) Where, pursuant to a transitional provisions order, the Tribunal reconsiders an appeal which was originally determined by an adjudicator, Section 2 of Part 3 shall apply to the reconsideration, subject to paragraph (7).

(7) Where—

    (a) a party has been granted permission to appeal to the Immigration Appeal Tribunal against an adjudicator's determination before 4th April 2005, but the appeal has not been determined by that date; and

    (b) by virtue of a transitional provisions order the grant of permission to appeal is treated as an order for the Tribunal to reconsider the adjudicator's determination, the reconsideration shall be limited to the grounds upon which the Immigration Appeal Tribunal granted permission to appeal unless the Tribunal directs otherwise.

(8) Any time limit in these Rules for the Tribunal to do anything shall not apply in relation to proceedings to which these Rules apply by virtue of paragraph (1) of this rule.

(9) In relation to proceedings which were pending immediately before 4th April 2005—

    (a) unless the Tribunal directs otherwise—

        (i) anything done or any directions given before 4th April 2005 under the 2003 Rules (including anything which, pursuant to rule 61(3) of those Rules, was

>> treated as if done or given under those Rules) shall continue to have effect on and after that date;

(ii) anything done or any directions given by the appellate authority shall be treated as if done or given by the Tribunal; and

(iii) any document served on the appellate authority shall be treated as if served on the Tribunal;

(b) unless the context requires otherwise, any reference in a document to an adjudicator, the Immigration Appeal Tribunal or the appellate authority shall, insofar as it relates to an event on or after 4th April 2005, be treated as a reference to the Tribunal.

(10) In this rule—

(a) 'the 2003 Rules' means the Immigration and Asylum Appeals (Procedure) Rules 2003;

(b) 'adjudicator' and 'appellate authority' have the same meaning as in the 2003 Rules; and

(c) 'a transitional provisions order' means an order under section 48(3)(a) of the 2004 Act containing transitional provisions.

Falconer of Thoroton Dated 6th February 2005

Explanatory Note
(*This note is not part of the Rules*)

These Rules prescribe the procedure to be followed for appeals and applications to the Asylum and Immigration Tribunal created under section 81 of and Schedule 4 to the Nationality, Immigration and Asylum Act 2002, as substituted by section 26(1) of and Schedule 1 to the Asylum and Immigration (Treatment of Claimants, etc) Act 2004. The Rules come into force on 4th April 2005.

Part 1 of these Rules contains introductory provisions.

Part 2 contains rules about appeals to the Tribunal. Subject to various exceptions and limitations in Part 5 of the 2002 Act, a right of appeal lies to the Tribunal—

(a) under section 82 of the 2002 Act, against an immigration decision;

(b) under section 83 of the 2002 Act, in certain circumstances, against a decision to reject an asylum claim; and

(c) under section 40A of the British Nationality Act 1981, against a decision to make an order depriving a person of a British citizenship status.

Part 3 contains rules about—

(a) applications under section 103A of the 2002 Act (as inserted by section 26(6) of the 2004 Act) for the review of a decision of the Tribunal, which are considered by a member of the Tribunal under the transitional filter provision in paragraph 30 of Schedule 2 to the 2004 Act;

(b) reconsideration by the Tribunal of appeals pursuant to an order under section 103A of the 2002 Act or an order of an appellate court;

(c) applications to the Tribunal for permission to appeal to the Court of Appeal, Court of Session or Court of Appeal in Northern Ireland.

Part 4 contains rules about applications to the Tribunal for bail. Such applications may be made under Schedule 2 to the <u>Immigration Act 1971</u>.

Part 5 contains general provisions which apply to proceedings under these Rules.

Part 6 revokes the Immigration and Asylum Appeals (Procedure) Rules 2003 and contains transitional provisions for appeals and applications to an adjudicator or the Immigration Appeal Tribunal which are pending immediately before 4th April 2005.

APPENDIX 7

The Asylum and Immigration Tribunal (Fast Track Procedure) (Amendment) Rules 2005, Amended on 13.11.06

PART 1
INTRODUCTION

Citation and commencement

1. These Rules may be cited as the Asylum and Immigration Tribunal (Fast Track Procedure) Rules 2005 and shall come into force on 4th April 2005.

Interpretation

2.—(1) In these Rules, 'the Principal Rules' means the Asylum and Immigration Tribunal (Procedure) Rules 2005[4].

(2) Subject to paragraph (3), words and expressions used in these Rules which are defined in rule 2 of the Principal Rules have the same meaning in these Rules as in the Principal Rules.

(3) In these Rules, and in any provision of the Principal Rules which applies by virtue of these Rules, 'business day' means any day other than a Saturday or Sunday, a bank holiday, 24th to 31st December, Maundy Thursday, Good Friday or the Tuesday after the last Monday in May.

(4) In a provision of the Principal Rules which applies by virtue of these Rules, a reference to an 'appropriate prescribed form' means, in relation to a notice of appeal or an application notice for permission to appeal to the appropriate appellate court, the appropriate form in Schedule 1 to these Rules, or that form with any variations that the circumstances may require.[1]

(5) Where a provision of the Principal Rules applies by virtue of these Rules-
   (a) any reference in that provision to the Principal Rules is to be interpreted as including a reference to these Rules; and
   (b) any reference in that provision to a specific Part or rule in the Principal Rules is to be interpreted as including a reference to any equivalent Part or rule in these Rules.

Scope of these Rules

3.—(1) Part 2 of these Rules applies to appeals to the Tribunal in the circumstances specified in rule 5.

(2) Part 3 applies to proceedings before the Tribunal of the types described in rule 24 of the Principal Rules in the circumstances specified in rule 15.

(3) Part 4 applies to proceedings before the Tribunal to which Part 2 or 3 applies.

---

[1] Omitted by AIT (Fast Track Procedure) Rules 2006, 13.11.06.

(4) Part 5 applies to proceedings before the Tribunal to which Part 2 or 3 applies or has applied.

(5) For the purpose of rules 5 and 15, a party does not cease to satisfy a condition that he must have been continuously in detention under the Immigration Acts at a place or places specified in Schedule 2 to these Rules by reason only of—

    (a) being transported from one place of detention specified in that Schedule to another place which is so specified; or

    (b) leaving and returning to such a place of detention for any purpose between the hours of 6 a.m. and 10 p.m.

Application of the Principal Rules

4.—(1) Rule 4 of the Principal Rules (Overriding objective) applies to these Rules.

(2) Where Part 2 or 3 of these Rules applies to proceedings before the Tribunal, the Principal Rules also apply to the extent specified in rules 6, 16, 20, 24 and 27 of these Rules.

PART 2
APPEALS TO THE TRIBUNAL

Scope of this Part

5.—(1) This Part applies to an appeal to the Tribunal where the person giving notice of appeal—

    (a) was in detention under the Immigration Acts at a place specified in Schedule 2 when he was served with notice of the immigration decision against which he is appealing; and

    (b) has been continuously in detention under the Immigration Acts at a place or places specified in Schedule 2 since that notice was served on him.

(2) This Part shall cease to apply if the Tribunal makes an order under rule 30(1).

Application of Part 2 of the Principal Rules

6. Where this Part applies to an appeal, the following provisions of Part 2 of the Principal Rules apply—

    (a) rule 6(1) to (3), omitting the reference to rule 6(4) in rule 6(2);

    (b) rule 8;

    (c) rule 10(1);

    (d) rule 13(1) and (4);

    (e) rule 14; and

    (f) rules 17 to 19.

Giving notice of appeal

7. Where a notice of appeal is served on a custodian under rule 6(3)(b) of the Principal Rules, the custodian must—

    (a) endorse on the notice the date that it is served on him; and

    (b) forward it to the Tribunal immediately.

Time limit

8.—(1) A person who wishes to appeal must give a notice of appeal not later than 2 days after the day on which he is served with notice of the immigration decision against which he is appealing.

(2) Where a notice of appeal is given outside the time limit in paragraph (1), the Tribunal must not extend the time for appealing unless it is satisfied that, because of circumstances outside the control of the person giving notice of appeal or his representative, it was not practicable for the notice of appeal to be given within that time limit.

Service of notice of appeal on respondent

9. When the Tribunal receives a notice of appeal it shall immediately serve a copy upon the respondent.

Filing of documents by respondent

10. The respondent must file the documents listed in rule 13(1) of the Principal Rules not later than 2 days after the day on which the Tribunal serves the respondent with the notice of appeal.

Listing

11.—(1) The Tribunal shall fix a hearing date which is—
   (a) not later than 2 days after the day on which the respondent files the documents under rule 10; or
   (b) if the Tribunal is unable to arrange a hearing within that time, as soon as practicable thereafter.
(2) The Tribunal must serve notice of the date, time and place of the hearing on every party as soon as practicable, and in any event not later than noon on the business day before the hearing.

Deciding timeliness issues

12.—(1) The Tribunal shall consider any issue as to—
   (a) whether a notice of appeal was given outside the applicable time limit; and
   (b) whether to extend the time for appealing where the notice of appeal was given outside that time limit, as a preliminary issue at the hearing fixed under rule 11, subject to paragraph (2) of this rule.
(2) Rule 13 applies to the consideration and decision of such an issue as it applies to the consideration and determination of an appeal.
(3) Where the notice of appeal was given outside the applicable time limit and the Tribunal does not grant an extension of time, the Tribunal must take no further action in relation to the notice of appeal, except that it must serve 'on every party' [inserted by AIT (Fast Track Procedure) Amendment Rules 2006] written notice of its decision under this rule 'including its reasons which may be in summary form' not later than 1 day after the day on which that decision is made.

Method of determining appeal

13. The Tribunal must consider the appeal at the hearing fixed under rule 11 except where—
   (a) the appeal—
      (i) lapses pursuant to section 99 of the 2002 Act;
      (ii) is treated as abandoned pursuant to section 104(4) 'or (4A)' of the 2002 Act;
      (iii) is treated as finally determined pursuant to section 104(5) of the 2002 Act; or
      (iv) is withdrawn by the appellant or treated as withdrawn in accordance with rule 17 of the Principal Rules;

(b) the Tribunal adjourns the hearing under rule 28 or 30(2)(a) of these Rules; or

(c) all of the parties to the appeal consent to the Tribunal determining the appeal without a hearing.

Giving of determination

14.—(1) Where the Tribunal determines an appeal, it must give a written determination containing its decision and the reasons for it.

(2) The Tribunal must serve its determination on every party to the appeal—

(a) if the appeal is considered at a hearing, not later than 2 days after the day on which the hearing of the appeal finishes; or

(b) if the appeal is determined without a hearing, not later than 2 days after the day on which it is determined.

PART 3
RECONSIDERATION OF APPEALS, ETC.

Scope of this Part

15.—(1) This Part applies to proceedings before the Tribunal of a type specified in rule 24 of the Principal Rules, where—

(a) Part 2 of these Rules applied at all times to the appeal to the Tribunal;

(b) Part 3 of these Rules applied at all times to any other proceedings before the Tribunal of a type specified in rule 24 of the Principal Rules which related to that appeal; and

(c) the appellant has been continuously in detention under the Immigration Acts at a place or places specified in Schedule 2 to these Rules since being served with notice of the immigration decision against which he is appealing.

(2) This Part shall cease to apply if the Tribunal makes an order under rule 30(1).

SECTION 1
SECTION 103A APPLICATIONS CONSIDERED BY
MEMBERS OF THE TRIBUNAL

Application of Section 1 of Part 3 of the Principal Rules

16. Where this Part applies to a section 103A application, the following provisions of Section 1 of Part 3 of the Principal Rules apply—

(a) rule 25;

(b) rule 26, omitting paragraphs (2) and (4) of that rule;

(c) rule 27(1) and (2); and

(d) rule 28.

Service of application and response

17. Where a section 103A application to which this Part applies is filed with the Tribunal—

(a) the Tribunal must serve copies of the application notice and any documents which were attached to it on the party to the appeal other than the party who made the section 103A application as soon as practicable; and

(b) the party to the appeal other than the party who made the section 103A application may file submissions in response to the application not later than 1 day after the day on which it is served with the application.

Method of deciding applications for review

18. The immigration judge shall decide the application without a hearing, and by reference only to—
    (a) the applicant's written submissions and the documents filed with the application notice; and
    (b) any submissions filed in response to the application under rule 17(b).

Service of decision

19. The Tribunal must serve a copy of the notice of decision and any directions given under rule 27(2)(b) of the Principal Rules on every party to the appeal—
    (a) if submissions were filed in response to the application under rule 17(b), not later than 1 day after they were filed; or
    (b) if no submissions were filed within the period specified in rule 17(b), not later than 1 day after the end of that period.

SECTION 2
RECONSIDERATION OF APPEALS

Application of the Principal Rules

20.—(1) Where this Part applies to the reconsideration of an appeal, the following provisions of Section 2 of Part 3 of the Principal Rules apply—
    (a) rule 31(2) to (5); and
    (b) rule 32(1).

(2) Rules 17 to 19 and Part 5 of the Principal Rules apply, with any necessary modifications, to the reconsideration of an appeal under this Part to the extent that they would apply to the initial determination of an appeal under Part 2 of these Rules.

Procedure for reconsideration of appeal

21.—(1) Where an order for reconsideration has been made, the Tribunal must fix a hearing date for the reconsideration of its decision on the appeal which is—
    (a) not later than 2 days after the day on which that order has been served on both parties to the appeal; or
    (b) if the Tribunal is unable to arrange a hearing within that time, as soon as practicable thereafter.

(2) The Tribunal must serve notice of the date, time and place of the reconsideration hearing on every party not later than noon on the business day before the hearing.

Fresh evidence on reconsideration of appeal

22.—(1) If a party wishes to ask the Tribunal to consider evidence which was not submitted on any previous occasion when it considered the appeal, he must notify the Tribunal and the other party of—
    (a) the nature of the evidence; and
    (b) the reasons why it was not submitted on any previous occasion.

(2) Wherever practicable, notification under paragraph (1) must be given before the date fixed for the reconsideration hearing under rule 21.

Determination on reconsideration

23.—(1) The Tribunal must reconsider its decision on the appeal at the hearing fixed under rule 21 except where—

(a) any of the circumstances set out in rule 13 applies;

(b) a party has failed to comply with a provision of these Rules or a direction of the Tribunal, and the Tribunal is satisfied that in all the circumstances, including the extent of the failure and any reasons for it, it is appropriate to reconsider its decision on the appeal without a hearing; or

(c) the Tribunal is satisfied, having regard to the material before it and the nature of the issues raised, that its decision on the appeal can be justly reconsidered without a hearing.

(2) Rule 14 applies to the reconsideration of an appeal as it applies to the initial determination of an appeal.

Section 3

Applications for permission to appeal to the appropriate appellate court

Application of Section 3 of Part 3 of the Principal Rules

24. Where this Part applies to an application for permission to appeal to the appropriate appellate court, the following provisions of Section 3 of Part 3 of the Principal Rules apply—

(a) rule 34(1) to (3); and

(b) rule 36.

Time limits for filing and serving application

25.—(1) An application notice for permission to appeal must be filed not later than 2 days after the day on which the appellant is served with the Tribunal's determination.

(2) The Tribunal may not extend the time limit in paragraph (1).

(3) Immediately upon an application notice for permission to appeal being filed, the Tribunal must notify the other party to the appeal to the Tribunal that it has been filed.

Time limit for determining the application

26. The Tribunal must determine the application for permission to appeal, and serve its determination on every party, not later than 1 day after the day on which the Tribunal receives the application notice.

Part 4

General Provisions

Application of Part 5 of the Principal Rules

27. Where this Part applies, Part 5 of the Principal Rules applies, except that—

(a) rule 47 applies subject to rule 28 of these Rules; and

(b) rule 60(2) does not apply.

Adjournment

28. The Tribunal may only adjourn a hearing where—
    (a) it is necessary to do so because there is insufficient time to hear the appeal or application which is before the Tribunal;
    (b) a party has not been served with notice of the hearing in accordance with these Rules;
    (c) the Tribunal is satisfied by evidence filed or given by or on behalf of a party that—
        (i) the appeal or application cannot be justly determined on the date on which it is listed for hearing; and
        (ii) there is an identifiable future date, not more than 10 days after the date on which the appeal or application is listed for hearing, by which it can be justly determined; or
    (d) the Tribunal makes an order under rule 30.

Correction of orders and determinations

29. Where an order, notice of decision or determination is amended under rule 60(1) of the Principal Rules, the Tribunal must, not later than 1 day after making the amendment, serve an amended version on every party on whom it served the original.

   'Correction of administrative errors 29A. Where an order, notice of decision or determination is set aside and the President, Deputy President or senior immigration judge orders that the relevant proceedings be dealt with again by the Tribunal under rule 60(1A) of the Principal Rules, the Tribunal must, not later than 1 day after making the order, notify every party of its decision'.

PART 5
REMOVAL OF PENDING PROCEEDINGS FROM FAST TRACK

Transfer out of fast track procedure

30.—(1) Where Part 2 or 3 of these Rules applies to an appeal or application, the Tribunal must order that that Part shall cease to apply—
    (a) if all the parties consent;
    (b) if it is satisfied by evidence filed or given by or on behalf of a party that there are exceptional circumstances which mean that the appeal or application cannot otherwise be justly determined; or
    (c) if—
        (i) the respondent to the appeal has failed to comply with a provision of these Rules, or the Principal Rules as applied by these Rules, or a direction of the Tribunal; and
        (ii) the Tribunal is satisfied that the appellant would be prejudiced by that failure if the appeal or application were determined in accordance with these Rules.
(2) When making an order under paragraph (1), the Tribunal may—
    (a) adjourn any hearing of the appeal or application; and
    (b) give directions relating to the further conduct of the appeal or application.
(3) Where the Tribunal adjourns a hearing under paragraph (2)(a)—
    (a) it must fix a new date, time and place for the hearing; and
    (b) in the case of an adjournment of an appeal, rule 21(4) of the Principal Rules shall apply.

Application of the Principal Rules on transfer out of fast track

31.—(1) This rule applies where Part 2 or 3 of these Rules ceases to apply to an appeal or application because—

    (a) the conditions in rule 5 or 15 cease to apply; or

    (b) the Tribunal makes an order under rule 30(1).

(2) Subject to paragraph (3), the Principal Rules shall apply to the appeal or application from the date on which these Rules cease to apply.

(3) Where—

    (a) a period of time for doing something has started to run under a provision of these Rules; and

    (b) that provision ceases to apply, if the Principal Rules contain a time limit for doing the same thing, the time limit in the Principal Rules shall apply, and the relevant period of time shall be treated as running from the date on which the period of time under these Rules started to run.

PART 6
REVOCATION AND TRANSITIONAL PROVISIONS

Revocation

32. The Immigration and Asylum Appeals (Fast Track Procedure) Rules 2003[5] are revoked.

Transitional provisions

33.—(1) Subject to the following paragraphs of this rule, these Rules apply to any pending appeal or application to an adjudicator or the Immigration Appeal Tribunal which was subject to the 2003 Fast Track Rules immediately before 4th April 2005, and which continues on or after that date as if it had been made to the Tribunal by virtue of a transitional provisions order.

(2) Where a notice of a relevant decision has been served before 4th April 2005 and the recipient gives notice of appeal against the decision on or after 4th April 2005—

    (a) rules 7 to 10 of these Rules, and rules 6(1) to (3), 8 and 13(1) and (4) of the Principal Rules, shall not apply; and

    (b) rule 6 of the 2003 Fast Track Rules and rules 6 and 8 of the 2003 Principal Rules shall continue to apply as if those rules had not been revoked, with the modification that references to an adjudicator or the appellate authority shall be treated as referring to the Tribunal.

(3) Where a notice of appeal to an adjudicator has been given before 4th April 2005, but the respondent has not filed the notice of appeal with the appellate authority in accordance with rule 6(3)(a) of the 2003 Fast Track Rules—

    (a) rules 9 and 10 of these Rules, and rule 13(1) and (4) of the Principal Rules, shall not apply; and

    (b) rule 6(3) of the 2003 Fast Track Rules shall continue to apply as if it had not been revoked, with the modification that the reference to the appellate authority shall be treated as referring to the Tribunal.

(4) Where, pursuant to a transitional provisions order, the Tribunal reconsiders an appeal which was originally determined by an adjudicator, Section 2 of Part 3 shall apply to the reconsideration, subject to paragraph (5).

(5) Where—

  (a) a party has been granted permission to appeal to the Immigration Appeal Tribunal against an adjudicator's determination before 4th April 2005, but the appeal has not been determined by that date; and

  (b) by virtue of a transitional provisions order the grant of permission to appeal is treated as an order for the Tribunal to reconsider the adjudicator's determination, the reconsideration shall be limited to the grounds upon which the Immigration Appeal Tribunal granted permission to appeal.

(6) In relation to proceedings which were pending immediately before 4th April 2005—

  (a) unless the Tribunal directs otherwise—

    (i) anything done or any directions given before 4th April 2005 under the 2003 Fast Track Rules shall continue to have effect on and after that date;

    (ii) anything done or any directions given by the appellate authority shall be treated as if done or given by the Tribunal; and

    (iii) any document served on the appellate authority shall be treated as if served on the Tribunal;

  (b) unless the context requires otherwise, any reference in a document to an adjudicator, the Immigration Appeal Tribunal or the appellate authority shall, insofar as it relates to an event on or after 4th April 2005, be treated as a reference to the Tribunal.

(7) In this rule—

  (a) 'the 2003 Fast Track Rules' means the Immigration and Asylum Appeals (Fast Track Procedure) Rules 2003;

  (b) 'the 2003 Principal Rules' means the Immigration and Asylum Appeals (Procedure) Rules 2003[6];

  (c) 'adjudicator' and 'appellate authority' have the same meaning as in the 2003 Fast Track Rules and 2003 Principal Rules; and

  (d) 'a transitional provisions order' means an order under section 48(3)(a) of the 2004 Act containing transitional provisions.

Falconer of Thoroton, C.

7th March 2005

Specified Places of Detention

Campsfield House Immigration Removal Centre, Kidlington, Oxfordshire Colnbrook House Immigration Removal Centre, Harmondsworth, Middlesex Harmondsworth Immigration Removal Centre, Harmondsworth, Middlesex Yarls Wood Immigration Removal Centre, Clapham, Bedfordshire.

Explanatory Note
(*This note is not part of the Rules*)

These Rules prescribe a 'fast track' procedure for appeals and applications to the Asylum and Immigration Tribunal, where the appellant is in detention under the Immigration Acts at the locations listed in Schedule 2. The Rules come into force on 4th April 2005.

The Tribunal is established under section 81 of and Schedule 4 to the Nationality, Immigration and Asylum Act 2002, as substituted by section 26(1) of and Schedule 1 to the Asylum and

Immigration (Treatment of Claimants, etc.) Act 2004. The general procedures for appeals and applications to the Tribunal are set out in the Asylum and Immigration Tribunal (Procedure) Rules 2005 ('the Principal Rules').

Parts 1 to 4 of these Rules specify the extent to which the Principal Rules apply to fast track appeals and applications, modify certain provisions of the Principal Rules and make different provision for certain matters. The circumstances in which those Parts apply are set out in rules 3, 5 and 15.

The procedure under these Rules differs from that under the Principal Rules principally in the following ways—

(a) there are shorter time limits for the parties and the Tribunal to take certain steps (rules 7 to 12, 14, 19, 21, 23, 25 and 26);

(b) the procedures for deciding certain issues are simplified or modified to reflect the shorter timetable in fast track proceedings (rules 12, 13, 22 and 28);

(c) in all fast track cases, including cases where the appeal relates in whole or in part to an asylum claim, the Tribunal must serve its determinations and decisions on every party to the appeal (rules 14, 19 and 23); and

(d) in the fast track, an application under section 103A of the 2002 Act must be served on the party to the appeal other than the applicant, who may file submissions in response to the application, which the immigration judge must consider (rules 17 and 18).

Part 5 specifies the circumstances in which the Tribunal may direct that an appeal or application is to be taken out of the fast track procedure, and the rules which apply when the fast track procedure ceases to apply. Part 6 revokes the Immigration and Asylum Appeals (Fast Track Procedure) Rules 2003 and contains transitional provisions.

Where these Rules apply, the time limits for applications under section 103A of the 2002 Act are varied by the Asylum and Immigration (Fast Track Time Limits) Order 2005.

Notes

[1] 2002 c. 41. Sections 106(1)–(3) were amended by paragraph 21 of Schedule 2 to the Asylum and Immigration (Treatment of Claimants, etc.) Act 2004 (c. 19).

[2] 1981 c. 61. Section 40A was inserted by section 4(1) of the Nationality, Immigration and Asylum Act 2002 (c. 41) and amended by paragraph 4 of Schedule 2 to the Asylum and Immigration (Treatment of Claimants, etc.) Act 2004 (c. 19).

[3] 1992 c. 53.

[4] SI 2005/230.

[5] SI 2003/801.

[6] SI 2003/652.

APPENDIX 8

Discretionary Leave

TABLE OF CONTENTS

INTRODUCTION

Humanitarian Protection and Discretionary Leave were introduced on 1 April 2003 to replace exceptional leave. Where an asylum applicant does not qualify for refugee status, the caseworker should always consider whether they qualify for leave on the basis of Humanitarian Protection and if not, then consider whether they qualify for Discretionary Leave (see the Asylum Instruction on Considering the Asylum Claim). A stand alone human rights claim may also result in a grant of Discretionary Leave if the qualifying criteria are met. This instruction explains the limited circumstances in which it would be appropriate to grant Discretionary Leave. For guidance on Humanitarian Protection please refer to the Asylum Instruction on Humanitarian Protection.

For details on family reunion and on dependants accompanying an applicant who is granted Discretionary Leave, please refer to the Children and Family Asylum Policy Unit (CFAPT) via a senior caseworker.

Non-asylum cases may qualify for Discretionary Leave only in the limited circumstances outlined in this instruction (see 'Criteria for granting DL' below, for the relevant categories). Where a non-asylum case does not meet the criteria for a grant of Discretionary Leave (or Humanitarian Protection leave) but the caseworker is still considering granting leave outside the Rules, they should refer to Chapter 1 section 14 of the IDIs on Leave Outside the Rules. Separate instructions may be issued in relation to the handling of applications for Discretionary Leave. The instructions will be in the form of APU Notices, Country Bulletins or Operational Guidance Notes (OGNs). Where such instructions are in force, they will take precedence over the contents of this instruction, to the extent that they make different provisions.

Key points

- Discretionary Leave is to be granted only if a case falls within the limited categories set out below in the section below 'Criteria for granting DL'. It is intended to be used sparingly.
- Discretionary leave is to be granted only where the Secretary of State is satisfied that neither an enforced nor voluntary return is possible without material prejudice to the rights protected under this instruction. References to 'return' are to be read accordingly.
- Discretionary Leave is granted outside the Immigration Rules.
- Discretionary Leave should not be granted where a person qualifies for asylum or Humanitarian Protection, or where there is another category within the Immigration Rules under which they qualify.
- Discretionary Leave should not be granted to EEA nationals (and their third-country national family members) who are exercising treaty rights.

- Discretionary Leave should not be granted where another EU Member State or Norway/ Iceland has accepted responsibility for an asylum claim under the Dublin arrangements or where an individual is otherwise removable on third country grounds.
- Discretionary Leave is not to be granted on the basis that, for the time being, practical obstacles prevent a person from leaving the UK or being removed, e.g. an absence of route or travel document.
- The period of leave granted will vary depending on the basis on which the grant of Discretionary Leave was made. An initial grant of leave will be no longer than three years and will sometimes be less—see section below on 'Duration of grants of DL'.
- Where an extension of leave is sought after a period of Discretionary Leave the request will be subject to an active review. A person will not become eligible for settlement until they have completed six years' Discretionary Leave. This period will be longer, at least ten years and potentially never, for those in the excluded category (see sections below on Exclusion from HP/DL). For further guidance see the Asylum Instruction on Active Review.
- For details on family reunion and dependants accompanying an applicant who is granted Discretionary Leave refer to CFAPT via a senior caseworker.
- Those granted Discretionary Leave have access to public funds and are entitled to work.

CRITERIA FOR GRANTING DISCRETIONARY LEAVE

Cases where return would breach Article 8 of the ECHR

Where the return of an individual would involve a breach of Article 8 of the ECHR (right to respect for private and family life) on the basis of family life established in the UK, they should be granted Discretionary Leave. Leave should not be granted on this basis without a full consideration of the Article 8 issues. Please refer to the Asylum Instruction on the Considering Human Rights.

This category applies to both asylum and non-asylum cases. In non-asylum cases it is most likely to arise in the context of a marriage or civil partnership application where, although the requirements of the Rules are not met (e.g. because the correct entry clearance is not held), there are genuine Article 8 reasons which would make return inappropriate. Discretionary Leave should not be granted under Article 8 in non-asylum cases without reference to a senior caseworker.

Policy on the consideration of cases of those who are persons liable to be removed as illegal entrants or deported and who have married a person settled in the UK involves special considerations. Immigration control issues weigh particularly heavily in such cases. The policy is contained in the Asylum Instruction on Processing Hybrid Applications. Similar considerations apply where the parties have contracted a civil partnership.

Cases Where Return Would Breach Article 3 of the ECHR but Where Humanitarian Protection is not Applicable

Where a person's return would be contrary to Article 3 of the ECHR (see the Asylum Instruction on Considering Human Rights for further details) based on a protection need arising from a real risk that the person would suffer serious harm on return, they will normally qualify for Humanitarian Protection unless they fall to be excluded from those provisions—see the Asylum Instruction on Humanitarian Protection. However, there are some cases where the Article 3 breach does not arise from a need for protection as such, e.g. where a person's medical condition or severe humanitarian conditions in the country of return would make return contrary to Article 3. Persons falling into this category should be granted Discretionary Leave rather than Humanitarian Protection.

Medical Cases

This category applies to both asylum and non-asylum cases.

It can in exceptional cases be a breach of Article 3 to remove someone from the UK if to do so would amount to inhuman or degrading treatment owing to the acute suffering which would be caused because of that person's medical condition. The threshold for inhuman and degrading treatment in such cases is extremely high and will only be reached in truly exceptional cases involving extreme circumstances. The fact that the applicant is suffering from a distressing medical condition (e.g. a condition which involves a limited life expectancy or affecting their mental health), may not, in itself, be sufficient to meet this threshold. Discretionary Leave should not be granted if the claimant could avoid the risk of acute suffering by leaving the UK voluntarily. For further guidance please refer to the Asylum Instruction on Considering Human Rights and Chapter 1 Section 8 of the IDIs (Medical).

Where it is proposed to grant leave under this category the case should be referred to a senior caseworker.

Severe Humanitarian Conditions

There may be some extreme cases (although such cases are likely to be rare) where a person would face such poor conditions if returned—e.g. absence of water, food or basic shelter—that removal could be a breach of the UK's Article 3 obligations. Discretionary Leave should not be granted if the claimant could avoid the risk of suffering by leaving the UK voluntarily. Where it is proposed to grant leave under this category the case should be referred to a senior caseworker.

Other Cases Where Return Would Breach the ECHR

This category applies to asylum and non-asylum cases where the breach would not give rise to a grant of Humanitarian Protection and is not covered above. For example, where return would result in a flagrant denial of the right in question in the person's country of origin. For guidance on the consideration of other ECHR claims, please refer to the Asylum Instruction on Considering Human Rights.

It will be rare for return to breach another Article of the ECHR without also breaching Article 3 and/or Article 8. Cases falling under this category should be referred to a senior caseworker for approval before a grant of Discretionary Leave is made.

Unaccompanied Asylum Seeking Children (UASCs)

Where an unaccompanied child applies for asylum, caseworkers should, as with any other applicant, first consider whether they qualify for asylum and if they do not, whether they qualify for Humanitarian Protection. If they do, leave should be granted accordingly. If they do not, they will qualify for Discretionary Leave if there are inadequate reception arrangements available in their own country. See the Children Asylum Instruction for further guidance.

Where an unaccompanied child qualifies for Discretionary Leave on more than one ground (i.e. on the ground of inadequate reception arrangements and also on another ground) they should be granted leave on the basis of the ground that provides the longer period of stay.

However, all grounds which might have led to a grant of leave should be recorded in the file minute.

Other Cases

This category applies only to asylum cases. Caseworkers should refer to Chapter 1 section 14 of the IDIs on Leave Outside the Rules for guidance on granting leave in non-asylum cases where there are particularly compelling circumstances.

The categories under which it would normally be appropriate to grant Discretionary Leave are set out above. There are likely to be very few other cases in which it would be appropriate to grant Discretionary Leave to an unsuccessful asylum seeker. However, it is not possible to anticipate every eventuality that may arise, so there remains scope to grant Discretionary Leave where individual circumstances, although not meeting the criteria of any of the other categories listed above, are so compelling that it is considered appropriate to grant some form of leave.

Discretionary Leave should not be granted on this basis without discussion with a senior caseworker. Detailed file minutes will be required to keep accurate records of what has been decided and for what reasons.

From time to time separate instructions may be issued describing a category of case for which Discretionary Leave might be granted under this heading. Such instructions would set out any other relevant information for handling such cases. See also the section on Short Periods of Stay or Deferred Decision/Removal.

Applicants Excluded From Refugee Status, Humanitarian Protection or Discretionary Leave

Exclusion from refugee status

Where an applicant would have established that they were a refugee under the 1951 Convention or eligible for a grant of Humanitarian Protection but for the fact that they were excluded from that protection, they should normally be granted Discretionary Leave for 6 months. Cases in which article 33(2) of the 1951 Convention applies should be treated in the same way. The criteria for exclusion from refugee status and the operation of article 33(2) are explained in the Asylum Instruction on Exclusion.

Exclusion from Humanitarian Protection

Individuals excluded from Humanitarian Protection will usually be granted Discretionary Leave for 6 months. See the Humanitarian Protection Asylum Instruction for the grounds of exclusion from Humanitarian Protection. The Asylum Instruction on Exclusion may also be helpful.

Exclusion from Discretionary Leave

The grounds for exclusion from Humanitarian Protection will apply to Discretionary Leave. See the Asylum Instruction on Humanitarian Protection for the relevant grounds. A person who is excluded from Discretionary Leave will be expected to leave the UK. Where neither enforced nor voluntary return is possible without material prejudice to the rights protected under this instruction, Discretionary Leave will usually be granted for six months.

Any decision that a UASC is excluded from Discretionary Leave should be referred to the Children and Families Asylum Policy Team (CFAPT).

NB: Where an individual has been excluded under this instruction, Ministers must be advised of any proposal to grant Discretionary Leave.

GRANTING OR REFUSING DISCRETIONARY LEAVE IN ASYLUM CASES

Granting Discretionary Leave

Asylum applicants who are granted Discretionary Leave should be issued with a Reasons For Refusal Letter (RFRL) which explains why the asylum application has been refused and why Humanitarian Protection has not been granted. The reasons for granting Discretionary Leave should also be set out. These reasons do not need to be detailed, but it should be clear under which of the categories listed above that the person qualifies. If someone qualifies under two headings they should benefit from the one that provides the longer period of stay. The letter should only refer to the basis on which leave was granted but the file minutes will need to be clear that both were considered applicable. If the grant of Discretionary Leave has been made on the basis of a fear of ill treatment by the authorities in the country of nationality, then the RFRL should make reference to this. Unless a fear of the authorities in the country of nationality is accepted, individuals with Discretionary Leave should apply for a national passport rather than a Home Office travel document if they wish to travel abroad.

Refusing Discretionary Leave

Applicants who are refused outright should be issued with a Reasons For Refusal Letter which explains why the asylum claim has been refused, why Humanitarian Protection has not been granted. If not already fully covered by the reasons for refusing asylum and Humanitarian Protection, the letter should explain why removal would not breach the United Kingdom's obligations under the ECHR, or why it is considered that the applicant can reasonably be expected to return voluntarily. Any matters raised by an applicant which relate to or rely on the contents of this policy instruction should be addressed in the refusal letter. See the Asylum Instruction on Considering Human Rights for further details about addressing ECHR issues. Further guidance is also provided in the Asylum Instruction on Article 8 of the ECHR.

REQUEST FOR DISCRETIONARY LEAVE AFTER THE INITIAL DECISION AND APPEAL STAGES

Occasions may arise when, following the refusal of asylum and exhaustion of all appeal rights, a request is nonetheless made for Discretionary Leave, usually in the form of a human rights claim.

By the time all rights of appeal have been exhausted, there will be very few cases that would merit a grant of Discretionary Leave because the relevant factors are likely to have been considered at an earlier stage. However, caseworkers should give full and careful consideration to the reasons provided for requesting such leave, and decide whether such a grant would be appropriate.

Further Representations/Fresh Claims

If refused, a request for DL in such a case should either be treated as further representations or, if treated as a fresh claim, be considered for certification under section 96 of the Nationality, Immigration and Asylum Act 2002 (as amended).

For more information see the Asylum Instruction on Further Representations and Fresh Claims. See also the IDI on Appeals—certification under section 96.

Asylum and Immigration Tribunal (AIT) Determinations

In some cases, the Asylum and Immigration Tribunal (AIT) may dismiss an asylum appeal but suggest that Discretionary Leave is granted in an individual case. In such instances the case is to be considered in accordance with guidance in the IDI on Appeals.

DURATION OF GRANTS OF DISCRETIONARY LEAVE

Standard Period for Different Categories of Discretionary Leave

It will normally be appropriate to grant the following periods of Discretionary Leave to those qualifying under the categories set out above. All categories will need to complete at least six years in total, or at least ten years in excluded cases, before being eligible to apply for ILR.

Article 8 cases—three years.

Article 3 cases—three years.

Other ECHR Articles—three years.

UASCs

Where leave is granted to a UASC on the basis of inadequate reception arrangements in their home country, the UASC should be granted DL. For decisions made before 1st April 2007 this grant of DL will be for three years or leave until age 18, whichever is the shorter; or the shorter of 12 months or leave until age 18 in certain specified countries (see the Children's Asylum Instruction). For all decisions made on or after 1 st April 2007 (where asylum/HP is being refused) DL must only be granted to 17.5 years or 3 years, (or 12 months for certain countries) which ever is the shorter period of time.

Other cases—three years (but this category is probably more likely than others to qualify for a non-standard grant period—see the section below).

Excluded from Humanitarian Protection or Discretionary Leave—six months. This period applies to the first grant and any subsequent grants following an active review.

See Duration of grants and Recording the consideration on the Minute in the Considering Human Rights claim instructions.

Non-Standard Grant Periods

There may be some cases—for example, some of those qualifying under Article 8 or the section on other cases—where it is clear from the individual circumstances of the case that the factors leading to Discretionary Leave being granted are going to be short lived. For example:

- an Article 8 case where a person is permitted to stay because of the presence of a family member in the United Kingdom and where it is known that the family member will be able to leave the United Kingdom within, say, 12 months;
- or a case where a grant of leave is appropriate to enable a person to stay in the UK to participate in a court case.

In these cases it will be appropriate to grant shorter periods of leave. Non-standard grants should be used only where the information relating to the specific case clearly points to a shorter period being applicable. Reasons for granting a shorter period shouldbe included in the letter to the applicant. Shorter periods of leave should only be granted after reference to a senior caseworker.

Short Periods of Stay or Deferred Decision/Removal

There will be some cases where the factors meriting a grant of Discretionary Leave are expected to be sufficiently short lived that the question arises whether to grant a short period of leave or to refuse the application outright whilst giving an undertaking not to remove the individual or expect them to return until the circumstances preventing their return have changed. Such cases could arise at the initial decision-making stage or following an appeal.

Where it is considered that return would be possible within six months of the date of decision it will normally be appropriate to refuse the claim outright, not to grant a period of Discretionary Leave, and to defer any removal until such time as it is possible.

CURTAILING DISCRETIONARY LEAVE

A grant of Discretionary Leave will not normally be actively reviewed during its currency. This paragraph sets out the circumstances when consideration should be given to curtailing such leave. Further guidance on curtailment of Discretionary Leave can be found in chapter 9, section 5, paragraph 3 of the IDIs.

Voluntary Actions Leading to Curtailment

It will not usually be appropriate to curtail a person's leave simply because they have returned to their own country or have travelled on their own national passport (people granted Discretionary Leave will normally be expected to keep their own national passport valid). This is because we will usually not have accepted that a person has a fear of return to their own country or a fear of their own authorities and will have granted Discretionary Leave for reasons other than protection.

However, there may be some occasions where leave should be curtailed because an individual has demonstrated by their own actions that the reasons on which they were granted Discretionary Leave no longer persist: for example, where a person with Discretionary Leave based on fear in the country of nationality obtains a national passport and uses it to return, or where someone was granted Discretionary Leave under Article 8 based on their marriage or civil partnership and that marriage or partnership has broken down.

Curtailment As A Result of A Change in Country Conditions

A grant of Discretionary Leave should not be reviewed on these grounds before it ends, unless there is a specific instruction to do so in relation to a particular country or to a category of cases in respect of a particular country. Any such instruction will provide details of the review process to be undertaken. These instructions may be separate from any instructions on reviewing limited leave as a refugee or Humanitarian Protection granted on or after 30 August 2005 based on a significant and non-temporary change in country conditions. Any consideration of whether to curtail Discretionary Leave would need to take into account the effect of the change in country circumstances on the individual.

It may be less likely for a change in country circumstances to have an effect on those with Discretionary Leave than those with refugee status or Humanitarian Protection. But there could be situations where such a change is relevant to those with Discretionary Leave under certain categories—for example any claims based on severe humanitarian conditions.

Curtailment/Variation of Leave on the Grounds of Character or Conduct (Including Deception)

Discretionary Leave should normally be curtailed if a person becomes subject to any of the grounds of exclusion criteria set out in the Asylum Instruction on Humanitarian Protection. This will usually apply where a person's actions after the grant of Discretionary Leave bring them within the scope of those grounds. There may also be some situations where we become aware that a person is subject to one of the grounds of exclusion only after the grant of Discretionary Leave. Again, it would normally be appropriate to curtail leave in such cases.

If the individual is liable to deportation and a deportation order is made, it will have the effect of invalidating any extant leave. Action to curtail or vary leave will only be necessary, therefore, where a person is liable to deportation but it is not possible to make a deportation order (e.g. for Article 3 ECHR reasons).

A person who obtains leave to enter by deception under the Discretionary Leave policy is an illegal entrant. If it is decided to take illegal entry action against that person (under Schedule 2 to the Immigration Act 1971) their leave is no longer valid. Where a person has obtained leave to remain by deception under this policy, that person is liable to removal under section 10 of the Immigration and Asylum Act 1999. A decision to remove under this section will invalidate the leave that has been given previously.

Separate action to vary Discretionary Leave will be required only where a decision to remove cannot be made or removal directions set (e.g. for Article 3 ECHR reasons).

If a person who falls into an exclusion category cannot return without material prejudice to the rights protected under this instruction, their leave should usually be varied and replaced with a maximum period of six months' Discretionary Leave in accordance with the guidelines set out in the sub-section of this instruction on 'Applicants excluded from Refugee Status, Humanitarian Protection or Discretionary Leave'.

If return is likely to be possible in the near future a shorter period of Discretionary Leave, or no leave, should be granted.

Other Situations Where the Basis for the Grant of Leave has Ceased to Exist

There may be other occasions where due to a change in circumstances it would be appropriate to curtail Discretionary Leave. For example, it would be appropriate where a child who was granted leave under the UASC policy is subsequently contacted by an adult family member who can care for them in their own country or where someone was granted leave on Article 8 grounds because of their relationship with a person settled here and that person subsequently leaves the United Kingdom or the relationship otherwise ends.

A senior caseworker should always be consulted before any action is undertaken to consider revocation of Discretionary Leave under this category.

APPLICATIONS FOR FURTHER LEAVE

A person will not become eligible for consideration for settlement until they have completed six years of Discretionary Leave or, in the case of persons subject to the exclusion criteria, until they have completed at least ten years of Discretionary Leave. Anyone granted Discretionary Leave will therefore have to have at least one active review before they become eligible for consideration for settlement.

An individual should apply for an extension of Discretionary Leave shortly before it expires. The application will be considered in the light of circumstances prevailing at that time.

Where the request for leave amounts to a request for an upgrade from Discretionary Leave to Humanitarian Protection status, see the Asylum Instruction on Humanitarian Protection.

Consideration of The Extension Request

Extension requests will normally be the subject of an active review, to decide whether the person still qualifies for Discretionary Leave (or any other form of leave that is requested). This review will take account of the information on the extension request form, present country information and any other information of which we are aware and which is relevant to the claim, including any relevant information provided at the time of the original grant of Discretionary Leave.

In many cases an active review will be conducted on the papers without the need for interview. However an interview may be necessary where further information is required in order to make a decision on the application.

The nature of the active review will depend on the reasons why Discretionary Leave was granted. It may, for example, involve consideration of the current family situation of the applicant, the conditions in the country of origin, whether reception arrangements for a child are still unavailable or whether there is still a barrier to the return of an excluded person. For further guidance see the Asylum Instruction on Active Review.

Granting An Extension

Where an individual still qualifies for Discretionary Leave (and does not qualify for leave on another basis—i.e. under the Immigration Rules) they should normally be given an extension of stay for a period in accordance with the 'Duration of grants . . .' section below. The exception is that a shorter period should be granted if such an extension would take the person beyond the time when they would become eligible for consideration for settlement (i.e. six or ten years). The shorter period should be such as to bring the person's aggregate stay on Discretionary Leave up to six or ten years, as appropriate.

Refusing An Extension

Where, following review, it is decided that an individual no longer qualifies for Discretionary Leave and that they do not qualify for any other form of leave their extension request should be refused.

APPLICATIONS FOR SETTLEMENT

A person will normally become eligible for consideration for settlement after completing six continuous years of Discretionary Leave. However, where a person is covered by one of the exclusion categories they will not become eligible for consideration for settlement until they have completed ten continuous years of Discretionary Leave. Any time spent in prison in connection with a criminal conviction would not count towards the six or ten years. An individual may apply for ILR/settlement at the six or ten year stage shortly before Discretionary Leave expires. The application will be considered in the light of circumstances prevailing at that time.

Consideration of Application

As with an extension request, the application should be subject to an active review to consider whether or not they still qualify for Discretionary Leave (or some other form of leave).

Granting Settlement

Where a person has held Discretionary Leave for an appropriate period and continues to qualify for Discretionary Leave, they should be granted ILR/settlement.

Further Grants of Discretionary Leave

There may be some cases where it is clear that the basis for the (continuing) grant of Discretionary Leave is temporary. If there is a clear basis for considering that within twelve months the factors giving rise to the grant of Discretionary Leave will have ceased to apply then settlement should not be granted—for example, an Article 8 case in which it is considered that a person who has been granted Discretionary Leave may not be removed for six months because of the family life they have established with someone in the United Kingdom who will be leaving the United Kingdom in six months' time. Instead a shorter further period of Discretionary Leave should be granted. A person may not be denied settlement under this section for more than twelve months beyond the normal qualifying period.

Personal Decision by Ministers

Where a person who is subject to the grounds of exclusion has completed ten years of Discretionary Leave they may be denied settlement where Ministers decide in the light of all the circumstances of the case, that the person's presence in the United Kingdom is not conducive to the public good (this may be decided in the individual circumstances of a case, or for a category of cases). Reasons for this decision should be given. A further period of Discretionary Leave should be granted where it is not possible to remove the person. In such a case, for so long as the individual remains in the United Kingdom, a fresh decision will need to be taken at least every three years on whether settlement should continue to be denied.

Refusal of Settlement and Further Leave

Where a person no longer qualifies for Discretionary Leave or any other form of leave, their application for settlement should be refused.

Appeal Rights

See the Rights of Appeal in Asylum Cases.

Issuing of Travel Documents

A person granted Discretionary Leave will normally be expected to keep their own national passport valid. This is because we will usually not have accepted that a person has a fear of return to their own country or a fear of their own authorities and will have granted Discretionary Leave for reasons other than protection. However, a person who has leave on grounds of Discretionary Leave may apply for a Home Office Certificate of Identity on the appropriate application form. Applicants must normally show that they have been formally and unreasonably refused a national passport, unless IND has accepted that they have a well-founded fear of their national authorities. It is not usually necessary for those applying for a Certificate of

Identity to provide a compelling reason for travelling. Where the applicant has ILR, the document will be valid for 5 years. Otherwise it will expire when the holder's current leave to enter or remain expires.

TRANSITIONAL ARRANGEMENTS

Up until 2007 there will be individuals granted exceptional leave under the old system whose leave will be ending and who will be seeking to extend their stay.

Those applicants who were granted a four-year period of exceptional leave in one block and who then apply for ILR at the end of that period should be considered for settlement with background character and conduct checks and war crimes screening, but without a full active review. In other words, those who pass such checks and screening will not need to show that they would necessarily qualify for Humanitarian Protection or Discretionary Leave at the time of the ILR decision.

Where a person seeks an extension of stay having spent fewer than four years on exceptional leave (or where they have spent four years on exceptional leave granted in more than one block), their application should be examined to determine whether a grant of Humanitarian Protection, Discretionary Leave or leave on another basis is appropriate. If they do not qualify for Humanitarian Protection or Discretionary Leave or for leave on any other basis (such as under the Immigration Rules), their claim for an extension of stay should be refused. (Further guidance is contained in the Asylum Instruction on Active Review.)

If they do qualify for Discretionary Leave (but not Humanitarian Protection) they should be granted leave in accordance with this instruction. Periods spent on exceptional leave will count towards the six or ten years qualifying period for settlement applicable to those with Discretionary Leave.

APPENDIX 9

Humanitarian Protection

CONTENTS

1. Introduction

Humanitarian Protection and Discretionary Leave were introduced on 1 April 2003 following the abolition of exceptional leave on 31 March 2003. On 30 August 2005, the policy on Humanitarian Protection was revised in line with new policies on the granting of refugee leave. On 9 October 2006, the policy changed again to reflect the requirements of Council Directive 2004/83/EC on minimum standards for the qualification and status of third country nationals or stateless persons as refugees or as persons who otherwise need international protection and the content of the protection granted (the 'Qualification Directive'). The UK should apply the provisions of the Directive to all live claims in the system, including those at appeal, on 9th October 2006.

Where an asylum applicant does not qualify for refugee status, the caseworker should always consider whether they qualify for a grant of Humanitarian Protection and, if not, consideration should be given as to whether they qualify for Discretionary Leave (see the **API** on *Assessing the Claim*). It is important that claims should be considered for asylum first, then for Humanitarian Protection and finally for Discretionary Leave.

This instruction explains the limited circumstances in which it would be appropriate to grant Humanitarian Protection. For guidance on Discretionary Leave please refer to the **API** on *Discretionary Leave*.

For details on family reunion and on dependants accompanying an applicant who is granted Humanitarian Protection, see the **APIs** on *Family Reunion* and *Dependants* respectively. Broadly speaking, anyone who is granted leave on Humanitarian Protection grounds on or after 30 August 2005 is entitled to apply for family reunion immediately.

The great majority of claims for Humanitarian Protection are likely to arise in the context of asylum claims. However, where an individual claims that although they are in need of international protection they are not seeking asylum and the reasons given clearly do not engage our obligations under the Refugee Convention (i.e. the fear of persecution is clearly not for one of the five Convention reasons), then this should be accepted as a standalone claim for Humanitarian Protection.

Separate instructions may be issued by AAPD in relation to handling of claims for Humanitarian Protection. For example, particular circumstances may arise in a country which may give rise to alternative arrangements such as differing periods of leave to be granted. The instructions will be in the form of APU Notices, Country Policy Bulletins or Operational Guidance Notes (OGNs). Where such instructions are in force, they will take precedence over the contents of these instructions, to the extent that they make different provisions.

1.1 Key points

Qualifying criteria

- Under paragraphs 339C and D of the Immigration Rules, Humanitarian Protection may be granted to a person who is in the United Kingdom and is not a refugee if:
  - there are substantial grounds for believing that the person would face a real risk of suffering serious harm in the country of return (this refers to a country or territory listed in paragraph 8(1)(c) of Schedule 2 to the Immigration Act 1971 (see section 3 below)); and
  - the person cannot obtain effective protection from the authorities of that country (or will not because of the risk of suffering serious harm).
- 'Serious harm' means:
  - the death penalty or execution; or
  - unlawful killing; or
  - torture or inhuman or degrading treatment or punishment in the country of return; or
  - serious and individual threat to a civilian's life or person by reason of indiscriminate violence in situations of international or internal armed conflict.

A person who cannot be removed from the UK on these grounds but who it is reasonably believed can make a voluntary return to the country of return without facing a real risk of serious harm will not be eligible for a grant of Humanitarian Protection. On that basis a reference in this instruction to a return (in whatever form and unless otherwise stated) includes a voluntary return and an enforced return.

Leave to be granted

- Those granted Humanitarian Protection will be granted leave to enter or remain for a period of five years.
- There will be an avenue for settlement (ILR) after 5 years of leave subject to checks detailed in the API on **Refugee Leave** and any other requirements that may be imposed by the settlement policy in force at the time.
- A review of Humanitarian Protection will only be conducted during a period of leave in specified circumstances. These are listed in section 8 below, but see also the **API on Refugee Leave**.

Other considerations

- In assessing whether a person qualifies for Humanitarian Protection the principles of internal relocation and sufficiency of state protection should be applied. See the **APIs** on *Internal Relocation* and *Assessing the Claim*.
- Humanitarian Protection is not the same as and is separate from Temporary Protection. Temporary Protection will be granted only to individuals in a category of persons covered by a declaration of the Council of the European Union on the existence of a mass influx situation. Further guidance can be from APU via a senior caseworker.

- Leave should not be granted on Humanitarian Protection grounds to EU nationals or their third country national family members who are exercising treaty rights.
- Humanitarian Protection leave should not be granted where another EU Member State or Norway / Iceland has accepted responsibility for an asylum claim under the Dublin arrangements or where an individual may otherwise removed on third country grounds.
- Those granted leave on Humanitarian Protection grounds have access to public funds and are entitled to work. Those granted such leave after 30 August 2005 also have the right to family reunion. Further enquiries should normally be made in writing to the Children and Family Asylum Policy Team (CFAPT) via a senior caseworker.

Family Reunion for those granted Humanitarian Protection
Pre August 30th 2005

- Where the sponsor was granted HP before 30 August 2005 family members will normally not benefit from the family reunion policy until the sponsor has obtained ILR (normally after three years).
- Similarly, if the family are seeking entry clearance it would normally be granted if the sponsor has been granted ILR. Applications for entry clearance may be considered before the sponsor has obtained ILR but will be granted only where there are exceptional compassionate circumstances.

Post August 30th 2005

- Where the sponsor was granted HP on or after August 30th 2005 family members who are abroad may seek entry clearance for immediate family reunion.

Dependants and Eligibility

- From the 9th October 2006 dependants eligible to apply for family reunion are spouses, minor children, civil partners, same sex or unmarried partners, who are related as claimed to the principal applicant, formed part of the pre-existing family unit abroad and were wholly dependent on the principal applicant immediately prior to arrival in the UK.
- It should be noted that to be eligible as a dependant an unmarried or same sex partner, is a person who has been living together with the principal applicant in a subsisting relationship akin to marriage or a civil partnership for two years or more.

2. Humanitarian Protection and the Qualification Directive

The Qualification Directive, agreed by the European Union in 2004, is a key step towards a Common European Asylum System. The provisions of the Directive required the UK to bring into force laws implementing the Directive by 9 October 2006, when the Immigration Rules and Regulations implementing the Qualification Directive came into force. They apply to all live applications from 9 October, including those at appeal. The Directive establishes common European qualifying standards for refugees and a new category of persons eligible for subsidiary protection, as well as setting out the minimum rights and benefits that must attach to these categories across Member States.

The provisions on subsidiary protection are similar to the UK's former provisions on Humanitarian Protection, which have been amended and incorporated into the Immigration Rules to meet the new requirements. Changes in the qualifying criteria were required under Article 15 of the Qualification Directive, and are set out in paragraphs 339C and D of the Immigration Rules. The main changes are to the criteria on torture and ill treatment and on situations of international and internal armed conflict. They are discussed below, but we do not anticipate that either change will result in a significant increase in grants of Humanitarian Protection leave.

3. Eligibility for Humanitarian Protection

Eligibility for humanitarian protection should be considered after consideration of the application for asylum, if the applicant has made one. A person will be granted Humanitarian Protection in the United Kingdom if the Secretary of State is satisfied that the following eligibility requirements, as set out in paragraphs 339C and D of the Immigration Rules, are met:

(i) he is in the United Kingdom or has arrived at a port of entry in the United Kingdom; and

(ii) he does not qualify as a refugee as defined in regulation 2 of The Refugee or Person in Need of International Protection (Qualification) Regulations 2006; and

(iii) substantial grounds have been shown for believing that the person concerned, if he returned to the country of return, would face a real risk of suffering serious harm and is unable, or, owing to such a risk, unwilling to avail himself of the protection of that country; and

(iv) he is not excluded from a grant of humanitarian protection.

Serious harm consists of:

(i) the death penalty or execution: or

(ii) unlawful killing; or

(iii) torture or inhuman or degrading treatment or punishment of a person in the country of return; or

(iv) serious and individual threat to a civilian's life or person by reason of indiscriminate violence in situations of international armed conflict. This is a new category included into the Immigration Rules to implement article 15(c) of the Qualification Directive. To qualify for Humanitarian Protection on this basis the applicant must establish substantial grounds for believing that if returned to the country of return he would face a real-risk of a serious and individual threat to his life or person by reason of indiscriminate violence in situations of international or internal armed conflict.

Country of return means a country or territory listed in paragraph 8(1)(c) of Schedule 2 to the Immigration Act 1971:

(i) a country of which the applicant is national or citizen; or

(ii) a country or territory in which the applicant has obtained a passport or other document of identity; or

(iii) a country or territory in which the applicant embarked for the United Kingdom; or

(iv) a country or territory to which there is reason to believe that the claimant will be admitted.

3.1 Standard of proof

In considering whether there are substantial grounds for believing that a person would face a real risk of suffering serious harm, the standard of proof to be applied is that which applies in asylum and ECHR Article 3 cases—i.e. a *reasonable degree of likelihood* or a *real risk* (these two tests reflect the same standard of proof).

3.2 Death penalty or execution

Where there are substantial grounds for believing that, a person if they returned, would face a real risk of the death penalty being imposed **and** carried out they will, subject to section 3.6, qualify for Humanitarian Protection.

3.3 Unlawful killing

Where a person satisfies us that, if they returned, they would face a real risk of being unlawfully killed they will, subject to section 3.6, qualify for Humanitarian Protection.

This would include a person who if returned to a war/conflict situation would face a real risk of being killed (and therefore overlaps with category 3.5 below).

Examples of cases that would not be included are where the threat to life is:

(a) in defence of any person from unlawful violence;
(b) in order to effect lawful arrest or to prevent the escape of a person lawfully detained;
(c) in action lawfully taken for the purpose of quelling a riot or insurrection.

Applications from those who face a real risk of being unlawfully killed on return should be considered in the same way as those from people who face a real risk of torture or inhuman or degrading treatment or punishment. If there is a real risk that a person, if they returned to the country of return, would be unlawfully killed by the state (or by agents of the state), or by non-state agents where there is no sufficiency of protection, then Humanitarian Protection should be granted, subject to section 3.6.

Decision makers should see the **APIs** on *European Convention on Human Rights* and *Assessing the Claim* for further information on the application of this element of the definition.

3.4 Return that would expose a person to torture or inhuman or degrading treatment

The terms in this section are based upon Article 3 of the ECHR which states that:

No one shall be subjected to torture or to inhuman or degrading treatment or punishment.

Relationship between Article 3 and Persecution

In the starred determination of *Kacaj* in July 2001, the Immigration Appeal Tribunal noted the close link between asylum and Article 3. It said that:

We recognise the possibility that Article 3 could be violated by actions which did not have a sufficiently systemic character to amount to persecution, although we doubt that this refinement would be likely to be determinative in any but a very small minority of cases. But apart from this and a case where conduct amounting to persecution but not for a Convention reason was established, we find it difficult to envisage a sensible possibility that a breach of Article 3 could be established where an asylum claim failed.

There are two types of case where a person whose asylum claim is unsuccessful may qualify for Humanitarian Protection by virtue of the application of Article 3. Namely:

• The treatment feared amounts to persecution but is not for one of the five Convention reasons.
• The treatment or punishment is in the narrow category of actions which are of a severity and nature to amount to Article 3 treatment but not to amount to persecution–for example, where the actions feared do not have a sufficiently systemic character to amount to persecution. As the Tribunal noted in *Kacaj*, few cases are likely to fit this description.

A person may establish that if they returned they would, in the country of return, be subject to treatment contrary to Article 3 yet have failed in their asylum claim because they are excluded by virtue of Article 1F or 33(2) of the Refugee Convention. However, all such persons would also be excluded from Humanitarian Protection (see section 3.6 below). They may instead qualify for Discretionary Leave (see the **API** on *Discretionary Leave*).

Prison conditions

Poor prison conditions may reach the threshold for Article 3 where they attain a minimum level of severity.

Where an applicant states that they face a real-risk of imprisonment on return, decision makers should first look at the reasons why the applicant faces imprisonment. If the reason is because the applicant falls within the exclusion criteria in section 3.6, the decision maker should not grant Humanitarian Protection as the applicant will *not* be eligible for a grant of Humanitarian Protection. If the decision maker considers that although an applicant is excluded from a grant of Humanitarian Protection s/he does face a real risk of imprisonment on return and prison conditions reach the threshold of Article 3, they should propose to grant Discretionary Leave in accordance with the provisions in the **API** on *Discretionary Leave*. The proposal to grant should be referred to a Senior Caseworker.

If the decision maker is satisfied that the reasons for imprisonment given by the applicant do not result in exclusion from Humanitarian Protection, then they should consider whether there are substantial grounds for believing that there is a real risk that the applicant will be imprisoned on return. If so, decision makers should go on to consider whether the conditions of detention the applicant will face are likely to reach the Article 3 threshold.

Section 7.2 of the **API** on ***European Convention on Human Rights*** sets out the issues for consideration. See the exclusion criteria in section 3.6 below.

Deliberate ill treatment/ill treatment in the country of return

Before 9 October 2006, Humanitarian Protection was granted where there was a serious risk of 'torture or inhuman or degrading treatment arising from the deliberate infliction of ill treatment.'

The new definition removes the need for the applicant to show deliberate ill treatment but only applies to 'torture or inhuman or degrading treatment or punishment of a person *in the country of return*' (paragraph 339C of the Immigration Rules, with emphasis added). Due to this geographical limitation, the new definition should not result in a significant increase in grants of Humanitarian Protection leave. Where a person can show that removal from the UK will involve ill treatment in the UK then of course removal would be unlawful and cannot proceed. However, a claim that succeeds on this ground will attract Discretionary Leave instead of Humanitarian Protection (see the ***Discretionary Leave API*** for further guidance).

Medical cases

Where a person claims that their return would be in breach of Article 3 of the ECHR because of their medical condition, they are not in need of international protection and are not eligible for Humanitarian Protection. The breach of Article 3 arises because the healthcare available to the applicant in the UK is not available in the country of return and because of the applicant's own exceptional circumstances. Individuals who cannot return for this reason may qualify for Discretionary Leave but the threshold for establishing an Article 3 breach in such cases is very high.

For more details see section 7.2 of the **API** on *European Convention on Human Rights*, section 3.4 of **Chapter 1 Section 8** of the IDIs on *Medical Examination* and the **API** on *Discretionary Leave.*

Other severe humanitarian conditions meeting the Article 3 threshold

There may be some cases (although any such cases are likely to be rare) where the general conditions in the country—for example, absence of water, food or basic shelter–are so poor that return in itself could, in extreme cases, constitute ill treatment under the Immigration Rules. Decision makers need to consider how those conditions would impact upon the individual if they were returned. Any such cases, if granted, would qualify for Discretionary Leave rather than Humanitarian Protection (because they are not protection-related cases), but leave should not be granted without reference to a senior caseworker. See the **API** on *Discretionary Leave.*

3.5 Serious and individual threat to a civilian's life or person by reason of indiscriminate violence in situations of international or internal armed conflict

This is a new category included into the Immigration Rules to implement article 15(c) of the Qualification Directive (see the definition of serious harm in paragraph 339C of the Immigration Rules).

To qualify for Humanitarian Protection on this basis, the applicant must show that there are substantial grounds for believing that if they returned to the country of return, they would face a real risk of a serious and individual threat to life or person by reason of indiscriminate violence in a situation of international or internal armed conflict.

The main effect of this provision is to clarify the instances in which Article 3 of the ECHR can be engaged in a situation of armed conflict. It reflects existing European caselaw in that respect (notably the cases of Vivaharajah and HLR cited below). Article 15(c) makes it clear that, whilst a situation of international or internal armed conflict does not, in itself, give rise to a claim for protection, it can provide the basis for such a claim where applicants can show that they are individually at risk.

Paragraph 26 of the recitals to the Qualification Directive states that

> 'risks to which a population of a country or a section of the population is generally exposed do not normally create in themselves an individual threat which would qualify as serious harm'.

Applicants cannot rely on the assertion that this ground is met simply because in the country of return there is an international or internal armed conflict where there is indiscriminate violence. The examination of the threatened return (enforced or voluntary) must focus on its foreseeable consequences, taking into account the personal circumstances of the applicant *(Vilvaharajah v United Kingdom (1991) 14 EHRR)*, and the risk posed must be specific to the individual. A general situation of violence in the receiving state is not sufficient *(HLR v France (1997) 26 E.H.R.R 29)*. Decision makers should consult Home Office country information and Operational Guidance Notes in each case on the question of whether a situation of international or internal armed conflict exists.

This is a narrow category. Humanitarian Protection is only likely to be granted on this basis in exceptional circumstances.

3.6 Exclusion Criteria

A person will not be eligible for a grant of Humanitarian Protection if he is excluded from it because one of the following provisions in paragraph 339D of the Immigration Rules apply:

  (i) there are serious reasons for considering that he has committed a crime against peace, a war crime, a crime against humanity, or any other serious crime or instigated or otherwise participated in such crimes; or

 (ii) there are serious reasons for considering that he is guilty of acts contrary to the purposes and principles of the United Nations or has committed, prepared or instigated such acts or induced others to commit, prepare or instigate such acts; or

(iii) there are serious reasons for considering that he constitutes a danger to the community or to the security of the United Kingdom; or

(iv) prior to his admission to the United Kingdom the person committed a crime outside the scope of (i) and (ii) that would be punishable by imprisonment were it committed in the United Kingdom and the person left his country of origin solely to avoid sanctions resulting from the crime.

A 'serious crime' for these purposes is:

* one for which a custodial sentence of at least twelve months has been imposed in the United Kingdom; or
* a crime considered serious enough to exclude the person from being a refugee in accordance with Article 1F(b) of the Convention (see the **API** on **Exclusion**); or
* conviction for an offence listed in an order made under section 72 of the Nationality, Immigration and Asylum Act 2002 (see the **Asylum Policy Notice** *Section 72 of the NIA Act 2002: Particularly Serious Crimes*).

People who may represent 'a danger to the community or to the security of the UK' include:

* those included on the Sex Offenders Register (this would apply to those convicted of an offence after 1997).
* those whose presence in the United Kingdom is deemed not conducive to the public good by the Secretary of State, for example on national security grounds, because of their character, conduct or associations.
* those who engage in one or more unacceptable behaviours (whether in the UK or abroad). The list of unacceptable behaviours includes using any means or medium including:
  * writing, producing, publishing or distributing material
  * public speaking including preaching
  * running a website or
  * using a position of responsibility such as teacher, community or youth leader
  to express views which:
  * foment, justify or glorify terrorist violence in furtherance of particular beliefs
  * seek to provoke others to terrorist acts
  * foment other serious criminal activity or seek to provoke others to serious criminal acts, or
  * foster hatred which may lead to inter-community violence in the UK.

This list is indicative, not exhaustive.

A person may also be regarded as a danger to the community or to the security of the United Kingdom in the light of their character, conduct or associations, insofar as this is not covered by the categories listed above. For example, where deportation action has been considered and has not been pursued or has been abandoned only because Article 2 or Article 3 considerations render return impossible for the time being. Where a person is excluded from Humanitarian

Protection, consideration should be given to whether they qualify for Discretionary Leave (see the **API** on *Discretionary Leave*).

3.7 ECHR claims that fall outside the scope of asylum and Humanitarian Protection

ECHR considerations falling outside the scope of asylum and Humanitarian Protection should be considered after consideration of eligibility for status in those categories. Other claims under the ECHR, such as those involving a flagrant denial of a non-article 3 right, should be considered in accordance with the *API* on *Discretionary Leave*.

4. OTHER ISSUES RELEVANT TO THE CONSIDERATION OF THE CLAIM

The general principles involved in considering a claim for Humanitarian Protection, either after considering an asylum claim or as a free-standing application, are broadly similar to those involved in assessing an asylum claim. Subject to the different criteria set out above, decision makers should conduct their examination in the same way. Two of the main considerations are mentioned below, but for detailed guidance on the decision making process as a whole, see the **API** on *Assessing the claim*.

4.1 Sufficiency of protection

In deciding whether a person qualifies for Humanitarian Protection, the sufficiency of protection test should be applied in the same way as it is applied in considering asylum claims. For further information on the sufficiency of protection test, see the **API** on *Assessing the Claim*. The **API** on *ECHR* also contains guidance on the question of effective protection in human rights cases.

4.2 Internal Relocation

In considering whether a person qualifies for Humanitarian Protection, the internal relocation test set out in paragraph 339O of the Immigration Rules should be applied. If there is a place in the country of return where the person would not face a real risk of serious harm and they can reasonably be expected to stay there, then they will not be eligible for a grant of Humanitarian Protection. Both the general circumstances prevailing in that part of the country and the personal circumstances of the person concerned should be taken into account, but the fact that there may be technical obstacles to return, such as re-documentation problems, does not prevent internal relocation from being applied. See the **API** on *Internal Relocation*.

5. GRANTING OR REFUSING HUMANITARIAN PROTECTION

5.1 Granting Humanitarian Protection

A grant of Humanitarian Protection grounds should only be considered *after* any asylum claim has been substantively considered, and it has been decided that asylum should be refused. In cases where Humanitarian Protection is granted, applicants should be issued with full reasons for refusal of asylum.

The Reasons for Refusal Letter (RFRL) should briefly set out the reasons why a person is being granted leave on Humanitarian Protection grounds. It should also state clearly whether the grant of Humanitarian Protection leave has been made on the basis of a fear of mistreatment by the national authorities or by non-state actors. This is important because, unless we accept that the individual has a fear of their own national authorities, we will expect those without a travel document at the time of decision to apply for a national passport rather than a Home Office travel document should they wish to travel abroad.

5.2 Refusing Humanitarian Protection

An asylum claim will always be deemed to be a claim for Humanitarian Protection. Therefore where it is decided that an applicant does not qualify for Humanitarian Protection the RFRL, as well as setting out why the asylum claim has been refused, should provide reasons why Humanitarian Protection is being refused.

The reasons for refusing any aspect of a human rights claim which are not covered by the reasons for refusing the Humanitarian Protection claim should also be given where no leave is being granted (this will normally be done, where applicable, when setting out why Discretionary Leave is also not being granted).

Where we are refusing Humanitarian Protection but granting Discretionary Leave, the reasons for refusing to grant Humanitarian Protection should still be addressed in the letter. There will be no need in such cases to address aspects of any human rights claim except in so far as this is done in explaining why asylum and Humanitarian Protection are being refused.

6. REQUEST FOR HUMANITARIAN PROTECTION AFTER THE INITIAL DECISION AND APPEAL STAGE

Occasions may arise when, following the refusal of asylum and exhaustion of all appeal rights, a request is nonetheless made for Humanitarian Protection, probably in the form of a human rights claim.

By the time all rights of appeal have been exhausted, there will be very few cases that would merit a grant of Humanitarian Protection because the relevant factors will have been considered at an earlier stage. However, caseworkers should give full and careful consideration to the reasons given for requesting such leave, and decide whether Humanitarian Protection leave or Discretionary Leave would be appropriate. See the **API** on *Further Representations and Fresh Claims* for further guidance.

6.1 Requests for Humanitarian Protection at removal stage

Those whose asylum and/or human rights claims were refused before April 2003 did not have the possibility of being granted leave on Humanitarian Protection grounds at the time of refusal. Those whose claims were refused before 9 October 2006 did not have their claims considered under the revised framework introduced to implement the Qualification Directive. However, in both cases applicants would have had the opportunity to raise all issues relevant to their asylum and/or human rights claim and leave to enter or remain would have been granted in circumstances where Humanitarian Protection would now be granted under the terms of this instruction.

Paragraph 353 of the Immigration Rules should therefore be applied to a request for Humanitarian Protection in such a case, in order to determine whether the request should be treated as further representations or a fresh claim. If treated as a fresh claim, consideration should be given to certifying the request under section 96 of the Nationality, Immigration and Asylum Act 2002.

These cases should be treated in accordance with normal principles since the individuals concerned have had the opportunity to raise any facts relevant to the present Humanitarian Protection request at the time of their original claim (on asylum/human rights grounds).

For more information see the **API** on *Further Representations and Fresh Claims*. See also the **API** on *Appeals*.

6.2 Requests to upgrade from Discretionary Leave to Humanitarian Protection

Situations may arise where a person previously refused leave on Humanitarian Protection grounds but granted Discretionary Leave seeks to 'upgrade' their status to Humanitarian Protection. Such requests should be considered.

6.3 Tribunal determinations and court judgments

Where the Asylum and Immigration Tribunal or a court hears an appeal and finds that the appellant qualifies for Humanitarian Protection, leave should be granted on Humanitarian Protection grounds (subject to any appeal against that determination being lodged) provided the provisions in section 3.6 do not apply. An appellant whose proposed removal is found to be unlawful will not be granted leave if that person can reasonably be expected to return voluntarily. In such cases, which it is believed will be relatively rare, IND will give effect to the court's decision by not enforcing removal.

7. Duration of Humanitarian Protection

Where Humanitarian Protection has been granted under paragraph 339C of the Immigration Rules, leave should be granted for a period of five years (339E).

8. Revocation of Humanitarian Protection

Humanitarian Protection granted under paragraph 339C will be revoked or not renewed if the Secretary of State is satisfied that at least one of the provisions in paragraph 339G of the Immigration Rules applies.

A grant of leave on Humanitarian Protection grounds will normally be reviewed during its currency only when certain events occur to trigger such a review. The triggers are discussed further in section 5 of the **API** on *Refugee Leave*.

8.1 Paragraph 339G (i) of the Immigration Rules

Where the circumstances which led to the grant of humanitarian protection have ceased to exist or have changed to such a degree that such protection is no longer required.

8.1.1 Where the actions of the individual suggest that the need for protection has ceased

This criterion will only apply where the change of circumstances is of such a significant and 'non-temporary' nature that the person no longer faces a real risk of serious harm. Given that the majority of grants of leave on Humanitarian Protection will have been made on the grounds of fear of persecution by nonstate actors, it is unlikely that the Humanitarian Protection criteria will cease to apply simply because the holder accepts the protection of the country of nationality in some temporary or limited way. Obtaining a passport is the obvious example. A refugee who obtains a national passport risks ceasing to be regarded as a refugee (though that is by no means an inevitable consequence), but a person with Humanitarian Protection does not normally run a similar risk. However, each case that arises will need to be considered on its individual merits to see whether the actions of the person provide clear grounds for concluding that they no longer qualify for Humanitarian Protection.

For example, where a person has taken to spending periods of time in the country where they previously feared serious harm, that would be very strong evidence that they no longer qualified. On the other hand, if a person has merely re-acquired the nationality of their country that will not necessarily mean they no longer qualify for Humanitarian Protection. For instance, that person may continue to fear treatment contrary to Article 3 from non-state actors against which the state is unable to protect them, and may not have claimed that the state was ever persecuting or mistreating them.

Caseworkers should also refer to the **API** on *Cessation, Cancellation and Revocation of Refugee Status*, especially in Humanitarian Protection cases involving a fear of the state as opposed to non-state agents.

8.1.2 *Where there is a significant and non-temporary change in the conditions in a particular country*

The details of this trigger are set out in section 6 of the **API** on *Refugee Leave*. When Ministers decide to review the refugee status of people from a particular country, the Humanitarian Protection status of people from that country should also be reviewed. A person will no longer be eligible for Humanitarian Protection where the change of circumstances is of such a significant and non-temporary nature that there are no longer substantial grounds for believing that the person faces a real risk of serious harm. Note that this test is worded slightly differently to that in refugee cases.

8.2 Paragraph 339G (ii)–(vi) of the Immigration Rules

Where protection should not be continued because of a person's actions

Under paragraph 339G Humanitarian Protection will be revoked or not renewed if the Secretary of State is satisfied that one of the following applies:

 (i) the person granted humanitarian protection should have been or is excluded from humanitarian protection because there are serious reasons for considering that he has committed a crime against peace, a war crime, a crime against humanity, or any other serious crime or instigated or otherwise participated in such crimes; or

 (ii) the person granted humanitarian protection should have been or is excluded from humanitarian protection because there are serious reasons for considering that he is guilty of acts contrary to the purposes and principles of the United Nations or has committed or prepared or instigated such acts; or

 (iii) the person granted humanitarian protection should have been or is excluded from humanitarian protection because there are serious reasons for considering that he constitutes a danger to the community or to the security of the United Kingdom; or

 (iv) the person granted humanitarian protection misrepresented or omitted facts, including the use of false documents, which were decisive to the grant of humanitarian protection; or

 (v) the person granted humanitarian protection should have been or is excluded from humanitarian protection because prior to his admission to the United Kingdom the person committed a crime outside the scope of (ii) and (iii) that would be punishable by imprisonment had it been committed in the United Kingdom and the person left his country of origin solely in order to avoid sanctions resulting from the crime.

See section 3.6 above for definitions of 'serious crime' and examples of cases in which the claimant should be regarded as a danger to the community or to the security of the United Kingdom. Further guidance is available in the **API** on *Refugee Leave*. Cases in which these exclusions may apply range from crimes against peace and acts contrary to the purposes and principles of the United Nations to extradition requests and court recommendations for deportation.

Limited leave should normally be curtailed if Humanitarian Protection is revoked or not renewed under any of the exclusion criteria set out above (paragraph 339H of the Immigration Rules). This will usually cover situations where a person's actions after the grant of Humanitarian Protection leave bring them within the scope of those criteria. There may also be some situations where we become aware that a person is already subject to one of the disqualifying criteria only after the grant of leave on Humanitarian Protection grounds. Again, it will normally be appropriate to curtail any leave granted in such cases.

If the individual is liable to deportation, the deportation order will have the effect of cancelling leave. Separate action to revoke or vary leave will only be necessary, therefore, where a person is liable to deportation but deportation action is not possible (e.g. for Article 3 ECHR reasons).

If it transpires that a person has obtained their Humanitarian Protection leave by deception (paragraph 339G(v)) then they are liable to removal either as an illegal entrant under Schedule 2 to the Immigration Act 1971 or under section 10 of the Immigration and Asylum Act 1999. The decision to remove someone under either section 10 or Schedule 2 invalidates any leave given previously. In these deception cases, separate action to curtail leave granted on Humanitarian Protection grounds will only be required where a person may not be removed (e.g. for Article 3 ECHR reasons).

Where evidence emerges indicating that an individual acquired leave by deception

Please see section 8.2 above for guidance.

8.3 Consequences

When a person no longer qualifies for Humanitarian Protection, the expectation is that leave granted on that basis will be curtailed and that either the person will leave voluntarily or removal will follow, subject to any appeal. However, there may be cases where return is not appropriate as the person qualifies for leave under the Immigration Rules or under another policy. There may also be cases where return is intended but is prevented for the time being— for example, because of ECHR barriers. In such cases consideration will need to be given to granting Discretionary Leave, but note that practical obstacles to return (such as difficulty in obtaining a passport and absence for the time being of a viable route of return) would not, in themselves, justify Discretionary Leave.

Chapter 9, section 5 of the **IDI** on General grounds for the refusal of entry clearance, leave to enter or variation of leave to enter or remain provides further guidance on curtailing leave. Paragraph 3 of that instruction covers the curtailment of leave granted outside the Immigration Rules.

9. Five Year Review: Granting or Refusing Settlement

People who have completed five years' Humanitarian Protection leave will be eligible to apply for Indefinite Leave to Remain (ILR), also known as settlement.

The individual should apply for settlement shortly before the expiry of their leave. It will not normally be necessary to conduct an in-depth review to determine whether the individual is still entitled to Humanitarian Protection, as long as the application is made before the existing leave expires. Background character and conduct checks will usually suffice, unless the individual concerned should have been subject to a previous case review on the grounds of the triggers listed in section 8 above.

If the application for settlement is made out of time, however, a full review should be conducted to determine whether the individual still qualifies for Humanitarian Protection.

The Five Year Strategy included a proposal to introduce English language and knowledge of British life tests, which applicants granted limited leave should be required to pass before qualifying for ILR. The policy on this is still being developed. This API will be updated once the tests are introduced.

Where a person has held leave on grounds other than Humanitarian Protection, the following are the qualifying periods for settlement purposes:

- Leave on Humanitarian Protection grounds and Refugee Leave in any combination: five years' leave
- Leave on Humanitarian Protection grounds and Discretionary Leave in any combination: six years' leave. However where a person is granted Discretionary Leave after having been excluded from Humanitarian Protection, they will have to complete a cumulative total of ten years' leave before being eligible to apply for settlement.

The criteria to be applied on considering an application for settlement are those relevant to the category in which the applicant currently holds leave. So a person who holds Discretionary Leave that has been 'upgraded' to leave on Humanitarian Protection grounds should be considered for settlement after six years in accordance with the criteria on Humanitarian Protection.

Leave on other grounds (for instance, under the Immigration Rules) will not count towards the qualifying periods for settlement under this policy.

Where settlement is refused, consideration will need to be given to whether or not the applicant qualifies for leave on any other basis, including Discretionary Leave.

10. Appeal Rights

See the **IDI** on *Appeals*.

11. Issuing of Travel Documents

Paragraph 344A of the Immigration Rules sets out the criteria under which a travel document may be issued to a person granted Humanitarian Protection leave. A person who holds leave on Humanitarian Protection grounds should in most cases travel on a national passport. They may be eligible to apply for a Home Office Certificate of Identity (CID) if they can show that they have been formally and unreasonably refused a national passport.

Alternatively, where IND has accepted that they have a well-founded fear of their national authorities, they will not be required to approach these authorities for a passport before becoming eligible for a CID. A CID may also be issued where a person has made reasonable attempts to obtain a national passport or identity document, particularly where there are serious humanitarian reasons for travel. For further information, see the guidance on applying for travel documents on the IND website.

12. Transitional Arrangements for Cases in Which Exceptional Leave was Granted Before 1 April 2003

Up until 2007 there will be individuals who were granted exceptional leave before April 2003 whose leave will be ending and who will be seeking to extend their stay.

Those applicants who were granted a four-year period of exceptional leave in one block and who apply for ILR at the end of that period should be considered for settlement with background character and conduct checks and war crimes screening, but without a full review. In other words, they will not need to show that they would necessarily qualify for Humanitarian Protection or Discretionary Leave at the time of the ILR decision.

Where a person seeks an extension of stay having spent less than four years on exceptional leave (or where they have spent four years on exceptional leave and this has been granted in more than one block), their application should be subject to a full active review. It will be necessary for them to show that they qualify for Humanitarian Protection or Discretionary Leave at the time of the decision on their extension request. If they do not qualify on either of these grounds or qualify for leave on any other basis (such as under the Immigration Rules) their claim for an extension of stay should be refused.

If they do qualify for Humanitarian Protection the period of leave granted will depend on how long they have already spent on exceptional leave. Where the period spent on exceptional leave is:

- One year or under—grant three years' HP leave.
- Over one year—grant the balance of leave to take the total leave to four years (e.g. where the person has spent two years on exceptional leave, grant two years' HP leave).

See section 4.9 of the **API** on *Active Reviews* for further instructions on handling cases of this kind.

Enquiries: Further enquiries should normally be made in writing to the Asylum Policy Unit and via a senior caseworker.

Annex A

NOTE THAT THIS INSTRUCTION *ONLY* APPLIES IN CASES WHERE HUMANITARIAN PROTECTION WAS GRANTED BEFORE 30 AUGUST 2005. WHERE HUMANITARIAN PROTECTION WAS GRANTED AFTER THAT DATE, CASEWORKERS SHOULD REFER TO THE API ON HUMANITARIAN PROTECTION

1. Introduction

Humanitarian Protection and Discretionary Leave were introduced on 1 April 2003 following the abolition of exceptional leave on 31 March 2003.

On 30 August 2005, the policy on Humanitarian Protection was revised in line with new policies on the granting of refugee leave. Although the criteria for granting Humanitarian Protection have not changed, people who are found to qualify on or after 30 August 2005 should usually be granted five years' limited leave in the first instance, rather than three years as previously. The arrangements for reviewing these cases are also different from those in place before 30 August 2005.

However, where leave was granted on Humanitarian Protection grounds before 30 August 2005, the review arrangements remain as they were before that date and the new arrangements do not apply. This annex explains how caseworkers should review these 'old' cases. Under the 'old' arrangements, people will be continue to be able to apply for ILR after three years' Humanitarian Protection leave, but these applications for settlement will always be subject to an active review. The new review category of 'a significant and non-temporary change in the conditions in a particular country' (see section 7 below and the *API* on *Refugee Leave*) will not be applied in these cases. On the other hand, note that the new arrangements for Home Office travel documents will apply even where Humanitarian Protection was granted before 30 August 2005 (see the main **API** on *Humanitarian Protection* for details).

Note that the relevant appeal rights will be whatever rights are current at the date of decision. See section 5 below and the **API** on *Appeals—Rights of Appeal*.

2. Revocation of Humanitarian Protection

A grant of Humanitarian Protection will not normally be actively reviewed during its currency. This paragraph sets out the circumstances when consideration should be given to revoking or varying leave granted on that basis.

In line with normal practice leave should not normally be curtailed if the leave will expire in less than six months unless the applicant falls into one of the excluded categories at paragraph 2.5 and removal action can be taken.

Any decision to revoke or vary leave should not be taken without reference to a senior caseworker.

2.1 Voluntary actions leading to revocation

There will be occasions where a person shows through their own actions that they no longer fear treatment that originally qualified them for Humanitarian Protection, or that even if they do continue to have such a fear another country is now better placed than the United Kingdom to provide protection against it. Reasons for revocation of refugee status based on actions of an individual are provided for in Article 1C (1–4) of the 1951 Refugee Convention. They are:

- voluntary re-availment of national protection;
- voluntary re-acquisition of nationality;
- acquisition of a new nationality;
- voluntary re-establishment in the country where persecution was feared.

These situations will normally be applicable to considering whether to revoke Humanitarian Protection. However as Humanitarian Protection is not identical to refugee status the above reasons may not always be relevant to whether Humanitarian Protection should be revoked (or varied) or not. Each case that arises will need to be considered on its individual merits to see whether the actions of the person provide clear grounds for concluding that they no longer qualify for Humanitarian Protection.

For example, where a person has taken to spending periods of time in the country where they previously feared treatment which qualified them for Humanitarian Protection that would be very strong evidence that they no longer qualified for it. On the other hand, if a person has re-acquired the nationality of their country that will not necessarily mean they no longer qualify for Humanitarian Protection if, for instance, they continue to fear treatment contrary to Article 3 from non-state actors against which the State is unable to protect them, and that person did not originally claim that the state was persecuting or mistreating them.

2.2 Revocation as a result of a change in country conditions

A grant of Humanitarian Protection should not be reviewed on these grounds before it ends, unless there is a specific instruction from AAPD in relation to a particular country or to a category of cases in respect of a particular country. Any such instruction will provide details of what cases should be reviewed and how that review should be undertaken. Since all Humanitarian Protection grants will be given on an individual basis, any consideration to revoke such leave following a change in country conditions would need to take into account the effect of that change on the circumstances of the individual.

2.3 Revocation on the grounds of character or conduct (including deception)

Leave granted on the basis of Humanitarian Protection should normally be revoked or varied if a person becomes subject to any of the exclusion criteria set out in paragraph 2.5 above. This will usually cover situations where a person's actions after the grant of Humanitarian Protection bring them within the scope of those criteria. There may also be some situations where we become aware that a person is subject to one of the disqualifying criteria only after the grant of Humanitarian Protection. Again, it would normally be appropriate to revoke or vary any leave granted in such cases.

If the individual was liable to deportation, the deportation order would have the effect of cancelling leave. Separate action to revoke or vary leave would, therefore, only be necessary where a person was liable to deportation but the initiation of deportation action was not possible (e.g. for Article 3 ECHR reasons).

If it transpires that a person has obtained their Humanitarian Protection by deception they will be liable to having removal directions set as an illegal entrant or in accordance with section 10 of the 1999 Immigration and Asylum Act. The setting of such directions under section 10 of the 1999 Act invalidates any leave given previously, but in the case of an illegal entrant it may be necessary to cancel the leave separately when the person is removed. Separate action to revoke Humanitarian Protection will only be required where removal directions cannot be set (e.g. for Article 3 ECHR reasons).

2.4 Action following revocation

When Humanitarian Protection is revoked the expectation is that removal will follow, subject to any appeal. However, there will be some cases where removal is not appropriate as the person qualifies for leave under the Immigration Rules. There may also be cases (most likely in the paragraph 7.3 category) where removal is intended but is prevented for the time being–for example, because of ECHR barriers. In such cases consideration will need to be given to the granting of Discretionary Leave.

So occasions may arise where leave is in effect being varied (e.g. one form of leave (Humanitarian Protection) being replaced with another, shorter, form of leave (Discretionary Leave)) rather than being revoked.

3. 3 Year Review: Granting or Refusing Settlement

People who have completed 3 years on Humanitarian Protection will be eligible to apply for Indefinite Leave to Remain (ILR), also known as settlement.

The individual should apply for settlement shortly before the expiry of their Humanitarian Protection leave. The application for settlement should be considered in the light of the circumstances prevailing at that time.

Note that any time spent on Discretionary Leave (or under a category of the Immigration Rules) does not count towards the three year qualifying period for settlement under the Humanitarian Protection scheme.

3.1 Consideration of application for settlement

All applications for ILR will be the subject of an active review, to decide whether the person still qualifies for Humanitarian Protection (or any leave on any other basis that is requested). This review will take account of the information on the extension request form, present country information and any relevant information provided at the time of the original grant of Humanitarian Protection. It will normally be carried out on the papers but there will be discretion to conduct an interview to ascertain further information where this is considered appropriate.

Where it comes to light at the time of the active review or otherwise that a person has conducted one of the 'voluntary actions' (see paragraph 7.1 above) the reasons for this will need to be sought.

Where there has been a change in the applicant's country of return (see paragraph 7.2 above) this may mean the basis for fearing mistreatment no longer subsists. Consideration will need to be given to the basis on which leave was originally granted and to any information provided by the applicant to consider whether they are still in need of Humanitarian Protection.

Where an applicant is identified as falling within the scope of the exclusion criteria (see paragraph 2.5 above) at the time of the active review, ILR should be refused (as should any extension of Humanitarian Protection—if the person cannot be removed for ECHR reasons any leave granted should be Discretionary Leave).

3.2 Granting settlement

Where a person has completed three years Humanitarian Protection and the review confirms that such protection is still appropriate they will qualify for ILR unless the case is subject to any other instruction (see introduction).

3.3 Refusing settlement and/or further Humanitarian Protection

Where settlement or (if a separate instruction is in force) any further Humanitarian Protection is refused consideration will need to be given to whether or not the applicant qualifies for leave on any other basis, including Discretionary Leave.

4. Reviews Where Less Than 3 Years Humanitarian Protection was Initially Granted

A person may have been granted less than 3 years in accordance with a separate instruction which may have been issued. When that leave expires and the person seeks an extension to their stay an active review should be conducted.

Where it is decided that the need for Humanitarian Protection continues a further period of leave should be granted. The period should bring the total time on Humanitarian Protection to 3 years or, if a separate instruction in regard to this category of claim is still in force, for a period of time in accordance with that instruction. However, where granting a further period of leave in accordance with the instruction would lead to more than 3 years being spent on Humanitarian Protection, a shorter period of time should instead be granted to complete the 3 years.

Where it is decided that the need for Humanitarian Protection has ceased the application should be refused unless the person qualifies for leave on another basis.

5. Appeal Rights

Note that the relevant appeal rights will be whatever rights are current at the date of decision. For instance, if ILR is refused following a period of Humanitarian Protection leave granted before 30 August 2005, the decision will be subject to appeal rights as they stand at the date of decision, not as they stood on 29 August 2005.

For full details of appeal rights see the **API** on *Appeals—Rights of Appeal.*

6. Transitional Arrangements

Up until 2007 there will be individuals granted exceptional leave before April 2003 whose leave will be ending and who will be seeking to extend their stay.

Those applicants who were granted a four-year period of exceptional leave in one block and who apply for ILR at the end of that period should be considered for settlement with background character and conduct checks, but without a full review. In other words, they will not need to show that they would necessarily qualify for Humanitarian Protection or Discretionary Leave at the time of the ILR decision.

Where a person seeks an extension of stay having spent less than four years on exceptional leave (or where they have spent four years on exceptional leave and this has been granted in more than one block), their application should be subject to a full active review. It will be necessary for them to show that they qualify for Humanitarian Protection or Discretionary Leave at the time of the ILR decision. If they do not qualify on either of these grounds or qualify for leave on any other basis (such as under the Immigration Rules) their claim for an extension of stay should be refused.

If they do qualify for Humanitarian Protection the period of leave granted will depend on how long they have already spent on exceptional leave. Where the period spent on exceptional leave is:

• One year or under—grant three years' Humanitarian Protection.
• Over one year—grant the balance of leave to take the total leave to four years (e.g. where the person has spent two years on exceptional leave, grant two years' Humanitarian Protection).

A person granted Humanitarian Protection for less than 3 years in accordance with this paragraph (i.e. because they have spent over 1 year on exceptional leave) should be considered for settlement at the point they have spent 4 years in total with Humanitarian Protection leave and ELE/R.

APPENDIX 10

DP 3/96—Marriage Policy

DP 3/96
and instruction to IES(1)
and IES(2)

INTRODUCTION

This notice provides guidance, in general terms, on the consideration of cases of those persons liable to be removed as illegal entrants or deported who have married a person settled in the United Kingdom. *This notice supersedes DP2/93 which is hereby cancelled,* subject to the transitional provisions set out in paragraph 10 of this instruction. Deportation cases fall to be considered within the framework of the Immigration Rules and the attached guidance should be read in conjunction with those Rules. Although illegal entry cases are considered outside the Rules, any relevant compassionate circumstances, including those referred to below, should be considered before a decision to remove is taken.

POLICY

2. Paragraph 364 of the Immigration Rules explains that deportation will normally be the proper course where a person has failed to comply with or has contravened, a condition or has remained here without authority but that all the known relevant factors must be taken into account before a decision is reached. These include:
    i) age;
    ii) length of residence in the United Kingdom;
    iii) strength of connections with the United Kingdom;
    iv) personal history, including character, conduct and employment record;
    v) domestic circumstances;
    vi) previous criminal record and the nature of any offence;
    vii) compassionate circumstances;
    viii) any representations.
3. Where persons do not qualify for leave to remain under the Immigration Rules and are to be considered for deportation, or where they are illegal entrants liable to removal, but seek nevertheless to remain on the basis of marriage in the United Kingdom, the following paragraphs of this guidance apply.
4. Where enforcement action is under consideration and the offender is married to someone settled here a judgement will need to be reached on the weight to be attached to the marriage as a compassionate factor. Caseworkers should bear in mind that paragraph 284 of the Immigration Rules, which sets out the requirements to be met for an extension of stay as the spouse of a person present and settled in the United Kingdom, specifically requires, amongst other things, a person to have a limited leave to remain here and to have not remained here in breach of the immigration laws, in order to obtain leave to remain on

that basis. Therefore, the fact that an offender is married to a person settled here does not give him/her any right to remain under the Rules.

Marriages that Pre-Date Enforcement Action

5. As a *general rule*, deportation action under 3(5)(a) or (3)(5)(b) (in non-criminal cases) or illegal entry action should not normally be initiated in the following circumstances (but see notes below):

   a) where the subject has a genuine and subsisting marriage with someone settled here and the couple have lived together in this country continuously since their marriage for at least 2 years before the commencement of enforcement action;
   and

   b) it is unreasonable to expect the settled spouse to accompany his/her spouse on removal.

Notes

i) In this instruction, "settled" refers to British citizens who live in the United Kingdom or to other nationals who have ILE or ILR here.

ii) In considering whether or not, under paragraph 5(b) above, it would be unreasonable for a settled spouse to accompany the subject of enforcement action on removal the onus rests with the settled spouse to make out a case with supporting evidence as to why it is unreasonable for him/her to live outside the United Kingdom. Factors which caseworkers should take into account, if. they are made known to them, will include whether the United Kingdom settled spouse:

   a. has very strong and close family ties in the United Kingdom such as older children from a previous relationship that form part of the family unit; or

   b. has been settled and living in the United Kingdom for at least the preceding 10 years; or

   c. suffers from ill-health and medical evidence conclusively shows that his/her life would be significantly impaired or endangered if he/she were to accompany his/her spouse on removal.

iii) In this instruction commencement of enforcement action is to be taken as either:-

   a. a specific instruction to leave with a warning of liability to deportation if the subject fails to do so; or

   b. service of a notice of intention to deport or service of illegal entry papers (including the service of papers during a previous stay in the United Kingdom where the subject has returned illegally); or

   c. a recommendation by a court that a person should be deported following a conviction.

iv) The commencement of enforcement action "stops the clock" in terms of the 2 year qualifying period referred to in paragraph 5(a) above in which a marriage must have subsisted. No further time can then be accrued to meet this criterion, eg, whilst making representations, appealing against the decision or applying for judicial review.

v) This notice contains guidance as to the approach to be adopted in the generality of cases but it must be remembered that each case is to be decided on its individual merits and, for instance, a particularly poor immigration history may warrant the offender's enforced departure from the UK notwithstanding the factors referred to above.

CRIMINAL CONVICTIONS

6. In cases where someone liable to immigration control has family ties here which would normally benefit him/her under paragraph 4 above but has criminal convictions, the severity of the offence should be balanced against the strength of the family ties. Serious crimes which are punishable with imprisonment or a series of lesser crimes which show a propensity to re-offend, would normally outweigh the family ties. A very poor immigration history may also be taken into account. Caseworkers must use their judgement to decide what is reasonable in any individual case.

CHILDREN

7. The presence of children with the right of abode in the UK (see note below) is a factor to be taken into account. In cases involving children who have the right of abode, the crucial question is whether it is reasonable for the child to accompany his/her parents abroad. Factors to be considered include:
   a) the age of the child (in most cases a child of 10 or younger could reasonably be expected to adapt to life abroad);
   b) serious ill-health for which treatment is not available in the country to which the family is going.

NOTE

i) Children will have the right of abode most commonly as a result of having been born in the United Kingdom to a parent settled here. It should be noted that under the British Nationality Act 1981 an illegitimate child born in the United Kingdom obtains British citizenship only if the mother is a British citizen or is settled in the United Kingdom. Under the 1981 Act the status of the father of a child born illegitimate has no bearing on the nationality of the child unless he subsequently marries the mother and thus legitimises the child.

MARRIAGES THAT POST-DATE ENFORCEMENT ACTION

8. Where a person marries *after* the commencement of enforcement action removal should normally be enforced. The criteria set out in paragraph 5 do *not* apply in such cases. Paragraph 284 of the Immigration Rules makes it clear that one of the requirements for an extension of stay as the spouse of a person present and settled in the United Kingdom is that "the marriage has not taken place after a decision has been made to deport the applicant or he has been recommended for deportation or has been given notice under Section 6(2) of the Immigration Act 1971". Marriage cannot therefore, in itself be considered a sufficiently compassionate factor to militate against removal. Detailed enquiries in order to ascertain whether the marriage is genuine and subsisting should *not* normally be undertaken. The onus is on the subject to put forward any compelling compassionate factors that he/she wishes to be considered which must be supported by documentary evidence. Only in the most *exceptional circumstances* should removal action be stopped and the person allowed to stay.

Marriage to European Economic Area (EEA) nationals

9. Any foreign national who contracts a marriage to an EEA national should have his/her case considered in the first instance by EC group, B6 Division to whom the case must be referred, irrespective of whether the marriage took place before or after the initiation of enforcement action.

Transitional Arrangements

10. This instruction will not apply retrospectively. It has immediate effect in cases where the marriage came to the notice, of the Immigration and Nationality Department after 13 March 1996 irrespective of the date on which the marriage took place. Cases where the marriage came to notice on or prior to 13 March 1996 should be considered under the terms of DP 2/93.

Enquiries

11. Any enquiries about this instruction should be addressed to the Enforcement Policy Group in Room 301 Apollo House. (Ext 8408/8409).

Enforcement Policy Group
13 March 1996

IMG 89 47/558/5

FLOW CHART

This flow chart should be used as a *guide* only. There will occasionally be cases which fall outside the guidelines.

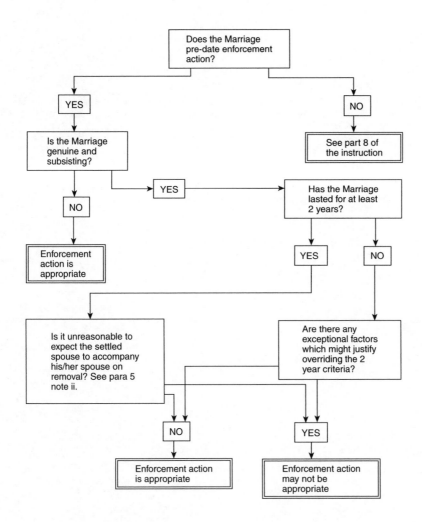

FLOW CHART

INDEX